Personalized Learning!

In *MyManagementLab* you are treated as an individual with specific learning needs.

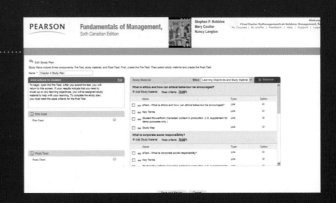

Personalized Study Plan

MyManagementLab treats you as an individual with specific learning needs. You have limited study time so you need to be effective during the time you have. A personalized Study Plan is generated from your results on Sample Tests and instructor assignments. You can clearly see which topics you have mastered and, more importantly, which ones you still need to work on.

Pearson eText

Access the eText while you study—without leaving the online environment! You can highlight passages and make notes.

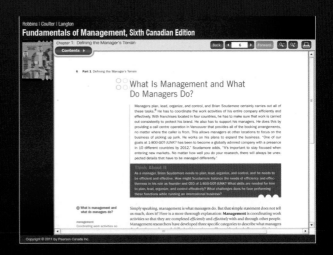

Annotated Figures and Tables from the Text

Detailed explanations—in addition to what's in the text—help you understand the concepts.

Self-Assessment Library

The Self-Assessment Library is an interactive library of 51 behavioural questionnaires that will help you discover yourself and give you insight into how you might behave as a manager.

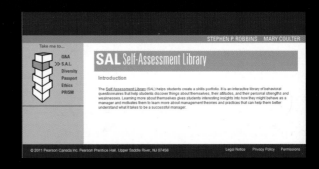

Save Time. Improve Results. www.pearsoned.ca/mymanagementlab

Sixth Canadian Edition

Fundamentals of Management

Stephen P. Robbins
San Diego State University

Mary Coulter
Southwest Missouri State University

Nancy Langton
Sauder School of Business
University of British Columbia

Pearson Canada
Toronto

Library and Archives Canada Cataloguing in Publication

Robbins, Stephen P., 1943–
Fundamentals of management / Stephen P. Robbins, Mary Coulter, Nancy Langton.—6th Canadian ed.

Canadian ed. 3rd Canadian ed. written by Stephen P. Robbins, David A. De Cenzo, Robin Stuart-Kotze. 4th Canadian ed. written by Stephen P. Robbins . . . [et al.].

Includes index.
ISBN 978-0-13-207461-2

1. Management—Textbooks.   I. Coulter, Mary   II. Langton, Nancy   III. Title.

HD31.R5643 2011   658.4   C2009-904326-2

ISBN 978-0-13-207461-2

Vice-President, Editorial Director: Gary Bennett
Acquisitions Editor: Karen Elliott
Executive Marketing Manager: Cas Shields
Developmental Editor: Su Mei Ku
Production Editor: Imee Salumbides
Copy Editor: Martin Tooke
Proofreader: Deborah Cooper-Bullock
Production Coordinator: Andrea Falkenberg
Compositor: MPS Limited, A Macmillan Company
Photo and Literary Permissions Researcher: Lisa Brant
Art Director: Julia Hall
Cover and Interior Designer: Anthony Leung
Cover Image: Veer Inc.

1 2 3 4 5   13 12 11 10 09

Printed and bound in the United States of America.

Brief Contents

Contents

PART TWO
Planning   66

PART THREE
Organizing 138

PART FOUR
Leading 232

CHAPTER 8
Leadership 232

CHAPTER 9
Motivating Employees 264

PART FIVE
Controlling 324

Preface

Welcome to the sixth Canadian edition of *Fundamentals of Management*, by Stephen Robbins, Mary Coulter, and Nancy Langton. This edition continues its fresh approach to management coverage through

- more relevant examples

- updated theory coverage

- a more pedagogically sound design

The underlying philosophy in carrying out this revision was to put additional emphasis on the idea that "Management Is for Everyone." Students who are not managers, or who do not envision themselves as managers, do not always understand why studying management is important or relevant. We use examples from a variety of settings and have introduced a new end-of-chapter feature, *Management for You Today*, to help students understand the relevance of studying management for their day-to-day lives.

Chapter Pedagogical Features

We have continued to enhance the sixth Canadian edition through a rich variety of pedagogical features, including the following:

- Outcomes-based questions at the opening of each chapter guide student learning. These questions are repeated at the start of each major chapter section to reinforce the learning outcome.

- A vignette opens each chapter and is threaded throughout the chapter to help students apply a story to the concepts they are learning.

- The vignette is followed by *Think About It* questions that give students a chance to put themselves into the shoes of managers in various situations.

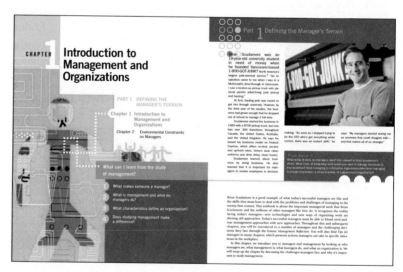

- Integrated questions (in the form of light green notes) throughout the chapters help students relate management to their everyday lives

- References in the margin to *Q&A*, *PRISM*, and *Diversity in Action* throughout the chapters enhance students' learning. These references send students to the MyManagementLab website (**www.pearsoned.ca/mymanagementlab**) where students can complete exercises to better their understanding or learn more about a management concept or issue. For example, the *Q&A* feature anticipates questions that students might have about specific areas of management. The answers to these questions are found on the MyManagementLab website.

Q&A 2.1

PRISM 6

Diversity in Action 5

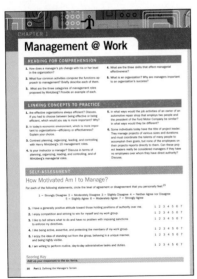

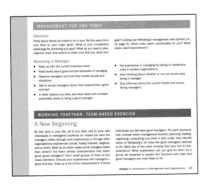

- *Tips for Managers* provides "take-aways" from the chapter—things that managers and would-be managers can start to put into action right now, based on what they have learned in the chapter.

- A *Management Reflection* feature appears in appropriate chapters. These are longer examples designed to enhance student learning.

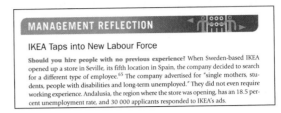

- *Summary and Implications* provides responses to the outcomes-based questions identified at the beginning of each chapter. Accompanying this is a *Snapshot Summary* that provides a quick look at the organization of the chapter topics.

End-of-Chapter Applications

The end-of-chapter section, *Management @ Work*, continues to provide a wealth of applications.

- *Reading for Comprehension* allows students to review their understanding of the chapter content.

- *Linking Concepts to Practice* helps students see the application of theory to management situations.

- *Self-Assessment* gives students an opportunity to discover things about themselves, their attitudes, and their personal strengths and weaknesses. Each chapter includes one self-assessment exercise that students can fill out and refers students to the MyManagementLab website where they can access additional interactive self-assessment exercises. (For more details, see the Supplements section on pages xv–xvi.)

- NEW structure! *Management for You Today* lets students apply material to their daily lives, helping them see that planning, leading, organizing, and controlling are useful in one's day-to-day life too. This feature is divided into two parts:

  - *Dilemma*, which presents an everyday scenario for students to resolve using management tools

  - *Becoming a Manager*, which provides suggestions for students on activities and actions they can do right now to help them in preparing to become a manager

- *Working Together: Team-Based Exercise* gives students a chance to work together in groups to solve a management challenge.

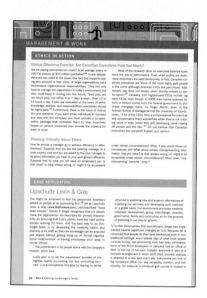

- NEW structure! *Ethics in Action* provides students with an opportunity to consider ethical issues that relate to chapter material. It has two parts:

  - *Ethical Dilemma Exercise*, which focuses on ethical dilemmas that employees of organizations may face

  - *Thinking Critically About Ethics*, which encourages students to think critically about ethical issues they may encounter

- *Case Application* is a decision-focused case that asks students to determine what they would do if they were in the situation described.

- *Developing Your Diagnostic and Analytical Skills* asks students to apply chapter material to analyze a case.

- *Developing Your Interpersonal Skills* emphasizes the importance of skills.

- *Managing Workforce Diversity* appears in some of the chapters and informs students about what can be done to make workplaces more inclusive.

 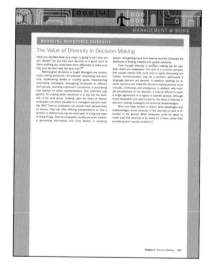

New to the Sixth Canadian Edition

In addition to the new pedagogical features highlighted on previous pages, we have introduced other new learning aids and made significant changes to content.

MyManagementLab

An access code to MyManagementLab at **www.pearsoned.ca/mymanagementlab** is included with the textbook. MyManagementLab is an online study tool for students and an online homework and assessment tool for faculty. Also on the site is the Robbins *OnLine Learning System (R.O.L.L.S.)*, with the *Q&A* feature and additional exercises on managing diversity, ethics, and global management. A MyManagementLab box at the end of each part in the textbook directs students to these additional exercises. The site also includes the Self-Assessment Library.

New Cases

Our reviews tell us that management courses need more cases. Besides offering cases at the end of each chapter (*Case Application* and *Developing Your Diagnostic and Analytical Skills*), we have responded to this request in other ways.

End-of-Part Case

NEW! A case featuring Starbucks appears at the end of each part of the text. The five parts of the case illustrate how the concepts and functions of management can be applied to a real-life corporation. The case can be used in parts, or it can serve as an integrating case at the end of the term.

End-of-Part Video Cases

Two video cases appear at the end of each part, for a total of 10 videos. A number of these come from CBC programs. The videos generally focus on several management issues within a part. The cases were carefully selected by Janina Kon (University of British Columbia) to provide instructors with audiovisual material to engage their students' attention. The videos are available in VHS (ISBN 978-0-13-511764-4) and DVD format (ISBN 978-0-13-511763-7).

End-of-Book Cases

NEW! Two longer cases, "The YMCA of London, Ontario," written by Pat MacDonald of the University of Western Ontario, and "Sarnia Food Fresh Grocery Store: The Icing on the Cake," written by J. David Whitehead and Jennifer Baker of Brock University, have been included at the end of the book. These two cases are lengthier and integrate a number of management issues.

Chapter-by-Chapter Highlight

Below, we highlight the new material that has been added to this edition.

Chapter 1: Introduction to Management and Organizations

- Updated examples and data
- Added a new exhibit on efficiency and effectiveness in management (Exhibit 1-2)
- Shortened chapter by deleting the section "The Challenges Managers Face" and moving the discussion of social responsibility to Chapter 4

Supplement 1: History of Management Trends

- Added a new section called "Historical Background of Management"

Chapter 2: Environmental Constraints on Managers

- Expanded the discussion of Hofstede's five dimensions of national culture, including a new exhibit (Exhibit 2-3)
- Significantly revised the section "Doing Business Globally," which includes the following new discussions:
  - multidomestic corporations
  - global companies
  - born globals
  - global sourcing
  - a new exhibit on how organizations go global (Exhibit 2-4)

- Shortened the section on stakeholder relationship management
- Added a discussion called "The Pros and Cons of Globalization" including a new exhibit (Exhibit 2-7)

Chapter 3: Planning and Strategic Management

- Introduced the concept of business model
- Increased depth and greater clarification of the strategic management process
- Revised the section on corporate strategy, including new discussions of renewal strategy and turnaround strategy

Chapter 4: Decision Making

- Updated examples and data
- Moved the topic of corporate social responsibility from Chapter 1 to this chapter

Chapter 5: Organizational Structure and Design

- Provided a greater emphasis on "today's view" of the six key elements of organizational structure
- Added a new section called "Today's Organizational Design Challenges," which includes the following topics:
  - Keeping Employees Connected
  - Building a Learning Organization
  - Managing Global Structural Issues

Chapter 6: Communication and Information Technology

- Shortened chapter by removing discussions of older communications technologies, such as voice mail and fax, and intranet and extranet
- Updated the chapter with new examples and data, including a discussion of social networking websites

Chapter 7: Human Resource Management

- Updated chapter content
- Elaborated the discussion of multiperson comparisons
- Added a new exhibit on what college and university graduates want from their jobs (Exhibit 7-11)

Chapter 8: Leadership

- Replaced the exhibit on path-goal theory with a new exhibit on path-goal situations and preferred leader behaviours (Exhibit 8-7)
- Reorganized the discussions of charismatic and transformational leaderships, including the addition of a new "Tip for Managers: How to Be a Transformational Leader"
- Provided a new "Tips for Managers: Being a Better Leader"

Chapter 9: Motivating Employees

- Introduced the concepts of procedural justice and distributive justice
- Developed a new discussion "Motivating Contingent Workers"
- Updated chapter examples and data

Chapter 10: Understanding Groups and Teams

- Created a new exhibit to highlight the differences between groups and teams (Exhibit 10-2)
- Added a new section called "Current Challenges in Managing Teams," which includes a new exhibit on the drawbacks and benefits of global teams (Exhibit 10-8)

Chapter 11: Foundations of Control

- Completely reorganized this chapter, significantly increasing the depth of discussion on control
- Added three new exhibits:
  - Exhibit 11-14 The Balanced Scorecard
  - Exhibit 11-15 Twenty-First Century Governance Principles for Public Companies
  - Exhibit 11-18 The Service Profit Chain

Chapter 12: Managing Change

- Updated chapter content, including new discussions of the following:
  - Global OD (organizational development)
  - Karoshi in Japan (death from overwork)

Supplements

With this edition of *Fundamentals of Management*, we have introduced MyManagement-Lab, which provides students with an assortment of tools to help enrich and expedite learning. MyManagementLab lets students assess their understanding through auto-graded tests and assignments, develop a personalized study plan to address areas of weakness, and practise a variety of learning tools to master management principles. Some of these tools are described below:

- *Personalized Study Plan* In MyManagementLab, students are treated as individuals with specific learning needs. Students have limited study time so it is important for them to use it effectively. A personalized study plan is generated from each student's results on the Pre-Tests for each chapter. Students can clearly see the topics they have mastered—and, more importantly, the concepts they need to work on. The Pre-Tests and Post-Test were prepared by Sandi Findlay at Mount Saint Vincent University.

- *Auto-Graded Tests and Assignments* MyManagementLab comes with Mini-Cases and Chapter Quizzes. These were prepared by Ian Anderson of Algonquin College and Richard Yipchuck of Humber College, respectively. Students can complete the Mini-Case activity to help them see key concepts applied in real-life scenarios and to test their understanding of the material covered. Instructors can also assign sample tests or create assignments, quizzes, or tests using a mix of publisher-supplied content and their own custom exercises.

- *Pearson eText* Students can study without leaving the online environment. They can access the Pearson eText online and use the new highlighting and notes features, as well as view media assets, which includes annotated text figures prepared by Cathy Heyland of Selkirk College.

- *Robbins OnLine Learning System (R.O.L.L.S.)* features the following tools:

  - *Robbins Self-Assessment Library.* The Self-Assessment Library helps students create a skills portfolio. It is an interactive library of 51 behavioural questionnaires that help students discover things about themselves, their attitudes, and their personal strengths and weaknesses. Learning more about themselves gives students interesting insights into how they might behave as a manager and motivates them to learn more about management theories and practices that can help them better understand what it takes to be a successful manager.

  - *Q&A.* The questions from each chapter that students ask most frequently are answered by the authors in both written and audio format. It's like having an instructor standing over their shoulder at the times students need it the most.

  - *Diversity in Action.* These interactive exercises put students in the challenging role of a manager making decisions related to age, gender, or ethnic diversity.

  - *Passport: Managing in a Global Environment.* This multimedia module illustrates the globalization challenges that managers face. There are three or four global case scenarios that students can examine at the end of each part. These cases span 13 different countries. Students will find a map and click a desired country to get information about that country (video and written information is provided). Using this information, students make decisions about the most appropriate ways to handle the managerial problems described in the case scenarios.

  - *Ethics.* In these interactive exercises, students are put in the role of a manager making decisions about current ethical issues.

  - *Practical Interactive Skills Modules (PRISM).* This module consists of 12 interactive decision-treestyle comprehensive exercises that provide students with an opportunity to try out different management skills and learn why certain approaches are better than others.

- *Glossary Flashcards* This study aid is useful for students' review of key concepts.

- *Management in the News* These mini-cases were developed from current news articles and include questions for students to answer.

- *MySearchLab* MySearchLab helps students quickly and efficiently make the most of their research time by providing four exclusive databases of reliable source content, including the EBSCO Academic Journal and Abstract Database, Google Scholar, "Best of the Web" Link Library, and Financial Times Article Archive and Company Financials.

For instructors, we have created an outstanding supplements package, all conveniently available online through MyManagementLab in the special instructor area, downloadable from our product catalogue at **www.pearsoncanada.ca**, or available on a single CD-ROM. The Instructor's Resource CD-ROM (ISBN 978-0-13-246951-7) contains the following:

- Instructor's Resource Manual (includes video teaching notes and detailed lecture outlines), prepared by Floyd Simpkins of St. Clair College

- PowerPoint Slides, prepared by Carolyn Stern of Capilano University

- TestGen, prepared by George Dracopoulos of Vanier College

The video cases are available in VHS (ISBN 978-0-13-511764-4) and DVD format (ISBN 978-0-13-511763-7). These cases were prepared by Janina Kon of the University of British Columbia.

Acknowledgments

A number of people worked hard to give this sixth Canadian edition of *Fundamentals of Management* a new look. Su Mei Ku was developmental editor on this project. Her wit, good humour, helpfulness, support, and organizational skills made working on this textbook immensely easier. She also played a valuable role in handling many aspects of the editorial work needed during the production process.

I received incredible support for this project from a variety of people at Pearson Canada. Karen Elliott, acquisitions editor, was simply terrific in encouraging a fresh look for this book. Anthony Leung translated my thoughts about what this book should look like, creating an exciting new design. I particularly appreciate his responsiveness to suggestions for changes. I appreciated working with Imee Salumbides in her role as the production editor for this project. Her professionalism, goodwill, and cheerfulness made the production process a surprisingly enjoyable task. Steve O'Hearn, president of higher education, and Gary Bennett, vice-president, editorial director, are extremely supportive on the management side of Pearson Canada, and this kind of support makes it much easier for an author to get work done and meet dreams and goals. Lisa Brant once again was very helpful in doing the photo research, and made some incredible finds in her search for photos to highlight management concepts. There are a variety of others at Pearson who also had their hand in making sure that the manuscript would be transformed into this book, and then delivered to your hands. To all of them I extend my thanks for jobs well done. The Pearson sales team is an exceptional group, and I know they will do everything possible to make this book successful. I continue to appreciate and value their support and interaction, particularly that of Cas Shields, executive marketing manager, and Ewan French, my local sales representative.

Martin Tooke was the copy editor for the project and did an amazing job of making sure everything was in place and written clearly. Deborah Cooper-Bullock was the proofreader and was extremely diligent about checking for consistency throughout the text. I enjoyed the opportunity to work with both of them. Their keen eyes helped to make the pages as clean as they are. They also help me remember the necessary qualities of virtual teams.

Finally, I want to acknowledge the many reviewers of this textbook for their detailed and helpful comments: Jody Merritt, St. Clair College; Susan Thompson, Trent University; James Voulakos, George Brown College; and Vasile Zamfirescu, Kwantlen University College.

I dedicate this book to my father, Peter X. Langton. He was a man of many talents, and his understanding of organizations may have been greater than my own. To my family I give silent acknowledgment for everything else.

Nancy Langton
July 2009

About the Authors

Stephen P. Robbins received his PhD from the University of Arizona and has taught at the University of Nebraska at Omaha, Concordia University in Montreal, the University of Baltimore, Southern Illinois University at Edwardsville, and San Diego State University. Dr. Robbins' research interests have focused on conflict, power, and politics in organizations, as well as on the development of effective interpersonal skills. His articles on these and other topics have appeared in journals such as *Business Horizons, California Management Review, Business and Economic Perspectives, International Management, Management Review, Canadian Personnel and Industrial Relations,* and *The Journal of Management Education.*

Dr. Robbins is the world's bestselling textbook author in the areas of management and organizational behaviour. His most recent textbooks include *Organizational Behavior,* 13th ed. (Prentice Hall, 2009), *Essentials of Organizational Behavior,* 9th ed. (Prentice Hall, 2008), *Fundamentals of Management,* 6th ed., with David DeCenzo (Prentice Hall, 2008), and *Supervision Today!,* 5th ed., with David DeCenzo (Prentice Hall, 2007). In addition, Dr. Robbins is the author of the global bestsellers *The Truth About Managing People,* 2nd ed. (Financial Times Press, 2008) and *Decide & Conquer* (Financial Times Press, 2004).

In his "other life," Dr. Robbins actively participates in masters' track competitions. Since turning 50 in 1993, he's won 18 national championships, won 12 world titles, and set numerous U.S. and world age-group records at 60, 100, 200, and 400 metres. In 2005, Dr. Robbins was elected into the USA Masters' Track & Field Hall of Fame.

Mary Coulter received her PhD in Management from the University of Arkansas in Fayetteville. Before completing her graduate work, she held different jobs, including high school teacher, legal assistant, and government program planner. She has taught at Drury University, the University of Arkansas, Trinity University, and, since 1983, Missouri State University. Dr. Coulter's research interests have focused on competitive strategies for not-for-profit arts organizations and the use of new media in the educational process. Her research on these and other topics has appeared in such journals as *International Journal of Business Disciplines, Journal of Business Strategies, Journal of Business Research, Journal of Nonprofit and Public Sector Marketing,* and *Case Research Journal.* In addition to *Management,* Dr. Coulter has published other books including *Strategic Management in Action,* 5th ed. (Prentice Hall, 2010) and *Entrepreneurship in Action,* 2nd ed. (Prentice Hall, 2003). When she is not busy teaching or writing, she enjoys puttering around in her flower gardens, trying new recipes, reading different types of books, and enjoying many different activities with Ron, Sarah and James, and Katie and Matt.

Nancy Langton received her PhD from Stanford University. Since completing her graduate studies, Dr. Langton has taught at the University of Oklahoma and the University of British Columbia (UBC). Currently a member of the Organizational Behaviour and Human Resources division in the Sauder School of Business, UBC, she teaches at the undergraduate, MBA, and PhD level and conducts executive programs on attracting and retaining employees, time management, family business issues, as well as women and management issues. Dr. Langton has received several major three-year research grants from the Social Sciences and Humanities Research Council of Canada, and her research interests have focused on human resource issues in the workplace, including pay equity, gender equity, and leadership and communication styles. She is currently conducting longitudinal research with entrepreneurs in the Greater Vancouver Region, trying to understand the relationship between their human resource practices and the success of their businesses. Her articles on these and other topics have appeared in such journals as *Administrative Science Quarterly, American Sociological Review, Sociological Quarterly, Journal of Management Education,* and *Gender, Work and Organizations.* She has won Best Paper

commendations from both the Academy of Management and the Administrative Sciences Association of Canada.

Dr. Langton routinely wins high marks from her students for teaching. She has been nominated many times for the Commerce Undergraduate Society Awards and has won several honourable mention plaques. She has also won the Sauder School of Business' most prestigious award for teaching innovation, The Talking Stick. The award was given for Dr. Langton's redesign of the undergraduate organizational behaviour course as well as for the many activities that were spin-offs of this effort. She was also part of the UBC MBA core design team that won the Alan Blizzard Award, a national award that recognizes innovation in teaching.

Dr. Langton's passion for teaching has taken a new direction in recent years through the Sauder School of Business's Africa Initiative. Specifically, she is the faculty advisor for Social Entrepreneurship 101 (SE101), a three-week program where UBC and Kenyan university students teach young people living in Nairobi how to write business plans. She took her fourth student team to Nairobi in summer 2009. You can read more about the project at **www.africa.sauder.ubc.ca**.

In Dr. Langton's "other life," she is fascinated with the artistry of quilting, and one day hopes to win first prize at *Visions*, the juried show for quilts as works of art. When she is not designing quilts, she is either reading novels (often suggested by a favourite correspondent), or studying cookbooks for new ideas. All of her friends would say that she makes from scratch the best pizza in all of Vancouver.

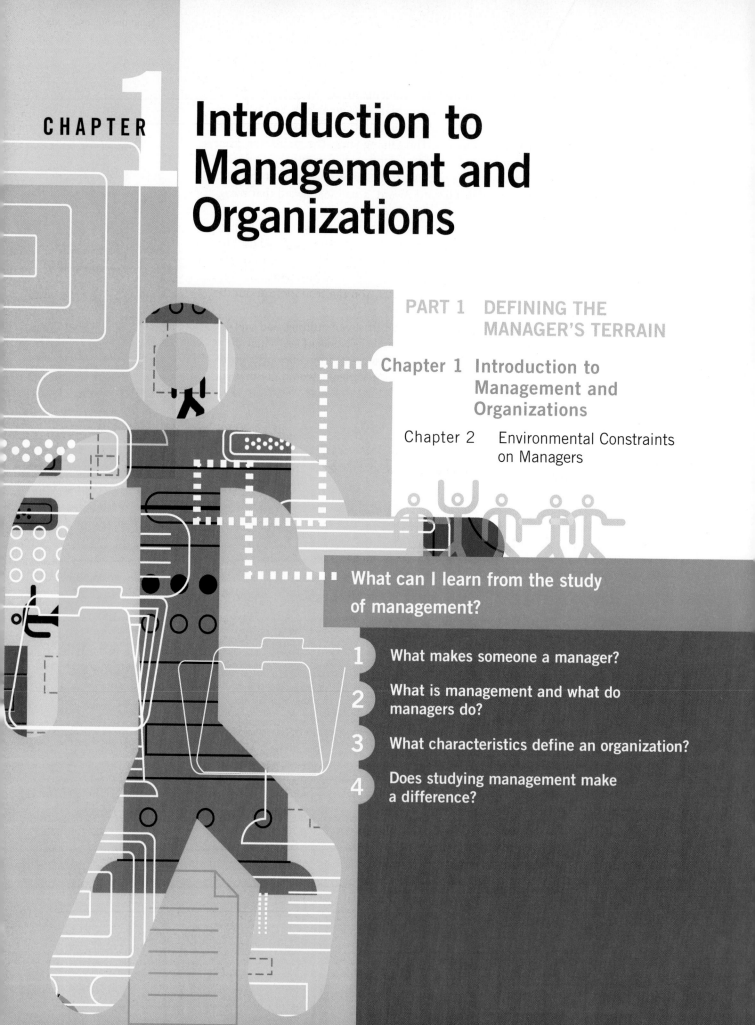

CHAPTER **1**

Introduction to Management and Organizations

**What can I learn from the study
of management?**

1 What makes someone a manager?

2 What is management and what do
managers do?

3 What characteristics define an organization?

4 Does studying management make
a difference?

Brian Scudamore was an 18-year-old university student in need of money when he founded Vancouver-based 1-800-GOT-JUNK? North America's largest junk-removal service.[1] "An inspiration came to me when I was in a McDonald's drive-through in Vancouver. I saw a beaten-up pickup truck with plywood panels advertising junk pickup and hauling."

At first, hauling junk was meant to get him through university. However, by the third year of his studies, the business had grown enough that he dropped out of school to manage it full time.

Scudamore started his business in 1989 with a $700 pickup truck, but now has over 300 franchises throughout Canada, the United States, Australia, and the United Kingdom. He says he based his business model on Federal Express, which offers on-time service and up-front rates. Drivers wear clean uniforms and drive shiny, clean trucks.

Scudamore learned about business by doing business. He also learned that it is important for managers to involve employees in decision making: "As soon as I stopped trying to be the CEO who's got everything under control, there was an instant shift," he says. "My managers started seeing me as someone they could disagree with—and that makes all of us stronger."

Think About It

What kinds of skills do managers need? Put yourself in Brian Scudamore's shoes. What kinds of leadership skills would you need to manage franchises in four countries? Does managing in a franchise organization differ from managing in a large corporation, a small business, or a government organization?

Brian Scudamore is a good example of what today's successful managers are like and the skills they must have to deal with the problems and challenges of managing in the twenty-first century. This textbook is about the important managerial work that Brian Scudamore and the millions of other managers like him do. It recognizes the reality facing today's managers—new technologies and new ways of organizing work are altering old approaches. Today's successful managers must be able to blend tried-and-true management approaches with new approaches. Throughout this and subsequent chapters, you will be introduced to a number of managers and the challenging decisions they face through the feature *Management Reflection*. You will also find *Tips for Managers* in many chapters, which presents actions managers can take in specific situations in the workplace.

In this chapter, we introduce you to managers and management by looking at who managers are, what management is, what managers do, and what an organization is. We will wrap up the chapter by discussing the challenges managers face and why it's important to study management.

○○○
○○○ # Who Are Managers?

As founder of 1-800-GOT-JUNK? Brian Scudamore manages the largest junk removal service in North America.[2] He attended Dawson College in Montreal, and then spent one year each at Concordia and the University of British Columbia studying business before dropping out to run his business full-time. Part of his job is making sure that those who run the 1-800-GOT-JUNK? franchises around the world are successful in carrying out his business model. "By relying on franchise owners to come in and share some of the risk, I realized I could expand the firm without having to turn to outside investors or other funding sources," Scudamore said. "To me, this was a solid plan for growth."

Think About It
What makes Brian Scudamore a manager?

① What makes someone a manager?

Managers may not be who or what you might expect. They're under age 18 to over age 80. They run large corporations as well as entrepreneurial start-ups. They're found in government departments, hospitals, small businesses, not-for-profit agencies, museums, schools, and even such nontraditional organizations as political campaigns and consumer cooperatives. Managers can also be found doing managerial work in every country around the globe. In addition, some managers are top-level managers, while others are first-line managers.

No matter where managers are found or what gender they are, the fact is that managers have exciting and challenging jobs. And organizations need managers more than ever in these uncertain, complex, and chaotic times. *Managers do matter!* How do we know that? The Gallup Organization, which has polled millions of employees and tens of thousands of managers, has found that the single most important variable in employee productivity and loyalty isn't pay or benefits or workplace environment; it's the quality of the relationship between employees and their direct supervisors.[3] A recent KPMG/Ipsos Reid study found that many Canadian companies that scored high in great human resource practices also scored high on financial performance and best long-term investment value.[4] In addition, global consulting firm Watson Wyatt Worldwide found that the way a company manages its people can significantly affect its financial performance.[5] We can conclude from such reports that managers *do* matter!

It used to be fairly simple to define who managers were: They were the organizational members who told others what to do and how to do it. It was easy to differentiate *managers* from *nonmanagerial employees*. But it isn't quite so simple anymore. In many organizations, the changing nature of work has blurred the distinction between managers and

Q&A 1.1

nonmanagerial employees. Many nonmanagerial jobs now include managerial activities.[6] For example, at General Cable Corporation's facility in Moose Jaw, Saskatchewan, managerial responsibilities are shared by managers and team members. Most of the employees at Moose Jaw are cross-trained and multiskilled. Within a single shift, an employee may be a team leader, an equipment operator, a maintenance technician, a quality inspector, and an improvement planner.[7]

How do we define who managers are? A **manager** is someone who works with and through other people by coordinating their work activities in order to accomplish organizational goals. A manager's job is not about *personal* achievement—it's about helping *others* do their work and achieve.

manager
Someone who works with and through other people by coordinating their work activities in order to accomplish organizational goals.

Types of Managers

Is there some way to classify managers in organizations? In traditionally structured organizations (often pictured as shaped like a pyramid in which the number of employees is greater at the bottom than at the top), managers are often described as first-line, middle, or top (see Exhibit 1-1). Identifying exactly who the managers are in these organizations isn't difficult, although they may have a variety of titles. **First-line managers** are at the lowest level of management and manage the work of nonmanagerial employees who are directly or indirectly involved with the production or creation of the organization's

first-line managers
Managers at the lowest level of the organization who manage the work of nonmanagerial employees who are directly or indirectly involved with the production or creation of the organization's products.

Exhibit 1-1

Managerial Levels

Top Managers

Middle Managers

First-Line Managers

Nonmanagerial Employees

products. They are often called *supervisors* but may also be called *shift managers, district managers, department managers,* or *office managers.* **Middle managers** include all levels of management between the first-line level and the top level of the organization. These managers manage the work of first-line managers and may have titles such as *regional manager, project leader, plant manager,* or *division manager.* At or near the top of the organization are the **top managers,** who are responsible for making organization-wide decisions and establishing the plans and goals that affect the entire organization. These individuals typically have titles such as *executive vice-president, president, managing director, chief operating officer, chief executive officer,* or *chair of the board.* In the chapter-opening case, Brian Scudamore is a top-level manager for 1-800-GOT-JUNK? He is involved in creating and implementing broad and comprehensive changes that affect the entire organization.

Not all organizations get work done using this traditional pyramidal form, however. Some organizations, for example, are more flexible and loosely structured with work being done by ever-changing teams of employees who move from one project to another as work demands arise. Although it's not as easy to tell who the managers are in these organizations, we do know that someone must fulfill that role—that is, there must be someone who works with and through other people by coordinating their work to accomplish organizational goals.

middle managers
Managers between the first-line level and the top level of the organization who manage the work of first-line managers.

top managers
Managers at or near the top level of the organization who are responsible for making organization-wide decisions and establishing the plans and goals that affect the entire organization.

Q&A 1.2

Allyson Koteski loves her job as the manager of the Toys "R" Us store in Annapolis, Maryland. She loves the chaos created by lots of kids, toys, and noise. She even loves the long and variable hours during hectic holiday seasons. Because employee turnover is a huge issue in the retail world, Allyson enjoys the challenge of keeping her employees motivated and engaged so they won't quit. And the occasional disgruntled customers don't faze her either. She patiently listens to their problems and tries to resolve them satisfactorily. That's what Allyson's life as a manager is like.

What Is Management and What Do Managers Do?

Managers plan, lead, organize, and control, and Brian Scudamore certainly carries out all of these tasks.[8] He has to coordinate the work activities of his entire company efficiently and effectively. With franchises located in four countries, he has to make sure that work is carried out consistently to protect his brand. He also has to support his managers. He does this by providing a call centre operation in Vancouver that provides all of the booking arrangements, no matter where the caller is from. This allows managers at other locations to focus on the business of picking up junk. He works on his plans to expand the business. "One of our goals at 1-800-GOT-JUNK? has been to become a globally admired company with a presence in 10 different countries by 2012." Scudamore adds, "It's important to stay focused when entering new markets. No matter how well you do your research, there will always be unexpected details that have to be managed differently."

> **Think About It**
>
> As a manager, Brian Scudamore needs to plan, lead, organize, and control, and he needs to be efficient and effective. How might Scudamore balance the needs of efficiency and effectiveness in his role as founder and CEO of 1-800-GOT-JUNK? What skills are needed for him to plan, lead, organize, and control effectively? What challenges does he face performing these functions while running an international business?

2 What is management and what do managers do?

management
Coordinating work activities so that they are completed *efficiently* and *effectively* with and through other people.

Simply speaking, management is what managers do. But that simple statement does not tell us much, does it? Here is a more thorough explanation: **Management** is coordinating work activities so that they are completed *efficiently* and *effectively* with and through other people. Management researchers have developed three specific categories to describe what managers do: functions, roles, and skills. In this section, we'll consider the challenges of balancing efficiency and effectiveness, and then examine the approaches that look at what managers do. In reviewing these categories, it might be helpful to understand that management is something that is a learned talent, rather than something that comes "naturally." Many people do not know how to be a manager when they first are appointed to that role.

Efficiency and Effectiveness

efficiency
Getting the most output from the least amount of inputs; referred to as "doing things right."

effectiveness
Completing activities so that organizational goals are achieved; referred to as "doing the right things."

Efficiency refers to getting the most output from the least amount of inputs, or as management expert Peter Drucker explained, "doing things right."[9] Because managers deal with scarce inputs—including resources such as people, money, and equipment—they are concerned with the efficient use of those resources by getting things done at the least cost.

It's not enough just to be efficient, however. Management is also concerned with being effective, completing activities so that organizational goals are achieved. **Effectiveness** is often described as "doing the right things"—that is, those work activities that will help the organization reach its goals. Hospitals might try to be efficient by reducing the number of days that patients stay in hospital. However, they may not be effective if patients get sick at home shortly after being released.

While efficiency is concerned with the means of getting things done, effectiveness is concerned with the ends, or attaining organizational goals (see Exhibit 1-2). Management is concerned, then, not only with completing activities to meet organizational goals (effectiveness), but also with doing so as efficiently as possible. In successful organizations, high efficiency and high effectiveness typically go hand in hand. Poor management is most often due to both inefficiency and ineffectiveness or to effectiveness achieved through inefficiency.

Q&A 1.3

Management Functions

According to the functions approach, managers perform certain activities or duties as they efficiently and effectively coordinate the work of others. What are these activities, or

Exhibit 1-2

Efficiency and Effectiveness in Management

Planning

If you have no particular destination in mind, then you can take any road. However, if you have someplace in particular you want to go, you have got to plan the best way to get there. Because organizations exist to achieve some particular purpose, someone must clearly define that purpose and the means for its achievement. Managers performing the **planning** function define goals, establish an overall strategy for achieving those goals, and develop plans to integrate and coordinate activities. This can be done by the CEO and senior management team for the overall organization. Middle managers often have a planning role within their units. Planning, by the way, is not just for managers. As a student, for example, you need to plan for exams and your financial needs.

Think about a manager you have had, and identify the extent to which he or she engaged in planning, organizing, leading, and controlling.

functions? In the early part of the twentieth century, French industrialist Henri Fayol first proposed that all managers perform five functions: planning, organizing, commanding, coordinating, and controlling.[10] Today, most management textbooks (including this one) are organized around four **management functions**: planning, organizing, leading, and controlling (see Exhibit 1-3). But you do not have to be a manager in order to have a need to plan, organize, lead, and control, so understanding these processes is important for everyone. Let's briefly define what each of these functions encompasses.

management functions
Planning, organizing, leading, and controlling.

planning
A management function that involves defining goals, establishing a strategy for achieving those goals, and developing plans to integrate and coordinate activities.

Exhibit 1-3

Management Functions

Planning	Organizing	Leading	Controlling	Lead to
Defining goals, establishing strategy, and developing subplans to coordinate activities	Determining what needs to be done, how it will be done, and who is to do it	Directing and motivating all involved parties and resolving conflicts	Monitoring activities to ensure that they are accomplished as planned	Achieving the organization's stated purpose

Organizing

organizing
A management function that involves determining what tasks are to be done, who is to do them, how the tasks are to be grouped, who reports to whom, and where decisions are to be made.

Managers are also responsible for arranging work to accomplish the organization's goals. We call this function **organizing**. When managers organize, they determine what tasks are to be done, who is to do them, how the tasks are to be grouped, who reports to whom (that is, they define authority relationships), and where decisions are to be made. When you work in a student group, you engage in some of these same organizing activities—deciding on a division of labour, and what tasks will be carried out to get an assignment completed.

Leading

leading
A management function that involves motivating subordinates, directing the work of individuals or teams, selecting the most effective communication channels, and resolving employee behaviour issues.

Every organization contains people. Part of a manager's job is to work with and through people to accomplish organizational goals. This is the **leading** function. When managers motivate subordinates, direct the work of individuals or teams, select the most effective communication channel, or resolve behaviour issues, they are leading. Knowing how to manage and lead effectively is an important, and sometimes difficult, skill as it requires the ability to successfully communicate. Leading is not just for managers, however. As a student, you might want to practise leadership skills when working in groups or club activities. You might also want to evaluate whether you need to improve your leadership skills in anticipation of the needs of future jobs.

Controlling

controlling
A management function that involves monitoring actual performance, comparing actual performance to a standard, and taking corrective action when necessary.

The final management function is **controlling**. After the goals are set (planning), the plans formulated (planning), the structural arrangements determined (organizing), and the people hired, trained, and motivated (leading), there has to be some evaluation of whether things are going as planned (controlling). To ensure that work is going as it should, managers must monitor and evaluate employees' performance. Actual performance must be compared with the previously set goals. If performance of individuals or units does not match the goals set, it's the manager's job to get performance back on track. This process of monitoring, comparing, and correcting is what we mean by the controlling function. Individuals, whether working in groups or alone, also face the responsibility of controlling; that is, they must make sure the goals and actions are achieved and take corrective action when necessary.

Just how well does the functions approach describe what managers do? Do managers always plan, organize, lead, and then control? In reality, what a manager does may not always happen in this logical and sequential order. But that does not negate the importance of the basic functions that managers perform. Regardless of the order in which the functions are performed, the fact is that managers do plan, organize, lead, and control as they manage.

The continued popularity of the functions approach is a tribute to its clarity and simplicity. But some have argued that this approach is not appropriate or relevant.[11] So let's look at another perspective.

Management Roles

management roles
Specific categories of managerial behaviour.

interpersonal roles
Management roles that involve working with people or performing duties that are ceremonial and symbolic in nature.

Henry Mintzberg, a prominent management researcher at McGill University, has studied actual managers at work. He says that what managers do can best be understood by looking at the roles they play at work. His studies allowed him to conclude that managers perform 10 different but highly interrelated management roles.[12] The term **management roles** refers to specific categories of managerial behaviour. (Think of the different roles you play and the different behaviours you are expected to perform in the roles of student, sibling, employee, volunteer, and so forth.) As shown in Exhibit 1-4, Mintzberg's 10 management roles are grouped around interpersonal relationships, the transfer of information, and decision making.

The **interpersonal roles** involve working with people (subordinates and persons outside the organization) or performing duties that are ceremonial and symbolic in nature. The three interpersonal roles include being a figurehead, leader, and liaison. The informational

Exhibit 1-4

Mintzberg's Management Roles

Role	Description	Examples of Identifiable Activities
Interpersonal		
Figurehead	Symbolic head; obliged to perform a number of routine duties of a legal or social nature	Greeting visitors; signing legal documents
Leader	Responsible for the motivation of subordinates; responsible for staffing, training, and associated duties	Performing virtually all activities that involve subordinates
Liaison	Maintains self-developed network of outside contacts and informers who provide favours and information	Acknowledging mail; doing external board work; performing other activities that involve outsiders
Informational		
Monitor	Seeks and receives a wide variety of internal and external information to develop a thorough understanding of organization and environment	Reading periodicals and reports; maintaining personal contacts
Disseminator	Transmits information received from outsiders or from subordinates to members of the organization	Holding informational meetings; making phone calls to relay information
Spokesperson	Transmits information to outsiders on organization's plans, policies, actions, results, etc.	Holding board meetings; giving information to the media
Decisional		
Entrepreneur	Searches organization and its environment for opportunities and initiates "improvement projects" to bring about changes	Organizing strategy and review sessions to develop new programs
Disturbance handler	Responsible for corrective action when organization faces important, unexpected disturbances	Organizing strategy and review sessions that involve disturbances and crises
Resource allocator	Responsible for the allocation of organizational resources of all kinds—making or approving all significant organizational decisions	Scheduling; requesting authorization; performing any activity that involves budgeting and the programming of subordinates' work
Negotiator	Responsible for representing the organization at major negotiations	Participating in union contract negotiations

Source: H. Mintzberg, *The Nature of Managerial Work* (New York: Harper and Row, 1973), pp. 93–94. Copyright © 1973 by Henry Mintzberg. Reprinted by permission of Harper & Row, Publishers, Inc.

roles involve receiving, collecting, and disseminating information. The three **informational roles** include monitor, disseminator, and spokesperson. Finally, the **decisional roles** involve making significant choices that affect the organization. The four decisional roles include entrepreneur, disturbance handler, resource allocator, and negotiator.

Functions vs. Roles

So which approach to describing what managers do is correct—functions or roles? Each has merit. However, the functions approach still represents the most useful way of conceptualizing the manager's job. "The classical functions provide clear and discrete methods of classifying the thousands of activities that managers carry out and the techniques they use in terms of the functions they perform for the achievement of goals."[13] Many of Mintzberg's roles align well with one or more of the functions. For example, resource allocation is part of planning, as is the entrepreneurial role, and all three of the interpersonal roles are part of the leading function. Although most of the other roles fit into one or more of the four functions, not all of them do. The difference can be explained by the fact that all managers do some work that is not purely managerial.[14]

informational roles
Management roles that involve receiving, collecting, and disseminating information.

decisional roles
Management roles that involve making significant choices that affect the organization.

Management Skills

Dell Inc. is one company that understands the importance of management skills.[15] It started an intensive five-day offsite skills training program for first-line managers as a way to improve its operations. One of Dell's directors of learning and development thought this was the best way to develop "leaders who can build that strong relationship with their front-line employees." What have the supervisors learned from the skills training? Some things they have mentioned were how to communicate more effectively and how to refrain from jumping to conclusions when discussing a problem with a worker.

What types of skills does a manager need? Research by Robert L. Katz found that managers needed three essential skills: technical skills, human skills, and conceptual skills.[16]

technical skills
Knowledge of and expertise in a specialized field.

Technical skills include knowledge of and expertise in a certain specialized field, such as engineering, computers, accounting, or manufacturing. These skills are more important at lower levels of management since these managers are dealing directly with employees doing the organization's work.

human skills
The ability to work well with other people both individually and in a group.

Human skills involve the ability to work well with other people both individually and in a group. Because managers deal directly with people, this skill is crucial! Managers with good human skills are able to get the best out of their people. They know how to communicate, motivate, lead, and inspire enthusiasm and trust. These skills are equally important at all levels of management. According to management professor Jin Nam Choi, of McGill University, 40 percent of managers either leave or stop performing within 18 months of starting at an organization "because they have failed to develop relationships with bosses, colleagues or subordinates."[17] Choi's comment underscores the importance of developing human skills.

conceptual skills
The mental ability to analyze and generate ideas about abstract and complex situations.

Finally, **conceptual skills** refer to the mental ability to analyze and generate ideas about abstract and complex situations. These skills help managers see the organization as a whole, understand the relationships among various subunits, and visualize how the organization fits into its broader environment. These skills are most important at the top manager level. Exhibit 1-5 shows the relationship of the three skills to each level of management. Note that the three skills are important to more than one level. Additionally, in very flat organizations, with little hierarchy, human, technical, and conceptual skills would be needed throughout the organization.

As you study the management functions in more depth, the exercises in *Developing Your Diagnostic and Analytical Skills* and *Developing Your Interpersonal Skills*, found at the end of most chapters, will give you the opportunity to practise some of the key skills that are part of doing what a manager does. Skill-building exercises cannot make you an instant managerial expert, but they can provide you with a basic understanding of some of the skills you will need to master to become an effective manager. To learn more about becoming a better mentor, see *Developing Your Interpersonal Skills—Mentoring* on pages 20–21, at the end of the chapter.

Exhibit 1-5

Skills Needed at Different Management Levels

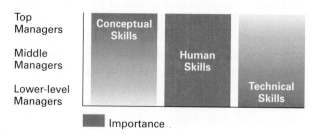

What Is an Organization?

Brian Scudamore is the founder of 1-800-GOT-JUNK?. Though he has a board of advisors, he is the sole shareholder of the company. Therefore he gets to set his own plans and goals. The company has over 250 franchises in four countries, which means his management skills have to include awareness of the challenges of managing in other countries.

Think About It

Do managers act differently when they work for large organizations rather than smaller ones? How does owning a franchise business affect the role of the manager?

Managers work in organizations. But what is an organization? An **organization** is a deliberate arrangement of people who act together to accomplish some specific purpose. Your college or university is an organization; so are fraternities and sororities, government departments, churches, Amazon.ca, your neighbourhood video store, the United Way, the Toronto Raptors basketball team, and the Hudson's Bay Company. These are all organizations because they have three common characteristics, as shown in Exhibit 1-6:

- *Distinct purpose.* This purpose is typically expressed in terms of a goal or a set of goals that the organization hopes to accomplish.

- *People.* One person working alone is not an organization. It takes people to perform the work that is necessary for the organization to achieve its goals.

- *Deliberate structure.* Whether that structure is open and flexible or traditional and clearly defined, the structure defines members' work relationships.

In summary, the term *organization* refers to an entity that has a distinct purpose, includes people or members, and has some type of deliberate structure.

Although these three characteristics are important to our definition of *what* an organization is, the concept of an organization is changing. It is no longer appropriate to assume that all organizations are going to be structured like Air Canada, Petro-Canada, or General Motors, with clearly identifiable divisions, departments, and work units. Just how is the concept of an organization changing? Exhibit 1-7 on page 12 lists some differences between traditional organizations and new organizations. As these lists show, today's organizations are becoming more open, flexible, and responsive to change.[18]

3 What characteristics define an organization?

organization
A deliberate arrangement of people who act together to accomplish some specific purpose.

Exhibit 1-6

Characteristics of Organizations

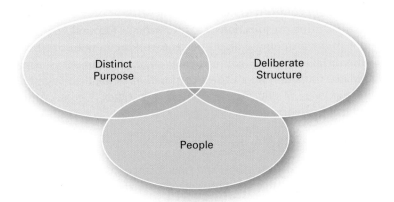

Exhibit 1-7

The Changing Organization

Traditional Organization	New Organization
• Stable	• Dynamic
• Inflexible	• Flexible
• Job-focused	• Skills-focused
• Work is defined by job positions	• Work is defined in terms of tasks to be done
• Individual-oriented	• Team-oriented
• Permanent jobs	• Temporary jobs
• Command-oriented	• Involvement-oriented
• Managers always make decisions	• Employees participate in decision making
• Rule-oriented	• Customer-oriented
• Relatively homogeneous workforce	• Diverse workforce
• Workdays defined as 9 to 5	• Workdays have no time boundaries
• Hierarchical relationships	• Lateral and networked relationships
• Work at organizational facility during specific hours	• Work anywhere, anytime

Does your college or university or an organization in which you have worked represent a "new organization"? Why or why not?

Why are organizations changing? Because the world around them has changed and continues to change. Societal, economic, political, global, and technological changes have created an environment in which successful organizations (those that consistently attain their goals) must embrace new ways of getting work done. As we stated earlier, even though the concept of an organization may be changing, managers and management continue to be important to organizations.

The Size of Organizations

Managers do not just manage in large organizations, which represent only about 2 percent of all organizations in Canada. Small businesses (those that employ fewer than 100 individuals) represent 98 percent of all Canadian companies. These businesses employ almost half of all Canadian workers. Small businesses also contribute significantly to the economy. Businesses employing 50 or fewer individuals generated about 22 percent of total GDP in 2005.[19] Organizations of every size need managers. Moreover, in 2007, about 16 percent of the labour force was self-employed, meaning that these people were managing themselves.[20]

Managers are also not confined to manufacturing work, as only 13 percent of Canadians work in manufacturing organizations. Most Canadians (around 76 percent) work in the service sector of the economy, with 19 percent working in public sector jobs (those in the local, provincial, or federal government).[21] The government is actually a large employer in Canada. Canada Post, a Crown corporation, is the fifth-largest employer in Canada, employing over 77 000 people, behind only Onex, George Weston, Loblaw Companies, and Magna International.[22]

The Types of Organizations

Managers work in a variety of situations, and thus the people to whom they are held accountable vary considerably. Large organizations in the **private sector** are often **publicly held**, which means that their shares are available on the stock exchange for public trading. Managers of publicly held companies report to a board of directors that is responsible to

private sector
The part of the economy that is run by organizations that are free from direct government control; operations in this sector operate to make a profit.

publicly held organization
A company whose shares are available on the stock exchange for public trading by brokers/dealers.

Canada Post is a Crown corporation that has been in operation for more than 150 years. Its 77 000+ full- and part-time employees run the country's most extensive distribution network, which includes 6600 postal outlets, 20 sorting plants, 500 letter carrier depots, and about 6800 vehicles.

shareholders (also known as stockholders). There are also numerous **privately held organizations** (whose shares are not available on the stock exchange), both large and small. Privately held organizations can be individually owned, family-owned, or owned by some other group of individuals. A number of managers work in the **nonprofit sector**, where the emphasis is on providing charity or services rather than on making a profit. Examples of such organizations include the SPCA (Society for the Prevention of Cruelty to Animals), Toronto's Royal Ontario Museum, and Vancouver's Bard on the Beach Festival. Other organizational forms such as **NGO**s (nongovernmental organizations), partnerships, and cooperatives also require managers.

Many managers work in the **public sector** as **civil servants** for the local, provincial, or federal government. The challenges of managing within government departments can be quite different from the challenges of managing in publicly held organizations. Critics argue that it is less demanding to work for governments because there are few measurable performance objectives, allowing employees to feel less accountable for their actions.

Some managers and employees work for **Crown corporations** such as Canada Post, the CBC, and the Business Development Bank of Canada. Crown corporations are structured like private sector corporations and have boards of directors, CEOs, and so on, but are owned by governments rather than shareholders. Employees in Crown corporations are not civil servants, and managers in Crown corporations are more independent than the senior bureaucrats who manage government departments.

Many of Canada's larger organizations are actually subsidiaries of American parent organizations (e.g., Sears, Safeway, General Motors, and Ford Motor Company). Their managers often report to American top managers, and are not always free to set their own goals and targets. Conflicts can arise when Canadian managers and the American managers to whom they report do not agree on how things should be done.

privately held organizations
Companies whose shares are not available on the stock exchange but are privately held.

nonprofit sector
The part of the economy that is run by organizations that operate for purposes other than making a profit (that is, providing charity or services).

NGO
A nongovernmental organization that emphasizes humanitarian issues, development, and sustainability.

public sector
The part of the economy that is directly controlled by government.

civil servants
People who work in a local, provincial, or federal government department.

Crown corporations
Commercial companies owned by the government but independently managed.

Why Study Management?

You may be wondering why you need to study management. If you are an accounting major, a marketing major, or any major other than management, you may not understand how studying management is going to help you in your career. We can explain the value of studying management by looking at the universality of management, the reality of work, and how management applies to anyone wanting to be self-employed.

4 Does studying management make a difference?

Q&A 1.4

Exhibit 1-8

Universal Need for Management

The Universality of Management

Just how universal is the need for management in organizations? We can say with absolute certainty that management is needed in all types and sizes of organizations, at all organizational levels, in all organizational work areas, and in all organizations, no matter what countries they are located in. This is known as the **universality of management** (see Exhibit 1-8). Managers in all these settings will plan, organize, lead, and control. However, this is not to say that management is done the same way in all settings. The differences in what a supervisor in a software applications–testing facility at Microsoft does versus what the CEO of Microsoft does are a matter of degree and emphasis, not of function. Because both are managers, both will plan, organize, lead, and control, but how they do so will differ.

Since management is universally needed in all organizations, we have a vested interest in improving the way organizations are managed. Why? We interact with organizations every single day of our lives. Are you irritated when none of the salespeople in a department store seems interested in helping you? Do you get annoyed when you call your computer's technical help desk because your CD-ROM drive is no longer working, go through seven voice menus, and then get put on hold for 15 minutes? These are examples of problems created by poor management. Organizations that are well managed—and we will share many examples of these—develop a loyal customer base, grow, and prosper. Those that are poorly managed find themselves with a declining customer base and reduced revenues. By studying management, you will be able to recognize poor management and work to get it corrected. In addition, you will be able to recognize good management and encourage it, whether it's in an organization with which you are simply interacting or whether it's in an organization in which you are employed.

The Reality of Work

Another reason for studying management is the reality that most of you, once you graduate and begin your careers, will either manage or be managed. For those who plan on management careers, an understanding of the management process forms the foundation on which to build your management skills. For those of you who do not see yourselves in management positions, you are still likely to have to work with managers. Also, assuming that you will have to work for a living and recognizing that you are very likely

universality of management
The reality that management is needed in all types and sizes of organizations, at all organizational levels, in all organizational work areas, and in organizations in all countries around the globe.

to work in an organization, you will probably have some managerial responsibilities even if you are not managers. Our experience tells us that you can gain a great deal of insight into the way your manager behaves and the internal workings of organizations by studying management. Our point is that you do not have to aspire to be a manager to gain something valuable from a course in management.

Self-Employment

You may decide that you want to run your own business rather than work for someone else. This will require that you manage yourself, and may involve managing other people as well. Thus, an understanding of management is equally important, whether you are a manager in someone else's business or running your own business. To find out whether management might be something of interest to you, see *Self-Assessment—How Motivated Am I to Manage?* on pages 16–17, at the end of the chapter.

SUMMARY AND IMPLICATIONS

1 **What makes someone a manager?** Managers work with and through other people by coordinating employee work activity in order to accomplish organizational goals. Managers may have personal goals, but management is not about *personal* achievement— it's about helping *others* achieve for the benefit of the organization as a whole.

As we saw with Brian Scudamore, he sees his role as a cheerleader to help everyone in the organization do a better job.

2 **What is management and what do managers do?** Management is coordinating work activities of people so that they are done efficiently and effectively. Efficiency means "doing things right" and getting things done at the least cost. Effectiveness means "doing the right things" and completing activities that will help achieve the organization's goals. To do their jobs, managers plan, organize, lead, and control. This means they set goals and plan how to achieve those goals; they figure out what tasks need to be done, and who should do them; they motivate individuals to achieve goals, and communicate effectively with others; and they put accountability measures into place to make sure that goals are achieved efficiently and effectively.

In Brian Scudamore's role as CEO of 1-800-GOT-JUNK? he sets the goals for the overall organization, working with the various franchise partners. One of the challenges he faces is determining how rapidly his company can expand without diluting its brand.

3 **What characteristics define an organization?** There is no single type of organization. Managers work in a variety of organizations, both large and small. They also work in a variety of industries, including manufacturing and the service sector. The organizations they work for can be publicly held (meaning shares are traded on the stock exchange and managers are responsible to shareholders), privately held (meaning shares are not available to the public), public sector (where the government is the employer), or nonprofit (where the emphasis is on providing charity or services rather than on making a profit).

Brian Scudamore owns his company and thus is ultimately responsible to himself. Most managers report to someone else.

4 **Does studying management make a difference?** There are many reasons why students end up in management courses. Some of you are already managers and are hoping to learn more about the subject. Some of you hope to be managers someday. And some of you might not have ever thought about being managers. Career aspirations are only one reason to study management, however. Any organization you encounter will have managers, and it is often useful to understand their responsibilities, challenges, and experiences. Understanding management also helps us improve organizations.

Snapshot Summary

1 Who Are Managers?
Types of Managers

2 What Is Management and What Do Managers Do?
Efficiency and Effectiveness
Management Functions
Management Roles
Management Skills

3 What Is an Organization?
The Size of Organizations
The Types of Organizations

4 Why Study Management?
The Universality of Management
The Reality of Work
Self-Employment

Management @ Work

READING FOR COMPREHENSION

1. How does a manager's job change with his or her level in the organization?

2. What four common activities compose the functions approach to management? Briefly describe each of them.

3. What are the three categories of management roles proposed by Mintzberg? Provide an example of each.

4. What are the three skills that affect managerial effectiveness?

5. What is an organization? Why are managers important to an organization's success?

LINKING CONCEPTS TO PRACTICE

1. Are effective organizations always efficient? Discuss. If you had to choose between being effective or being efficient, which would you say is more important? Why?

2. In today's economic environment, which is more important to organizations—efficiency or effectiveness? Explain your choice.

3. Contrast planning, organizing, leading, and controlling with Mintzberg's 10 management roles.

4. Is your instructor a manager? Discuss in terms of planning, organizing, leading, and controlling, and of Mintzberg's managerial roles.

5. In what ways would the job activities of an owner of an automotive repair shop that employs two people and the president of the Ford Motor Company be similar? In what ways would they be different?

6. Some individuals today have the title of project leader. They manage projects of various sizes and durations and must coordinate the talents of many people to accomplish their goals, but none of the employees on their projects reports directly to them. Can these project leaders really be considered managers if they have no employees over whom they have direct authority? Discuss.

SELF-ASSESSMENT

How Motivated Am I to Manage?

For each of the following statements, circle the level of agreement or disagreement that you personally feel:[23]

1 = Strongly Disagree 2 = Moderately Disagree 3 = Slightly Disagree 4 = Neither Agree nor Disagree
5 = Slightly Agree 6 = Moderately Agree 7 = Strongly Agree

1. I have a generally positive attitude toward those holding positions of authority over me.   1 2 3 4 5 6 7

2. I enjoy competition and striving to win for myself and my work group.   1 2 3 4 5 6 7

3. I like to tell others what to do and have no problem with imposing sanctions to enforce my directives.   1 2 3 4 5 6 7

4. I like being active, assertive, and protecting the members of my work group.   1 2 3 4 5 6 7

5. I enjoy the idea of standing out from the group, behaving in a unique manner, and being highly visible.   1 2 3 4 5 6 7

6. I am willing to perform routine, day-to-day administrative tasks and duties.   1 2 3 4 5 6 7

Scoring Key

Add up your responses to the six items.

Analysis and Interpretation

Not everyone is motivated to perform managerial functions. This instrument taps six components that have been found to be related to managerial success, especially in larger organizations. These are a favourable attitude toward authority; a desire to compete; a desire to exercise power; assertiveness; a desire for a distinctive position; and a willingness to engage in repetitive tasks.

Scores on this instrument will range from 6 to 42. Arbitrary cut-offs suggest that scores of 6 to 18 indicate low motivation to manage; 19 to 29 is moderate motivation; and 30 and above is high motivation.

What meaning can you draw from your score? It gives you an idea of how comfortable you would be doing managerial activities. Note, however, that this instrument emphasizes tasks associated with managing in larger and more bureaucratic organizations. A low or moderate score may indicate that you are more suited to managing in a small firm, in an organic organization, or in entrepreneurial situations.

More Self-Assessments

To learn more about your skills, abilities, and interests, take the following self-assessments on MyManagementLab at www.pearsoned.ca/mymanagementlab:

- I.A.4.—How Well Do I Handle Ambiguity?
- I.E.1.—What's My Emotional Intelligence Score?
- I.E.4.—Am I Likely to Become an Entrepreneur?
- III.C.1.—How Well Do I Respond to Turbulent Change? (This exercise also appears in Chapter 12 on pages 379–380.)

MANAGEMENT FOR YOU TODAY

Dilemma

Think about where you hope to be in your life five years from now (that is, your major goal). What is your competitive advantage for achieving your goal? What do you need to plan, organize, lead, and control to make sure that you reach your goal? Looking over Mintzberg's management roles (Exhibit 1-4, on page 9), which roles seem comfortable for you? What areas need improvement?

Becoming a Manager

- Keep up with the current business news.
- Read books about good and bad examples of managing.
- Observe managers and how they handle people and situations.
- Talk to actual managers about their experiences—good and bad.
- In other classes you take, see what ideas and concepts potentially relate to being a good manager.
- Get experience in managing by taking on leadership roles in student organizations.
- Start thinking about whether or not you would enjoy being a manager.
- Stay informed about the current trends and issues facing managers.

WORKING TOGETHER: TEAM-BASED EXERCISE

A New Beginning

By this time in your life, all of you have had to work with individuals in managerial positions (or maybe you were the manager), either through work experiences or through other organizational experiences (social, hobby/interest, religious, and so forth). What do you think makes some managers better than others? Are there certain characteristics that distinguish good managers? Form small groups of 3 or 4 class members. Discuss your experiences with managers—good and bad. Draw up a list of the characteristics of those individuals you felt were good managers. For each characteristic, indicate which management function (planning, leading, organizing, controlling) you think it falls under. Also identify which of Mintzberg's 10 roles the good managers seemed to fill. Were any of the roles missing from your list of characteristics? What explanation can you give for this? As a group, be prepared to explain the functions and roles that good managers are most likely to fill.

ETHICS IN ACTION

Ethical Dilemma Exercise: Are Canadian Executives Paid Too Much?

Are we paying executives too much? Is an average salary in 2007 in excess of $10 million justifiable?[24] In any debate, there are two sides to the issue. One fact that supports paying this amount is that CEOs of large organizations have tremendous organizational responsibilities. They not only have to manage the organization in today's environment, but also must keep it moving into the future. Their jobs are not 9-to-5 jobs, but rather 6 to 7 days a week, often 10 to 14 hours a day. If jobs are evaluated on the basis of skills, knowledge, abilities, and responsibilities, executives should be highly paid.[25] Furthermore, there is the issue of motivation and retention. If you want these individuals to succeed and stay with the company, you must provide a compensation package that motivates them to stay. Incentives based on various measures also provide the impetus for them to excel.

Most of the research done on executive salaries questions the link to performance. Even when profits are down, many executives are paid handsomely. In fact, Canadian corporate executives are some of the most highly paid people in the world (although American CEOs are paid more). Additionally, pay does not always seem directly related to performance.[26] Canada's 100 highest-paid CEOs include big bank CEOs, even though in 2008 their banks received billions in bailout money from the federal government to purchase mortgage loans. As Roger Martin, dean of the Rotman School of Management at the University of Toronto, notes, "A lot of the CEOs have a compensation formula that still compensates them wonderfully while they're not creating value or even [when they are] destroying value—laying off people and the like."[27]

Do you believe that Canadian executives are overpaid? Explain your opinion.

Thinking Critically About Ethics

How far should a manager go to achieve efficiency or effectiveness? Suppose that you are the catering manager at a local country club and you are asked by the club manager to lie about information you have on your work group's efficiency. Suppose that by lying you will save an employee's job. Is that okay? Is lying always wrong, or might it be acceptable under certain circumstances? What, if any, would those circumstances be? What about simply misrepresenting information that you have? Is that always wrong, or might it be acceptable under certain circumstances? When does "misrepresenting" become "lying"?

CASE APPLICATION

Lipschultz Levin & Gray

You might be surprised to find the passionate emphasis placed on people at an accounting firm.[28] Yet at Lipschultz Levin & Gray (**www.thethinkers.com**), self-described "head bean counter" Steven P. Siegel recognizes that his people make the organization. He describes his primary responsibility as ensuring that LLG's clients have the best professionals working for them. And the best way to do this, Siegel feels, is by developing the creativity, talent, and diversity of its staff so that new knowledge can be acquired and shared without getting hung up on formal organizational relationships or having employees shut away in corner offices.

The commitment to its people starts with the company's mission, which says,

LLG's goal is to be the pre-eminent provider of the highest quality accounting, tax and consulting services. LLG accomplishes this goal by leaving no stone unturned in exploring new and superior alternatives of supplying our services, and developing such methods on a global basis. Our environment promotes creativity, individual development, group interchange, diversity, good humor, family and community, all for the purpose of assisting in our clients' growth.

To further demonstrate that commitment, Siegel has implemented several significant changes at LLG. Because he is convinced that people do their best intellectual work in nontraditional settings, every telltale sign of what most people consider boring, dull accounting work has been eliminated. None of the firm's employees or partners has an office or desk to call his or her own. Instead, everyone is part of a nomadic arrangement in which stuff (files, phones, laptops) is wheeled to a new spot every day. Everywhere you look in the company's office, you see versatility, comfort, and individuality. For instance, a miniature golf course is located in the middle of everything. The motivation behind this open office design is to create opportunities for professionals to gather—on purpose or by accident—without walls, cubicles, or offices to get in the way.

Visitors to LLG realize that the firm is different as soon as they walk in the door. A giant, wall-mounted abacus (remember the image of bean counters) decorates the interior. And visitors are greeted by a "Welcome Wall" with a big-screen television that flashes a continuous slide show of one-liners about business, life, and innovation. The setting may be fun and lighthearted, but the LLG team is seriously committed to serving its clients. So serious, in fact, that they state,

> We have one goal. To "Delight" you. Good, even great, is not enough any more. We will "Dazzle" you and we will guarantee it; We will deliver our service with integrity, honesty and openness in everything we do

for you and with you; We will absolutely respect the confidentiality of our working relationship; We will return your phone calls, facsimiles and e-mails within 24 hours; We will always provide exceptional service, designed to help you add significant value to your business; We will meet the deadlines we set together with you; We will communicate with you frequently, building a win-win relationship with you; You will always know in advance our fee arrangement for any service.

Yesterday, one of Siegel's new employees complained in an email to him that the work environment is too informal and that employees need their own desks. This employee has done well in her first few months on the job. Siegel is meeting with her in an hour. What should he say to her?

DEVELOPING YOUR DIAGNOSTIC AND ANALYTICAL SKILLS

Managing the Virus Hunters

Imagine what life would be like if your product were never finished, if your work were never done, if your market shifted 30 times a day.[29] The computer-virus hunters at Symantec don't have to imagine. That is the reality of their daily work life. At the company's Response Lab in Santa Monica, California, described as the "dirtiest of all our networks at Symantec," software analysts collect viruses and other suspicious code and try to figure out how they work so security updates can be provided to the company's customers. By the door to the lab, there is even a hazardous materials box marked "Danger," where they put all the discs, tapes, and hard drives with the nasty viruses that need to be carefully and completely disposed of. Symantec's situation may seem unique, but the company, which makes content and network security software for both consumers and businesses, reflects the realities facing many organizations today: quickly shifting customer expectations and continuously emerging global competitors that have drastically shortened product life cycles. Managing talented people in such an environment can be quite challenging as well.

Vincent Weafer, a native of Ireland, has been the leader of Symantec's virus-hunting team since 1999. Back then, he said, "There were less than two dozen people, and . . . nothing really happened. We'd see maybe five new viruses a day, and they would spread in a matter of months, not minutes." Now, Symantec's virus hunters around the world deal with some 20 000 virus samples each month, not all of which are unique, stand-alone viruses. To make the hunters' jobs even more interesting, computer attacks are increasingly

being spread by criminals wanting to steal information, whether corporate data or personal user account information that can be used in fraud. The response-centre team is a diverse group whose members were not easy to find. Says Weafer, "It's not as if colleges are creating thousands of anti-malware or security experts every year that we can hire. If you find them in any part of the world, you just go after them." The response-centre team's makeup reflects that. One senior researcher is from Hungary; another is from Iceland; and another works out of her home in Melbourne, Florida. But they all share something in common: They are all motivated by solving problems.

The launch of the Blaster.B worm changed the company's approach to dealing with viruses. The domino effect of Blaster.B and other viruses spawned by it meant the front-line software analysts were working around the clock for almost two weeks. The "employee burnout" potential made the company realize that its virus-hunting team would now have to be much deeper talent-wise. Now, the response centre's team numbers in the hundreds, and managers can rotate people from the front lines, where they are responsible for responding to new security threats that crop up, into groups where they can help with new-product development. Others write internal research papers. Still others are assigned to develop new tools that will help their colleagues battle the next wave of threats. There is even an individual who tries to figure out what makes the virus writers tick—and the day never ends for these virus hunters. When Santa Monica's team finishes its day, colleagues in Tokyo take over. When the Japanese team finishes its day, it hands off to Dublin, who then hands back to Santa Monica for the new day. It's a frenetic, chaotic, challenging work environment that spans the entire globe. But Weafer says his goals are to "try to take the chaos out, to make the exciting boring," to have a predictable and well-defined process for dealing with the virus threats, and to spread work evenly among the company's facilities around the world. It's a managerial challenge that Weafer has embraced.

Questions

1. Keeping professionals excited about work that is routine and standardized *and* chaotic is a major challenge for Vincent Weafer. How could he use technical, human, and conceptual skills to maintain an environment that encourages innovation and professionalism among the virus hunters?

2. What management roles is Weafer playing as he (a) has weekly security briefing conference calls with co-workers around the globe, (b) assesses the feasibility of adding a new network security consulting service, and (c) keeps employees focused on the company's commitments to customers?

3. Go to Symantec's website (**www.symantec.com**) and look up information about the company. What can you tell about its emphasis on customer service and innovation? In what ways does the organization support its employees in servicing customers and being innovative?

4. What could other managers learn from Weafer's and Symantec's approach?

DEVELOPING YOUR INTERPERSONAL SKILLS

Mentoring

About the Skill

A mentor is someone in the organization, usually older, more experienced, and in a higher-level position, who sponsors or supports another employee (a protégé) who is in a lower-level position in the organization. A mentor can teach, guide, and encourage. Some organizations have formal mentoring programs, but even if your organization does not, mentoring should be an important skill for you to develop.

Steps in Developing the Skill

You can be more effective at mentoring if you use the following six suggestions as you mentor another person:[30]

1. **Communicate honestly and openly with your protégé.** If your protégé is going to learn from you and benefit from your experience and knowledge, you are going to have to be open and honest as you talk about what you have done. Bring up the failures as well as the successes. Remember that mentoring is a learning process, and in order for learning to take place you are going to have to be open and honest in "telling it like it is."

2. **Encourage honest and open communication from your protégé.** As the mentor, you need to know what your protégé hopes to gain from this relationship. You should encourage the protégé to ask for information and be specific about what he or she wants to gain.

3. **Treat the relationship with the protégé as a learning opportunity.** Do not pretend to have all the answers and all the knowledge, but do share what you have learned through your experiences. In your conversations and interactions with your protégé, you may be able to learn as much from that person as he or she does from you. So be open to listening to what your protégé has to say.

4. **Take the time to get to know your protégé.** As a mentor, you should be willing to take the time to get to know your protégé and his or her interests. If you are not willing to spend that extra time, you should probably not embark on a mentoring relationship.

5. **Remind your protégé that there is no substitute for effective work performance.** In any job, effective work performance is absolutely essential for success. It does not matter how much information you provide as a mentor if the protégé is not willing to strive for effective work performance.

6. **Know when it's time to let go.** Successful mentors know when it's time to let the protégé begin standing on his or her own. If the mentoring relationship has been effective, the protégé will be comfortable and confident in handling new and increasing work responsibilities. Just because the mentoring relationship is over does not mean that you never have contact with your protégé. It just means that the relationship becomes one of equals, not one of teacher and student.

Practising the Skill

Lora Slovinsky has worked for your department in a software design firm longer than any other of your employees. You value her skills and commitment, and you frequently ask for her judgment on difficult issues. Very often, her ideas have been better than yours and you have let her know through both praise and pay increases how much you appreciate her contributions. Recently, though, you have begun to question Lora's judgment. The fundamental problem is in the distinct difference in the ways you each approach your work. Your strengths lie in getting things done on time and under budget. Although Lora is aware of these constraints, her creativity and perfectionism sometimes make her prolong projects, continuously looking for the best approaches. On her most recent assignment, Lora seemed more intent than ever on doing things her way. Despite what you felt were clear guidelines, she was two weeks late in meeting an important customer deadline. While her product quality was high, as always, the software design was far more elaborate than what was needed at this stage of development. Looking over her work in your office, you feel more than a little frustrated and certain that you need to address matters with Lora. What will you say?

History of Management Trends

Walk down almost any street in Vancouver, and you will spot a number of people carrying paper cups of coffee, picked up from one of the many local coffee shops found on many corners.[1] Per-capita coffee consumption in Canada is high—an average of 402 cups of coffee per year, almost 25 percent more than Americans, and 161 percent more than Europeans. Vancouverites do their share to keep the numbers up.

Christine Corkan noticed the number of coffee drinkers and the coffee shops in Vancouver and realized that there were lots of places where one could not easily get a cup of coffee in the city. Trendy coffee shops tend not to be located next door to community parks, for instance, where people play soccer, baseball, and field hockey. From that observation, her business, Java Jazz Mobile Café, was born.

Java Jazz offers coffee, tea, and cold drinks, as well as baked goods, smoothies, and fresh fruit from the side of a cube van outfitted with a small kitchen run on a generator. Corkan aims to fill the niche where other concessions are not available, and can be hired for any private event in the area that wants to have coffee and beverages available on-site.

Corkan started developing her business with $35 000, almost all of it loaned to her by a friend at 5 percent interest. With the money, she had to purchase and furnish the van and buy beverages and serving cups.

In August, two months after starting the business, Corkan felt she was doing well. Her previous job was with Air Canada. "I made more in two days with Java Jazz than I make in a month at the airport," she said. "I have the first payment already saved for my loan and it's not due until November."

It is important for managers such as Corkan to understand how to run a business—a new experience for her, compared with working for Air Canada. Corkan would do well to learn more about different management theories, as they provide a framework for managing one's business, dealing with employees when she brings them on, and understanding the environment of the business. One of the keys to her success will be understanding as much as she can about how management works. Below we review the history of management thought. As you read through it, you may want to identify some of the tips that would help you be a better manager.

Looking at management history can help us understand today's management theory and practice. It can help us see what did work and what did not. In this supplement, we introduce you to the origins of many contemporary management concepts and show how they have evolved to reflect the changing needs of organizations and society as a whole.   Q&A S1.1

Historical Background of Management

Organized endeavours directed by people responsible for planning, organizing, leading, and controlling activities have existed for thousands of years. The Egyptian pyramids and the Great Wall of China are tangible evidence that projects of tremendous scope, employing tens of thousands of people, were undertaken well before modern times. The pyramids are a particularly interesting example. The construction of a single pyramid occupied more than 100 000 workers for 20 years.[2] Who told each worker what to do? Who ensured that there would be enough stones at the site to keep workers busy? The answer to such questions is managers. Regardless of what managers were called at the time, someone had to plan what was to be done, organize people and materials to do it, lead and direct the workers, and impose some controls to ensure that everything was done as planned.

While organizations and managers have been around for thousands of years, two pre-twentieth-century events are particularly significant to the study of management. First, in 1776 Adam Smith published *The Wealth of Nations*, in which he argued for the economic advantages that organizations and society would gain from the **division of labour**—the breakdown of jobs into narrow and repetitive tasks. Using the pin industry as an example, Smith claimed that 10 individuals, each doing a specialized task, could together produce about 48 000 pins a day. However, if each person worked alone performing each task separately, it would be quite an accomplishment to produce even 10 pins a day! Smith concluded that the division of labour increased productivity by increasing each person's skill and dexterity, by saving time lost in changing tasks, and by creating labour-saving inventions and machinery. The continued popularity of job specialization—for example, specific tasks performed by members of a hospital surgery team, specific meal preparation tasks done by employees in restaurant kitchens, or specific positions played by players on a hockey team—is undoubtedly due to the economic advantages cited by Adam Smith.

The second important pre-twentieth-century influence on management is the **Industrial Revolution**. Starting in the eighteenth century in Great Britain, the revolution eventually crossed the Atlantic to North America. What the Industrial Revolution did was substitute machine power for human power. This made it more economical to manufacture goods in factories rather than at home. Managers were needed to forecast demand, ensure that enough material was on hand to make products, assign tasks to people, direct daily activities, and so forth. However, it was not until the early 1900s that the first major step was taken toward developing a formal theory to guide managers in running these large organizations.

In the next sections, we present the six major approaches to management: scientific management, general administrative theory, quantitative, organizational behaviour, systems, and contingency (see Exhibit S1-1 on page 24). Each of the six perspectives contributes to our overall understanding of management. However, each is also a limited view of a particular aspect of management. We begin our journey into management's past by looking at the first major theory of management—scientific management.

Scientific Management

If you had to pinpoint the year modern management theory was born, 1911 might be a logical choice. That was the year Frederick Winslow Taylor's *The Principles of Scientific Management* was published. Its contents were widely accepted by managers around the world. The book described the theory of **scientific management**: the use of the scientific method to define the "one best way" for a job to be done.

Important Contributions

Important contributions to scientific management theory were made by Frederick W. Taylor and Frank and Lillian Gilbreth. Let's look at what they did.

Frederick W. Taylor

Taylor did most of his work at the Midvale and Bethlehem Steel companies in Pennsylvania. As a mechanical engineer with a Quaker and Puritan

division of labour The breakdown of jobs into narrow and repetitive tasks.

Industrial Revolution A period during the late eighteenth century when machine power was substituted for human power, making it more economical to manufacture goods in factories than at home.

scientific management The use of the scientific method to determine the "one best way" for a job to be done.

Exhibit S1-1

Development of Major Management Theories

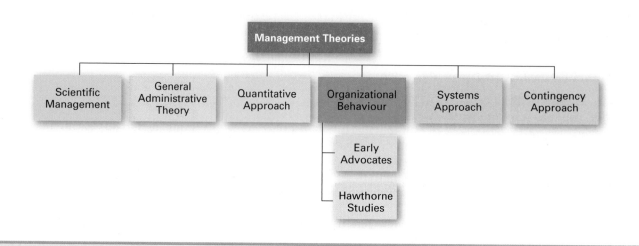

background, he was continually shocked at how employees performed. He observed that they used vastly different techniques to do the same job and were inclined to "take it easy" on the job. Taylor believed that employee output was only about one-third of what was possible. Virtually no work standards existed. Employees were placed in jobs with little or no concern for matching their abilities and aptitudes with the tasks they were required to do. Taylor set out to correct the situation by applying the scientific method to shop-floor jobs and spent more than two decades passionately pursuing the "one best way" for each job to be done.

Taylor's experiences at Midvale led him to define clear guidelines for improving production efficiency. He argued that four principles of management (see *Tips for Managers—Taylor's Four Principles of Management*) would result in prosperity for both employees and managers.[3] Through his studies of manual work using scientific principles, Taylor became known as the "father" of scientific management. His ideas spread in the United States, France, Germany, Russia, and Japan, and inspired others to study and develop

methods of scientific management. His most prominent followers were Frank and Lillian Gilbreth.

Frank and Lillian Gilbreth

A construction contractor by trade, Frank Gilbreth gave up that career to study scientific management after hearing Taylor speak at a professional meeting. Frank and his wife, Lillian, a psychologist, studied work to eliminate wasteful hand and body motions. The Gilbreths also experimented with the design and use of the proper tools and equipment for optimizing work performance.[4]

Frank is probably best known for his experiments in bricklaying. By carefully analyzing the bricklayer's job, he reduced the number of motions in laying exterior brick from 18 to about 5, and on laying interior brick the motions were reduced from 18 to 2. Using Gilbreth's techniques, the bricklayer could be more productive and less fatigued at the end of the day.

The Gilbreths were among the first researchers to use motion pictures to study hand and body motions. They invented a device called a micro-chronometer, which recorded an employee's motions and the amount of time spent doing each motion. Wasted motions missed by the naked eye

TIPS FOR MANAGERS

Taylor's Four Principles of Management

- Develop a **science for each element of an individual's work**, which will replace the old rule-of-thumb method.

- **Scientifically select** and then train, teach, and develop employees.

- **Heartily cooperate with employees** so as to ensure that all work is done in accordance with the principles of the science that has been developed.

- **Divide work and responsibility almost equally** between management and employees. Management takes over all work for which it is better fitted than the employees.

could be identified and eliminated. The Gilbreths also devised a classification scheme to label 17 basic hand motions (such as search, grasp, hold), which they called **therbligs** ("Gilbreth" spelled backward with the *th* transposed). This scheme allowed the Gilbreths a more precise way of analyzing an employee's exact hand movements.

How Do Today's Managers Use Scientific Management?

The guidelines that Taylor and others devised for improving production efficiency are still used in organizations today.[5] When managers analyze the basic work tasks that must be performed, use time-and-motion study to eliminate wasted motions, hire the best-qualified people for a job, and design incentive systems based on output, they are using the principles of scientific management. But current management practice is not restricted to scientific management. In fact, we can see ideas from the next major approach—general administrative theory—being used as well. **Q&A S1.2**

General Administrative Theory

Another group of writers looked at the subject of management but focused on the entire organization. These **general administrative theorists** developed more general theories of what managers do and what constitutes good management practice. Let's look at some important contributions that grew out of this perspective.

Important Contributions

The two most prominent theorists behind general administrative theory were Henri Fayol and Max Weber.

Henri Fayol

We mention Fayol in Chapter 1 because he described management as a universal set of functions that included planning, organizing, commanding, coordinating, and controlling. Because

TIPS FOR MANAGERS

Fayol's 14 Principles of Management

- **Division of work.** Specialization increases output by making employees more efficient.

- **Authority.** Managers must be able to give orders, and authority gives them this right.

- **Discipline.** Employees must obey and respect the rules that govern the organization.

- **Unity of command.** Every employee should receive orders from only one superior.

- **Unity of direction.** The organization should have a single plan of action to guide managers and employees.

- **Subordination of individual interests to the general interest.** The interests of any one employee or group of employees should not take precedence over the interests of the organization as a whole.

- **Remuneration.** Employees must be paid a fair wage for their services.

- **Centralization.** This term refers to the degree to which subordinates are involved in decision making.

- **Scalar chain.** The line of authority from top management to the lowest ranks is the scalar chain.

- **Order.** People and materials should be in the right place at the right time.

- **Equity.** Managers should be kind and fair to their subordinates.

- **Stability of tenure of personnel.** Management should provide orderly personnel planning and ensure that replacements are available to fill vacancies.

- **Initiative.** Employees who are allowed to originate and carry out plans will exert high levels of effort.

- **Esprit de corps.** Promoting team spirit will build harmony and unity within the organization.

his ideas were important, let's look more closely at what he had to say.[6]

Fayol wrote during the same time period as Taylor. While Taylor was concerned with first-line managers and the scientific method, Fayol's attention was directed at the activities of *all* managers. He wrote from personal experience because he was the managing director of a large French coal-mining firm.

Fayol described the practice of management as something distinct from accounting, finance, production, distribution, and other typical business functions. His belief that management was an activity common to all human endeavours in business, government,

therbligs A classification scheme for labelling 17 basic hand motions.

general administrative theorists Writers who developed general theories of what managers do and what constitutes good management practice.

Exhibit S1-2

Weber's Ideal Bureaucracy

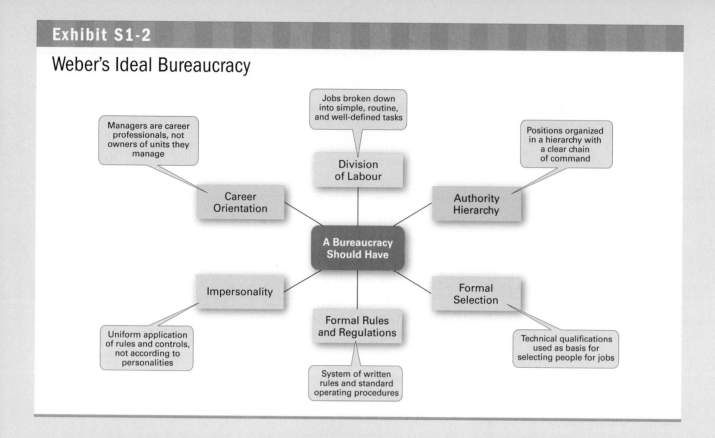

and even in the home led him to develop 14 **principles of management**—fundamental rules of management that could be taught in schools and applied in all organizational situations. These principles are shown in *Tips for Managers—Fayol's 14 Principles of Management.*   Q&A S1.3

Max Weber

Weber (pronounced VAY-ber) was a German sociologist who studied organizational activity. Writing in the early 1900s, he developed a theory of authority structures and relations.[7] Weber described an ideal type of organization that he called a **bureaucracy**—a form of organization characterized by division of labour, a clearly defined hierarchy, detailed rules and regulations, and impersonal relationships. Weber recognized that this "ideal bureaucracy" did not exist in reality. Instead, he intended it as a basis for theorizing about how work could be done in large groups. His theory became the model structural design for many of today's

large organizations. The features of Weber's ideal bureaucratic structure are outlined in Exhibit S1-2.

Bureaucracy, as described by Weber, is a lot like scientific management in its ideology. Both emphasize rationality, predictability, impersonality, technical competence, and authoritarianism. Although Weber's writings were less operational than Taylor's, the fact that his "ideal type" still describes many contemporary organizations attests to the importance of his work.

How Do Today's Managers Use General Administrative Theory?

Some of our current management ideas and practices can be directly traced to the contributions of the general administrative theorists. For instance,

the functional view of the manager's job can be attributed to Fayol. In addition, his 14 principles serve as a frame of reference from which many current management concepts have evolved.

Weber's bureaucracy was an attempt to formulate an ideal prototype for organizations. Although many characteristics of Weber's bureaucracy are still evident in large organizations, his model is not as popular today as it was in the twentieth century. Many contemporary managers feel that bureaucracy's emphasis on strict division of labour, adherence to formal rules and regulations, and impersonal application of rules and controls takes away the individual employee's creativity and the organization's ability to respond quickly to an increasingly dynamic environment. However, even in highly flexible organizations of talented professionals—such as Calgary-based

principles of management Fourteen fundamental rules of management that could be taught in schools and applied in all organizational situations.

bureaucracy A form of organization characterized by division of labour, a clearly defined hierarchy, detailed rules and regulations, and impersonal relationships.

WestJet Airlines, Toronto-based ING Bank of Canada, or Ottawa-based Corel—some bureaucratic mechanisms are necessary to ensure that resources are used efficiently and effectively.

The Quantitative Approach

The **quantitative approach** involves the use of quantitative techniques to improve decision making. This approach also has been called *operations research* or *management science*.

Important Contributions

The quantitative approach evolved out of the development of mathematical and statistical solutions to military problems during World War II. After the war was over, many of the techniques that had been used to solve military problems were applied to businesses. One group of military officers, nicknamed the Whiz Kids, joined Ford Motor Company in the mid-1940s and immediately began using statistical methods and quantitative models to improve decision making. Two of these individuals whose names you might recognize are Robert McNamara (who went on to become president of Ford, US Secretary of Defense, and head of the World Bank and was recently featured in the documentary *The Fog of War*) and Charles "Tex" Thornton (who founded Litton Industries).

What exactly does the quantitative approach do? It involves applications of statistics, optimization models, information models, and computer simulations to management activities. Linear programming, for example, is a technique that managers use to improve resource allocation decisions. Work scheduling can be more efficient as a result of critical-path scheduling analysis. The economic order quantity model helps managers determine optimum inventory levels. Each of these is an example of quantitative techniques being applied to improve managerial decision making.

How Do Today's Managers Use the Quantitative Approach?

The quantitative approach contributes directly to management decision making in the areas of planning and control. When managers make budgeting, scheduling, quality control, and similar decisions, they typically rely on quantitative techniques. The availability of software programs has made the use of quantitative techniques somewhat less intimidating for managers, although they must still be able to interpret the results.

The quantitative approach has not influenced management practice as much as the next approach we are going to discuss—organizational behaviour—for a number of reasons. These include the fact that many managers are unfamiliar with and intimidated by the quantitative tools, behavioural problems are more widespread and visible, and it is easier for most students and managers to relate to real, day-to-day people problems than to the more abstract activity of constructing quantitative models.

Organizational Behaviour

As we know, managers get things done by working with people. This explains why some writers have chosen to look at management by focusing on the organization's human resources.

The field of study concerned with the actions (behaviour) of people at work is called **organizational behaviour (OB)**. Much of what currently makes up the field of human resource management, as well as contemporary views on motivation, leadership, trust,

teamwork, and conflict management, has come out of OB research.

Early Advocates

Although a number of people in the late 1800s and early 1900s recognized the importance of the human factor to an organization's success, four stand out as early advocates of the OB approach: Robert Owen, Hugo Münsterberg, Mary Parker Follett, and Chester Barnard. The contributions of these individuals were varied and distinct, yet they all believed that people were the most important asset of the organization and should be managed accordingly. Their approach was very different from the emphasis on bureaucracy and structured arrangements to improve workflow. In particular, their ideas provided the foundation for such management practices as employee selection procedures, employee motivation programs, employee work teams, and organization–environment management techniques. Exhibit S1-3 (on page 28) summarizes the most important ideas of the early advocates of OB.

The Hawthorne Studies

Without question, the most important contribution to the developing OB field came out of the **Hawthorne Studies**, a series of studies conducted at the Western Electric Company Works in Cicero, Illinois. These studies, which started in 1924, were initially designed by Western Electric industrial engineers as a scientific management experiment. They wanted to examine the effect of various illumination levels on employee productivity. As in any good scientific experiment, control and experimental groups were set up, with the experimental group being exposed to various lighting intensities, and the

quantitative approach The use of quantitative techniques to improve decision making.

organizational behaviour (OB) The field of study concerned with the actions (behaviour) of people at work.

Hawthorne Studies A series of studies during the 1920s and 1930s that provided new insights into individual and group behaviour.

Exhibit S1-3

Early Advocates of OB

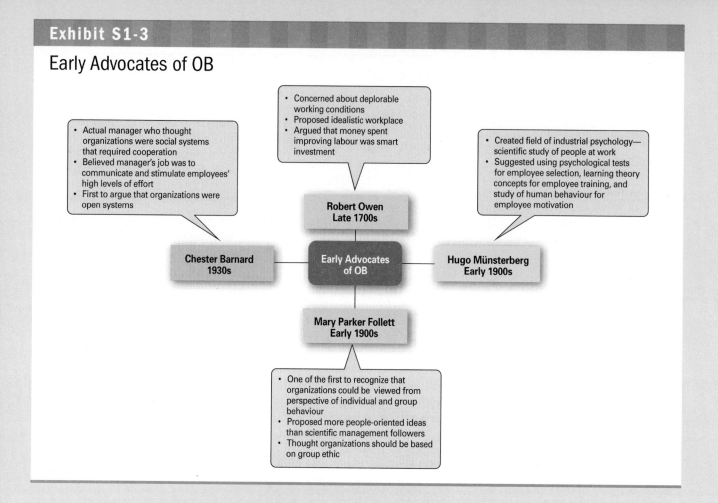

- Actual manager who thought organizations were social systems that required cooperation
- Believed manager's job was to communicate and stimulate employees' high levels of effort
- First to argue that organizations were open systems

- Concerned about deplorable working conditions
- Proposed idealistic workplace
- Argued that money spent improving labour was smart investment

- Created field of industrial psychology—scientific study of people at work
- Suggested using psychological tests for employee selection, learning theory concepts for employee training, and study of human behaviour for employee motivation

Robert Owen Late 1700s

Chester Barnard 1930s

Early Advocates of OB

Hugo Münsterberg Early 1900s

Mary Parker Follett Early 1900s

- One of the first to recognize that organizations could be viewed from perspective of individual and group behaviour
- Proposed more people-oriented ideas than scientific management followers
- Thought organizations should be based on group ethic

control group working under a constant intensity. If you were the industrial engineers in charge of this experiment, what would you have expected to happen? It's logical to think that individual output in the experimental group would be directly related to the intensity of the light.

However, they found that as the level of light was increased in the experimental group, output for both groups increased. Then, much to the surprise of the engineers, as the light level was decreased in the experimental group, productivity continued to increase in both groups. In fact, a productivity decrease was observed in the experimental group *only* when the level of light was reduced to that of a moonlit night. What would explain these unexpected results? The engineers were not sure, but concluded that illumination intensity was not directly related to group productivity, and that something

else must have contributed to the results. They were not able to pinpoint what that "something else" was, though.

In 1927, the Western Electric engineers asked Harvard professor Elton Mayo and his associates to join the study as consultants. Thus began a relationship that would last through 1932 and encompass numerous experiments in the redesign of jobs, changes in workday and workweek length, introduction of rest periods, and individual vs. group wage plans.[8] For example, one experiment was designed to evaluate the effect of a group piecework incentive pay system on group productivity. The results indicated that the incentive plan had less effect on an employee's output than did group pressure, acceptance, and security. The researchers concluded that social norms, or group standards, were the key determinants of individual work behaviour.

Scholars generally agree that the Hawthorne Studies had a dramatic impact on management beliefs about the role of human behaviour in organizations. Mayo concluded that behaviour and attitudes are closely related, that group influences significantly affect individual behaviour, that group standards establish individual employee output, and that money is less a factor in determining output than are group standards, group attitudes, and security. These conclusions led to a new emphasis on the human behaviour factor in the management of organizations and the attainment of goals.

However, these conclusions were criticized. Critics attacked the research procedures, analyses of findings, and conclusions.[9] From a historical standpoint, it's of little importance whether the studies were academically sound or their conclusions justified. What *is* important is that they stimulated an interest in human behaviour in organizations.   Q&A S1.4

How Do Today's Managers Use the Behavioural Approach?

The behavioural approach has largely shaped today's organizations. From the way managers design motivating jobs to the way they work with employee teams to the way they use open communication, we can see elements of the behavioural approach. Much of what the early OB advocates proposed and the conclusions from the Hawthorne Studies provided the foundation for our current theories of motivation, leadership, group behaviour and development, and numerous other behavioural topics that we address fully in later chapters.

The Systems Approach

During the 1960s, researchers began to analyze organizations from a systems perspective, a concept taken from the physical sciences. A **system** is a set of interrelated and interdependent parts

arranged in a manner that produces a unified whole. The two basic types of systems are closed and open. **Closed systems** are not influenced by and do not interact with their environment. This is very much how Air Canada operated when it was a Crown corporation. Because it was in a regulated industry, it did not need to worry about competition. When the Canadian airline industry was deregulated, Air Canada was slow to adapt to the new competitive environment and went into bankruptcy protection in order to restructure its operations and attempt to become a more open system.[10]

Open systems dynamically interact with their environment. Today, when we describe organizations as systems, we mean open systems. Exhibit S1-4 shows a diagram of an organization from an open systems perspective. As you can see, an organization takes in inputs (resources) from the environment and transforms or processes these resources into outputs that are distributed into

the environment. The organization is "open" to its environment and interacts with that environment.

The Systems Approach and Managers

How does the systems approach contribute to our understanding of management thinking? Systems researchers envisioned an organization as being made up of "interdependent factors, including individuals, groups, attitudes, motives, formal structure, interactions, goals, status, and authority."[11] What this means is that managers coordinate the work activities of the various parts of the organization and ensure that all the interdependent parts of the organization are working together so that the organization's goals can be achieved. For example, the systems approach would recognize that, no matter how efficient the production department might be, if the marketing department does not anticipate changes in customer tastes

---

system A set of interrelated and interdependent parts arranged in a manner that produces a unified whole.

closed systems Systems that are not influenced by and do not interact with their environment.

open systems Systems that dynamically interact with their environment.

Exhibit S1-4

The Organization as an Open System

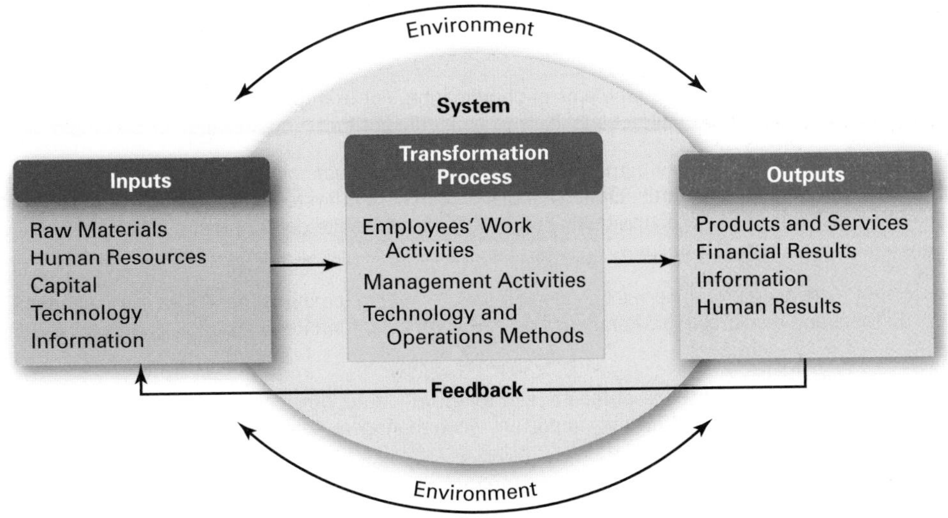

and work with the product development department to create products customers want, the organization's overall performance will suffer. This approach is very different from the "silo" approach in some organizations, where each individual unit operates almost in isolation from other units.

In addition, the systems approach implies that decisions and actions taken in one organizational area will affect others and vice versa. For example, if the purchasing department does not acquire the right quantity and quality of inputs, the production department will not be able to do its job effectively.

Finally, the systems approach recognizes that organizations are not self-contained. They rely on their environments for essential inputs and as sources to absorb their outputs. No organization can survive for long if it ignores government regulations, supplier relations, or the varied external constituencies on which it depends. (We cover these external forces in Chapter 2.)

How relevant is the systems approach to management? Quite relevant. Think, for example, of a day-shift manager at a local Harvey's restaurant who every day must coordinate the work of employees filling customer orders at the front counter and the drive-through windows, direct the delivery and unloading of food supplies, and address any customer concerns that come up. This manager "manages" all parts of the "system" so that the restaurant meets its daily sales goals.   Q&A S1.5

The Contingency Approach

Early management thinkers such as Taylor, Fayol, and Weber gave us principles of management that they generally assumed to be universally applicable. Later research found exceptions to many of their principles. For example, division of labour is valuable and widely used, but jobs can become *too* specialized. Bureaucracy is desirable in many situations, but in other circumstances, other structural designs are *more* effective. Management is not (and cannot be) based on simplistic principles to be applied in all situations. Different and changing situations require managers to use different approaches and techniques. The **contingency approach** (sometimes called the *situational approach*) says that organizations are different, face different situations (contingencies), and require different ways of managing.

The Contingency Approach and Managers

A contingency approach to management is intuitively logical because organizations and even units within the same organization are diverse—in size, goals, work, and the like. It would be surprising to find universally applicable management rules that would work in *all* situations. But, of course, it's one thing to say that the method of managing "depends on the situation" and another to say what the situation is. Management researchers have been working to identify these "what" variables. Exhibit S1-5 describes four popular contingency variables. The list is by no means comprehensive—more than 100 different "what" variables have been identified—but it represents those most widely used and gives you an idea of what we mean by the term *contingency variable*. As you can see, the contingency variables can have a significant impact on managers. The primary value of the contingency approach is that it stresses

contingency approach An approach that says that organizations are different, face different situations (contingencies), and require different ways of managing.

Exhibit S1-5

Popular Contingency Variables

Organization Size. As size increases, so do the problems of coordination. For example, the type of organization structure appropriate for an organization of 50 000 employees is likely to be inefficient for an organization of 50 employees.

Routineness of Task Technology. To achieve its purpose, an organization uses technology. Routine technologies, such as assembly lines, require organizational structures, leadership styles, and control systems that differ from those required by customized or nonroutine technologies where individuals continually have to make decisions about how their jobs are to be done, such as in the emergency room of a hospital.

Environmental Uncertainty. The degree of uncertainty caused by environmental changes influences the management process. What works best in a stable and predictable environment may be totally inappropriate in a rapidly changing and unpredictable environment.

Individual Differences. Individuals differ in terms of their desire for growth, autonomy, tolerance of ambiguity, and expectations. These and other individual differences are particularly important when managers select motivation techniques, leadership styles, and job designs.

there are no simplistic or universal rules for managers to follow. Q&A S1.6

Summarizing Management Theory

It would not be unusual for you to read through this supplement on the history of management theory and wonder whether any of it is relevant to you. Theoretical perspectives and the research that is generated to help examine theories lead us to a more solid understanding of how managers should manage. The theories we present above appear in a historical sequence, but that does not mean that as a new theory was developed, the previous one became irrelevant. Instead, if you carefully consider the theories, you will note that they are somewhat self-contained, each addressing a separate aspect of the various considerations that managers face. Exhibit S1-6 highlights for you the different emphases of these theories, so that you can see how each contributes to a better understanding of management as a whole.

Exhibit S1-6

Emphases of Major Management Theories

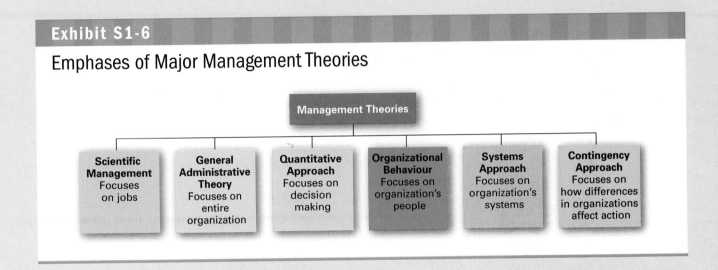

Environmental Constraints on Managers

What constraints do managers face?

1 How much control do managers have?

2 What is the external environment for managers?

3 What challenges do managers face in a global environment?

4 How do organizations do business globally?

5 How does the environment affect managers?

Concern over pet food contamination swept across North America in February and March of 2007, upon news that at least 15 cats and 1 dog had died after eating possibly poisoned food.[1] There were also unconfirmed reports that hundreds of pets in Canada had suffered kidney failure. Though pet owners were reporting pet illnesses in February, the first recall of pet food did not occur until March 16, 2007, when Mississauga, Ontario-based Menu Foods asked retailers to remove 60 million packages of its wet pet foods off grocery and pet food store shelves. At the time, the company was not entirely sure why pets were getting sick, but something seemed to be wrong with its pet food.

For consumers, the pet food recall caused immediate confusion. There is no brand called "Menu Foods" on pet food shelves. Instead, 889 separate items under 100 different brand names had to be taken off grocery shelves. Menu Foods processes most of North America's most popular brands of wet pet food packaged in cans and foil pouches. It produces about 75 percent of private-label pet food brands in Canada (for companies such as Walmart Canada, Sobeys, and Pet Valu) and between 40 and 50 percent of private-label pet food brands in the United States (for companies such as PetSmart, Safeway, and Walmart).

At the time of the recall, Menu Foods was a virtually unknown company, particularly to consumers. Suddenly, this Canadian company had Americans worried about the wisdom of importing food from foreign sources, including Canada. Ironically, the contaminated ingredient in the recalled pet food came from an American company, Nevada-based ChemNutra, that had purchased the ingredient from a company in China.

Think About It
Should large corporations have to report the source of all ingredients in the food products they manufacture? Put yourself in the shoes of Menu Foods' CEO. What responsibilities do organizations have when sourcing food ingredients globally?

Managers at Menu Foods are responsible for overseeing the production of pet food and other products. But how much actual impact does a manager have on an organization's success or failure? Can managers do anything they want? These questions raise more general questions: Do managers control their environment, or are they controlled by it? Are they affected more by circumstances outside or inside the organization? In this chapter, we consider the impact of an organization's external environment on the ability of managers to act. We begin our exploration by considering the degree of control managers have over an organization's performance.

The Manager: How Much Control?

① How much control do managers have?

omnipotent view of management
The view that managers are directly responsible for an organization's success or failure.

Q&A 2.1

symbolic view of management
The view that managers have only a limited effect on substantive organizational outcomes because of the large number of factors outside their control.

Q&A 2.2

The dominant view in management theory and society in general is that managers are directly responsible for an organization's success or failure. We will call this perspective the **omnipotent view of management**. The view of managers as omnipotent is consistent with the stereotypical picture of the take-charge business executive who can overcome any obstacle in carrying out the organization's goals. In the omnipotent view, when organizations perform poorly, someone has to be held accountable regardless of the reasons, and in our society that "someone" is the manager. Of course, when things go well, we need someone to praise. So managers also get the credit—even if they had little to do with achieving positive outcomes.

In contrast, some observers have argued that much of an organization's success or failure is due to external forces outside managers' control. For example, when tunnelling for the Canada Line transit system began tearing up Vancouver's Cambie Street, the street became noisy, there was no parking, and the area was a traffic nightmare. Once a busy shopping area, customers stopped coming to the stores and restaurants. The **symbolic view of management** would suggest that the loss of sales was not the managers' fault. The symbolic view says that a manager's ability to affect outcomes is influenced and constrained by external factors.[2] In this view, it's unreasonable to expect managers to significantly affect an organization's performance. Instead, an organization's results are strongly influenced by factors outside the control of managers. These factors include, for example, the economy, customers, government policies, competitors' actions, industry conditions, control over proprietary technology, and decisions made by previous managers.

In reality, managers are neither helpless nor all-powerful. Internal and external constraints that restrict a manager's decision-making options exist within every organization. Internal constraints arise from the organization's culture (which we discuss in Chapter 11) and external constraints come from the organization's environment, as shown in Exhibit 2-1.

In our chapter-opening vignette we saw how the external environment can place constraints on managers' ability to control the success of an organization. In the remainder of this chapter, we will explore the idea of how an organization's internal and external environment imposes constraints on managers. In other chapters, however, we will learn that these constraints do not mean that a manager's hands are tied; managers can and do influence their culture and environment.

When both Home Hardware and Army and Navy closed their stores in downtown Regina, Blue Mantle, a thrift store in the same area, faced a loss of customer traffic and sales. As a result, Dave Barrett, the store's manager at the time, closed Blue Mantle soon after. He explained his decision: "When Home Hardware closed, and department store Army and Navy closed, that cut away a lot of our traffic to the store. We used to have lots of seniors that would swing over to our place." He also noted that the state of the economy was a factor in the store closing.[3] The Roman Catholic Archdiocese of Regina eventually re-opened Blue Mantle after receiving numerous requests from customers, and now runs the store with volunteers.

Exhibit 2-1

Parameters of Managerial Discretion

Organizational Environment → **Managerial Discretion** → Organizational Culture

The External Environment

After Menu Foods recalled its pet food, one legislator reminded Americans that it might not be safe to rely on foreign sources of food.[4] "We really don't know what else is out there and yet we've increased food imports and reduced inspections," says Bob Etheridge, a Democratic representative from North Carolina.

Some US legislators and farm groups have called for fewer imports, a reconsideration of the free-trade agreement, fees from Canada and other countries so that the United States can conduct more inspections of food, and labels indicating country of origin on all food products. Should such legislation be passed, Menu Foods may find its dominant role in the pet food market shrinking.

The immediate impact of the pet food recall affects Menu Foods, but some are worried that the scandal could affect Canada's economy, which saw about $15.5 billion in sales of food to the United States in 2006. "This is an ongoing issue that we have anxiety over," says Canadian Minister of Trade David Emerson.

Think About It

How might the tainted pet food scandal affect the Canadian pet food industry's trade relations with the United States and Mexico?

As we discussed in Chapter 1, management is no longer constrained by national borders. Managers in all sizes and types of organizations are faced with the opportunities and challenges of managing in a global environment. Managers at Menu Foods capitalized on the opportunity of the global environment by buying ingredients from companies around the world. This allowed them to expand their company into a leading pet food manufacturer in North America. However, their reliance on ingredients that originated in China, a country that did not have the same food product inspection standards as North American countries, has proven to be extremely costly.

The term **external environment** refers to forces and institutions outside the organization that potentially can affect its performance. The external environment is made up of three components, as shown in Exhibit 2-2 on page 36: the specific environment, the general environment, and the global environment.

Anyone who questions the impact of the external environment on managing should consider the following:

- Canadians spent $652.7 million on bottled water in 2005 and sales of bottled water increased 20 percent in 2006, but complaints by environmentalist David Suzuki and others that bottled water is not good for the environment started to change individuals' views about drinking bottled water.[5]

- In 2008, the impact of defaults on subprime mortgages in the United States started to have a ripple effect throughout the world. The impact on employment and earnings in Canada was huge, even though Canadian bankers had been far more conservative in their mortgage products.

2 What is the external environment for managers?

external environment
Outside forces and institutions that potentially can affect the organization's performance.

Exhibit 2-2

The External Environment

As these two examples show, there are forces in the environment that play a major role in shaping managers' actions. In this section, we identify some of the critical environmental forces that affect managers and show how they constrain managerial discretion.

The Specific Environment

specific environment
The part of the external environment that is directly relevant to the achievement of an organization's goals.

The **specific environment** includes those external forces that have a direct and immediate impact on managers' decisions and actions and are directly relevant to the achievement of the organization's goals. Each organization's specific environment is unique and changes with conditions. For example, Timex and Rolex both make watches, but their specific environments differ because they operate in distinctly different market niches. What forces make up the specific environment? The main ones are customers, suppliers, competitors, and public pressure groups.

Customers

An organization exists to meet the needs of customers who use its output. Customers represent potential uncertainty to an organization. Their tastes can change, or they can become dissatisfied with the organization's products or service. For example, shoppers are confused by different food rating systems—"Smart Choices," "Sensible Solution," "Best Life," and so forth. Grocery chains are taking steps to help them by creating simpler ways to assess the foods they are buying.[6]

Suppliers

Managers seek to ensure a steady flow of needed inputs (supplies) at the lowest price possible. An organization's supplies being limited or delayed in delivery can constrain managers' decisions and actions. Disney World, for example, must make sure it has supplies of soft drinks, computers, food, flowers and other nursery stock, concrete, paper products, and so forth. Suppliers also provide financial and labour inputs. For example, a lack of qualified nurses continues to be a serious problem plaguing health care providers, affecting their ability to meet demand and keep service levels high.

Competitors

All organizations—profit and nonprofit—have one or more competitors. The three major broadcast networks—ABC, CBS, and NBC—used to control what you watched on television. Now, they face competition from digital cable, satellite, DVDs, and the Internet, all of which offer customers a much broader choice.

Public Pressure Groups

Managers must recognize the special-interest groups that attempt to influence the actions of organizations. Both Walmart and Home Depot have had difficulty getting approval to build stores in Vancouver. Neighbourhood activists worry about traffic density brought about by big-box stores, and in the case of both stores there is concern that local businesses will fail if the stores move in. Home Depot's director of real estate called Vancouver city hall's review process "confusing and unfair" and "unlike anything in my experience."[7] Local hardware store owners and resident groups have lobbied against the store to city planners, hoping to keep big-box stores out of the Kitsilano neighbourhood.

As social and political attitudes change, so too does the power of public pressure groups. Through their persistent efforts, groups such as MADD (Mothers Against Drunk Driving) and SADD (Students Against Destructive Decisions) have managed to make changes in the alcoholic beverage and restaurant and bar industries, and raised public awareness about the problem of drunk drivers.

The General Environment

The **general environment** includes the broad economic, legal–political, socio-cultural, demographic, and technological conditions that *may* affect the organization. Changes in any of these areas usually do not have as large an impact as changes in the specific environment do, but managers must consider them as they plan, organize, lead, and control.

general environment
Broad external conditions that may affect the organization.

Economic Conditions

Interest rates, inflation, changes in disposable income, stock market fluctuations, and the stage of the general business cycle are some of the economic factors that can affect management practices in Canada. For example, many specialty retailers such as IKEA, Roots, Birks, and Williams-Sonoma are acutely aware of the impact consumer disposable income has on their sales. When consumers' incomes fall or confidence about job security declines, such as happened in 2009, consumers will postpone purchasing anything that is not a necessity. Even charitable organizations such as the United Way and the Heart and Stroke Foundation feel the impact of economic factors. During economic downturns, not only does the demand for their services increase, but also their contributions typically decrease.

Legal–Political Conditions

Federal, provincial, and local governments influence what organizations can and cannot do. Some federal legislation has significant implications. The Canadian Human Rights Act makes it illegal for any employer or provider of service that falls within federal jurisdiction to discriminate on the following grounds: race, national or ethnic origin, colour, religion, age, sex (including pregnancy and childbirth), marital status, family status, mental or physical disability (including previous or current drug or alcohol dependence), pardoned conviction, or sexual orientation. The Act covers federal departments and agencies; Crown corporations; chartered banks; national airlines; interprovincial communications and telephone companies; interprovincial transportation companies; and other federally regulated industries, including certain mining operations.

Canada's Employment Equity Act of 1995 protects several categories of employees from employment barriers: Aboriginal peoples (whether First Nation, Inuit, or Metis);

persons with disabilities; members of visible minorities (nonCaucasian in race or non-white in colour); and women. This legislation aims to ensure that members of these four groups are treated equitably. Employers covered by the Canadian Human Rights Act are also covered by the Employment Equity Act.

Many provinces have their own legislation, including employment equity acts, to cover employers in their provinces. Companies sometimes have difficulty complying with equity acts, as recent audits conducted by the Canadian Human Rights Commission show. In an audit of 180 companies, only Status of Women Canada; Elliot Lake, Ontario-based AJ Bus Lines; the National Parole Board; the Canadian Transportation Agency; Les Méchins, Quebec-based Verreault Navigation; and Nortel Networks were compliant on their first try.[8]

The Competition Act of 1985 created the Bureau of Competition Policy (now called the Competition Bureau) to oversee and encourage competition in Canada. For example, if two major competing companies consider merging, they will come under scrutiny from the bureau. Heather Reisman and Gerry Schwartz's purchase of Chapters in 2001 needed approval before they could merge Chapters with their Indigo bookstores. Before approving the merger, the bureau imposed a number of conditions, including the sale or closing of 20 stores and a code of conduct for dealing with publishers. The code of conduct was the result of publishers' complaints about the way Chapters had treated them in the past. These rules affected the way Indigo/Chapters could do business until 2006. Beyond that time, the bookseller was allowed to operate without restraint by the Competition Bureau.[9]

To protect farmers, the Canadian government has created marketing boards that regulate the pricing and production of such items as milk and eggs. Those who decide that they want to manufacture small amounts of cheese would have great difficulty doing so because the Canadian government does not open production quotas to new producers very often. Marketing boards restrict imports of some products, but the unintended result is that foreign governments oppose exports from Canada.

Organizations spend a great deal of time and money meeting government regulations, but the effects of these regulations go beyond time and money.[10] They can also reduce managerial discretion by limiting the choices available to managers. In a 2004 COMPAS survey of business leaders, most respondents cited interprovincial trade barriers as a significant hurdle to doing business in this country, calling the barriers "bad economics." One respondent to the survey noted that the federal government fails "to realize that in today's global economy, our real 'competitors' are no longer in the next province (or the next city), not even in the U.S. or Mexico but are the emerging economies of Asia and Europe."[11]

Not all regulations have a negative impact, however, as the following *Management Reflection* shows.

MANAGEMENT REFLECTION

Groupe Savoie Loses Market, Makes a Deal

Can regulations actually improve a company's business? New government regulations that could have put Saint Quentin, New Brunswick-based Groupe Savoie out of business instead turned out to be an opportunity to figure out something else for the company to do.[12] When the provincial government introduced local woodlot marketing boards in 1982 and changed the way buyers were required to purchase wood, Groupe Savoie lost its market, and had 25 000 cords of wood it could not sell. In response, Groupe Savoie made a deal with a local pulp mill that was converting from softwood to hardwood chips and provided a win-win solution for both. Groupe Savoie decided to move into the pallet manufacturing business, and the pulp mill agreed to finance a sawmill that could cut the lumber needed to build the pallets. In return, Groupe Savoie supplied the pulp mill with the hardwood chips it needed. Today Groupe Savoie has three locations and grosses $80 million a year. ■

Peter B. Moore, founder, chief executive, and chairman of Barrie, Ontario-based Moore Packaging, which makes corrugated boxes, knows how changes in the general environment can seriously affect one's business. For several years, the company experienced double-digit sales growth each year, but he does not expect this kind of success to continue for long. "The corrugated packaging market is kind of stagnating right now as far as growth is concerned," Moore says. "Manufacturing companies have shut down and we come and go as they come and go. I used to say everything made goes in a box but I didn't realize it would be going into a box in China."

Other legal–political conditions are the political climate, the general stability of a country in which an organization operates, and the attitudes that elected government officials hold toward business. In Canada, organizations have generally operated in a stable political environment. Managers in some other countries do not face such a stable environment, however.

Socio-cultural Conditions

In 2004, Cambridge, Ontario-based Frito Lay Canada announced that it was eliminating trans fatty acids (TFAs) from Doritos, Tostitos, and Sunchips (it had already done so for its Lay's, Ruffles, and Miss Vickie's chips). Marc Guay, president of Frito Lay Canada, explained his decision at the time: "Eliminating trans fat is a major step in Frito Lay Canada's on-going commitment to offer consumers a wide variety of great-tasting snacks made with more healthful oils."[13] Burlington, Ontario-based Voortman Cookies was the first Canadian cookie maker to drop TFAs from its products. President and co-founder Harry Voortman said he dropped the TFAs after his daughter, Lynn, a naturopathic doctor, became concerned enough that she stopped eating her father's cookies altogether.[14]

Why did Frito Lay Canada and Voortman Cookies change their products? Because health officials and consumers became increasingly anxious about the link between TFAs and heart disease.[15] Managers must adapt their practices to the changing expectations of the societies in which they operate. As societal values, customs, and tastes change, managers also must change. For example, as employees have begun seeking more balance in their lives, organizations have had to adjust by offering family leave policies, more flexible work hours, and even on-site child care facilities. These trends may pose a constraint on managers' decisions and actions. If an organization does business in other countries, managers need to be familiar with those countries' values and cultures and manage in ways that recognize and embrace those specific socio-cultural aspects.

Demographic Conditions

Demographic conditions encompass trends in the physical characteristics of a population such as gender, age, level of education, geographic location, income, family composition,

Diversity in Action 5

and so forth. Changes in these characteristics may constrain how managers plan, organize, lead, and control.

One population group that we all have heard a lot about is the Baby Boomers, a group that encompasses individuals born between the years 1947 and 1966. Other age cohorts besides Baby Boomers that have been identified include the Depression group (born 1912–1921), the World War II group (born 1922–1927), the Post-war group (born 1928–1945), Generation X (born 1965–1977), and Generation Y (born 1978–1994). Although each of these groups has its own unique characteristics, Gen Y is of particular interest because they are thinking, learning, creating, shopping, and playing in fundamentally different ways that are likely to greatly affect managers and organizations.

Technological Conditions

In terms of the general environment, the most rapid changes have occurred in technology. We live in a time of continuous technological change. For example, the human genetic code has been cracked. Just think of the implications of such an incredible breakthrough! Information gadgets are getting smaller and more powerful. We have automated offices, electronic meetings, robotic manufacturing, lasers, integrated circuits, faster and more powerful microprocessors, synthetic fuels, and entirely new models of doing business in an electronic age. Companies that capitalize on technology, such as Research In Motion (RIM), eBay, and Google, prosper. In addition, many successful retailers such as Walmart, use sophisticated information systems to keep on top of current sales trends. Similarly, hospitals, universities, airports, police departments, and even military organizations that adapt to major technological advances have a competitive edge over those that do not. The whole area of technology is radically changing the fundamental ways that organizations are structured and the way that managers manage.

Understanding the Global Environment

Menu Foods was founded in 1971, and bought its first US factory in New Jersey in 1977, hoping to use that factory to launch an expansion into the US market.[16] Today the global company has four pet food processing plants: one in Canada (Mississauga, Ontario) and three in the United States (Emporia, Kansas; Pennsauken, New Jersey; and North Sioux City, South Dakota). The company's Canadian and American plants operate close to the areas they serve, which reduces shipping expenses. According to the company's website, "Menu's ability to serve [retailers] from four locations provides it with service and freight cost advantages compared to other single or two plant private-label competitors."

Menu Foods buys the ingredients for its pet food products from a variety of companies, and those companies in turn may buy ingredients for their products from other companies around the world. As the tainted pet food investigation found, an ingredient that originated in China was responsible for the deaths caused by Menu Foods' various pet foods. Menu Foods gets some of its ingredients from suppliers, who may themselves rely on external suppliers. As a result, Menu Foods may not always be aware of the original source of every ingredient it uses.

Think About It

How is Menu Foods structured to do business globally? Would it make sense for Menu Foods to form a strategic alliance or a joint venture, or create a foreign subsidiary in a country that produces its ingredients? How might it choose partners to do so, if that strategy were chosen?

3 What challenges do managers face in a global environment?

Historically, Canada has been slow to face the global challenge, although the relatively small size of many Canadian firms may be partly a factor in this.[17] The *Fortune* list of the "Top 100 Global Companies of 2006" does not include any Canadian firms (although there are 14 in the Top 500).[18] The majority of the firms listed are American, but there are several entries from Britain, France, Germany, Japan, and China.[19]

The global environment presents both opportunities and challenges for managers. With the entire world as a market and national borders becoming increasingly irrelevant, the potential for organizations to grow is expanding dramatically. To evaluate your fit for an international position, see *Self-Assessment—Am I Well-Suited for a Career as a Global Manager?* on pages 54–55, at the end of the chapter.

However, even large successful organizations with talented managers face challenges in managing in the global environment. Managers must deal with cultural, economic, and political differences. Meanwhile, new competitors can suddenly appear at any time from any place on the globe. Managers who make no attempt to learn and adapt to changes in the global environment end up reacting rather than innovating. As a result, their organizations often become uncompetitive and fail.[20] Below, we discuss the issues managers have to face in managing in a global environment.

Global Trade

What is the global environment like? An important feature is global trade. Global trade is not new. Countries and organizations have been trading with each other for centuries. "Trade is central to human health, prosperity, and social welfare."[21] When trade is allowed to flow freely, countries benefit from economic growth and productivity gains because they specialize in producing the goods they are best at and importing goods that are more efficiently produced elsewhere. Global trade is being shaped by two forces: regional trading alliances and the agreements negotiated through the World Trade Organization.

Regional Trading Alliances

The major regional trading alliances are as follows:

- The **European Union (EU)**: The signing of the Maastricht Treaty (named for the Dutch town where the treaty was signed) in February 1992 created the European Union (EU), a unified economic and trade entity with 12 member countries— Belgium, Denmark, France, Greece, Ireland, Italy, Luxembourg, the Netherlands, Portugal, Spain, the United Kingdom, and Germany. By 2007, the EU comprised 27 countries. Three other countries (Croatia, the former Yugoslav Republic of Macedonia, and Turkey) have submitted applications to join the EU.[22] The economic power represented by the EU is considerable, with the current EU membership encompassing more than 490 million people.[23]

  European Union (EU)
  A union of 27 European countries that forms an economic and political entity.

- The **North American Free Trade Agreement (NAFTA)**: When agreements in key issues covered by the North American Free Trade Agreement (NAFTA) were reached by the Canadian, US, and Mexican governments in August 1992, a vast economic bloc was created in which barriers to free trade were reduced. Since NAFTA went into effect, Canada has become the United States' number-one trading partner.[24] In 2006, Canadian exports to the United States were $362 billion, which accounted for almost 79 percent of our total exports.[25] Canada's exports to Mexico have quadrupled since the NAFTA agreement was signed, and its foreign investments in Mexico increased by a factor of five.[26] Westcoast Energy, Scotiabank, and BCE are just a few Canadian companies that have expanded their operations to Mexico. Many economists argue that reducing the barriers to trade (tariffs, import licensing requirements, customs user fees) has resulted in a strengthening of the economic power of all three countries. Free trade did not eliminate all trade problems between Canada and the United States, however, as the ongoing softwood lumber negotiations show.

  North American Free Trade Agreement (NAFTA)
  An agreement among the Canadian, American, and Mexican governments in which barriers to free trade were reduced.

- The **Association of Southeast Asian Nations (ASEAN)**: A trading alliance of 10 Southeast Asian countries. The ASEAN region has a population of about 500 million and a combined gross domestic product of $1174 billion.[27] During the years ahead, the Southeast Asian region promises to be one of the fastest-growing economic regions of the world. It will be an increasingly important regional economic and political alliance whose impact eventually could rival that of both NAFTA and the EU.

  Association of Southeast Asian Nations (ASEAN)
  A trading alliance of 10 Southeast Asian countries.

The World Trade Organization

World Trade Organization (WTO)
A global organization of 153 member countries that deals with the rules of trade among nations.

The **World Trade Organization (WTO)** is a global organization that sets rules for international trade and helps countries negotiate trade problems and settle trade disputes.[28]

The WTO was formed in 1995 and evolved from the General Agreement on Tariffs and Trade (GATT), an agreement in effect since the end of World War II. Today, the WTO is the only *global* organization dealing with the rules of trade among nations. Its membership consists of 153 member countries and 31 observer governments (which have a specific time frame within which they must apply to become members). At its core are various trade agreements negotiated and ratified by the vast majority of the world's trading nations. The goal of the WTO is to help businesses conduct trade between countries (importing and exporting) without undesired side effects. Although a number of vocal critics have staged highly visible protests and criticized the WTO, claiming that it destroys jobs and the natural environment, the WTO appears to play an important role in monitoring and promoting global trade.

The Legal–Political Environment

Canadian managers are accustomed to stable legal and political systems. Changes are slow, and legal and political procedures are well established. The stability of laws governing the actions of individuals and institutions allows for accurate predictions. The same cannot be said for all countries. Managers in a global organization must stay informed of the specific laws in countries where they do business.

Also, some countries have a history of unstable governments. Managers of businesses in these countries face dramatically greater uncertainty as a result of political instability or interference. The Chinese government controls what organizations do and how they do it within China's borders. Google has struggled with determining how to manage its website in China. "Figuring out how to deal with China has been a difficult exercise for Google," said Elliot Schrage, former vice-president of global communications and public affairs at Google. "The requirements of doing business in China include self-censorship—something that runs counter to Google's most basic values and commitments as a company."[29]

The legal–political environment does not have to be unstable or revolutionary to be a concern to managers. Just the fact that a country's laws and political system differ from those of Canada is important. Managers must recognize these differences to understand the constraints under which they operate and the opportunities that exist.

The Economic Environment

market economy
An economic system in which resources are primarily owned and controlled by the private sector.

planned economy
An economic system in which all economic decisions are planned by a central government.

The global manager must be aware of economic issues when doing business in other countries. First, it's important to have an understanding of the type of economic system under which the country operates. The two major types are a market economy and a planned economy. A **market economy** is one in which resources are primarily owned and controlled by the private sector. A **planned economy** is one in which all economic decisions are planned by a central government. In actuality, no economy is purely market or planned. Canada and the United States are two countries at the market end of the spectrum, but they do have some governmental control. The economies of Vietnam and North Korea, however, are more planned-based. Then there is China, a country that has utilized a planned economy for decades but is moving toward becoming more market-based. Why would managers need to know about a country's economic system? Because it has the potential to constrain decisions and actions. Other economic issues a manager would need to understand include currency exchange rates, inflation rates, and diverse tax policies.

The Cultural Environment

Which is more important to a manager—national culture or organizational culture? Research by Geert Hofstede, a professor at Maastricht University in the Netherlands, indicates that national culture has a greater effect on employees than does their organization's culture.[30] For example, German employees at an IBM facility in Munich will be influenced more by German culture than by IBM's culture. This means that as influential as organizational culture may be on managerial practice, **national culture** is even more influential.

national culture
The values and attitudes shared by individuals from a specific country that shape their behaviour and beliefs about what is important.

Hofstede developed one of the most widely referenced approaches to helping managers better understand differences between national cultures. His research found that managers and employees vary on five dimensions of national culture, which are as follows:

In what ways do you think culture affects doing business in other countries?

- *Individualism vs. collectivism.* Individualism is the degree to which people in a country prefer to act as individuals rather than as members of groups. In an individualistic society, people are supposed to look after their own interests and those of their immediate family and do so because of the large amount of freedom that an individualistic society allows its citizens. The opposite is collectivism, which is characterized by a social framework in which people prefer to act as members of groups and expect others in groups of which they are a part (such as a family or an organization) to look after them and to protect them.

- *Power distance.* Hofstede used the term *power distance* as a measure of the extent to which a society accepts the fact that power in institutions and organizations is distributed unequally. A high power distance society accepts wide differences in power in organizations. Employees show a great deal of respect for those in authority. Titles, rank, and status carry a lot of weight. In contrast, a low power distance society plays down inequalities as much as possible. Superiors still have authority, but employees are not afraid of or in awe of the boss.

- *Uncertainty avoidance.* Uncertainty avoidance describes the degree to which people tolerate risk and prefer structured over unstructured situations. People in low uncertainty avoidance societies are relatively comfortable with risks. They are also relatively tolerant of behaviour and opinions that differ from their own because they do not feel threatened by them. On the other hand, people in a society that is high in uncertainty avoidance feel threatened by uncertainty and ambiguity and experience high levels of anxiety, which manifests itself in nervousness, high stress, and aggressiveness.

- *Achievement vs. nurturing.* The fourth cultural dimension, like individualism/
collectivism, is a dichotomy. Achievement is the degree to which values such as assertiveness, the acquisition of money and material goods, and competition prevail. Nurturing is a national cultural attribute that emphasizes relationships and concern for others.[31]

- *Long-term and short-term orientation.* This cultural attribute looks at a country's orientation toward life and work. People in cultures with long-term orientation look to the future and value thrift and persistence. Also, in these cultures, leisure time is not so important and it is believed that the most important events in life will occur in the future. A short-term orientation values the past and present and emphasizes respect for tradition and fulfilling social obligations. Leisure time is important, and it is believed that the most important events in life happened in the past or occur in the present.

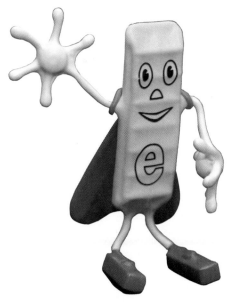

When managers at W.R. Grace & Company introduced the pink Eraser Man, the cartoon mascot was meant to convey a simple message to employees: "Erase" waste. However, the message perplexed and annoyed the company's staff in China. To them, "erase" means "invisible." Did the company really want this program to be invisible? As well, the colour pink is considered feminine in China—no self-respecting man would want to be associated with this colour. While the company quickly corrected this cross-cultural blunder, it also learned an important lesson about managing globally.

Exhibit 2-3

Hofstede's Five Dimensions of National Culture

(1) *Individualistic*—People look after their own and family interests
Collectivistic—People expect group to look after and protect them

Individualistic		*Collectivistic*
United States, Canada, Australia	Japan	Mexico, Thailand

(2) *High power distance*—Accepts wide differences in power, great deal of respect for those in authority
Low power distance—Plays down inequalities: employees are not afraid to approach nor are they in awe of the boss

High power distance		*Low power distance*
Mexico, Singapore, France	Italy, Japan	United States, Sweden

(3) *High uncertainty avoidance*—Threatened with ambiguity and experience high levels of anxiety
Low uncertainty avoidance—Comfortable with risks; tolerant of different behaviour and opinions

High uncertainty avoidance		*Low uncertainty avoidance*
Italy, Mexico, France	United Kingdom	Canada, United States, Singapore

(4) *Achievement*—Values such as assertiveness, acquiring money and goods, and - competition prevail
Nurturing—Values such as relationships and concern for others prevail

Achievement		*Nurturing*
United States, Japan, Mexico	Canada, Greece	France, Sweden

(5) *Long-term orientation*—People look to the future and value thrift and persistence
Short-term orientation—People value tradition and the past

Short-term thinking		*Long-term thinking*
Germany, Australia, United States, Canada		China, Taiwan, Japan

These dimensions are described in Exhibit 2-3, which also shows some of the countries characterized by those dimensions.

PRISM 6   Hofstede's findings are based on research that is nearly three decades old, and has been subject to some criticism, which he refutes.[32] In addition, he has recently updated his research, and included studies from a variety of disciplines that support his findings.[33] *Developing Your Interpersonal Skills—Becoming More Culturally Aware,* on pages 58–59, encourages you to think about how to become more comfortable when interacting with people from different cultures.

Doing Business Globally

Menu Foods was forced to remove 60 million packages of its wet pet foods off grocery and pet food store shelves in March 2007.[34] The pet food had been contaminated with melamine, a non food product. Investigators found that the melamine had been mixed with wheat gluten (an ingredient in pet food) at Xuzhou Anying factory in China. Employees apparently deliberately mixed the melamine into the wheat gluten because melamine mimics protein when mixed with gluten. The resulting product would then appear to have a higher nutrient value than it actually did.

China's animal feed producer had been supplementing the feed with melamine for a number of years. "Many companies buy melamine scrap to make animal feed, such as fish feed," says Ji Denghui, general manager of the Fujian Sanming Dinghui Chemical Company, which sells melamine. The additive is inexpensive, thus it reduces product costs. Ji also explains, "I don't know if there's a regulation on it. Probably not. No law or regulation says 'don't do it,' so everyone's doing it. The laws in China are like that, aren't they? If there's no accident, there won't be any regulation."

Think About It

How have the global legal–political and economic environments affected Menu Foods' ability to produce its pet food? What could Menu Foods do to protect itself from importing tainted ingredients from countries that have fewer regulations about food processing than Canada or the United States?

Organizations in different industries and from different countries are pursuing global opportunities. In this section, we look at different types of global organizations and how they do business in the global marketplace.

④ How do organizations do business globally?

Different Types of International Organizations

Despite the fact that doing business internationally is widespread, there is no one generally accepted approach to describing the different types of international companies—they are called different things by different authors. We use the terms *multinational, multidomestic, global,* and *transnational* to describe the various types of international organizations.[35]

Multinational Corporations

Organizations doing business globally are not anything new. DuPont started doing business in China in 1863. H.J. Heinz Company was manufacturing food products in the United Kingdom in 1905. Ford Motor Company set up its first overseas sales branch in France in 1908. But it was not until the mid-1960s that international companies became commonplace. A **multinational corporation (MNC)** is a broad term usually used to refer to any and all types of companies that maintain operations in multiple countries but manages them from a base in the home country. Today, most companies have some type of international dealings.

multinational corporation (MNC)
A broad term that refers to any and all types of international companies that maintain operations in multiple countries.

Multidomestic Corporations

A **multidomestic corporation** is an MNC that maintains significant operations in more than one country but decentralizes management to the local country. This type of organization does not attempt to manage foreign operations from its home country. Instead, local employees typically are hired to manage the business, and marketing strategies are tailored to that country's unique characteristics. Switzerland-based Nestlé can be described as a multidomestic corporation. With operations in almost every country on the globe, its managers match the company's products to its consumers. In parts of Europe, Nestlé sells products that are not available in North America or Latin America. Another example of a multidomestic corporation is Frito-Lay, a division of PepsiCo, which markets a Doritos chip in the British market that differs in both taste and texture from the Canadian and US versions. Many consumer companies manage their global businesses using this approach because they must adapt their products and services to meet the needs of the local markets.

multidomestic corporation
An international company that decentralizes management and other decisions to the local country.

Global Companies

A **global company** is international in scope but centralizes its management and other decisions in the home country. These companies treat the world market as an integrated whole and focus on the need for global efficiency. Although these companies may have considerable global holdings, management decisions with company-wide implications are made from headquarters in the home country. Some examples of companies that can be considered global companies include Montreal-based transport manufacturer Bombardier, Montreal-based aluminum producer Rio Tinto Alcan, Tokyo-based consumer

global company
An international company that centralizes management and other decisions in the home country.

electronics firm Sony, Frankfurt-based Deutsche Bank AG, and New York City–based financial services provider Merrill Lynch.

Transnational or Borderless Organizations

Many companies are going global by eliminating structural divisions that impose artificial geographical barriers. This type of global organization is called a **transnational** or **borderless organization**. For example, IBM dropped its organizational structure based on country and reorganized into industry groups such as business solutions, software, IT services, and financing. Borderless management is an attempt by organizations to increase efficiency and effectiveness in a competitive global marketplace.[36]

Born Globals

Our classification of different types of international organizations tends to describe large international businesses. However, there is an increasing number of businesses, called **born globals**, that choose to go global from inception.[37] These companies (also known as *international new ventures* or *INVs*) commit resources upfront (material, people, financing) to doing business in more than one country and are likely to continue to play an increasingly important role in international business.

How Organizations Go Global

When organizations do go global, they often use different approaches depending on whether they are just starting or whether they have been doing business internationally for awhile (see Exhibit 2-4). During the initial stages of going global, managers look at ways to get into a global market without having to invest a lot of capital. At this stage, companies may start with **global sourcing** (also called *global outsourcing*), which refers to the purchasing of materials or labour from around the world, wherever it is cheapest. The goal is to take advantage of lower costs in order to be more competitive. In 2006, for example, Montreal-based Bell Canada contracted with Sitel India and two other Indian companies to provide technical support and customer care to Canadian customers.[38] Although global sourcing is often the first step to going global, many organizations continue to use this approach even as they become more international, because of the competitive advantages it offers. Beyond global sourcing, however, each successive stage of becoming more international requires more investment and thus entails more risk for the organization.

Exhibit 2-4

How Organizations Go Global

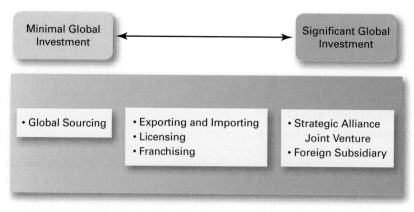

Importing and Exporting

If a company wants to do business in other countries, what choices does it have?

An organization can go global by **exporting** its products to other countries—that is, by making products at home and selling them overseas. In addition, an organization can go global by **importing** products—that is, by selling products at home that are made abroad. Both exporting and importing are small steps toward being a global business and usually involve minimal investment and minimal risk. Many organizations start doing business globally this way. Many, especially small businesses, continue with exporting or importing as the way they do business globally. For example, Haribhai's Spice Emporium, a small business in Durban, South Africa, exports spices and rice to customers all over Africa, Europe, and the United States. Montreal-based Mega Brands (formerly Mega Bloks), with sales in over 100 countries, focuses on exporting. The company holds the number-one position in Canada and Spain, and has a 43 percent share of the UK market.[39] The company operates in eight countries, with more than 1000 employees. Mega Brands is only one example of Canada's increasing reliance on export business. The value of merchandise exported from Canada totalled $489.5 billion in 2008, up 36 percent from 2002.[40] Transportation equipment manufacturing, primary metal manufacturing, and paper manufacturing account for the largest volume of Canadian exports.

exporting
An approach to going global that involves making products at home and selling them abroad.

importing
An approach to going global that involves acquiring products made abroad and selling them at home.

Licensing and Franchising

Some managers use licensing or franchising in the early stages of doing business internationally. Licensing and franchising are similar in that they both involve one organization giving another the right to use its brand name, technology, or product specifications in return for a lump-sum payment or a fee that is usually based on sales. The only difference is that **licensing** is primarily used by manufacturing organizations that make or sell another company's products and **franchising** is primarily used by service organizations that want to use another company's name and operating methods. For example, Russian consumers can enjoy McDonald's hamburgers because McDonald's Canada opened the first Russian franchise in Moscow. Franchises have also made it possible for Mexicans to dine on Richmond, BC-based Boston Pizza and Koreans to consume frozen yogourt from Markham, Ontario-based Coolbrands' Yogen Früz. Anheuser-Busch licenses the right to brew and market Budweiser beer to other brewers, such as Labatt in Canada, Modelo in Mexico, and Kirin in Japan. Licensing and franchising involve more investment and risk than exporting and importing because the company's brand is more at stake.

licensing
An approach to going global in which a manufacturer gives another organization the right to use its brand name, technology, or product specifications.

franchising
An approach to going global in which a service organization gives a person or group the right to sell a product, using specific business methods and practices that are standardized.

Fast-food giant KFC, like many big franchise firms, is opening more new outlets overseas. Along the way, the company is making appropriate changes in its menu offerings, such as substituting juice and fruit for Coke and fries. This Shanghai promotion features egg tarts.

Strategic Alliance

strategic alliance
An approach to going global that involves a partnership between a domestic and a foreign company in which both share resources and knowledge in developing new products or building production facilities.

Typically, once an organization has been doing business internationally for awhile and has gained experience in international markets, managers may decide to make more of a direct investment. One way they can do this is through a **strategic alliance**, which is a partnership between a domestic and a foreign company in which both share resources and knowledge in developing new products or building production facilities. The partners also share the risks and rewards of this alliance. It is not always easy to find a partner, however. When Starbucks decided to open coffee shops in France, it was turned down by four major French food companies it approached as possible joint venture partners. Jean-Paul Brayer, former head of one of the food companies Starbucks approached, commented, "Their contract was way too expensive. It was a win-win situation—but only for Starbucks."[41] Starbucks ended up partnering with a Spanish firm, Grupo VIPS, and together they opened the first Parisian Starbucks in January 2004.

joint venture
An approach to going global in which the partners agree to form a separate, independent organization for some business purpose; it is a type of strategic alliance.

A specific type of strategic alliance in which the partners agree to form a separate, independent organization for some business purpose is called a **joint venture**. Hewlett-Packard has had numerous joint ventures with various suppliers around the globe to develop different components for its computer equipment, such as Tokyo-based Hitachi, which supplies hard drives for HP. These partnerships provide a faster and more inexpensive way for companies to compete globally than doing it on their own.

Foreign Subsidiary

foreign subsidiary
An approach to going global that involves a direct investment in a foreign country by setting up a separate and independent production facility or office.

Managers can make a direct investment in a foreign country by setting up a **foreign subsidiary**, a separate and independent production facility or office. This subsidiary can be managed as an MNC (domestic control), a TNC (foreign control), or as a borderless organization (global control). As you can probably guess, this arrangement involves the greatest commitment of resources and poses the greatest amount of risk. Many of the larger companies operating in Canada are actually subsidiaries of US corporations, including GM Canada, Procter & Gamble Canada, and McDonald's Canada. Canadian subsidiaries manage their operations and set their own targets and goals, but they also report to head office in the United States.

How the Environment Affects Managers

⑤ How does the environment affect managers?

Knowing *what* the various components of the environment are is important to managers. However, understanding *how* the environment affects managers is equally important. The environment affects managers through the degree of environmental uncertainty that is present; through the various stakeholder relationships that exist between the organization and its external constituencies; and through the challenges of managing in a global environment.

Assessing Environmental Uncertainty

environmental uncertainty
The degree of change and the degree of complexity in an organization's environment.

Not all environments are the same. They differ by what we call their degree of **environmental uncertainty**, which is the degree of change and the degree of complexity in an organization's environment (see Exhibit 2-5).

The first of these dimensions is the degree of change. If the components in an organization's environment change frequently, we call it a *dynamic* environment. If change is minimal, we call it a *stable* one. A stable environment might be one in which there are no new competitors, few technological breakthroughs by current competitors, little activity by pressure groups to influence the organization, and so forth. Zippo Canada, best known for its Zippo lighters, faces a relatively stable environment. There are few competitors and there is little technological change. Probably the main environmental concern for the company is the declining trend in tobacco smokers, although the company's lighters have other uses and global markets remain attractive.

Exhibit 2-5

Environmental Uncertainty Matrix

		Degree of Change	
		Stable	**Dynamic**
Degree of Complexity	**Simple**	**Cell 1** Stable and predictable environment Few components in environment Components are somewhat similar and remain basically the same Minimal need for sophisticated knowledge of components	**Cell 2** Dynamic and unpredictable environment Few components in environment Components are somewhat similar but are in continual process of change Minimal need for sophisticated knowledge of components
	Complex	**Cell 3** Stable and predictable environment Many components in environment Components are not similar to one another and remain basically the same High need for sophisticated knowledge of components	**Cell 4** Dynamic and unpredictable environment Many components in environment Components are not similar to one another and are in continual process of change High need for sophisticated knowledge of components

In contrast, the recorded music industry faces a highly uncertain and unpredictable environment. Digital formats such as MP3, music-swapping Internet services, and the ability to buy individual songs from companies such as iTunes have turned the industry upside down. Although music companies traditionally earned revenues by selling physical products such as LP records, cassettes, and CDs, the digital future represents chaos and uncertainty. This environment can definitely be described as dynamic.

What about rapid change that is predictable? Is that considered a dynamic environment? Bricks-and-mortar retail department stores provide a good example. They typically make one-quarter to one-third of their sales in December. The drop-off from December to January is significant. However, because the change is predictable, we do not consider the environment to be dynamic. When we talk about degree of change, we mean change that is unpredictable. If change can be accurately anticipated, it's not an uncertainty that managers must confront.

The other dimension of uncertainty describes the degree of **environmental complexity**. The degree of complexity refers to the number of components in an organization's environment and the extent of the knowledge that the organization has about those components. For example, Hasbro, the world's second-largest toy manufacturer (behind Mattel) has simplified its environment by acquiring many of its competitors such as Tiger Electronics, Wizards of the Coast, Kenner Toys, Parker Brothers, and Tonka Toys. The fewer competitors, customers, suppliers, government agencies, and so forth that an organization must deal with, the less complexity and, therefore, the less uncertainty there is in its environment.

Complexity is also measured in terms of the knowledge an organization needs to have about its environment. For example, managers at the online brokerage E*TRADE must know a great deal about their Internet service provider's operations if they want to ensure that their website is available, reliable, and secure for their stock-trading customers. On the other hand, managers of grocery stores have a minimal need for sophisticated knowledge about their suppliers.

How does the concept of environmental uncertainty influence managers? Looking again at Exhibit 2-5, each of the four cells represents different combinations of degree of complexity and degree of change. Cell 1 (an environment that is stable and simple) represents the lowest level of environmental uncertainty. Cell 4 (an environment that is

environmental complexity
The number of components in an organization's environment and the extent of the organization's knowledge about those components.

dynamic and complex) represents the highest. Not surprisingly, managers' influence on organizational outcomes is greatest in cell 1 and least in cell 4.

Because uncertainty is a threat to an organization's effectiveness, managers try to minimize it. Given a choice, managers would prefer to operate in environments such as those in cell 1. However, they rarely have full control over that choice. In addition, most industries today are facing more dynamic change, making their environments more uncertain. Thus, managers, as planners, need to consider the environment they currently face, as well as thinking ahead about possible changes in the environment, and act accordingly. In a simple, stable environment, a manager may decide to continue doing things in the usual way. In a dynamic, complex environment, a manager may want to develop plans that will keep the organization ahead of competitors, or develop new niches in which to operate.

Managing Stakeholder Relationships

Managers are also affected by the nature of the relationships they have with external stakeholders. The more obvious and secure these relationships become, the more influence managers will have over organizational outcomes.

stakeholders
Any constituencies in the organization's external environment that are affected by the organization's decisions and actions.

Who are **stakeholders**? We define them as groups in the organization's external environment that are affected by and/or have an effect on the organization's decisions and actions. These groups have a stake in or are significantly influenced by what the organization does. In turn, these groups can influence the organization. For example, think of the groups that might be affected by the decisions and actions of Starbucks' managers—coffee bean farmers, employees, specialty-coffee competitors, local communities, and so forth. Some of these stakeholders also may affect the decisions and actions of Starbucks' managers. For example, Starbucks recently changed the way it purchased coffee beans after activists pressured the company to stop buying from plantations that treated their workers poorly. The idea that organizations have stakeholders is now widely accepted by both management academics and practising managers.[42] *Stakeholders* should not be confused with *shareholders*, although shareholders are also stakeholders in an organization. **Shareholders** (also known as stockholders) own one or more shares of stock in a company.

Q&A 2.9

shareholders
Individuals or companies that own stocks in a business.

With what types of stakeholders might an organization have to deal? Exhibit 2-6 identifies some of the most common. Note that these stakeholders include internal and

Organizational Stakeholders

external groups. Why? Because both can affect what an organization does and how it operates. In this chapter, we are primarily interested in the external groups and their impact on managers' discretion in planning, organizing, leading, and controlling. This does not mean that internal stakeholders are not important; we address internal stakeholders, primarily employees, throughout the rest of the textbook.

Why is stakeholder-relationship management important? Why should managers care about stakeholders?[43] One reason is that it can lead to organizational outcomes such as improved predictability of environmental changes, more successful innovations, a greater degree of trust among stakeholders, and greater organizational flexibility to reduce the impact of change. But does it affect organizational performance? The answer is yes! Management researchers who have looked at this issue are finding that managers of high-performing companies tend to consider the interests of all major stakeholder groups as they make decisions.[44]

Another reason given for managing external stakeholder relationships is that it's the "right" thing to do. What does this mean? It means that an organization depends on these external groups as sources of inputs (resources) and as outlets for outputs (goods and services), and managers should consider their interests as they make decisions and take actions.

The more critical the stakeholder and the more uncertain the environment, the more managers need to rely on establishing explicit stakeholder partnerships rather than just acknowledging their existence.

The Pros and Cons of Globalization

What is your attitude toward globalization? Is it favourable or unfavourable?

Doing business globally today isn't easy! Advocates praise the economic and social benefits that come from globalization. Yet that very globalization has created challenges and controversy because of the potential negative impact it can have on the world's poor. Instances of the use of child labour to produce North American goods have come to light. Also, globalization has led to the economic interdependence of trading countries. If one country's economy falters, it could potentially have a domino effect on other countries with which it does business.

Some have predicted that globalization is dead, including Canadian philosopher John Ralston Saul. However, Joel Bakan, a University of British Columbia law professor who wrote *The Corporation* and co-produced the documentary of the same name, claims, "It's overly optimistic to say globalization is dead."[45]

Although supporters of globalization praise it for its economic benefits, there are those who think that it is simply a euphemism for "Americanization"—that is, the spread of US cultural values and business philosophy throughout the world.[46] Critics claim that this attitude of the "almighty American dollar wanting to spread the American way to every single country" has created many problems.[47] Exhibit 2-7 on page 52 outlines the major pro- and anti-globalization arguments. Some of the dominant opponents of globalization include the International Institute for Sustainable Development; the International Forum on Globalization; Greenpeace; the Canadian-based Centre for Research on Globalization; and Canadian author, journalist, and activist Naomi Klein, who is well known for her book *No Logo: Taking Aim at the Brand Bullies*. Some of the main supporters of globalization include London-based International Policy Network, and Washington-based Competitive Enterprise Institute and the Cato Institute.

Because Canada is not seen as a country that wants to spread Canadian values and culture, Canadian managers may have some advantages over their American counterparts in doing business internationally. Managers will need to be aware of how their decisions and actions will be viewed, not only by those who may agree, but, more importantly, by those who may disagree. They will need to adjust their leadership styles and management approaches to accommodate these diverse views. Yet, as always, they will need to do this while still being as efficient and effective as possible in reaching the organization's goals.

Exhibit 2-7

Sample Positions of Anti- and Pro-Globalization Groups

Anti-Globalization Positions	Pro-Globalization Positions
• Globalization is a synonym for Western imperialism.	• Globalization promotes economic prosperity; it offers access to foreign capital, export markets, and advanced technology.
• Trade liberalization may hinder economic development for poorer countries.	• Globalization encourages the efficient use of natural resources and raises environmental awareness and, thus, helps protect the environment.
• There are environmental, social, and economic costs to globalization.	
• Globalization erodes the power of local organizations and local decision-making methods.	• Globalization minimizes government intervention, which can hinder development, in business and in people's lives.
• Globalization can lead to the exploitation of workers' rights and human rights.	• Globalization is a positive force that has encouraged the development of markets, which can bring about prosperity.
• Globalization usually benefits wealthy countries at the expense of poor countries.	
• Lessening or removing trade regulations hurts the poor by pushing up the price of necessities, such as seeds for planting crops and medicine.	

Source: Based on "Who Are the Players?" *Globalisation Guide,* www.globalisationguide.org/02.html (accessed June 7, 2009).

SUMMARY AND IMPLICATIONS

❶ **How much control do managers have?** The omnipotent view of management suggests that managers are directly responsible for an organization's success or failure. While this is the dominant view of managers, there is another perspective. The symbolic view of management argues that much of an organization's success or failure is due to external forces outside managers' control. The reality is probably somewhere in between these two views, with managers often able to exert control, but also facing situations over which they have no control.

Menu Foods purchased many of its pet food ingredients from external suppliers, who in turn also used suppliers for their production needs. Because of this, the company was not initially aware that some of its food product was coming from China, a country with less stringent food safety regulations. With multiple partners, it becomes more difficult to control the various situations managers may face.

❷ **What is the external environment for managers?** The external environment plays a major role in shaping managers' actions. In the specific environment, managers have to be responsive to customers and suppliers while being aware of competitors and public pressure groups. As well, economic, legal–political, socio-cultural, demographic, and technological conditions in the general environment affect the issues managers face in doing their job.

❸ **What challenges do managers face in a global environment?** When managers do business in other countries, they will be affected by the global legal–political and economic environments of those countries. Differing laws and political systems can create constraints as well as opportunities for managers. The type of economic system in some countries can place restrictions on how foreign companies are able to conduct business there. In addition, managers must be aware of the culture of the countries in which they do business to understand *how* business is done and what customers expect.

Menu Foods learned the challenge of relying on pet food ingredients that originate in countries with different food safety standards and regulations. Though Menu Foods' ingredient supplier was American, that company was merely a distributor for Chinese-produced goods. As Menu Foods discovered, in a very unfortunate way, the wheat gluten its company had used in numerous brands was not produced according to the same food safety standards and regulations that exist in Canada and the United States.

④ How do organizations do business globally? Organizations can take on a variety of structures when they go global, including multinational corporations, multidomestic corporations, global companies, and transnational or borderless organizations. An organization can take lower-risk and lower-investment strategies for going global through importing or exporting, hiring foreign representation, or contracting with foreign manufacturers. It can also increase its presence in another country by joining with another business to form a strategic alliance or joint venture. Or it can set up a foreign subsidiary in order to have a full presence in the foreign country.

Menu Foods is a global company that produces private-label and brand-name pet foods for retailers in Canada, the United States, and Mexico. Its headquarters are in Canada, and it has four manufacturing facilities in Canada and the United States. It processes pet food products close to the areas it serves to reduce product costs, such as freight costs, so that it can remain competitive.

⑤ How does the environment affect managers? Because environments can change, sometimes even unexpectedly, managers have to be aware of the degree of environmental uncertainty they face. They also have to be aware of the complexity of the environment that they face. Managers need to manage relationships with their stakeholders—individuals who are influenced by and have an influence on the organization's decisions and actions. Successfully managing in today's global environment requires incredible sensitivity and understanding. Canadian managers may have some advantages over their American counterparts in doing business internationally, because American companies are sometimes viewed as trying to impose American culture on foreign countries.

CHAPTER 2

Management @ Work

READING FOR COMPREHENSION

1. Describe the components of the specific and general environments.

2. Describe the role of the World Trade Organization.

3. Contrast multinational corporations, multidomestic corporations, global companies, and transnational or borderless organizations.

4. Define exporting, importing, licensing, and franchising.

5. Define global strategic alliances, joint ventures, and foreign subsidiaries.

6. Discuss the two dimensions of environmental uncertainty.

7. Identify the most common organizational stakeholders.

LINKING CONCEPTS TO PRACTICE

1. Why is it important for managers to understand the external forces that act on them and their organizations?

2. "Businesses are built on relationships." What do you think this statement means? What are the implications for managing the external environment?

3. What would be the drawbacks in not managing stake-holder relationships?

4. What are the managerial implications of a borderless organization?

5. Compare the advantages and disadvantages of the various approaches to going global.

6. What challenges might confront a Mexican manager transferred to Canada to manage a manufacturing plant in Winnipeg? Will these be the same for a Canadian manager transferred to Guadalajara, Mexico? Explain.

SELF-ASSESSMENT

Am I Well-Suited for a Career as a Global Manager?

For each of the following statements, circle the level of agreement or disagreement according to how well the statement describes you:[48]

1 = Strongly Disagree 2 = Moderately Disagree 3 = Slightly Disagree 4 = Neither Agree nor Disagree
5 = Slightly Agree 6 = Moderately Agree 7 = Strongly Agree

1. When working with people from other cultures, I work hard to understand their perspectives. 1 2 3 4 5 6 7
2. I have a solid understanding of my organization's products and services. 1 2 3 4 5 6 7
3. I am willing to take a stand on issues. 1 2 3 4 5 6 7
4. I have a special talent for dealing with people. 1 2 3 4 5 6 7
5. I can be depended on to tell the truth regardless of circumstances. 1 2 3 4 5 6 7
6. I am good at identifying the most important part of a complex problem or issue. 1 2 3 4 5 6 7
7. I clearly demonstrate commitment to seeing the organization succeed. 1 2 3 4 5 6 7
8. I take personal as well as business risks. 1 2 3 4 5 6 7
9. I have changed as a result of feedback from others. 1 2 3 4 5 6 7
10. I enjoy the challenge of working in countries other than my own. 1 2 3 4 5 6 7
11. I take advantage of opportunities to do new things. 1 2 3 4 5 6 7
12. I find criticism hard to take. 1 2 3 4 5 6 7
13. I seek feedback even when others are reluctant to give it. 1 2 3 4 5 6 7
14. I don't get so invested in things that I cannot change when something does not work. 1 2 3 4 5 6 7

Scoring Key

Reverse your scoring for item 12 (that is, 1 = 7, 2 = 6, 3 = 5, etc.), and then add up your total score.

Analysis and Interpretation

Your total score will range from 14 to 98. The higher your score, the greater your potential for success as an international manager.

In today's global economy, being a manager often means being a global manager. But unfortunately, not all managers are able to transfer their skills smoothly from domestic environments to global ones. Your results here can

help you assess whether your skills align with those needed to succeed as an international manager.

More Self-Assessments

To learn more about your skills, abilities, and interests, take the following self-assessment on MyManagementLab at www.pearsoned.ca/mymanagementlab:

- III.B.3.—Am I Experiencing Work/Family Conflict?

MANAGEMENT FOR YOU TODAY

Dilemma

You are considering organizing an event to raise funds for a special cause (children living in poverty, breast cancer research, illiteracy, or another cause of your choice). Think about who you might invite to this event (that is, your "customers"—those who will buy tickets to the event). What

type of event might appeal to them? What suppliers might you approach for help in organizing the event? What legal issues might you face in setting up this event? After considering all these specific environmental forces, describe the challenges you could face in holding this event.

Becoming a Manager

- Familiarize yourself with current global political, economic, and cultural issues.

- If given the opportunity, try to have your class projects or reports (in this class and other classes) cover global issues or global companies.

- Talk to instructors or students who may be from other countries and ask them what the business world is like in their countries.

- When you evaluate companies for class assignments (for this class and others you may be enrolled in), get in the habit of looking at the stakeholders that might be affected by these companies' decisions and actions.

WORKING TOGETHER: TEAM-BASED EXERCISE

Assessing Employees' Global Aptitudes

Moving to a foreign country is not easy, no matter how many times you have done it or how receptive you are to new experiences. Successful global organizations are able to identify the best candidates for global assignments, and one of the ways they do this is through individual assessments prior to assigning people to global facilities. Form groups of 3 to 5 individuals. Your newly formed team, the Global Assignment Task Force, has been given the responsibility for developing a global aptitude assessment form for Zara, the successful European clothing retailer.[49] Although the company is not well known in North America, Zara's managers have positioned the company for continued global success. That success is based on a simple principle— in fashion, nothing is as important as time to market.

Zara's store managers (more than 600 worldwide) offer suggestions every day on cuts, fabrics, and even new lines. After reviewing the ideas, a team at headquarters in La Coruna, Spain, decides what to make. Designers draw up

the ideas and send them over the company's intranet to nearby factories. Within days, the cutting, dyeing, sewing, and assembling start. In three weeks, the clothes will be in stores from Barcelona to Berlin to Buenos Aires. That is 12 times faster than its competitors. Zara has a twice-a-week delivery schedule that restocks old styles and brings in new designs. Competitors tend to get new designs once or twice a season.

Because Zara is expanding its global operations significantly, management wants to make sure they are sending the best possible people to the various global locations. Your team's assignment is to come up with a rough draft of a form to assess people's global aptitudes. Think about the characteristics, skills, attitudes, and so on, that you think a successful global employee would need. Your team's draft should be at least a half page but not longer than 1 page. Be prepared to present your ideas to your classmates and instructor.

ETHICS IN ACTION

Ethical Dilemma Exercise: What Should a Company Do When It Faces Opposition to Expansion in Another Country?

Montreal-based Rio Tinto Alcan (formerly Alcan) is the world's largest primary aluminum producer.[50] The company has some 68 000 employees and 430 facilities in 61 countries; it posted a profit of $129 million in 2005. The company plans to develop a $1.8-billion strip mine and refinery in Orissa state, 1200 kilometres southeast of New Delhi, India.

The company has only recently been given permission to begin developing the mine. For a number of years, local people have expressed concern that the mining activities will uproot the Adivasis, some of India's indigenous tribes. Several years ago the protests against developing the mine grew violent when state police fired guns at the Adivasis, killing three protesters. Rio Tinto Alcan's plans were put on hold while government officials conducted an inquiry into the deaths. The government concluded that tribal areas "cannot afford to remain backward for the sake of so-called environmental protection."

Bhagawan Majhi serves as sarpanch (chief) of Kucheipadar village, where the violence took place. He has led the opposition to the mines since he was a teen, and says, "Our fight will continue until the government revokes its agreement with the company."

Rio Tinto Alcan insists on carrying through with the mine, even though one of its partners in the project, Norway-based Norsk Hydro, decided to quit the project after three of its employees were kidnapped by tribe members.

Rio Tinto Alcan spokespeople claim that the mine can actually improve the life of the Adivasis. The company promises to create more than 1000 jobs, and each tribal family will be given at least one. Employees will get a health clinic that others in the area can use. Majhi does not believe that the Adivasis will be better off with the mine. For one thing, the Baphlimali Hill, which is sacred to their tribe, will be ruined. He also says that land is more important than jobs. "What will we do with the money? We don't know how to do business," he notes. He also talks about how the lives of villagers who accepted money from Rio Tinto Alcan in exchange for drilling rights have been ruined: "They spent it on alcohol, they married two or three women, they bought wristwatches and motorcycles," Majhi says.

Rio Tinto Alcan's CEO at the time, Travis Engen, was given notice two weeks before the annual general meeting that several shareholders would protest the company's plans to develop the mine on Adivasis land. He knew that he would have to respond to their complaints at the meeting. Would it have made sense to simply abandon the mining plans in the face of protests? What should he have told shareholders at the meeting about Rio Tinto Alcan's future plans for the region?

Thinking Critically About Ethics

Foreign countries often have lax product labelling laws. As the international product manager for a Canadian pharmaceutical company, you are responsible for the profitability of a new drug to be sold outside Canada. The drug's side effects can be serious, although not fatal. Adding this information to the label or even putting an informational insert into the package will add to the product's cost, threatening profitability margins. What will you do? Why? What factors will influence your decision?

CASE APPLICATION

National Basketball Association

Using an exceptionally well-executed game plan, the National Basketball Association (NBA) has emerged as the first truly global sports league.[51] During the 2008–2009 season, viewers in 215 countries watched NBA basketball games broadcast in 41 different languages.[52] The game was invented in 1891 by Canadian James Naismith, from Almonte, Ontario, and the Toronto Raptors and Vancouver Grizzlies were the first non-US cities to join the league, during the 1995–1996 season.

The desire to transform the once-faltering domestic sport into a global commercial success reflects a keen understanding of managing in a global environment. Much of the credit should go to NBA commissioner David Stern, who has been consciously building the NBA into a global brand.

Professional basketball sparked the interest of fans and players around the globe in the mid-1990s. At one time, if you had asked someone in China what the most popular basketball team was, the answer would have been the "Red Oxen" from Chicago (the Bulls). Today, the NBA's centre of attention comes from China. Yao Ming, the 2.2-metre-tall centerpiece of the Houston Rockets, has a personality that

appeals to fans around the world. But he is not the only foreign player in the league. Others include Andrea Bargnani of the Toronto Raptors (from Italy); Dirk Nowitzki of the Dallas Mavericks (from Germany); Pau Gasol of the Los Angeles Lakers (from Spain); Tony Parker of the San Antonio Spurs (from France); Nenê Hilario of the Denver Nuggets (from Brazil); and Gordan Giricek of the Phoenix Suns (from Croatia). What started as a trickle in the 1980s, with occasional foreign stars such as Hakeem Olajuwon (Nigeria) and the late Dražen Petrović (Croatia), has turned into a flood. A total of 60 players from 28 countries and territories outside the United States were playing in the NBA as of July 2007. These include Canadian players Jamaal Magloire of the Miami Heat and Steve Nash of the Phoenix Suns. Seventeen Canadian basketball players have played in the NBA over the years. The NBA wants to prove that one day there can be affiliated teams throughout the world.

What strategies can Stern use to increase consumer familiarity with basketball both domestically and globally? How can he develop a greater basketball presence in Canada?

DEVELOPING YOUR DIAGNOSTIC AND ANALYTICAL SKILLS

When Yes Does Not Always Mean Yes, and No Does Not Always Mean No

When a major chip-manufacturing project ran more than a month late, David Sommers, vice-president for engineering at Adaptec, felt that perhaps the company's Indian engineers "didn't understand the sense of urgency" in getting the project completed.[53] In the Scottish Highlands, Bill Matthews, the general manager of McTavish's Kitchens, is quite satisfied with his non-Scottish employees—cooks who are German, Swedish, and Slovak and waitresses who are mostly Polish. Other Highland hotels and restaurants also have a large number of Eastern European staff. Despite the obvious language barriers, these Scottish employers are finding ways to help their foreign employees adapt and be successful. When Lee Epting, the US-born vice-president of Forum Nokia, gave a presentation to a Finnish audience and asked for feedback, she was told, "That was good." Based on his interpretation of that phrase, he assumed that it must have been just an okay presentation . . . nothing spectacular. However, because Finns tend to be generally much quieter and more reserved than North Americans, that response actually meant, "That was great, off the scale."

It's not easy being a successful global manager, especially when it comes to dealing with cultural differences. Research by Wilson Learning Worldwide says there is an "iceberg of culture, of which we can only see the top 15 percent—food, appearance, and language." Although these elements themselves can be complicated, it's the other 85 percent of the "iceberg" that is not apparent initially that managers need to be especially concerned about. What does that include? Workplace issues such as communication styles, prioritizing, role expectations, work tempo, negotiation styles, nonverbal communication, attitudes toward planning, and so forth. Understanding these issues requires developing a global mindset and skill set. Many organizations are relying on cultural awareness training to help them do just that.

Having outsourced some engineering jobs to India, Axcelis Technologies had its North American–based employees go through a training program in which they role-played scenarios with one person pretending to be Indian and the other his or her North American co-worker. One of the company's human resources directors said, "At first I was skeptical and wondered what I'd get out of the class, but it was enlightening for me. Not everyone operates like we do in North America." In our global world, successful managers must learn to recognize and appreciate cultural differences and to understand how to work effectively and efficiently with employees, no matter what their nationality is.

Questions

1. What global attitude do you think would most support, promote, and encourage cultural awareness? Explain.

2. Would legal–political and economic differences play a role as companies design appropriate cultural awareness training for employees? Explain.

3. Pick one of the countries mentioned in the case and do some cultural research on it. What did you find out about the culture of that country? How might this information affect the way a manager in that country plans, organizes, leads, and controls?

4. UK-based company Kwintessential has several cultural awareness "quizzes" on its website (**www.kwintessential. co.uk/resources/culture-tests.html**). Go to the company's website and try 2 or 3 of these. Were you surprised at your score? What does your score tell you about your cultural awareness?

5. What advice might you give to a manager who has little experience working with people in other countries?

Becoming More Culturally Aware

About the Skill

"Understanding and managing people who are similar to us are challenges—but understanding and managing those who are *dissimilar from us and from each other* can be even tougher." Workplaces around the world are becoming increasingly diverse. Thus, managers need to recognize that not all employees want the same thing, act in the same manner, and can be managed in the same way. What is a diverse workforce? It's one that is heterogeneous in terms of gender, race, ethnicity, age, and other characteristics that reflect differences. Valuing diversity and helping a diverse workforce achieve its maximum potential are becoming indispensable skills for more and more managers.

Steps in Developing the Skill

The diversity issues an individual manager might face are many. They might include communicating with employees whose familiarity with the language might be limited; creating career development programs that fit the skills, needs, and values of a variety of employees; helping a diverse team cope with a conflict over goals or work assignments; or learning which rewards are valued by different groups of employees. You can improve your handling of diversity issues by following these eight behaviours:[54]

1. **Fully accept diversity.** Successfully valuing diversity starts with each individual's accepting the principle of multiculturalism. Accept the value of diversity for its own sake—not simply because you have to. Accepting and valuing diversity is important because it's the right thing to do. And it's important that you reflect your acceptance in all you say and do.

2. **Recruit broadly.** When you have job openings, work to get a diverse applicant pool. Although referrals from current employees can be a good source of applicants, they tend to produce candidates similar to the current workforce.

3. **Select fairly.** Make sure that the selection process does not discriminate. One suggestion is to use job-specific tests rather than general aptitude or knowledge tests. Such tests measure specific skills, not subjective characteristics.

4. **Provide orientation and training for minorities.** Making the transition from outsider to insider can be particularly difficult for an employee who belongs to a minority group. Provide support either through a group or through a mentoring arrangement.

5. **Sensitize nonminorities.** Not only do you personally need to accept and value diversity, but as a manager you need to encourage all your employees to do so. Many organizations do this through diversity training programs, in which employees examine the cultural norms of different groups. The most important thing a manager can do is show by his or her actions that diversity is valued.

6. **Strive to be flexible.** Part of valuing diversity is recognizing that different groups have different needs and values. Be flexible in accommodating employees' requests.

7. **Seek to motivate individually.** Motivating employees is an important skill for any manager; motivating a diverse workforce has its own special challenges. Managers must be more in tune with the background, cultures, and values of employees. What motivates a single mother with two young children and who is working full time to support her family is likely to be different from the needs of a young, single, part-time employee or an older employee who is working to supplement his or her retirement income.

8. **Reinforce employee differences.** Encourage individuals to embrace and value diverse views. Create traditions and ceremonies that promote diversity. Celebrate diversity by accentuating its positive aspects. However, also be prepared to deal with the challenges of diversity such as mistrust, miscommunication, lack of cohesiveness, attitudinal differences, and stress.

Practising the Skill

Read the descriptions of the following employees who work for the same organization. After reading each description, write a short paragraph describing what you think the goals and priorities of each employee might be. With what types of employee issues might the manager of each employee have to deal? How could these managers exhibit the value of diversity?

Lester is 57 years old, a college graduate, and a vice-president of the firm. His two children are married, and he is a grandparent of three grandchildren. He lives in a condo with his wife who does volunteer work and is active in their church. Lester is healthy and likes to stay active, both physically and mentally.

Sanjyot is a 30-year-old clerical worker who came to Canada from Indonesia 10 years ago. She completed high school after moving to Canada and has begun to attend evening classes at a local college. Sanjyot is a single parent with two children under the age of eight. Although her health is excellent, one of her children suffers from a severe learning disability.

Yuri is a recent immigrant from one of the former Soviet republics. He is 42 years old and his English communication skills are quite limited. He has an engineering degree from his country but since he is not licensed to practise in Canada, he works as a parts clerk. He is unmarried and has no children but feels an obligation to his relatives back in his home country. He sends much of his paycheque to them.

Continuing Case: Starbucks

Community. Connection. Caring. Committed. Coffee.[1] Five Cs that describe the essence of Starbucks Corporation—what it stands for and what it wants to be as a business. With over 15 000 outlets in 44 countries, Starbucks is the world's number-one specialty coffee retailer. It's also a company that truly epitomizes the challenges facing managers in today's globally competitive environment. To help you better understand these challenges, we are going to take an in-depth look at Starbucks through these continuing cases, which you will find at the end of every part in the textbook. Each of these five part-ending continuing cases will look at Starbucks from the perspective of the material presented in that part. Although each case "stands alone," you will be able to see the progression of the management process as you work through each one.

So how does Starbucks epitomize the five Cs—community, connection, caring, committed, and coffee? That is what you will discover as you complete the remaining continuing cases. Keep in mind that as you do the other cases, there may be information included in this introduction you might want to review.

The Beginning

"We aren't in the coffee business, serving people. We're in the people business, serving coffee." That is the philosophy of Howard Schultz, chair, president, and CEO of Starbucks. It's a philosophy that has shaped—and continues to shape—the company.

The first Starbucks, which opened in Seattle's famous Pike Place Market in 1971, was founded by Gordon Bowker, Jerry Baldwin, and Zev Siegl. The company was named for the coffee-loving first mate in the book Moby Dick, which also influenced the design of Starbucks' distinctive two-tailed siren logo. Schultz, a successful New York City businessperson, first walked into Starbucks in 1981 as a sales representative for a Swedish kitchenware manufacturer. He was hooked immediately. He knew that he wanted to work for this company, but it took almost a year before he could persuade the owners to hire him. After all, he was from New York and he had not grown up with the values of the company. The owners thought Schultz's style and high energy would clash with the existing culture. But Schultz was quite persuasive and was able to allay the owners' fears. They asked him to join the company as director of retail operations and marketing, which he enthusiastically did. Schultz's passion for the coffee business was obvious. Although some of the company's employees resented the fact that he was an "outsider," Schultz had found his niche and he had lots of ideas for the company. As he says, "I wanted to make a positive impact."

About a year after joining the company, while on a business trip to Milan, Schultz walked into an espresso bar and right away knew that this concept could be successful in the United States. He said, "There was nothing like this in America. It was an extension of people's front porch. It was an emotional experience. I believed intuitively we could do it. I felt it in my bones." Schultz recognized that although Starbucks treated coffee as produce, something to be bagged and sent home with the groceries, the Italian coffee bars were more like an experience . . . a warm, community experience. That is what Schultz wanted to recreate in the United States. However, Starbucks' owners were not really interested in making Starbucks big and did not really want to give the idea a try. So Schultz left the company in 1985 to start his own small chain of espresso bars in Seattle and Vancouver called Il Giornale. Two years later, when Starbucks' owners finally wanted to sell, Schultz raised $3.8 million from local investors to buy them out. That small investment has made him a very wealthy person indeed, and allowed him to open his first Canadian store in Vancouver in 1987. In 1996, Starbucks went east, opening five stores in the greater Toronto area. By 2007, Starbucks had over 500 stores across Canada.

Company Facts

Starbucks' main product is coffee . . . more than 30 blends and single-origin coffees. In addition to fresh-brewed coffee, here is a sampling of other products the company offers:

- *Handcrafted beverages:* Hot and iced espresso beverages, coffee and noncoffee blended beverages, and Tazo® teas
- *Merchandise:* Home espresso machines, coffee brewers and grinders, premium chocolates, coffee mugs and coffee accessories, compact discs, and other assorted items
- *Fresh food:* Baked pastries, sandwiches, and salads

Pike Place Market was the site of the first Starbucks coffee shop, opened in 1971, in Seattle, Washington.

- *Global consumer products:* Starbucks Frappuccino® coffee drinks, Starbucks Iced Coffee drinks, Starbucks Coffee Liqueurs, Starbucks Discoveries® coffee drinks (in Japan and Taiwan), Starbucks DoubleShot® espresso drinks, and a line of super-premium ice creams
- *Starbucks Card:* A reloadable stored-value card
- *Starbucks Entertainment:* A selection of music, books, and film from new and established talent
- *Brand portfolio:* Starbucks Entertainment, Ethos™ Water, Seattle's Best Coffee, Tazo® teas, Starbucks Hear Music, and Torrefazione Italia Coffee

At the end of 2006, the company had over 145 000 full- and part-time partners (employees) around the world. Starbucks also has "interesting" top-level executive positions: senior vice-president of total pay, senior vice-president of coffee and global procurement, senior vice-president of global business systems solutions, senior vice-president of culture and leadership development, and senior vice-president of corporate social responsibility.

Starbucks Culture and Environment

As managers manage, they must be aware of the terrain or broad environment within which they plan, organize, lead, and control. The characteristics and nature of this "terrain" will influence what managers and other employees do and how they do it. More importantly, it will affect how efficiently and effectively managers do their job of coordinating and overseeing the work of other people so that goals—organizational and work-level or work unit—can be accomplished. What does Starbucks' terrain look like and how is the company adapting to that terrain?

An organization's culture is a mix of written and unwritten values, beliefs, and codes of behaviour that influence the way work gets done and the way that people behave in the organization. The distinct flavour of Starbucks' culture can be traced to the original founders' philosophies and Schultz's unique beliefs about how a company should be run. The three friends (Bowker, Baldwin, and Siegl) who founded Starbucks in 1971 as a store in Seattle's historic Pike Place Market district did so for one reason: They loved coffee and tea and wanted Seattle to have access to the best. They had no intention of building a business empire. Their business philosophy, although never written down, was simple: "Every company must stand for something; don't just give customers what they ask for or what they think they want; and assume that your customers are intelligent and seekers of knowledge." The original Starbucks was a company passionately committed to world-class coffee and dedicated to educating its customers, one on one, about what great coffee can be. It was these qualities that ignited Schultz's passion for the coffee business and inspired him to envision what Starbucks could become. Schultz continues to have that passion for his business—he is the visionary and soul behind Starbucks. He visits at least 30 to 40 stores a week, talking to partners (employees) and to customers. His ideas for running a business have been called "unconventional," but Schultz does not care. He says, "We can be extremely profitable and competitive, with a highly regarded brand, and also be respected for treating our people well." One member of the company's board of directors says about him, "Howard is consumed with his vision of Starbucks. That means showing the good that a corporation can do for its workers, shareholders, and customers."

The company's mission is as follows: "To establish Starbucks as the premier purveyor of the finest coffee in the world while maintaining our uncompromising principles as we grow." What are those principles that guide the decisions and actions of company partners from top to bottom?

- "Provide a great work environment and treat each other with respect and dignity."
- "Embrace diversity as an essential component in the way we do business."

Starbucks chair, president, and CEO Howard Schultz (on left).

- "Apply the highest standards of excellence to the purchasing, roasting, and fresh delivery of our coffee."
- "Develop enthusiastically satisfied customers all of the time."
- "Contribute positively to our communities and our environment."
- "Recognize that profitability is essential to our future success."

Starbucks' culture emphasizes keeping employees motivated and content. One thing that has been important to Schultz from day one is the relationship that he has with his employees. He treasures those relationships and feels that they are critically important to the way the company develops its relationships with its customers and the way it is viewed by the public. He says, "We know that our people are the heart and soul of our success." Starbucks' employees worldwide serve millions of customers each week. That is a lot of opportunities to either satisfy or disappoint the customer. The experiences customers have in the stores ultimately affect the company's relationships with its customers. That is why Starbucks has created a unique relationship with its employees. Starbucks provides all employees who work more than 20 hours a week health care benefits and stock options. Schultz says, "The most important thing I ever did was give our partners [employees] bean stock [options to buy the company's stock]. That's what sets us apart and gives us a higher-quality employee, an employee that cares more." And Starbucks does care about its employees. For example, when a manager of a downtown Vancouver outlet was murdered while saving the life of a fellow employee who was being attacked by a man with a butcher's knife, Schultz attended the memorial service. In addition, about a dozen Starbucks stores were closed for that evening, allowing about 400 Starbucks employees to attend the service. Schultz spoke at the ceremony and later read a statement to the media: "I have been incredibly moved by the words and gestures from the many people who were touched by Tony's life. . . . We will never forget

Tony. His heroism and joyful spirit will touch us forever." It probably should not come as a surprise that Starbucks has the lowest level of employee attrition (leaving) of any comparable retailer.

As a global company with annual revenues well over $7 billion, Starbucks' executives recognize they must be aware of the impact the environment has on their decisions and actions. The company recently began lobbying legislators in Washington, DC, on issues including lowering trade barriers, health care costs, and tax breaks. It's something that Schultz did not really want to do, but he recognizes that such efforts could be important to the company's future.

Global Challenges

Although Starbucks does business in 42 countries, about 85 percent of Starbucks' revenues come from the US market. Much of the company's future growth, however, is likely to be global. In fact, the company has targeted four markets for major global expansion: China, Brazil, India, and Russia. As Starbucks continues its global push, it has to be concerned not only with the product, but also with staffing issues. The president of Starbucks Coffee International says, "These emerging markets have a great deal to offer. They are rich in culture, heritage, and untapped resources, possessing, in many cases, an eager workforce keen to better their lives, which in turn improves the social and economic situation in their respective country."

Starbucks entered the Chinese market in 1999 and currently has 140 stores there, which it feels is an accomplishment, given the fact that this is a country of tea drinkers. However, Starbucks feels there are untapped opportunities as China becomes a stronger economic force and as young, newly affluent urban Chinese workers embrace drinking quality coffee products. One of the major problems that Starbucks encountered in China—an imitator by the name of Shanghai Xing Ba Ke coffee shops (loosely translated as "Shanghai Starbucks") that was creating customer confusion—has been resolved. A Chinese court ordered the imitator to pay Starbucks rmb500 000 (approximately $62 000) for copying the Starbucks name and logo. This trademark protection victory was an important one for Starbucks.

Corporate Social Responsibility and Ethics

Good coffee is important to Starbucks, but equally important is doing good. Starbucks takes that commitment seriously. Its website states, "Corporate Social Responsibility. It's the way we do business. Contributing positively to our communities and environment is so important to Starbucks that it's a guiding principle of our mission statement. We jointly fulfill this commitment with partners [employees], at all levels of the company, by getting involved together to help build stronger communities and conserve natural resources." Here is a list of some of the things that Starbucks has done in relation to its corporate social responsibilities:

- Requires its stores to donate to local causes and charities
- Made part-time employees eligible for health and pension benefits
- Works to protect the rainforest
- Introduced recycled-content paper cups in early 2006
- Introduced a bottled-water product called Ethos and will donate 5 cents per bottle sold to boost clean-water supplies in poorer countries
- Provided assistance to coffee farmers and their families in southwest Mexico and northwest Guatemala after Hurricane Stan in October 2005
- Launched an international program to offer better pay to coffee farmers who treat their workers and the environment decently

In 2001, the company began issuing an annual corporate social responsibility report, which addresses the company's decisions and actions in relation to its products, society, the environment, and the workplace. These reports are not simply a way for Starbucks to brag about its socially responsible actions, but are intended to stress the importance of doing business in a responsible way and to hold employees and managers accountable for their actions.

Starbucks also takes its ethical commitments seriously. Each top-level manager who has financial responsibilities signs a "Code of Ethics" that affirms his or her commitment to balancing, protecting, and preserving stakeholders' interests. All store employees (partners) have resources ("Standards of Business Conduct"; the Partner Guide; the Safety, Security and Health Standards Manual) to help them in doing their jobs ethically. And the company created a process for employees to raise complaints and concerns they may have over questionable accounting and internal accounting controls.

Questions

1. What management skills do you think would be most important for Howard Schultz to have? Why? What skills do you think would be most important for a Starbucks store manager to have? Why?
2. How might the following management theories/approaches be useful to Starbucks: scientific management, organizational behaviour, quantitative approach, systems approach?
3. Choose three of the current trends and issues facing managers and explain how Starbucks might be affected. What might be the implications for first-line managers? Middle managers? Top managers?

4. Give examples of how Howard Schultz might perform the interpersonal roles, the informational roles, and the decisional roles.
5. Look at Howard Schultz's philosophy of Starbucks. How will this affect the way the company is managed?
6. Go to the company's website (**www.starbucks.com**) and find the list of senior officers. Pick one of those positions and describe what you think that job might involve. Try to envision what types of planning, organizing, leading, and controlling this person would have to do.
7. What do you think of the company's guiding principles? Describe how the company's guiding principles would influence how a barista at a local Starbucks store does his or her job. Describe how these principles would influence how one of the company's top executives does his or her job.
8. Do you think Howard Schultz views his role more from the omnipotent or from the symbolic perspective? Explain.
9. What has made Starbucks' culture what it is? How is that culture maintained?
10. Does Starbucks encourage a customer-responsive culture? An ethical culture? Explain.
11. Describe some of the specific and general environmental components that are likely to affect Starbucks.
12. How would you classify the uncertainty of the environment in which Starbucks operates? Explain.
13. What stakeholders do you think Starbucks might be most concerned with? Why? What issue(s) might each of these stakeholders want Starbucks to address?
14. Why do you think Howard Schultz is uncomfortable with the idea of legislative lobbying? Do you think his discomfort is appropriate? Why or why not?
15. What types of global economic and legal–political issues might Starbucks face?
16. You are responsible for developing a global cultural awareness program for Starbucks' executives who are leading the company's international expansion efforts. Describe what you think will be important for these executives to know.
17. Go to the company's website (**www.starbucks.com**) and find the latest corporate social responsibility annual report. Choose one of the key areas in the report (or your instructor may assign one of these areas). Describe and evaluate what the company has done in this key area.
18. What do you think the company's use of the term *partners* instead of *employees* implies? What is your reaction to this? Do you think it matters what companies call their employees? (For example, Walmart calls its employees associates.) Why or why not?
19. What does Starbucks' terrain look like and how is the company adapting to that terrain?
20. How effective is Starbucks at recognizing and managing its terrain? Explain.

VIDEO CASE INCIDENTS

CBC 🕸 Video Case Incident

Greenlite

With growing concern over climate change, governments around the world are looking for ways to reduce greenhouse gases and consumption of fossil fuels. One simple solution that has garnered government support is phasing out energy-inefficient light bulbs and replacing them with energy-efficient ones. The most popular commercially available and affordable bulbs are compact fluorescent light bulbs (CFLs). CFLs use approximately 75 percent less energy than regular incandescent light bulbs. CFLs also have a long lifespan, typically 6000 to 15 000 hours, as compared to the 750- to 1000-hour lifespan of a normal incandescent bulb.

Beginning in 2006, the Government of Canada began replacing light bulbs in all federal government buildings with CFLs. In April 2007, the Government of Canada announced it would legislate a complete ban on the sale of inefficient light bulbs by 2012. According to the Minister of Natural Resources, Gary Lunn, the ban will reduce greenhouse gas emissions by over 6 million tonnes a year.

Canada was not the only country to phase out energy-inefficient light bulbs. In 2007, the United States government signed the Clean Energy Act into law. This legislation effectively phases out the sale of incandescent bulbs in the United States by January 2014.

Canadian Nina Gupta viewed these developments as a business opportunity. Her father owned a factory in India that made halogen bulbs for cars. She founded Greenlite Lighting Corporation, managed the transition in her father's factory to the production of CFLs, and began selling CFLs in India, Canada, and the United States. "We recognized that the green movement was the wave of the future," she says, "so we found a product that was ecologically and environmentally friendly and focused on that."

Greenlite is now one of the leading producers of CFLs in the world, selling over 30 million CFLs a year.

QUESTIONS

1. *For analysis:* How did the general environment influence Nina Gupta's decision to sell energy-efficient light bulbs in North America?

2. *For application:* Greenlite plans to expand its business by building a factory in India, at a cost of $250 million, that will produce solar energy. Greenlite also intends to manage the employees in this factory. The company speculates it will be able to sell energy to consumers in the United States, China, and India. What challenges do you anticipate the corporation could face in carrying out these plans for globalization?

3. *For application:* Explain how the specific environment will change for Greenlite if it decides to sell solar energy to customers in the United States, China, and India.

4. *For debate:* Some university researchers have noted a number of health risks associated with CFL bulbs. These bulbs often contain a large amount of mercury, which can be dangerous for children if the bulbs are broken and the mercury is released into the air. Furthermore, some research has shown that emission of UV radiation from CFLs may be related to skin rashes, headaches, and depression in adults who are sensitive to UV radiation exposure. These problems should not be of concern to the management of Greenlite, as their only responsibility is to maximize the profits of the business. Do you agree? Why or why not?

Sources: "Greenlite," *Fortune Hunters, My First Million,* February 28, 2009; Greenlite Lighting Corporation website, www.greenlite.ca (accessed August 13, 2009); Petition filed with the Office of the Auditor General of Canada, www.oag-bvg.gc.ca/internet/English/pet_254_e_31427.html (accessed August 24, 2009); "Lights Go Out On Inefficient Bulbs by 2012," *CBC News,* April 25, 2007, www.cbc.ca/canada/story/2007/04/25/lunn-bulbs.html (accessed August 27, 2009); "Health Canada Testing Compact Fluorescent Bulbs For Harmful Radiation," *CBC News,* January 21, 2009, www.cbc.ca/health/story/2009/01/21/bulbs.html (accessed August 24, 2009).

Mountain Equipment Co-op

In 1971, Mountain Equipment Co-op (MEC) was founded in Vancouver by a group of Canadian rock climbers who needed a store to buy gear that other, more conventional retailers did not carry, including gear for mountaineering, rock climbing, and hiking. MEC is a cooperative in which members employ their shared purchasing power to obtain goods and services for outdoor activities. Anyone can become a member at MEC by buying a $5 membership share. MEC now ranks as the largest retail cooperative in Canada and sells a broad range of outdoor gear, clothing, and services.

In its first 30 years, MEC focused on the sale of clothing made only in Canada. MEC billed its "made in Canada" strategy as an initiative promoting corporate social responsibility that supported the local economy and created jobs for Canadians. In recent years, however, the cooperative's commitment to this strategy has lagged. In 2002, 70 percent of the clothing it sold was made in Canada, while in 2007 only 50 percent of the clothing in its stores was made locally.

The stated reason for this change in strategy is that locally made clothing is too costly. MEC's major foreign suppliers are now located in India and China, and these suppliers sell their products at lower prices due to the lower cost of labour in these countries. Some foreign-made products can be sold to members for nearly half the cost of the same products made in Canada. Former MEC CEO Steve Robinson reported that to sell more Canadian-produced goods the organization would have to "eat the profit margin" in order to make these goods affordable for its members. The company's latest research shows that, in general, most members will pay only slightly more for clothing made in Canada. Beyond a certain point, MEC is likely to lose the sale.

This change in strategy is bad news for Canadian outdoor clothing manufacturers.

QUESTIONS

1. *For analysis:* Identify the stakeholders affected by MEC's decision to sell fewer goods manufactured in Canada and more goods manufactured abroad.

2. *For application:* Explain how each stakeholder is affected and identify which stakeholders are the most critical to MEC.

3. *For application:* Explain how MEC is "going global" and describe what degree of risk and investment is involved in this endeavour.

4. *For debate:* As a company created in Canada, managed in Canada, and selling goods exclusively in Canada, MEC has a social responsibility to sell primarily Canadian manufactured goods. Do you agree? Why or why not?

Sources: "MEC," *The National*, May 30, 2007; Mountain Equipment Co-op website, www.mec.ca (accessed August 25, 2009).

After you have completed your study of Part 1, do the following exercises on MyManagementLab at www.pearsoned.ca/mymanagementlab:

- *You're the Manager: Putting Ethics into Action* (**Lindblad Expeditions**)

- *Passport, Scenario 1* (**Paula Seeger, Java World**), *Scenario 2* (**Charles Mathidi, QSI**), and *Scenario 3* (**André Fasset, PhenomGaming**)

CHAPTER **3**

Planning and Strategic Management

How do I make plans to carry out decisions?

1 What does planning involve?

2 How do managers set goals and develop plans?

3 What are the steps in strategic management?

4 What kinds of strategies can managers use?

5 How can quality be a competitive advantage?

Heather Reisman and husband Gary Schwartz, owners of Toronto-based Indigo Books & Music, opened their first store in Burlington, Ontario, in September 1997.[1] By 2000, there were 14 locations across Canada. Indigo was the first book retailer in Canada to sell music and gifts and to include licensed cafés in their stores. The company faced stiff competition from Chapters, however, which was formed by the merger of SmithBooks and Coles in 1995. By 2000, Chapters was the top retail book brand in Canada, having achieved that rank from consumers for four consecutive years (from 1997 to 2000).

In November 2000, Reisman and Schwartz announced their bid to buy Chapters, and though a bitter battle ensued, the two companies merged in August 2001.

The merger was not a smooth one. Before the merger could be approved, the Competition Bureau imposed a number of conditions, including the sale or closing of 20 stores and a code of conduct for dealing with publishers. These rules affected the way Indigo/Chapters could do business until 2006.

Reisman has taken Canada's biggest book chain from a $48-million loss in 2002 to a $30-million profit in 2006, which represents an increase of

18 percent over 2005. With profit firmly part of her business plan, Reisman is now trying to determine a strategy that will lead to more growth.

Think About It

How does a bookselling company choose a strategy for growth in the digital age? Put yourself in Heather Reisman's shoes. What kinds of analyses can Reisman use to help her make good decisions that will lead to growth?

Managers everywhere need to plan. In this chapter, we present the basics of planning: what it is, why managers plan, and how they plan. We will also discuss the importance of strategic management and choosing effective strategies to develop a competitive advantage.

What Is Planning?

As we stated in Chapter 1, **planning** involves defining goals, establishing an overall strategy for achieving those goals, and developing a comprehensive set of plans to integrate and coordinate the work needed to achieve the goals. It is concerned with both ends (what is to be done) and means (how it is to be done). For example, you and your classmates may want to organize a large graduation dinner dance. To do so, you would consider the goals, the strategy, the plans, and assign committees to get the work done.

1 What does planning involve?

planning
A management function that involves defining goals, establishing a strategy for achieving those goals, and developing plans to integrate and coordinate activities.

Planning can either be formal or informal. In informal planning, nothing is written down, and there is little or no sharing of goals with others. Informal planning is general and lacks continuity. Although it is more common in smaller organizations, where the owner-manager has a vision of where he or she wants the business to go and how to get there, informal planning does exist in some large organizations as well. At the same time, some small businesses may have very sophisticated planning processes and formal plans. For a look at your response to planning, see *Self-Assessment—How Good Am I at Personal Planning?* on pages 94–95, at the end of the chapter.

When we use the term *planning* in this book, we mean *formal* planning. In formal planning, specific goals covering a period of years are defined. These goals are written and shared with organization members. Then a specific action program for the achievement of these goals is developed; that is, managers clearly define the path they want to take to get the organization and the various work units from where they are to where they want them to be.

Setting goals, establishing a strategy to achieve those goals, and developing a set of plans to integrate and coordinate activities seems pretty complicated. So why would managers want to plan? Does planning affect performance? We address these issues next.

Q&A 6.1

Purposes of Planning

Are you a planner or a doer? Do you prefer to make plans or just act?

We can identify at least four reasons for planning:

- *Planning provides direction to managers and nonmanagers alike.* When employees know where the organization or work unit is going and what they must contribute to reach goals, they can coordinate their activities, cooperate with each other, and do what it takes to accomplish those goals. Without planning, departments and individuals might work at cross purposes, preventing the organization from moving efficiently toward its goals. This would also be true if you and your friends were planning your grad party— if you did not coordinate and cooperate, you might not actually get the party organized in time.

- *Planning reduces uncertainty by forcing managers to look ahead, anticipate change, consider the impact of change, and develop appropriate responses.* Even though planning cannot eliminate change or uncertainty, managers plan in order to anticipate change and develop the most effective response to it. Similarly, by planning a grad party ahead of time, you can make sure that it is held at a desired location, rather than at the only one that was left because you waited until the last minute.

- *Planning reduces overlapping and wasteful activities.* When work activities are coordinated around established plans, redundancy can be minimized. Furthermore, when means and ends are made clear through planning, inefficiencies become obvious and can be corrected or eliminated.

- *Planning establishes the goals or standards that are used in controlling.* If we are unsure of what we are trying to accomplish, how can we determine whether we have actually achieved it? In planning, we develop the goals and the plans. Then, through controlling, we compare actual performance against the goals, identify any significant deviations, and take any necessary corrective action. Without planning, there would be no way to control outcomes.

Renato Zambonini, board chair of Ottawa-based Cognos, notes that planning went out of fashion during the dot-com years. He found that in both California and Ottawa, entrepreneurs worked "90 hours a week, but the whole goal [was] not to build a business or a company. [All they really wanted was] someone to buy them out."[2] Unfortunately, many of those companies were not bought out, but folded. Planning might have helped them be more successful.

Planning and Performance

Are you skeptical of planning? Do you wonder whether planning really pays off?

Is planning worthwhile? Do managers and organizations that plan outperform those that don't? Intuitively, you would expect the answer to be a resounding yes. While studies of performance in organizations that plan are generally positive, we cannot say that organizations that formally plan *always* outperform those that don't plan.

Numerous studies have looked at the relationship between planning and performance.[3] We can draw the following four conclusions from these studies. First, generally speaking, formal planning is associated with higher profits, higher return on assets, and other positive financial results. Second, the quality of the planning process and the appropriate implementation of the plans probably contribute more to high performance than does the extent of planning. Third, in those studies in which formal planning did not lead to higher performance, the external environment often was the culprit. Government regulations, powerful labour unions, and other critical environmental forces constrain managers' options and reduce the impact of planning on an organization's performance. Fourth, the planning/performance relationship is influenced by the planning time frame. Organizations need at least four years of systematic formal planning before performance is affected.

Planning is definitely not just for managers. When families in the *Vancouver Sun*'s distribution area were asked to take the newspaper's "car free challenge" for a month, they learned that planning became a much greater part of their lives. The three families pictured above took the challenge and found that figuring out how long a journey took and the best way to get there required being more aware of their schedules than when they could just grab their car keys and drive off.

Q&A 6.2

How Do Managers Plan?

Planning is often called the primary management function because it establishes the basis for all the other functions that managers perform. Without planning, managers would not know what to organize, lead, or control. In fact, without plans, there would not be anything to organize, lead, or control! So how do managers plan?

Planning involves two important elements: goals and plans. **Goals (objectives)** are the desired outcomes for individuals, groups, or entire organizations.[4] Goals are objectives, and we use the two terms interchangeably. They provide the direction for all management decisions and form the criteria against which actual work accomplishments can be measured. That is why they are often called the foundation of planning. You have to know the desired target or outcome before you can establish plans for reaching it. **Plans** are documents that outline how goals are going to be met and that typically describe resource allocations, schedules, and other necessary actions to accomplish the goals. As managers plan, they are developing both goals and plans.

In the next section, we consider how to establish goals.

Approaches to Establishing Goals

Goals provide the direction for all management decisions and actions and form the criteria against which actual accomplishments are measured. Everything organizational members

2 How do managers set goals and develop plans?

goals (objectives)
Desired outcomes for individuals, groups, or entire organizations.

plans
Documents that outline how goals are going to be met and describe resource allocations, schedules, and other necessary actions to accomplish the goals.

do should be oriented toward helping their work units and the organization achieve its goals. Goals can be established through a process of traditional goal setting or management by objectives.

Traditional Goal Setting

In **traditional goal setting**, goals are set at the top of the organization and then broken into subgoals for each organizational level. This works reasonably well when an organization is hierarchically structured. This traditional perspective assumes that top managers know what is best because they see "the big picture." Thus, the goals that are established and passed down to each succeeding level serve to direct and guide, and in some ways constrain, individual employees' work behaviours. Employees work to meet the goals that have been assigned in their areas of responsibility.

In traditional goal setting, if top management wants to increase sales by 10 percent for the year, the marketing and sales departments need to develop action plans that will yield these results. The manufacturing department needs to develop plans for how to produce more product. An individual salesperson may need to make more calls to new clients, or convince current clients that they need more product. Thus, each of the lower levels (individual employee, sales, marketing, production) becomes a means to achieving the corporate end of increasing sales.

Management by Objectives

Instead of traditional goal setting, many organizations use **management by objectives (MBO)**, an approach in which specific performance goals are jointly determined by employees and their managers, progress toward accomplishing these goals is periodically reviewed, and rewards are allocated on the basis of this progress. Rather than using goals only as controls, MBO uses them to motivate employees as well. Employees will be more committed to goals that they help set.

Management by objectives consists of four elements: goal specificity, participative decision making, an explicit time period, and performance feedback.[5] Its appeal lies in its focus on the accomplishment of participatively set objectives as the reason for and motivation behind individuals' work efforts. Exhibit 3-1 lists the steps in a typical MBO program.

Exhibit 3-1

Steps in a Typical MBO Program

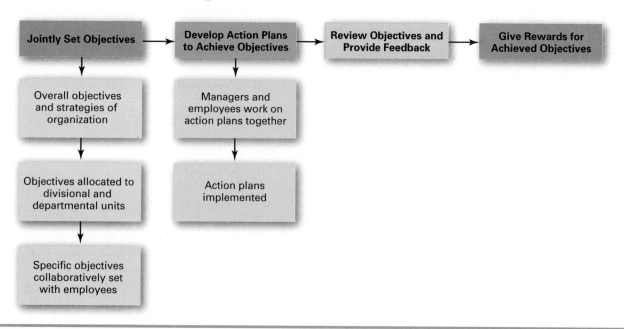

Exhibit 3-2

Characteristics of Well-Designed Goals

- Written in terms of outcomes rather than actions
- Measurable and quantifiable
- Clear time frame

- Challenging yet attainable
- Written down
- Communicated to all necessary organizational members

Do MBO programs work? Studies of actual MBO programs confirm that MBO increases employee performance and organizational productivity. A review of 70 programs, for example, found organizational productivity gains in 68 of them.[6] This same review also identified top management commitment and involvement as important conditions for MBO to succeed.

Characteristics of Well-Designed Goals

Have you occasionally failed at your goals? How can you develop more achievable goals?

Goals are not all created equal. Some goals are better than others. How can you tell the difference? What makes a "well-designed" goal?[7] Exhibit 3-2 outlines the characteristics of well-designed goals.

Steps in Goal Setting

What steps should managers follow in setting goals? The goal-setting process consists of five steps.

1. *Review the organization's mission.* The **mission** is the purpose of an organization. The broad statement of what the organization's purpose is and what it hopes to accomplish provides an overall guide to what organizational members think is important. It's important to review these statements before writing goals because the goals should reflect what the mission statement says.

   mission
   The purpose of an organization.

2. *Evaluate available resources.* You don't want to set goals that are impossible to achieve given your available resources. Even though goals should be challenging, they should be realistic. After all, if the resources you have to work with will not allow you to achieve a goal no matter how hard you try or how much effort is exerted, that goal should not be set. That would be like the person with a $50 000 annual income and no other financial resources setting a goal of building an investment portfolio worth $1 million in three years. No matter how hard he or she works at it, it's not going to happen.

3. *Determine the goals individually or with input from others.* The goals reflect desired outcomes and should be consistent with the organization's mission and goals in other organizational areas. These goals should be measurable, specific, and include a time frame for accomplishment.

4. *Write down the goals and communicate them to all who need to know.* We have already explained the benefit of writing down and communicating goals.

5. *Review results and whether goals are being met.* Make changes as needed. For any plan to be effective, reviews need to be done.

Developing Plans

Once goals have been established, written down, and communicated, a manager is ready to develop plans for pursuing the goals.

What are the advantages of specifying the plans to achieve goals? Jean-Marc Eustache, president and CEO of Montreal-based Transat A.T., knows he cannot relax just because he has one of the largest international travel and tourism companies in the world. He recently told shareholders that he plans "to double [Transat's] revenues during the next three-and-a-half years."[8] To do this, he plans to do the following: increase the company's share of the leisure travel business into and out of Ontario; increase the company's share of the leisure travel business in France; increase flights between Canada and the United Kingdom; move into the United States and offer flights to Mexico and the Caribbean; and increase the company's ownership and management of hotels in the Caribbean and Mexico. By specifying the plans to achieve his goal to double revenues, Eustache let Transat employees know where to focus attention when helping people make their travel plans.

Types of Plans

The most popular ways to describe an organization's plans are by their breadth (strategic vs. operational), time frame (short term vs. long term), specificity (directional vs. specific), and frequency of use (single use vs. standing). These planning classifications are not independent. As Exhibit 3-3 illustrates, strategic plans are long-term, directional, and single-use. Operational plans are short-term, specific, and standing. Let's examine each of these types of plans.

Strategic plans are plans that apply to the entire organization, establish the organization's overall goals, and seek to position the organization in terms of its environment.

strategic plans
Plans that apply to the entire organization, establish the organization's overall goals, and seek to position the organization in terms of its environment.

Exhibit 3-3

Types of Plans

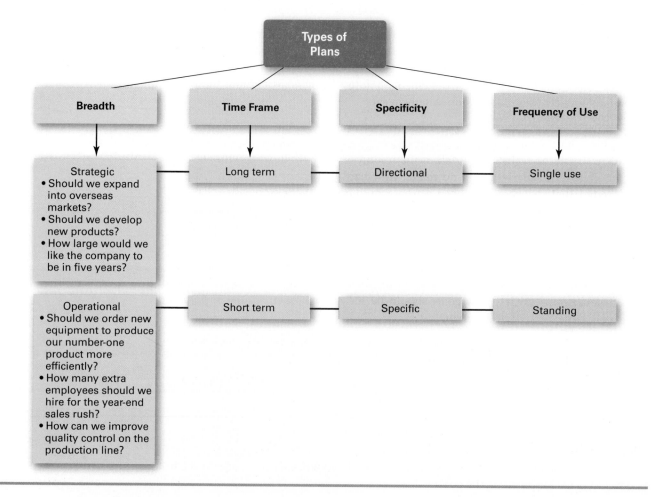

Plans that specify the details of how the overall goals are to be achieved are called **operational plans**. How do the two types of plans differ? Strategic plans tend to cover a longer time frame and a broader view of the organization. Strategic plans also include the formulation of goals, whereas operational plans define ways to achieve the goals. Also, operational plans tend to cover short time periods—monthly, weekly, and day-to-day.

The difference in years between short term and long term has shortened considerably. It used to be that long term meant anything more than seven years. Try to imagine what you would like to be doing in seven years, and you can begin to appreciate how difficult it was for managers to establish plans that far in the future. As organizational environments have become more uncertain, the definition of *long term* has changed. We define **long-term plans** as those with a time frame beyond three years.[9] For example, an organization may develop a five-year plan for increasing its sales in Asia. We define **short-term plans** as those with a time frame of one year or less. For example, a company may decide that it will increase sales by 10 percent over the next year. The *intermediate term* is any time period in between. Although these time classifications are fairly common, an organization can designate any time frame it wants for planning purposes.

Intuitively, it would seem that specific plans would be preferable to directional, or loosely guided, plans. **Specific plans** are plans that are clearly defined and that leave no room for interpretation. They have clearly defined objectives. There is no ambiguity and no problem with misunderstanding. For example, a manager who seeks to increase his or her unit's work output by 8 percent over a given 12-month period might establish specific procedures, budget allocations, and schedules of activities to reach that goal. The drawbacks of specific plans are that they require clarity and a sense of predictability that often do not exist.

When uncertainty is high and managers must be flexible in order to respond to unexpected changes, directional plans are preferable. **Directional plans** are flexible plans that set out general guidelines. They provide focus but don't lock managers into specific goals or courses of action. (Exhibit 3-4 illustrates how specific and directional plans differ, with the directional plan indicating only the *intent* to get from "A" to "B" and the specific plan *identifying the exact route* that one would take to get from "A" to "B.") Instead of detailing a specific plan to cut costs by 4 percent and increase revenues by 6 percent in the next six months, managers might formulate a directional plan for improving profits by 5 to 10 percent over the next six months. The flexibility inherent in directional plans must be weighed against the loss of clarity provided by specific plans.

Some plans that managers develop are ongoing, while others are used only once. A **single-use plan** is a one-time plan specifically designed to meet the needs of a unique situation. For example, when Charles Schwab introduced its online discount stockbrokerage service, top-level executives used a single-use plan to guide the creation and

operational plans
Plans that specify the details of how the overall goals are to be achieved.

long-term plans
Plans with a time frame beyond three years.

short-term plans
Plans with a time frame of one year or less.

specific plans
Plans that are clearly defined and leave no room for interpretation.

directional plans
Plans that are flexible and that set out general guidelines.

single-use plan
A one-time plan specifically designed to meet the needs of a unique situation.

Exhibit 3-4

Specific vs. Directional Plans

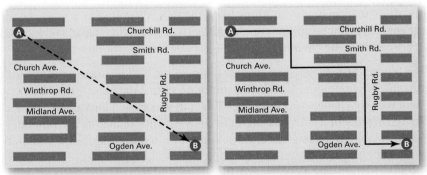

Directional Plan   **Specific Plan**

standing plans
Ongoing plans that provide
guidance for activities performed
repeatedly.

Q&A 6.5

implementation of the new service. In contrast, standing plans are ongoing and provide guidance for activities performed repeatedly. **Standing plans** include policies, rules, and procedures, which we define in Chapter 4. An example of a standing plan would be the discrimination and harassment policy developed by the University of British Columbia. It provides guidance to university administrators, faculty, and staff as they perform their job duties.

Contingency Factors in Planning

What kinds of plans are needed in a given situation? Will strategic or operational plans be needed? How about specific or directional plans? In some situations, long-term plans make sense; in others they do not. What are these situations? The process of developing plans is influenced by two contingency factors—the degree of environmental uncertainty and the length of future commitments—and by the planning approach followed.[10]

When environmental uncertainty is high, plans should be specific, but flexible. Managers must be prepared to amend plans as they are implemented. At times, managers may even have to abandon their plans.[11] As CEO of Continental Airlines, Gordon M. Bethune, together with his management team, established the specific goal of focusing on a key concern of customers—on-time flights—to help the company become more competitive in the highly uncertain airline industry. Because of the high level of uncertainty, the management team identified a "destination, but not a flight plan," and changed plans as necessary to achieve that goal of on-time service. Also, it's important for managers to continue formal planning efforts through periods of environmental uncertainty because studies have shown that it takes at least four years of such efforts before any positive impact on organizational performance is seen.[12]

The second contingency factor that affects planning is the time frame of plans. The more that current plans affect future commitments, the longer the time frame for which managers should plan. This means that plans should extend far enough ahead to meet those future commitments made when the plans were developed. Planning for too long or too short a time period is inefficient and ineffective.

Criticisms of Planning

What if you really don't like to make plans?

Formalized organizational planning became popular in the 1960s and, for the most part, it is still popular today. It makes sense for an organization to establish some direction. But critics have challenged some of the basic assumptions underlying planning. What are the primary criticisms directed at formal planning?

- *Planning may create rigidity.*[13] Formal planning efforts can lock an organization into specific goals to be achieved within specific timetables. When these goals are set, the assumption may be that the environment will not change during the time period the goals cover. If that assumption is faulty, managers who follow a plan may face trouble. Rather than remaining flexible—and possibly throwing out the plan—managers who continue to do the things required to achieve the original goals may not be able to cope with the changed environment. Forcing a course of action when the environment is fluid can be a recipe for disaster.

Q&A 6.6

- *Plans cannot be developed for a dynamic environment.*[14] Most organizations today face dynamic environments. If a basic assumption of making plans—that the environment will not change—is faulty, then how can you make plans at all? Today's business environment is often chaotic at best. By definition, that means random and unpredictable. Managing under those conditions requires flexibility, and that may mean not being tied to formal plans.

- *Formal plans cannot replace intuition and creativity.*[15] Successful organizations are typically the result of someone's innovative vision. But visions have a tendency to become formalized as they evolve. Formal planning efforts typically involve a thorough investigation of the organization's capabilities and opportunities and a mechanical analysis that reduces the vision to some type of programmed routine. That approach can spell disaster for an organization. Apple Computer learned this the hard way. In the late 1970s and throughout the 1980s Apple's success was attributed, in part, to the innovative and creative approaches of co-founder Steve Jobs. Eventually, Jobs was forced to leave, and with his departure came increased organizational formality, including detailed planning—the same things that Jobs despised so much because he felt that they hampered creativity. During the 1990s, the situation at Apple became so bad that Jobs was brought back as CEO to get Apple back on track. The company's renewed focus on innovation led to the debut of the iMac in 1998, the iPod in 2001, a radically new look for the iMac in 2002, and an online music store in 2003.

- *Planning focuses managers' attention on today's competition, not on tomorrow's survival.*[16] Formal planning has a tendency to focus on how to capitalize on existing business opportunities within an industry. It often does not allow managers to consider creating or reinventing an industry. Consequently, formal plans may result in costly blunders and high catch-up costs when other competitors take the lead. On the other hand, companies such as Intel, General Electric, Nokia, and Sony have found success by forging into uncharted waters, spawning new industries as they go.

- *Formal planning reinforces success, which may lead to failure.*[17] It's hard to change or discard previously successful plans—to leave the comfort of what works for the anxiety of the unknown. Successful plans, however, may provide a false sense of security, generating more confidence in the formal plans than is warranted. Many managers will not face the unknown until they are forced to do so by environmental changes. By then, it may be too late!

Q&A 6.7

How valid are these criticisms? Should managers forget about planning? No! Although the criticisms have merit when directed at rigid, inflexible planning, today's managers can be effective planners if they understand the need to be flexible in responding to environmental change.

The following *Management Reflection* shows what can happen when an organization does not set goals and targets that match its overall plans.

MANAGEMENT REFLECTION

Kicking Horse Coffee Learns to Plan

Can a company have too much success? For Canada's top seller of organic coffee, Invermere, BC-based Kicking Horse Coffee, rapid growth and expansion meant that the company could not meet the demand for its product.[18] As they started expanding into markets east of Manitoba, Kicking Horse founders Elana Rosenfeld (CEO) and Leo Johnson (president) did not really consider whether they had the capacity to meet an increase in demand. Rather, they focused on getting into new markets.

Unable to meet the soaring demand for their coffee, the owners got a wake-up call about the need for planning. As a result, they developed detailed sales forecasts, and considered capital needs. They also started to examine space, people, and equipment needs. The owners realized that they needed to be more disciplined about the opportunities they pursued, such as their decision not to supply ground coffee to grocery stores.

The new strategic plan makes sure that demand for coffee can be met, and that Kicking Horse can grow rapidly, while still keeping a promise to employees: "never any overtime." Rosenfeld explains why she has become so committed to planning: "Part of planning is articulating who you are and what you believe in so you can stay on the path." ∎

⦿⦿⦿ Organizational Strategy: Choosing a Niche

As Heather Reisman considers the future of Indigo Books & Music, she recognizes that consumers have changed the way in which they get information and entertainment.[19] Book reading is down, as is television watching, while Internet use is up. Thus, Reisman has to respond to this new reality by figuring out ways to attract more consumers to Chapters/Indigo bookstores and websites. Reisman is considering starting the equivalent of Facebook for book lovers, which would be housed on the chapters.indigo.ca website. By creating a community of book lovers, she hopes to entice people to buy more books.

Think About It

What other strategies could Heather Reisman use to create more crossovers between books and the Internet? Would some strategies be more effective than others?

❸ What are the steps in strategic management?

Q&A 7.1

To begin to understand why organizational strategy matters, you need look no further than at what has happened in the discount retail industry in Canada. The industry's two largest competitors—Walmart and Zellers—have battled for market dominance since Walmart entered Canada in 1992. The two chains have some striking similarities: store atmosphere, markets served, and organizational purpose. Yet Walmart's performance (financial and otherwise) has taken market share from Zellers every single year. Walmart is the world's largest and most successful retailer, and Zellers is the second-largest discount retailer in Canada. Why the difference in performance? Organizations vary in how well they perform because of differences in their strategies and differences in competitive abilities.[20] Walmart excels at strategic management, while Zellers struggles to find the right niche.

strategic management
What managers do to develop the organization's strategies.

Strategic management is what managers do to develop the organization's strategies. What are an organization's **strategies**? They are the plans for how the organization will do whatever it's in business to do, how it will compete successfully, and how it will attract and satisfy its customers in order to achieve its goals.[21]

strategies
The decisions and actions that determine the long-run performance of an organization.

One term that is often used in conjunction with strategic management and strategies is **business model**, which is a strategic design for how a company intends to profit from its strategies, work processes, and work activities. A company's business model focuses on two things: (1) whether customers will value what the company is providing and (2) whether the company can make any money doing that.[22] Dell pioneered a new business model for selling computers to consumers directly on the Internet instead of selling its computers, like all the other computer manufacturers, through computer retailers. Did customers "value" that? Absolutely! Did Dell make money doing it that way? Absolutely! As managers think about strategies for their businesses, they need to give some thought to the economic viability of their business model.

business model
A strategic design for how a company intends to profit from its strategies, work processes, and work activities.

strategic management process
A six-step process that encompasses strategic planning, implementation, and evaluation.

The **strategic management process**, as illustrated in Exhibit 3-5, is a six-step process that encompasses strategic planning, implementation, and evaluation. Although the first four steps describe the planning that must take place, implementation and evaluation are just as important. Even the best strategies can fail if management does not implement or evaluate them properly. Let's examine the six steps in detail.

Step 1: Identify the Organization's Current Mission, Goals, and Strategies

Every organization needs a mission—a statement of the purpose of an organization. The mission answers the question, What is our reason for being in business? Defining the organization's mission forces managers to carefully identify the scope of their products or services. Indigo's mission statement is "to provide a service-driven, stress-free approach to satisfying the booklover." The mission of WorkSafeBC (the Workers' Compensation

Exhibit 3-5

The Strategic Management Process

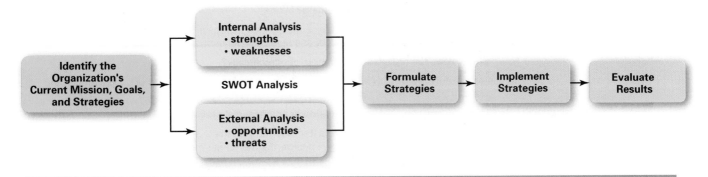

Q&A 7.2

How would you develop a strategic plan for the next five or ten years of your life? What would be your mission, goals, and strategies?

Board of British Columbia) is to "promot[e] workplace health and safety for the workers and employers of [the] province."[23] The mission of eBay is "to build an online marketplace that enables practically anyone to trade practically anything almost anywhere in the world." These statements provide clues to what these organizations see as their reason for being in business. Exhibit 3-6 on page 78 describes the typical components of a mission statement.

It's important for managers to identify goals and strategies consistent with the mission being pursued. For example, based on its mission statement, the Workers' Compensation Board established the following goals:[24]

- Promote the prevention of workplace injury, illness, and disease

- Rehabilitate those who are injured and provide timely return to work

- Provide fair compensation to replace workers' loss of wages while recovering from injuries

- Ensure sound financial management for a viable workers' compensation system

Step 2: Do an Internal Analysis

Now we move from looking outside the organization to looking inside. The internal analysis provides important information about an organization's specific resources and capabilities. An organization's **resources** are its assets—financial, physical, human, intangible—that are used by the organization to develop, manufacture, and deliver products or services to its customers. Its **capabilities** are its skills and abilities in doing the work activities needed in its business. The major value-creating capabilities and skills of the organization are known as its **core competencies**.[25] Both resources and core competencies can determine the organization's competitive weapons. Fujio Cho, Toyota Motor Corporation's chair, called the Toyota Prius "a giant leap into the future," but the highly popular car is simply one more example of the company's resources and core competencies in product research and design, manufacturing, marketing, and managing its human resources. Toyota is renowned worldwide for its effectiveness and efficiency. Experts who have studied the company point to its ability to nourish and preserve employee creativity and flexibility in a work environment that is fairly rigid and controlled.[26]

After doing the internal analysis, managers should be able to identify organizational strengths and weaknesses. **Strengths** are any activities the organization does well or any unique resources that it has. **Weaknesses** are activities the organization does not do well or resources it needs but does not possess. This step forces managers to recognize

resources
An organization's assets—financial, physical, human, intangible—that are used to develop, manufacture, and deliver products or services to customers.

capabilities
An organization's skills and abilities that enable it to do the work activities needed in its business.

core competencies
An organization's major value-creating skills, capabilities, and resources that determine its competitive weapons.

Q&A 7.3

strengths
Any activities the organization does well or any unique resources that it has.

weaknesses
Activities the organization does not do well or resources it needs but does not possess.

Exhibit 3-6

Components of a Mission Statement

Customers:	**Who are the organization's customers?**
	We believe our first responsibility is to the doctors, nurses and patients, to mothers, fathers and all others who use our products and services. (Johnson & Johnson)
Markets:	**Where does the organization compete geographically?**
	To invoke the senses, evoke the imagination and provoke the emotions of people around the world! (Cirque du Soleil)
Concern for survival, growth, and profitability:	**Is the organization committed to growth and financial stability?**
	We expand our thinking and grow faster than the industry average, and we enjoy being seen as a young aggressive company. We believe that we do not have to compromise our integrity to be profit driven. (G.A.P Adventures)
Philosophy:	**What are the organization's basic beliefs, values, and ethical priorities?**
	Ducks Unlimited Canada (DUC) envisions Canada as a nation that can sustain use by people and wildlife without endangering the amount or functions of natural lands. DUC leads wetland conservation for waterfowl, other wildlife and people in North America. (Ducks Unlimited Canada)
Concern for public image:	**How responsive is the organization to societal and environmental concerns?**
	As a vital measure of integrity, we will ensure the health and safety of our communities, and protect the environment in all we do. (Dow Chemical)
Products or services:	**What are the organization's major products or services?**
	To enrich the lives of everyone in WestJet's world by providing safe, friendly and affordable air travel. (WestJet Airlines)
Technology:	**Is the organization's technologically current?**
	Pushing the limits of what technology can accomplish: Pushing the limits means focusing more of our resources and attention on what we do not know rather than on controlling what we already know. The fact that something has not worked in the past does not mean that it cannot be made to work in the future; and the fact that something did work in the past doesn't mean that it can't be improved upon. (Syncrude Canada)
Self-concept:	**What are the organization's major competitive advantage and core competencies?**
	CBC Television, as Canada's national public television broadcaster, has a cultural mandate to tell compelling, original, audacious and entertaining Canadian stories in a way that Canadians want to watch, and in large numbers. (CBC Television)
Concern for employees:	**Are employees a valuable asset of the organization?**
	We recognize contributions and celebrate accomplishments. (Tourism BC)

Sources: Based on company websites; and F. David, *Strategic Management,* 11th ed. (Upper Saddle River, NJ: Prentice Hall, 2007), p. 70.

What are your strengths and weaknesses for developing a successful career?

Q&A 7.4
PRISM 3

that their organizations, no matter how large or successful, are constrained by the resources and capabilities they have.

Doing an internal analysis of an organization's financial and physical assets is fairly easy because information on those areas is readily available. However, evaluating an organization's intangible assets—things such as employees' skills, talents, and knowledge; databases and other IT assets; organizational culture; and so forth—is a bit more challenging. Organizational culture, specifically, is one crucial part of the internal analysis that is often overlooked.[27] It's crucial because strong and weak cultures have different effects on strategy and the content of a culture has a major effect on strategies pursued. What is a strategically appropriate culture? It's one that supports the firm's chosen strategy. For a number of years, Avis, the number-two US car rental company, has stood at the top of its category in an annual survey of brand loyalty. By creating a culture in which employees obsess over every step of the rental car experience, Avis has built an unmatched record for customer loyalty.[28]

Another intangible asset that is important, but difficult to assess during an internal analysis, is corporate reputation. Does the fact that Montreal-based aluminum producer Rio Tinto Alcan is ranked as one of Canada's "most admired corporations" make a difference? Does the fact that Calgary-based WestJet Airlines often makes the list of "Canada's 10 Most Admired Corporate Cultures™" mean anything? Does the fact that Coca-Cola has the world's most powerful global brand give it any edge? Studies of reputation on corporate performance show that it can have a positive impact.[29] As one researcher stated, ". . . a strong, well-managed reputation can and should be an asset for any organization."[30]

Step 3: Do an External Analysis

> *What changes in the world are happening that might affect how your career might unfold over time? How might this affect your strategic plan?*

In Chapter 2, we described the external environment as an important constraint on a manager's actions. Analyzing that environment is a critical step in the strategic management process. Managers in every organization need to do an external analysis. They need to know, for example, what the competition is doing, what pending legislation might affect the organization, or what the labour supply is like in locations where it operates. In analyzing the external environment, managers should examine both the specific and general environments to see what trends and changes are occurring. As previously mentioned, managers at Indigo Books & Music noted that individuals were reading fewer books, and using the Internet more. This observation required Indigo to rethink how to encourage more people to rely on Indigo stores for gift items and connections with other book lovers. (To learn more about analyzing the environment, see *Developing Your Interpersonal Skills—Scanning the Environment* on page 98, at the end of the chapter.)

Q&A 7.5

After analyzing the environment, managers need to assess what they have learned in terms of opportunities that the organization can exploit, and threats that it must counteract. **Opportunities** are positive trends in external environmental factors; **threats** are negative trends. For Indigo Books & Music managers, one opportunity is the increased use of the Internet, and managers have looked for ways to get more revenue from this medium. Threats to Indigo include a decreasing number of people who read books and greater competition from alternative sources of entertainment, including movies, radio, and television programs.

opportunities
Positive trends in external environmental factors.

threats
Negative trends in external environmental factors.

One last thing to understand about external analysis is that the same environment can present opportunities to one organization and pose threats to another in the same industry because of their different resources and capabilities. For example, WestJet Airlines has prospered in a turbulent industry, while Air Canada has struggled.

Paul Holland, CEO of Vancouver-based A&W, celebrates with employee Fatemeh Divsaler Mohajer. Despite the downturn in the economic environment, A&W's sales increased 10 percent in 2008, due to Holland's strategy of focusing on Baby Boomers' taste for nostalgia.

Exhibit 3-7

Identifying the Organization's Opportunities

Organization's
Resources/Capabilities

Organization's
Opportunities

Opportunities in
the Environment

SWOT analysis

An analysis of the organization's strengths, weaknesses, opportunities, and threats.

The combined external and internal analyses are called the **SWOT analysis** because it's an analysis of the organization's *strengths*, *weaknesses*, *opportunities*, and *threats*. Based on the SWOT analysis, managers can identify a strategic niche that the organization might exploit (see Exhibit 3-7). For example, owner Leonard Lee started Ottawa-based Lee Valley Tools in 1982 to help individual woodworkers, and later gardeners, find just the right tools for their tasks. This niche strategy enabled Lee to grow Lee Valley into one of North America's leading garden and woodworking catalogue companies.

SWOT analysis was very effective in keeping jobs at Proctor & Gamble Canada's Brockville, Ontario, plant, as the following *Management Reflection* shows.

MANAGEMENT REFLECTION

Loss of Detergent Production Turns into Victory

How does a Canadian CEO convince his American bosses that there is advantage to staying in Canada? SWOT analysis saved the jobs of employees at Proctor & Gamble (P&G) Canada's Brockville, Ontario, plant.[31] Tim Penner, president of the Toronto-based company, knew that the parent company (based in Cincinnati, Ohio) planned to consolidate the production of laundry detergent in the United States, which would have eliminated the jobs of the Brockville employees. Penner, in search of a new opportunity, suggested to head office that P&G move the manufacture of fabric softener sheets and electrostatic cleaning sheets for the Swiffer sweeper to Brockville. Penner outlined the strengths of the Ontario plant, including a highly educated workforce known for its commitment and productivity. With Penner's strategic thinking, Brockville's loss of laundry detergent production turned into a victory for Canadian jobs. More recently, Penner convinced the US head office to allow the Brockville plant to produce Tide to Go. Penner says his job includes "aggressively selling Canada [to US head office] as a possible site for new products and reorganized operations." Penner's strategy has paid off. When he became CEO in 1999, P&G Canada was the seventh-largest revenue generator in the world for the US multinational. By 2007, Penner had taken the Canadian subsidiary to third place, and increased annual sales from $1.5 billion to over $2.9 billion. ∎

Step 4: Formulate Strategies

Q&A 7.6

Once the SWOT analysis is complete, managers need to develop and evaluate strategic alternatives and then select strategies that either capitalize on the organization's strengths and exploit environmental opportunities or correct the organization's weaknesses and buffer it against threats. Strategies need to be established for the corporate, business, and functional levels of the organization, which we will describe shortly. This step is complete when managers have developed a set of strategies that gives the organization a relative advantage over its rivals. Professor Henry Mintzberg of McGill Business School notes that strategies often emerge from actions that organizations take rather than simply reflect the original strategic intent of the organization.[32]

Step 5: Implement Strategies

After strategies are formulated, they must be implemented. No matter how effectively an organization has planned its strategies, it cannot succeed if the strategies are not implemented properly. Involving all members of the organization in strategic planning is also important.

Q&A 7.7

Step 6: Evaluate Results

The final step in the strategic management process is evaluating results. How effective have the strategies been? What adjustments, if any, are necessary? We discuss this step in our coverage of the control process in Chapter 11.

Q&A 7.8

Types of Organizational Strategies

Indigo Books & Music first started to implement its expansion plans in 2001, by buying its major competitor, Chapters (and chapters.ca).[33] This move gave Indigo a broader market base with a number of new stores, as well as the platform to launch a successful online business.

The plans Reisman contemplated in 2007 sought to further grow the company. Reisman planned to open at least 12 new stores by the end of 2008, with 6 of them being the large superstore format. She also hoped to expand some stores in Toronto and Montreal. To build stronger ties with consumers, she planned to create a social-networking site for book lovers. She also planned to launch Indigo TV, a channel that would broadcast author interviews and book-related programming throughout certain stores, and host an online photo album site where people can upload and display their pictures.

Think About It

Indigo Books & Music has chosen a growth strategy. In what other ways might the company grow? What other strategies might you recommend to Heather Reisman?

There are three types of organizational strategy: corporate, business, and functional (see Exhibit 3-8). They relate to the particular level of the organization that introduces the strategy. Managers at the top level of the organization typically are responsible for corporate strategies; for example, Heather Reisman plans Indigo Books & Music's growth

4 What kinds of strategies can managers use?

Exhibit 3-8

Types of Organizational Strategy

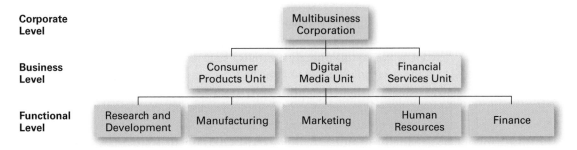

strategy. Managers at the middle level typically are responsible for business strategies; for example, Indigo's senior vice-president, Online, is responsible for the company's Internet business. Departmental managers typically are responsible for functional strategies; for example, Indigo's senior vice-president, Human Resource/Organization Development, is responsible for human resource policies, employee training, and staffing. Let's look at each type of organizational strategy.

Corporate Strategy

corporate strategy
An organizational strategy that evaluates what businesses a company is in, should be in, or wants to be in, and what it wants to do with those businesses.

If you were to develop your own company, what business would it be in? Why?

Corporate strategy is a strategy that evaluates what businesses a company is in, should be in, or wants to be in, and what it wants to do with those businesses. It's based on the mission and goals of the organization and the roles that each business unit of the organization will play. Take PepsiCo, for example. Its mission is to be a successful producer and marketer of beverage and packaged food products, and its strategy for pursuing that mission and various goals is through its different businesses including North American Soft Drinks, Frito-Lay, Gatorade, Tropicana Products, and PepsiCo International. At one time, PepsiCo had a restaurant division that included Taco Bell, Pizza Hut, and KFC, but because of intense competitive pressures in the restaurant industry and the division's inability to contribute to corporate growth, PepsiCo made a strategic decision to spin off that division as a separate and independent business entity, now known as YUM! Brands, Inc. What types of corporate strategies do organizations, such as PepsiCo, use?

In choosing what businesses to be in, senior management can choose among three main types of corporate strategies: growth, stability, and renewal. To illustrate, Walmart, Cadbury Schweppes, and General Motors are companies that seem to be going in different directions. Walmart is rapidly expanding its operations and developing new business and retailing concepts. Cadbury's managers, on the other hand, are content to maintain the status quo and focus on the candy industry. Meanwhile, sluggish sales and an uncertain outlook in the automobile industry have prompted GM to take drastic measures in dealing with its problems. Each of these organizations is using a different type of corporate strategy. Let's look closer at each type.

Growth

Even though it's the world's number-one retailer, Walmart continues to grow and over the next five years will concentrate its growth efforts internationally. Because it plans to open 142 to 157 new stores in 2010 in the United States, its corporate strategy is definitely growth! Walmart's international operations included more than 3400 stores in 2009, and these stores account for about 25 percent of the company's revenue.[34] A **growth strategy** is used when an organization wants to grow and does so by expanding the number of products offered or markets served, either through its current business(es) or through new business(es). As a result of its growth strategy, the organization may increase sales revenues, number of employees, market share, or other quantitative measures. How can organizations grow? Through concentration, vertical integration, horizontal integration, or diversification.

growth strategy
A corporate strategy that is used when an organization wants to grow and does so by expanding the number of products offered or markets served, either through its current business(es) or through new business(es).

Concentration Growth through *concentration* is achieved when an organization concentrates on its primary line of business and increases the number of products offered or markets served in this primary business. No other firms are acquired or merged with; instead the company chooses to grow by increasing its own business operations. For example, Oakville, Ontario-based Tim Hortons opens about 200 new stores a year, and is currently focusing most of its new openings on small-town western Canada, Quebec, and the United States, where it had 184 stores in 2004.[35] Montreal-based Jean Coutu Group recognized that, to grow, the company needed to open stores in the United States, which has a much larger market than Canada. So it bought 1539 Eckerd drugstores in the eastern

United States.[36] That was followed by the merger of the company's US subsidiary into Rite Aid Corporation, the third-largest drugstore chain in North America in 2007.[37]

Vertical Integration A company also might choose to grow by *vertical integration*, which is an attempt to gain control of inputs (backward vertical integration), outputs (forward vertical integration), or both. In backward vertical integration, the organization attempts to gain control of its inputs by becoming its own supplier. For example, French hospitality giant Accor, which owns Motel 6, Red Roof Inns, and numerous other lodging properties, also owns a majority of Carlson Wagonlit Travel, one of the world's largest travel agencies. In forward vertical integration, the organization gains control of its outputs (products or services) by becoming its own distributor. For example, several manufacturers with strong brands—including Coach, Apple, LaCoste, and Lego—have opened select stores where customers can buy products. In other words, they have become their own distributors.

Horizontal Integration In *horizontal integration*, a company grows by combining with other organizations in the same industry—that is, combining operations with competitors. Inbev of Belgium, which owns Alexander Keith's and Labatt, is the leading brewer in the world; it is a dominant player in North America, South America, Europe, Australia, and parts of Asia and Africa because of its acquisition of local breweries. Horizontal integration has been considered frequently in the Canadian banking industry in recent years as well.

When Stewart Gilliland took over as CEO of Labatt Breweries in January 2004, he discovered that with its concentration strategy, the company had been more of a follower than a leader. He vowed to change that immediately by putting a "fresh emphasis on quality, brewing process and taste among his company's many products, including its flagship Blue brand."

Because combining with competitors might decrease the amount of competition in an industry, Competition Bureau Canada assesses the impact of proposed horizontal integration strategies and must approve such plans before they are allowed to go forward in this country. Other countries have similar bodies that protect fair competition. For example, the Federal Trade Commission examines proposals for horizontal integration in the United States. In early 2007, Sirius Satellite Radio and XM Satellite Radio announced that they would merge to create a single satellite radio network in the United States and Canada. The companies face significant hurdles in the United States to finalizing their agreement because the merger would create a monopoly in satellite radio. The merger is not guaranteed for the companies' satellite services in Canada either. In this case, both the Competition Bureau Canada and the Canadian Radio-television and Telecommunications Commission (CRTC) would need to approve any merger between Sirius Canada and XM Canada before it could happen.

Diversification Finally, an organization can grow through *diversification*, either related or unrelated. In **related diversification** a company grows by merging with or acquiring firms in different, but related, industries. For example, Toronto-based Weston Foods is involved in the baking and dairy industries, while its ownership of Loblaw Companies Limited ("Loblaw") provides for the distribution of Weston's food products. In **unrelated diversification** a company grows by merging with or acquiring firms in different and unrelated industries. Toronto-based Brookfield Asset Management (formerly Brascan) is one of the few Canadian conglomerates that pursues a diversified strategy. Under CEO Bruce Flatt, Brascan has focused its development in three areas: real estate (Brookfield Properties), financial services (Brookfield Asset Management), and power generation (Brookfield Power). The company also owns 49 percent of Fraser Papers, a leading manufacturer of specialized printing, publishing, and converting papers; 38 percent of Norbord, a paperboard company; and 23 percent of Stelco, a steel producer.[38] However, unrelated diversification has fallen out of favour in recent years because too much diversification can cause managers to lose control of their organizations' core business. This can reduce value rather than create it.[39]

related diversification
When a company grows by combining with firms in different, but related, industries.

unrelated diversification
When a company grows by combining with firms in different and unrelated industries.

Many companies use a combination of these approaches to grow. McDonald's has grown using the concentration strategy by opening more than 32 000 outlets in more than 100 countries, of which about 30 percent are company-owned. In addition, it has used horizontal integration by purchasing Boston Market, Chipotle Mexican Grill (which it spun off as a separate entity in 2006), and Donato's Pizza chains (which it sold in late 2003). It also has a minority stake in the UK-based sandwich shops Pret A Manger. McDonald's newest twist on its growth strategy is a move into the premium coffee market with its McCafe coffee shops.

Stability

stability strategy
A corporate strategy characterized by an absence of significant change in what the organization is currently doing.

A **stability strategy** is a corporate strategy characterized by an absence of significant change in what the organization is currently doing. Examples of this strategy include continuing to serve the same clients by offering the same product or service, maintaining market share, and sustaining the organization's business operations. The organization does not grow, but it doesn't fall behind, either.

Although it may seem strange that an organization might not want to grow, there are times when its resources, capabilities, and core competencies are stretched to their limits, and expanding operations further might jeopardize its future success. When might managers decide that a stability strategy is the most appropriate choice? One situation might be that the industry is in a period of rapid upheaval with external forces drastically changing and making the future uncertain. At times like these, managers might decide that the prudent course of action is to sit tight and wait to see what happens.

Another situation where a stability strategy might be appropriate is if the industry is facing slow- or no-growth opportunities. In such situations, managers might decide to keep the organization operating at its current levels before making any strategic moves. This period of stability would allow them time to analyze their strategic options. The grocery industry is growing very slowly. This fact, plus the all-out push of Walmart into grocery retailing, for example, led managers at Etobicoke, Ontario-based grocery chain A&P to use a stability strategy.

Finally, owners and managers of small businesses, such as small neighbourhood grocers, often purposefully choose to follow a stability strategy. Why? They may feel that their business is successful enough as it is, that it adequately meets their personal goals, and that they don't want the hassles of a growing business.

Renewal

renewal strategies
Corporate strategies designed to address organizational weaknesses that are leading to performance declines.

retrenchment strategy
A short-term renewal strategy that reduces the organization's activities or operations.

The popular business periodicals frequently report stories of organizations that are not meeting their goals or whose performance is declining. When an organization is in trouble, something needs to be done. Managers need to develop strategies that address organizational weaknesses that are leading to performance declines. These strategies are called **renewal strategies**. There are two main types of renewal strategies, retrenchment and turnaround.

A **retrenchment strategy** reduces the organization's activities or operations. Retrenchment strategies include cost reductions, layoffs, closure of underperforming units, or closure of entire product lines or services.[40] There is no shortage of companies that have pursued a retrenchment strategy. A partial list includes some big corporate names: Procter & Gamble, Sears Canada, Corel, and Nortel Networks. When an organization is facing minor performance setbacks, a retrenchment strategy helps it stabilize operations, revitalize organizational resources and capabilities, and prepare to compete once again. Brampton, Ontario-based Loblaw Cos. is hoping that reducing office staff by 20 percent and centralizing procurement and merchandising operations will help offset problems the supermarket chain has had in expanding its stores to better compete with Walmart's supercentres.[41]

turnaround strategy
A renewal strategy for situations in which the organization's performance problems are more serious.

What happens if an organization's problems are more serious? What if the organization's profits are not just declining, but instead there are no profits, just losses? General Motors reported a net loss in 2005 of $3.6 billion; Kodak had a $1.3 billion loss for 2005. These types of situations call for a more drastic strategy. The **turnaround strategy**

Steven Shore (on left in photo) and Barry Prevor (on right, in checkered shirt) of retailer Steve & Barry's fuelled their company's growth through low-cost operations. The two CEOs saved money on everything from the low rent they paid in mid-size malls hungry for tenants to hefty allowances they earned for building the interiors of their stores. Buying direct from overseas factories also cut expenses as did word-of-mouth advertising. However, despite their low-cost approach, the tough economic climate in 2008 led to the company's filing for bankruptcy. A turnaround specialist bought the company and plans to continue operating the 276 stores.

is a renewal strategy for times when the organization's performance problems are more critical.

For both renewal strategies, managers cut costs and restructure organizational operations. However, a turnaround strategy typically involves a more extensive use of these measures than does a retrenchment strategy. One of GM's more drastic measures in its turnaround strategy was making buyout offers to about 113 000 workers. GM hoped that at least 30 000 employees would accept the offer so it could get to 100 percent plant capacity by 2008 and avoid having to potentially file for bankruptcy.

Business Strategy

What might be the competitive advantage of a business you would like to create?

The selection of a corporate strategy sets the direction for the entire organization. Subsequently, each unit within the organization has to translate this corporate strategy into a set of business strategies that will give the organization a competitive advantage. **Competitive advantage** is what sets an organization apart: that is, its distinct edge. That distinct edge comes from the organization's core competencies—what the organization does that others cannot do or what it does better than others can do.

competitive advantage
What sets an organization apart; its distinct edge.

Competitive Strategies

Many important ideas in strategic management have come from the work of Michael Porter.[42] His competitive strategies framework identifies three generic strategies from which managers can choose. Success depends on selecting the right strategy—one that fits the competitive strengths (resources and capabilities) of the organization and the industry it's in. Porter's major contribution has been to explain how managers can create and sustain a competitive advantage that will give a company above-average profitability. An important element in doing this is an industry analysis.

Porter proposes that some industries are inherently more profitable (and, therefore, more attractive to enter and remain in) than others. For example, the pharmaceutical industry is one with historically high profit margins, and the airline industry is one with notoriously low ones. But a company can still make a lot of money in a "dull" industry and lose money in a "glamorous" industry. The key is to exploit a competitive advantage.

In any industry, five competitive forces dictate the rules of competition. Together, these five forces (see Exhibit 3-9 on page 86) determine industry attractiveness and profitability. Managers assess an industry's attractiveness using these forces:

- *Threat of new entrants.* Factors such as economies of scale, brand loyalty, and capital requirements determine how easy or hard it is for new competitors to enter an industry.

Exhibit 3-9

Forces in an Industry Analysis

Source: Based on M. E. Porter, *Competitive Strategy: Techniques for Analyzing Industries and Competitors* (New York: Free Press, 1980).

- *Threat of substitutes.* Factors such as switching costs and buyer loyalty determine the degree to which customers are likely to buy a substitute product.

- *Bargaining power of buyers.* Factors such as number of customers in the market, customer information, and the availability of substitutes determine the amount of influence that buyers have in an industry.

- *Bargaining power of suppliers.* Factors such as the degree of supplier concentration and availability of substitute inputs determine the amount of power that suppliers have over firms in the industry.

- *Current-competitor rivalry.* Factors such as industry growth rate, increasing or falling demand, and product differences determine how intense the competitive rivalry will be among firms currently in the industry.

Once managers have assessed the five forces and determined what threats and opportunities exist, they are ready to select an appropriate competitive strategy. According to Porter, no firm can be successful by trying to be all things to all people. He proposes that managers select a strategy that will give the organization a competitive advantage, which he says arises out of either having lower costs than all other industry competitors or by being significantly different from competitors. On that basis, managers can choose one of three strategies: cost leadership, differentiation, or focus. Which one managers select depends on the organization's strengths and core competencies and its competitors' weaknesses (see Exhibit 3-10).

Cost Leadership Strategy When an organization sets out to be the lowest-cost producer in its industry, it's following a **cost leadership strategy**. A low-cost leader aggressively searches out efficiencies in production, marketing, and other areas of operation. Overhead is kept to a minimum, and the firm does everything it can to cut costs. You will not find expensive art or interior décor at offices of low-cost leaders. For example, at Walmart's headquarters in Bentonville, Arkansas, office furnishings are sparse and drab but functional.

cost leadership strategy
A business strategy in which the organization sets out to be the lowest-cost producer in its industry.

In trying to find a niche for his bread-making company, Dokse Perklin, founder of Mississauga, Ontario-based Le Bon Croissant, realized that he could do something that grocery stores and restaurants could not: ensure high-quality bakery products while controlling costs. "Hotels, grocery chains, restaurant chains [and] institutions just can't afford to bake on-premises anymore," Perklin says. "They can't find the staff, they can't effectively control overheads, they can't ensure consistent quality." So Perklin filled that need, and has created a bread-baking business that ships frozen unbaked and baked goods throughout Canada, the United States, the Caribbean, Hong Kong, and Great Britain.

Exhibit 3-10

Requirements for Successfully Pursuing Porter's Competitive Strategies

Generic Strategy	Commonly Required Skills and Resources	Common Organizational Requirements
Cost leadership	Sustained capital investment and access to capital Process engineering skills Intense supervision of labour Products designed for ease in manufacture Low-cost distribution system	Tight cost control Frequent, detailed control reports Structured organization and responsibilities Incentives based on meeting strict quantitative targets
Differentiation	Strong marketing abilities Product engineering Creative flair Strong capability in basic research Corporate reputation for quality or technological leadership Long tradition in the industry or unique combination of skills drawn from other businesses Strong cooperation from channels	Strong coordination among functions in R & D, product development, and marketing Subjective measurement and incentives instead of quantitative measures Amenities to attract highly skilled labour, scientists, or creative people
Focus	Combination of the foregoing skills and resources directed at the particular strategic target	Combination of the foregoing organizational requirements directed at the particular strategic target

Source: Reprinted from M. E. Porter, *Competitive Strategy: Techniques for Analyzing Industries and Competitors* (New York: Free Press, 1980), pp. 40–41.

Although low-cost leaders do not place a lot of emphasis on "frills," the product or service being sold must be perceived as comparable in quality to that offered by rivals or at least be acceptable to buyers. Examples of companies that have used a low-cost leadership strategy include Zellers, Hyundai, and WestJet Airlines.

differentiation strategy
A business strategy in which a company seeks to offer unique products that are widely valued by customers.

Differentiation Strategy The company that seeks to offer unique products that are widely valued by customers is following a **differentiation strategy**. Sources of differentiation might be exceptionally high quality, extraordinary service, innovative design, technological capability, or an unusually positive brand image. The key to this competitive strategy is that whatever product or service attribute is chosen for differentiating must set the firm apart from its competitors and be significant enough to justify a price premium that exceeds the cost of differentiating. St. Stephen, New Brunswick-based Ganong Bros., a small chocolate maker, differentiates itself from bigger boxed-chocolate makers by focusing on the assorted chocolates market. This enables it to rank second in Canada in that market. Its Fruitfull brand, made with real fruit purée and packaged like chocolates, had a 43 percent share of fruit jelly sales in 2003.[43] Vancouver-based Vancouver City Savings Credit Union differentiates itself from competitors through a focus on the community and the customer, as the following *Management Reflection* shows.

MANAGEMENT REFLECTION

Vancity Champions the Underdog

How does a small bank compete against the larger ones? Vancouver City Savings Credit Union (Vancity) does not hope to be like the country's Big Five banks.[44] It is much smaller, for one thing. Profit is not the bank's only goal, and only 20 percent of executive compensation is based on profit. Even so, the bank makes enough profit each year to return 30 percent of the profits to its members and the community. When Tamara Vrooman assumed the role of CEO in September 2007, she emphasized how Vancity is not simply about profit. "I am thrilled to be joining an organization that is well-known, successful, not afraid to take risks, and is thoughtful in terms of what it means to be a co-operative, a banker, an employer, and a member of the community."[45]

Vancity is sometimes mocked for its "left coast ways," but it is not afraid to be clear about its mission: The bank is committed to the community, social responsibility, and the environment. This is also what makes the bank unique. "Every day of our lives we're trading on our differentiation," former CEO Dave Mowat noted. "We have to do it a little bit different, a little bit better to give value-added to draw people to our organization. There isn't an end point where we can win on scale." What they can win on is customer service. As Mowat explains, "We're always looking to provide that extra bit of customization."

While Vancity has many wealthy clients, it likes to work with the less fortunate. It has set up a branch in Canada's poorest neighbourhood, East Vancouver, something other banks were reluctant to do. Mowat believes these clients can be just as trustworthy when you take the time to get to know them. Vancity is so dedicated to customer service that its customer satisfaction rating is at 85 percent, compared with 60 percent for the big banks. ■

By looking at successful consumer products or services, a company's differentiation strategy is often clear: Calgary-based WestJet Airlines—customer service; Ottawa-based Research In Motion, the maker of the BlackBerry—quality and innovative design; Vancouver-based Martha Sturdy—sleek furniture design and brand image; and Ottawa-based Lee Valley Tools—quality product design.

focus strategy
A business strategy in which a company pursues a cost or differentiation advantage in a narrow industry segment.

Focus Strategy The first two of Porter's competitive strategies seek a competitive advantage in the broad marketplace. However, the **focus strategy** involves a cost advantage

How can a Canadian company compete against imports from low-labour-cost countries such as China? Mississauga, Ontario-based Dahl Brothers Canada, which makes valves and fittings for plumbing and hot-water heating systems, found a way. "Where we compete is on design, quality, response time and choice," president Jannike Godfrey says. "By doing that, we can hold our own against imports."

(cost leadership focus) or a differentiation advantage (differentiation focus) in a narrow industry segment. That is, managers select a market segment in an industry and tailor their strategy to serve it rather than the broad market. Segments can be based on product variety, type of end buyer, distribution channel, or geographical location of buyers. For example, at Compania Chilena de Fosforos SA, a large Chilean wood products manufacturer, Vice-Chair Gustavo Romero Zapata devised a focus strategy to sell chopsticks in Japan. Competitors, and even other company managers, thought he was crazy. However, by focusing on this segment, Romero's strategy managed to create more demand for his company's chopsticks than it had mature trees with which to make the products. Whether a focus strategy is feasible depends on the size of the segment and whether the organization can support the additional cost of focusing. Research suggests that the focus strategy may be the most effective choice for small businesses because they typically do not have the economies of scale or internal resources to successfully pursue one of the other two strategies.[46]

Stuck in the Middle What happens if an organization is unable to develop a competitive advantage through either cost or differentiation? Porter uses the term **stuck in the middle** to describe those organizations that find it very difficult to achieve long-term success. He goes on to note that successful organizations frequently get into trouble by reaching beyond their competitive advantage and end up stuck in the middle. The Hudson's Bay Company department store in recent years seems to have had this strategy, avoiding the low-cost strategy of its sister store, Zellers, and avoiding the strategies of higher-end fashion boutiques such as Holt Renfrew.

We now realize organizations *can* achieve competitive advantage by pursuing a cost-leadership and a differentiation strategy at the same time. Studies have shown that such a dual emphasis can result in high performance.[47] However, an organization must be strongly committed to quality products or services, and consumers of those products or services must value quality. By providing high-quality products or services, an organization differentiates itself from its rivals. Consumers who value high quality will purchase more of the organization's products, and the increased demand will lead to economies of scale and lower per-unit costs. For example, companies such as Molson, Toyota, Intel, and Coca-Cola differentiate their products while at the same time maintaining low-cost operations.

stuck in the middle
A situation in which an organization is unable to develop a competitive advantage through cost or differentiation.

Functional Strategy

Functional strategies are the strategies used by an organization's various functional departments to support the business strategy. For organizations that have traditional functional departments such as manufacturing, marketing, human resources, research and development, and finance, these strategies must support the business strategy. Problems arise when employees and customers do not understand a company's strategy. For example, Air Canada did not articulate a clear strategy in creating Tango and Zip to operate alongside the parent airline. By spring 2004, Tango had become a fare category rather than a brand, and it was announced that Zip would no longer operate as a separate carrier. By contrast, WestJet Airlines communicates a very clear strategy to its employees: enjoyable flights and an affordable experience for travellers. Employees are to ensure these by working to keep costs down and improve turnaround time. Aware of the strategy, all WestJet employees know what is expected of them in a crisis, and all employees help in whatever ways are necessary to meet this strategy.

Quality as a Competitive Advantage

5 How can quality be a competitive advantage?

A quality revolution swept through both the business and public sectors during the 1980s and 1990s.[48] The generic term used to describe this revolution was *total quality management*, or *TQM*.

Quality management describes management's commitment to constantly improving the quality of products and services and responding to customer needs and expectations (see Exhibit 3-11). The term *customer* generally includes anyone who interacts with the organization's product or services internally or externally, such as employees, suppliers, and the people who purchase the organization's goods or services.

If implemented properly, quality can be a way for an organization to create a sustainable competitive advantage.[49] That is why many organizations apply quality management concepts to their operations in an attempt to set themselves apart from competitors. Constant improvement in the quality and reliability of an organization's products or services may result in a competitive advantage that cannot be taken away.[50] Kerry Shapansky, president of Toronto-based Pareto, a marketing services company, emphasizes the value of quality as a competitive advantage. "You can do 984 things right and just one thing wrong for it all to come apart," he says. "Nobody remembers the 984 things you did right; all focus is on that one thing you did wrong."

How Can Benchmarking Help Promote Quality?

Benchmarking involves the search for the best practices among competitors or noncompetitors that lead to their superior performance.[51] The basic idea underlying benchmarking is that management can improve quality by analyzing and then copying the methods of the leaders in various fields.

To illustrate benchmarking in practice, let's look at an application at Ford Motor Company. Ford used benchmarking in early 2000 to develop its highly promising Range Rover line. The company compiled a lengthy list of features that its customers said were the most important and then set about finding vehicles with the best of each. Then it tried to match or top the best of the competition in an effort to produce the world's best sport utility vehicle.[52]

What Is the ISO 9000 Series?

During the 1980s, there was an increasing push among global corporations to improve their quality. They knew that to compete in the global village they had to offer some assurances to purchasers of their products and

At Luxottica's factory in Agordo, Italy, designer-brand eyeglass frames are carefully inspected for scratches or other imperfections before being shipped to stores all over the world. Quality has remained a top priority at the company even as it has grown dramatically in the last several years. The focus begins in the design phase and extends all the way through production, 80 percent of which is still done in Italy in the heart of the mountainous areas where artisans have specialized in eyeglasses for generations.

Exhibit 3-11

Characteristics of Quality Management

1. Intense focus on the *customer*.
2. Concern for *continual improvement*.
3. Attention to the *work process*.
4. Improvement in the *quality of everything* the organization does.
5. *Accurate measurement* of all critical variables in the organization's operations.
6. *Empowered employees*.

---

services that what they were buying was of the quality they expected. To address this concern, the International Organization for Standardization, based in Geneva, Switzerland, designed the **ISO 9000 series** in 1987.[53] The ISO standards reflect a process whereby independent auditors attest that a company's factory, laboratory, or office has met quality management requirements.[54] These standards, once met, assure customers that a company uses specific steps to test the products it sells; continuously trains its employees to ensure they have up-to-date skills, knowledge, and abilities; maintains satisfactory records of its operations; and corrects problems when they occur. Some of the multinational and transnational companies that have met these standards are British Airways; Shanghai Foxboro Company; Braas Company; Betz Laboratories; Hong Kong Mass Transit Railway Corporation; BP Chemicals International; Borg Warner Automotive; Standard Aero Alliance; Taiwan Synthetic Rubber Corporation; and Weyerhaeuser.[55]

Achieving ISO certification is far from cost-free. Most organizations that want certification spend nearly one year and incur several hundreds of thousands of dollars in costs to achieve that goal. This type of certification is quickly becoming a necessity for exporting goods to organizations in the nations that support the ISO 9000 series standards.[56]

ISO 9000 series
A series of international quality management standards that sets uniform guidelines for processes to ensure that products conform to customer requirements.

How Can Attaining Six Sigma Signify Quality?

Wander around organizations such as London, Ontario-based 3M Canada; Morristown, New Jersey-based Honeywell; and Toronto-based Maple Leaf Foods, and you are likely to find green and black belts. Karate classes? Hardly. These green and black belts signify individuals trained in six sigma processes.[57]

Six sigma is a quality standard developed in the 1980s at Motorola.[58] The premise behind six sigma is to design, measure, analyze, and control the input side of a production process to achieve the goal of no more than 3.4 defects per million parts or procedures.[59] That is, rather than measuring the quality of a product after it is produced, six sigma attempts to design quality in as the product is being made (see Exhibit 3-12 on page 92 for the six sigma process steps). It is a process that uses statistical models, coupled with specific quality-measurement tools, high levels of rigour, and know-how when improving processes.[60] How effective is six sigma at ensuring quality? Let's answer that by posing a question. In your opinion, is 99.9 percent effective sufficient? Consider this: At 99.9 percent effectiveness, 12 babies would be given to the wrong parents each day; 22 000 cheques would be deducted from the incorrect chequing accounts each hour; and 2 planes a day would fail to land safely at Chicago's O'Hare International Airport.[61]

Six sigma applications can also be useful on the service side of the business—especially in identifying cost savings. At General Electric, the company spent more than $137 million in an effort to find more than $2.75 billion in cost-cutting savings. These savings came from reduced personnel, reduced inventories, and increased procurement and sales activities. General Electric also assisted two of its customers—Walmart and Dell—by lending these organizations its six sigma expertise in an effort to eliminate more than $1.1 billion in inefficiencies in the two organizations.[62]

six sigma
A quality standard that establishes a goal of no more than 3.4 defects per million parts or procedures.

Exhibit 3-12

Six Sigma Process Steps

- Select the critical-to-quality characteristics.
- Define the required performance standards.
- Validate measurement system, methods, and procedures.
- Establish the current processes' capability.
- Define upper and lower performance limits.
- Identify sources of variation.
- Screen potential causes of variation to identify the vital few variables needing control.
- Discover variation relationship for the vital variables.
- Establish operating tolerances on each of the vital variables.
- Validate the measurement system's ability to produce repeatable data.
- Determine the capability of the process to control the vital variables.
- Implement statistical process control on the vital variables.

Source: Cited in D. Harold and F. J. Bartos, "Optimize Existing Processes to Achieve Six Sigma Capability," reprinted from *Control Engineering Practice,* © 1998, p. 87.

SUMMARY AND IMPLICATIONS

❶ What does planning involve? Planning is the process of defining goals and assessing how those goals can best be achieved. The goals are written and shared with organizational members. Once the goals are agreed on, specific action plans are created to achieve the goals. Planning's purpose is to provide direction, reduce uncertainty, reduce overlapping and wasteful activities, and establish the goals or standards used in controlling. Without planning, managers would not know what to organize, lead, or control.

❷ How do managers set goals and develop plans? Planning involves two important elements: goals and plans. Goals are the desired outcomes for individuals, groups, or entire organizations. They provide the direction for all management decisions and form the criteria against which actual work accomplishments can be measured. Goals can be set at the top of the organization, or through management by objectives (MBO), in which employees and managers jointly develop goals. Once goals have been established, managers develop plans to achieve them, either on their own, or with the help of employees. Plans outline how goals are going to be met. They typically describe resource allocations, schedules, and other necessary actions to accomplish the goals. Planning can lock people into a particular way of behaving, which might not be appropriate at a later point. Therefore, plans need to be somewhat flexible so that managers can respond to environmental changes.

❸ What are the steps in strategic management? The strategic management process is a six-step process that encompasses strategic planning, implementation, and evaluation. The first four steps involve planning: identifying the organization's current mission, goals, and strategies; analyzing the internal environment; analyzing the external environment; and formulating strategies. The fifth step is implementing strategies, and the sixth step is evaluating the results. Even the best strategies can fail if management does not implement or evaluate them properly.

Heather Reisman, CEO of Indigo Books & Music, announced a new growth strategy in June 2007 that recognizes the influence of the digital age on book sales. She hopes that the strategy she has chosen will pay off. Indigo is currently building on its use of the Internet to help increase sales. The company will want to evaluate the success of its strategy over time and may want to reconsider it if online purchases do not increase significantly or if they fall.

❹ What kinds of strategies can managers use? There are three types of organizational strategy: corporate, business, and functional. They relate to the particular level of the organization that introduces the strategy. At the corporate level, organizations can engage in growth, stability, and renewal strategies. At the business level, strategies look at how an organization should compete in each of its businesses: through cost leadership, differentiation, or focus. At the functional level, strategies of the various functional departments support the business strategy.

○○○
○○○ Indigo is trying a differentiation strategy primarily by offering consumers a unique social-networking site for book lovers.

❺ How can quality be a competitive advantage? To the degree that an organization can satisfy customers' needs for quality, it can differentiate itself from competitors and attract a loyal customer base. Moreover, constant improvement in the quality and reliability of an organization's products or services is something that other organizations cannot necessarily copy. Three ways of managing quality are identified in this chapter: benchmarking, by which management improves quality by analyzing best practices of the leaders in various fields; meeting ISO 9000 series standards for quality management; and using six sigma to achieve the goal of no more than 3.4 defects per million parts or procedures.

Management @ Work

READING FOR COMPREHENSION

1. Contrast formal with informal planning.

2. Under what circumstances are short-term plans preferred? Under what circumstances are specific plans preferred?

3. Describe the differences between (a) strategic and operational plans, (b) short- and long-term plans, and (c) specific and directional plans.

4. If planning is so crucial, why do some managers choose not to do it? What would you advise these managers about planning?

5. Will planning become more or less important to managers in the future? Why?

6. Compare an organization's mission with its goals.

7. Describe the six-step strategic management process.

8. What is a SWOT analysis?

9. How can quality provide a competitive advantage? Give an example.

LINKING CONCEPTS TO PRACTICE

1. "Organizations that fail to plan are planning to fail." Do you agree or disagree with this statement? Explain your position.

2. Under what circumstances do you believe management by objectives and traditional goal setting would be most useful? Discuss.

3. Using Michael Porter's generic strategies (cost leadership, differentiation, and focus), describe the strategy used by each of the following companies to develop a competitive advantage in its industry: Walmart, Home Depot, Holt Renfrew, and WestJet Airlines. Provide specific examples.

4. How might planning in a nonprofit organization such as the Canadian Cancer Society differ from planning in a for-profit organization such as Molson?

5. "The primary means of sustaining a competitive advantage is to adjust faster to the environment than your competitors do." Do you agree or disagree with this statement? Explain your position.

6. "Benchmarking, six sigma, and ISO 9000 series all have the effect of assisting a company to develop a competitive advantage." Do you agree? Why or why not? Cite specific examples.

SELF-ASSESSMENT

How Good Am I at Personal Planning?

Indicate how much you agree or disagree with each of the six statements as they relate to your school and personal life. Use the following scale to record your answers:[63]

1 = Strongly Disagree 2 = Disagree 3 = Neither Agree nor Disagree 4 = Agree 5 = Strongly Agree

1. I am proactive rather than reactive.   1 2 3 4 5

2. I set aside enough time and resources to study and complete projects.   1 2 3 4 5

3. I am able to budget money to buy the things I really want without going broke.   1 2 3 4 5

4. I have thought through what I want to do in school.   1 2 3 4 5

5. I have a plan for completing my major.   1 2 3 4 5

6. My goals for the future are realistic.   1 2 3 4 5

Scoring Key

A score of 5 on any item means that you are doing well in planning and goal setting in that area. The authors of this instrument suggest that scores of 3 or less on any item indicate you need to gain a better understanding of the importance of goal setting and what is involved in the process.

Analysis and Interpretation

Successful people have goals and establish plans to help them achieve those goals. This exercise is designed to get you to think about goal setting as it relates to your school and personal life.

If your performance on this instrument was less than you desire, consider practising skills related to goal setting and time management. Toward that end, you might want to read one or more of the following books: D. K. Smith, *Make Success Measurable! A Mindbook-Workbook for Setting Goals and Taking Action* (New York: Wiley, 1999); G. R. Blair, *Goal Setting 101: How to Set and Achieve a Goal!* (Syracuse, NY: GoalsGuy Learning, 2000); and M. Leboeuf, *Working Smart:*

How to Accomplish More in Half the Time (New York: Warner Books, 1993).

More Self-Assessments

To learn more about your own skills, abilities, and interests, take the following self-assessments on MyManagementLab at www.pearsoned.ca/mymanagementlab:

- I.E.2.—What Time of Day Am I Most Productive?
- I.E.3.—How Good Am I at Personal Planning?
- III.C.1.—How Well Do I Respond to Turbulent Change? (This exercise also appears in Chapter 12 on pages 379–380.)

MANAGEMENT FOR YOU TODAY

Dilemma

Think ahead to five years from now, to consider what it is that you might like to be doing with your life. Develop your own vision and mission statements. Establish a set of goals that will help you achieve your vision and mission. Develop a five-year plan that maps out the steps you need to take in order to get to where you want to be with your life at that time.

Becoming a Manager

- Practise setting goals by doing so for various aspects of your life, such as academic studies, career preparation, family, and so forth.
- Be prepared to change your goals as circumstances change.
- For goals that you have set, write out plans for achieving those goals.

- Write a personal mission statement.
- If you are employed, talk to your manager(s) about the types of planning they do. Ask them for suggestions on how to be a better planner.

WORKING TOGETHER: TEAM-BASED EXERCISE

Your College or University's Mission

You might not pay much attention to the goals and objectives of your college or university because you are focusing on your studies. But your college or university had to carve out its niche in an effort to provide something of value to its students, and it must continue to monitor its performance.

For this exercise, break up into small groups. The task of each small group is to prepare responses to the following questions and present its findings to the class.

1. What is your college or university's mission? What resources does your college or university have that support its mission?

2. How would you describe your college or university's environment in terms of technology and government regulations?

3. What do you believe are the strengths and weaknesses of your college or university? Its opportunities and threats?

4. Which corporate strategy is your college or university following? How does this relate to its strengths, weaknesses, opportunities, and threats?

5. Which of Porter's generic strategies is evident at your college or university?

6. What do you believe is your college or university's competitive advantage? What do you think your college or university should do to sustain its competitive advantage?

ETHICS IN ACTION

Ethical Dilemma Exercise: What Should Managers Do When Pressured to Deliver Results?

Some lower- and mid-level managers go to great lengths to achieve their goals rather than disrupt the means–ends chain that supports the accomplishment of higher-level goals. But how far is too far? Coca-Cola has admitted that some employees acted improperly when they took steps to manipulate the results of a product test at Burger King restaurants in Richmond, Virginia. If the test succeeded, the product—Frozen Coke—would have been introduced in more Burger King outlets. In turn, the prospect of higher sales would have been a milestone toward meeting Coca-Cola's overall revenue and profit goals.

Burger King executives and franchisees were not pleased when they found out about the manipulated test results. Coca-Cola's president sent a written apology to Burger King, noting: "These actions were wrong and inconsistent with the values of the Coca-Cola Company. Our relationships with Burger King and all our customers are of the utmost importance to us and should be firmly grounded in only the highest-integrity actions."[64] Did Coca-Cola managers feel too much pressure to deliver results?

Imagine that you are a district manager with Coca-Cola and you are being promoted to a new position at the end of the month. Your area's sales are an important component of the corporation's provincial and national sales goals. However, this month's sales are running below the planned level. Should you ask area supermarkets to double their current monthly order and promise that any unsold Coca-Cola products can be returned during the following month?

Thinking Critically About Ethics

"I'm telling you. After my talk with my manager today about my work goals for the next quarter, I think our company's MBO program actually stands for 'manipulating by objectives,' not management by objectives," Carlos complained to his friend Sabrina. He went on, "She came in and outlined what she thought I should be working on, and then asked me what I thought of it. I guess that's her way of getting me to participate in the goal setting."

Is it unethical for a manager to enter a participative goal-setting session with a pre-established set of goals that he or she wants the employee to accept? Why or why not? Is it unethical for a manager to use his or her formal position to impose specific goals on an employee? Why or why not?

CASE APPLICATION

Haier Group

You may not be familiar with the Haier Group (sounds like "higher"), but if you have ever shopped for a refrigerator, microwave, wine cellar, or air conditioner at Walmart, Sears, or Home Depot you have undoubtedly seen, if not purchased, the company's products.[65] Haier's name surfaced in North American headlines in late 2005, when it made a bid to purchase domestic appliance maker Maytag, which operates in both Canada and the United States. Haier exports its products to more than 100 countries and regions, and its revenue in 2005 was over $14 billion.

Haier Group is China's largest home-appliance maker and CEO Zhang Ruimin has ambitious goals for his company. Whereas the United States has General Electric, Germany has Mercedes-Benz, and Japan has Sony, China has yet to produce a comparable global competitor. Zhang is hoping to change that. Haier enjoys enviable prestige in China (a survey of "young, fashionable" Chinese ranked

Haier as the country's third most popular brand behind Shanghai Volkswagen and Motorola, with Coca-Cola fourth), but Zhang is not satisfied. He wants to gain worldwide recognition, build the company into China's first truly global brand, and be listed on the *Fortune* Global 500. But accomplishing those goals may mean losing its "Chineseness." In an online survey conducted in 2005 by Interbrand, 79 percent of the respondents believed that a "made in China" label hurts Chinese brands, with the biggest challenge to Chinese companies being to change the impression of Chinese products as cheap, poor value, poor quality, and unreliable. Product recalls during the period 2007–2009 have increased concern about products manufactured in China.

What can Zhang do to build his brand globally, while addressing the concerns of those who worry about the quality and safety of Chinese products?

DEVELOPING YOUR DIAGNOSTIC AND ANALYTICAL SKILLS

Living Large

Although the music business is struggling, Live Nation is sitting pretty.[66] It's the world's largest events and live music promoter, with more than 64 million people attending some 28 000 of those events each year. The company also owns the House of Blues chain of venues, where customers can enjoy different genres of live music. CEO Michael Rapino has guided the company since it was spun off as a separate business in 2005 from radio giant Clear Channel Communications.

On its website, Live Nation describes itself as the "future of the music business." Through live concerts, music venues and festivals, and the most comprehensive concert search engine on the web, Live Nation is revolutionizing the music industry both onstage and online. Its strategy is to connect the artists to the fans. And Rapino isn't satisfied with dominating only the concert business. Although Live Nation will continue to focus on its live music assets, Rapino is going after the record labels' most important assets—the music stars. He's offering them a one-stop operation that handles their every musical need. That offer is: "We already operate your tours. Why not let us make

your albums, sell your merchandise, run your website, and produce your videos and a range of other products you haven't yet thought of." In October 2007, Rapino landed a big name when he signed a first-of-its-kind deal with Madonna, who left her long-time label Warner Records and signed a 10-year contract worth an estimated $120 million to let Live Nation handle every part of her business except publishing. Madonna's manager said, "The labels are in a jam. For a company to do well in music now, it's got to be in all aspects of the business. And Live Nation is the risk-taker. It's leading the charge." Live Nation has signed Shakira, Jay-Z, and Nickelback to similar deals and hopes to add more superstars to its roster.

The key to Live Nation's growth strategy is the ability to connect to those millions of people who attend shows every year. The company's valuable database containing contact information for those fans gives it an efficient way to offer them additional music-related products and services. Will Rapino's strategy live or die?

Questions

1. What growth strategy does Live Nation appear to be using? What competitive advantage do you think Live Nation has?

2. How might SWOT analysis be useful to Mike Rapino?

3. Find Live Nation's most current annual report. What goals is the company pursuing? What strategies is it using? Do its strategies appear to be helping it reach these goals?

4. What do you think of Rapino's strategic direction for Live Nation?

DEVELOPING YOUR INTERPERSONAL SKILLS

Scanning the Environment

About the Skill

Anticipating and interpreting changes that are taking place in the environment is an important skill that managers need. Information that comes from scanning the environment can be used in making decisions and taking actions. Managers at all levels of an organization need to know how to scan the environment for important information and trends.

Steps in Developing the Skill

You can be more effective at scanning the environment if you use the following five suggestions:[67]

1. **Decide which type of environmental information is important to your work.** Perhaps you need to know changes in customers' needs and desires, or perhaps you need to know what your competitors are doing. Once you know the type of information that you would like to have, you can look at the best ways to get that information.

2. **Regularly read and monitor pertinent information.** There is no scarcity of information to scan, but what you need to do is read those information sources that are pertinent. How do you know information sources are pertinent? They are pertinent if they provide you with the information that you identified as important.

3. **Incorporate the information that you get from your environmental scanning into your decisions and actions.** Unless you use the information you are getting, you are wasting your time getting it. Also, the more that you find

you are using information from your environmental scanning, the more likely it is that you will want to continue to invest time and other resources into gathering it. You will see that this information is important to your being able to manage effectively and efficiently.

4. **Regularly review your environmental scanning activities.** If you find that you are spending too much time getting nonuseful information, or if you are not using the pertinent information that you have gathered, you need to make some adjustments.

5. **Encourage your subordinates to be alert to information that is important.** Your employees can be your "eyes and ears" as well. Emphasize to them the importance of gathering and sharing information that may affect your work unit's performance.

Practising the Skill

Read the following scenario. Write some notes about how you would handle the situation described. Be sure to refer to the five suggestions for scanning the environment.

You are the assistant to the president at your college or university. You have been asked to prepare a report outlining the external information that you think is important for her to monitor. Think of the types of information that the president would need in order to do an effective job of managing the college or university right now and over the next three years. Be as specific as you can in describing this information. Also, identify where this information could be found.

CHAPTER **4** Decision Making

How do I make good decisions?

1 What are the steps in the decision-making process?

2 What factors affect how decisions are made?

3 How do ethics and social responsibility relate to decision making?

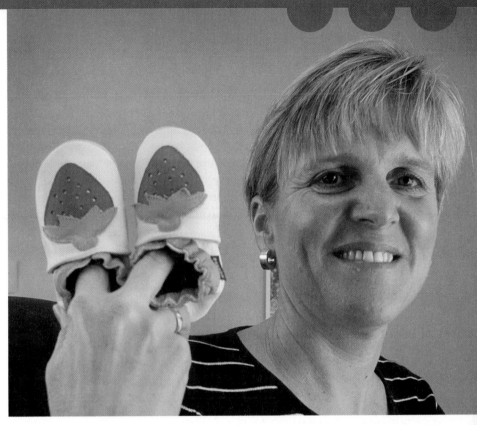

Sandra Wilson, chair and CEO of Burnaby, BC-based Robeez Footwear, faced a very big decision in spring 2006.[1] At the time, Robeez was the leading worldwide manufacturer of soft-soled leather footwear for young children. Wilson wondered what the company should do next. Robeez was poised for growth, but needed outside capital in order to expand. Was it time to take on a new partnership or sell the company? Would bringing in an outside investor take the company, which she considered her baby, out of her hands? Was there a company to which Wilson might sell Robeez that had the desire, drive, and expertise to achieve her vision for growth?

Wilson started her home-based business after she "stumbled across the idea to design baby shoes by watching [her] son and [her] friend's young children." She received immediate encouragement from friends who saw her shoes. To test her idea in the marketplace, she made 20 pairs of shoes by hand, and took them to a retailer gift show. From that show she received orders from 15 retailers. This was enough to launch her business, Robeez Footwear, named for her young son, Robert.

Initially Wilson handled all aspects of her business herself, from design to production to marketing and distribution. By 2006, however, 20 years after she had started the company, she employed 400 people and sold shoes in North America, Europe, and Australia. It was time for Wilson to decide on the next steps for her business. "We experienced significant growth at Robeez, particularly over the last three or four years," said Wilson. "We have a real vision about where we want to take the Robeez brand and we feel there is a lot of potential for growth with the brand."

Think About It

How do CEOs make important decisions? Put yourself in Sandra Wilson's shoes. What steps would you take to determine whether Robeez should take on a partner or be sold to another company? How could Wilson evaluate the effectiveness of the decision she is about to make? What decision criteria might she use?

Sandra Wilson needs to make good decisions. Making good decisions is something that every manager strives to do, since the overall quality of managerial decisions has a major influence on organizational success or failure. In this chapter, we examine the concept of decision making and how managers can make ethical decisions.

The Decision-Making Process

While watching a sports competition, have you ever felt that you could make better decisions than the coaches on the field or court? Soccer fans outside Helsinki, Finland, get to do just that, as the following *Management Reflection* shows.

❶ What are the steps in the decision-making process?

MANAGEMENT REFLECTION

Fans Help Soccer Coach Make Decisions

Can you really coach a team by getting input from 300 fans? In the Helsinki suburb of Pukinmaki, the fans of PK-35, an amateur soccer team, get that chance![2] The coach does not make decisions about what to do on the field by himself, but instead relies on 300 fans who text message their instructions via their cellphones. Each week, the coach posts between 3 and 10 questions about training, team selection, and game tactics to the fans. They have three minutes to respond via cellphone text messaging, and they receive immediate feedback on what others think.

Does shared decision making work? During the first season of the experiment, the team won first place in its division and was promoted to the next higher division. Although we are unlikely to see this type of wireless interactive decision making any time soon in organizations, it does illustrate that decisions, and maybe even how they are made, play a role in performance. ■

decision
A choice from two or more alternatives.

Individuals must continually make **decisions**. Although decision making is typically described as "choosing among alternatives," that view is simplistic. Why? Because decision making is a comprehensive process, not just a simple act of choosing among alternatives.[3] Even for something as straightforward as deciding where to go for lunch, you do more than just choose burgers or pizza. You may consider various restaurants, how you will get there, who might go with you. Granted, you may not spend a lot of time contemplating a lunch decision, but you still go through a process when making that decision. What *does* the decision-making process involve?

decision-making process
A set of eight steps that includes identifying a problem, selecting an alternative, and evaluating the decision's effectiveness.

Exhibit 4-1 illustrates the **decision-making process**, a set of eight steps that begins with identifying a problem, the decision criteria, and the weights for those criteria; moves to developing, analyzing, and selecting an alternative that can resolve the problem; then moves to implementing the alternative; and concludes with evaluating the decision's effectiveness. Many individuals use most or all of the steps implicitly, if not explicitly. Often, when a poor decision is made, it is because one of the steps was not carefully considered.

This process is as relevant to your personal decision about what movie to see on a Friday night as it is to a corporate action such as a decision to use technology in managing client relationships. The process can also be used to describe both individual and group decisions. Let's take a closer look at the process in order to understand what each step involves. We will use an example—a manager deciding what laptop computers are best to purchase—to illustrate these steps.

Step 1: Identify a Problem

problem
A discrepancy between an existing and a desired state of affairs.

The decision-making process begins with the existence of a **problem** or, more specifically, a discrepancy between an existing and a desired state of affairs.[4] Take Amanda, a sales manager whose sales representatives need new laptops because their old ones are inadequate to do their jobs efficiently and effectively. For simplicity's sake, assume that Amanda has determined that it's not economical to simply add memory to the old computers and that it's the organization's policy that managers purchase new computers rather than lease them. Now we have a problem. There is a disparity between the capabilities of the sales reps' current computers and the capabilities that the sales reps require of their computers in order to do their jobs properly. Amanda has a decision to make.

Step 2: Identify Decision Criteria

decision criteria
Criteria that define what is relevant in making a decision.

Once a manager has identified a problem, the **decision criteria** important to resolving the problem must be identified. That is, managers must determine what is relevant in making a decision. Whether explicitly stated or not, every decision maker has criteria that guide his or her decisions. These criteria are generally determined by one's objectives. For example, when you buy a car, your objective might be to have a car that shouts "status

Exhibit 4-1

The Decision-Making Process

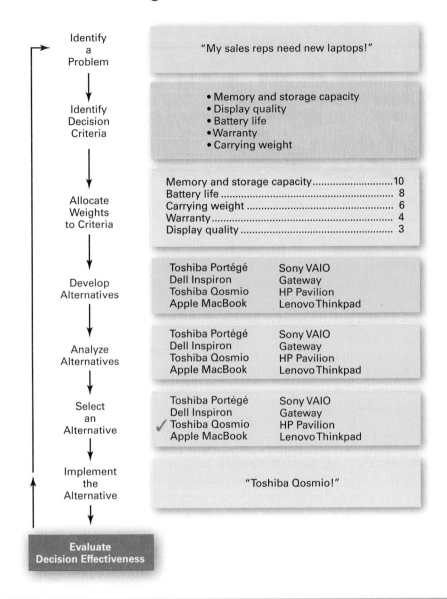

Identify a Problem
"My sales reps need new laptops!"

Identify Decision Criteria
- Memory and storage capacity
- Display quality
- Battery life
- Warranty
- Carrying weight

Allocate Weights to Criteria

Memory and storage capacity 10
Battery life 8
Carrying weight 6
Warranty.. 4
Display quality 3

Develop Alternatives

Toshiba Portégé	Sony VAIO
Dell Inspiron	Gateway
Toshiba Qosmio	HP Pavilion
Apple MacBook	Lenovo Thinkpad

Analyze Alternatives

Toshiba Portégé	Sony VAIO
Dell Inspiron	Gateway
Toshiba Qosmio	HP Pavilion
Apple MacBook	Lenovo Thinkpad

Select an Alternative

Toshiba Portégé	Sony VAIO
Dell Inspiron	Gateway
✓ Toshiba Qosmio	HP Pavilion
Apple MacBook	Lenovo Thinkpad

Implement the Alternative
"Toshiba Qosmio!"

Evaluate Decision Effectiveness

symbol." Or you might want a car that is low maintenance. With your objective in mind, you might consider speed, fuel efficiency, colour, manufacturer, size, and so on as criteria on which to evaluate which car to buy. In our laptop purchase example, Amanda has to assess what factors are relevant to her decision. These might include criteria such as price, convenience, multimedia capability, memory and storage capabilities, display quality, battery life, expansion capability, warranty, and carrying weight. After careful consideration, she decides that memory and storage capabilities, display quality, battery life, warranty, and carrying weight are the relevant criteria in her decision.

Step 3: Allocate Weights to Criteria

If the criteria identified in Step 2 are not equally important, the decision maker must weight the items in order to give them the correct priority in the decision. How do you weight criteria? A simple approach is to give the most important criterion a weight of 10 and then assign weights to the rest against that standard. Thus, a criterion with a weight of 10 would be twice as important as one given a 5. Of course, you could use 100 or 1000

The choice of a new laptop computer relies on specific decision criteria such as price, convenience, memory and storage capacity, display quality, battery life, and even carrying weight.

Q&A 5.1

or any number you select as the highest weight. The idea is to prioritize the criteria you identified in Step 2 by assigning a weight to each.

Exhibit 4-2 lists the criteria and weights that Amanda developed for her computer replacement decision. As you can see, memory and storage capability is the most important criterion in her decision, and display quality is the least important.

Step 4: Develop Alternatives

The fourth step requires the decision maker to list viable alternatives that could resolve the problem. No attempt is made to evaluate the alternatives, only to list them. Our sales manager, Amanda, identified eight laptops as possible choices, including Toshiba Portégé, Dell Inspiron, Toshiba Qosmio, Apple MacBook, Sony VAIO, Gateway, HP Pavilion, and Lenovo Thinkpad.

PRISM 12

Step 5: Analyze Alternatives

Once the alternatives have been identified, a decision maker must analyze each one. How? By appraising each against the criteria established in steps 2 and 3. From this comparison, the strengths and weaknesses of each alternative become evident. Exhibit 4-3 shows the assessed values that Amanda gave each of her eight alternatives after she had talked to some computer experts and read the latest information from computer magazines and from the web.

Keep in mind that carrying weight is easy to determine by looking at descriptions online or in computer magazines. However, the assessment of display quality is more of a personal judgment. The point is that most decisions by managers involve judgments—the criteria chosen in Step 2, the weights given to the criteria in Step 3, and the analysis of alternatives in Step 5. This explains why two computer buyers with the same amount of money may look at two totally different sets of alternatives or even rate the same alternatives differently.

Exhibit 4-2

Criteria and Weights for Laptop Replacement Decision

Criterion	Weight
Memory and storage capacity	10
Battery life	8
Carrying weight	6
Warranty	4
Display quality	3

Exhibit 4-3

Assessed Values of Laptops Using Decision Criteria

	Memory and Storage Capacity	Battery Life	Carrying Weight	Warranty	Display Quality
Toshiba Portégé	10	3	10	8	5
Dell Inspiron	8	7	7	8	7
HP Pavilion	8	5	7	10	10
Apple MacBook	8	7	7	8	7
Sony VAIO	7	8	7	8	7
Gateway	8	3	6	10	8
Toshiba Qosmio	10	7	8	6	7
Lenovo Thinkpad	4	10	4	8	10

Exhibit 4-3 represents only an assessment of the eight alternatives against the decision criteria. It does not reflect the weighting done in Step 3. If you multiply each alternative's assessed value (Exhibit 4-3) by its weight (Exhibit 4-2), you get the scores presented in Exhibit 4-4 on page 106. The sum of these scores represents an evaluation of each alternative against both the established criteria and weights. At times a decision maker might not have to take this step. If one choice had scored 10 on every criterion, you would not need to consider the weights. Similarly, if the weights were all equal, you could evaluate each alternative merely by summing up the appropriate lines in Exhibit 4-3. In this instance, for example, the score for the Toshiba Protégé would be 36 and the score for Gateway would be 35.

Step 6: Select an Alternative

What does it mean if the "best" alternative does not feel right to you after going through the decision-making steps?

Step 6 is choosing the best alternative from among those considered. Once all the pertinent criteria in the decision have been weighted and viable alternatives analyzed, we simply choose the alternative that generated the highest total in Step 5. In our example (Exhibit 4-4), Amanda would choose the Toshiba Qosmio because it scored highest (249 total) on the basis of the criteria identified, the weights given to the criteria, and her assessment of each laptop's ranking on the criteria.

That said, occasionally when one gets to this step, the alternative that looks best according to the numbers may not feel like the best solution (e.g., your intuition might suggest some other alternative). Often the reason is that the individual did not give the correct weight to one or more criteria (perhaps because one criteria was actually much more important than the individual realized initially, when assigning weights). Thus, if the individual finds that the "best alternative" does not seem like the right alternative, the decision maker needs to decide before implementing the alternative if a review of the criteria is necessary.

Step 7: Implement the Alternative

Step 7 is concerned with putting the decision into action. This involves conveying the decision to those affected by it and getting their commitment to it. Managers often fail to get buy-in from those around them before making a decision, even though successful implementation requires participation. One study found that managers used participation in only 20 percent of decisions, even though broad participation in decisions led to successful implementation 80 percent of the time. The same study found that managers most commonly tried to implement decisions through power or persuasion (used in 60 percent of decisions). These tactics were successful in only one of three decisions, however.[5] If the people who must carry out a decision participate in the process, they are

Q&A 5.2

Exhibit 4-4

Evaluation of Laptop Alternatives Against Weighted Criteria

	Memory and Storage Capacity	Battery Life	Carrying Weight	Warranty	Display Quality	Total
Toshiba Portégé	100	24	60	32	15	231
Dell Inspiron	80	56	42	32	21	231
HP Pavilion	80	40	42	40	30	232
Apple MacBook	80	56	42	32	21	231
Sony VAIO	70	64	42	32	21	229
Gateway	80	24	36	40	24	204
Toshiba Qosmio	100	56	48	24	21	249
Lenovo Thinkpad	40	80	24	32	30	206

more likely to enthusiastically support the outcome than if they are just told what to do. Parts 3, 4, and 5 of this book discuss how decisions are implemented by effective organizing, leading, and controlling.

Step 8: Evaluate Decision Effectiveness

The last step in the decision-making process involves evaluating the outcome of the decision to see if the problem has been resolved. Did the alternative chosen in Step 6 and implemented in Step 7 accomplish the desired result? In Part 5 of this book, in which we look at the controlling function, we will see how to evaluate the results of decisions.

Q&A 5.3

What if the evaluation shows the problem still exists? The manager would need to assess what went wrong. Was the problem incorrectly defined? Were errors made in the evaluation of the various alternatives? Was the right alternative selected but poorly implemented? Answers to questions such as these might send the manager back to one of the earlier steps. It might even require re-doing the whole decision process. To learn more about creativity and decision making, see *Developing Your Interpersonal Skills—Solving Problems Creatively* on page 130, at the end of the chapter.

The Manager as Decision Maker

As chair and CEO, Sandra Wilson needed to make a decision about the future of Robeez Footwear.[6] "We recognized that if we wanted to execute the plans and achieve the vision for where we could take this company we needed to look for . . . someone with the financial backing and expertise to help us continue to build Robeez," says Wilson.

Should Wilson seek a new partner for Robeez or sell the company? She weighed the pros and cons of each choice. For example, taking on a new partner would provide the company with the money to expand to more markets. The downside would be the possibility of losing control over the quality of the product. Selling Robeez to another company could provide Robeez with the resources and experience necessary to continue its momentum of growth. However, if Robeez were manufactured by another company, the corporate culture that underlies Robeez' success might change and negatively affect the brand.

Think About It

What biases might enter into Sandra Wilson's decision making, and how might she overcome these? How can Wilson improve her decision making, given that she is dealing with uncertainty and risk? How might escalation of commitment affect her decision?

Exhibit 4-5

Decisions in the Management Functions

Planning

- What are the organization's long-term objectives?
- What strategies will best achieve those objectives?
- What should the organization's short-term objectives be?
- How difficult should individual goals be?

Leading

- How do I handle employees who appear to be low in motivation?
- What is the most effective leadership style in a given situation?
- How will a specific change affect worker productivity?
- When is the right time to stimulate conflict?

Organizing

- How many employees should I have report directly to me?
- How much centralization should there be in the organization?
- How should jobs be designed?
- When should the organization implement a different structure?

Controlling

- What activities in the organization need to be controlled?
- How should those activities be controlled?
- When is a performance deviation significant?
- What type of management information system should the organization have?

Everyone in an organization makes decisions, but decision making is particularly important in a manager's job. As Exhibit 4-5 shows, decision making is part of all four managerial functions. That's why managers—when they plan, organize, lead, and control—are frequently called *decision makers.*

The decision-making process described in Exhibit 4-1 on page 103 suggests that individuals make rational, carefully scripted decisions. But, is *rational* the best word to describe the decision-making process and the person who actually makes the decisions? We look at these issues in this section. We start by looking at three perspectives on how decisions are made.

> **2 What factors affect how decisions are made?**

Making Decisions: Rationality, Bounded Rationality, and Intuition

Our model of the decision-making process implies that individuals engage in **rational decision making**. By that we mean that people make consistent, value-maximizing choices within specified constraints.[7] What are the underlying assumptions of rationality, and how valid are those assumptions?

rational decision making
Making decisions that are consistent and value-maximizing within specified constraints.

Assumptions of Rationality

Would you say you make decisions rationally or do you rely on gut instinct?

A decision maker who was perfectly rational would be fully objective and logical. He or she would carefully define a problem and would have a clear and specific goal. Moreover, making decisions using rationality would consistently lead to selecting the alternative that maximizes the likelihood of achieving that goal. Exhibit 4-6 on page 108 summarizes the assumptions of rationality.

The assumptions of rationality apply to any decision—personal or managerial. However, because we are concerned with managerial decision making, we need to add one further assumption. Rational managerial decision making assumes that decisions are made in the best interests of the organization. That is, the decision maker is assumed to be maximizing the organization's interests, not his or her own interests.

How realistic are these assumptions? Not all problems are simple, with clear goals and limited alternatives. Often time pressures are involved in decision making. There can be high costs in seeking out and evaluating alternatives. For these reasons, most decisions that managers face in the real world do not meet the assumptions of rationality.[8] So how

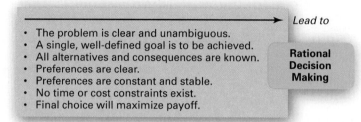

Exhibit 4-6

Assumptions of Rationality

- The problem is clear and unambiguous.
- A single, well-defined goal is to be achieved.
- All alternatives and consequences are known.
- Preferences are clear.
- Preferences are constant and stable.
- No time or cost constraints exist.
- Final choice will maximize payoff.

Lead to → **Rational Decision Making**

are most decisions in organizations usually made? The concept of bounded rationality can help answer that question.

Bounded Rationality

bounded rationality
Limitations on a person's ability to interpret, process, and act on information.

Managers tend to operate under assumptions of **bounded rationality**. That is, they make decisions rationally but are limited (bounded) by their ability to interpret, process, and act on information.[9]

satisfice
To accept solutions that are "good enough."

Because they cannot possibly analyze all information on all alternatives, managers **satisfice** rather than maximize. That is, they accept a solution that is both satisfactory and sufficient. When managers satisfice, they limit their review of alternatives to some of the more conspicuous ones. Rather than carefully evaluate each alternative in great detail, managers settle on an alternative that is "good enough"—one that meets an acceptable level of performance. The first alternative that meets the "good enough" criterion ends the search.

Q&A 5.4

Let's look at an example. Suppose that you are a finance major and upon graduation you want a job, preferably as a personal financial planner, with a minimum annual salary of $50 000 and a location within 100 kilometres of your hometown. You are in a hurry to get a job, so you accept a job offer as a business credit analyst—not exactly a personal financial planner but still in the finance field—at a bank 50 kilometres from your hometown at a starting salary of $55 000. A more comprehensive job search would have revealed a job in personal financial planning at a trust company only 25 kilometres from your hometown with a starting salary of $57 000. Because the first job offer was satisfactory (or "good enough"), you behaved in a boundedly rational manner by accepting it, although according to the assumptions of perfect rationality you did not maximize your decision by searching all possible alternatives and then choosing the best.

Q&A 5.5

Intuition

Do you prefer to make decisions intuitively? Are these good decisions?

When managers at stapler-maker Swingline saw the company's market share declining, they decided to use a logical scientific approach to help them address the issue. For three years, they exhaustively researched stapler users before deciding what new products to develop. However, at newcomer Accentra, Inc., founder Todd Moses used a more intuitive decision approach to come up with his line of unique PaperPro staplers. His stapler sold 1 million units in 6 months in a market that sells only 25 million units annually in total—a pretty good result for a new product.[10]

intuitive decision making
Making decisions on the basis of experience, feelings, and accumulated judgment.

Like Todd Moses, managers regularly use their intuition, which may actually help improve their decision making.[11] What is **intuitive decision making**? It's making decisions

Exhibit 4-7

What Is Intuition?

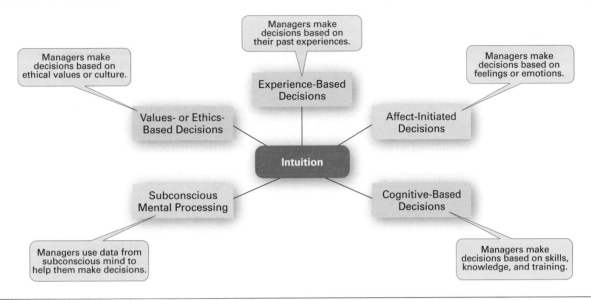

Source: Based on L. A. Burke and M. K. Miller, "Taking the Mystery Out of Intuitive Decision Making." *Academy of Management Executive*, October 1999, pp. 91–99.

on the basis of experience, feelings, and accumulated judgment. Researchers studying managers' use of intuitive decision making identified five different aspects of intuition, which are described in Exhibit 4-7.

Making a decision on intuition or "gut feeling" does not necessarily happen independently of rational analysis; rather, the two complement each other. A manager who has had experience with a particular, or even similar, type of problem or situation often can act quickly with what appears to be limited information. Such a manager does not rely on a systematic and thorough analysis of the problem or identification and evaluation of alternatives but instead uses his or her experience and judgment to make a decision.

How accurate is intuitive decision making? A recent study suggests that complex decisions may be better if made "in the absence of attentive deliberation."[12] To discover your own intuitive abilities, see *Self-Assessment—How Intuitive Am I?* on pages 125–126, at the end of the chapter.

Q&A 5.6

Types of Problems and Decisions

Managers at eating establishments in Whitehorse, Yukon, make decisions weekly about purchasing food supplies and scheduling employee work shifts. It is something they have done countless times. But in 2007, they faced a decision they had never encountered—how to adapt to a newly enacted no-smoking bylaw in public places, which includes restaurants and bars. This situation is not all that unusual. Managers in all kinds of organizations will face different types of problems and decisions as they do their jobs. Depending on the nature of the problem, a manager can use different types of decisions.

Structured Problems and Programmed Decisions

Some problems are straightforward. The goal of the decision maker is clear, the problem is familiar, and information about the problem is easily defined and complete. Examples of these types of problems could include what to do when a customer returns a purchase to a store, a supplier delivers an important product late, a news team wants to respond to a fast-breaking event, or a student wants to drop a class. Such situations are called **structured problems** because they are straightforward, familiar, and easily defined. When situations are structured, there is probably some standardized routine for handling problems that may arise. For example, when a restaurant server spills a drink on a customer's coat, the manager offers to have the coat cleaned at the restaurant's expense. This is what we call a **programmed decision**—a repetitive decision that can be handled by a routine approach. Because the problem is structured, the manager does not have to go to the trouble and expense of following an involved decision process.

Programmed decisions can have negative consequences, however, particularly when decision makers deal with diverse populations/clients/customers. For example, it may be difficult to have one's coat cleaned immediately if one is away from home on a business trip in the middle of winter. Employees of Ottawa-based JDS Uniphase were not happy with the programmed decision they received from the Canada Revenue Agency about hefty taxes they were asked to pay on their company stock options. When JDS stock was trading at $300 per share, employees were saddled with tax bills of several hundred thousand dollars for their stock options, even though they had not cashed them in. When employees asked the Canada Revenue Agency how they could be expected to pay such big tax bills when they earned only $50 000 per year, the agency responded unsympathetically that they had to pay up.[13]

Managers make programmed decisions by falling back on procedures, rules, and policies.

A **procedure** is a series of interrelated sequential steps that a decision maker can use to respond to a structured problem. The only real difficulty is in identifying the problem. Once it's clear, so is the procedure. When bad weather grounds airplanes, airlines have procedures for helping customers who miss their flights. Customers may request that they be put up in a hotel for the night. The customer service agent knows how to make this decision—follow the established airline procedure for dealing with customers when flights are grounded.

A **rule** is an explicit statement that tells a decision maker what he or she can or cannot do. Rules are frequently used because they are simple to follow and ensure consistency. For example, rules about lateness and absenteeism permit supervisors to make disciplinary decisions rapidly and fairly.

A **policy** is a guideline for making a decision. In contrast to a rule, a policy establishes general parameters for the decision maker rather than specifically stating what should or should not be done. Policies typically contain an ambiguous term that leaves interpretation up to the decision maker. "The customer always comes first and should always be *satisfied*" is an example of a policy statement. While ambiguity of policies is often intended to allow more flexibility in action, not all employees and customers are comfortable with flexibly determined policies.

Unstructured Problems and Nonprogrammed Decisions

Many organizational situations involve **unstructured problems**, which are problems that are new or unusual and for which information is ambiguous or incomplete. Whether to build a new manufacturing facility in Beijing is an example of an unstructured problem.

Nonprogrammed decisions are unique and nonrecurring and require custom-made solutions. For example, if an office building were to be flooded because sprinklers went off accidentally, CEOs with businesses in the buildings would have to decide when and how to start operating again, and what to do for employees whose offices were completely ruined. When a manager confronts an unstructured problem, there is no cut-and-dried solution. It requires a custom-made response through nonprogrammed decision making.

Few managerial decisions in the real world are either fully programmed or nonprogrammed. These are extremes, and most decisions fall somewhere in between. Few

structured problems
Problems that are straightforward, familiar, and easily defined.

programmed decision
A repetitive decision that can be handled by a routine approach.

procedure
A series of interrelated sequential steps that a decision maker can use to respond to a structured problem.

rule
An explicit statement that tells a decision maker what he or she can or cannot do.

policy
A guideline for making a decision.

Q&A 5.7

unstructured problems
Problems that are new or unusual and for which information is ambiguous or incomplete.

nonprogrammed decisions
Decisions that are unique and nonrecurring and require custom-made solutions.

Many people believe that China will become the next big market for powerful brand-name products, and Zong Qinghou, founder of China's Wahaha beverage group, is ready. But brand names are a new concept in Chinese markets, and Zong prefers his own first-hand information to market research. He will face many nonprogrammed decisions as he tries to make his brand strong at home and abroad.

programmed decisions are designed to eliminate individual judgment completely. At the other extreme, even a unique situation requiring a nonprogrammed decision can be helped by programmed routines. It's best to think of decisions as *mainly* programmed or *mainly* nonprogrammed, rather than as completely one or the other.

The problems confronting managers usually become more unstructured as they move up the organizational hierarchy. Why? Because lower-level managers handle the routine decisions themselves and let upper-level managers deal with the decisions they find unusual or difficult. Similarly, higher-level managers delegate routine decisions to their subordinates so they can deal with more difficult issues.[14]

One of the more challenging tasks facing managers as they make decisions is analyzing decision alternatives (Step 5 in the decision-making process). In the next section, we look at analyzing alternatives under different conditions.

Decision-Making Conditions

When managers make decisions, they face three conditions: certainty, risk, and uncertainty. What are the characteristics of each?

Certainty

The ideal condition for making decisions is one of **certainty**, that is, a condition in which a decision maker can make accurate decisions because the outcome of every alternative is known. For example, when Alberta's finance minister is deciding in which bank to deposit excess provincial funds, he knows the exact interest rate being offered by each bank and the amount that will be earned on the funds. He is certain about the outcomes of each alternative. As you might expect, most managerial decisions are not like this.

certainty
A condition in which a decision maker can make accurate decisions because the outcome of every alternative is known.

Risk

How much do uncertainty and risk affect your decisions?

A far more common condition is one of **risk**, a condition in which a decision maker is able to estimate the likelihood of certain outcomes. The ability to assign probabilities to outcomes may be the result of personal experiences or secondary information. With risk, managers have historical data that let them assign probabilities to different alternatives. Let's work through an example.

Suppose that you manage a ski resort in Whistler, BC. You are thinking about adding another lift to your current facility. Obviously, your decision will be influenced by the additional revenue that the new lift would generate, and additional revenue will depend on snowfall. The decision is made somewhat clearer because you have fairly reliable weather data from the past 10 years on snowfall levels in your area—3 years of heavy snowfall, 5 years of normal

risk
A condition in which a decision maker is able to estimate the likelihood of certain outcomes.

Exhibit 4-8

Expected Value for Revenues From the Addition of One Ski Lift

Event	Expected Revenues	×	Probability	=	Expected Value of Each Alternative
Heavy snowfall	$850 000		0.3		$255 000
Normal snowfall	725 000		0.5		362 500
Light snowfall	350 000		0.2		70 000
					$687 500

snowfall, and 2 years of light snowfall. Can you use this information to help you make your decision about adding the new lift? If you have good information on the amount of revenues generated during each level of snowfall, the answer is yes.

You can calculate expected value—the expected return from each possible outcome—by multiplying expected revenues by snowfall probabilities. The result is the average revenue you can expect over time if the given probabilities hold. As Exhibit 4-8 shows, the expected revenue from adding a new ski lift is $687 500. Of course, whether that justifies a decision to build or not depends on the costs involved in generating that revenue, such as the cost to build the lift, the additional annual operating expenses for the lift, the interest rate for borrowing money, and so forth.

Uncertainty

What happens if you have a decision of which you are not certain about the outcomes and cannot even make reasonable probability estimates? We call such a condition **uncertainty**. Managers do face decision-making situations of uncertainty. Under these conditions, the choice of alternative is influenced by the limited amount of information available to the decision maker and by the psychological orientation of the decision maker. The optimistic manager will follow a *maximax* choice (maximizing the maximum possible payoff) in order to get the largest possible gain. The pessimist will follow a *maximin* choice (maximizing the minimum possible payoff) to make the best of a situation should the worst possible outcome occur. The manager who desires to minimize his maximum "regret" will opt for a *minimax* choice, to avoid having big regrets after decisions play out.

Decision-Making Styles

Suppose that you are a new manager at Sony or at the local YMCA. How would you make decisions? Decision-making styles differ along two dimensions.[15] The first dimension is an individual's *way of thinking*. Some of us are more rational and logical in the way we process information. A rational type processes information in order and makes sure that it's logical and consistent before making a decision. Others tend to be creative and intuitive. An intuitive type does not have to process information in a certain order and is comfortable looking at it as a whole.

The other dimension is an individual's *tolerance for ambiguity*. Some of us have a low tolerance for ambiguity. These types need consistency and order in the way they structure information so that ambiguity is minimized. On the other hand, some of us can tolerate high levels of ambiguity and are able to process many thoughts at the same time. When we diagram these two dimensions, four decision-making styles are evident: directive, analytic, conceptual, and behavioural (see Exhibit 4-9). Let's look more closely at each style.

- *Directive style.* Individuals with a **directive style** have low tolerance for ambiguity and are rational in their way of thinking. They are efficient and logical. Directive types make fast decisions and focus on the short run. Their efficiency and speed

Exhibit 4-9

Decision-Making Styles

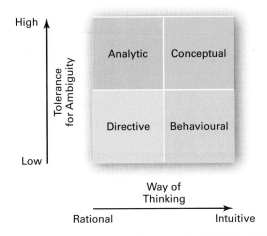

Source: Robbins, Stephen P., and David A. DeCenzo, *Supervision Today!*, 2nd ed., © 1998. Electronically reproduced by permission of Pearson Education, Inc., Upper Saddle River, New Jersey.

in making decisions often result in decisions that are made with minimal information and assessment of few alternatives.

- *Analytic style.* Individuals with an **analytic style** have much greater tolerance for ambiguity than do directive types. They want more information before making a decision and consider more alternatives than directive-style decision makers do. Analytic-style decision makers are characterized as careful decision makers with the ability to adapt to or cope with unique situations.

- *Conceptual style.* Individuals with a **conceptual style** tend to be very broad in their outlook and consider many alternatives. They are intuitive, focus on the long run, and are very good at finding creative solutions to problems. They are also adaptive and flexible.

- *Behavioural style.* Individuals with a **behavioural style** have a low tolerance for ambiguity and an intuitive way of thinking. They are sociable, friendly, and supportive. They work well with others, are concerned about the achievements of those around them, and are receptive to suggestions from others. They often use meetings to communicate, although they try to avoid conflict. Acceptance by others is important in this decision-making style.

Although these four decision-making styles are distinct, most managers have characteristics of more than one style. It's probably more realistic to think of a manager's dominant style and his or her alternative styles. Although some managers will rely almost exclusively on their dominant style, others are more flexible and can shift their style depending on the situation.

Managers should also recognize that their employees may use different decision-making styles. Some employees may take their time, carefully weighing alternatives and considering riskier options (analytic style), while other employees may be more concerned about getting suggestions from others before making decisions (behavioural style). This does not make one approach better than the other. It just means that their decision-making styles are different. For a look at the issues associated with diversity and making decisions, see *Managing Workforce Diversity—The Value of Diversity in Decision Making* on page 131, at the end of the chapter.

analytic style
A decision-making style characterized by a high tolerance for ambiguity and a rational way of thinking.

conceptual style
A decision-making style characterized by a high tolerance for ambiguity and an intuitive way of thinking.

behavioural style
A decision-making style characterized by a low tolerance for ambiguity and an intuitive way of thinking.

Q&A 5.8, Q&A 5.9

Group Decision Making

Do you think individuals or groups make better decisions?

Many organizational decisions are made by groups. It's a rare organization that does not at some time use committees, task forces, review panels, study teams, or similar groups to make decisions. In addition, studies show that managers may spend up to 30 hours a week in group meetings.[16] Undoubtedly, a large portion of that time is spent identifying problems, developing solutions, and determining how to implement the solutions. It's possible, in fact, for groups to be assigned any of the eight steps in the decision-making process. In this section, we look at the advantages and disadvantages of group decision making, discuss when groups would be preferred, and review some techniques for improving group decision making.

What advantages do group decisions have over individual decisions?

- *More complete information and knowledge.* A group brings a diversity of experience and perspectives to the decision process that an individual cannot.

- *More diverse alternatives.* Because groups have a greater amount and diversity of information, they can identify more diverse alternatives than an individual.

- *Increased acceptance of a solution.* Group members are reluctant to fight or undermine a decision they have helped develop.

- *Increased legitimacy.* Decisions made by groups may be perceived as more legitimate than decisions made unilaterally by one person.

If groups are so good at making decisions, how did the phrase "A camel is a horse put together by a committee" become so popular? The answer, of course, is that group decisions also have disadvantages:

- *Increased time to reach a solution.* Groups almost always take more time to reach a solution than it would take an individual.

- *Opportunity for minority domination.* The inequality of group members creates the opportunity for one or more members to dominate others. A dominant and vocal minority frequently can have an excessive influence on the final decision.

- *Ambiguous responsibility.* Group members share responsibility, but the responsibility of any single member is diluted.

- *Pressures to conform.* There can be pressures to conform in groups. This pressure undermines critical thinking in the group and eventually harms the quality of the final decision.[17]

groupthink
The withholding by group members of different views in order to appear to be in agreement.

Groupthink

The pressure to conform is what Irving Janis called the "groupthink" phenomenon. Have you ever been in a situation in which several people were sitting around discussing a particular item and you had something to say that ran contrary to the consensus views of the group, but you remained silent? Were you surprised to learn later that others shared your views and also had remained silent? What you experienced is what Janis termed **groupthink**.[18] This is a form of conformity in which group members withhold deviant, minority, or unpopular views in order to give the appearance of

The choice of an advertising agency is often made by those with a conceptual approach to decision making. Marketing executives from Virgin Atlantic Airways saw presentations from five ad agencies before choosing Crispin Porter & Bogusky, a small firm whose inventive proposal showed how efficiently the airline's $19 million ad budget could be spent. The marketing team from Virgin allowed 10 weeks to make a decision; it took 4 days. The winning team is pictured here with the paper airplanes that played a part in their pitch.

agreement. As a result, groupthink undermines critical thinking in the group and eventually harms the quality of the final decision.

Groupthink applies to a situation in which a group's ability to appraise alternatives objectively and arrive at a quality decision is jeopardized. Because of pressures for conformity, groups often deter individuals from critically appraising unusual, minority, or unpopular views. Consequently, an individual's mental efficiency, reality testing, and moral judgment deteriorate.

How does groupthink occur? The following are examples of situations in which groupthink is evident:

- Group members rationalize any resistance to the assumptions they have made.

- Members apply direct pressure on those who momentarily express doubts about any of the group's shared views or who question the validity of arguments favoured by the majority.

- Those members who have doubts or hold differing points of view seek to avoid going against what appears to be group consensus.

- There is an illusion of unanimity. If someone does not speak, it is assumed that he or she is in full agreement.

Does groupthink really hinder decision making? Yes. Several research studies have found that groupthink symptoms were associated with poorer-quality decision outcomes. But groupthink can be minimized if the group is cohesive, fosters open discussion, and has an impartial leader who seeks input from all members.[19]

Individual vs. Group Decision Making

Determining whether a group or an individual will be more effective in making a particular decision depends on the criteria you use to assess effectiveness.[20] Exhibit 4-10 indicates when group decisions are preferable to those made by an individual.

Keep in mind, however, that the effectiveness of group decision making is also influenced by the size of the group. Although a larger group provides greater opportunity for diverse representation, it also requires more coordination and more time for members to contribute their ideas. So groups probably should not be too large. Evidence indicates, in fact, that groups of five, and to a lesser extent, seven, are the most effective.[21] Having an odd number in the group helps avoid decision deadlocks. Also, these groups are large enough for members to shift roles and withdraw from unfavourable positions but still small enough for quieter members to participate actively in discussions.

Decision-Making Biases and Errors

When managers make decisions, not only do they use their own particular style, but many use "rules of thumb," or **heuristics**, to simplify their decision making. Rules of thumb can be useful to decision makers because they help make sense of complex,

heuristics
Rules of thumb that managers use to simplify decision making.

Exhibit 4-10		
Group vs. Individual Decision Making		
Criteria of Effectiveness	Groups	Individuals
Accuracy	✔	
Speed		✔
Creativity	✔	
Degree of acceptance	✔	
Efficiency		✔

Exhibit 4-11

Common Decision-Making Biases and Errors

uncertain, and ambiguous information.[22] Even though managers may use rules of thumb, that does not mean those rules are reliable. Why? Because they may lead to errors and biases in processing and evaluating information. Exhibit 4-11 identifies seven common decision-making biases and errors. Let's take a quick look at each.[23]

- *Overconfidence bias.* Decision makers tend to think they know more than they do or hold unrealistically positive views of themselves and their performance. For example, a sales manager brags that his presentation was so good that there is no doubt the sale will be his. Later he learns that he lost the sale because the client found him obnoxious.

- *Selective perception bias.* Decision makers selectively organize and interpret events based on their biased perceptions. This influences the information they pay attention to, the problems they identify, and the alternatives they develop. For example, before John meets with two job candidates, he learns that one went to his alma mater. He does not seriously consider the other job candidate because he believes that graduating from the same university as he did makes the candidate superior.

- *Confirmation bias.* Decision makers seek out information that reaffirms their past choices and discount information that contradicts past judgments. These people tend to accept at face value information that confirms their preconceived views and are critical and skeptical of information that challenges these views. For example, Pierre continues to give business to the same supplier, even though the supplier has been late on several deliveries. Pierre thinks the supplier is a nice person, and the supplier keeps promising to deliver on time.

- *Sunk-costs error.* Decision makers forget that current choices cannot correct the past. They incorrectly fixate on past expenditures of time, money, or effort in assessing choices rather than on future consequences. For example, Hakan has spent thousands of dollars and several months introducing new procedures for handling customer complaints. Both customers and employees are complaining about the new procedures. Hakan does not want to consider the possibility that the procedures are needlessly complicated because of the investment in time and money he has already made.

- *Escalation-of-commitment error.* Decisions can also be influenced by a phenomenon called **escalation of commitment**, which is an increased commitment to

escalation of commitment
An increased commitment to a previous decision despite evidence that the decision might have been wrong.

a previous decision despite evidence that it might have been wrong.[24] For example, studies of the events leading up to the space shuttle *Columbia* disaster in 2003 point to an escalation of commitment by decision makers to ignore the possible damage that foam striking the shuttle at takeoff might have had, even though the decision was questioned by some individuals. Why would decision makers want to escalate commitment to a bad decision? Because they don't want to admit that their initial decision might have been flawed. Rather than search for new alternatives, they simply increase their commitment to the original solution.

- *Self-serving bias.* Decision makers take credit for their successes and blame failure on outside factors. For example, Jesse dismisses his team's efforts when he wins a contract, although he blames them for the small error that was in the final report.

- *Hindsight bias.* Decision makers falsely believe that they would have accurately predicted the outcome of an event once that outcome is actually known. For example, after a client cancelled a contract that had been drawn up, Cindy tells her manager she knew ahead of time that was going to happen, even though she'd had no such thoughts before the contract was cancelled. After the fact, some outcomes seem more obvious than they did beforehand.

How can managers avoid the negative effects of these decision errors and biases? The main thing is being aware of them and then trying not to exhibit them. Beyond that, managers also should pay attention to "how" they make decisions and try to identify the heuristics they typically use and critically evaluate how appropriate those are. Finally, managers might want to ask those around them to help identify weaknesses in their decision-making style and try to improve on them.

Ethics, Corporate Social Responsibility, and Decision Making

When you see top managers such as those formerly at Merrill-Lynch, AIG, and some of the other major financial institutions being greedy and using financial manipulations, lying, and group pressure to deceive others, you might conclude that corporations have no ethics. Although that is by no means true, what *is* true is that managers—at all levels, in all areas, and in all kinds of organizations—will face ethical issues and dilemmas. As managers plan, organize, lead, and control, they must consider ethical dimensions.

What do we mean by ethics? The term **ethics** refers to rules and principles that define right and wrong behaviour.[25] Unfortunately, the ethics of a situation are not always black and white. For some decisions, you can make choices exercising complete freedom of choice, with no regard for others. For other decisions, there is a set of laws that guides your behaviour. In between, there is a set of situations where you might want to consider the impact of your decision on others, even though there are no laws regarding your behaviour. This is the grey area of behaviour. Laws often develop because people did not act responsibly when they had a choice. For example, not too long ago drinking and driving did not have the penalties that it does now. Many people have talked about laws banning cellphones in various situations for much the same reason: Individuals do not think about the impact of their use on others.

In this section, we examine the ethical dimensions of managerial decisions. Many decisions that managers make require them to consider who may be affected—in terms of the result as well as the process.[26] To better understand the complicated issues involved in managerial ethics, we will look at four different views of ethics and the factors that influence a person's ethics, and offer some suggestions for what organizations can do to improve the ethical behaviour of employees.

3 How do ethics and social responsibility relate to decision making?

ethics
Rules and principles that define right and wrong behaviour.

Four Views of Ethics

There are four views of ethics: the utilitarian view, the rights view, the theory of justice view, and the integrative social contracts theory.[27]

The Utilitarian View of Ethics

The **utilitarian view of ethics** says that ethical decisions are made solely on the basis of their outcomes or consequences. Utilitarian theory uses a quantitative method for making ethical decisions by looking at how to provide the greatest good for the greatest number. Following the utilitarian view, a manager might conclude that laying off 20 percent of the workforce in her plant is justified because it will increase the plant's profitability, improve job security for the remaining 80 percent, and be in the best interest of stockholders. Utilitarianism encourages efficiency and productivity and is consistent with the goal of profit maximization. However, it can result in biased allocations of resources, especially when some of those affected by the decision lack representation or a voice in the decision. Utilitarianism can also result in the rights of some stakeholders being ignored.

The Rights View of Ethics

The **rights view of ethics** is concerned with respecting and protecting individual liberties and privileges such as the rights to privacy, freedom of conscience, free speech, life and safety, and due process. This would include, for example, protecting the free speech rights of employees who report legal violations by their employers. The positive side of the rights perspective is that it protects individuals' basic rights, but the drawback is that it can hinder productivity and efficiency by creating a work climate that is more concerned with protecting individuals' rights than with getting the job done. For example, an individual's right to privacy might make it difficult to make special arrangements for an employee whose illness is preventing them from carrying out all of their job responsibilities.

The Theory of Justice View of Ethics

According to the **theory of justice view of ethics**, managers impose and enforce rules fairly and impartially and do so by following all legal rules and regulations. A manager following this view would decide to provide the same rate of pay to individuals who are similar in their levels of skills, performance, or responsibility and not base that decision on arbitrary differences such as gender, personality, race, or personal favourites. Using standards of justice also has pluses and minuses. It protects the interests of those stakeholders who may be underrepresented or lack power, but it can encourage a sense of entitlement that might make employees reduce risk-taking, innovation, and productivity.

The Integrative Social Contracts Theory

The **integrative social contracts theory** proposes that ethical decisions be based on existing ethical norms in industries and communities in order to determine what constitutes right and wrong. This view of ethics is based on the integration of two "contracts": the general social contract that allows businesses to operate and defines the acceptable ground rules, and a more specific contract among members of a community that addresses acceptable ways of behaving. In deciding what wage to pay employees in a new factory in Ciudad Juarez, Mexico, Canadian managers following the integrative social contracts theory would base the decision on existing wage levels in the community, rather than paying what Canadians might consider a "fair wage" in that context. Although this theory focuses on looking at existing practices, the problem is that some of these practices may be unethical.[28]

Which approach to ethics do most businesspeople follow? Not surprisingly, most follow the utilitarian approach. Why? It's consistent with such business goals as efficiency, productivity, and profits. However, that perspective needs to change because of the changing world facing managers. Trends toward individual rights, social justice, and community standards mean that managers need ethical standards based on nonutilitarian criteria. This is an obvious challenge for managers because making decisions based on such criteria involves far more ambiguities than using utilitarian criteria such as efficiency and profits. The result, of course, is that managers increasingly find themselves struggling with the question of the right thing to do.

Improving Ethical Behaviour

Managers can do a number of things if they are serious about reducing unethical behaviour in their organizations. They can seek to hire individuals with high ethical standards, establish codes of ethics and decision rules, lead by example, delineate job goals and performance appraisal mechanisms, provide ethics training, conduct independent social audits, and provide support to individuals facing ethical dilemmas. Taken individually, these actions will probably not have much impact. But when all or most of them are implemented as part of a comprehensive ethics program, they have the potential to significantly improve an organization's ethical climate. The key term here, however, is *potential*. There are no guarantees that a well-designed ethics program will lead to the desired outcome.

Sometimes corporate ethics programs can be little more than public relations gestures, having minimal influence on managers and employees. Retailer Sears has a long history of encouraging ethical business practices and, in fact, has a corporate Office of Compliance and Ethics. However, the company's ethics programs did not stop managers from illegally trying to collect payments from bankrupt charge-account holders or from routinely deceiving automotive–service centre customers in California into thinking they needed unnecessary repairs.

Codes of Ethics and Decision Rules

Toronto-based Royal Bank of Canada has had a corporate code of conduct for more than 25 years. Christina Donely, the bank's senior adviser on employee relations and policy governance, says that the code "focuses on outlining behaviours that support honesty and integrity . . . and covers environmental [and] social issues."[29] However, that is not the way it is in all organizations. The US government passed the Sarbanes–Oxley Act in 2002 to crack down on business wrongdoing in publicly traded companies. Following the American example, the Canadian Securities Administrators put best corporate governance practices into effect in March 2004, although these are not as tough as the American rules.[30] As well, the securities regulators of all 10 provinces and 3 territories have proposed that all public companies adopt written codes of ethics and conduct, or explain why they do not have them.[31] But these proposals carry no enforcement requirements or mechanisms.

Ambiguity about what is and is not ethical can be a problem for employees. A **code of ethics**—a formal statement of an organization's primary values and the ethical rules it expects its employees to follow—is a popular choice for reducing that ambiguity. About 60 percent of Canada's 650 largest corporations have some sort of ethics code.[32] Codes of ethics are also becoming more popular globally. A survey of business organizations in 22 countries found that 78 percent have formally stated ethics standards and codes of ethics.[33]

What should a code of ethics look like? It has been suggested that codes should be specific enough to show employees the spirit in which they are supposed to do things yet loose enough to allow for freedom of judgment.[34] A survey of companies' codes of ethics found their content tended to fall into three categories: (1) Be a dependable organizational citizen; (2) don't do anything unlawful or improper that will harm the organization; and (3) be good to customers.[35]

How well do codes of ethics work? The reality is they are not always effective in encouraging ethical behaviour in organizations. While no comparable Canadian data are available, a survey of employees in US businesses with ethics codes found that 75 percent of those surveyed had observed ethical or legal violations in the previous 12 months, including such things as deceptive sales practices, unsafe working conditions, sexual

code of ethics
A formal statement of an organization's primary values and the ethical rules it expects its employees to follow.

> ### Exhibit 4-12
>
> ## 12 Questions for Examining the Ethics of a Business Decision
>
> 1. Have you defined the problem accurately?
> 2. How would you define the problem if you stood on the other side of the fence?
> 3. How did this situation occur in the first place?
> 4. To whom and to what do you give your loyalty as a person and as a member of the corporation?
> 5. What is your intention in making this decision?
> 6. How does this intention compare with the probable results?
> 7. Whom could your decision or action injure?
> 8. Can you discuss the problem with the affected parties before you make the decision?
> 9. Are you confident that your position will be as valid over a long period of time as it seems now?
> 10. Could you disclose without qualm your decision or action to your boss, your chief executive officer, the board of directors, your family, society as a whole?
> 11. What is the symbolic potential of your action if understood? If misunderstood?
> 12. Under what conditions would you allow exceptions to your stand?
>
> *Source:* An exhibit from "Ethics Without the Sermon" by L. L. Nash. November–December 1981, p. 81. With permission from Harvard Business School Publishing.

harassment, conflicts of interest, and environmental violations.[36] Companies with codes of ethics may not do enough monitoring. For example, David Nitkin, president of Toronto-based EthicScan Canada, an ethics consultancy, notes that "only about 15% of [larger Canadian corporations with codes of ethics] have designated an ethics officer or ombudsman" or provide an ethics hotline, and that less than 10 percent offer whistle-blower protection.[37] Vancouver public employees were concerned enough about whistle-blower protection that it was one of the major stumbling blocks in reaching an agreement for a new collective agreement in summer 2007, leading to a 12-week strike.

Does this mean that codes of ethics should not be developed? No. But there are some suggestions managers can follow. First, an organization's code of ethics should be developed and then communicated clearly to employees. Second, all levels of management should continually reaffirm the importance of the ethics code and the organization's commitment to it, and consistently discipline those who break it. When managers consider the code of ethics important, regularly affirm its content, and publicly reprimand rule breakers, ethics codes can supply a strong foundation for an effective corporate ethics program.[38] Finally, an organization's code of ethics might be designed around the 12 questions listed in Exhibit 4-12, which can be used as decision rules in guiding managers as they handle ethical dilemmas in decision making.[39]

Corporate Social Responsibility

corporate social responsibility
A business's obligation, beyond that required by law and economics, to do the right things and act in ways that are good for society.

We define **corporate social responsibility** as a business's obligation, beyond that required by law and economics, to do the right things and act in ways that are good for society.[40] Note that this definition assumes that a business obeys laws and pursues economic interests. But also note that this definition views business as a moral agent. That is, in its effort to do good for society, it must differentiate between right and wrong. A great deal of attention has been focused on the extent to which organizations and management should act in socially responsible ways. On one side, there is the classical—or purely economic—view, and on the other side is the socio-economic view.

The Classical View

The **classical view** says that management's only social responsibility is to maximize profits. The most outspoken advocate of this approach is the late economist and Nobel laureate Milton Friedman.[41] He argues that managers' primary responsibility is to operate the business in the best interests of the stockholders (the owners of a corporation). What are those interests? Friedman contends that stockholders have a single concern: financial return. He also argues that any time managers decide to spend the organization's resources for "social good," they are adding to the costs of doing business. These costs have to be passed on to consumers either through higher prices or absorbed by stockholders through a smaller profit returned as dividends. We must be clear that Friedman is not saying that organizations should *not* be socially responsible; he thinks they should. But the extent of that responsibility is to maximize organizational profits for stockholders.

Joel Bakan, professor of law at the University of British Columbia, author of *The Corporation*, and co-director of the documentary of the same name, is more critical of organizations than Friedman, though he finds that current laws support corporate behaviour that some might find troubling. Bakan suggests that today's corporations have many of the same characteristics as a psychopathic personality (that is, self-interested, lacking empathy, manipulative, and reckless in one's disregard of others). Bakan notes that even though companies have a tendency to act psychopathically, this is not why they are fixated on profits. Rather, though they may have social responsibilities, the only *legal* responsibility corporations have is to maximize organizational profits for stockholders.[42] He suggests that more laws and more restraints need to be put in place if corporations are to behave more socially responsibly, as current laws direct corporations to be responsible to their shareholders, and make little mention of responsibility toward other stakeholders.

> **classical view**
> The view that management's only social responsibility is to maximize profits.

The Socio-economic View

> *Is it wrong for Canadian companies to employ children to work in factories in countries where child labour is legal?*

The **socio-economic view** says that management's social responsibility goes beyond making profits to include protecting and improving society's welfare. This position is based on the belief that corporations are *not* independent entities responsible only to stockholders. They also have a responsibility to the larger society that endorses their creation through various laws and regulations and supports them by purchasing their products and services. In addition, proponents of this view believe that business organizations are not mere economic institutions. Society expects and even encourages businesses to become involved in social, political, and legal issues. Proponents of the socio-economic view would say that Avon Products was being socially responsible when it initiated its Breast Cancer Crusade to provide women with breast cancer education and early detection screening services, and which, after 14 years, has raised more than $400 million worldwide.[43]

Educational programs implemented by Brazilian cosmetics manufacturer Natura Cosméticos SA in public primary schools in São Paulo to improve children's literacy and decision-making skills are also viewed as socially responsible.[44] Why? Through these programs, the managers are protecting and improving society's welfare. More and more organizations around the world are taking their social responsibilities seriously, especially in Europe, where the view that businesses need to focus on more than just profits has a stronger tradition than in North America.[45] Some even try to measure their "Triple Bottom Line," which takes into account not only financial responsibilities, but social and environmental ones as well.[46]

> **socio-economic view**
> The view that management's social responsibility goes beyond making profits to include protecting and improving society's welfare.

Comparing the Two Views

The key differences between the two views of corporate social responsibility are easier to understand if we think in terms of the people to whom organizations are responsible.

Exhibit 4-13

Approaches to Corporate Social Responsibility

Obstructionist Approach	Defensive Approach	Accommodative Approach	Proactive Approach
Disregard for social responsibility	Minimal commitment to social responsibility	Moderate commitment to social responsibility	Strong commitment to social responsibility

No Social Responsibility   High Social Responsibility

Classicists would say that shareholders, or owners, are the only legitimate concern. Those supporting the socio-economic view would respond that managers should be responsible to any group affected by the organization's decisions and actions—that is, the stakeholders (such as employees and community members).[47] Exhibit 4-13 shows four different approaches that an organization can take toward corporate social responsibility.[48] The defensive approach is consistent with the classical view, while the accommodative and proactive approaches are consistent with the socio-economic view.

Those who avoid corporate social responsibility altogether take an **obstructionist approach**. Obstructionist managers engage in unethical and illegal behaviour, and try to hide their behaviour from organizational stakeholders and society at large.

Those taking the minimal position toward corporate social responsibility use a **defensive approach**. These organizations have a commitment to ethical behaviour, making sure that employees behave legally and no harm is done to others. The claims and interests of shareholders come first with this approach, and little attention is paid to other stakeholders. Managers taking a defensive perspective rely only on legally established rules to guide their behaviour. They do not believe that they should make socially responsible choices that are not spelled out in laws and regulations. For example, a company that meets pollution control standards established by the federal government or that does not discriminate against employees over the age of 40 in promotion decisions is meeting its social obligation and nothing more because there are laws mandating these actions.

Some managers go beyond legal requirements, choosing to support corporate social responsibility in a balanced fashion. These managers take an **accommodative approach** to corporate social responsibility. Accommodative managers make choices that try to balance the interests of shareholders with those of other stakeholders. Corporate social responsibility goals for suppliers and customers might include fair prices, high-quality products and services, safe products, good supplier relations, and similar actions. Their philosophy is that they can meet their responsibilities to stockholders only by meeting the needs of these other stakeholders.

Finally, some managers take an active interest in corporate social responsibility. These managers take a **proactive approach** to find out about and meet the needs of different stakeholder groups. They promote the interests of shareholders *and* stakeholders, using organizational resources to do so. These managers feel a responsibility to society as a whole. They view their business as a public entity and feel a responsibility to advance the public good, even if such actions may decrease profits. The acceptance of such responsibility means that managers actively promote social justice, preserve the environment, and

obstructionist approach
The avoidance of corporate social responsibility; managers engage in unethical and illegal behaviour that they try to hide from organizational stakeholders and society.

defensive approach
Managers rely only on legally established rules to take the minimal position toward corporate social responsibility.

accommodative approach
Managers make choices that try to balance the interests of shareholders with those of other stakeholders.

proactive approach
Managers go out of their way to actively promote the interests of stockholders and stakeholders, using organizational resources to do so.

Would you be willing to stop eating your favourite snack if you found out the company did not use environmentally friendly packaging for its products?

support social and cultural activities. For example, Vancouver-based Weyerhaeuser Canada is committed to sustainable forestry practices and has a formal policy for building relationships with Canada's Aboriginal peoples.

Corporate Social Responsibility and Economic Performance

How do socially responsible activities affect a company's economic performance? Findings from a number of research studies can help us answer this question.[49] The majority of these studies show a positive relationship between social involvement and economic performance. One study found that firms' corporate social performance was positively associated with both *prior* and *future* financial performance.[50] But we should be cautious about making any compelling assumptions from these findings because of methodological questions associated with trying to measure "corporate social responsibility" and "economic performance."[51] Most of these studies determined a company's social performance by analyzing the content of annual

Richard Kouwenhoven, manager of digital services of Burnaby, BC-based Hemlock Printers, founded by his father, has been one of the leaders of his generation's push to have the company, already known for its green practices, become a leader in sustainable paper use.

reports, citations of social actions in news articles on the company, or "reputation" indexes based on public perception. Such criteria certainly have drawbacks as reliable measures of corporate social responsibility.

We can also look at what consumers say about corporate social responsibility. A recent survey conducted by GlobeScan, which specializes in corporate issues, found that "83 percent of Canadians believe that corporations should go beyond their traditional economic role; 51 percent say they have punished a socially irresponsible company in the past year."[52] As for naming a socially responsible company, 43 percent of Canadians said they could not do so.

What conclusion can we draw from all of this? Corporate social responsibility is generally good for the bottom line. It matters to consumers and there is little evidence to say that a company's social actions hurt its long-term economic performance. Given political and societal pressures on business to be socially involved, managers would be wise to take social goals into consideration as they plan, organize, lead, and control.

SUMMARY AND IMPLICATIONS

❶ What are the steps in the decision-making process? The steps include identifying a problem and the decision criteria; allocating weights to those criteria; developing, analyzing, and selecting an alternative that can resolve the problem; implementing the alternative; and evaluating the decision's effectiveness.

Sandra Wilson, Robeez Footwear chair and CEO, recognized that her company was poised for growth. She had to determine the relevant criteria and their weights to make a decision about whether or not to seek a new partner or sell the company. Which would be the best alternative?

❷ What factors affect how decisions are made? It is often assumed that managers make decisions that follow the steps of the rational decision-making process. However, not all decisions follow that process for a variety of reasons. Often managers work with bounded rationality, because they are not able to collect and process all the information on all possible alternatives. Or they might make a satisficing decision—one that is "good enough" rather than the "best." Managers sometimes use intuition to enhance their decision-making process. Managers also need to decide whether they should make decisions themselves, or encourage a team to help make the decision. Teams can make better decisions in many cases, but the time to make the decision generally increases. Managers are affected by a variety of biases and errors: overconfidence bias, selective perception bias, confirmation bias, sunk-costs error, escalation of commitment error, self-serving bias, and hindsight bias.

Sandra Wilson was aware of a variety of positives and negatives in the decision to either bring in a new partner or sell Robeez. It was important for her to recognize that her preference for growth and the desire to see her creative vision for the brand continue might affect how she made her decision.

③ How do ethics and social responsibility relate to decision making? Ethics refers to rules and principles that define right and wrong conduct. There are four views of ethics: the utilitarian view, the rights view, the theory of justice view, and the integrative social contracts theory. The utilitarian view of ethics says that ethical decisions are made solely on the basis of their outcomes or consequences. The rights view of ethics is concerned with respecting and protecting individual liberties and privileges. According to the theory of justice view of ethics, managers impose and enforce rules fairly and impartially, following all legal rules and regulations. The integrative social contracts theory proposes that ethical decisions be based on existing ethical norms in industries and communities.

To improve ethical behaviour, managers can hire individuals with high ethical standards, design and implement a code of ethics, lead by example, undertake performance appraisals, provide ethics training, conduct independent social audits, and provide formal protective mechanisms for employees who face ethical dilemmas.

Beyond ethics, managers are increasingly being asked to be more socially responsible in the decisions they make. In doing so, some organizations are likely to simply give lip service to social responsibility, while others are much more committed to actually being socially responsible.

Management @ Work

READING FOR COMPREHENSION

1. Why is decision making often described as the essence of a manager's job?

2. How is implementation important to the decision-making process?

3. What is a satisficing decision? How does it differ from a maximizing decision?

4. How do certainty, risk, and uncertainty affect decision making?

5. What is groupthink? How does it affect decision making?

6. Describe the decision-making biases and errors managers may exhibit.

7. How does escalation of commitment affect decision making? Why would managers make this type of error?

8. Define the four views of ethics.

9. Contrast the classical and socio-economic views of corporate social responsibility.

10. Discuss the role that stakeholders play in the four approaches to corporate social responsibility.

LINKING CONCEPTS TO PRACTICE

1. Describe a decision you have made that closely aligns with the assumptions of perfect rationality. Compare this with the process you used to select your major. Is there a departure from the rational model in your choice of major? Explain.

2. Is the order in which alternatives are considered more critical under assumptions of perfect rationality or bounded rationality? Why?

3. Explain how a manager might deal with making decisions under conditions of uncertainty.

4. "With more and more managers using computers, they'll be able to make more rational decisions."

Do you agree or disagree with the statement? Why?

5. Why do you think organizations have increased the use of groups for making decisions during the past 20 years? When would you recommend using groups to make decisions?

6. Do you think it's difficult to make ethical decisions when a company focuses primarily on the bottom line?

7. What does corporate social responsibility mean to you personally? Do you think business organizations should be socially responsible? Explain.

SELF-ASSESSMENT

How Intuitive Am I?

For each of the following questions, select the response that first appeals to you:[53]

1. When working on a project, I prefer to
   a. be told what the problem is, but left free to decide how to solve it.
   b. get very clear instructions about how to go about solving the problem before I start.

2. When working on a project, I prefer to work with colleagues who are
   a. realistic.
   b. imaginative.

3. I most admire people who are
   a. creative.
   b. careful.

4. The friends I choose tend to be
   a. serious and hard-working.
   b. exciting and often emotional.

5. When I ask a colleague for advice on a problem I have, I
   a. seldom or never get upset if he/she questions my basic assumptions.
   b. often get upset if he/she questions my basic assumptions.

6. When I start my day, I
   a. seldom make or follow a specific plan.
   b. usually make a plan first to follow.

7. When working with numbers, I find that I
   a. seldom or never make factual errors.
   b. often make factual errors.

8. I find that I
   a. seldom daydream during the day and really don't enjoy doing so when I do it.
   b. frequently daydream during the day and enjoy doing so.

9. When working on a problem, I
   a. prefer to follow the instructions or rules when they are given to me.
   b. often enjoy circumventing the instructions or rules when they are given to me.

10. When I try to put something together, I prefer to have
   a. step-by-step written instructions on how to assemble the item.
   b. a picture of how the item is supposed to look once assembled.

11. I find that the person who irritates me the most is the one who appears to be
   a. disorganized.
   b. organized.

12. When an unexpected crisis comes up that I have to deal with, I
   a. feel anxious about the situation.
   b. feel excited by the challenge of the situation.

Scoring Key

For items 1, 3, 5, 6, and 11, score as follows: a = 1, b = 0.
For items 2, 4, 7, 8, 9, 10, and 12, score as follows: a = 0, b = 1.
Your total score will range between 0 and 12.

Analysis and Interpretation

Decision making isn't all systematic logic. Good decision makers also have developed, through experience, an intuitive ability that complements rational analysis. This ability is particularly valuable when decision makers face high levels of uncertainty, when facts are limited, when there is little previous precedent, when time is pressing, or when there are multiple plausible alternatives to choose among and there are good arguments for each.

If you have an intuitive score greater than 8, you prefer situations where there is a lack of structure and rules. You can handle uncertainty, spontaneity, and openness. Whether this ability is a plus in your job depends to a great extent on the culture of your organization. Where rationality is highly valued, reliance on intuition is likely to be seen as a negative quality. In open and creative-type cultures, intuitive ability is more likely to be valued.

More Self-Assessments

To learn more about your skills, abilities, and interests, take the following self-assessments on the MyManagementLab at www.pearsoned.ca/mymanagementlab:

- I.A.4.—How Well Do I Handle Ambiguity?
- I.D.1.—Am I a Procrastinator?
- I.D.2.—How Do My Ethics Rate?
- III.C.1.—How Well Do I Respond to Turbulent Change? (This exercise also appears in Chapter 12 on pages 379–380.)
- IV.A.2.—Am I a Deliberate Decision Maker?

MANAGEMENT FOR YOU TODAY

Dilemma

Suppose your uncle said that he would help you open your own business. You are not sure whether you really want to run your own business, or work for a large consulting firm. However, you have always been interested in running a restaurant. How would you go about making a decision on what kind of restaurant you might open? How would you decide whether you should take your uncle up on his offer?

Becoming a Manager

- Pay close attention to decisions you make and how you make them.

- When you feel you have not made a good decision, assess how you could have made a better one. Which step of the decision-making process could you have improved?

- Work at developing good decision-making skills.

- Read books about decision making.

- Ask people you admire for advice on how they make good decisions.

WORKING TOGETHER: TEAM-BASED EXERCISE

Individual vs. Group Decisions

Objective To contrast individual and group decision making.
Time 15 minutes.

Step 1 You have 5 minutes to read the following story and individually respond to each of the 11 statements as either true, false, or unknown.

The Story

A salesclerk had just turned off the lights in the store when a man appeared and demanded money. The owner opened a cash register. The contents of the cash register were scooped up, and the man sped away. A member of the police force was notified promptly.

Statements About the Story

1. A man appeared after the owner had turned off his store lights. True, false, or unknown?

2. The robber was a man. True, false, or unknown?

3. The man did not demand money. True, false, or unknown?

4. The man who opened the cash register was the owner. True, false, or unknown?

5. The store owner scooped up the contents of the cash register and ran away. True, false, or unknown?

6. Someone opened a cash register. True, false, or unknown?

7. After the man who demanded the money scooped up the contents of the cash register, he ran away. True, false, or unknown?

8. The cash register contained money, but the story does not state how much. True, false, or unknown?

9. The robber demanded money of the owner. True, false, or unknown?

10. The story concerns a series of events in which only three persons are referred to: the owner of the store, a man who demanded money, and a member of the police force. True, false, or unknown?

11. The following events in the story are true: Someone demanded money; a cash register was opened; its contents were scooped up; a man dashed out of the store. True, false, or unknown?

Step 2 After you have answered the 11 questions individually, form groups of 4 or 5 members each. The groups have 10 minutes to discuss their answers and agree on the correct answers to each of the 11 statements.

Step 3 Your instructor will give you the correct answers. How many correct answers did you get at the conclusion of Step 1? How many did your group achieve at the conclusion of Step 2? Did the group outperform the average individual? The best individual? Discuss the implications of these results.

ETHICS IN ACTION

Ethical Dilemma Exercise: Can Investment Advice Be "Perfectly Objective"?

Competitive problems are rarely well structured, as the managers at Greenfield Brokerage know.[54] Over the years, the firm has successfully competed with well-established rivals by making nonprogrammed decisions. For example, management decided to charge customers less for trading stocks, bonds, and mutual funds and to implement technology giving customers more trading choices. Because the competitive environment is constantly changing, Greenfield's advertising managers can never be certain about the outcome of decisions concerning how to promote the firm's competitive advantages.

Not long ago, some competing brokerage firms paid hefty fines to settle charges stemming from conflicts of interest involving their research and recommendations to customers. In the aftermath of these scandals, Greenfield's managers decided on an advertising campaign to stress that Greenfield does things differently. One tongue-in-cheek commercial took viewers behind the scenes at a fictitious competitor's office, where brokers chanted "Buy, buy, buy." A broker looked at a restaurant takeout menu as he told a customer on the phone, "I have your portfolio right here, and I think you should buy." Some networks rejected these aggressive commercials. The ads also raised questions about potential conflicts of interest created by Greenfield brokers steering business to in-house traders and mutual funds.

Imagine you are an advertising manager at Greenfield. Your advertising agency has suggested a newspaper ad in which a fictitious competing broker is quoted as saying, "My investment advice is perfectly objective, even though I work on commission." A Greenfield broker is then quoted as saying, "I don't work on commission like other brokers do, so my investment advice is perfectly objective." How certain are you that your advice is perfectly objective when Greenfield benefits from every client it gets? (Review Exhibit 4-11 on page 116 as you think about this dilemma.)

Thinking Critically About Ethics

You are in charge of hiring a new employee to work in your area of responsibility, and one of your friends from college needs a job. You think he is minimally qualified for the position, and you feel that you could find a better-qualified and more experienced candidate if you kept looking. What will you do? What factors will influence your decision? What will you tell your friend?

CASE APPLICATION

C. F. Martin Guitar Company

The C. F. Martin Guitar Company (www.mguitar.com) has been producing acoustic instruments since 1833.[55] A Martin guitar is among the best that money can buy. Current CEO Christian Frederick Martin IV—better known as Chris—continues to be committed to the guitar maker's craft. During 2002, the company sold about 77 000 instruments and hit a record $77 million in revenue. Despite this success, Chris is facing some serious issues.

Martin Guitar is an interesting blend of old and new. Although the equipment and tools may have changed over the years, employees remain true to the principle of high standards of musical excellence. In a 1904 catalogue, a family member explained, "How to build a guitar to give this tone is not a secret. It takes care and patience." Now well over a century later, this statement is still an accurate reflection of the company's philosophy.

From the very beginning, quality has played an important role in everything that Martin Guitar does. Part of that quality approach includes a long-standing ecological policy. The company depends on natural-wood products to make its guitars, but a lot of the wood supply is vanishing. Chris has long embraced the responsible use of traditional wood materials, going so far as to encourage suppliers to find alternative species. Based on thorough customer research, Martin Guitar introduced guitars that used structurally sound woods with natural cosmetic defects that were once considered unacceptable. In addition, Martin Guitar follows the directives of CITES, the Convention on International Trade in Endangered Species of Wild Fauna and Flora (www.cites.org), even though it has the potential to affect Martin Guitar's ability to produce the type of quality products it has in the past. This treaty barred the export of the much-desired Brazilian rosewood, which is considered endangered. A guitar built from the remaining supply of this popular wood has a hefty price tag— $39 999 and up. Similar prices may be in line for the leading alternative, Honduras mahogany. Chris says, "All of us who use wood for the tone [it makes] are scrambling. Options are limited."

Although the company is rooted in its past, Chris is wondering whether he should go in new directions. For example, he could try selling guitars in the under-$800 market, a segment that accounts for 65 percent of the acoustic guitar industry's sales. A less expensive guitar would not look, smell, or feel like the company's pricier models. But Chris thinks that it would sound better than guitars in that price range made by other companies. Chris explains, "My fear is that if we don't look at alternatives, we'll be the company making guitars for doctors and lawyers. If Martin just worships its past without trying anything new, there won't be a Martin left to worship."

What should Chris do? Why?

DEVELOPING YOUR DIAGNOSTIC AND ANALYTICAL SKILLS

Designing for Dollars

Great product design is absolutely critical for most consumer products companies.[56] But how do these companies know when a design feature will pay off, especially when every dollar counts? How do they make those tough decisions? That's the challenge that faced Whirlpool's chief designer, Chuck Jones. He knew he had to come up with a better way.

Chuck's realization that the whole process of making design decisions needed to be improved came after a meeting with Whirlpool's resource allocation team. Chuck wanted to add some ornamentation to a KitchenAid refrigerator that was being redesigned, but it would have added about $5 in extra cost. When the team asked him to estimate the return on investment (that is, would it pay off financially to add this cost?), he couldn't give them any data. His "trust me, I'm a designer" argument didn't sway them either. Chuck resolved to improve the approach to investing in design.

His first step was to survey other "design-centric" companies, including BMW, Nike, and Nokia. Surprisingly, only a few had a system for forecasting return on design. Most of them simply based future investments on past performance. Chuck said, "No one had really figured this stuff out." With so many smart, talented people in this field, why had no one been able to come up with a good way to make those decisions? According to two accounting professors, one reason is that it's incredibly difficult to discern design's contribution from all the other business functions (marketing, manufacturing, distribution, etc.). Even the design profession could not agree on how to approach this problem. Despite the obstacles, Chuck continued his quest to find a way to objectively measure the benefits of design.

He eventually concluded that a focus on customer preferences would work better than a focus on bottom-line returns. If his team could objectively measure what customers want in a product and then meet those needs, the company could realize financial returns. Chuck's design team created a standardized company-wide process that puts design prototypes in front of customer focus groups and then gets detailed measurements of their preferences about aesthetics, craftsmanship, technical performance, ergonomics, and usability. They chart the results against competing products and the company's own products. This metrics-based approach gives decision makers a baseline of objective evidence from which to make investment decisions. Design investment decisions are now based on fact, not opinion. The "new" decision-making approach has transformed the company's culture and led to bolder designs because the designers can now make a strong case for making those investments.

Questions

1. Would you characterize product design decisions as structured or unstructured problems?

2. Describe and evaluate the process Chuck went through to change the way design decisions were made. Describe and evaluate the company's new design decision process.

3. What criteria does Whirlpool's design team use in design decisions? What do you think each of these criteria involves?

DEVELOPING YOUR INTERPERSONAL SKILLS

Solving Problems Creatively

Creativity is a frame of mind. You need to expand your mind's capabilities—that is, open up your mind to new ideas. Every individual has the ability to improve his or her creativity, but many people simply don't try to develop that ability. In a global business environment, where changes are fast and furious, organizations desperately need creative people. The uniqueness and variety of problems that managers face demand that they be able to solve problems creatively.

Steps in Developing the Skill

You can be more effective at solving problems creatively if you use the following 10 suggestions:[57]

1. **Think of yourself as creative.** Although this may be a simple suggestion, research shows that if you think you cannot be creative, you won't be. Believing in your ability to be creative is the first step in becoming more creative.

2. **Pay attention to your intuition.** Every individual has a subconscious mind that works well. Sometimes answers will come to you when you least expect them. Listen to that "inner voice." In fact, most creative people keep notepads near their beds and write down ideas when the thoughts come to them. That way they don't forget them.

3. **Move away from your comfort zone.** Every individual has a comfort zone in which certainty exists. But creativity and the known often do not mix. To be creative, you need to move away from the status quo and focus your mind on something new.

4. **Determine what you want to do.** This includes taking time to understand a problem before beginning to try to resolve it, getting all the facts in mind, and trying to identify the most important facts.

5. **Look for ways to tackle the problem.** This can be accomplished by setting aside a block of time to focus on it; working out a plan for attacking it; establishing subgoals; imagining or actually using analogies wherever possible (e.g., could you approach your problem like a fish out of water and look at what the fish does to cope? Or can you use the things you have to do to find your way when it's foggy to help you solve your problem?); using different problem-solving strategies

such as verbal, visual, mathematical, theatrical (e.g., you might draw a diagram of the decision or problem to help you visualize it better or you might talk to yourself out loud about the problem, telling it as you would tell a story to someone); trusting your intuition; and playing with possible ideas and approaches (e.g., look at your problem from a different perspective or ask yourself what someone else, such as your grandmother, might do if faced with the same situation).

6. **Look for ways to do things better.** This may involve trying consciously to be original, not worrying about looking foolish, eliminating cultural taboos (such as gender stereotypes) that might influence your possible solutions, keeping an open mind, being alert to odd or puzzling facts, thinking of unconventional ways to use objects and the environment (e.g., thinking about how you could use newspaper or magazine headlines to help you be a better problem solver), discarding usual or habitual ways of doing things, and striving for objectivity by being as critical of your own ideas as you would be of those of someone else.

7. **Find several right answers.** Being creative means continuing to look for other solutions even when you think you have solved the problem. A better, more creative solution just might be found.

8. **Believe in finding a workable solution.** Like believing in yourself, you also need to believe in your ideas. If you don't think you can find a solution, you probably won't.

9. **Brainstorm with others.** Creativity is not an isolated activity. Bouncing ideas off others creates synergy.

10. **Turn creative ideas into action.** Coming up with creative ideas is only part of the process. Once the ideas are generated, they must be implemented. Keeping great ideas in your mind, or on papers that no one will read, does little to expand your creative abilities.

Practising the Skill

How many words can you make using the letters in the word *brainstorm*? (There are at least 95.)

MANAGING WORKFORCE DIVERSITY

The Value of Diversity in Decision Making

Have you decided what your major is going to be? How did you decide? Do you feel your decision is a good one? Is there anything you could have done differently to make sure that your decision was the best one?[58]

Making good decisions is tough! Managers are continuously making decisions—for example, developing new products, establishing weekly or monthly goals, implementing advertising campaigns, reassigning employees to different work groups, resolving customers' complaints, or purchasing new laptops for sales representatives. One important suggestion for making better decisions is to tap into the diversity of the work group. Drawing upon the ideas of diverse employees can prove valuable to a manager's decision making. Why? Diverse employees can provide fresh perspectives on issues. They can offer differing interpretations on how a problem is defined and may be more open to trying new ways of doing things. Diverse employees usually are more creative in generating alternatives and more flexible in resolving issues. And getting input from diverse sources increases the likelihood of finding creative and unique solutions.

Even though diversity in decision making can be valuable, there are drawbacks. The lack of a common perspective usually means that more time is spent discussing the issues. Communication may be a problem, particularly if language barriers are present. In addition, seeking out diverse opinions can make the decision-making process more complex, confusing, and ambiguous. In addition, with multiple perspectives on the decision, it may be difficult to reach a single agreement or to agree on specific actions. Although these drawbacks are valid concerns, the value of diversity in decision making outweighs the potential disadvantages.

When you have worked in teams, what advantages and disadvantages arose because of the diversity (or lack of diversity) in the group? What measures could be taken to make sure that diversity is an asset for a team, rather than something that causes problems?

Continuing Case: Starbucks

One thing that all managers do is plan.[1] The planning they do may be extensive or it may be limited. It might be for the next week or month or it might be for the next couple of years. It might cover a work group or it might cover an entire division. No matter what type or extent of planning a manager does, the important thing is that planning takes place. Without planning, there would be nothing for managers to organize, lead, or control. Based on the numerous accomplishments that Starbucks has achieved through the efforts of its employees, managers, no doubt, have done their planning.

Company Goals

As of June 2009, Starbucks had over 15 000 outlets in 44 countries, and the company plans continued growth. Chair, president, and CEO Howard Schultz told those attending the 2009 annual shareholders meeting that "Despite the challenging economic environment, Starbucks is profitable, has a strong balance sheet and generates solid cash from operations." The company will continue to meet customer's needs for value and quality, and expand into global markets, with a disciplined growth strategy.

In addition to its financial and other growth goals, Starbucks has an even "glitzier" goal. It wants to have a hand in helping define society's pop culture menu. Although this goal takes Starbucks beyond its coffee roots, it seems to fit well with the unconventional approach to business that Schultz has followed from the beginning.

Company Strategies

Starbucks has been called the most dynamic retail brand conceived over the last two decades. It has been able to rise above the commodity nature of its product and become a global brand leader by reinventing the coffee experience. Millions of times each week, a customer receives a drink from a Starbucks barista. It's a reflection of the success that Schultz has had in creating something that never really existed in North America—café life. Even though Toronto-based Second Cup started operating in 1975 and Starbucks did not come to Canada until 1987, Starbucks dominates the Canadian marketplace. Second Cup has 360 cafés across Canada (and over 50 cafés internationally), while Starbucks has over 500 stores across the country.

Schultz has created a cultural phenomenon. Starbucks is changing what we eat and drink. It's altering where we work and play. It's shaping how we spend time and money. No one is more surprised by this cultural impact than Schultz. He says, "It amazes all of us how we've become part of popular culture. Our customers have given us permission to extend the experience."

Starbucks has found a way to appeal to practically every customer demographic, as its customers cover a broad base. It's not just the affluent or the urban professionals, and it's not just the intellectuals or the creative types who frequent Starbucks. You will find soccer moms, construction workers, bank tellers, and clerical assistants at Starbucks. And despite the high price of its products, customers pay it because they think it's worth it. What they get for that price is some of the finest coffee available commercially, custom preparation, and, of course, that Starbucks ambience—the music, the comfy chairs, the aromas, the hissing steam from the espresso machine—all invoking that warm feeling of community and connection that Schultz experienced on his first business trip to Italy and knew instinctively could work elsewhere.

There is no hiding the fact that Starbucks' broad strategy is to grow into a global empire. Schultz says, "We are in the second inning of a nine-inning game. We are just beginning to tap into all sorts of new markets, new customers, and new products." But any growth that Starbucks pursues is done with great care and planning, with a focus on maintaining quality. If there is any uncertainty about quality, a new strategy will not fly, no matter how good it might seem. Starbucks has designed its growth strategies to exploit the customer connections it has so carefully nurtured and the brand equity it has so masterfully built. And company executives have taken the company in new directions even while continuing to grow store numbers and locations and increasing same-store sales.

As the world's number-one specialty coffee retailer, Starbucks sells coffee drinks, food items, coffee beans, and coffee-related accessories and equipment. In addition,

Starbucks sells whole-bean coffees through a specialty sales group and grocery stores. Starbucks has grown beyond coffee into related businesses such as coffee-flavoured ice cream and ready-to-drink coffee beverages. These Starbucks-branded products have been developed with other companies. For example, its Frappuccino® and DoubleShot™ coffee drinks were developed with Pepsi-Cola. Its Starbucks Ice Cream was developed with Dreyer's. In 2006, Starbucks launched its ready-to-drink coffee drink, Starbucks Iced Coffee, through a joint venture with Pepsi-Cola. The company extended its success at brand extensions to selected global markets when it launched a fresh Starbucks-branded premium ready-to-drink chilled coffee called Starbucks Discoveries™ in convenience stores in Taiwan and Japan. This product was enthusiastically embraced by customers immediately. In addition, Starbucks markets a selection of premium tea products since its acquisition of Tazo, LLC.

Starbucks has also pursued other strategic initiatives to enhance its core business. For example, in November 2001, the company launched the Starbucks Card, a prepaid card. Since that time, more than 193 million Starbucks Cards have been activated and loaded in North America with more than $2.5 billion. Because of its success in North America, the Starbucks Card has been introduced in other countries, including Mexico, Hong Kong, Australia, Thailand, Greece, and the United Kingdom. The director of Starbucks global card services says, "We've been pleasantly surprised by the card business, by how fast it's grown in percentage of tender, and how people use the card. It offers so many opportunities to grow from there. It's one of our fastest-growing channels." Industry experts say that part of the reason for its success is its dual use—as gift cards and for customer loyalty. Also important to its success, however, is the fact that the company has made it easy to purchase, reload, and use. The company is on the leading edge in finding innovative ways to get the prepaid cards into potential customers' hands, such as parent–student cards, gift-card malls, and business gifts and incentives.

Having conquered the coffee business, one of the company's most interesting brand extensions has been music. Selling music at Starbucks began when a store manager made tapes for his store. These tapes proved to be so popular that the company began licensing music compilation CDs for sale. Initially, Schultz had to be persuaded about this product and recalls, "I began to understand that our customers looked to Starbucks as a kind of editor. It was

like . . . we trust you. Help us choose." And if you think about it, music has always been part of the café or coffee-house experience. In addition to selling its private-label CDs, the company launched the HearMusic Café in Santa Monica, California, in March 2004. At these stores, customers burn their own compilation CDs. After sampling selections, if they choose to buy, customers can walk up to a music "bar" and order a custom CD with any variation of songs and have it delivered to their table when it's completed. Based on the success Starbucks has had with music, it decided to selectively link the Starbucks brand with certain kinds of movies, the first being *Akeelah and the Bee*. The president of Starbucks entertainment division says, "Movies are a very important part of our entertainment strategy. The thought was to start with music, build some success, establish credibility, and then move into films." Eventually, the company wants to be a destination not just for java but also for music, movies, books, and more.

Not everything that Starbucks touches turns to gold. One of its big flops was a magazine called *Joe*, launched by the company and *Time*. It lasted three issues before being called off. A carbonated coffee beverage product called Mazagran, developed with Pepsi-Cola, never made it to market. As well, Starbucks decided to close its Torrefazione Italia cafés when they did not meet the goals set for them.

A customer selects songs for burning to a CD as another orders coffee at a Starbucks' HearMusic Café.

There is no doubt that Schultz has built and continues to build Starbucks to be big. Growth has been funded through cash flow, not by selling stock or by using debt financing. Some of the new ideas to be implemented include an aggressive rollout of drive-through windows, which now number 2800 North American locations; a co-branded website between Yahoo! and Starbucks where online daters can arrange to meet and drink free coffee; a partnership between Starbucks and Kellogg that created a hot breakfast product; and two new banana-based blended drinks.

Questions

1. Starbucks has some specific goals it wants to achieve. Given this, do you think managers would be more likely to make rational decisions, bounded rationality decisions, or intuitive decisions? Explain.

2. Give examples of decisions that Starbucks managers might make under conditions of certainty. Under conditions of risk. Under conditions of uncertainty.

3. Make a list of Starbucks' goals. Describe what type of goal each is. Then, describe how that stated goal might affect how the following employees do their jobs: (a) a part-time store employee—a barista—in Winnipeg; (b) a quality assurance technician at one of the company's roasting plants; (c) a regional sales manager; (d) the senior vice-president of new markets; and (e) the president and CEO.

4. Discuss the types of growth strategies that Starbucks has used. Be specific.

5. Evaluate the growth strategies Starbucks is using. What do you think it will take for these strategies to be successful?

6. What competitive advantage(s) do you think Starbucks has? What will it have to do to maintain that (those) competitive advantage(s)?

7. Do you think the Starbucks brand can become too saturated—that is, extended to too many different products? Why or why not?

8. What companies might be good benchmarks for Starbucks? Why? What companies might want to benchmark Starbucks? Why?

9. Describe how the following Starbucks managers might use forecasting, budgeting, and scheduling (be specific): (a) a retail store manager; (b) a regional marketing manager; (c) the manager of global trends; and (d) the president and CEO.

10. Describe Howard Schultz as a strategic leader.

11. Is Starbucks "living" its mission? Explain. (You can find the company mission on its website [**www.starbucks.com**] or in the continuing case found at the end of Part 1.)

VIDEO CASE INCIDENTS

Joe Six-Pack and Four Canadian Entrepreneurs

Today, Canada's brewing industry comprises two dominant companies: Labatt Breweries of Canada, established in 1847, brewing 60 quality beers, employing 3200 Canadians, and operating six breweries from coast to coast; and Molson Breweries, Canada's oldest brewing company, established in 1786, employing 3000 employees across the country, and operating six breweries. Molson Canada is now an integral part of the Molson Coors Brewing Company, which was formed by the 2005 merger of Molson and Coors.

In recent times, the Canadian market has seen the development of over 40 microbreweries and an endless influx of international beers. Risks for new market entrants are high. How could another start-up beer company and a micro-distillery promoting coolers ever hope to make it?

Black Fly Beverage Company

Black Fly Beverage Company is Ontario's first micro-distillery, founded by husband and wife team Rob Kelly and Cathy Siskind-Kelly in May 2005. Black Fly Coolers are made and bottled in London, Ontario. Setting up the enterprise required considerable funds, and major lenders were reluctant due to the very real risk of failure; most of the start-up funds were raised by the Kellys themselves. The production capacity of their 3300 square foot "pilot" plant is limited to 2.5 million 400-millilitre bottles per year.

In January 2006, Black Fly's original cranberry–blueberry cooler was selling in 140 Liquor Control Board of Ontario (LCBO) outlets and bars in the London area. Today the LCBO distributes the "all Canadian produced" cooler to 450 of its 600 stores. The Kellys are looking for a new plant with at least 10 times the capacity of the existing plant, and are considering expanding their market into all parts of Canada.

Mountain Crest Brewing Company

Meet Manjit and Ravinder Minhas, petroleum-engineering graduates from the University of Calgary. The 20-something siblings started Calgary-based Mountain Crest Brewing Company in 2002. Their strategy is to underprice Molson and Labatt. To do so, they outsourced their brewing to Huber Brewing in Monroe, Wisconsin. Huber offered lower prices than any of the Canadian brewers they approached. In 2006, the siblings bought Huber Brewing to have long-term production stability, renaming it Minhas Craft Brewery in October 2007.

Mountain Crest beer is mainly sold in Alberta and other western provinces. In an effort to have a presence in eastern Canada, the Minhases incorporated Lakeshore Creek Brewing in Ontario in the summer of 2004, wanting to crack the large, highly competitive Ontario market with their Lakeshore Creek brand of premium but inexpensive beer. Statistics Canada reports that Canadians bought around $7.9 billion worth of beer in 2003; it is estimated that 20 percent of that was spent on value beer. Ontario craft brewers such as Brick Brewery are posting record sales numbers. This is good news for the Minhases!

QUESTIONS

1. *For discussion:* Compare and contrast the Mountain Crest Brewing Company with the Black Fly Beverage Company using the strategic management process.

2. *For debate:* "The weakest part of the strategic management process undertaken by both the Mountain Crest Brewing Company and the Black Fly Beverage Company in their entry into the Ontario market was in their assessment of threats, or in the external analysis process." Do you agree or disagree with this statement? Explain.

3. *For analysis:* Which growth strategies would be best suited to each company in the long and short term?

4. *For application:* Using the Internet and other sources, identify two key competitors for both the Mountain Crest Brewing Company (in Ontario) and the Black Fly Beverage Company, and identify each company's sustainable competitive advantage over its key competitors.

Sources: "Joe Six Pack," *CBC Venture*, January 22, 2006, 6, NEP-14756; Black Fly Beverage Company website, www.blackflycoolers.com (accessed August 31, 2009); "Entrepreneur: Black Fly Beverage Co.," *National Post*, January 15, 2007, FP12, www.roynatentrepreneur.com/pdf/profile/BlackflyBeverages-011506.pdf (accessed August 31, 2009); D. Izenberg, "Freezies that kick," *Macleans.ca*, www.macleans.ca/business/companies/article.jsp?content=20060529_127754_127754 (accessed August 31, 2009); T. Daykin, "Crafting Success," *Milwaukee Journal Sentinel*, September 30, 2007, www.jsonline.com/business/29477899.html (accessed August 31, 2009); H. Daniszewski, "Black Fly Grips Sales," *The London Free Press*, January 18, 2006, www.lfpress.ca/cgi-bin/publish.cgi?p=120093&x=articles&s=shopping (accessed August 31, 2009); M. Magnan, "Beer War," *Canadian Business Online*, July 18, 2005, www.canadianbusiness.com/shared/print.jsp?content=20050718_69548_69548 (accessed August 31, 2009); "Siblings Brew Up Attack Plan on Big Beer," *Business Edge*, March 31, 2005, www.businessedge.ca/article.cfm/newsID/8963.cfm (accessed August 31, 2009); and Mountain Crest Brewing Company website, www.damngoodbeer.ca (accessed August 31, 2009).

Ben & Jerry's in Canada

In May 1978, Ben Cohen and Jerry Greenfield completed a $5 correspondence course on ice-cream making and started Ben & Jerry's in a converted abandoned gas station in Burlington, Vermont. They gambled their life savings of $8000 on a dream of making Vermont's best ice cream. By 1985, Ben & Jerry's had sales of more than $9 million, reaching almost $20 million the following year. Sales hit $237 million by the end of 1999, before the company was acquired by the Anglo-Dutch corporation Unilever in August 2000.

Ben & Jerry's operates on a corporate concept of *linked prosperity* anchored in three key parts to its mission statement. Its *product mission* calls for making, distributing, and selling "the finest quality all natural ice cream . . . with a continued commitment to incorporating wholesome, natural ingredients and promoting business practices that respect the earth . . . " Its *economic mission* is "to operate the company on a sustainable financial basis of profitable growth . . . " and its *social mission* is "to operate the company in a way that actively recognizes the central role that business plays in society by initiating innovative ways to improve the quality of life locally, nationally, and internationally."

Perhaps this is why Morrie Baker and his real estate partner were willing to risk over $1 million of their own money to develop Ben & Jerry's in Canada. But investors were worried that their $1 million could be eaten up very quickly. According to TheFranchiseMall.com, the total investment to open a single Ben & Jerry's franchise could run from $147 000 to $396 000. Planning and decision making is critical. Where should the franchises be set up? How much should be spent on a location? How much customer traffic is necessary to be profitable? Do the locations offer exclusivity or would the location manager offer a site to competitors?

Morrie Baker now owns 20 Canadian shops and takes the view that success comes from execution and proper location choice. While Baker appears to be succeeding in Canada, it seems that elsewhere 10 percent of Ben & Jerry's shops close each year. Baker knows that a winning strategy requires the right decisions at the right times . . . within the confines of rationality!

QUESTIONS

1. *For discussion:* Which step of the decision making process presents the greatest risk?

2. *For debate:* "Given the advances of information and communications technology, managerial decision making today is much easier since so much information is so quickly and easily available to aid in the decision-making process." Do you agree or disagree with this statement?

3. *For analysis:* In your view, which of the common decision-making biases and errors would most likely present the greatest risk to a manager deciding on a location for a Ben & Jerry's franchise?

4. *For application:* Using the Internet and other sources, identify some of the corporate social responsibility activities Ben & Jerry's has undertaken as a member of the Unilever company. What do you feel are the most important issues that affect the decision of the company to invest in these activities?

Sources: "Ben & Jerry's Ice Cream Moves into Canada," *CBC Venture*, January 30, 2005, 935, VA-2100 F; Ben & Jerry's website, www.benjerry.com/company/history (accessed August 31, 2009); "Ben & Jerry's and Unilever to Join Forces," www.benjerry.com/company/media-center/press/join-forces.html (accessed August 31, 2009); "Ben & Jerry's," Unilever, www.unileverusa.com/ourbrands/foods/benandjerrys.asp?linkid=dropdown (accessed August 31, 2009); "Ben & Jerry's," TheFranchiseMall.com, www.thefranchisemall.com/franchises/details/10816-0-Ben_and_Jerrys.htm (accessed August 31, 2009); and "Ben and Jerry's Franchise," FranchiseMarketplace.com, www.franchisemarketplace.com/franchisedetail.asp?aid=147&franchise=Ben_and_Jerry (accessed August 31, 2009).

After you have completed your study of Part 2, do the following exercises on MyManagementLab at www.pearsoned.ca/mymanagementlab:

- *You're the Manager: Putting Ethics into Action* (**HealthSouth**)
- *Passport, Scenario 1* (**Luke Castillo, Deere & Company**), *Scenario 2* (**Yoko Sato, Toys "R" Us International**), and *Scenario 3* (**Tomasso Perelli, Benito Sportswear**)

Organizational Structure and Design

What kind of organizational structure do I need?

1 What are the major elements of organizational structure?

2 What factors affect organizational structure?

3 Beyond traditional organizational designs, how else can organizations be structured?

Richard A. Peddie is the president and CEO of Maple Leaf Sports & Entertainment (MLSE), which owns the NHL's Toronto Maple Leafs, the NBA's Toronto Raptors, Major League Soccer's Toronto FC, the AHL's Toronto Marlies, Leafs TV, and Raptors NBA TV.[1] MLSE also owns Air Canada Centre (where the Maple Leafs and Raptors play their home games) and is a major investor in BMO Field (where the Toronto FC play their home games). Peddie's job is complex—it includes responsibility for the business affairs of each team ("team operations, sales, marketing, finance, administration, event operations, broadcast, communications, and community development"). Peddie is also responsible for the operation of Air Canada Centre, BMO Field, Ricoh Coliseum in Toronto, and General Motors Centre in Oshawa, Ontario.

To perform his job, Peddie needs a variety of people and departments to help him. One of his jobs, then, is to create an organizational structure for MLSE that supports the operations of the sports teams and the sports facilities. He has a great deal of flexibility in determining some parts of the structure, and less flexibility in determining others. For example, the number of athletes that can fill positions on a hockey team is determined by the NHL. Through

the draft and trades, Peddie and his coaches have some ability to choose the particular players who fill these positions, however.

Peddie also oversees ticket sales for the four teams. In determining how to manage ticket sales, Peddie can consider

whether there should be separate ticket sales departments for each team, whether marketing should be included with or separate from ticket sales, and whether ticket salespeople should be subdivided into specialties: corporate sales, season tickets, playoff tickets, and so forth.

Think About It
How do you run four sports teams and four sports facilities? Put yourself in Richard Peddie's shoes. He wants to continue to make Maple Leaf Sports & Entertainment successful. What can he do so that MLSE continues to adapt and change? What organizational structure can best ensure his goals?

Richard Peddie's desire to make Maple Leaf Sports & Entertainment successful illustrates how important it is for managers to design an organizational structure that helps accomplish organizational goals and objectives. In this chapter, we present information about designing appropriate organizational structures. We look at the various elements of organizational structure and the factors that influence their design. We also look at some traditional and contemporary organizational designs, as well as organizational design challenges that today's managers face.

Q&A 9.1

Defining Organizational Structure

No other topic in management has undergone as much change in the past few years as that of organizing and organizational structure. Traditional approaches to organizing work are being questioned and re-evaluated as managers search out organizational

❶ What are the major elements of organizational structure?

Exhibit 5-1

Purposes of Organizing

- Divides work to be done into specific jobs and departments.
- Assigns tasks and responsibilities associated with individual jobs.
- Coordinates diverse organizational tasks.
- Clusters jobs into units.
- Establishes relationships among individuals, groups, and departments.
- Establishes formal lines of authority.
- Allocates and deploys organizational resources.

organizing
A management function that involves determining what tasks are to be done, who is to do them, how the tasks are to be grouped, who reports to whom, and where decisions are to be made.

organizational structure
How job tasks are formally divided, grouped, and coordinated within an organization.

organizational design
The process of developing or changing an organization's structure.

structures that will best support and facilitate employees' doing the organization's work—approaches that can achieve efficiency but also have the flexibility that is necessary for success in today's dynamic environment. Recall from Chapter 1 that **organizing** is defined as the process of creating an organization's structure. That process is important and serves many purposes (see Exhibit 5-1). The challenge for managers is to design an organizational structure that allows employees to do their work effectively and efficiently.

Just what is **organizational structure**? It's how job tasks are formally divided, grouped, and coordinated within an organization. When managers develop or change the structure, they are engaged in **organizational design**, a process that involves decisions about six key elements: work specialization, departmentalization, chain of command, span of control, centralization and decentralization, and formalization.[2]

Work Specialization

work specialization
The degree to which tasks in an organization are subdivided into separate jobs; also known as *division of labour*.

When you are working in a team on a course project, does it make sense to specialize tasks? What are the advantages and disadvantages?

Adam Smith first identified division of labour and concluded that it contributed to increased employee productivity. Early in the twentieth century, Henry Ford applied this concept in an assembly line where every Ford employee was assigned a specific, repetitive task.

Today we use the term **work specialization** to describe the degree to which tasks in an organization are subdivided into separate jobs. The essence of work specialization is that an entire job is not done by one individual but instead is broken down into steps, and each step is completed by a different person. Individual employees specialize in doing part of an activity rather than the entire activity.

Q&A 9.2

During the first half of the twentieth century, managers viewed work specialization as an unending source of increased productivity, and for a time it was. Because it was not widely used, when work specialization *was* implemented, employee productivity rose. By the 1960s, however, it had become evident that a good thing could be carried too far. The point had been reached in some jobs where human diseconomies from work specialization—boredom, fatigue, stress, poor quality, increased absenteeism, and higher turnover—more than offset the economic advantages.

Today's View

Most managers today see work specialization as an important organizing mechanism but not as a source of ever-increasing productivity. They recognize the economies it provides in certain types of jobs, but they also recognize the problems it creates when it's carried to extremes, including job dissatisfaction, poor mental health, and a low sense of accomplishment.[3] McDonald's uses high work specialization to efficiently make and sell its products, and most employees in health care organizations are specialized. However, other organizations, such as Bolton, Ontario-based Husky Injection Molding Systems, and Ford Australia have successfully increased job breadth and reduced work specialization. Still, specialization has its place in some organizations. No hockey team has anyone play both goalie and centre positions. Rather, players tend to specialize in their positions.

Departmentalization

Does your college or university have an office of student affairs? A financial aid or student housing department? Once jobs have been divided up through work specialization, they have to be grouped back together so that common tasks can be coordinated. The basis on which jobs are grouped together is called **departmentalization**. Every organization will have its own specific way of classifying and grouping work activities. Exhibit 5-2 on page 142 shows the five common forms of departmentalization.

Functional departmentalization groups jobs by functions performed. This approach can be used in all types of organizations, although the functions change to reflect the organization's purpose and work. **Product departmentalization** groups jobs by product line. In this approach, each major product area is placed under the authority of a manager who is responsible for everything having to do with that product line. For example, Estée Lauder sells lipstick, eyeshadow, blush, and a variety of other cosmetics, represented by different product lines. The company's lines include Clinique, Prescriptives, and Origins, in addition to Canadian-created MAC Cosmetics and its own original line of Estée Lauder products, each of which operates as a distinct company. Similarly, while Richard Peddie is the president and CEO of both the Raptors and the Maple Leafs, each team is treated as a separate product line in terms of the rest of its management and operations, with each team being led by its own general manager.

Geographical departmentalization groups jobs on the basis of territory or geography such as the East Coast, western Canada, or central Ontario, or maybe by US, European, Latin American, and Asia–Pacific regions. **Process departmentalization** groups jobs on the basis of product or customer flow. In this approach, work activities follow a natural processing flow of products or even of customers. For example, many beauty salons have separate employees for shampooing, colouring, and cutting hair, all different processes for having one's hair styled. Finally, **customer departmentalization** groups jobs on the basis of customers who have common needs or problems that can best be met by having specialists for each. There are advantages to matching departmentalization to customer needs.

Large organizations often combine forms of departmentalization. For example, a major Japanese electronics firm organizes each of its divisions along functional lines: its manufacturing units around processes, its sales units around seven geographic regions, and sales regions into four customer groupings.

Today's View

Two popular trends in departmentalization are the use of customer departmentalization and the use of cross-functional teams. Managers use customer departmentalization to monitor customers' needs and to respond to changes in those needs. Toronto-based Dell Canada is organized around four customer-oriented business units: home and home office; small business; medium and large business; and government, education, and health care. Burnaby, BC-based TELUS is structured around four customer-oriented business units: consumer solutions (focused on services to homes and individuals); business solutions (focused on services to small and medium-sized businesses and entrepreneurs); TELUS Québec (a TELUS company focused on services for the Quebec marketplace); and partner solutions (focused on services to wholesale customers, such as telecommunications carriers and wireless communications companies). Customer-oriented structures enable companies to better understand their customers and to respond faster to their needs.

Managers use **cross-functional teams**—teams made up groups of individuals who are experts in various specialties and who work together—to increase knowledge and understanding for some organizational tasks.

departmentalization
The basis on which jobs are grouped together.

functional departmentalization
Groups jobs by functions performed.

product departmentalization
Groups jobs by product line.

geographical departmentalization
Groups jobs on the basis of territory or geography.

process departmentalization
Groups jobs on the basis of product or customer flow.

customer departmentalization
Groups jobs on the basis of customers who have common needs or problems.

cross-functional teams
Work teams made up of individuals who are experts in various functional specialties.

TELUS, one of Canada's leading telecommunication companies, is structured around customer-oriented business units. A goal of this structure is to help the company improve customer response times.

Exhibit 5-2

The Five Common Forms of Departmentalization

Functional Departmentalization

```
                    Plant Manager
   ┌──────────┬──────────┬──────────┬──────────┐
 Manager,    Manager,   Manager,    Manager,        Manager,
 Engineering Accounting Manufacturing Human Resources Purchasing
```

+ Efficiencies from putting together similar specialties and
   people with common skills, knowledge, and orientations
+ Coordination within functional area
+ In-depth specialization
− Poor communication across functional areas
− Limited view of organizational goals

Geographical Departmentalization

```
                 Vice-President
                   for Sales
   ┌──────────┬──────────┬──────────┐
 Sales Director, Sales Director, Sales Director, Sales Director,
 Western Region  Prairies Region Central Region  Eastern Region
```

+ More effective and efficient handling of specific regional
   issues that arise
+ Better service of needs of unique geographic markets
− Duplication of functions
− Feelings of isolation from other organizational areas possible

Product Departmentalization
Source: Bombardier Annual Report

```
                        Bombardier
        ┌──────────────────────────┐
  Bombardier                    Bombardier
  Aerospace                     Transportation

  Commercial Aircraft           Rail Vehicles
  Regional Aircraft             Total Transit Systems
  Business Aircraft             Propulsion and Controls
  Amphibious Aircraft           Services
  Military Aviation Training    Retail Control Solutions
  Flexjet                       Bogies
  Skyjet
```

+ Specialization in particular products and services possible
+ Managers able to become experts in their industry
+ Closer to customers
− Duplication of functions
− Limited view of organizational goals

Process Departmentalization

```
                        Plant
                     Superintendent
   ┌────────┬─────────┬─────────┬─────────┬─────────┐
 Sawing    Planing   Assembling Lacquering Finishing  Inspection
 Department and Milling Department and Sanding Department and Shipping
 Manager   Department  Manager   Department  Manager   Department
           Manager              Manager               Manager
```

+ More efficient flow of work activities
− Use possible only with certain types of products

Customer Departmentalization

```
                   Director
                   of Sales
   ┌──────────┬──────────┐
 Manager,    Manager,    Manager,
 Retail Accounts Wholesale Accounts Government Accounts
```

+ Specialists able to meet customers' needs and problems
− Duplication of functions
− Limited view of organizational goals

Scarborough, Ontario-based Aviva Canada, a leading property and casualty insurance group, puts together cross-functional catastrophe teams, with trained representatives from all relevant departments, to more quickly help policyholders when a crisis occurs. During the BC wildfires of summer 2003, the catastrophe team worked on both local and corporate issues, including managing information technology, internal and external communication, tracking, resourcing, and vendors. This made it easier to meet the needs of policyholders as quickly as possible.[4] We discuss the use of cross-functional teams more fully in Chapter 10.

Chain of Command

Have you ever worked in an organization where the chain of command was not clear? What effect did this have on employees?

For many years, the chain-of-command concept was a cornerstone of organizational design. As you will see, it has far less importance today. But contemporary managers still need to consider its implications when deciding how best to structure their organizations.

The **chain of command** is the continuous line of authority that extends from upper organizational levels to the lowest levels and clarifies who reports to whom. It helps employees answer questions such as "Who do I go to if I have a problem?" or "To whom am I responsible?"

You cannot discuss the chain of command without discussing these other concepts: authority, responsibility, accountability, unity of command, and delegation. **Authority** refers to the rights inherent in a managerial position to tell people what to do and to expect them to do it.[5] To facilitate decision making and coordination, an organization's managers are part of the chain of command and are granted a certain degree of authority to meet their responsibilities. Some senior managers and CEOs are better at granting authority than others. For example, when Richard Peddie hired Rob Babcock to be the general manager of the Raptors in 2004, some sports writers raised concerns over whether Babcock would have enough autonomy to do his job. It was noted that Peddie "has a reputation for meddling with basketball operations."[6] When Babcock was fired in 2006, sports writers observed that many of his decisions were actually made by senior management.[7]

As managers coordinate and integrate the work of employees, those employees assume an obligation to perform any assigned duties. This obligation or expectation to perform is known as **responsibility**. Responsibility brings with it **accountability**, which is the need to report and justify work to a manager's superiors. When John Muckler was dismissed as general manager of the Ottawa Senators in 2007, the team owner was signalling that he held Muckler accountable for failing to land top players that could have helped the team in their run at the Stanley Cup.[8]

The **unity of command** principle (one of Fayol's 14 principles of management discussed in the supplement *History of Management Trends* on page 25) helps preserve the concept of a continuous line of authority. It states that every employee should receive orders from only one superior. Without unity of command, conflicting demands and priorities from multiple managers can create problems.

Because managers have limited time and knowledge, they may delegate some of their responsibilities to other employees. **Delegation** is the assignment of authority to another person to carry out specific duties, allowing the employee to make some of the decisions. Delegation is an important part of a manager's job, as it can ensure that the right people are part of the decision-making process. *Tips for Managers—How to Delegate Effectively* gives tips for doing a better job of delegating.

To learn more about being an effective delegator, see *Developing Your Interpersonal Skills—Delegating*, on pages 164–165, at the end of the chapter.

chain of command
The continuous line of authority that extends from the top of the organization to the lowest level and clarifies who reports to whom.

authority
The rights inherent in a managerial position to tell people what to do and to expect them to do it.

responsibility
The obligation or expectation to perform any assigned duties.

accountability
The need to report and justify work to a manager's superiors.

unity of command
The management principle that states every employee should receive orders from only one superior.

delegation
The assignment of authority to another person to carry out specific duties, allowing the employee to make some of the decisions.

Q&A 9.3

PRISM 10

TIPS FOR MANAGERS

How to Delegate Effectively

- Delegate **the whole task**.
- Select **the right person**.
- Ensure that **authority equals responsibility**.
- Give **thorough instructions**.
- Maintain **feedback**.
- **Evaluate** and **reward** performance.[9]

Line and Staff Authority

In many organizations there is a distinction between line and staff authority. **Line managers** are responsible for the essential activities of the organization, including production and sales. Line managers have the authority to issue orders to those in the chain of command. The president, the production manager, and the sales manager are examples of line managers. **Staff managers** work in the supporting activities of the organizations (such as human resources or accounting). Staff managers have advisory authority, and cannot issue orders to those in the chain of command (except those in their own department). The vice-president of accounting, the human resource manager, and the marketing research manager are examples of staff managers. Mardi Walker, senior vice-president, People, for Maple Leaf Sports & Entertainment, may have recommendations about how the Raptors might win more games, but cannot expect that such recommendations to current general manager Bryan Colangelo will be followed. However, as senior vice-president, People, Walker can give advice about managing employee benefits.

Today's View

Although early management theorists (Fayol, Weber, Taylor, and others) were enamoured with the concepts of chain of command, authority, responsibility, and unity of command, times have changed,[10] and these concepts are far less important today. For example, at the Michelin plant in Tours, France, managers have replaced the top-down chain of command with "birdhouse" meetings, in which employees meet for five minutes at regular intervals throughout the day at a column on the shop floor and study simple tables and charts to identify production bottlenecks. Instead of being bosses, shop managers are enablers.[11] In addition, information technology has made such concepts less relevant today. In a matter of a few seconds, employees can access information that used to be available only to managers. And employees can communicate with anyone else in the organization without going through the chain of command.

Span of Control

How many employees can a manager efficiently and effectively manage? This question of **span of control** is important because, to a large degree, it determines the number of levels and managers an organization has. All things being equal, the wider or larger the span, the more efficient the organization. An example can show why.

Assume that we have two organizations, both of which have almost 4100 employees. As Exhibit 5-3 shows, if one organization has a uniform span of four and the other a span of eight, the wider span will have two fewer levels and approximately 800 fewer managers.

line managers
Managers responsible for the essential activities of the organization, including production and sales.

staff managers
Managers who work in the supporting activities of the organizations (such as human resources or accounting).

span of control
The number of employees a manager can efficiently and effectively manage.

Exhibit 5-3

Contrasting Spans of Control

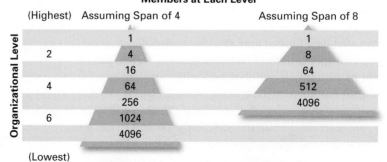

Members at Each Level

(Highest)	Assuming Span of 4	Assuming Span of 8
1	1	1
2	4	8
	16	64
4	64	512
	256	4096
6	1024	
	4096	

Organizational Level

(Lowest)

Span of 4:
Employees: = 4096
Managers (levels 1–6) = 1365

Span of 8:
Employees: = 4096
Managers (levels 1–4) = 585

If the average manager made $50 000 a year, the organization with the wider span would save more than $40 million a year in management salaries alone! Obviously, wider spans are more efficient in terms of cost. However, at some point, wider spans reduce *effectiveness*. When the span becomes too large, employee performance can suffer because managers may no longer have the time to provide the necessary leadership and support.

Q&A 9.4

Today's View

The contemporary view of span of control recognizes that many factors influence the appropriate number of employees a manager can efficiently *and* effectively manage. These factors include the skills and abilities of the manager and the employees, and characteristics of the work being done. For example, the more training and experience employees have, the less direct supervision they need. Therefore, managers with well-trained and experienced employees can function quite well with a wider span. Other contingency variables that determine the appropriate span include similarity of employee tasks, the complexity of those tasks, the physical proximity of subordinates, the degree to which standardized procedures are in place, the sophistication of the organization's information system, the strength of the organization's culture, and the preferred style of the manager.[12] Wider spans of control are also possible due to technology—it is easier for managers and their subordinates to communicate with each other, and there is often more information readily available to help employees perform their jobs.

The trend in recent years has been toward larger spans of control, which are consistent with managers' efforts to reduce costs, speed up decision making, increase flexibility, get closer to customers, and empower employees. However, to ensure that performance does not suffer because of these wider spans, organizations are investing heavily in employee training. Managers recognize that they can handle a wider span when employees know their jobs well or can turn to co-workers if they have questions.

Q&A 9.5

Centralization and Decentralization

In some organizations, top managers make all the decisions and lower-level managers and employees simply carry out their orders. At the other extreme are organizations in which decision making is pushed down to the managers who are closest to the action. The former organizations are centralized, and the latter are decentralized.

Centralization describes the degree to which decision making is concentrated at a single point in the organization. If top managers make the organization's key decisions with little or no input from below, then the organization is centralized. We noted above that Richard Peddie tends to be closely involved in decisions regarding the Raptors. In contrast, the more that lower-level employees provide input or actually make decisions, the more **decentralization** there is. Keep in mind that the concept of centralization/decentralization is relative, not absolute—that is, an organization is never completely centralized or decentralized. Few organizations could function effectively if all decisions were made by only a select group of top managers; nor could they function if all decisions were delegated to employees at the lowest levels.

centralization
The degree to which decision making is concentrated at a single point in the organization.

decentralization
The degree to which lower-level employees provide input or actually make decisions.

Today's View

As organizations become more flexible and responsive, there is a distinct trend toward decentralizing decision making. In large companies especially, lower-level managers are "closer to the action" and typically have more detailed knowledge about problems and how best to solve them than do top managers. For example, the Bank of Montreal's some 1000 branches are organized into "communities"—a group of branches within a limited geographical area. Each community is led by a community area manager, who typically works within a 20-minute drive of the other branches. This area manager can respond faster and more intelligently to problems in his or her community than could some senior executive in Toronto. The following *Management Reflection* considers the case of Cascades, a pulp-and-paper company, which illustrates a few of the reasons for having a decentralized structure.

MANAGEMENT REFLECTION

Brothers Decentralize to Increase Entrepreneurial Management

Does decentralization lead to better management? Kingsey Falls, Quebec-based Cascades, a leading manufacturer of packaging products and tissue paper, has more than 100 operating units located in Canada, the United States, and Europe.[13] Alain Lemaire is president and CEO, and his two brothers, Bernard and Laurent, are also senior executives in the business.

Four autonomous units form Cascades: the Boxboard Group, the Containerboard Group–Norampac, the Specialty Products Group, and the Tissue Group. The companies produce coated boxboard and folding cartons, container-board packaging, specialty paper products, and tissues. Boralex, a company affiliated with Cascades, produces energy and is headed by Bernard Lemaire. The companies are treated as separate entities, based on product, and operate like a federation of small and medium-sized businesses. Each mill within a subsidiary operates as a separate business unit and is accountable for its own bottom line.

The company motivates its employees through profit sharing, although employees share only in the profits generated by their own mill. Because each mill is evaluated separately, managers have to be both more responsible and more accountable for their operations, and encourage employees to take more ownership of their job perform-ance. The Lemaires' emphasis on decentralized, entrepreneurial management has been copied by other Canadian forest products companies, such as Domtar. ∎

employee empowerment
Giving more authority to employees to make decisions.

Another term for increased decentralization is **employee empowerment**, which is giving more authority to employees to make decisions.

What determines whether an organization will move toward more centralization or decentralization? Exhibit 5-4 lists some of the factors that influence the amount of centralization or decentralization an organization uses.[14]

formalization
The degree to which jobs within the organization are standardized and the extent to which employee behaviour is guided by rules and procedures.

Formalization

Formalization refers to the degree to which jobs within the organization are standardized and the extent to which employee behaviour is guided by rules and procedures. If a job is highly formalized, then the person doing that job has little freedom to choose what

Exhibit 5-4

Factors That Influence the Amount of Centralization and Decentralization

More Centralization	More Decentralization
• Environment is stable.	• Environment is complex, uncertain.
• Lower-level managers are not as capable or experienced at making decisions as upper-level managers.	• Lower-level managers are capable and experienced at making decisions.
• Lower-level managers do not want to have a say in decisions.	• Lower-level managers want a voice in decisions.
• Decisions are significant.	• Decisions are relatively minor.
• Organization is facing a crisis or the risk of company failure.	• Corporate culture is open to allowing managers to have a say in what happens.
• Company is large.	• Company is geographically dispersed.
• Effective implementation of company strategies depends on managers retaining say over what happens.	• Effective implementation of company strategies depends on managers having involvement and flexibility to make decisions.

Nordstrom employees are well known for their exceptional customer focus and the freedom they are given to go above and beyond the call of duty to help their customers. Recently a business consultant arrived late one evening at a distant city where he was to make a presentation the following morning. Unfortunately, after checking into his hotel, the man realized that he had failed to pack any ties. With his meeting set for 10 o'clock, he raced to the nearest Nordstrom store at 9 the next morning but found the store still locked. Panicked, he spotted an employee arriving for work at a side entrance and asked for help. The employee unlocked the doors early and brought the man to the menswear department to make his purchase. That is exceptional customer service!

is to be done, when it is to be done, and how he or she does it. Employees can be expected to handle the same input in exactly the same way, resulting in consistent and uniform output. In organizations with high formalization, there are explicit job descriptions, numerous organizational rules, and clearly defined procedures covering work processes. On the other hand, where formalization is low, job behaviours are relatively unstructured and employees have a great deal of freedom in how they do their work.

Q&A 9.6

The degree of formalization varies widely between organizations and even within organizations. For example, at a newspaper, news reporters often have a great deal of discretion in their jobs. They may pick their news topics, find their own stories, research them the way they want, and write them up, usually within minimal guidelines. On the other hand, employees who lay out the newspaper pages do not have that type of freedom. They have constraints—both time and space—that standardize how they do their work.

Today's View

Although some formalization is important and necessary for consistency and control, many of today's organizations seem to be less reliant on strict rules and standardization to guide and regulate employee behaviour. Consider the following situation:

> It is 2:37 p.m. and a customer at a branch of a large national drugstore chain is trying to drop off a roll of film for same-day developing. Store policy states that film must be dropped off by 2:00 p.m. for this service. The clerk knows that rules like this are supposed to be followed. At the same time, he wants to be accommodating to the customer, and he knows that the film could, in fact, be processed that day. He decides to accept the film and, in so doing, to violate the policy. He just hopes that his manager does not find out.[15]

Has this employee done something wrong? He did "break" the rule. But by breaking the rule, he actually brought in revenue and provided the customer good service: so good, in fact, that the customer may be satisfied enough to come back in the future.

Considering the fact that there are numerous situations like these where rules may be too restrictive, many organizations have allowed employees some freedom to make those decisions that they feel are best under the circumstances. It does not mean that all organizational rules are thrown out the window; there *will* be rules that are important for employees to follow, and these rules should be explained so employees understand why it's important to adhere to them. But for other rules, employees may be given some leeway in application.[16]

Organizational Design Decisions

All organizations do not have the same structures. A company with 30 employees is not going to look like one with 30 000 employees. But even organizations of comparable size do not necessarily have similar structures. What works for one organization may not

2 What factors affect organizational structure?

work for another. How do managers decide what organizational structure to use? Organizational design decisions depend on certain contingency factors. In this section, we look at two generic models of organizational design and then at the contingency factors that favour each.

Mechanistic and Organic Organizations

Dining in Vancouver can get you two very different experiences. At McDonald's, you will find a limited selection of menu items, most available daily. Employees are not expected to be decision makers. Rather, they are closely supervised and follow well-defined rules and standard operating procedures. Only one employee helps each customer. At Blue Water Café in downtown Vancouver, by contrast, there is no division of labour, and management does not dictate what the kitchen serves. Instead, the chef on duty creates a meal of his choice while you sit at the sushi bar and watch. The chef chooses the meal from the fresh fish of the day that he bought at the market earlier, so each day's menu can be quite original. Waiters work collaboratively, helping each other serve all customers, rather than being assigned to specific tables.

mechanistic organization
An organizational design that is rigid and tightly controlled.

Exhibit 5-5 describes two organizational forms.[17] A **mechanistic organization** is a rigid and tightly controlled structure, much like that of McDonald's. It's characterized by high specialization, rigid departmentalization, a limited information network (mostly downward communication), narrow spans of control, little participation in decision making by lower-level employees, and high formalization.

Mechanistic organizational structures tend to be efficiency machines and rely heavily on rules, regulations, standardized tasks, and similar controls. This organizational structure tries to minimize the impact of differing personalities, judgments, and ambiguity because these human traits are seen as inefficient and inconsistent. Although there is no totally mechanistic organization, almost all large corporations and government agencies have some of these mechanistic characteristics.

organic organization
An organizational design that is highly adaptive and flexible.

In direct contrast to the mechanistic form of organization is the **organic organization**, which is as highly adaptive and flexible a structure as the mechanistic organization is rigid and stable. Organic organizations have a division of labour, but the jobs people do are not standardized. Employees are highly trained and empowered to handle diverse job activities and problems, and these organizations frequently use cross-functional and cross-hierarchical teams. Employees in organic organizations require minimal formal rules and little direct supervision; instead, they rely on a free flow of information and a wide span of control. Their high levels of skills and training and the support provided by other team members make formalization and tight managerial controls unnecessary.

Exhibit 5-5

Mechanistic vs. Organic Organization

Mechanistic	Organic
• High Specialization	• Cross-Functional Teams
• Rigid Departmentalization	• Cross-Hierarchical Teams
• Clear Chain of Command	• Free Flow of Information
• Narrow Spans of Control	• Wide Spans of Control
• Centralization	• Decentralization
• High Formalization	• Low Formalization

An organizational redesign at GlaxoSmithKline, a London-based pharmaceutical company, resulted in a more organic structure for the company. Before the restructuring, product research was hampered by slow-moving bureaucracy. Decisions about which drugs to fund were made by a committee of research and development executives far removed from the research labs—a time-consuming process not at all appropriate for a company dependent on scientific breakthroughs. Now, lab scientists set the priorities and allocate the resources. The change has "helped produce an entrepreneurial environment akin to a smaller, biotechnology outfit."[18]

Organizations can display a mix of mechanistic and organic features. Wikipedia, the online encyclopedia, is known for its creation and editing of entries by anyone who has Internet access. In this way, it displays a very organic structure. However, behind the scenes there is a more mechanistic structure, where individuals have some authority to monitor abuse and perform other functions to safeguard the credibility of entries and the website overall, as the following *Management Reflection* shows.

MANAGEMENT REFLECTION

Structure in the Face of Anarchy

Why would a decentralized, free-wheeling website need an organizational structure?
Even a seemingly democratic organization such as Wikipedia has an organizational structure.[19] The structure serves to help the online encyclopedia be as accurate as possible. At the bottom of that structure are the 4.6 million registered English-language users. These users are overseen by a group of about 1200 administrators, who have the power to "block other users from the site, either temporarily or permanently." One of their roles is to make sure that users are not vandalizing the site by deliberately adding incorrect information. To become an administrator, one must first be nominated, and then answer a series of five questions. Users then have seven days to register their approval or disapproval of the nominee. The administrators are overseen by a group called "bureaucrats." The bureaucrats can appoint administrators once they determine that users approve of a particular administrator nominee (this requires about a 70 percent approval rating by users). They can also change user names, and they make sure that bot policies (policies regarding automated or semi-automated processes that edit webpages) are followed. Above the bureaucrats are about 30 stewards, who are elected to this position. The stewards can provide (and take away) special access status to Wikipedia. Above the stewards is the seven-person Wikimedia Foundation board of trustees, who are "the ultimate corporate authority." At the top of the Wikipedia organizational chart is the "de-facto leader," Jimmy Wales, one of the co-founders of Wikipedia. ■

When is a mechanistic structure preferable, and when is an organic one more appropriate? Let's look at the main contingency factors that influence the decision.

Q&A 9.7

Contingency Factors

Top managers of most organizations typically put a great deal of thought into designing an appropriate structure. What that appropriate structure is depends on four contingency variables: the organization's strategy, size, technology, and degree of environmental uncertainty. It is important to remember that because these variables can change over the life cycle of the organization, managers should consider from time to time whether the current organizational structure is best suited for what the organization is facing.

Q&A 9.8

Strategy and Structure

An organization's structure should facilitate the achievement of goals. Because goals are influenced by the organization's strategies, it's only logical that strategy and structure should be closely linked. More specifically, structure should follow strategy. If managers significantly change the organization's strategy, they need to modify the structure to accommodate and support the change.

Most current strategy frameworks tend to focus on three dimensions:

- *Innovation.* This dimension reflects the organization's pursuit of meaningful and unique innovations.

- *Cost minimization.* This dimension reflects the organization's pursuit of tightly controlled costs.

- *Imitation.* This dimension reflects an organization's attempt to minimize risk and maximize profit opportunities by copying the market leaders.

What organizational structure works best with each?[20] Innovators need the flexibility and free-flowing information of the organic structure, whereas cost minimizers seek the efficiency, stability, and tight controls of the mechanistic structure. Imitators use structural characteristics of both—the mechanistic structure to maintain tight controls and low costs and the organic structure to mimic the industry's innovative directions.

Size and Structure

There is considerable evidence that an organization's size significantly affects its structure.[21] For example, large organizations—those with 2000 or more employees—tend to have more specialization, departmentalization, centralization, and rules and regulations than do small organizations. However, the relationship is not linear. Rather, beyond a certain point, size becomes a less important influence on structure as an organization grows. Why? Essentially, once an organization has around 2000 employees, it's already fairly mechanistic. Adding 500 employees to an organization with 2000 employees will not have much of an impact. On the other hand, adding 500 employees to an organization that has only 300 members is likely to result in a shift toward a more mechanistic structure.

Technology and Structure

Q&A 9.9

Every organization has at least one form of technology to convert its inputs into outputs. Employees at Whirlpool's Manaus, Brazil, facility build microwave ovens and air-conditioners on a standardized assembly line. Employees at FedEx Kinko's produce custom design and print jobs for individual customers. And employees at Bayer's facility in Karachi, Pakistan, make pharmaceutical products using a continuous-flow production line. Each of these organizations uses a different type of technology.

The initial interest in technology as a determinant of structure can be traced to the work of British scholar Joan Woodward.[22] She studied several small manufacturing firms in southern England to determine the extent to which organizational design elements were related to organizational success. Woodward was unable to find any consistent pattern until she segmented the firms into three categories based on the size of their production runs. The three categories, representing three distinct technologies, have increasing levels of complexity and sophistication. The first category, **unit production**, describes the production of items in units or small batches. The second category, **mass production**, describes large-batch manufacturing. Finally, the third and most technically complex group, **process production**, describes the production of items in continuous processes. A summary of her findings is shown in Exhibit 5-6.

Since Woodward's initial work, numerous studies have been done on the technology–structure relationship. These studies generally demonstrate that organizations adapt their structures to their technology.[23] The processes or methods that transform an organization's inputs into outputs differ by their degree of routineness or standardization. In general, the more routine the technology, the more mechanistic the structure can be. Organizations with more nonroutine technology, such as custom furniture building or online education, are more likely to have organic structures because the product delivery cannot be standardized.[24]

unit production
The production of items in units or small batches.

mass production
The production of items in large batches.

process production
The production of items in continuous processes.

Exhibit 5-6

Woodward's Findings on Technology, Structure, and Effectiveness

	Unit Production	Mass Production	Process Production
Structural characteristics	• Low vertical differentiation • Low horizontal differentiation • Low formalization	• Moderate vertical differentiation • High horizontal differentiation • High formalization	• High vertical differentiation • Low horizontal differentiation • Low formalization
Most effective structure	• Organic	• Mechanistic	• Organic

Source: Based on J. Woodward, *Industrial Organization: Theory and Practice* (London: Oxford University Press, 1965).

Environmental Uncertainty and Structure

In Chapter 2 we discussed the organization's environment and the amount of uncertainty in that environment as constraints on managerial discretion. Why should an organization's structure be affected by its environment? Because of environmental uncertainty! Some organizations face relatively stable and simple environments; others face dynamic and complex environments. Because uncertainty threatens an organization's effectiveness, managers will try to minimize it. One way to reduce environmental uncertainty is through adjustments in the organization's structure.[25] The greater the uncertainty, the more an organization needs the flexibility offered by an organic structure. On the other hand, in a stable, simple environment, a mechanistic structure tends to be most effective.

Today's View

The evidence on the environment–structure relationship helps explain why so many managers today are restructuring their organizations to be lean, fast, and flexible. Global competition, accelerated product innovation by competitors, and increased demands from customers for high quality and faster delivery are examples of dynamic environmental forces. Mechanistic organizations are not equipped to respond to rapid environmental change and environmental uncertainty. As a result, we are seeing a greater number of organizations designed to be more organic. However, a purely organic organization may not be ideal. One study found that organic structures may work more effectively if managers establish semistructures that govern "the pace, timing, and rhythm of organizational activities and processes." Thus, introducing a bit of structure while keeping most of the flexibility of the organic structure may reduce operating costs.[26]

Common Organizational Designs

Maple Leaf Sports & Entertainment (MLSE) is divided into four operating units: MLSE, Toronto Raptors, Toronto Maple Leafs (Toronto Marlies is an affiliate), and Toronto FC. Richard Peddie is the president and CEO of all four units.[27] The Raptors, the Maple Leafs, the Marlies, and Toronto FC each have their own general manager who manages the day-to-day operations of the team, develops recruiting plans, and oversees training. The general managers report to the CEO, and have a number of managers who report to them. MLSE has a divisional structure, whereby its businesses operate separately, on a daily basis.

Think About It

Why do organizations vary in the types of structures they have? How do organizations choose their structures? Why does Maple Leaf Sports & Entertainment have the structure it does?

Exhibit 5-7

Strengths and Weaknesses of Common Traditional Organizational Designs

Structure	Strengths	Weaknesses
Simple structure	Fast; flexible; inexpensive to maintain; clear accountability.	Not appropriate as organization grows; reliance on one person is risky.
Functional structure	Cost-saving advantages from specialization (economies of scale, minimal duplication of people and equipment) and employees are grouped with others who have similar tasks.	Pursuit of functional goals can cause managers to lose sight of what's best for overall organization; functional specialists become insulated and have little understanding of what other units are doing.
Divisional structure	Focuses on results—division managers are responsible for what happens to their products and services.	Duplication of activities and resources increases costs and reduces efficiency.

❸ Beyond traditional organizational designs, how else can organizations be structured?

What types of organizational designs exist in small businesses or in big companies such as Ford Canada, Corel, McCain Foods, Procter & Gamble, and eBay? When making organizational design decisions, managers can choose from traditional organizational designs and contemporary organizational designs.

Traditional Organizational Designs

In designing a structure to support the efficient and effective accomplishment of organizational goals, managers may choose to follow more traditional organizational designs. These designs—the simple structure, functional structure, and divisional structure—tend to be more mechanistic. Exhibit 5-7 summarizes the strengths and weaknesses of each design.

Simple Structure

simple structure
An organizational structure with low departmentalization, wide spans of control, authority centralized in a single person, and little formalization.

Most organizations start as entrepreneurial ventures with a simple structure consisting of owners and employees. A **simple structure** is an organizational structure with low departmentalization, wide spans of control, authority centralized in a single person, and little formalization.[28] This structure is most commonly used by small businesses in which the owner and manager are one and the same.

Most organizations do not remain simple structures. As an organization grows, it generally reaches a point where it has to add employees. As the number of employees rises, the structure tends to become more specialized and formalized. Rules and regulations are introduced, work becomes specialized, departments are created, levels of management are added, and the organization becomes increasingly bureaucratic. At this point, a manager might choose to organize around a functional structure or a divisional structure.

Q&A 9.10

Functional Structure

functional structure
An organizational structure that groups similar or related occupational specialties together.

A **functional structure** is an organizational structure that groups similar or related occupational specialties together. It's the functional approach to departmentalization applied to the entire organization. Revlon, for example, is organized around the functions of operations, finance, human resources, and product research and development.

Divisional Structure

divisional structure
An organizational structure that consists of separate business units or divisions.

The **divisional structure** is an organizational structure that consists of separate business units or divisions.[29] In this structure, each unit or division has relatively limited autonomy, with a division manager responsible for performance and with strategic and operational authority over his or her unit. In divisional structures, however, the parent corporation typically acts as an external overseer to coordinate and control the various divisions, and it often provides support services such as financial and legal. As we noted earlier, Maple Leaf Sports & Entertainment has three divisions, including the two sports teams the Raptors and the Maple Leafs.

Contemporary Organizational Designs

Managers in some contemporary organizations are finding that these traditional hierarchical designs often are not appropriate for the increasingly dynamic and complex environments they face. In response to marketplace demands for being lean, flexible, and innovative, managers are finding creative ways to structure and organize work and to make their organizations more responsive to the needs of customers, employees, and other organizational constituents.[30] At the Canada Revenue Agency, the workforce is spread out, and employees rely on shared workspaces, mobile computing, and virtual private networks to get work done. Nevertheless, work gets done effectively and efficiently.[31] Now, we want to introduce you to some of the newest concepts in organizational design. Exhibit 5-8 summarizes these contemporary organizational designs.

Team Structure

Larry Page and Sergey Brin, co-founders of Google, have created a corporate structure that "tackles most big projects in small, tightly focused teams."[32] In a **team structure**, the entire organization is made up of work groups or teams that perform the organization's work.[33] Needless to say, employee empowerment is crucial in a team structure because there is no line of managerial authority from top to bottom. Rather, employee teams are free to design work in the way they think is best. However, the teams are also held responsible for all work and performance results in their respective areas. Let's look at some examples of organizations that are organized around teams.

Whole Foods Market, the largest natural-foods grocer in the United States, opened its first Canadian outlet in Toronto in 2002, its second in North Vancouver in 2004, and its third in Oakville, Ontario, in 2005. The stores are structured around teams.[34] Each Whole Foods store is an autonomous profit centre composed of an average of 10 self-managed teams, each with a designated team leader. The team leaders in each store are a team; store leaders in each region are a team; and the company's six regional presidents are a team. At the Sun Life Assurance Company of Canada (US) office in Wellesley Hills, Massachusetts, customer representatives work in eight-person teams trained to expedite all customer

> **team structure**
> An organizational structure in which the entire organization is made up of work groups or teams.

> Q&A 9.11

Exhibit 5-8

Contemporary Organizational Designs

Structure	Description	Advantages	Disadvantages
Team	A structure in which the entire organization is made up of work groups or teams.	Employees are more involved and empowered. Reduced barriers among functional areas.	No clear chain of command. Pressure on teams to perform.
Matrix–Project	Matrix is a structure that assigns specialists from different functional areas to work on projects but who return to their areas when the project is completed. Project is a structure in which employees continuously work on projects. As one project is completed, employees move on to the next project.	Fluid and flexible design that can respond to environmental changes. Faster decision making.	Complexity of assigning people to projects. Task and personality conflicts.
Boundaryless	A structure that is not defined by or limited to artificial horizontal, vertical, or external boundaries; includes *virtual* and *networked* types of organizations.	Highly flexible and responsive. Draws on talent wherever it's found.	Lack of control. Communication difficulties.

requests. When customers call in, they are not switched from one specialist to another, but to one of the teams who takes care of every aspect of the customer's request.

In large organizations, the team structure complements what is typically a functional or divisional structure. This enables the organization to have the efficiency of a bureaucracy while providing the flexibility that teams provide. To improve productivity at the operating level, for example, Toyota's CAPTIN plant (based in Delta, BC), Motorola, and Xerox use self-managed teams extensively. Together, team members work to make resolving insurance difficulties after a disaster go much smoother.[35]

Matrix and Project Structures

matrix structure
An organizational structure that assigns specialists from different functional departments to work on one or more projects.

Have you ever had to work for two managers at the same time? Was this a positive or negative experience?

Other popular contemporary designs are the matrix and project structures. The **matrix structure** is an organizational structure that assigns specialists from different functional departments to work on one or more projects being led by project managers. Once a project is completed, the specialists return to their functional departments. Exhibit 5-9 shows an example of the matrix structure used in an aerospace firm. Along the top are the familiar organizational functions. The specific projects the firm is currently working on are listed along the left-hand side. Each project is managed by an individual who staffs his or her project with people from each of the functional departments. The addition of this vertical dimension to the traditional horizontal functional departments in effect "weaves together" elements of functional and product departmentalization, creating a matrix arrangement. One other unique aspect of this design is that it creates a *dual chain of command*. It explicitly violates the classical organizing principle of unity of command.

Q&A 9.12   How does a matrix structure work in reality?

Employees in a matrix organization have two managers: their functional department manager and their product or project manager, who share authority. The project managers have authority over the functional members who are part of their project team in areas relative to the project's goals. However, decisions such as promotions, salary recommendations, and annual reviews remain the functional manager's responsibility. To work effectively, project and functional managers have to communicate regularly, coordinate work demands on employees, and resolve conflicts together.

project structure
An organizational structure in which employees continuously work on projects.

Although the matrix structure continues to be an effective organizational structure choice for some organizations, many are using a **project structure**, in which employees continuously work on projects. Unlike the matrix structure, a project structure has no

Exhibit 5-9

A Matrix Organization in an Aerospace Firm

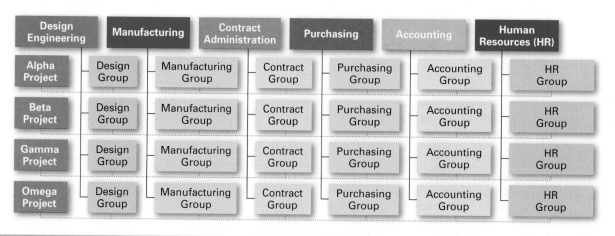

formal departments that employees return to at the completion of a project. Instead, employees take their specific skills, abilities, and experiences to other projects. In addition, all work in project structures is performed by teams of employees who become part of a project team because they have the appropriate work skills and abilities. For example, at Oticon A/S, a Danish hearing-aid manufacturer, there are no departments or employee job titles. All work is project-based, and these project teams form, disband, and form again as the work requires. Employees "join" project teams because they bring needed skills and abilities to that project. Once the project is completed, they move on to the next one.[36]

Project structures tend to be fluid and flexible organizational designs. There is no departmentalization or rigid organizational hierarchy to slow down decision making or taking actions. In this type of structure, managers serve as facilitators, mentors, and coaches. They "serve" the project teams by eliminating or minimizing organizational obstacles and by ensuring that the teams have the resources they need to effectively and efficiently complete their work.

Boundaryless Organizations

Another approach to contemporary organizational design is the concept of a **boundaryless organization**, an organization whose design is not defined by a predefined structure. Instead the organization seeks to eliminate the chain of command, places no limits on spans of control, and replaces departments with empowered teams.[37] The term was coined by Jack Welch, former chair of General Electric (GE), who wanted to eliminate vertical and horizontal boundaries within GE and break down external barriers between the company and its customers and suppliers. This idea may sound odd, yet many successful organizations are finding that they can operate more effectively in today's environment by remaining flexible and *unstructured*: the ideal structure for them is *not* having a rigid, predefined structure. Instead, the boundaryless organization seeks to eliminate the chain of command, to have limitless spans of control, and to replace departments with empowered teams.[38]

What do we mean by "boundaries"? In a typical organization there are internal boundaries—horizontal boundaries imposed by work specialization and departmentalization, and vertical boundaries that separate employees into organizational levels and hierarchies. Then there are external boundaries that separate the organization from its customers, suppliers, and other stakeholders. To minimize or eliminate these boundaries, managers might use virtual or network organizational structures.

So how does a boundaryless organization operate in practice? General Electric is made up of a number of companies including GE Money, which provides financial services to consumers and retailers; GE Water & Process Technologies, which provides water treatment, wastewater treatment, and process systems products; GE Energy, which supplies technology to the energy industry; and NBC Universal Studios, a leading media and entertainment company. One way that the boundaryless organization functions for employees is that anyone working in any division of GE can learn about opportunities available in the other business units, and how to move into those units, if so desired. Outside the company, the boundaryless structure means that some GE customers can send information to the factories to increase inventory when the customer needs more product. Thus, the customer makes a decision about inventory that was once made inside the organization. GE also encourages customers and suppliers to evaluate its service levels, giving direct and immediate feedback to employees.

Virtual Organizations A **virtual organization** has elements of a traditional organization, but also relies on recent developments in information technology to get work done.[39] Thus, the organization could consist of a small core of full-time employees that temporarily hires outside specialists to work on opportunities that arise.[40] The virtual organization could also be composed of employees who work from their own home offices—connected by technology, but perhaps getting together face-to-face only rarely. An example of a virtual organization is Strawberry Frog, an international advertising agency based in Amsterdam. The small administrative staff accesses a network of more than 100 people

boundaryless organization
An organization that is not defined by a chain of command, places no limits on spans of control, and replaces departments with empowered teams.

Q&A 9.13

virtual organization
An organization that has elements of a traditional organization, but also relies on recent developments in information technology to get work done.

around the globe to complete advertising projects. By relying on this web of free-lancers around the globe, the company enjoys a network of talent without all the over-head and structural complexity of a more traditional organization.

The inspiration for virtual organizations comes from the film industry. If you look at the film industry, people are essentially "free agents" who move from project to project applying their skills—directing, talent search, costuming, makeup, set design—as needed.

New Westminster, BC-based iGEN Knowledge Solutions uses its virtual form to bring technical solutions to its business clients. iGEN associates work from home offices, connected by wireless technologies, to solve client problems collaboratively. This structure allows faster idea implementation, product development, and service delivery. The company finds it easy to set up operations in different regions of the country without large overhead costs because of its virtual structure.

Organizations may be considering a new form of virtuality, using the virtual online world of *Second Life*, to create a different type of organization, as the following *Management Reflection* shows.

MANAGEMENT REFLECTION

Avatars and the Business World

Can a *Second Life* presence bring a company more clients? Vancouver-based Davis LLP is the first Canadian law firm to have a presence in the virtual online world of *Second Life*.[41] Lawyer Dani Lemon, whose online avatar (the digital versions of real people) is Lemon Darcy, said "the online world gives [Davis] an opportunity to interact with clients and meet new ones who are comfortable in that setting."

Lemon believes that being part of *Second Life* will bring new clients to Davis, giving them an opportunity to communicate in new ways. Several of her colleagues have joined her in this virtual office, including Sarah Dale-Harris (BarristerSolicitor Underwood), Pablo Guzman (PabloGuzman Little), Chris Bennett (IPand Teichmann), David Spratley (DaveS Blackadder), and Chris Metcalfe (IP Maximus).

The *Second City* office has a boardroom off the lobby, which can be used for online conferences, a room containing recruiting information from Davis, and a library that will house online legal information.

"I think it will be an evolving process," Lemon said of the online office. "We will use it as a networking tool and as a way to meet clients."

The law firm plans to hold online events in *Second Life*, conduct seminars, and give talks that might be of value to potential clients. ■

Bill Green, shown here at a press conference in Mumbai, India, is the CEO of Accenture, Ltd., the international consulting firm that is also a virtual organization. Green does not maintain a permanent office, and the company has no operational headquarters or branch offices. Its top-level executives are scattered around the world, and many of its employees spend their days travelling to or working with clients in their clients' offices. The company's culture is one of constant motion and its managers thrive on personal contact with clients. "We don't get to go down the hall to the coffee pot, ask someone how their weekend was, and then ask a business question," says Green, who logs hundreds of thousands of air miles in a typical year. "We spend time together in the countries where our clients are, which is more important if you're running a global company."

Network Organizations Another structural option for managers wanting to minimize or eliminate organizational boundaries is the **network organization**, which is a small core organization that outsources major business functions.[42] This approach allows organizations to concentrate on what they do best and to contract out other activities to companies that can do those activities best. Many large organizations use the network structure to outsource manufacturing. Companies such as Cisco Systems, Nike, Ericsson, L.L.Bean, and Reebok have found that they can do hundreds of millions of dollars of business without owning manufacturing facilities. San Jose, California-based Cisco Systems is essentially a research and development company that uses outside suppliers and independent manufacturers to assemble the Internet routers its engineers design. Beaverton, Oregon-based Nike is essentially a product development and marketing company that contracts with outside organizations to manufacture its athletic footwear. Stockholm, Sweden-based Ericsson contracts its manufacturing and even some of its research and development to more cost-effective contractors in New Delhi, Singapore, California, and other global locations.[43]

network organization
A small core organization that outsources major business functions.

While many companies use outsourcing, not all are successful at it. Managers should be aware of some of the problems involved in outsourcing, such as the following:

- Choosing the wrong activities to outsource
- Choosing the wrong vendor
- Writing a poor contract
- Failing to consider personnel issues
- Losing control over the activity
- Ignoring the hidden costs
- Failing to develop an exit strategy (for either moving to another vendor or deciding to bring the activity back in-house)

A review of 91 outsourcing activities found that the most likely reasons for an outsourcing venture to fail were writing a poor contract and losing control of the activity.[44] Canadian managers say they are reluctant to outsource.[45] In a 2004 survey of 603 Canadian companies by Ipsos Reid, 60 percent were not eager to ship software development overseas. While a number of managers said they were concerned with controlling costs (36 percent), almost the same number said they preferred to keep jobs in Canada (32 percent), and one-third were also concerned about losing control of projects that went overseas.

Today's Organizational Design Challenges

As managers look for organizational designs that will best support and facilitate employees doing their work efficiently and effectively in today's dynamic environment, there are certain challenges with which they must contend. These include keeping employees connected, building a learning organization, and managing global structural issues.

Keeping Employees Connected

Many organizational design concepts were developed during the twentieth century, when work tasks were fairly predictable and constant, most jobs were full time and continued indefinitely, and work was done at an employer's place of business under a manager's supervision.[46] That is not what it's like in many organizations today, as you saw in our preceding discussion of virtual and network organizations. A major structural design challenge for managers is finding a way to keep widely dispersed and mobile employees connected to the organization. We cover information on motivating these employees in Chapter 9.

Building a Learning Organization

Doing business in an intensely competitive global environment, managers at British retailer Tesco realize how important it is for stores to operate smoothly behind the scenes. And they do so through the use of a proven tool—a set of software applications called Tesco in a Box, which promotes consistency in operations and acts as a way to share innovations. Tesco is an example of a learning organization, an organization that has developed the capacity to constantly learn, adapt, and change.[47] In a learning organization, employees continually acquire and share new knowledge and apply that knowledge in making decisions or doing their work. Some organizational theorists even go so far as to say that an organization's ability to do this—that is, to learn and to apply that learning—may be the only sustainable source of competitive advantage.[48] What structural characteristics does a learning organization need?

Q&A 9.14
Q&A 9.15

First, it's critical for members in a learning organization to share information and collaborate on work activities throughout the entire organization—across different functional specialties and even at different organizational levels. To do this requires minimal structural and physical barriers. In such a boundaryless environment, employees can work together and collaborate in doing the organization's work the best way they can and learn from each other. Finally, because of this need to collaborate, teams also tend to be an important feature of a learning organization's structural design. Employees work in teams that are empowered to make decisions about doing whatever work needs to be done or resolving issues. With empowered employees and teams, there is little need for "bosses" to direct and control. Instead, managers serve as facilitators, supporters, and advocates.

Managing Global Structural Issues

Are there global differences in organizational structures? Are Australian organizations structured like those in Canada? Are German organizations structured like those in France or Mexico? Given the global nature of today's business environment, this is an issue with which managers need to be familiar. Researchers have concluded that the structures and strategies of organizations worldwide are similar, "while the behavior within them is maintaining its cultural uniqueness."[49] What does this mean for designing effective and efficient structures? When designing or changing structure, managers may need to think about the cultural implications of certain design elements. One study showed that formalization—rules and bureaucratic mechanisms—may be more important in less economically developed countries and less important in more economically developed countries where employees may have higher levels of professional education and skills.[50] Other structural design elements may be affected by cultural differences as well.

A Final Thought

No matter what structural design managers choose for their organization, it should help employees work in the most efficient and effective way possible to meet the organization's goals. After all, the structure is simply a means to an end. To understand your reaction to organizational structure, see *Self-Assessment—What Type of Organizational Structure Do I Prefer?* on pages 160–161, at the end of the chapter.

SUMMARY AND IMPLICATIONS

❶ **What are the major elements of organizational structure?** Organizational structure is the formal arrangement of jobs within an organization. Organizational structures are determined by six key elements: work specialization, departmentalization, chain of command, span of control, centralization and decentralization, and formalization. Decisions made about these elements define how work is organized; how many employees managers supervise; where in the organization decisions are made; and whether employees follow standardized operating procedures or have greater flexibility in how they do their work.

○ ○ ○
○ ○ ○ For Maple Leaf Sports & Entertainment, it makes sense to separate the operation of the four sports teams because of the work specialization involved. For example, the general manager of the Raptors would not necessarily make good decisions about what Maple Leafs players should do to improve their game.

❷ **What factors affect organizational structure?** There is no one best organizational structure. The appropriate structure depends on the organization's strategy (innovation, cost minimization, imitation), its size, the technology it uses (unit production, mass production, or process production), and the degree of environmental uncertainty the organization faces.

○ ○ ○
○ ○ ○ For Maple Leaf Sports & Entertainment, because hockey, basketball, and soccer are in different "industries" with different types of players, it makes sense to organize the teams by industry. Because sports teams are governed by formal rules, the teams have more of a mechanistic structure than an organic one. Each team has a similar organizational structure because size, technology, and environmental uncertainty would not differ in any meaningful way among the teams.

❸ **Beyond traditional organizational designs, how else can organizations be structured?** The traditional structures of organizations are simple, functional, and divisional. Contemporary organizational designs include team structure, matrix and project structures, and boundaryless organizations.

○ ○ ○
○ ○ ○ Maple Leaf Sports & Entertainment follows a traditional divisional structure for its sport teams. Other structures might be used to operate its sports facilities, such as a project structure or a boundaryless organization, because events and ticket sales can be managed in a variety of ways.

Management @ Work

READING FOR COMPREHENSION

1. Describe what is meant by the term *organizational design*.

2. In what ways can management departmentalize? When should one approach be considered over the others?

3. What is the difference between a mechanistic and an organic organization?

4. Why is a simple structure inadequate in large organizations?

5. Describe the characteristics of a boundaryless organization structure.

6. Describe the characteristics of a learning organization. What are its advantages?

LINKING CONCEPTS TO PRACTICE

1. Which do you think is more efficient: a wide or a narrow span of control? Support your decision.

2. "An organization can have no structure." Do you agree or disagree with this statement? Explain.

3. Show how both the functional and matrix structures might create conflict within an organization.

4. Do you think the concept of organizational structure, as described in this chapter, is appropriate for charitable organizations? If yes, which organizational design do you believe to be most appropriate? If no, why not? Explain your position.

5. What effects do you think the characteristics of the boundaryless organization have on employees in today's contemporary organizations?

SELF-ASSESSMENT

What Type of Organizational Structure Do I Prefer?

For each of the following statements, circle your level of agreement or disagreement:[51]

1 = Strongly Disagree 2 = Moderately Disagree 3 = Neither Agree nor Disagree 4 = Moderately Agree 5 = Strongly Agree

I prefer to work in an organization where:

1. Goals are defined by those at higher levels.	1 2 3 4 5
2. Clear job descriptions exist for every job.	1 2 3 4 5
3. Top management makes important decisions.	1 2 3 4 5
4. Promotions and pay increases are based as much on length of service as on level of performance.	1 2 3 4 5
5. Clear lines of authority and responsibility are established.	1 2 3 4 5
6. My career is pretty well laid out for me.	1 2 3 4 5
7. I have a great deal of job security.	1 2 3 4 5
8. I can specialize.	1 2 3 4 5
9. My boss is readily available.	1 2 3 4 5
10. Organization rules and regulations are clearly specified.	1 2 3 4 5
11. Information rigidly follows the chain of command.	1 2 3 4 5

12. There is a minimal number of new tasks for me to learn.　　1　2　3　4　5

13. Work groups incur little turnover in members.　　1　2　3　4　5

14. People accept the authority of a leader's position.　　1　2　3　4　5

15. I am part of a group whose training and skills are similar to mine.　　1　2　3　4　5

Scoring Key

Add up the numbers for each of your responses to get your total score.

Analysis and Interpretation

This instrument measures your preference for working in a mechanistic or an organic organizational structure.

Scores above 60 suggest that you prefer a mechanistic structure. Scores below 45 indicate a preference for an organic structure. Scores between 45 and 60 suggest no clear preference.

Because the trend in recent years has been toward more organic structures, you are more likely to find a good organizational match if you score low on this instrument. However, there are few, if any, pure organic structures. Therefore, very low scores may also mean that you are likely to be frustrated by what you perceive as overly rigid structures of rules, regulations, and boss-centred leadership. In general, however, low scores indicate that you prefer small, innovative, flexible, team-oriented organizations. High scores indicate a preference for stable, rule-oriented, more bureaucratic organizations.

More Self-Assessments

To learn more about your skills, abilities, and interests, take the following self-assessments on MyManagementLab at www.pearsoned.ca/mymanagementlab:

- III.A.2.—How Willing Am I to Delegate?
- III.A.3.—How Good Am I at Giving Performance Feedback?
- IV.F.1.—Is My Workplace Political?
- IV.F.2.—Do I Like Bureaucracy?

MANAGEMENT FOR YOU TODAY

Dilemma

Choose an organization for which you have worked. How did the structure of your job and the organization affect your job satisfaction? Did the tasks within your job make sense? In what ways could they be better organized? What structural changes would you make to this organization? Would you consider making this a taller or flatter organization (that is, would you increase or decrease the span of control)? How would the changes you have proposed improve responsiveness to customers and your job satisfaction?

Becoming a Manager

- If you belong to a student organization or are employed, notice how various activities and events are organized through the use of work specialization, chain of command, authority, responsibility, and so forth.

- As you read current business periodicals, note what types of organizational structures businesses use and whether or not they are effective.

- Talk to managers about how they organize work and what they have found to be effective.

- Since delegating is part of decentralizing and is an important management skill, complete the *Developing Your Interpersonal Skills—Delegating* module on pages 164–165. Then practise delegating in various situations.

- Look for examples of organizational charts (visual representations of organizations' structures), and use them to try to determine what structural design the organization is using.

How Is Your School Organized?

Every university or college displays a specific type of organization structure. For example, if you are a business major, your classes are often housed in a department, school, or faculty of business. But have you ever asked why? Or is it something you just take for granted?

In Chapter 3 you had an opportunity to assess your college or university's strengths, weaknesses, and competitive advantage and see how these fit into its strategy. Now, in this chapter, we have argued that structure follows strategy. Given your analysis in Chapter 3 (if you have not done so, you may want to refer to pages 95–96 for the strategy part of this exercise), analyze your college or university's overall structure in terms of its degree of formalization, centralization/ decentralization, and complexity. Furthermore, look at the departmentalization that exists. Is your college or university more organic or mechanistic? Now analyze how well your college or university's structure fits with its strategy. Do the same thing for your college or university's size, technology, and environment. That is, assess its size, degree of technological routineness, and environmental uncertainty. Based on these assessments, what kind of structure would you predict that your college or university has? Does it have this structure now? Compare your findings with those of other classmates. Are there similarities in how each viewed the college or university? Differences? To what do you attribute these findings?

ETHICS IN ACTION

Ethical Dilemma Exercise: Is "Just Following Orders" a Valid Defence?

Is a manager acting unethically by simply following orders within the chain of command?[52] One recent survey of human resource managers found that 52 percent of the respondents felt some pressure to bend ethical rules, often because of orders from above or to achieve ambitious goals. This might happen in any organization. At WorldCom, for example, Betty Vinson was a senior manager when she and others received orders, through the chain of command, to slash expenses through improper accounting. She argued against the move. Her manager said he had also objected and was told this was a one-time "fix" to make WorldCom's finances look better. Vinson reluctantly agreed, but she felt guilty and told her manager she wanted to resign. A senior executive persuaded her to stay, and she continued following orders to fudge the accounting.

Soon Vinson realized that the figures would need fudging for some time. After investigators started to probe WorldCom's finances, she and others cooperated with regulators and prosecutors. Ultimately, the company was forced into bankruptcy. Some managers were indicted; some (including Vinson) pleaded guilty to conspiracy and fraud.

Imagine that you are a salesperson at a major corporation. Your manager invites you to an expensive restaurant where she is entertaining several colleagues and their spouses. The manager orders you to put the meal on your expense account as a customer dinner. She says she will approve the expense so that you are reimbursed, and higher-level managers will not know that managers and their spouses were in attendance. What would you do? (Review this chapter's Chain of Command section, on pages 143–144, as you consider your decision.)

Thinking Critically About Ethics

Changes in technology have cut the shelf life of most employees' skills. A factory or clerical worker used to be able to learn one job and be reasonably sure that the skills acquired to do that job would be enough for most of his or her work years. That is no longer the case. What ethical obligation do organizations have to assist employees whose skills have become obsolete? What about employees? Do they have an obligation to keep their skills from becoming obsolete? What ethical guidelines might you suggest for dealing with employee skill obsolescence?

Hewlett-Packard

Best known for its printers, cameras, calculators, and computers, Hewlett-Packard (HP) has had its share of organizing challenges over the years.[53] Carly Fiorina, who was named CEO of HP in 1999—a move that made news headlines because HP was one of the first major US corporations to be headed by a woman—continued the company's strategy of growing by acquiring businesses. Her most controversial acquisition was the $25 billion purchase of rival Compaq Computers—a decision that was the beginning of the end for Fiorina. The combined companies experienced many problems—financial, cultural, and structural—resulting in poor performance. Her differences with the company's board of directors over the direction HP was going finally led to her firing in early February 2005. By the end of March 2005, Mark Hurd, CEO of NCR, had been selected by the board as the new CEO of HP.

A few weeks after arriving at HP, Hurd began hearing complaints about the company's sales force. At a retreat "with 25 top corporate customers, several of them told Hurd they didn't know whom to call at HP because of the company's confusing management layers." He also heard the same complaints inside the organization. The company's head of corporate technology told Hurd that "it once took her three months to get approval to hire 100 sales specialists." Another executive said that "his team of 700 salespeople typically spent 33 percent to 36 percent of their time with customers. The rest of the time was spent negotiating internal HP bureaucracy." Even the sales reps said that they did not get to spend time with customers because they were "often burdened with administrative tasks." Getting a price quote or a sample product to a customer became a time-consuming ordeal. It did not take Hurd long to realize that there was a "fundamental problem" that he had to address.

Delving into HP's sales structure, Hurd found 11 layers of management between him and customers—way too many, he decided. And the company's sales structure was highly inefficient. For example, in Europe, HP had four people from different departments working to close a sales deal while competitors typically had only three people. "That meant HP was slower to cut a deal and lost many bids." And the final issue Hurd uncovered: Of the 17 000 people working in corporate sales, less than 60 percent of them directly sold to customers. The rest were support staff or in management.

How should Hurd restructure HP to restore it to its former position as an industry leader?

A New Kind of Structure

Admit it.[54] Sometimes the projects you are working on (school, work, or both) can get pretty boring and monotonous. Wouldn't it be nice to have a magic button you could push to get someone else to do the boring, time-consuming stuff for you? At Pfizer, such a button is a reality for a large number of employees.

As a global pharmaceutical company, Pfizer is continually looking for ways to be more efficient and effective. The company's senior director of organizational effectiveness, Jordan Cohen, found that the "Harvard MBA staff we hired to develop strategies and innovate were instead Googling and making PowerPoints." Indeed, internal studies conducted to find out just how much time its valuable talent was spending on menial tasks was startling. The average Pfizer employee was spending 20 to 40 percent of his or her time on support work (creating documents, typing notes, doing research, manipulating data, scheduling meetings) and only 60 to 80 percent on knowledge work (strategy, innovation, networking, collaborating, critical thinking). And the problem wasn't just at lower levels. Even the highest-level employees were affected. That's when Cohen began looking for solutions. The solution he chose turned out to be the numerous knowledge-process outsourcing companies based in India.

Initial tests of outsourcing the support tasks did not go well at all. However, Cohen continued to tweak the process until everything worked. Now Pfizer employees can click the OOF (Office of the Future) button in Microsoft Outlook, and they are connected to an outsourcing company where a single worker in India receives the request and assigns it to a team. The team leader calls the employee to clarify the request. The team leader then emails back a cost specification for the requested work. At this point, the Pfizer employee can say yes or no. Cohen says that the benefits of OOF are unexpected. Time spent on analysis of data has been cut—sometimes in half. The financial benefits are also impressive. And Pfizer employees love it. Cohen says, "It's kind of amazing. I wonder what they used to do."

Questions

1. Describe and evaluate what Pfizer is doing.

2. What structural implications—good and bad—does this approach have? (Think in terms of the six organizational design elements.)

3. Do you think this arrangement would work for other types of organizations? Why or why not?

4. What role do you think organizational structure plays in an organization's efficiency and effectiveness? Explain.

DEVELOPING YOUR INTERPERSONAL SKILLS

Delegating

About the Skill

Managers get things done through other people. Because there are limits to any manager's time and knowledge, effective managers need to understand how to delegate. Delegation is the assignment of authority to another person to carry out specific duties. It allows an employee to make some of the decisions. Delegation should not be confused with participation. In participative decision making, there is a sharing of authority. In delegation, employees make decisions on their own.

Steps in Developing the Skill

A number of actions differentiate the effective delegator from the ineffective delegator. You can be more effective at delegating if you use the following five suggestions:[55]

1. **Clarify the assignment.** Determine what is to be delegated and to whom. You need to identify the person who is most capable of doing the task and then determine whether or not he or she has the time and motivation to do the task. If you have a willing and able employee, it's your responsibility to provide clear information on what is being delegated, the results you expect, and any time or performance expectations you may have. Unless there is an overriding need to adhere to specific methods, you should delegate only the results expected. Get agreement on what is to be done and the results expected, but let the employee decide the best way to complete the task.

2. **Specify the employee's range of discretion.** Every situation of delegation comes with constraints. Although you are delegating to an employee the authority to perform some task or tasks, you are not delegating unlimited authority. You are delegating authority to act on certain issues within certain parameters. You need to specify what those parameters are so that employees know, without any doubt, the range of their discretion.

3. **Allow the employee to participate.** One of the best ways to decide how much authority will be necessary to accomplish a task is to allow the employee who will be held accountable for that task to participate in that decision. Be aware, however, that allowing employees to participate can present its own set of potential problems as a result of employees' self-interests and biases in evaluating their own abilities.

4. **Inform others about the delegation.** Delegation should not take place behind the scenes. Not only do the manager and employee need to know specifically what has been delegated and how much authority has been given, but so does anyone else who is likely to be affected by the employee's decisions and actions. This includes people inside and outside the organization. Essentially, you need to communicate what has been delegated (the task and amount of authority) and to whom.

5. **Establish feedback channels.** To delegate without establishing feedback controls is to invite problems. The establishment of controls to monitor the employee's performance increases the likelihood that important problems will be identified and that the task will be completed on time and to the desired specifications. Ideally, these controls should be determined at the time of the initial assignment. Agree on a specific time for the completion of the task and then set progress

dates on which the employee will report back on how well he or she is doing and any major problems that may have arisen. These controls can be supplemented with periodic checks to ensure that authority guidelines are not being abused, organizational policies are being followed, proper procedures are being met, and the like.

Practising the Skill

Ricky Lee is the manager of the contracts group of a large regional office-supply distributor. His manager, Anne Zumwalt, has asked him to prepare, by the end of the month, the department's new procedures manual that will outline the steps followed in negotiating contracts with office products manufacturers who supply the organization's products. Because Ricky has another major project he is working on, he went to Anne and asked her if it would be possible to assign the rewriting of the procedures manual to Bill Harmon, one of his employees who has worked in the contracts group for about three years. Anne said she had no problems with Ricky reassigning the project as long as Bill knew the parameters and the expectations for the completion of the project. Ricky is preparing for his meeting in the morning with Bill regarding this assignment. Prepare an outline of what Ricky should discuss with Bill to ensure the new procedures manual meets expectations.

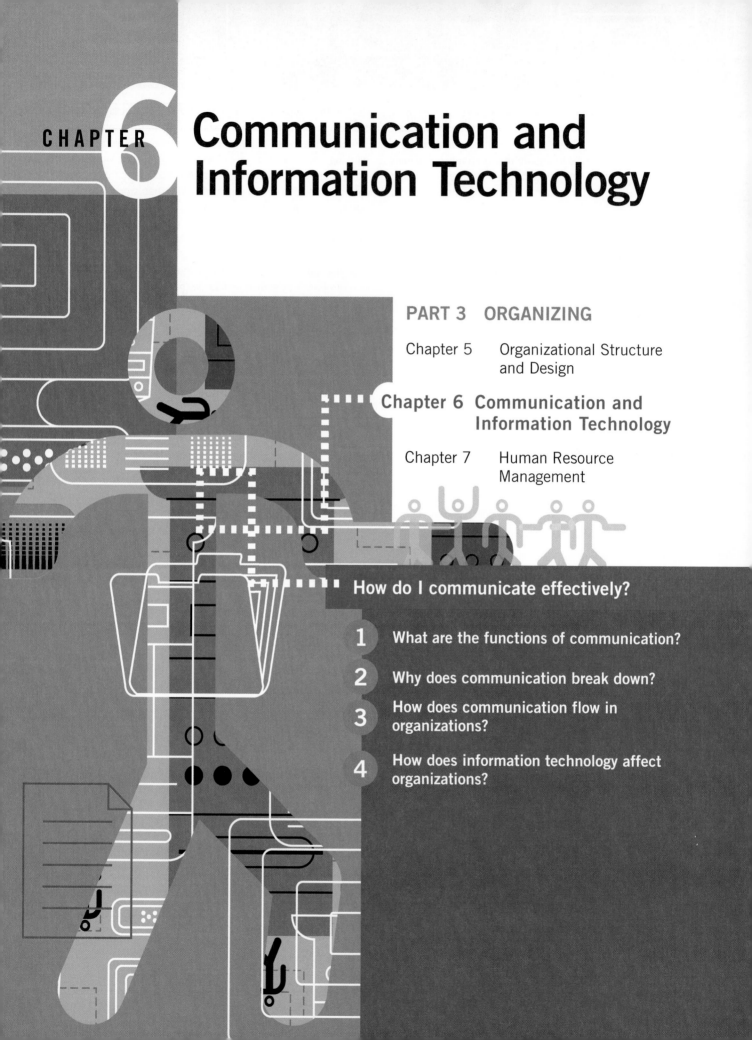

CHAPTER **6** Communication and Information Technology

How do I communicate effectively?

1 What are the functions of communication?

2 Why does communication break down?

3 How does communication flow in organizations?

4 How does information technology affect organizations?

Facebook, the social networking website, was started in 1995 as a way for university students to connect with each other online.[1] Users could post photos and information about themselves, and keep in contact with friends.

Currently, less than half of Facebook's 24 million members worldwide are in university. Nearly 3 million Canadians use Facebook, with more than half logging in daily. Canada is second only to the United States in the numbers of people on Facebook, and Toronto has the largest regional network in the world (637 956 members in 2007).

Facebook is starting to be recognized as a multi-faceted tool by the business community. Some employers pre-screen job applicants by searching their Facebook profile. "At its core, Facebook is a place to share information and communicate and people are really starting to see it as an effective utility in their lives," says Brandee Barker, director of communications for Facebook. Brian Drum, president of the New York–based executive search firm Drum Associates, says that sites such as Facebook make it easy to do "subtle" background checks. "Employers can go to these sites and see what people are saying about themselves," he says. Employers are also starting to create their own company networks on Facebook, where only those with the company's email address can join. This allows employees to use Facebook features to communicate.

Think About It

Can social networking websites enhance communication in the workplace? How might social networking websites affect communication in organizations? What risks might using Facebook pose to graduating students looking for their first major job?

Communication between managers and employees provides the information necessary to get work done effectively and efficiently in organizations. As such, there is no doubt that communication is fundamentally linked to managerial performance.[2] In this chapter, we present basic concepts in managerial communication. We describe the interpersonal communication process, distortions that can happen in interpersonal communication, the channels of communication, as well as the barriers to effective interpersonal communication and ways to overcome those barriers. We look at how communication flows in organizations, communication networks, and the effects of information technology on organizational communication.

Understanding Communication

If you have not studied communication before, you might think it's a pretty normal process, and that almost anyone can communicate effectively without much thought. So many things can go wrong with communication, though, that it's clear not everyone thinks about how to communicate effectively. For example, unlike the character Bill Murray plays in *Groundhog Day*, Neal L. Patterson, chair and CEO of Cerner, a health care

❶ What are the functions of communication?

software development company based in Kansas City, probably wishes he *could* do over one particular day. Upset with the fact that employees did not seem to be putting in enough hours, he sent an angry and emotional email to about 400 company managers that said, in part:

> We are getting less than 40 hours of work from a large number of our K.C.-based EMPLOYEES. The parking lot is sparsely used at 8 a.m.; likewise at 5 p.m. As managers, you either do not know what your EMPLOYEES are doing, or you do not CARE. You have created expectations on the work effort which allowed this to happen inside Cerner, creating a very unhealthy environment. In either case, you have a problem and you will fix it or I will replace you. . . . I will hold you accountable. You have allowed things to get to this state. You have two weeks. Tick, tock.[3]

Patterson had a message, and he wanted to get it out to his managers. Although the email was meant only for the company's managers, it was leaked and posted on a Yahoo! discussion site. The tone of the email surprised industry analysts, investors, and, of course, Cerner's managers and employees. The company's stock price dropped 22 percent over the next three days. Patterson apologized to his employees and acknowledged, "I lit a match and started a firestorm." This is a good example of why it's important for individuals to understand the impact of communication.

The importance of effective communication for managers cannot be overemphasized for one specific reason: Everything a manager does involves communicating. Not *some* things, but everything! A manager cannot make a decision without information. That information has to be communicated. Once a decision is made, communication must again take place. Otherwise, no one would know that a decision was made. The best idea, the most creative suggestion, the best plan, or the most effective job redesign cannot take shape without communication. Managers need effective communication skills. We are not suggesting that good communication skills alone make a successful manager. We can say, however, that ineffective communication skills can lead to a continuous stream of problems for a manager.

What Is Communication?

communication
The transfer and understanding of meaning.

Communication is the transfer and understanding of meaning. The first thing to note about this definition is the emphasis on the *transfer* of meaning. This means that if no information or ideas have been conveyed, communication has not taken place. The speaker who is not heard or the writer who is not read has not communicated.

More importantly, however, communication involves the *understanding* of meaning. For communication to be successful, the meaning must be conveyed and understood. A letter written in Portuguese addressed to a person who does not read Portuguese cannot be considered communication until it's translated into a language the person does read and understand. Perfect communication, if such a thing existed, occurs when the receiver understands a transmitted thought or idea exactly as it was intended by the sender.

Q&A 10.1

Another point to keep in mind is that *good* communication is often erroneously defined by the communicator as *agreement* with the message instead of clearly *understanding* the message.[4] If someone disagrees with us, many of us assume that the person just did not fully understand our position. In other words, many of us define good communication as having someone accept our views. But I can clearly understand what you mean and just *not* agree with what you say. In fact, many times when a conflict has gone on for a long time, people will say it's because the parties are not communicating effectively. That assumption reflects the tendency to think that effective communication equals agreement.

interpersonal communication
Communication between two or more people.

organizational communication
All the patterns, networks, and systems of communication within an organization.

The final point we want to make about communication is that it encompasses both **interpersonal communication**—communication between two or more people—and **organizational communication**—all the patterns, networks, and systems of communication within an organization. Both these types of communication are important to managers in organizations.

Functions of Communication

Why is communication important to managers and organizations? It serves four major functions: control, motivation, emotional expression, and information.[5]

Communication acts to *control* member behaviour in several ways. As we know from Chapter 5, organizations have authority hierarchies and formal guidelines that employees are required to follow. For example, when employees are required to communicate any job-related grievance first to their immediate manager, or to follow their job description, or to comply with company policies, communication is being used to control. But informal communication also controls behaviour. When work groups tease or harass a member who is working too hard or producing too much (making the rest of the group look bad), they are informally controlling the member's behaviour.

Communication encourages *motivation* by clarifying to employees what is to be done, how well they are doing, and what can be done to improve performance if it's not up to par. As employees set specific goals, work toward those goals, and receive feedback on their progress, communication is required. Managers motivate more effectively if they show support for the employee when communicating constructive feedback, rather than mere criticism.

For many employees, their work group is a primary source of social interaction. The communication that takes place within the group is a fundamental mechanism by which members share frustrations and feelings of satisfaction. Communication, therefore, provides a release for *emotional expression* of feelings and for fulfillment of social needs.

If you have ever had a bad haircut, you have probably never forgotten the experience. And you might never have returned to the stylist again. Dorys Belanger, owner of Montreal-based Au Premier Spa Urbain, says that a bad haircut should not be blamed on the stylist alone. Good communication is "50 percent up to the hairdresser, 50 percent up to the client," she says.

Finally, individuals and groups need *information* to get things done in organizations. Communication provides that information.

No one of these four functions is more important than the others. For groups to work effectively, they need to maintain some form of control over members, motivate members to perform, provide a means for emotional expression, and make decisions. You can assume that almost every communication interaction that takes place in a group or organization is fulfilling one or more of these four functions.

Interpersonal Communication

Facebook encourages online interaction rather than face-to-face communication.[6] Because Facebook users write rather than speak directly to each other, they may feel safer saying something on their Facebook page than they would in person. There is concern that these less personal interactions may lead to poorer-quality relationships with fewer emotional rewards.[7]

Individuals might also inadvertently incriminate themselves. The Ontario Provincial Police have used the site to find out about parties that might have illegal drug use and underage drinking. Facebook makes it easy—it makes such party plans instantly available and provides directions to the location on the site.

Following the lead of Queen's Park and Parliament Hill, the City of Toronto banned its employees from using Facebook while at work in May 2007, because it had become so popular. Managers wanted to remove the temptation to waste "an inordinate amount of time."

Think About It

What effect will the growing use of online social networking sites have on people's ability to communicate face to face? Can online social networking lead people to forget to consider the consequences of their communication?

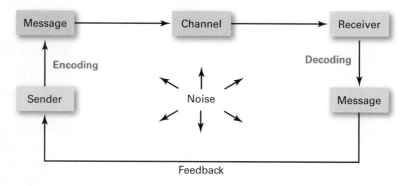

Exhibit 6-1

The Interpersonal Communication Process

2 Why does communication break down?

message
A purpose to be conveyed.

encoding
Converting a message into symbols.

channel
The medium a message travels along.

decoding
A receiver's translation of a sender's message.

communication process
The seven elements involved in transferring meaning from one person to another.

noise
Disturbances that interfere with the transmission, receipt, or feedback of a message.

Before communication can take place, a purpose, expressed as a **message** to be conveyed, must exist. It passes between a source (the sender) and a receiver. The message is converted into symbols (called **encoding**) and passed by way of some medium (**channel**) to the receiver, who translates the sender's message (called **decoding**). The result is the transfer of meaning from one person to another.[8] Exhibit 6-1 illustrates the seven elements of the interpersonal **communication process**: the sender, the message, encoding, the channel, the receiver, decoding, and feedback. In addition, note that **noise**—disturbances that interfere with the transmission, receipt, or feedback of a message—can affect the entire process. Typical examples of noise include external factors such as illegible print, phone static, or background sounds of machinery or co-workers. However, noise can be the result of internal factors such as inattention of the receiver, as well as perceptions and personality traits of the receiver. Remember that anything that interferes with understanding can be noise, and noise can create distortion at any point in the communication process.

How Distortions Can Happen in Interpersonal Communication

Distortions can happen with the sender, the message, the channel, the receiver, or the feedback loop. Let's look at each.

Sender

A *sender* initiates a message by *encoding* a thought. Four conditions influence the effectiveness of that encoded message: the skills, attitudes, and knowledge of the sender, and the socio-cultural system. How? We will use ourselves, as your textbook authors, as an example. If we do not have the required skills, our message will not reach you, the reader, in the form desired. Our success in communicating to you depends on our writing skills. In addition, any pre-existing ideas (attitudes) that we may have about numerous topics will affect how we communicate. For example, our attitudes about managerial ethics or the importance of managers to organizations influence our writing. Next, the amount of knowledge we have about a subject affects the message(s) we are transferring. We cannot communicate what we do not know; and if our knowledge is too extensive, it's possible that our writing will not be understood by the readers. Finally, the socio-cultural system in which we live influences us as communication senders. Our beliefs and values (all part of culture) act to influence what and how we communicate.

Message

The *message* itself can distort the communication process, regardless of the kinds of supporting tools or technologies used to convey it. A message is the actual physical product encoded by the source. It can be a written document, a speech, or even the gestures and facial expressions we make. The message is affected by the symbols used to transfer meaning (words, pictures, numbers, etc.), the content of the message itself, and the decisions that the sender makes in selecting and arranging both the symbols and the content. Noise can distort the communication process in any of these areas.

Channel

> Your instructor chooses to interact with all students via email, rather than hold office hours. How effective do you think email is as the channel of communication in this context?

The *channel* chosen to communicate the message also has the potential to be affected by noise. Whether it's a face-to-face conversation, an email message, or a company-wide memo, distortions can, and do, occur. Managers need to recognize that certain channels are more appropriate for certain messages. (Think back to how Cerner's CEO chose to communicate his frustration with his managers by email and whether that was an appropriate choice.) Obviously, if the office is on fire, a memo to convey that fact is inappropriate. And if something is important, such as an employee's performance appraisal, a manager might want to use multiple channels—perhaps an oral review followed by a written letter summarizing the points. Using multiple channels to communicate a message decreases the potential for distortion. In general, the type of channel chosen will affect the extent to which accurate emotional expression can be communicated. For example, individuals often make stronger negative statements when using email than they would in holding a face-to-face conversation.[9] Additionally, individuals often give little thought to how their emails might be interpreted, and assume that their intent will be readily apparent to the recipient, even though this is not always the case.[10]

Receiver

The *receiver* is the individual to whom the message is directed. Before the message can be received, however, the symbols in it must be translated into a form that the receiver can understand. This is the *decoding* of the message. Just as the sender was limited by his or her skills, attitudes, knowledge, and socio-cultural system, so is the receiver. And just as the sender must be skillful in writing or speaking, so the receiver must be skillful in reading or listening. A person's knowledge influences his or her ability to receive. Moreover, the receiver's attitudes and socio-cultural background can distort the message. *Managing Workforce Diversity—The Communication Styles of Men and Women* on page 193, at the end of the chapter, considers how men and women might hear messages differently.

Feedback Loop

The final link in the communication process is a *feedback loop*. Feedback returns the message to the sender and provides a check on whether understanding has been achieved. Because feedback can be transmitted along the same types of channels as the original message, it faces the same potential for distortion. Many receivers forget that there is a responsibility involved in communication: to give feedback. If you sit in a boring lecture but never discuss with the instructor ways that the delivery could be improved, you have not engaged in communication with your instructor.

When either the sender or the receiver fails to engage in the feedback process, the communication is effectively one-way communication. Two-way communication involves both talking and listening. Many managers communicate poorly because they fail to use two-way communication.[11]

Channels for Communicating Interpersonally

Managers have a wide variety of communication channels from which to choose. These include face-to-face, telephone, group meetings, formal presentations, memos, postal

Q&A 10.2

Are there any guidelines on which communication channel is best for a given circumstance?

(snail) mail, fax machines, employee publications, bulletin boards, other company publications, audio- and video-tapes, hotlines, email, computer conferences, voice mail, teleconferences, and videoconferences. All of these communication channels include oral or written symbols, or both. How do you know which to use? Managers can use 12 questions to help them evaluate appropriate communication channels for different circumstances.[12]

1. *Feedback.* How quickly can the receiver respond to the message?

2. *Complexity capacity.* Can the method effectively process complex messages?

3. *Breadth potential.* How many different messages can be transmitted using this method?

4. *Confidentiality.* Can communicators be reasonably sure their messages are received only by those for whom they are intended?

5. *Encoding ease.* Can the sender easily and quickly use this channel?

6. *Decoding ease.* Can the receiver easily and quickly decode messages?

7. *Time–space constraint.* Do senders and receivers need to communicate at the same time and in the same space?

8. *Cost.* How much does it cost to use this method?

9. *Interpersonal warmth.* How well does this method convey interpersonal warmth?

10. *Formality.* Does this method have the needed amount of formality?

11. *Scanability.* Does this method allow the message to be easily browsed or scanned for relevant information?

12. *Time of consumption.* Does the sender or receiver exercise the most control over when the message is dealt with?

Exhibit 6-2 provides a comparison of the various communication channels based on these 12 criteria. Which channel a manager ultimately chooses should reflect the needs of the sender, the attributes of the message, the attributes of the channel, and the needs of the receiver. For example, if you need to communicate to an employee the changes being made in her job, face-to-face communication would be a better choice than a memo, because you want to be able to immediately address any questions and concerns that she might have. To find out more about face-to-face communication, see *Self-Assessment—What's My Face-to-Face Communication Style?* on pages 187–189, at the end of the chapter.

We cannot leave the topic of interpersonal communication without looking at the role of **nonverbal communication**—that is, communication transmitted without words. Some of the most meaningful communications are neither spoken nor written. A loud siren or a red light at an intersection tells you something without words. When an instructor is teaching a class, she does not need words to tell her that her students are bored when their eyes are glazed over or they begin to read the school newspaper in the middle of class. Similarly, when students start putting their papers, notebooks, and books away, the message is clear: Class time is just about over. The size of a person's office or the clothes he or she wears also convey messages to others. These are all forms of nonverbal communication. The best-known types of nonverbal communication are body language and verbal intonation.

Body language refers to gestures, facial expressions, and other body movements that convey meaning. A person frowning "says" something different from one who is smiling. Hand motions, facial expressions, and other gestures can communicate emotions or temperaments such as aggression, fear, shyness, arrogance, joy, and anger. Knowing the meaning behind someone's body movements and learning how to put forth your best

nonverbal communication
Communication transmitted without words.

body language
Gestures, facial expressions, and other body movements that convey meaning.

Comparison of Communication Channels

Channel	Feedback Potential	Complexity Capacity	Breadth Potential	Confiden-tiality	Encoding Ease	Decoding Ease	Time–Space Constraint	Cost	Interpersonal Warmth	Formality	Scan-ability	Consumption Time
Face-to-face	1	1	1	1	1	1	1	2	1	4	4	S/R
Telephone	1	4	2	2	1	1	3	3	2	4	4	S/R
Group meetings	2	2	2	4	2	2	1	1	2	3	4	S/R
Formal presentations	4	2	2	4	3	2	1	1	3	3	5	Sender
Memos	4	4	2	3	4	3	5	3	5	2	1	Receiver
Postal mail	5	3	3	2	4	3	5	3	4	1	1	Receiver
Fax	3	4	2	4	3	3	5	3	3	3	1	Receiver
Publications	5	4	2	5	5	3	5	2	4	1	1	Receiver
Bulletin boards	4	5	1	5	3	2	2	4	5	3	1	Receiver
Audio files/DVD videos	4	4	3	5	4	2	3	2	3	3	5	Receiver
Hot lines	2	5	2	2	3	1	4	2	3	3	4	Receiver
Email	3	4	1	2	3	2	4	2	4	3	4	Receiver
Computer conference	1	2	2	4	3	2	3	2	3	3	4	S/R
Voice mail	2	4	2	1	2	1	5	3	2	4	4	Receiver
Teleconference	2	3	2	5	2	2	2	2	3	3	5	S/R
Videoconference	3	3	2	4	2	2	2	1	2	3	5	S/R

Note: Ratings are on a 1–5 scale where 1 = high and 5 = low. Consumption time refers to who controls the reception of communication. S/R means the sender and receiver share control.

Source: P. G. Clampitt, *Communicating for Managerial Effectiveness* (Newbury Park, CA: Sage Publications, 1991), p. 136.

Does body language really affect how communication is received?

body language can help you personally and profession-ally.[13] For example, studies indicate that those who main-tain eye contact while speaking are viewed with more credibility than those whose eyes wander. People who make eye contact are also deemed more competent than those who do not.

Be aware that what is communicated nonverbally may be quite different from what is communicated verbally. A manager may say it's a good time to discuss a raise, but then keep looking at the clock. This nonverbal signal may indicate that the manager has other things to do right now. Thus, actions can speak louder (and more accurately) than words.

A variety of popular books have been written to help one interpret body language. However, do use some care when interpreting these messages. For example, while it is often thought that crossing one's arms in front of one's chest shows resistance to a mes-sage, it might also mean the person is feeling cold.

verbal intonation
An emphasis given to words or phrases that conveys meaning.

filtering
The deliberate manipulation of information to make it appear more favourable to the receiver.

Verbal intonation (more appropriately called *paralinguistics*) refers to the emphasis someone gives to words or phrases that conveys meaning. To illustrate how intonation can change the meaning of a message, consider the student who asks the instructor a question. The instructor replies, "What do you mean by that?" The student's reaction will vary, depending on the tone of the instructor's response. A soft, smooth vocal tone con-veys interest and creates a different meaning from one that is abrasive and puts a strong emphasis on saying the last word. Most of us would view the first intonation as coming from someone sincerely interested in clarifying the student's concern, whereas the second suggests that the person is defensive or aggressive.

Q&A 10.3

The fact that every oral communication also has a nonverbal message cannot be overemphasized. Why? Because the nonverbal component usually carries the greatest im-pact. "It's not *what* you said, but *how* you said it." People respond to *how* something is said as well as *what* is said. Managers should remember this as they communicate.

Barriers to Effective Interpersonal Communication

In addition to the general distortions identified in the communication process, managers face other barriers to effective interpersonal communication.

Filtering

Filtering is the deliberate manipulation of information to make it appear more favourable to the receiver. For ex-ample, when a person tells his or her manager what the manager wants to hear, that individual is filtering infor-mation. Does this happen much in organizations? Yes, it does! As information is communicated up through organizational levels, it's condensed and synthesized by senders so those on top do not become overloaded with information. Those doing the condensing filter commu-nications through their personal interests and their per-ceptions of what is important.

Filtering, or shaping information to make it look good to the receiver, might not always be intentional. For John Seral, vice-president and chief information officer of GE Energy, the problem was that "when the CEO asked how the quarter was looking, he got a different answer depending on whom he asked." Seral solved the problem by building a continuously updated data-base of the company's most important financial information that gives not just the CEO but also 300 company managers instant access to sales and operating figures on their PCs and BlackBerrys. Instead of dozens of analysts compiling the information, the new system requires only six.

The extent of filtering tends to be a function of the number of vertical levels in the organization and the organizational culture. The more vertical levels there are in an organization, the more opportunities there are for filtering. As organizations become less dependent on strict hierarchical arrangements and instead use more col-laborative, cooperative work arrangements, information filtering may become less of a problem. In addition, the ever-increasing use of email to communicate in organizations reduces filtering because communication is more direct as intermediaries are bypassed. Finally, the organizational culture encourages or discourages filtering by the type of behaviour it rewards. The more that organizational rewards emphasize style and appearance, the more managers will be motivated to filter communications in their favour.

Q&A 10.4

Emotions

How a receiver feels when a message is received influences how he or she interprets it. You will often interpret the same message differently, depending on whether you are happy or upset. Extreme emotions are most likely to hinder effective communication. In such instances, we often disregard our rational and objective thinking processes and substitute emotional judgments. It's best to avoid reacting to a message when you are upset because you are not likely to be thinking clearly.

Information Overload

A marketing manager goes on a week-long trip to Spain and does not have access to his email. On his return, he is faced with 1000 email messages. It's not possible to fully read and respond to each and every one of those messages without facing **information overload**—a situation in which information exceeds a person's processing capacity. Today's typical executive frequently complains of information overload. Email has added considerably to the number of hours worked per week, according to a recent study by Christina Cavanagh, professor of management communications at the University of Western Ontario's Richard Ivey School of Business.[14] Researchers calculate that 141 billion email messages circulate the globe each day. In 2001, that number was 5.1 billion email messages.[15] One researcher suggests that knowledge workers devote about 28 percent of their days to email.[16] The demands of keeping up with email, phone calls, faxes, meetings, and professional reading create an onslaught of data that is nearly impossible to process and assimilate. What happens when individuals have more information than they can sort and use? They tend to select out, ignore, pass over, or forget information. Or they may put off further processing until the overload situation is over. Regardless, the result is lost information and less effective communication.

information overload
A situation in which information exceeds a person's processing capacity.

Q&A 10.5

Selective Perception

Individuals don't see reality; rather, they interpret what they see and call it "reality." These interpretations are based on an individual's needs, motivations, experience, background, and other personal characteristics. Individuals also project their interests and expectations when they are listening to others. For example, the employment interviewer who believes that young people spend too much time on leisure and social activities will have a hard time believing that young job applicants will work long hours.

Q&A 10.6

Defensiveness

When people feel that they are being threatened, they tend to react in ways that reduce their ability to achieve mutual understanding. That is, they become defensive—engaging in behaviours such as verbally attacking others, making sarcastic remarks, being overly judgmental, and questioning others' motives.[17] When individuals interpret another's message as threatening, they often respond in ways that hinder effective communication.

Language

Words mean different things to different people. Age, education, and cultural background are three of the more obvious variables that influence the language a person uses and the definitions he or she gives to words. Television news anchor Peter Mansbridge and rap artist Nelly both speak English, but the language each uses is vastly different.

In an organization, employees typically come from diverse backgrounds and have different patterns of speech. Even employees who work for the same organization but in different departments often have different **jargon**—specialized terminology or technical language that members of a group use to communicate among themselves. Keep in mind

jargon
Specialized terminology or technical language that members of a group use to communicate among themselves.

that while we may speak the same language, our use of that language is far from uniform. Senders tend to assume that the words and phrases they use mean the same to the receiver as they do to themselves. This, of course, is incorrect and creates communication barriers. Knowing how each of us modifies the language would help minimize those barriers.

Q&A 10.7

Executives at Montreal-based Yellow Pages learned that they could produce better printed telephone directories by studying how online users searched for things—demonstrating that customers and advertisers do not always think in the same categories, as this *Management Reflection* shows.

MANAGEMENT REFLECTION

Finding Sushi

Should we look under "sushi" or "restaurants—Japanese" in the phone book when we decide we want raw fish for dinner? Paying attention to how people search for information online can give clearer insights into what organizations need to do to communicate more effectively.[18] Executives at Montreal-based Yellow Pages Group learned this by recording how people searched for telephone listings.

Until recently, sushi restaurants were listed under "restaurants—Japanese" or "restaurants—seafood" in the hard-copy version of the Yellow Pages telephone directory. Online, however, people do not type in those search words to find sushi restaurants. They simply type in "sushi."

In 2007, Yellow Pages executives started reviewing how to more effectively present material in the next edition of their hard-copy phone book, so that it would make more sense to the end user. They did this by constructing categories that "reflect how people think, speak and search online." "Armouries" and "buttonhole makers" will be dropped from the directory categories, while new categories such as "tapas" and "wine cellars" will be added.

The company has been in the phone book business for 100 years, and with the help of advertisers has always determined the categories used by people searching the directory. The Internet has allowed Yellow Pages to better address user needs, however. "Now that we're seeing the trends through our online directories—the key words people use—it gives us a good idea of what they are looking for in the print book," said company spokeswoman Annie Marsolais. ∎

National Culture

Communication differences can also arise from the different languages that individuals use to communicate and the national cultures they are part of. Interpersonal communication is not conducted the same way around the world. For example, let's compare countries that place a higher value on individualism (such as Canada) with countries in which the emphasis is on collectivism (such as Japan).[19]

In Canada, communication patterns tend to be oriented to the individual and clearly spelled out. Canadian managers rely heavily on memos, announcements, position papers, and other formal forms of communication to state their positions on issues. Supervisors may hoard information in an attempt to make themselves look good and as a way of persuading their employees to accept decisions and plans. For their own protection, lower-level employees often engage in this practice as well.

In collectivist countries, such as Japan, there is more interaction for its own sake. The Japanese manager, in contrast to the Canadian manager, engages in extensive verbal consultation with subordinates over an issue first and draws up a formal document later to outline the agreement that was made. The Japanese value decisions by consensus, and open communication is an inherent part of the work setting. Also, face-to-face communication is encouraged.

Cultural differences can affect the way a manager chooses to communicate. These differences undoubtedly can be a barrier to effective communication if not recognized and taken into consideration.

Cultural differences also affect body language and such things as how closely people stand to each other. In China, it is not unusual for people to push in queues to get ahead, and even step ahead of someone who has left too much space in line. In North America, there is an expectation that people will maintain a greater distance between one another and stay in their position in a lineup.

Diversity in Action 7

Overcoming the Barriers

What can we do to overcome barriers to communication? The following suggestions should help make your interpersonal communication more effective.

Use Feedback

Many communication problems can be directly attributed to misunderstanding and inaccuracies. These problems are less likely to occur if individuals use the feedback loop in the communication process, either verbally or nonverbally.

If a speaker asks a receiver, "Did you understand what I said?" the response represents feedback. Good feedback should include more than yes-and-no answers. The speaker can ask a set of questions about a message to determine whether or not the message was received and understood as intended. Better yet, the speaker can ask the receiver to restate the message in his or her own words. If the speaker hears what was intended, understanding and accuracy should improve. Feedback includes subtler methods than directly asking questions or having the receiver summarize the message. General comments can give the speaker a sense of the receiver's reaction to a message. To learn more about giving feedback, see *Self-Assessment—How Good Am I at Giving Performance Feedback?* on pages 221–222, in Chapter 7.

Of course, feedback does not have to be conveyed in words. Actions *can* speak louder than words. A sales manager sends an email to his or her staff describing a new monthly sales report that all sales representatives will need to complete. If some of them do not turn in the new report, the sales manager has received feedback. This feedback suggests that the sales manager needs to clarify the initial communication. Similarly, when you are talking to people, you watch their eyes and look for other nonverbal clues to tell whether they are getting your message or not.

Simplify Language

Because language can be a barrier, managers should choose words and structure their messages in ways that will make those messages clear and understandable to the receiver. Remember, effective communication is achieved when a message is both received and *understood*. Understanding is improved by simplifying the language used in relation to the audience intended. This means, for example, that a hospital administrator should always try to communicate in clear, easily understood terms. The language used in messages to the emergency room staff should be purposefully different from that used with office employees. Jargon can facilitate understanding when it's used within a group of those who know what it means, but it can cause many problems when used outside that group.

Listen Actively

Do you know the difference between hearing and listening? When someone talks, we hear. But too often we do not listen. Listening is an active search for meaning, whereas hearing is passive. In listening, two people are engaged in thinking: the sender *and* the receiver.

Many of us are poor listeners. Why? Because careful listening is difficult, and it's usually more satisfying to be on the offensive, that is, to be the one doing the talking. Listening, in fact, is often more tiring than talking. It demands intellectual effort. Unlike hearing, **active listening**, which is listening for full meaning without making premature judgments or interpretations, demands total concentration. The average person normally speaks at a rate of about 125 to 200 words per minute. However, the average listener can

active listening
Listening for full meaning without making premature judgments or interpretations.

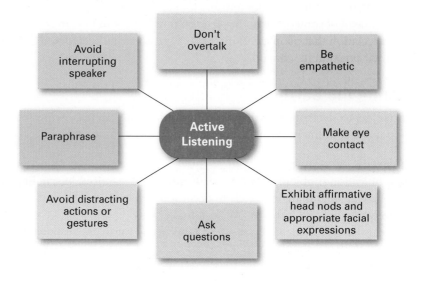

Exhibit 6-3

Active Listening Behaviours

Source: Based on P. L. Hunsaker, *Training in Management Skills* (Upper Saddle River, NJ: Prentice Hall, 2001).

comprehend up to 400 words per minute.[20] The difference obviously leaves lots of idle time for the brain and opportunities for the mind to wander.

Active listening is enhanced by developing empathy with the sender—that is, by placing yourself in the sender's position. Because senders differ in attitudes, interests, needs, and expectations, empathy makes it easier to understand the actual content of a message. An empathetic listener reserves judgment on the message's content and carefully listens to what is being said. The goal is to improve your ability to receive the full meaning of a communication without having it distorted by premature judgments or interpretations. Other specific behaviours that active listeners demonstrate are listed in Exhibit 6-3. To learn more about being an effective listener, see *Developing Your Interpersonal Skills—Active Listening* on pages 192–193, at the end of the chapter.

PRISM 11

Constrain Emotions

It would be naive to assume that managers always communicate in a rational manner. We know that emotions can severely cloud and distort the transference of meaning. A manager who is emotionally upset over an issue is more likely to misconstrue incoming messages and fail to communicate clearly and accurately. What can the manager do? The simplest answer is to refrain from communicating until he or she has regained composure.

Watch Nonverbal Cues

If actions speak louder than words, then it's important to watch your actions to make sure they align with and reinforce the words that go along with them. The effective communicator watches his or her nonverbal cues to ensure that they convey the desired message.

Organizational Communication

3 How does communication flow in organizations?

An understanding of managerial communication is not possible without looking at the fundamentals of organizational communication. In this section, we look at several important aspects of organizational communication including formal vs. informal communication, the direction of communication flow, and organizational communication networks.

Formal vs. Informal Communication

Communication within an organization is often described as either formal or informal. **Formal communication** refers to communication that follows the official chain of command or is part of the communication required to do one's job. When a manager asks an employee to complete a task, he or she is communicating formally. So is the employee who brings a problem to the attention of his or her manager. Any communication that takes place within prescribed organizational work arrangements would be classified as formal.

Informal communication is communication that is not defined by the organization's structural hierarchy. When employees talk with each other in the lunchroom, as they pass in hallways, or as they are working out at the company exercise facility, that is informal communication. Employees form friendships and communicate with each other. The informal communication system fulfills two purposes in organizations: (1) it permits employees to satisfy their need for social interaction; (2) it can improve an organization's performance by creating alternative, and frequently faster and more efficient, channels of communication.

formal communication
Communication that follows the official chain of command or is part of the communication required to do one's job.

informal communication
Communication that is not defined by the organization's structural hierarchy.

Diversity in Action 1

Direction of Communication Flow

Organizational communication can flow downward, upward, laterally, or diagonally. Let's look at each.

Downward Communication

Every morning and often several times a day, managers at UPS package delivery facilities gather workers for mandatory meetings that last precisely three minutes. During those 180 seconds, managers relay company announcements and go over local information such as traffic conditions or customer complaints. Then, each meeting ends with a safety tip. The three-minute meetings have proved so successful that many of the company's office workers are using the idea.[21]

Any communication that flows downward from managers to employees is **downward communication**. Downward communication is used to inform, direct, coordinate, and evaluate employees. When managers assign goals to their employees, they are using downward communication. Managers are also using downward communication when providing employees with job descriptions, informing them of organizational policies and procedures, pointing out problems that need attention, or evaluating and giving feedback on their performance. Downward communication can take place through any of the communication channels we described earlier. Managers can improve the quality of the feedback they give to employees if they follow the advice given in *Tips for Managers—Suggestions for Giving Feedback*.

downward communication
Communication that flows downward from managers to employees.

upward communication
Communication that flows upward from employees to managers.

Upward Communication

Any communication that flows upward from employees to managers is **upward communication**. Managers rely on their employees for information. Reports are given to managers to inform them of progress toward goals and any current problems. Upward communication keeps managers aware of how employees feel about their jobs, their co-workers, and the organization in general. Managers also rely on it for ideas on how things can be improved. Some examples of upward communication include performance reports prepared by employees, suggestion boxes, employee attitude surveys, grievance procedures, manager–employee discussions, and informal group sessions in which employees have the opportunity to identify and discuss problems with their manager or even representatives of top management.

TIPS FOR MANAGERS

Suggestions for Giving Feedback

Managers can use the following tips to give more effective feedback:

- "Relate feedback to existing **performance goals and clear expectations**."

- "Give **specific feedback** tied to observable behaviour or measurable results."

- "Channel feedback toward **key result areas**."

- "Give feedback **as soon as possible**."

- "Give positive **feedback for improvement**, not just final results."

- "**Focus feedback on performance**, not personalities."

- "Base feedback on **accurate and credible information**."[22]

The extent of upward communication depends on the organizational culture. If managers have created a climate of trust and respect and use participative decision making or empowerment, there will be considerable upward communication as employees provide input to decisions. Ernst & Young encourages employees to evaluate the principals, partners, and directors on how well they create a positive work climate. A partner in the Montreal office was surprised to learn that people in her office found her a poor role model, and she took care to more carefully explain her actions as a result.[23] In a highly structured and authoritarian environment, upward communication still takes place, but is limited in both style and content.

Lateral Communication

lateral communication
Communication that takes place among employees on the same organizational level.

Communication that takes place among employees on the same organizational level is called **lateral communication**. In today's often chaotic and rapidly changing environment, lateral communication is frequently needed to save time and facilitate coordination. Cross-functional teams, for example, rely heavily on this form of communication. However, it can create conflicts if employees do not keep their managers informed about decisions they have made or actions they have taken.

Diagonal Communication

diagonal communication
Communication that cuts across both work areas and organizational levels.

Communication that cuts across both work areas *and* organizational levels is **diagonal communication**. When an analyst in the credit department communicates directly with a regional marketing manager—note the different department and different organizational level—about a customer problem, that is diagonal communication. In the interest of efficiency and speed, diagonal communication can be beneficial. Email facilitates diagonal communication. In many organizations, any employee can communicate by email with any other employee, regardless of organizational work area or level. However, just as with lateral communication, diagonal communication has the potential to create problems if employees do not keep their managers informed.

Organizational Communication Networks

communication networks
The variety of patterns of vertical and horizontal flows of organizational communication.

The vertical and horizontal flows of organizational communication can be combined into a variety of patterns called **communication networks**. Exhibit 6-4 illustrates three common communication networks.

Exhibit 6-4

Three Common Organizational Communication Networks and How They Rate on Effectiveness Criteria

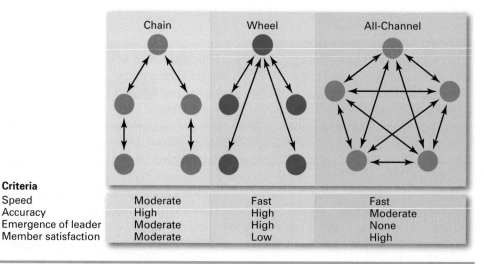

Criteria	Chain	Wheel	All-Channel
Speed	Moderate	Fast	Fast
Accuracy	High	High	Moderate
Emergence of leader	Moderate	High	None
Member satisfaction	Moderate	Low	High

Types of Communication Networks

In the *chain* network, communication flows according to the formal chain of command, both downward and upward. The *wheel* network represents communication flowing between a clearly identifiable and strong leader and others in a work group or team. The leader serves as the hub through whom all communication passes. Finally, in the *all-channel* network, communication flows freely among all members of a work team.

As a manager, which network should you use? The answer depends on your goal. Exhibit 6-4 also summarizes the effectiveness of the various networks according to four criteria: speed, accuracy, the probability that a leader will emerge, and the importance of member satisfaction. One observation is immediately apparent: No single network is best for all situations. If you are concerned with high member satisfaction, the all-channel network is best; if having a strong and identifiable leader is important, the wheel facilitates this; and if accuracy is most important, the chain and wheel networks work best.

The Grapevine We cannot leave our discussion of communication networks without discussing the **grapevine**—the informal organizational communication network. The grapevine is active in almost every organization. Is it an important source of information? You bet! One survey reported that 75 percent of employees hear about matters first through rumours on the grapevine.[24]

grapevine
The informal organizational communication network.

What are the implications for managers? Certainly, the grapevine is an important part of any group or organization communication network and well worth understanding.[25] It identifies for managers those bewildering issues that employees consider important and anxiety-producing. It acts as both a filter and a feedback mechanism, picking up on the issues employees consider relevant. More importantly, from a managerial point of view, it *is* possible to analyze what is happening on the grapevine—what information is being passed, how information seems to flow along the grapevine, and which individuals seem to be key conduits of information on the grapevine. By being aware of the grapevine's flow and patterns, managers can stay on top of issues that concern employees and, in turn, can use the grapevine to disseminate important information. Since the grapevine cannot be eliminated, managers should "manage" it as an important information network.

Rumours that flow along the grapevine also can never be eliminated entirely. Managers can minimize the negative consequences of rumours by limiting their range and impact. How? By communicating openly, fully, and honestly with employees, particularly in situations where employees may not like proposed or actual managerial decisions or actions. Open and honest communication with employees can affect the organization in various ways. A study by Watson Wyatt Worldwide concluded that effective communication "connects employees to the business, reinforces the organization's vision, fosters process improvement, facilitates change, and drives business results by changing employee behavior." For those companies that communicated effectively, total returns to shareholders were 57 percent higher over a five-year period than for companies with less effective communication. And the study also showed that companies that were highly effective communicators were 20 percent more likely to report lower turnover rates.[26]

Q&A 10.8

Understanding Information Technology

Social networking websites such as Facebook and LinkedIn have become resources for employers seeking job candidates.[27] Companies large and small are using these resources to do research, form relationships, and fill positions. More than 350 companies broadcast their job listings to more than 10 million registered users of LinkedIn. A manager looking to fill a key position can use LinkedIn to view posted résumés and read an individual's postings, and can even "check out a competitor's site for potential candidates."

Brian Drum, president of executive search firm Drum Associates, uses social networking sites such as MySpace to see if there is any information about a job candidate's character that might suggest an inability to perform reliably. "Sometimes all we find is meaningless chitchat," says Drum, "but once in a while we'll turn up something useful, like an unflattering picture or a piece of information that really shows what the person is made of."

Some businesses are not just using social networking sites for recruiting, however. They have also added their own company profiles at such sites, allowing employees to interact with each other. They realize that a number of younger employees are using social networking sites, so they might as well encourage productive use of the medium.

Think About It

What are the benefits to employers of using a source such as Facebook to screen job candidates? Should employers consider these postings just private musings and ignore them? Are there advantages to organizations in allowing employees to use social networking sites? If yes, do they outweigh the disadvantages?

4 How does information technology affect organizations?

Information technology is changing the way we live and work. Take the following three examples: In a number of countries, employees, managers, housewives, and teens use wireless interactive web phones to send email, surf the web, swap photos, and play computer games. Service technicians at Ajax, Ontario-based Pitney Bowes Canada use instant messaging rather than pagers, because "it's cheaper and it's two-way." The company knows when messages are received.[28] IBM's 398 000 employees regularly use instant messaging software for both communicating and workplace collaboration.[29]

The world of communication is not what it used to be. Managers are challenged to keep their organizations functioning smoothly while continually improving work operations *and* staying competitive even though both the organization and the environment are changing rapidly. Although changing technology has been a significant source of the environmental uncertainty facing organizations, these same technological advances have enabled managers to coordinate the work efforts of employees in ways that can lead to increased efficiency and effectiveness. Information technology now touches every aspect of almost every company's business. The implications for the ways individuals communicate are profound.

Q&A 10.9

How Information Technology Affects Communication

Information technology has radically changed the way organizational members communicate. For example, it has

- significantly improved a manager's ability to monitor individual or team performance

- allowed employees to have more complete information to make faster decisions

- provided employees with more opportunities to collaborate and share information

- made it possible for employees to be fully accessible, any time, regardless of where they are

Several developments in information technology seem to be having the most significant impact on current managerial communication: email, instant messaging, and social networking websites such as Facebook and LinkedIn.

Q&A 10.10

Email

Have you ever emailed or instant-messaged someone who was just in the next office? Does the reliance on technology make it harder or easier to communicate effectively with people?

Email is a quick and convenient way for organizational members to share information and communicate. However, many people complain about email overload, and it is not always used effectively. A recent study found that opening nasty messages from your boss can harm your health over time.[30] While negative email messages from anyone had health consequences, those from superiors showed the most significant increase in a person's blood pressure.

Individuals should remember that email tends to be permanent, which means that a message sent in anger could come back to hurt the sender later on. Email is also not necessarily private communication, and organizations often take the position that they have the right to read your email.

To construct more effective emails, you might want to consider the following tips for writing and sending email offered by Professor Christina Cavanagh of the University of Western Ontario's Richard Ivey School of Business:[31]

- Don't send emails without a subject line.

- Be careful in your use of emoticons and acronyms for business communication.

- Write your message clearly and briefly.

- Copy emails to others only if they really need the information.

- Sleep on angry emails before sending to be sure you are sending the right message.

Instant Messaging

Instant messaging (IM) first became popular among teens and preteens who wanted to communicate online immediately with their friends. Now, it has moved to the workplace. According to a 2007 survey by AP and AOL, 27 percent of IM users say they use instant messaging at work, and over half of that use is for personal, rather than business, matters.[32] However, there are drawbacks to IM. Unlike email, it requires users to be logged on to the organization's computer network in order to communicate with one another. This leaves the network open to security breaches, and some organizations have limited which employees can use IM in the workplace as a result.

Social Networking Websites

Social networking websites such as Facebook, MySpace, and LinkedIn have drawn millions of subscribers who voluntarily post information about themselves that can be viewed by any other subscriber, unless the user deliberately sets privacy restrictions.

Employers and search firms are starting to check the postings of clients, and some even monitor employees to see if there is anything questionable in their character. Despite the public's concern that the government is not doing enough to protect individual privacy, many people feel free to post information about themselves (flattering and unflattering) online that is readily accessible to anyone.

Some employers post job offerings on sites such as Facebook; others post recruitment videos on sites such as YouTube. In a recent twist, some employers have done virtual interviews through *Second Life*, the online virtual community.[33] Job seekers create an "avatar," a computer-generated image that represents themselves, and then communicate with prospective employers through instant messaging. A recent virtual job fair on *Second Life* included employers Hewlett-Packard, Microsoft, Verizon, and Sodexho Alliance SA, a food and facilities-management services company.

Individuals who use websites such as Facebook may want to consider the lack of privacy such sites afford when it comes to employers and evaluations. Individuals may forget that once it's written on the web, it's difficult to erase. So while it might seem like a good idea to post photos of drunken partying, this might not leave a good impression on potential employers. As Deanna MacDougal, a partner at Toronto-based IQ Partners notes, "If your potential employer Googles a name and sees your social life, that can be good but it can also hinder you. Even with password-protected sites, I think the youth need to be a little bit more careful." Geoff Bagg, president of Toronto-based The Bagg Group adds: "I don't think you can segment your life and say, 'This is my private life and this is my work life.' They're all intertwined."[34]

How Information Technology Affects Organizations

Employees—working in teams or as individuals—need information to make decisions and do their work. After describing the communications capabilities managers have at their disposal, it's clear that technology *can* significantly affect the way that

Technology need not always reduce face-to-face communication.
To make contact easier between
employees at its call centre and
in its information systems department, ASB, a New Zealand bank,
adopted an open layout encompassing five areas on three different floors. There is a landscaped
park area in the centre, a café, a
minigolf green, a TV room, and a
barbecue area, all of which help
bring people together. Since moving into the new design, bank
managers have noted that the volume of interdepartmental emails
has dropped, indicating that people are communicating in person
more.

organizational members communicate, share information, and do their work. Information technology also creates opportunities for organizations. For example, colleges and
universities now have the capability of offering online courses and degrees. Over time,
this could decrease the number of students taught in face-to-face settings, while increasing the overall number of students who can be reached because of online methods of
teaching.

The following *Management Reflection* explores how one Canadian firm reduced cost
and improved service for customers using Voice over Internet Protocol (VoIP) technology.

MANAGEMENT REFLECTION

VoIP Improves Communication and Customer Service

Can saving money increase service? Johnson, a St. John's, Newfoundland-based
national insurance company, founded in 1880, recently introduced the latest in long-
distance telephone technology: Voice over Internet Protocol (VoIP).[35] The technology,
purchased from Cisco Systems, treats long distance calls as if they were local ones.
With appropriate hardware, subscribers can use the same cable that connects their
computer to the Internet to connect their telephone to make calls. It is not just a cost-
saving measure, though. C. C. Huang, Johnson's president and CEO, says, "We really
believe in Voice over IP. It's helping us provide better customer service, improve our
productivity—and outperform the industry." The IP infrastructure allows voice, video,
and data to be transferred on a single network.

When customers call in, the network can direct calls to staff members who have the
appropriate skills and are available to handle the call. The network is also able to link a
caller's phone number to his or her electronic file, making it immediately available to
the employee handling the phone call. Employees are able to see their voice mail,
email, and faxes on their telephone screens. Huang is enthusiastic about the system because "we're actually spending less money—and doing more than we have before." ∎

Communication and the exchange of information among organizational members are
no longer constrained by geography or time. Collaborative work efforts among widely
dispersed individuals and teams, information sharing, and the integration of decisions
and work throughout an entire organization have the potential to increase organizational

David Breda, co-owner of Leader Plumbing and Heating, a mechanical contractor in Woodbridge, Ontario, finds online collaboration a major boon to his business. His employees, mostly plumbers, are able to exchange real-time information, and thus be more efficient in their work.

efficiency and effectiveness. While the economic benefits of information technology are obvious, managers must not forget to address the psychological drawbacks.[36] For example, what is the psychological cost of an employee's always being accessible? Will there be increased pressure for employees to "check in" even during their off hours? How important is it for employees to separate their work lives and their personal lives? While there are no easy answers to these questions, these are issues that managers will have to face.

The widespread use of voice mail and email at work has led to some ethical concerns as well. These forms of communication are not necessarily private, because employers have access to them. The federal Privacy Act (which protects the privacy of individuals and provides individuals with the right to access personal information about themselves) and the Access to Information Act (which allows individuals to access government information) apply to all federal government departments, most federal agencies, and some federal Crown corporations. However, many private sector employees are not covered by privacy legislation. Only Quebec's privacy act applies to the entire private sector. Managers need to clearly convey to employees the extent to which their communications will be monitored, and policies on such things as personal Internet and email use.

SUMMARY AND IMPLICATIONS

❶ What are the functions of communication? Communication serves four major functions: control, motivation, emotional expression, and information. In the control function, communication sets out the guidelines for behaviour. Communication motivates by clarifying to employees what is to be done, how well they are doing, and what can be done to improve performance if it's not up to par. Communication provides an opportunity to express feelings and also fulfills social needs. Finally, communication also provides the information to get things done in organizations.

Facebook has allowed employers to learn more about potential employees, and some organizations have set up Facebook sites for employees to communicate with each other.

❷ Why does communication break down? When a message passes between a sender and a receiver, it needs to be converted into symbols (called encoding) and passed to the receiver by some channel. The receiver translates (decodes) the sender's message. At any point in this process, communication can be distorted by noise. A variety of other factors can also affect whether the message is interpreted correctly, including the degree of filtering, the sender's or receiver's emotional state, and whether too much information is being sent (information overload).

The value of face-to-face communication is that one receives more information through body language. The rise of online communication, through such tools as email, as well as social networking sites such as Facebook, means that communication is often more ambiguous. It also becomes harder to know whether too much information has been revealed because feedback mechanisms may not be as direct.

3 **How does communication flow in organizations?** Communication can be of the formal or informal variety. Formal communication follows the official chain of command or is part of the communication required to do one's job. Informal communication is not defined by the organization's structural hierarchy. Communication can flow downward, upward, laterally to those at the same organizational level, or diagonally, which means that the communication cuts across both work areas and organizational levels. Communication can also flow through networks and through the grapevine.

4 **How does information technology affect organizations?** Information technology allows managers and employees more access to each other and to customers and clients. It provides more opportunities for monitoring, as well as a greater ability to share information. Information technology also increases flexibility and responsiveness.

Even though some workplaces have banned Facebook use, some employers have found ways to use Facebook as a source of information on job candidates and employees and as a business communication tool. Other organizations are exploring how to implement Facebook, knowing that their younger employees are widely using the social networking site already.

Management @ Work

READING FOR COMPREHENSION

1. What are the four functions of communication?

2. What steps can you take to make interpersonal communication more effective?

3. What can managers do to help them determine which communication channel to use in a given circumstance?

4. Describe the barriers to effective interpersonal communication. How can they be overcome?

5. Which do you think is more important for a manager: speaking accurately or listening actively? Why?

6. Identify four types of channels and when they might be best used.

7. How has information technology enhanced a manager's communication effectiveness?

LINKING CONCEPTS TO PRACTICE

1. "Ineffective communication is the fault of the sender." Do you agree or disagree with this statement? Explain your position.

2. Describe why effective communication is not synonymous with agreement between the communicating parties.

3. "As technology improves, employees will be working more, be more accessible to employers, and be suffering from information overload." Do you agree or disagree with this statement? Explain your position.

4. How might a manager use the grapevine to his or her advantage? Support your response.

5. Using what you have learned about active listening in this chapter, would you describe yourself as a good listener? Are there any areas in which you are deficient? If so, how could you improve your listening skills?

SELF-ASSESSMENT

What's My Face-to-Face Communication Style?

For each of the following statements, circle the level of agreement or disagreement that you personally feel:[37]

1 = Strongly Disagree 2 = Moderately Disagree 3 = Neither Agree nor Disagree 4 = Moderately Agree 5 = Strongly Agree

1. I am comfortable with all varieties of people.	1 2 3 4 5
2. I laugh easily.	1 2 3 4 5
3. I readily express admiration for others.	1 2 3 4 5
4. What I say usually leaves an impression on people.	1 2 3 4 5
5. I leave people with an impression of me which they definitely tend to remember.	1 2 3 4 5
6. To be friendly, I habitually acknowledge verbally others' contributions.	1 2 3 4 5
7. I have some nervous mannerisms in my speech.	1 2 3 4 5
8. I am a very relaxed communicator.	1 2 3 4 5
9. When I disagree with somebody, I am very quick to challenge them.	1 2 3 4 5
10. I can always repeat back to a person exactly what was meant.	1 2 3 4 5
11. The sound of my voice is very easy to recognize.	1 2 3 4 5

12. I leave a definite impression on people.　　　　　　　　　　　　　1　2　3　4　5

13. The rhythm or flow of my speech is sometimes affected by nervousness.　　1　2　3　4　5

14. Under pressure I come across as a relaxed speaker.　　　　　　　　　1　2　3　4　5

15. My eyes reflect exactly what I am feeling when I communicate.　　　　1　2　3　4　5

16. I dramatize a lot.　　　　　　　　　　　　　　　　　　　　　　1　2　3　4　5

17. Usually, I deliberately react in such a way that people know that I am listening to them.　　1　2　3　4　5

18. Usually, I do not tell people much about myself until I get to know them well.　　1　2　3　4　5

19. Regularly I tell jokes, anecdotes, and stories when I communicate.　　1　2　3　4　5

20. I tend to gesture constantly when I communicate.　　　　　　　　　1　2　3　4　5

21. I am an extremely open communicator.　　　　　　　　　　　　　1　2　3　4　5

22. I am vocally a loud communicator.　　　　　　　　　　　　　　　1　2　3　4　5

23. In arguments I insist on very precise definitions.　　　　　　　　　1　2　3　4　5

24. In most social situations I generally speak very frequently.　　　　　1　2　3　4　5

25. I like to be strictly accurate when I communicate.　　　　　　　　　1　2　3　4　5

26. Because I have a loud voice, I can easily break into a conversation.　　1　2　3　4　5

27. Often I physically and vocally act out when I want to communicate.　　1　2　3　4　5

28. I have an assertive voice.　　　　　　　　　　　　　　　　　　　1　2　3　4　5

29. I readily reveal personal things about myself.　　　　　　　　　　　1　2　3　4　5

30. I am dominant in social situations.　　　　　　　　　　　　　　　1　2　3　4　5

31. I am very argumentative.　　　　　　　　　　　　　　　　　　　1　2　3　4　5

32. Once I get wound up in a heated discussion, I have a hard time stopping myself.　　1　2　3　4　5

33. I am always an extremely friendly communicator.　　　　　　　　　1　2　3　4　5

34. I really like to listen very carefully to people.　　　　　　　　　　　1　2　3　4　5

35. Very often I insist that other people document or present some kind of proof for what they are arguing.　　1　2　3　4　5

36. I try to take charge of things when I am with people.　　　　　　　1　2　3　4　5

37. It bothers me to drop an argument that is not resolved.　　　　　　1　2　3　4　5

38. In most social situations I tend to come on strong.　　　　　　　　1　2　3　4　5

39. I am very expressive nonverbally in social situations.　　　　　　　1　2　3　4　5

40. The way I say something usually leaves an impression on people.　　1　2　3　4　5

41. Whenever I communicate, I tend to be very encouraging to people.　　1　2　3　4　5

42. I actively use a lot of facial expressions when I communicate.　　　1　2　3　4　5

43. I very frequently exaggerate verbally to emphasize a point.　　　　　1　2　3　4　5

44. I am an extremely attentive communicator.　　　　　　　　　　　　1　2　3　4　5

45. As a rule, I openly express my feelings and emotions.　　　　　　　1　2　3　4　5

Scoring Key

Step 1: Reverse the score on items 7, 13, and 18 (1 = 5, 2 = 4, 3 = 3, etc.).

Step 2: Add together the scores on the following items to get a final total for each dimension. (Not every item is included in determining the dimensions.)

1. 24, 30, 36, 38 = _____ (Dominant)

2. 16, 19, 27, 43 = _____ (Dramatic)

3. 9, 31, 32, 37 = _____ (Contentious)

4. 15, 20, 39, 42 = _____ (Animated)

5. 4, 5, 12, 40 = _____ (Impression-leaving)

6. 7, 8, 13, 14 = _____ (Relaxed)

7. 10, 17, 34, 44 = _____ (Attentive)

8. 18, 21, 29, 45 = _____ (Open)

9. 3, 6, 33, 41 = _____ (Friendly)

Analysis and Interpretation

This scale measures the following dimensions of communication style:

Dominant—Tends to take charge of social interactions.

Dramatic—Manipulates and exaggerates stories and uses other stylistic devices to highlight content.

Contentious—Is argumentative.

Animated—Uses frequent and sustained eye contact and many facial expressions and gestures often.

Impression-leaving—Is remembered because of the communicative stimuli that are projected.

Relaxed—Is relaxed and void of nervousness.

Attentive—Makes sure that the other person knows that he or she is being listened to.

Open—Is conversational, expansive, affable, convivial, gregarious, unreserved, somewhat frank, definitely extroverted, and obviously approachable.

Friendly—Ranges from being unhostile to showing deep intimacy.

For each dimension, your score will range from 5 to 25. The higher your score for any dimension, the more that dimension characterizes your communication style. When you review your results, consider to what degree your scores aid or hinder your communication effectiveness. High scores for being attentive and open would almost always be positive qualities. A high score for contentiousness, on the other hand, could be a negative in many situations.

More Self-Assessments

To learn more about your skills, abilities, and interests, take the following self-assessments on the MyManagementLab at **www.pearsoned.ca/mymanagementlab:**

- II.A.2.—How Good Are My Listening Skills?

- III.A.3.—How Good Am I at Giving Performance Feedback? (This exercise also appears in Chapter 7 on pages 221–222.)

MANAGEMENT FOR YOU TODAY

Dilemma

Think of a person with whom you have had difficulty communicating. Using the barriers to effective interpersonal communication as a start, analyze what has gone wrong with the communication process with that person. What can be done to improve communication? To what extent did sender and receiver problems contribute to the communication breakdown?

Becoming a Manager

- Practise being a good communicator—as a sender and a listener.

- When preparing to communicate, think about the most appropriate channel for your communication and why it may or may not be the most appropriate.

- Pay attention to your and others' nonverbal communication. Learn to notice the cues.

- Complete the *Developing Your Interpersonal Skills—Active Listening* module on pages 192–193.

WORKING TOGETHER: TEAM-BASED EXERCISE

Choosing the Right Communication Channel

Purpose

To reinforce the idea that some channels are more appropriate for certain communications than others.

Time Required

Approximately 20 minutes.

Procedure

Form groups of 5 or 6 individuals. Evaluate the most appropriate channel to use to deliver the following information to employees. Justify your choices.

1. The company has just been acquired by a large competitor, and 15 percent of the employees will be laid off within the next 3 months.

2. A customer has complained about an employee via email. You have investigated and found the complaint justified. How do you convey this to the employee?

3. The founder of the company, who is well liked, died of a heart attack last night.

4. Bonus decisions have been made. Not all individuals will receive a bonus.

5. An employee has gone above and beyond in meeting a customer's request. You want to acknowledge the employee's efforts.

ETHICS IN ACTION

Ethical Dilemma Exercise: Should CEOs Join the Blogger's World?

More and more organizational members are initiating messages through corporate blogs.[38] Officially known as *weblogs*, these are websites where an individual posts ideas, comments on contemporary issues, and offers other musings. Because anyone can visit the site and read the messages, companies have become concerned about messages that include sensitive data, criticize managers or competitors, use inflammatory language, or contain misrepresentations. Companies are also worried about the reaction of stakeholders who disagree with or are offended by blog postings. Corporate blogs are becoming so popular that companies such as Groove Networks have developed blog policies. In fact, CNN insisted that a reporter suspend a blog where he posted his conflicting thoughts about a career as a war correspondent, even though the reporter had a disclaimer saying the blog was "not affiliated with, endorsed by, or funded by CNN."

But what happens when a CEO sets up a blog? Jonathan Schwartz, CEO of Sun Microsystems, blogs about new technologies, management issues, and more (see http://blogs.sun.com/jonathan/). Alan Meckler, the CEO of Jupitermedia, started a blog as "a diary of the ups and downs of trying to do something monumental"—to create a new industry-wide technology conference. This event put Jupitermedia squarely in competition with a well-established event known as Comdex. In early blog entries, Meckler talked bluntly about the competing conference's management. Based on legal advice (and negative feedback from a few conference exhibitors), he softened his tone in later entries. Although he still blogs, Meckler notes, "I'm not stirring the pot anymore, which isn't my nature." What is the most ethical way to deal with a corporate blog, especially one by a senior manager?

Imagine that you are Jupitermedia's public relations director. The CEO has just posted a blog message saying your conference was more financially successful than the competing conference. Because neither company releases profitability details, you know this statement cannot be verified. You don't want Jupitermedia to look bad; you also know that your CEO likes to express himself. What should you do about the CEO's blog? (Review Exhibit 6-1 on page 170 as you think about the ethical challenge posed by this blog communication.)

Thinking Critically About Ethics

According to a survey by Websense, 58 percent of employees spend time at nonwork-related websites.[39] Another survey by Salary.com and AOL found that personal Internet surfing was the top method of goofing off at work. Funny stories, jokes, and pictures make their way from one employee's email inbox to another's, to another's, and so forth. An elf bowling game sent by email was a favourite diversion during the holiday season. Although these may seem like fun and

harmless activities, it's estimated that such Internet distractions cost businesses over $54 billion annually. While there is a high dollar cost associated with using the Internet at work for other than business reasons, is there a psychological benefit to be gained by letting employees do something to relieve the stress of pressure-packed jobs? What are the ethical issues associated with widely available Internet access at work for both employees and organizations?

CASE APPLICATION

Voyant Technologies

After a chance meeting in a headquarters hallway with his chief engineer, Bill Ernstrom, CEO of Voyant Technologies (a company that makes teleconferencing equipment), decided to have his engineers add streaming media to the company's flagship product.[40] Four months and $200 000 later, Ernstrom wishes he had never had that conversation. Last week, one of his product managers, who only recently learned of the project, produced a marketing report that showed most customers had little interest in streaming anything.

Ernstrom realizes that he has been ignoring a communication challenge for too long: The top engineers are not listening to the product managers, and vice versa. Ernstrom says, "We got a long way down the road, built the code, got

the engineers excited. Then we found out that we'd sell about 10 units."

Ernstrom recognizes that there may be communication barriers in high-tech organizations between engineers and product managers. He notes that cultural and language gaps between computer "geeks" and the more market/ business-oriented colleagues happen time and time again.

Ernstrom's not sure what to do. Usually, in a high-tech organization, the early stages of a new project belong to the engineers. It is crucial to get the technology right, but what they produce is "often elegant technology that has no market, is too complicated, or doesn't match customers' expectations." Ernstrom's challenge is to get the two competing groups to collaborate. What steps can he take to make this happen?

DEVELOPING YOUR DIAGNOSTIC AND ANALYTICAL SKILLS

English-Only Rules

Canada is a multicultural country. "One in six Canadians in their 20s are immigrants, and one in five are the children of at least one immigrant parent."[41] In 2006, 45.7 percent of Metropolitan Toronto's population, 39.6 percent of Vancouver's, and 20.6 percent of Montreal's were made up of immigrants.[42]

The 2006 census found that 40.3 percent of Vancouver's population spoke neither of the country's two official languages as their first language.[43] The largest number of people who speak neither English nor French as their preferred language speak Chinese (mainly Mandarin or Cantonese). The other dominant language in Vancouver is Punjabi, but many other languages are represented as well. Very few Vancouverites speak French, however.

Can an organization in BC require its employees to speak only English on the job?[44] There are many sides to

this issue. On the one hand, employers have identified the need to have a common language spoken in the workplace. Employers must be able to communicate effectively with all employees, especially when safety or productive efficiency matters are at stake. This, they claim, is a business necessity. Consequently, if it is a valid requirement of the job, the practice could be permitted. Furthermore, an employer's desire to have one language also stems from the fact that some employees may use bilingual capabilities to harass and insult other employees in a language they cannot understand. With today's increasing concern with protecting employees, especially women, from hostile environments, English-only rules serve as one means of reasonable care.

A counterpoint to this English-only rule firmly rests with the workforce diversity issue. Employees in today's organizations come from all nationalities and speak different languages. What about these individuals' desire to speak their languages, to communicate effectively with their peers, and to maintain their cultural heritages? To them, English-only rules are discriminatory in terms of national origin in that they have an adverse impact on non-English-speaking individuals. Moreover, promoting the languages of employees might be one way for organizations to avert marketing disasters. For example, marketing campaigns by Kentucky Fried Chicken and Coors have caused some embarrassment when these campaigns are translated in the global arena. Specifically, while Kentucky Fried Chicken's "Finger Licking Good" implies great-tasting fried chicken in North America, those same words in Chinese translate into "Eat Your Fingers Off." Likewise, Coors's marketing adage to "Turn It Loose," in Spanish means "Drink Coors and Get Diarrhea." Probably not the images the companies had in mind.

Questions

1. Should employers be permitted to require that only English be spoken in the workplace? Defend your position.

2. What suggestions for communication effectiveness, if any, would you give to organizations that market goods globally? Explain.

DEVELOPING YOUR INTERPERSONAL SKILLS

Active Listening

About the Skill

The ability to be an effective listener is often taken for granted. Hearing is often confused with listening, but hearing is merely recognizing sound vibrations. Listening is making sense of what we hear and requires paying attention, interpreting, and remembering. Effective listening is active rather than passive. Active listening is hard work and requires you to "get inside" the speaker's head in order to understand the communication from his or her point of view.

Steps in Developing the Skill

You can be more effective at active listening if you use the following eight suggestions:[45]

1. **Make eye contact.** Making eye contact with the speaker focuses your attention, reduces the likelihood that you will be distracted, and encourages the speaker.

2. **Exhibit affirmative nods and appropriate facial expressions.** The effective active listener shows interest in what is being said through nonverbal signals. Affirmative nods and appropriate facial expressions that signal interest in what is being said, when added to eye contact, convey to the speaker that you are really listening.

3. **Avoid distracting actions or gestures.** The other side of showing interest is avoiding actions that suggest your mind is elsewhere. When listening, don't look at your watch, shuffle papers, play with your pencil, or engage in similar distractions.

4. **Ask questions.** The serious active listener analyzes what he or she hears and asks questions. This behav-iour provides clarification, ensures understanding, and assures the speaker you are really listening.

5. **Paraphrase.** Restate in your own words what the speaker has said. The effective active listener uses phrases such as "What I hear you saying is . . ." or "Do you mean . . .?" Paraphrasing is an excellent control device to check whether or not you are listening carefully and it is also a control for accuracy of understanding.

6. **Avoid interrupting the speaker.** Let the speaker complete his or her thoughts before you try to respond. Don't try to second-guess where the speaker's thoughts are going. When the speaker is finished, you will know it.

7. **Don't overtalk.** Most of us would rather speak our own ideas than listen to what others say. While talking might be more fun and silence might be uncomfortable, you cannot talk and listen at the same time. The good active listener recognizes this fact and does not overtalk.

8. **Make smooth transitions between the roles of speaker and listener.** In most work situations, you are continually shifting back and forth between the roles of speaker and listener. The effective active listener makes transitions smoothly from speaker to listener and back to speaker.

Practising the Skill

Ben Lummis has always been one of the most reliable technicians at the car stereo shop you manage. Even on days when the frantic pace stressed most other employees, Ben was calm and finished his work efficiently and effectively. You don't know much about his personal life except that he likes to read books about model railroading during his lunch break and he has asked to listen to his favourite light jazz station on the shop radio for part of the day. Because his work has always been top-notch, you were happy to let him maintain his somewhat aloof attitude. But over the past month, you have wished you knew Ben better. He has been averaging about an absence a week, and he no longer spends his lunch break reading in the break room. When he returns from wherever it is he goes, he seems even more remote than when he left. You strongly suspect that something is wrong. Even his normally reliable work has changed. Several irate customers have returned with sound systems he installed improperly. At the time of these complaints, you reviewed each problem with him carefully, and each time he promised to be more careful. In addition, you checked the company's work absence records and found that Ben has enough time saved up to take seven more sick days this year. But things don't seem to be improving. Just this week Ben took another suspicious sick day, and another angry customer has demanded that his improperly installed sound system be fixed. How would you discuss the matter with Ben?

MANAGING WORKFORCE DIVERSITY

The Communication Styles of Men and Women

"You don't understand what I'm saying, and you never listen!" "You're making a big deal out of nothing." Have you said (or heard) these statements or ones like them made to friends of the opposite sex? Most of us probably have! Research shows us that men and women tend to have different communication styles.[46] Let's look more closely at these differing styles and the problems that can arise, and try to suggest ways to minimize the barriers.

Deborah Tannen has studied the ways that men and women communicate, and reports some interesting differences. The essence of her research is that men use talk to emphasize status, while women use it to create connection. She states that communication between the sexes can be a continual balancing act of juggling our conflicting needs for intimacy, which emphasizes closeness and commonality, and independence, which emphasizes separateness and differences. It's no wonder, then, that communication problems arise! Women hear and speak a language of connection and intimacy. Men hear and speak a language of status and independence. For many men, conversations are merely a way to preserve independence and maintain status in a hierarchical social order. Yet for many women, conversations are negotiations for closeness and seeking out support and confirmation. Let's look at a few examples of what Tannen has described.

Men frequently complain that women talk on and on about their problems. Women, however, criticize men for not listening. What is happening is that when a man hears a woman talking about a problem, he frequently asserts his desire for independence and control by offering solutions. Many women, in contrast, view conversing about a problem as a way to promote closeness. The woman talks about a problem to gain support and connection, not to get the male's advice.

Here is another example: Men are often more direct than women in conversation. A man might say, "I think you're wrong on that point." A woman might say, "Have you looked at the marketing department's research report on that issue?" The implication in the woman's comment is that the report will point out the error. Men frequently misread women's indirectness as "covert" or "sneaky," but women are not as concerned as men with the status and one-upmanship that directness often creates.

Finally, men often criticize women for seeming to apologize all the time. Men tend to see the phrase "I'm sorry" as a sign of weakness because they interpret the phrase to mean the woman is accepting blame, when he may know she's not to blame. The woman also knows she is not at fault. Yet she is typically using "I'm sorry" to express regret: "I know you must feel bad about this and I do, too."

What differences do you see in men's and women's communication styles? Have these differences ever gotten in the way of working together? Describe some of the issues you have encountered.

CHAPTER 7 **Human Resource Management**

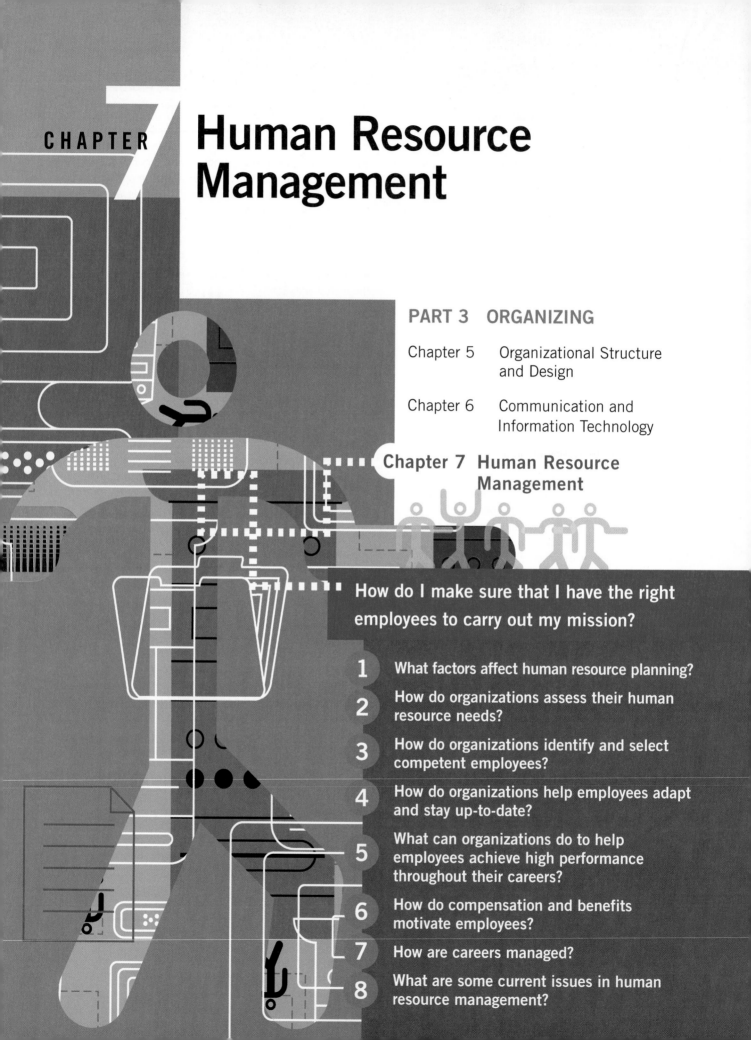

How do I make sure that I have the right
employees to carry out my mission?

1   What factors affect human resource planning?

2   How do organizations assess their human
resource needs?

3   How do organizations identify and select
competent employees?

4   How do organizations help employees adapt
and stay up-to-date?

5   What can organizations do to help
employees achieve high performance
throughout their careers?

6   How do compensation and benefits
motivate employees?

7   How are careers managed?

8   What are some current issues in human
resource management?

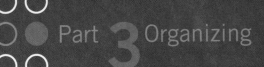

Toronto-based Bank of Nova Scotia (also called Scotiabank), Canada's second-largest bank, provides retail, corporate, and investment banking services worldwide.

Scotiabank has more than 970 domestic branches and offices in 50 countries, including Mexico, Ireland, and China.[1] In fiscal year 2006, the bank had total assets of over $379 billion, making it the number-two bank by market capitalization. From 1996 to 2006, Scotiabank grew earnings per share at a compound annual rate of 14 percent, and annual dividends more than doubled between 2002 and 2006. Scotiabank has close to 57 000 employees, but president and CEO Rick Waugh worries that too many will be leaving within the next 5 to 10 years. He expects about half of the bank's senior management—vice-presidents and those at higher levels—will retire during that time.

Managing human resources so that an organization has the right people in place at the right time is often thought of as a key role of human resource managers. Waugh thinks that is not enough, however. "Responsibility for leadership development must begin at the very top. HR can and does play an important role facilitating the process, but it must be owned and executed by current leaders," Waugh told attendees at a recent Conference Board of Canada National Leadership Summit.

Waugh also wants to make sure that Scotiabank taps the full potential of its workforce. For example, while women represent about 50 percent of Scotiabank's management-level employees, they have much less representation at the executive level. Waugh will be working with senior managers to make sure that more qualified women get opportunities in senior management.

Think About It

How do companies manage their human resources to achieve strong organizational performance? Put yourself in Rick Waugh's shoes. What policies and practices can he adopt to ensure that the bank has a high-quality workforce? What might he do to make sure that Scotiabank will have enough people to fill important roles as Baby Boomers retire?

Rick Waugh is faced with the challenge of making sure that Scotiabank recruits and retains high-quality employees. This type of human resource management challenge is just one of many facing today's managers. If an organization does not take its human resource management responsibilities seriously, work performance and goal accomplishment may suffer. The quality of an organization is, to a large degree, merely the sum of the quality of people it hires and retains. Getting and keeping competent employees is critical to the success of every organization, whether the organization is just starting out or has been in business for years. Therefore, part of every manager's job in the organizing function is human resource management.

Q&A 11.1

The Human Resource Management Process

1 What factors affect human resource planning?

"Our people are our most important asset." Many organizations use this phrase, or something close to it, to acknowledge the important role that employees play in organizational success. These organizations also recognize that *all* managers must engage in some human resource management (HRM) activities—even in large ones that have a separate HRM department. These managers interview job candidates, orient new employees, and evaluate their employees' work performance. Because HR also involves appropriate ways of treating co-workers, even nonmanagers must be aware of basic HR principles and practices.

Can HRM be an important strategic tool? *Can* it help establish an organization's sustainable competitive advantage? The answer to these questions seems to be yes. Various studies have concluded that an organization's human resources can be a significant source of competitive advantage.[2] And that is true for organizations around the world, not just Canadian firms. The Human Capital Index, a comprehensive global study of more than 2000 firms conducted by consulting firm Watson Wyatt Worldwide, concluded that people-oriented HR gives an organization an edge by creating superior shareholder value.[3]

Human resource management should not operate in a vacuum. Rather, it must support the organization's corporate strategy.[4] Thus, human resource practices must support the organization's distinctive competencies, its competitive advantage (e.g., superior customer service, innovation, efficient production), and the long-term objectives of the organization (such as growth or market share.)

Exhibit 7-1 introduces the key components of an organization's **human resource management process**, which consists of eight activities for staffing the organization and sustaining high employee performance. The first three activities ensure that competent employees are identified and selected; the next two activities involve providing employees with up-to-date knowledge and skills; and the final three activities entail making sure

human resource management process
Activities necessary for staffing the organization and sustaining high employee performance.

Exhibit 7-1

The Human Resource Management Process

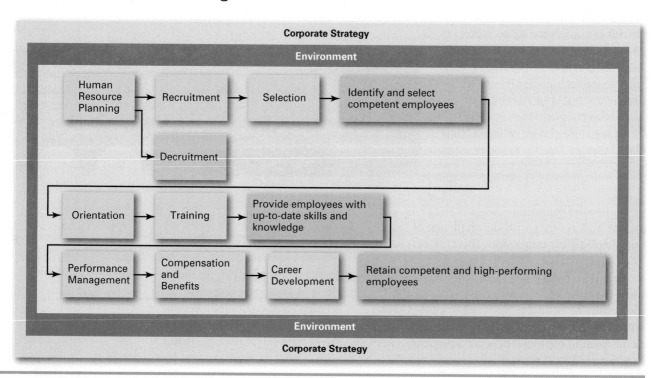

that the organization retains competent and high-performing employees who are capable of sustaining high performance.

Q&A 11.2

Environmental Factors Affecting HRM

Notice in Exhibit 7-1 that the entire HRM process is influenced by the external environment as well as the organization's strategy. Whatever effect the external environment has on the organization ultimately affects the organization's employees. We elaborated on the constraints that the environment puts on managers in Chapter 2. The environmental factors that most directly influence the HRM process are economic conditions, labour unions, and government legislation.

Economic Conditions

The ability of employers to recruit is dependent on local (and national) unemployment rates, competition in regional and local labour markets, and industry-specific labour market conditions. For example, BC is facing a shortage in skilled labour in the leadup to the 2010 Olympics because of the increasing number of jobs available, the decreasing number of people available because of demographic issues, such as the oldest Baby Boomers nearing the age of retirement, and Alberta's higher wage rates. Similarly, hospitals across the country are facing a shortage of nurses, so provinces compete with each other to recruit and retain nurses. When the unemployment rate is high, employers have more potential employees to choose from.

Labour Unions

The Canada Labour Code covers employment by the federal government and Crown corporations and establishes the right of employees to join labour unions if they desire. The provinces and territories have similar legislation to cover workplaces within their areas. This legislation provides a general framework for fair negotiations between management and labour unions and also provides guidelines to make sure that labour disputes do not unduly inconvenience the public.

A **labour union** is an organization that represents employees and seeks to protect their interests through collective bargaining. Labour unions try to improve pay and benefits and working conditions for members. They also try to have greater control over the rules and procedures covering issues such as promotions, layoffs, transfers, and outsourcing.

labour union
An organization that represents employees and seeks to protect their interests through collective bargaining.

In unionized organizations, many HRM decisions are regulated by the terms of collective agreements. These agreements usually define such things as recruitment sources; criteria for hiring, promotions, and layoffs; training eligibility; and disciplinary practices. About 31 percent of Canadian employees belong to labour unions, a figure that has been consistent for the past 20 years.[5] By comparison, only about 12.5 percent of the workforce in the United States is unionized, although that percentage is higher in other countries. In Japan and Germany, respectively, 19.6 percent and 27 percent of the labour force belong to a union. In Mexico, 19 percent of employees belong to a union.[6] Individuals join a labour union for any number of reasons.[7] Wages, working conditions, lack of respect by managers, unfair working hours, job security, and the desire for safer workplaces all contribute to unionization. For example, students working at Montreal's downtown Indigo Books, Music & Café were unhappy with their working conditions and voted to join the Confédération des syndicats nationaux in February 2003.[8]

Q&A 11.3

Government Legislation

The federal government has greatly expanded its influence over HRM by enacting a number of laws and regulations including the Canada Labour Code, employment standards legislation, the Charter of Rights and Freedoms, and the Canadian Human Rights Act. The provincial governments also have their own labour legislation that governs the workplace.

Legislation Affecting Workplace Conditions As noted above, the Canada Labour Code establishes the right of employees to join labour unions if they desire. Part II of this legislation outlines the health and safety obligations of federal employers to prevent accidents and injury to their employees.

Each province and territory has health and safety regulations that cover most nonfederal workplaces in its region. This legislation is typically called the Occupational Health and Safety Act, or something similar. The act generally does not cover work done in private homes or work done in farming operations (unless separate regulations have been added). There is separate legislation covering workplace hazards: the Workplace Hazardous Materials Information System (WHMIS). This is a comprehensive plan for providing information on the safe use of potentially hazardous materials in the workplace.

Q&A 11.4

Employment standards legislation sets minimum employment standards in the private sector in Canada. It covers such things as the minimum age of employees, hours of work and overtime pay, minimum wages, equal pay, general holidays and annual vacations with pay, parental leave, and termination of employment.

Anti-Discrimination Legislation The Charter of Rights and Freedoms and the Canadian Human Rights Act require employers to ensure that equal employment opportunities exist for job applicants and current employees. Decisions regarding who will be hired, for example, or which employees will be chosen for a management training program must

Diversity in Action 2, 4

be made without regard to race, sex, religion, age, colour, national origin, or disability.

Trying to balance the "shoulds and should-nots" of these laws often falls within the realm of employment equity. The Employment Equity Act creates four "protected categories"—women, Aboriginal peoples, people with disabilities, and visible minorities. These groups must not be discriminated against by federally regulated employers and all employers who receive federal contracts worth more than $200 000. Employment equity is intended to ensure that all citizens have an equal opportunity to obtain employment regardless of gender, race or ethnicity, or disabilities.

The intent of the Canada Labour Code, Occupational Health and Safety Act, employment standards legislation, the Charter of Rights and Freedoms, and the Canadian Human Rights Act is to ensure that all employees have a safe work environment, that they are not asked to work too many hours, that they have reasonable opportunities to be considered for jobs, and that pay for jobs is not discriminatory. Because an increasing number of workplace lawsuits are targeting supervisors, as well as their organizations, managers need to be aware of what they can and cannot do by law.[9]

Human Resource Planning

As president and CEO of Scotiabank, Rick Waugh recognizes that providing good service means having good employees.[10] Scotiabank needs to recruit more employees to replace those who move into senior management positions in the next few years.

Think About It

How will changes in the age of the population affect the way organizations hire people?
How can Scotiabank and other organizations respond successfully?

2 How do organizations assess their human resource needs?

Canada will experience a shortage of 1 million skilled workers over the next 20 years, according to The Conference Board of Canada.[11] Aware of these predictions, managers at many companies are developing plans to ensure that they will have enough qualified people to fulfill their human resource needs.

human resource planning
The process by which managers ensure that they have the right number and kinds of people in the right places, and at the right times, who are capable of effectively and efficiently performing assigned tasks.

Through **human resource planning**, managers ensure that they have the right number and kinds of people in the right places, and at the right times, who are capable of effectively and efficiently performing assigned tasks. Through planning, organizations can avoid sudden talent shortages and surpluses.[12] Human resource planning can be condensed into two steps: (1) assessing current human resources; and (2) assessing future human resource needs and developing a program to meet those future needs.

Assessing Current Human Resources

Managers begin human resource planning by reviewing the organization's current human resource status, usually through a *human resource inventory*. This information is taken from forms filled out by employees, and includes things such as name, education, training, prior employment, languages spoken, special capabilities, and specialized skills. Many firms have introduced HR management information systems (HRMIS) to track employee information for policy and strategic needs. For example, these systems can be used for salary and benefits administration. They can also be used to track absenteeism, turnover, and health and safety data. More strategically, HRMIS can be used to keep track of employee skills and education, and match these to ongoing needs of the organization.

Another part of the current assessment is the **job analysis**, which is an assessment that defines jobs and the behaviours necessary to perform them. Information for a job analysis can be gathered by directly observing or videotaping individuals on the job, interviewing employees individually or in a group, having employees complete a structured questionnaire, having job "experts" (usually managers) identify a job's specific characteristics, or having employees record their daily activities in a diary or notebook.

With information from the job analysis, managers develop or revise job descriptions and job specifications. A **job description** is a written statement of what a jobholder does, how the job is done, and why the job is done. It typically describes job content, environment, and conditions of employment. A **job specification** states the minimum qualifications that a person must possess to perform a given job successfully. It identifies the human traits, knowledge, skills, and attitudes needed to do the job effectively. The job description and the job specification are both important documents that aid managers in recruiting and selecting employees.

job analysis
An assessment that defines jobs and the behaviours necessary to perform them.

job description
A written statement of what a jobholder does, how the job is done, and why the job is done.

job specification
A statement of the minimum qualifications that a person must possess to perform a given job successfully.

Meeting Future Human Resource Needs

Future human resource needs are determined by the organization's mission, goals, and strategies. Demand for employees is a result of demand for the organization's products or services. On the basis of its estimate of total revenue, managers can attempt to establish the number and mix of employees needed to reach that revenue. In some cases, however, that situation may be reversed. When particular skills are necessary but in short supply, the availability of appropriate human resources determines revenues.

After they have assessed both current capabilities and future needs, managers are able to estimate human resource shortages—both in number and in type—and to highlight areas in which the organization will be overstaffed. Managers can then develop replacement charts for managerial positions, which outline what employees are available to fill future managerial needs, and can indicate who might be ready for promotion, and who might need more training to move into upper-level positions. With all of this information, managers are ready to proceed to the next step in the HRM process.

Staffing the Organization

To deal with recruiting issues, Scotiabank has developed a Careers webpage to target young graduates and encourage them to think about working for the bank.[13] "We looked at our audience and their primary medium is the Internet. We're matching the channels with the audience we're trying to attract," says Arlene Russell, vice-president of HR. The site gives corporate information, and users can do job searches and read about what makes Scotiabank a good employer.

Russell notes that e-recruiting is not the only way that the bank seeks job applicants. Scotiabank also uses print advertising and recruitment fairs, for example. "There are still strengths in all mediums and I think to really attract job seekers, you have to deliver on all the channels people want," says Russell. "The bottom line is you need to understand who you're speaking to and speak to them in the medium they're comfortable with."

Think About It
What kinds of selection techniques can Scotiabank use to choose suitable employees?

3 How do organizations identify and select competent employees?

recruitment
The process of locating, identifying, and attracting capable applicants.

decruitment
Reducing an organization's workforce.

Once managers know their current human resource status and their future needs, they can begin to do something about any shortages or excesses. If one or more vacancies exist, they can use the information gathered through job analysis to guide them in **recruitment**—that is, the process of locating, identifying, and attracting capable applicants.[14] On the other hand, if human resource planning shows a surplus of employees, management may want to reduce the organization's workforce through **decruitment**.[15]

Recruitment

How would you go about recruiting team members to work on a course project?

At a career fair and expo at Edmonton City Centre mall, the Edmonton Police Service tried to convince high school students that they should consider a career with the police force. To show that there are many different opportunities in police service, they brought their vehicles, including police motorcycles and dirt bikes. Explains spokesperson Dean Parthenis, "People may have thought that once you become a police officer, you stay in that position on patrol for the rest of your life. You can if you like. But there's lots of opportunity to move around once you become a police officer."[16] Potential job candidates can be found through several sources, as Exhibit 7-2 shows.[17]

Web-based recruiting, or e-recruiting, has become a popular choice for organizations and applicants. After the Vancouver Police Department (VPD) examined what kinds of recruits would be needed over the next several years, the department decided to launch a recruitment seminar inside *Second Life*, the online alternative universe. The police recruiters created their own avatars (*Second Life* persona) dressed "in a specially designed VPD uniform, badge, belt and radio." Inspector Kevin McQuiggen, head of the department's tech crimes division, explains why recruiting on *Second Life* makes sense: "If people are on *Second Life*, they're likely to be web-savvy, a quality the police department is looking for in new recruits." The department has seen an increasing number of Internet and technology-related crimes in recent years, and hiring people who can help detect those crimes would be an advantage to the Vancouver police.[18]

Although e-recruiting has been gaining in popularity (Scotiabank, for example, allows applicants to fill out information forms online and upload their résumés with the forms), employers use other recruitment sources as well. Burnaby, BC-based Electronic

Exhibit 7-2

Major Sources of Potential Job Candidates

Source	Advantages	Disadvantages
Internet	Reaches large numbers of people; can get immediate feedback	Generates many unqualified candidates
Employee referrals	Knowledge about the organization provided by current employee; can generate strong candidates because a good referral reflects on the recommender	May not increase the diversity and mix of employees
Company website	Wide distribution; can be targeted to specific groups	Generates many unqualified candidates
College/University recruiting	Large centralized body of candidates	Limited to entry-level positions
Professional recruiting organizations	Good knowledge of industry challenges and requirements	Little commitment to specific organization

Arts Canada, following the lead of some other Canadian companies, decided to recruit at universities in recent years to win "the best and the brightest" from computer science programs.[19] Pat York, director of human resources, is pleased with the results, as the interviews have led to hires more than one-third of the time.

Despite the popularity of new recruiting techniques, the majority of studies have found that employee referrals generally produce the best candidates.[20]

Decruitment

The other approach to controlling labour supply is through decruitment, which is not a pleasant task for any manager. The decruitment options are shown in Exhibit 7-3. Obviously people can be fired, but other choices may be more beneficial to the organization. Keep in mind that, regardless of the method used to reduce the number of employees in the organization, there is no easy way to do it, even though it may be absolutely necessary.

Selection

Once the recruiting effort has developed a pool of candidates, the next step in the HRM process is to determine who is best qualified for the job. This step is called the **selection process**, the process of screening job applicants to ensure that the most appropriate candidates are hired. Errors in hiring can have far-reaching implications. Hiring the right people pays off, however, as the following *Management Reflection* shows.

The Vancouver Police Department has started recruiting through an online presence on *Second Life*. They created special avatars (shown here) to interview prospective candidates.

selection process
The process of screening job applicants to ensure that the most appropriate candidates are hired.

Exhibit 7-3

Decruitment Options

Option	Description
Firing	Permanent involuntary termination
Layoffs	Temporary involuntary termination; may last only a few days or extend to years
Attrition	Not filling openings created by voluntary resignations or normal retirements
Transfers	Moving employees either laterally or downward; usually does not reduce costs but can reduce intraorganizational supply–demand imbalances
Reduced workweeks	Having employees work fewer hours per week, share jobs, or perform their jobs on a part-time basis
Early retirements	Providing incentives to older and more senior employees for retiring before their normal retirement dates
Job sharing	Having employees share one full-time position

MANAGEMENT REFLECTION

Hiring for Passion Decreases Turnover

How closely should companies look for "fit" in prospective employees? Earl Brewer, CEO of Greenarm, believes company fit makes a big difference. He makes sure Greenarm hires people who put people first.[21] "We don't want people working excessively and neglecting their families," he says of the Fredericton, New Brunswick-based developer and property management firm. Brewer says the low turnover at the firm is because they hire the right people: "They have to have passion for the job."

A *Progress* magazine survey of the employees found them raving about working for the company. The employees appreciate that senior management leads by example, and emphasize the importance of balancing work and family life. As one employee explains, "I tell people that my company expects hard, good quality work, but also expects me and others to have a family life and to be happy."

Greenarm, named by *Progress* magazine as a Best Company to Work for in Atlantic Canada, turns its hiring success into business success. The company is New Brunswick's largest private-sector property management company. ■

What Is Selection?

Selection is an exercise in prediction. It seeks to predict which applicants will be successful if hired. *Successful* in this case means performing well on the criteria the organization uses to evaluate employees. In filling a sales position, for example, the selection process should be able to predict which applicants will generate a high volume of sales; for a position as a network administrator, it should predict which applicants will be able to effectively oversee and manage the organization's computer network.

Consider, for a moment, that any selection decision can result in four possible outcomes. As shown in Exhibit 7-4, two of these outcomes would be correct, and two would indicate errors.

A decision is correct when the applicant was predicted to be successful and proved to be successful on the job, or when the applicant was predicted to be unsuccessful and would have been so if hired. In the first case, we have successfully accepted; in the second case, we have successfully rejected.

Problems arise when errors are made in rejecting candidates who would have performed successfully on the job (reject errors) or accepting those who ultimately perform poorly (accept errors). These problems can be significant. Given today's human resource

Exhibit 7-4

Selection Decision Outcomes

		Selection Decision	
		Accept	**Reject**
Later Job Performance	**Successful**	Correct decision	Reject error
	Unsuccessful	Accept error	Correct decision

laws and regulations, reject errors can cost more than the additional screening needed to find acceptable candidates. They can expose the organization to charges of discrimination, especially if applicants from protected groups are disproportionately rejected. The costs of accept errors include the cost of training the employee, the profits lost because of the employee's incompetence, the cost of severance, and the subsequent costs of further recruiting and screening. The major thrust of any selection activity should be to reduce the probability of making reject errors or accept errors while increasing the probability of making correct decisions. How do managers do this? By using selection procedures that are both valid and reliable.

Validity and Reliability

Any selection device that a manager uses should demonstrate **validity**, a proven relationship between the selection device and some relevant job criterion. For example, the law prohibits managers from using a test score as a selection device unless there is clear evidence that, once on the job, individuals with high scores on the test outperform individuals with low test scores. The burden is on managers to show that any selection device they use to differentiate between applicants is related to job performance.

In addition to being valid, a selection device must also demonstrate **reliability**, which indicates whether the device measures the same thing consistently. For example, if a test is reliable, any single individual's score should remain fairly consistent over time, assuming that the characteristics being measured are also stable. No selection device can be effective if it's low in reliability. Using such a device would be like weighing yourself every day on an erratic scale. If the scale is unreliable—randomly fluctuating, say, four to seven kilos every time you step on it—the results will not mean much. To be effective predictors, selection devices must possess an acceptable level of consistency.

validity
The proven relationship that exists between the selection device and some relevant job criterion.

reliability
The ability of a selection device to measure the same thing consistently.

Types of Selection Devices

Managers can use a number of selection devices to reduce accept and reject errors. The best-known include application forms, written tests, performance-simulation tests, interviews, background investigations, and, in some cases, physical examinations. Let's briefly review each of these devices. Exhibit 7-5 on page 204 lists the strengths and weaknesses of each of these devices.[22] We review these devices below.

Application Forms Almost all organizations require job candidates to fill out an application. The form might include space in which the candidate can write his or her name, address, and telephone number. Or it might be a comprehensive personal-history profile that details the candidate's activities, skills, and accomplishments.

Written Tests Typical written tests include tests of intelligence, aptitude, ability, and interest. Such tests have been used for years, although their popularity tends to run in cycles. Today, personality, behavioural, and aptitude assessment tests are popular among businesses. Managers need to be careful regarding their use, however, since legal challenges against such tests have been successful when the tests are not job related or when they elicit information concerning sex, race, age, or other areas protected by the Employment Equity Act.

Managers know that poor hiring decisions are costly and that properly designed tests can reduce the likelihood of poor decisions. In addition, the cost of developing and validating a set of written tests for a specific job has decreased significantly.

A review of the evidence finds that tests of intellectual ability, spatial and mechanical ability, perceptual accuracy, and motor ability are moderately valid predictors for many semiskilled and unskilled operative jobs in manufacturing.[23] However, an enduring criticism of written tests is that intelligence and other tested characteristics can be somewhat removed from the actual performance of the job itself.[24] For example, a high score on an intelligence test is not necessarily a good indicator that the applicant will perform well as a computer programmer. This criticism has led to an increased use of performance-simulation tests.

Exhibit 7-5

Selection Devices

Selection Device	Strengths	Weaknesses
Application forms	Relevant biographical data and facts that can be verified have been shown to be valid performance measures for some jobs. When items on the form have been weighted to reflect job relatedness, this device has proved to be a valid predictor for diverse groups.	Usually only a couple of items on the form prove to be valid predictors of job performance and then only for a specific job. Weighted-item applications are difficult and expensive to create and maintain.
Written tests	Tests of intellectual ability, spatial and mechanical ability, perceptual accuracy, and motor ability are moderately valid predictors for many semi-skilled and unskilled lower-level jobs in manufacturing. Intelligence tests are reasonably good predictors for supervisory positions.	Intelligence and other tested characteristics can be somewhat removed from actual job performance, thus reducing their validity.
Performance-simulation tests	Tests are based on job analysis data and easily meet the requirement of job relatedness. Tests have proven to be valid predictors of job performance.	They are expensive to create and administer.
Interviews	Interviews must be structured and well organized to be effective predictors. Interviewers must use common questions to be effective predictors.	Interviewers must be aware of the legality of certain questions. Interviews are subject to potential biases, especially if they are not well structured and standardized.
Background investigations	Verifications of background data are valuable sources of information.	Reference checks are essentially worthless as a selection tool.
Physical examinations	Physical exams have some validity for jobs with certain physical requirements.	Managers must be sure that physical requirements are job related and do not discriminate.

Performance-Simulation Tests What better way is there to find out whether an applicant for a technical writing position at Matsushita can write technical manuals than by having him or her do it? Performance-simulation tests are made up of actual job behaviours. The best-known performance-simulation tests are **work sampling** (a miniature model of a job) and **assessment centres** (a set of varied exercises that simulate different aspects of the work environment).

The advantage of performance simulation over traditional testing methods should be obvious. Because content is essentially identical to job content, performance simulation should be a better predictor of short-term job performance and should minimize potential employment discrimination allegations. Additionally, because of the nature of their content and the methods used to determine content, well-constructed performance-simulation tests are valid predictors.

work sampling
A performance-simulation test in which job applicants are presented with a miniature model of a job and are asked to perform a representative set of tasks that are central to the job.

assessment centres
A set of varied exercises that simulate different aspects of the work environment and are used to assess job candidates.

Interviews The interview, like the application form, is an almost universal selection device.[25] Not many of us have ever been hired without one or more interviews. Because there are so many variables that can influence interviewer judgment, the value of the interview as a selection device has been of considerable debate.[26] Managers can make interviews more valid and reliable by following the approach presented in *Tips for Managers—Some Suggestions for Interviewing*. See also *Developing Your Interpersonal Skills—Interviewing*, on page 225, at the end of the chapter.

Q&A 11.5
Q&A 11.6

Another important factor in interviewing job candidates is the legality of certain interview questions. Employment law attorneys warn managers to be extremely cautious in the types of questions they ask candidates. Questions about age, marital status, and child-bearing plans, for example, are not appropriate.

A new approach that some companies are using is *situational interviews* in which candidates role-play in mock scenarios. For example, at a Bay Street bank in Toronto, a prospective account representative might be asked to role-play dealing with a customer who has an account discrepancy. The interviewers watch the candidate's reaction: how he or she processes the information, how he or she interacts with the "client," his or her body language, and which words he or she chooses.[28] Some companies also use group interviews, in which job candidates are interviewed by multiple people at once. In some settings, the interviews are conducted by different people across the organization to assess whether the candidate fits in with the organizational culture. In other settings, the work team in which the candidate will work conducts the interview to determine whether the candidate will fit into the work team. Candidates may even be asked to perform tasks with the team to better assess how the candidate works with the team members.

Background Investigations If managers at Lucent Technologies had done a thorough background check, they might have discovered that the individual who eventually became director of recruitment (who is no longer with the company) was imprisoned for stealing money from student funds while a principal at a California high school and had lied about earning a doctorate at Stanford.[29]

Background investigations are of two types: verifications of application data and reference checks. The first type has proved to be a valuable source of selection information and can lower turnover, which saves the company the headaches and additional costs of continually hiring.[30] For instance, Angus Stewart notes that "education fraud is the most common" thing he finds on background checks. He is vice-president of forensics and leader of corporate intelligence at KPMG LLP in Toronto. Quite a lot of people lie "about the degree they received or the institutions they attended," he adds.[31] The second type can be worthless as a selection tool because applicants' references tend to be almost universally positive. Employers should consider contacting the previous employer to get further information, although employers have become reluctant to reveal negative information in recent years.

Physical Examinations This selection device would be useful for only a small number of jobs that have certain physical requirements.

What Works Best and When?

Many selection devices are of limited value to managers in making selection decisions. Exhibit 7-6 on page 206 summarizes the validity of these devices for particular types of jobs. Managers should use those devices that effectively predict success for a given job.

In addition, managers who treat the recruiting and hiring of employees as if the applicants must be sold on the job and exposed only to an organization's positive characteristics are likely to have a workforce that is dissatisfied and has higher turnover.[32] During the hiring process, every job applicant develops a set of expectations about the company and about the job for which he or she is interviewing. When the positive information an applicant receives is excessively inflated, a number of things happen that have potentially negative effects on the company. First, mismatched applicants are less likely to withdraw from the selection process. Second, because inflated information builds unrealistic expectations, new employees are likely to become quickly dissatisfied and leave the organization. Third, new hires are likely to become disillusioned and less committed to the organization when they face the unexpected harsh realities of the job. In many cases, these individuals may feel that they were misled during the hiring process and may become problem employees.

TIPS FOR MANAGERS

Some Suggestions for Interviewing

- Structure a **fixed set of questions** for all applicants.
- Have **detailed information about the job** for which applicants are interviewing.
- **Minimize any prior knowledge** of applicants' backgrounds, experience, interests, test scores, or other characteristics.
- **Ask behavioural questions** that require applicants to give detailed accounts of actual job behaviours.
- Use a **standardized evaluation form**.
- **Take notes** during the interview.
- **Avoid short interviews** that encourage premature decision making.[27]

Exhibit 7-6

Quality of Selection Devices as Predictors

Selection Device	Position			
	Senior Management	Middle and Lower Management	Complex Nonmanagerial	Routine Work
Application forms	2	2	2	2
Written tests	1	1	2	3
Work sampling	—	—	4	4
Assessment centres	5	5	—	—
Interviews	4	3	2	2
Verification of application data	3	3	3	3
Reference checks	1	1	1	1
Physical exams	1	1	1	2

Note: Validity is measured on a scale from 5 (highest) to 1 (lowest). A dash means "not applicable."

realistic job preview (RJP)
A preview of a job that includes both positive and negative information about the job and the company.

To increase job satisfaction among employees and reduce turnover, you should consider providing a **realistic job preview (RJP)**. An RJP includes both positive and negative information about the job and the company. For example, in addition to the positive comments typically expressed during an interview, the job applicant might be told that there are limited opportunities to talk to co-workers during work hours, that promotional advancement is slim, or that work hours fluctuate so erratically that employees may be required to work during what are usually off hours (nights and weekends). Research indicates that applicants who have been given a realistic job preview hold lower and more realistic job expectations for the jobs they will be performing and are better able to cope with the frustrating elements of the job than are applicants who have been given only positive information.

Orientation and Skill Development

Thirty-year-old Roxann Linton is enthusiastic about her career at Scotiabank.[33] "Working with an international and diverse organization like Scotiabank, there are so many opportunities," says Linton. The young woman was chosen for Leading Edge, Scotiabank's fast-track leadership program. In the application process, she had to prepare a challenging business case analysis, go through psychometric testing, and be interviewed twice by a total of eight executives. The Leading Edge program prepares employees for senior management positions by rotating them through a series of assignments.

Linton worked for the bank for about five years in the bank's internal audit department in Kingston, Jamaica. She then transferred to Halifax and worked in commercial banking. During the first 15 months of the Leading Edge program, Linton managed more than 100 people in the electronic banking contact centre. Her next assignment was as director of special projects at Scotia Cassels Investment Counsel, part of the bank's wealth management division. She launched a new corporate bond fund during her first three months in that assignment. She will have one more 12- to 18-month assignment in another part of the bank, and then she can start applying for vice-president positions.

Think About It

What kinds of orientation and training methods do organizations use to help employees develop their skills and learn about their organizations?

Organizations have to introduce new members to the work they will do and the organization. They do this through their orientation programs. As time goes by, employees may need to increase their skills. This is handled through training. We review the strategies that organizations use for orientation and training below.

4 How do organizations help employees adapt and stay up-to-date?

Orientation

Did you participate in some type of organized introduction to campus life when you started college or university? If so, you might have been told about your school's rules and regulations, the procedures for activities such as applying for financial aid, cashing a cheque, or registering for classes, and you were probably introduced to some of the campus administrators. A person starting a new job needs the same type of introduction to his or her job and the organization. This introduction is called **orientation**.

orientation
The introduction of a new employee to his or her job and the organization.

There are two types of orientation. *Work unit orientation* familiarizes the employee with the goals of the work unit, clarifies how his or her job contributes to the unit's goals, and includes an introduction to his or her new co-workers. *Organization orientation* informs the new employee about the organization's objectives, history, philosophy, procedures, and rules. This should include relevant human resource policies and benefits such as work hours, pay procedures, overtime requirements, and fringe benefits. In addition, a tour of the organization's work facilities is often part of the organization orientation.

Managers have an obligation to make the integration of the new employee into the organization as smooth and as free of anxiety as possible. They need to openly discuss employee beliefs regarding mutual obligations of the organization and the employee.[34] It's in the best interests of the organization and the new employee to get the person up and running in the job as soon as possible. Successful orientation, whether formal or informal, results in an outsider–insider transition that makes the new member feel comfortable and fairly well adjusted, lowers the likelihood of poor work performance, and reduces the probability of a surprise resignation by the new employee only a week or two into the job.

Training

Employee training is an important HRM activity. As job demands change, employee skills have to be altered and updated. In 2006, US business firms budgeted over $55 billion on workforce formal training.[35] Canadian companies spend far less than American firms on training and development, about $852 per employee compared with $1273 by the

Infosys Technologies, India's fast-growing software company, has created Infosys University, one of the largest training centres in the world, to train the new employees the company hires each year. The $120 million campus-like facility bans alcohol and offers only single-sex dorms, but there are three movie theatres, a pool, a gym, and dozens of instructors as well as online courses to teach recruits everything from technical skills and team building to interpersonal communication and corporate etiquette. Says CEO Nandan Nilekani, "Companies haven't been investing enough in people. Rather than train them, they let them go. Our people are our capital. The more we invest in them, the more they can be effective."

Exhibit 7-7

Types of Training

Type	Includes
General	Communication skills, computer systems application and programming, customer service, executive development, management skills and development, personal growth, sales, supervisory skills, and technological skills and knowledge
Specific	Basic life/work skills, creativity, customer education, diversity/cultural awareness, remedial writing, managing change, leadership, product knowledge, public speaking/presentation skills, safety, ethics, sexual harassment, team building, wellness, and others

Source: Based on "2005 Industry Report—Types of Training," *Training*, December 2005, p. 22.

Americans in 2006.[36] Managers, of course, are responsible for deciding what type of training employees need, when they need it, and what form that training should take.

Types of Training

When organizations invest in employee training, what are they offering? Exhibit 7-7 describes the major types of training that organizations provide.[37] Some of the most popular types of training that organizations provide include sexual harassment, safety, management skills and development, and supervisory skills.[38] For many organizations, employee interpersonal skills training—communication, conflict resolution, team building, customer service, and so forth—is a high priority. Shannon Washbrook, director of training and development for Vancouver-based Boston Pizza International, says, "Our people know the Boston Pizza concept; they have all the hard skills. It's the soft skills they lack." To address that, Washbrook launched Boston Pizza College, a training initiative that uses hands-on, scenario-based learning about many interpersonal skills topics.[39] SaskPower, like Scotiabank, uses training to develop leadership potential, as the following *Management Reflection* shows.

Is college or university education enough for the workplace, or do you need more training?

MANAGEMENT REFLECTION

SaskPower Sends Its Leaders to Leadership School

Are leaders made or born? Managers at Regina-based SaskPower believe that leaders are developed, not born.[40] The company has developed a leadership program that is similar to a mini-MBA. It introduces participants to leadership skills and other areas of business. The company selects employees for the program based on leadership potential. Individuals can nominate themselves for the leadership-training program by persuading management with examples of why they would make great managers.

The program works better than the way managers were chosen previously at SaskPower. "It was unorganized, and the 'old boys network' was still at work," said Bill Hyde, former vice-president of human resources. The program also ensures that SaskPower continues to have a skilled workforce and trained managers for the future, when Baby Boomers start retiring in large numbers. ■

Training Methods

Employee training can be delivered in traditional ways including on-the-job training, job rotation, mentoring and coaching, experiential exercises, workbooks and manuals, classroom lectures, or videos. Toronto-based Labatt Breweries has created its own beer school at

Exhibit 7-8

Employee Training Methods

Traditional Training Methods

- *On-the-job*—Employees learn how to do tasks simply by performing them, usually after an initial introduction to the task.
- *Job rotation*—Employees work at different jobs in a particular area, getting exposure to a variety of tasks.
- *Mentoring and coaching*—Employees work with an experienced worker who provides information, support, and encouragement; also called apprenticing in certain industries.
- *Experiential exercises*—Employees participate in role playing, simulations, or other face-to-face types of training.
- *Workbooks/manuals*—Employees refer to training workbooks and manuals for information.
- *Classroom lectures*—Employees attend lectures designed to convey specific information.

Technology-Based Training Methods

- *CD-ROM/DVD/videotapes/audiotapes*—Employees listen to or watch selected media that convey information or demonstrate certain techniques.
- *Videoconferencing/teleconferencing/satellite TV*—Employees listen to or participate as information is conveyed or techniques demonstrated.
- *E-learning*—Internet-based learning in which employees participate in multimedia simulations or other interactive modules.

an on-site pub at company headquarters to teach employees about the qualities of beer.[41] It might seem obvious that those in sales should know the product, but even accountants and human resource specialists from head office learn how to change a keg and clean the lines. They learn that "Keith's is a fast-pouring beer, that Stella Artois is best served in a glass with a stem and that foam bubbles should be sliced from the heads of some beers because 'large CO_2 bubbles will bloat us.'" Labatt's senior management feels that all employees need to be beer experts so that they can help sell the product, even if they are not officially salespeople.

Many organizations are relying more on technology-based training methods because of their accessibility, lower cost, and ability to deliver information. For example, a computer-based simulation called Virtual Leader by SimuLearn provides trainees with realistic leadership scenarios, including the following:

> "Be in the boardroom in 10 minutes," reads the email from Senior Vice President Alan Young. The CEO is out on his boat, and a storm has knocked out all communication. Worse, there has been a massive fire in the call centre in South America. "We could lose billions," Young says. The board has given senior staff emergency powers. You're a top manager who has been called in to help. What do you do?[42]

Exhibit 7-8 provides a description of the various traditional and technology-based employee training methods that managers might use. Although web-based or online training had been predicted to become the most popular method of training, it simply has not lived up to expectations, Julie Kaufman, an industry analyst with Toronto-based IDC Canada, told attendees at a training and development conference. Most organizations have not yet figured out how to make use of this type of training.[43]

Managing and Rewarding Performance

Managers need to know whether their employees are performing their jobs efficiently and effectively or whether there is need for improvement. Employees are often compensated based on those evaluations. For more on giving evaluations, see *Self-Assessment—How Good Am I at Giving Performance Feedback?* on pages 221–222, at the end of the chapter.

5 What can organizations do to help employees achieve high performance throughout their careers?

Performance Management

performance management system
A process of establishing performance standards and evaluating performance in order to arrive at objective human resource decisions, as well as to provide documentation to support those decisions.

Evaluating employee performance is part of a **performance management system**, which is a process of establishing performance standards and appraising employee performance in order to arrive at objective human resource decisions as well as to provide documentation to support those decisions. Performance appraisal is a critical part of a performance management system. Some companies invest far more effort in it than others.

What techniques might you want to use if you had to evaluate the members of your student project group?

Performance appraisal is not easy to do, and many managers do it poorly. Both managers and employees often dread the appraisal process. A survey found that 41 percent of employees report having had a least one incident of being demotivated after feedback from their managers.[44] Performance appraisal can also be subject to politics, not unlike the 2002 Olympic Winter Games ice skating controversy in which the French judge was accused of manipulating her scores to enable the Russian skaters to win the gold over Canadians Jamie Salé and David Pelletier. Let's look at some different methods of doing performance appraisal.

Performance Appraisal Methods

Managers can choose from seven major performance appraisal methods. The advantages and disadvantages of each of these methods are shown in Exhibit 7-9.

written essay
A performance appraisal method in which the evaluator writes out a description of an employee's strengths and weaknesses, past performance, and potential.

Written Essays The **written essay** is a performance appraisal method in which the evaluator writes out a description of an employee's strengths and weaknesses, past performance, and potential. The evaluator also makes suggestions for improvement.

critical incidents
A performance appraisal method in which the evaluator focuses on the critical, or key, behaviours that separate effective from ineffective job performance.

Critical Incidents The use of **critical incidents** focuses the evaluator's attention on critical, or key, behaviours that separate effective from ineffective job performance. The evaluator writes down anecdotes that describe what an employee did that was especially effective or ineffective. The key here is that only specific behaviours, not vaguely defined personality traits, are cited.

graphic rating scales
A performance appraisal method in which the evaluator rates an employee on a set of performance factors.

Graphic Rating Scales One of the most popular performance appraisal methods is **graphic rating scales**. This method lists a set of performance factors such as quantity and quality of work, job knowledge, cooperation, loyalty, attendance, honesty, and initiative. The evaluator then goes down the list and rates the employee on each factor using an incremental scale, which usually specifies five points. A factor such as job knowledge,

Exhibit 7-9

Advantages and Disadvantages of Performance Appraisal Methods

Method	Advantage	Disadvantage
Written essays	Simple to use	More a measure of evaluator's writing ability than of employee's actual performance
Critical incidents	Rich examples; behaviourally based	Time-consuming; lack quantification
Graphic rating scales	Provide quantitative data; less time-consuming than others	Do not provide depth of job behaviour assessed
BARS	Focus on specific and measurable behaviours	Time-consuming; difficult to develop job behaviours
Multiperson comparisons	Compare employees with one another	Unwieldy with large number of employees; legal concerns
MBO	Focuses on end goals; results oriented	Time-consuming
360-degree feedback	Thorough	Time-consuming

for example, might be rated from 1 ("poorly informed about work duties") to 5 ("has complete mastery of all phases of the job").

Behaviourally Anchored Rating Scales Another popular performance appraisal method is **behaviourally anchored rating scales (BARS)**. These scales combine major elements from the critical incident and graphic rating scale approaches. The evaluator rates an employee according to items along a numeric scale, but the items are examples of actual job behaviours rather than general descriptions or traits.

behaviourally anchored rating scales (BARS)
A performance appraisal method in which the evaluator rates an employee on examples of actual job behaviours.

Multiperson Comparisons **Multiperson comparisons** compare one individual's performance with that of others.[45] Made popular by former General Electric (GE) CEO Jack Welch, employees were rated as top performers (20 percent), middle performers (70 percent), or bottom performers (10 percent). It was believed that by using this type of "rank and yank" appraisal, the company would rid itself of slackers and thus be more productive. However, critics of such systems say that they unfairly penalize groups made up of star performers and hinder risk-taking and collaboration.[46] For example, Sprint used forced rankings for a year and discontinued the program because it found more effective ways to differentiate performance.[47] Are forced rankings a good idea or a bad idea? Research has shown that in companies that used forced rankings and fired the bottom 5 percent to 10 percent of employees, productivity increased an impressive 16 percent over the first couple of years. But then in subsequent years, productivity gains dropped off considerably.[48] So, companies are questioning the wisdom of strict forced ranking. Even GE has been looking at ways to make its system more flexible and has encouraged its managers to use more common sense in assigning rankings.[49]

multiperson comparisons
A performance appraisal method by which one individual's performance is compared with that of others.

Management by Objectives We previously introduced management by objectives (MBO) when we discussed planning in Chapter 3. MBO is also a mechanism for appraising performance. In fact, it's often used for assessing managers and professional employees.[50] With MBO, employees are evaluated according to how well they accomplish specific goals that have been established by them and their managers.

360-Degree Feedback **360-degree feedback** is a performance appraisal method that uses feedback from supervisors, employees, and co-workers. In other words, this appraisal uses information from the full circle of people with whom the manager interacts. Of the 101 large Canadian organizations surveyed by professors Mehrdad Debrayen and Stephane Brutus of the John Molson School of Business at Concordia University, 43 percent used 360-degree feedback.[51] Toronto-based Hill & Knowlton Canada, a public relations firm, uses 360-degree feedback to help employees learn what they need to get to the next level of the organization. The feedback has had the added benefit of reducing turnover to 18 percent.[52]

360-degree feedback
A performance appraisal method that uses feedback from supervisors, employees, and co-workers.

Users caution that, although it's effective for career coaching and helping a manager recognize his or her strengths and weaknesses, this method is not appropriate for determining pay, promotions, or terminations. Managers using 360-degree feedback also have to carefully consider the pros and cons of using anonymous evaluations.[53]

Not all organizations conduct performance evaluations; in particular, smaller organizations often do not. Consequently, it can be useful as an employee to ask your manager for an annual appraisal, if you do not routinely receive one. The feedback will allow you to determine your goals for the following year, and identify anything for which you need improvement or training.

What Happens When Performance Falls Short?

So far, our discussion has focused on the performance management system. But what if an employee is not performing in a satisfactory manner? What can you do?

If, for some reason, an employee is not meeting his or her performance goals, a manager needs to find out why. If it is because the employee is mismatched for the job (a hiring error) or because he or she does not have adequate training, something relatively simple can be done: The manager can either reassign the individual to a job that better matches his or her skills or train the employee to do the job more effectively. If the problem is associated not with the employee's abilities but with his or her desire to do the job, it becomes a **discipline** problem. In that case, a manager can try counselling and, if necessary, can take disciplinary action such as oral and written warnings, suspensions, and even termination.

Employee counselling is a process designed to help employees overcome performance-related problems. Rather than viewing the performance problem as something that needs to be punished (discipline), employee counselling attempts to uncover why employees have lost their desire or ability to work productively. More important, it is designed to find ways to fix the problem. In many cases, employees do not go from being productive one day to being unproductive the next. Rather, the change happens gradually and may be a function of what is occurring in their personal lives. Employee counselling attempts to assist employees in getting help to resolve whatever is bothering them.

discipline
Actions taken by a manager to enforce an organization's standards and regulations.

employee counselling
A process designed to help employees overcome performance-related problems.

Compensation and Benefits

6 How do compensation and benefits motivate employees?

How would you know whether your employer was paying you fairly?

Q&A 11.7

Most of us expect to receive appropriate compensation from our employers. Therefore, developing an effective and appropriate compensation system is an important part of the HRM process.[54] Why? Because it helps attract and retain competent and talented individuals who help the organization accomplish its mission and goals. In addition, an organization's compensation system has been shown to have an impact on its strategic performance.[55]

Managers must develop a compensation system that reflects the changing nature of work and the workplace in order to keep people motivated. Organizational compensation can include many different types of rewards and benefits such as base wages and salaries, wage and salary add-ons, incentive payments, as well as other benefits and services such as vacation time, extended health care, training allowances and pensions. Benefits can often amount to one-third or more of an individual's base salary and should be viewed by the employee as part of the total compensation package.

How do managers determine who gets paid $9 an hour and who gets $350 000 a year? Several factors influence the differences in compensation and benefit packages for different employees. Exhibit 7-10 summarizes these factors, which are both job-based and business- or industry-based.

Many organizations use an alternative approach to determining compensation called **skill-based pay**. In a skill-based pay system, an employee's job title does not define his or her pay category; skills do.[56] Research shows that these types of pay systems seem to be more successful in manufacturing organizations than in service organizations and organizations pursuing technical innovations.[57] Skill-based pay systems seem to mesh nicely with the changing nature of jobs and today's work environment. As one expert noted, "Slowly, but surely, we're becoming a skill-based society where your market value is tied to what you can do and what your skill set is. In this new world where skills and knowledge are what really count, it doesn't make sense to treat people as jobholders. It makes sense to treat them as people with specific skills and to pay them for these skills."[58] On the other hand, many organizations are using **variable pay** systems, in which an individual's compensation is contingent on performance—81 percent of Canadian and Taiwanese organizations use variable pay plans, and 78 percent of US organizations do.[59]

Although many factors influence the design of an organization's compensation system, flexibility is a key consideration. The traditional approach to paying people reflected a time of job stability when an employee's pay was largely determined by seniority and job level. Given the dynamic environments that many organizations face in which the

skill-based pay
A pay system that rewards employees for the job skills and competencies they can demonstrate.

variable pay
A pay system in which an individual's compensation is contingent on performance.

Exhibit 7-10

Factors That Influence Compensation and Benefits

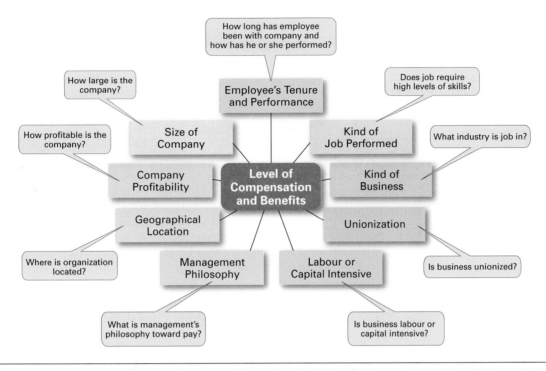

Sources: Based on R. I. Henderson, *Compensation Management*, 6th ed. (Upper Saddle River, NJ: Prentice Hall, 1994), pp. 3–24; and A. Murray, "Mom, Apple Pie, and Small Business," *Wall Street Journal*, August 15, 1994, p. A1.

skills that are absolutely critical to organizational success can change in a matter of months, the trend is to make pay systems more flexible and to reduce the number of pay levels. However, whatever approach managers take, they must establish a fair, equitable, and motivating compensation system that allows the organization to recruit and keep a productive workforce.

Career Development

The term *career* has several meanings. In popular usage, it can mean advancement ("she is on a management career track"), a profession ("he has chosen a career in accounting"), or a lifelong sequence of jobs ("his career has included 12 jobs in 6 organizations"). For our purposes, we define a **career** as the sequence of positions held by a person during his or her lifetime.[60] Using this definition, it's apparent that we all have, or will have, a career. Moreover, the concept is as relevant to unskilled labourers as it is to software designers or physicians.

7 How are careers managed?

career
A sequence of positions held by a person during his or her lifetime.

Managing One's Career

Downsizing, restructuring, and other organizational adjustments have brought us to one significant conclusion about career development: The individual—not the organization—is responsible for his or her own career! Individuals need to assume primary responsibility for career planning, career goal setting, and education and training.[61]

One of the first career decisions you have to make is career choice. The optimum career choice is one that offers the best match between what you want out of life and your interests, abilities, and market opportunities. Good career choice outcomes should result in a series of positions that give you an opportunity to be a good performer, make you

Q&A 11.8

Exhibit 7-11

What Do College and University Grads Want From Their Jobs?

Top Factors for Canadian Students

- Opportunities for advancement in position
- Good people to work with
- Good people to report to
- Work–life balance
- Initial salary

Top Factors for US Students

- Work–life balance
- Annual base salary
- Job stability and security
- Recognition for a job done well
- Increasingly challenging tasks
- Rotational programs

Top Factors for UK Students

- International career opportunities
- Flexible working hours
- Variety of assignments
- Paid overtime

Sources: Based on E. Pooley, "Hire Education: How to Recruit Top University Graduates," *Canadian Business*, September 11–24, 2006; S. Shellenbarger, "Avoiding the Next Enron: Today's Crop of Soon-to-Be Grads Seeks Job Security," *Wall Street Journal*, February 16, 2006; "MBAs Eye Financial Services and Management Consulting," *HRMarketer.com*, June 7, 2005; and J. Boone, "Students Set Tighter Terms for Work," *FinancialTimes.com*, May 21, 2005.

want to maintain your commitment to your career, lead to highly satisfying work, and give you the proper balance between work and personal life. A good career match, then, is one in which you are able to develop a positive self-concept, to do work that you think is important, and to lead the kind of life you desire.[62] Exhibit 7-11 describes the factors Canadian, American, and UK college and university students and graduates are looking for in their jobs. As you look at these results, think about what is important to you. How would you have ranked these items?

Q&A 11.9   Once you have identified a career choice, it's time to initiate the job search. We are not going to get into the specifics of job hunting, writing a résumé, or interviewing successfully, although those career actions are important. Let's fast forward through all that and assume that your job search was successful. It's time to go to work! How do you survive and excel in your career? See *Tips for Managers—Some Suggestions for a Successful Management Career.*[63] By taking an active role in managing your career, your work life can be more exciting, enjoyable, and satisfying.

⃝⃝⃝ Current Issues in Human Resource Management

Scotiabank prides itself on its work with the Aboriginal community.[64] The bank sponsors scholarships, events, and programs for community members, and also supports Aboriginal business initiatives.

The bank actively recruits from the Aboriginal community. Scotiabank's recruiting strategy is based "on the medicine wheel and the teachings of the medicine wheel, in terms of all the components [of the medicine wheel] need to exist in balance together," says Michele Baptiste, national manager of Aboriginal relations with Scotiabank. The bank has also approached the Aboriginal Human Resource Development Council of Canada to assist "in recruitment and retention of Aboriginal people across the country," according to Baptiste.

Think About It

How are companies managing diversity in their workplaces? To what extent are they addressing issues such as work–life balance? Should they be doing so?

8 What are some current issues in human resource management?

We conclude this chapter by looking at some contemporary human resource issues facing today's managers—workforce diversity, sexual harassment, work–life balance, and layoff-survivor sickness.

Workforce Diversity

We have discussed the changing makeup of the workforce in several places throughout this textbook and provided insights in our *Managing Workforce Diversity* feature in several chapters. In this section, we discuss how workforce diversity is directly affected by basic HRM activities including recruitment, selection, and orientation and training.

Recruitment

To improve workforce diversity, managers need to widen their recruiting net. For example, the popular practice of relying on employee referrals as a source of job applicants tends to produce candidates who are similar to present employees. However, some organizations, such as Toronto-based TELUS Mobility, have recruited and hired diverse individuals by relying on referrals from their current employees. But not every organization has the employee resources needed to achieve workforce diversity through employee referrals. So managers may have to look for job applicants in places where they might not have looked before. To increase diversity, managers from such companies as Calgary-based Suncor Energy, Saskatoon, Saskatchewan-based Cameco, and Toronto-based Scotiabank and TELUS Mobility are increasingly turning to nontraditional recruitment sources such as women's job networks, over-50 clubs, urban job banks, disabled people's training centres, ethnic newspapers, and gay rights organizations. This type of outreach should enable the organization to broaden its pool of diverse applicants. When IKEA went to Seville, Spain, it followed an alternative recruiting strategy, as the following *Management Reflection* shows.

MANAGEMENT REFLECTION

IKEA Taps into New Labour Force

Should you hire people with no previous experience? When Sweden-based IKEA opened up a store in Seville, its fifth location in Spain, the company decided to search for a different type of employee.[65] The company advertised for "single mothers, students, people with disabilities and long-term unemployed." They did not even require working experience. Andalusia, the region where the store was opening, has an 18.5 percent unemployment rate, and 30 000 applicants responded to IKEA's ads.

Employers in Spain had never recruited from these categories of workers before. IKEA's model for employment is unique: It targets people who really need jobs. The company provides training to its employees to help them overcome any initial hurdles from lack of experience. People with disabilities were hired for customer service, administration, and logistics. Juvencio Maeztu, the store manager, explained the store's hiring policy: "We were more interested in finding people with the right motivation than with the right college degrees."

IKEA's strategy of hiring the previously "unhirable" may well pay off in Spain. With high unemployment rates and IKEA's plan to open 22 new stores, those in Spain looking for jobs have renewed hope they will be able to find work. ■

Selection

Once a diverse set of applicants exists, efforts must be made to ensure that the selection process does not discriminate. Moreover, applicants need to be made comfortable with the organization's culture and be made aware of management's desire to accommo-date their needs. For example, at TD Canada Trust, managers are trained to respond pos-itively to requests by employees who need a prayer room or whose religion requires them to stop working by sundown.[66]

Orientation and Training

The outsider–insider transition is often more challenging for women and minorities than for white males. Many organizations provide special workshops to raise diversity aware-ness issues. However, some organizations pursue diversity efforts only after being hit with legal claims. For instance, the Denny's restaurant chain was hit with a series of legal claims in the early 1990s. It responded with aggressive minority hiring and a supplier-diversity effort. The company has been ranked in the top 10 of *Fortune* magazine's "America's 50 Best Companies for Minorities" for eight years straight. Coca-Cola, which settled a class-action suit by black employees for more than $287 million in November 2000, has made strides in its diversity efforts, including launching a formal mentoring program and required diversity training for employees.[67]

Diversity in Action 6

Sexual Harassment

Sexual harassment is a serious issue in both public and private sector organizations. A survey by York University found that 48 percent of working women in Canada reported they had experienced some form of "gender harassment" in the year before they were surveyed.[68] A 1996 RCMP survey found that 6 out of every 10 female Mounties said they had experienced sexual harassment and in the decade following that report female RCMP members have launched lawsuits in Saskatchewan, Alberta, BC, Manitoba, and Ontario.[69] In 2006, Nancy Sulz, who worked as an RCMP officer in BC, was awarded $950 000 for her complaint against the detachment, which included claims of sexual harassment.[70] Barbara Orser, a research affiliate with The Conference Board of Canada, notes that "sexual harassment is more likely to occur in workplace environments that tolerate bullying, intimidation, yelling, innuendo and other forms of discourteous behaviour."[71]

Sexual harassment is not a problem just in Canada. During 2007, more than 12 500 com-plaints were filed with the Equal Employment Opportunity Commission (EEOC) in the United States. Although most complaints are filed by women, in 2007 the percentage of charges filed by males in the United States reached an all-time high of 16 percent.[72] Charges have also been filed against employers in such countries as Japan, Australia, the Netherlands, Belgium, New Zealand, Sweden, Ireland, and Mexico.[73]

Even though discussions of sexual harassment cases often focus on the large awards granted by a court, there are other concerns for employers. Sexual harassment creates an unpleasant work environment and undermines employees' ability to perform their jobs.

Sexual harassment is defined by the Supreme Court of Canada as unwelcome behav-iour of a sexual nature in the workplace that negatively affects the work environment or leads to adverse job-related consequences for the employee.[74] Sexual harassment can occur between members of the opposite sex or of the same sex. By most accounts, prior to the mid-1980s instances of sexual harassment were generally viewed as isolated inci-dents, with the individual at fault being solely responsible (if at all) for his or her actions. Little, if any, emphasis was placed on the problem of offensive or hostile work environ-ments. Although sexual harassment is generally covered under employment discrimina-tion laws, in recent years this problem has gained wider recognition.

Many problems associated with sexual harassment involve interpreting the Supreme Court's definition to determine exactly what constitutes illegal behaviour. For many organ-izations, conveying what an offensive or hostile environment looks like is not completely black and white. While it is relatively easy to focus on the issue of an individual employee being harassed, this may not address more systemic problems in the workplace. Other employees can also be negatively affected when they witness offensive conduct.[75] Thus

sexual harassment
Any unwelcome behaviour of a sexual nature in the workplace that negatively affects the work environment or leads to adverse job-related consequences for the employee.

managers need to be attuned to what makes fellow employees uncomfortable—and if they don't know, they should ask.[76]

What can an organization do to protect itself against sexual harassment claims?[77] The courts want to know two things: Did the organization know about, or should it have known about, the alleged behaviour? and What did management do to stop it? With the number and dollar amounts of the awards against organizations increasing, organizations should develop sexual harassment policies, educate all employees on sexual harassment matters, and have mechanisms in place to monitor employees and deal with complaints, should they arise.

Work–Life Balance

> *What kinds of work–life balance issues are affecting your life right now?*

Professors Linda Duxbury of the Sprott School of Business at Carleton University and Chris Higgins of the University of Western Ontario are the leading Canadian researchers on the issue of work–life balance. Their research shows that employees are working long hours, and are also increasingly being asked to work a number of unpaid hours a week. This affects employees' abilities to manage their family lives.

What kinds of work–life balance issues can arise that might affect an employee's job performance? Here are some examples:

- Is it okay for someone to bring his baby to work because of an emergency crisis with normal child care arrangements?

- Is it okay to expect an employee to work 60 or more hours a week?

- Should an employee be given the day off to watch her child perform in a school event?

family-friendly benefits
Benefits that accommodate employees' needs for work–life balance.

In the 1980s, organizations began to recognize that employees do not leave their families and personal lives behind when they walk into work. An organization hires a person who has a personal life outside the office, personal problems, and family commitments. Although managers cannot be sympathetic to every detail of an employee's family life, we *are* seeing organizations more aware of the fact that employees have sick children, elderly parents who need special care, and other family issues that may require special arrangements. In response, most major organizations have taken actions to make their workplaces more family-friendly by offering **family-friendly benefits**, which include a wide range of work and family programs to help employees.[78] They have introduced programs such as on-site child care, summer day camps, flextime, job sharing, leaves for school functions, telecommuting, and part-time employment.

Work–life conflicts are as relevant to male employees with children and female employees without children as they are to female employees with children. Heavy workloads and increased travel demands, for example, are making it increasingly hard for many employees, male and female, to meet both work and personal responsibilities. A *Fortune* survey found that 84 percent of male executives surveyed said that "they'd like job options that let them realize their professional aspirations while having more time for things outside work." Also,

Does being rigid about not offering flextime harm employers? Surrey, BC, mom Sheila Whitehead thinks so. She quit her job as a marketing manager for a pharmaceuticals company when she could not get the flextime she needed to spend more time with her four-year-old daughter Abigail and her other two young children. She says that employers are "missing out on incredibly talented people who simply don't want the rigid nine-to-five hours." She created a website, Beyond9to5.com, to help match employers with employees who want to have more flexible work hours.

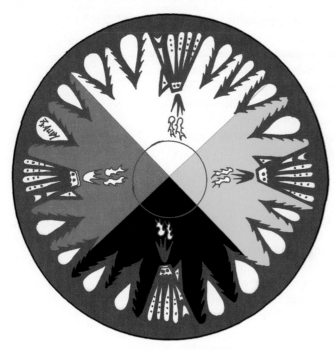

Michele Baptiste, national manager of Aboriginal relations with Scotiabank, created the bank's Aboriginal employment strategy. It is based on the teachings of the medicine wheel (an example of which is shown here). The idea behind the medicine wheel is that the four major components of an individual (mental, spiritual, emotional, physical) have to be in balance. Baptiste emphasizes that Scotiabank takes a holistic approach to Aboriginal relations, bringing together employment, business, and community involvement.

87 percent of these executives believed that any company that restructured top-level management jobs in ways that would both increase productivity and make more time available for life outside the office would have a competitive advantage in attracting talented employees.[79] Younger employees, particularly, put a higher priority on family and a lower priority on jobs and are looking for organizations that give them more work flexibility.[80]

Today's progressive workplace is becoming more accommodating of the varied needs of a diverse workforce. It provides a wide range of scheduling options and benefits that give employees more flexibility at work and allow employees to better balance or integrate their work and personal lives. Despite these organizational efforts, work–life programs have room for improvement. Workplace surveys still show high levels of employee stress stemming from work–life conflicts. And large groups of women and minority employees remain unemployed or underemployed because of family responsibilities and bias in the workplace.[81] So what can managers do?

Research on work–life balance has provided some new insights. For example, we are beginning to see evidence that there are positive outcomes when individuals are able to combine work and family roles.[82] As one study participant noted, "I think being a mother and having patience and watching someone else grow has made me a better manager. I am better able to be patient with other people and let them grow and develop in a way that is good for them."[83] In addition, individuals who have family-friendly workplace support appear to be more satisfied on the job.[84] This seems to strengthen the notion that organizations benefit by creating a workplace in which employee work–life balance is possible. And the benefits show up in financial results as well. Research has shown a significant, positive relationship between work–family initiatives and an organization's stock price.[85]

However, managers need to understand that people do differ in their preferences for work–family life scheduling options and benefits.[86] Some people prefer organizational initiatives that better *segment* work from their personal lives. Others prefer programs that facilitate *integration*. Flextime schedules segment because they allow employees to schedule work hours that are less likely to conflict with personal responsibilities. On the other hand, on-site child care integrates by blurring the boundaries between work and family responsibilities. People who prefer segmentation are more likely to be satisfied and committed to their jobs when offered options such as flextime, job sharing, and part-time hours. People who prefer integration are more likely to respond positively to options such as on-site child care, gym facilities, and company-sponsored family picnics.

Diversity in Action 5

Helping Survivors Respond to Layoffs

As a result of the financial crisis that swept North America in 2008 and 2009, Canadians started losing jobs at increasing rates. Between October 2008 and March 2009, 357 000 jobs were lost (a drop of 2.1 percent), the largest decline in percentage terms in a five-month period since the 1982 recession.[87] Employers, because of financial stress, were engaging in **downsizing**, the planned elimination of jobs in an organization. How can managers best manage a downsized workplace? Expect disruptions in the workplace and in employees' personal lives. Stress, frustration, anxiety, and anger are typical reactions of both individuals being laid off and the job survivors. But are there things managers can do to lessen the pain? Yes.[88]

downsizing
The planned elimination of jobs in an organization.

Open and honest communication is critical. Individuals who are being let go need to be informed as soon as possible. In providing assistance to employees being downsized, the law requires some form of severance pay in lieu of proper notice. Benefit extensions to help employees while they find new plans must also be covered for a specified period of time. Managers want to be sure to follow any laws that might affect the length of time that pay and benefits must be offered. In addition, many organizations provide job search assistance.

It may surprise you to learn that both victims and survivors experience feelings of frustration, anxiety, and loss.[89] But layoff victims get to start over with a clean slate and a clear conscience. Survivors do not. A new syndrome seems to be popping up in more and more organizations: **layoff-survivor sickness**, a set of attitudes, perceptions, and behaviours of employees who survive involuntary staff reductions.[90] Symptoms include job insecurity, perceptions of unfairness, guilt, depression, stress from increased workload, fear of change, loss of loyalty and commitment, reduced effort, and an unwillingness to do anything beyond the required minimum.

To address this survivor syndrome, managers may want to provide opportunities for employees to talk to counsellors about their guilt, anger, and anxiety.[91] Group discussions can also provide an opportunity for the survivors to vent their feelings. Some organizations have used downsizing as the spark to implement increased employee participation programs such as empowerment and self-managed work teams. In short, to keep morale and productivity high, every attempt should be made to ensure that those individuals who are still working in the organization know that they are valuable and much-needed resources.

Diversity in Action 8

layoff-survivor sickness
A set of attitudes, perceptions, and behaviours of employees who remain after involuntary employee reductions; it includes insecurity, guilt, depression, stress, fear, loss of loyalty, and reduced effort.

SUMMARY AND IMPLICATIONS

❶ **What factors affect human resource planning?** The human resource management (HRM) process consists of eight activities for staffing the organization and sustaining high employee performance. These include making sure that competent employees are identified and selected; trained appropriately; and motivated to stay with the organization and perform at a high level. The entire HRM process is influenced by the external environment, particularly economic conditions, labour unions, and government legislation. When managers hire employees, they must follow laws that have been written to protect employees and the workplace, including the Canada Labour Code, employment standards legislation, the Charter of Rights and Freedoms, and the Canadian Human Rights Act. Therefore, managers are not completely free to choose whom they hire, promote, or fire.

Practically speaking, managers such as Rick Waugh of Scotiabank cannot simply hire their friends, or decide to exclude from hire a particular ethnic group. While Scotiabank's employees are not unionized, managers within a unionized environment are obligated to uphold the collective agreement negotiated with the labour union.

❷ **How do organizations assess their human resource needs?** Human resource managers do a human resource inventory to discover what skills and capabilities current employees have. They map that inventory against what might be needed in the future, based on the organization's mission, goals, and strategies.

Because president and CEO Rick Waugh would like to see more women in senior management positions, Scotiabank needs to assess which of its female employees have the skills and leadership qualities to move into senior management.

❸ **How do organizations identify and select competent employees?** Organizations first need to assess their current and future needs for employees, to make sure they have enough of the right people to accomplish the organization's goals. When selecting new employees, organizations need to determine whether potential employees will be successful once they are on the job. To do this, managers use application forms, written tests, performance-simulation tests, interviews, background investigations, and, in some cases, physical examinations to screen employees. Managers also need to make sure that they do not engage in discrimination in the hiring process.

One way that Scotiabank identifies potential employees is through applications that come in through its Careers webpage, which targets young graduates and encourages them to think about working for the bank.

4 How do organizations help employees adapt and stay up-to-date? Organizations, particularly larger ones, have orientation programs for new employees. The orientation introduces the new employee to his or her job, and also to the organization. As job demands change, employees may need to have their skills updated through training programs. Companies use a variety of training methods, from on-the-job training to classroom work to technology-based training.

Among other programs, Scotiabank has Leading Edge, the bank's fast-track leadership program.

5 What can organizations do to help employees achieve high performance throughout their careers? Organizations should develop performance standards for employees, and then evaluate employees on a regular basis. Through performance appraisal, employees learn whether they are performing effectively, or whether they need help to improve, including getting additional training.

6 How do compensation and benefits motivate employees? Organizations develop compensation and benefit programs that will motivate employees to achieve high performance. Many organizations have implemented skill-based pay systems, which reward employees for the job skills and competencies they can demonstrate.

7 How are careers managed? A career is the sequence of positions held by a person during his or her lifetime. Employees are encouraged to create their own development programs, in addition to whatever their companies provide, because often employees work for multiple organizations during their careers.

8 What are some current issues in human resource management? The major current issues in human resource management include workforce diversity, sexual harassment, work–life balance, and layoff-survivor sickness.

Scotiabank prides itself on its work with the Aboriginal community, sponsoring scholarships, events, and programs for community members and also supporting Aboriginal business initiatives. The bank also permits flex hours, flex days, job sharing, and telecommuting so that employees can find the right "work life" to match their personal needs.

Management @ Work

READING FOR COMPREHENSION

1. Describe the environmental factors that most directly influence the human resource management process.

2. Contrast reject errors and accept errors. Which are more likely to open an employer to charges of discrimination? Why?

3. What is the relationship among job analysis, recruitment, and selection?

4. What are the major problems of the interview as a selection device?

5. What are the benefits and drawbacks of realistic job previews? (Consider this question from the perspective of both the organization and the employee.)

6. How are orientation and employee training alike? How are they different?

7. Describe three performance appraisal methods as well as the advantages and disadvantages of each.

8. What is skill-based pay?

9. How do recruitment, selection, orientation, and training directly affect workforce diversity?

LINKING CONCEPTS TO PRACTICE

1. Should an employer have the right to choose employees without government interference in the hiring process? Explain your position.

2. Do you think there are moral limits on how far a prospective employer should delve into an applicant's life by means of interviews, tests, and background investigations? Explain your position.

3. Studies show that women's salaries still lag behind men's, and even with equal opportunity laws and regulations women are paid about 73 percent of what men are paid. How would you design a compensation system that would address this issue?

4. What in your view constitutes sexual harassment? Describe how companies can minimize sexual harassment in the workplace.

5. Why should managers be concerned with diversity in the workplace? What special human resource management issues does diversity raise?

6. "Victims of downsizing are not those employees who were let go. Rather, the victims are the ones who have kept their jobs." Do you agree or disagree with this statement? Defend your position.

SELF-ASSESSMENT

How Good Am I at Giving Performance Feedback?

For each of the following pairs, identify the statement that most closely matches what you normally do when you give feedback to someone else.[92]

1. **a.** Describe the behaviour.
   b. Evaluate the behaviour.

2. **a.** Focus on the feelings that the behaviour evokes.
   b. Tell the person what he or she should be doing differently.

3. **a.** Give specific instances of the behaviour.
   b. Generalize.

4. **a.** Deal only with behaviour that the person can control.
   b. Sometimes focus on something the person can do nothing about.

5. **a.** Tell the person as soon as possible after the behaviour.
   b. Sometimes wait too long.

6. **a.** Focus on the effect the behaviour has on me.
   b. Try to figure out why the individual did what he or she did.

7. **a.** Balance negative feedback with positive feedback.
   b. Sometimes focus only on the negative.

8. **a.** Do some soul searching to make sure that the reason I am giving the feedback is to help the other person or to strengthen our relationship.
   b. Sometimes give feedback to punish, win, or dominate the other person.

Scoring Key

Total the number of "a" responses, and then total the number of "b" responses, and then form an a/b ratio. For instance, if you have 6 "a" responses and 2 "b" responses, your a/b ratio would be 6/2.

Analysis and Interpretation

Along with listening skills, feedback skills comprise the other primary component of effective communication. This instrument is designed to assess how good you are at providing feedback.

In this assessment instrument, the "a" responses are your self-perceived strengths and the "b" responses are your self-perceived weaknesses. By looking at the proportion of your "a" and "b" responses, you will be able to see how effective you feel you are when giving feedback and determine where your strengths and weaknesses lie. For instance, an a/b ratio of 8/0, 7/1, or 6/2 suggests relatively strong feedback skills. In contrast, ratios of 3/5, 2/6, 1/7, or 0/8 indicate significant self-perceived weaknesses that can be improved upon. To work on improving your feedback skills, see M. London, *Job Feedback: Giving, Seeking, and Using Feedback for Performance Improvement* (Lawrence Erlbaum, 2003).

More Self-Assessments

To learn more about your skills, abilities, and interests, take the following self-assessments on MyManagementLab at www.pearsoned.ca/mymanagementlab:

- I.B.3.—How Satisfied Am I With My Job?
- III.B.3.—Am I Experiencing Work–Family Conflict?

MANAGEMENT FOR YOU TODAY

Dilemma

Your instructor has asked class members to form teams to work on a major class project. You have worked on teams before, and have not always been pleased with the results. This time you are determined to have a good team experience. You have reason to believe that how people are recruited to and selected for teams might make a difference.

You also know that evaluating performance and giving feedback are important. You have also heard that training can make a difference. With all of this in mind, write up a plan that indicates how you might recruit an excellent set of team members, and make sure that they perform well throughout.

Becoming a Manager

- Using the Internet, research different companies that interest you and check out what they say about careers or their people.
- If you are working, note what types of human resource management activities your managers do. What do they do that seems to be effective? Ineffective? What can you learn from this?

- Do career research in your chosen career by finding out what it's going to take to be successful in that career.
- Complete the *Developing Your Interpersonal Skills—Interviewing* module on page 225 and the *Developing Your Interpersonal Skills—Becoming More Culturally Aware* module on pages 58–59, in Chapter 2.

WORKING TOGETHER: TEAM-BASED EXERCISE

Laying Off Workers

Every manager, at some point in his or her career, is likely to be faced with the difficult task of laying off employees. Assume that you are the manager in the internal auditing department of a 4500-member corporation. You have been notified by top management that you must permanently reduce your staff of five by two. Following are some data about your five employees.

Emma Liu: Chinese Canadian female, age 32. Emma has been employed with your company for five years in the accounting department. Her evaluations over the past three years have been above average and outstanding. Emma has an MBA from a top business school. She has been on maternity leave for the past few weeks because of the birth of her second child and is expected to return to work in 20 weeks.

Ron Johnson: White male, age 49. Ron has been with you for 4 months and has 11 years of experience in the company in payroll. He has a B.Comm. and an MBA, and he specialized in accounting during both degree programs. He is also a CGA. Ron's evaluations over the past three years in payroll have been average, but he did save the company $150 000 on a suggestion he made regarding the use of electronic time sheets.

Satish Patel: Indo-Canadian male, age 31. Satish has been with the company for almost four years. His evaluations over the past three years in your department have been outstanding. He is committed to getting the job done and doing whatever it takes. He has also shown initiative by taking job assignments that no one else wanted, and he has recovered a number of overdue and uncollected accounts that you had simply thought should be written off as a loss.

Julie Sapp: White female, age 35. Julie has been with your company for seven years. Four years ago, Julie was in an automobile accident while travelling on business to a customer's location. As a result of the accident, she was disabled and is wheelchair-bound. Rumours have it that she is about to receive several million dollars from the insurance company of the driver who hit her. Her performance during the past two years has been above average. She has a B.Comm. in accounting and has developed considerable expertise in computer information systems.

Bobby Hayden: African Canadian male, age 43. Bobby just completed his double master's degree in taxation and law and recently passed the bar exam. He has been with your department for four years. His evaluations have been good to above average. Five years ago, Bobby won a lawsuit against your company for discriminating against him in a promotion to a supervisory position. Rumours have it that now, with his new degree, Bobby is actively pursuing another job outside the company.

In a group of 3 to 5 students, seek consensus on the questions that follow. Given the 5 brief descriptions above, which 2 employees should be laid off? Are there any other options that can be used to meet the requirement of downsizing by 2 employees without resorting to layoffs? What will you do to assist the 2 individuals who have been let go and to assist the remaining 3 employees? Be prepared to defend your actions.

ETHICS IN ACTION

Ethical Dilemma Exercise: But I Deserve an "A"!

Everybody wants an A ranking; nobody wants a C ranking. Yet the multiperson ranking system used by Goodyear Tire & Rubber Company forced managers to rank 10 percent of the workforce as A performers, 80 percent as B performers, and 10 percent as C performers. Those ranked as A performers were rewarded with promotions; those ranked as C performers were told they could be demoted or fired for a second C rating. Goodyear abandoned its 10-80-10 system just before some C employees who had been fired filed a lawsuit claiming age discrimination. "It is very unfair to start with the assumption that a certain percentage of your employees are unsatisfactory," said one of the plaintiffs. "It was very subjective and designed to weed out the older people."

Like Goodyear, a growing number of companies have followed the lead of General Electric in regularly ranking employees. Many companies give poor performers an opportunity to improve before taking action. However, critics say the ranking system forces managers to penalize employees on poorly performing teams. They also say the ranking system can lead to age, gender, or race discrimination. In response, companies are training managers to use more objective measures for appraisals, such as monitoring progress toward preset goals.[93]

Imagine that you must rank 20 percent of your subordinate managers as top performers, 70 percent as average, and 10 percent as needing improvement. Retaining incompetent or unmotivated managers is unfair to the rest of the staff and sends mixed signals. On the other hand, even if all your managers are competent, you must put 10 percent into the bottom category. Now it's appraisal time and you do not feel that any of your employees deserve to be in the bottom category. What should you do? (Review Exhibit 7-9 on page 210 as you consider this ethical challenge.)

Thinking Critically About Ethics

What you say online *can* come back to haunt you. Organizations are using Google, MySpace, and Facebook to check out applicants and current employees. In fact, some organizations see Google as a way to get "around discrimination laws, inasmuch as employers can find out all manner of information—some of it for a nominal fee—that is legally off-limits in interviews: your age, your marital status, fraternity pranks, stuff you wrote in college, political affiliations and so forth." And for those individuals who like to rant and rave about employers, there might be later consequences. That is why some individuals pull their Facebook profiles. What do you think of what these companies are doing? What positives and negatives are there to such behaviour? What are the ethical implications? What guidelines might you suggest for an organization's selection process?

Mitsubishi Motors North America

When Rich Gilligan took over as plant manager at Mitsubishi Motors North America's (MMNA) manufacturing facility in Normal, Illinois, in 1998 the plant had two notorious distinctions: It was one of the most automated yet least productive plants in the industry, and it was known as the place sued by the US government for the sexual harassment of its female employees.[94] That lawsuit was what most people knew about Mitsubishi Motors.

The high-profile case told the story of a dismal workplace: "sexual graffiti written on fenders about to pass female line employees; pornographic pictures taped on walls; male employees taunting women with wrenches and air compressors; women asked by male employees to bare their breasts; other women fondled; and women who complained of being fired or passed over for promotion." Almost from the beginning, the plant had a bad reputation regarding the employment of women. People in the local community looked with suspicion at plant employees. One of the shift managers said, "We had guys who had no bad marks asked to stop coaching girls' softball teams just because they worked at that plant." After numerous employee complaints, the Equal Employment Opportunity Commission (EEOC) entered the picture and filed suit on behalf of 500 female employees, charging the company with sexual harassment. The case dragged on for three years, further draining employee morale and damaging an already distant relationship between American employees and Japanese managers. That is the environment that Gilligan inherited.

Right before Gilligan was hired, MMNA settled the EEOC lawsuit for more than $50 million—still the largest sexual harassment settlement in US history. The money was distributed to more than 400 women, many of whom still work at the plant. The EEOC settlement also dictated a makeover of the work environment.

Gilligan needs to change the culture of the plant, and improve productivity and quality. He knows that Mitsubishi's mission statement is "We are a spirited, diverse workforce. We are a culture that looks for, and rewards, hard work and dedication. We are winners." Although each member of the Mitsubishi Group is independent, they are supposed to share the guiding principles of the Sankoryo, first announced in the 1930s by founder Mr. Koyata Iwasaki and revised to reflect today's realities:

- Shoki Hoko: Strive to enrich society, both materially and spiritually, while contributing toward the preservation of the environment.

- Shoji Komei: Maintain principles of transparency and openness, conducting business with integrity and fairness.

- Ritsugyo Boeki: Expand business, based on an all-encompassing global perspective.

Conduct like this was not happening at MMNA when Gilligan took over. What should he do to improve the culture and increase productivity?

The Benefits of Benefits

Can the benefits offered to employees be a factor in encouraging individuals to apply for and accept jobs in an organization? Would your response to a job viewed as less than desirable, in which the work hours are long and the pay is low, be the same if it had benefits? For some people, benefits are critical to whether they take and keep a job. Take the case of Patsy Sechrest.

Patsy Sechrest is among a growing number of contemporary employees who cannot afford to retire. She is in her twenty-eighth year as an employee at a family restaurant in BC. She works more than 50 hours a week, earning $9.00 per hour and arriving to work at 4:05 a.m. each day. Sechrest, like many others more than 50 years old, continues to work simply because she needs the money and the extended health benefits (eye care, dental care, prescription drugs, massage, and physiotherapy) that working provides. Compounding this issue is the fact that Sechrest and her husband live in a depressed area that was hit hard by the closing of a local pulp-and-paper mill.

Sechrest is also dealing with health ailments that have created a financial burden for her family. Making just over $20 000 annually, she is one of the more fortunate ones. Her employer provides generous extended health benefits. Without it, she would be financially devastated and in physical pain. Due to arthritis she needs to see a massage therapist and a physiotherapist regularly. Her health insurance pays most of the costs. Without the health insurance coverage, she simply could not have afforded the alternative medical treatments she receives.

For Patsy Sechrest, work and therapist visits have become a way of life. She is not bitter at the hand she has been dealt, but rather she is thankful for what her employer has provided—a paying job and extended health benefits. She expects to hang on to both for as long as she can!

Questions

1. How do benefits, such as those that the family restaurant provides, assist organizations in competing for and retaining employees?

2. Do you believe employee benefits should be membership-based (you get them simply because you work for the company) or performance-based (you earn them)? Defend your position.

3. Do you believe providing extended health care benefits for employees is a competitive necessity or a socially responsible action by the organization? Defend your position.

DEVELOPING YOUR INTERPERSONAL SKILLS

Interviewing

About the Skill

The interview is used almost universally as part of the employee selection process. Not many of us have ever been hired without having gone through one or more interviews. Interviews can be valid and reliable selection tools, but they need to be structured and well organized.

Steps in Developing the Skill

You can be an effective interviewer by using the following seven suggestions for interviewing job candidates:[95]

1. **Review the job description and job specifications.** Be sure that prior to the interview you have reviewed pertinent information about the job. Why? Because this will provide you with valuable information with which to assess the job candidate. Furthermore, knowing the relevant job requirements will help eliminate interview bias.

2. **Prepare a structured set of questions you want to ask all job applicants.** By having a set of prepared questions, you ensure that you will get the information you want. Furthermore, by asking similar questions, you are able to better compare all candidates' answers against a common base.

3. **Before meeting a candidate, review his or her application form and résumé.** By doing this, you will be able to create a complete picture of the candidate in terms of what is represented on the résumé or application and what the job requires. You can also begin to identify areas to explore during the interview; that is, areas that are not clearly defined on the résumé or application but that are essential to the job can become a focal point in your discussion with the candidate.

4. **Open the interview by putting the applicant at ease and by providing a brief preview of the topics to be discussed.** Interviews are stressful for job candidates. Opening the discussion with small talk, such as the weather, can give the candidate time to adjust to the interview setting. By providing a preview of topics to come, you are giving the candidate an agenda. This helps the candidate begin framing what he or she will say in response to your questions.

5. **Ask your questions and listen carefully to the candidate's answers.** Select follow-up questions that flow naturally from the answers given. Focus on the candidate's responses as they relate to information you need to ensure that the person meets your job requirements. If you are still uncertain, use a follow-up question to probe further for information.

6. **Close the interview by telling the applicant what is going to happen next.** Applicants are anxious about the status of your hiring decision. Be upfront with candidates regarding others who will be interviewed and the remaining steps in the hiring process. Let the person know your time frame for making a decision. In addition, tell the applicant how you will notify him or her about your decision.

7. **Write your evaluation of the applicant while the interview is still fresh in your mind.** Do not wait until the end of the day, after interviewing several people, to write your analysis of each person. Memory can (and often will) fail you! The sooner you write down your impressions after an interview, the better chance you have of accurately noting what occurred in the interview and your perceptions of the candidate.

Practising the Skill

Review and update your résumé. Then have several friends critique it who are employed in management-level positions or in management training programs. Ask them to explain their comments and make any changes to your résumé that they think will improve it.

Now inventory your interpersonal and technical skills and any practical experiences that do not show up in your résumé. Draft a set of leading questions you would like to be asked in an interview that would give you a chance to discuss the unique qualities and attributes you could bring to the job.

PART Three

Organizing

Continuing Case: Starbucks

Organizing is an important task of managers.[1] Once the organization's goals and plans are in place, the organizing function sets in motion the process of seeing that those goals and plans are pursued. When managers organize, they are defining what work needs to get done and creating a structure that enables work activities to be completed efficiently and effectively by organizational members hired to do that work. As Starbucks continues its global expansion and pursues innovative strategic initiatives, managers must deal with the realities of continually organizing and reorganizing its work efforts.

Structuring Starbucks

Like many start-up businesses, Starbucks' original founders organized their company around a simple structure based on each person's unique strengths: Zev Siegl became the retail expert; Jerry Baldwin took over the administrative functions; and Gordon Bowker was the dreamer who called himself "the magic, mystery, and romance man" and recognized from the start that a visit to Starbucks could "evoke a brief escape to a distant world." As Starbucks grew to the point where Jerry recognized that he needed to hire professional and experienced managers, Howard Schultz joined the company, bringing his skills in sales, marketing, and merchandising. When the original owners eventually sold the company to Schultz, he was able to take the company on the path to becoming what it is today and what he hopes it will become in the future.

As Starbucks has expanded, its organizational structure has changed to accommodate that growth. However, the company prides itself on its "lean" corporate structure—Howard Schultz is chair, president, and CEO. Schultz has focused on hiring a team of executives from companies such as Walmart, Dell, and PepsiCo. He says, "I wanted to bring in people who had experience working at $10 billion companies." These senior corporate officers include the following: president of Starbucks Coffee US, president of Starbucks Coffee International, 4 executive vice-presidents, and 29 senior vice-presidents. In addition to the president of Starbucks Coffee Canada, Colin Moore, the senior vice-president positions include senior vice-president of finance,

senior vice-president of coffee and global procurement, and senior vice-president of corporate social responsibility. (A complete list of upper-level managers can be found in the company's annual report on its website: **www. starbucks.com**.)

Although the executive team provides the all-important strategic direction, the "real" work of Starbucks gets done at the company's support centre, zone offices, retail stores, and roasting plants. The support centre provides support to and assists all other aspects of corporate operations in the areas of accounting, finance, information technology, and sales and supply chain management.

The zone offices oversee the regional operations of the retail stores and provide support in human resource management, facilities management, account management, financial management, and sales management. The essential link between the zone offices and each retail store is the district manager, each of whom oversees 8 to 10 stores, which is down from the dozen or so stores they used to oversee. Since district managers need to be out working with the stores, most use mobile technology that allows them to spend more time in the stores and still remain connected to their own office. A company executive says, "These are the most important people in the company. And while their primary job is outside the office and in those stores, they still need to be connected."

In the retail stores, hourly employees (baristas) service customers under the direction of assistant store managers and store managers. These managers are responsible for the day-to-day operations of each Starbucks location. One of the organizational challenges for many store managers has been the company's decision to add more drive-through windows to retail stores, which appears to be a smart strategic move since the average annual volume at a store with a drive-through window is about 30 percent higher than a store without one. However, a drive-through window often takes up to four people to operate: one to take orders, one to operate the cash register, one to work the espresso machine, and a "floater" who can fill in where needed. And these people have to work rapidly and carefully to get the cars in and out in a timely manner, since the drive-through lane can get congested quickly.

Finally, without coffee to sell, there would be no Starbucks. The coffee beans are processed at the company's domestic roasting plants in Washington, Pennsylvania, Nevada, and internationally in Amsterdam. At each roasting plant, the production team produces the coffee and the distribution team manages the inventory and distribution of products and equipment to company stores. Because product quality is so essential to Starbucks' success, each person in the roasting plants must be focused on maintaining quality control at every step in the process.

Communication at Starbucks

Keeping organizational communication flowing in all directions is important to Starbucks. It's a commitment that starts at the top: Howard Schultz visits at least 30 to 40 stores a week. Not only does this give him an upfront view of what is happening out in the field, it gives partners a chance to talk with the top guy in the company. Despite these efforts, results from the most current employee survey indicated communication needed improvement. Managers listened and made some changes.

An initial endeavour was the creation of Starbucks Broadcast News, an internal video newsletter that conveys information to partners about company news and announcements. Another change was the implementation of an internal communication audit that asks randomly selected partners for feedback on how to make company communication more effective. In addition, partners can voice concerns to the mission review team about actions or decisions where they "believe the company is not operating in a manner consistent with Starbucks' Guiding Principles." The mission review team was formed in 1991 and is made up of company managers and partners. In 2005, more than 4200 contacts were made with this team in North America. The concept has worked so well that many of Starbucks' international units have provided similar communication forums to their partners.

People Management at Starbucks

"Our ability to accomplish what we set out to do is based primarily on the people we hire. . . . We recognize that the right people, offering their ideas and expertise, will enable us to continue our success," says Starbucks' website.

Since the beginning, Starbucks has strived to be an employer that nurtured employees and gave them opportunities to grow and be challenged. The company says it is "pro-partner" and has always been committed to providing a flexible and progressive work environment and treating all employees with respect and dignity.

As Starbucks continues its expansion, it needs to make sure it has the right number of the right people in the right place at the right time. What kinds of people are "right" for Starbucks? The company states that it wants "people who are adaptable, self-motivated, passionate, creative team players." Starbucks uses a variety of methods to attract potential partners. The company has an interactive and easy-to-use online career centre. Job seekers—who must be at least 16 years old—can search and apply online for jobs in any geographic location. Starbucks also has recruiting events in various locations in Canada throughout the year, which allow job seekers to talk to recruiters and partners face-to-face about working at Starbucks. In addition, job seekers for part-time and full-time hourly positions can submit an application at any Starbucks store location. The company also has a limited number of internship opportunities for students during the summer.

Starbucks' workplace policies provide for employment equity and strictly prohibit discrimination. Diversity and inclusion are very important to Starbucks. That commitment to diversity starts at the top. During 2005, 13 senior executives participated in a 360-degree diversity assessment to identify their strengths and areas that needed improvement. Also during 2005, an executive diversity learning series was developed for individuals at the vice-president level and above to build their diversity competencies. In 2006, a full-day diversity immersion exercise was launched.

Although diversity training is important to Starbucks, it is not the only training provided. The company continually invests in training programs and career development initiatives: baristas, who get a "green apron book" that exhorts them to be genuine and considerate, receive 23 hours of initial training; an additional 29 hours of training as shift supervisor; 112 hours as assistant store manager; and 320 hours as store manager. District manager trainees receive 200 hours of training. And every partner takes a class on coffee education, which focuses on Starbucks' passion for coffee and understanding the core product. In addition, Starbucks offers a variety of classes ranging from basic computer skills to conflict resolution to management training. Starbucks' partners are not "stuck" in their jobs.

The company's rapid growth creates tremendous opportunities for promotion and advancement for all store partners. If they desire, they can utilize career counselling, executive coaching, job rotation, mentoring, and leadership development to help them create a career path that meets their needs. In 2006, Starbucks was named one of *Training* magazine's Top 100. One example of the company's training efforts: When oxygen levels in coffee bags were too high in one of the company's roasting plants (which affected product freshness), partners were retrained on procedures and given additional coaching. After the training, the number of bags of coffee placed on "quality hold" declined by 99 percent.

One human resource issue that has haunted Starbucks is its position on labour unions. The company states on its website, "We firmly believe that the direct employment relationship which we currently have with our partners is the best way to help ensure a great work environment. We believe we do not need a third party to act on behalf of our partners. We prefer to deal directly with them in a fair and respectful manner, just as we have throughout our history." Starbucks prides itself on how it treats its employees. However, the Canadian Auto Workers represents about 140 Starbucks workers at 10 stores in Vancouver.

Change and Innovation at Starbucks

Starbucks has always thought "outside the box." It took the concept of the corner coffee shop and completely revamped the coffee experience. The company has always had the ability to roll out new products relatively quickly. If a new product seems like it would appeal to customers—the popular pumpkin spice latte is one example—Starbucks often skips product testing and does not use focus groups to assess the product. Innovation is so important, in fact, that the category management group is responsible for changing the items on the shelves every six weeks. And Starbucks relies heavily on its partners to be the driving force behind innovations. As we said earlier, Starbucks is firmly committed to its belief that "We recognize that the right people, offering their ideas and expertise, will enable us to continue our success."

Questions

1. What types of departmentalization are being used? Explain your choices. (Hint: In addition to information in the case, you might want to look at the list of corporate executives on the company's website.)

2. Do you think it's a good idea to have a president for the US division and for the international divisions? What are the advantages of such an arrangement? Disadvantages?

3. What examples of the six organizational structural elements do you see discussed in the case? Describe.

4. Considering the expense associated with having more managers, what are some reasons why you think Starbucks decided to decrease the number of stores each district manager was responsible for, thus increasing the number of managers needed? Other than the expense, can you think of any disadvantages to this decision?

5. Give some examples of the types of communication taking place at Starbucks.

6. Suppose that you are a Starbucks store manager in St. John's, Newfoundland and Labrador. How do you find out what is going on in the company? How might you communicate concerns or issues that you have?

7. Starbucks' long-term goal is to have 15 000 US stores and 30 000 stores globally. In addition, the company has set a financial goal of attaining total net revenue growth of 20 percent and earnings per share growth of 20 to 25 percent. How will the organizing function contribute to the accomplishment of these goals?

8. Starbucks has said that it wants people who are "adaptable, self-motivated, passionate, and creative team players." How does the company ensure that its hiring and selection process identifies those kinds of people?

9. Select one of the job openings posted on the company's website. Do you think the job description and job

specifications for this job are adequate? Why or why not? What changes might you suggest?

10. Evaluate Starbucks' training efforts. What types of training are available?

11. Pretend that you are a local Starbucks' store manager. You have three new hourly partners (baristas) joining your team. Describe the orientation you would provide these new hires.

12. Which of the company's Guiding Principles affect the organizing function of management? Explain how the one(s) you chose would affect how Starbucks' managers deal with: (a) structural issues; (b) communication issues; and (c) HRM issues. (Hint: The Guiding Principles can be found on the company's website or, in the continuing case in Part 1 of this textbook, under "Starbucks Culture and Environment" on pages 61–62.)

VIDEO CASE INCIDENTS

Emails

Using email away from the office has become a way of life for many employees in Canada. Companies now provide employees with BlackBerrys and set up Virtual Private Networks that enable staff to access email accounts from home. This technology blurs the line between "work time" and "personal time." The implementation of this technology has produced a workplace with no boundaries. Many employees draft and send email communications from home well into the night.

Pfizer Inc. is the world's largest research-based biomedical and pharmaceutical company. At a division of Pfizer Inc. located in Markham, Ontario, a group of employees convinced management to put in place a policy that forbids staff to send email between 6 p.m. and 6 a.m., unless doing so is absolutely necessary for the performance of their job functions. Management agreed that "email addiction" has a detrimental impact on employee stress, workplace morale, and work–life balance. The policy encourages employees to put their BlackBerrys and laptops away and spend time with their families when they leave the office.

One employee at Pfizer, Graham Robertson, was identified as the "worst offender" of email use outside of work hours. He typed emails during family meals and while attending his son's soccer games. The purpose of the new corporate policy is to persuade Graham and others to change their ways.

Management in the Markham office claim that the new policy not only decreased the volume of emails sent by employees over the company network but also increased employee productivity.

QUESTIONS

1. *For analysis:* What impacts have recent advances in information technology had on communication in organizations?

2. *For application:* Identify potentially detrimental effects to Pfizer of Graham Robertson sending so many email messages outside of work hours.

3. *For application:* In order to ensure effective communication, what factors should a manager consider when deciding whether or not to deliver a message by email?

4. *For debate:* A policy banning email between certain hours is fair to all employees. Implementing such a policy would benefit most organizations. Do you agree with this statement? Why or why not?

Sources: "E-mails," *The National*, March 2, 2006; Pfizer Inc., www.pfizer.com (accessed August 13, 2009).

Flair Bartending

Part bartender, part circus performer, Toronto's Gavin McMillan serves up drinks with flash and style. Gavin has worked in restaurants and bars in cities ranging from London and Birmingham to Singapore and Bangkok. His accumulated experience encompasses concepts and lessons learned at hundreds of restaurants and bars from around the world. Gavin has been featured in music videos and media outlets such as the Travel Channel, A&E, E! Entertainment Television, *The Toronto Sun*, *Metro News*, and *Bar and Beverage* magazine. In 2005, he was the top-ranked Canadian bartender at the world championships in Las Vegas.

Gavin modelled his style of bartending, known as Flair Bartending, on the character played by Tom Cruise in the movie *Cocktail*. Gavin's expertise provides the foundation for a series of schools across Canada in which students learn his unique bartending style. His new company is called Bartender One. Bartender One holds its training classes in actual bars in which up to 60 students can be trained at one time with the help of several expert instructors. In these classes students watch bartending "stunts" performed by the instructors, and learn how to mix popular drinks. They then practice stunt work, and mix drinks on their own, except that, rather than using glass bottles, students practise with props.

The demand for Bartender One's classes is increasing rapidly. Gavin faces the challenge of hiring enough qualified instructors to meet this demand; only 40 people in Canada are trained in the Flair Bartending style. As a first step in meeting this challenge, Gavin is considering hiring recent graduates from his courses as instructors. However, this will naturally take time, and Gavin is worried about meeting the current demand for his classes.

QUESTIONS

1. *For analysis:* How important is human resource management to the success of Bartender One?

2. *For application:* What steps do you recommend the organization take to recruit instructors?

3. *For application:* What selection devices do you recommend the organization use to select between the applicants for the instructor positions?

4. *For debate:* The greatest human resource management challenges Bartender One faces are in the areas of recruitment and selection. These are the areas where the company should focus its attention and resources. Other areas of managing the employment relationship, such as performance management and training, will be less important.

Sources: "Flair Bartending," *CBC Venture*, November 8, 2006, 5, NEP-15568; Bartender One, www.bartenderone.com (accessed August 10, 2009); Wikipedia, http://en.wikipedia.org/wiki/Flair_bartending (accessed August 18, 2009).

After you have completed your study of Part 3, do the following exercises on MyManagementLab at www.pearsoned.ca/mymanagementlab:

- *You're the Manager: Putting Ethics into Action* (**General Electric**)
- *Passport, Scenario 1* (**Patrick Hollis, Grupo Bimbo**), *Scenario 2* (**Scott Estes, Reebok International**), and *Scenario 3* (**Paul Souza, Ernst & Young**)

What does it take to be a good leader?

1 How do leaders and managers differ?

2 What do trait and behavioural theories tell us about leadership?

3 How do contingency theories of leadership improve our understanding of leadership?

4 What do charismatic and transformational leaders do?

5 What are some current issues in leadership?

When Rossana Di Zio Magnotta first started Vaughan, Ontario-based Festa Juice with her husband Gabe, the company sold imported grape juice to people who were making wine at home.[1] A scientist by training, she helped with the technical side of the business, by applying biochemistry and microbiology to winemaking. Her intention was to offer free advice about winemaking to her customers, even testing some of their samples to see how they could improve their wine.

Her scientific background did not impress her customers, however, who were mainly first-generation Italian and Portuguese men. They had trouble believing a Canadian woman (even if she had Italian ancestry) could possibly know how to make wine. "They would say they were 'born in the grapes,' and start talking to me about the old country," she said.

Rather than feel undermined by the questioning of her winemaking ability, Magnotta decided to win over her customers by writing a step-by-step guide to winemaking, "Making Wine the Festa Way." The booklet was translated into Italian and Spanish, and was given away to every Festa Juice purchaser.

Because of the helpful advice Magnotta provided, it was not too long before customers started asking the company to sell wine, rather than juice and advice. After much consideration, the husband and wife team decided to buy Charal Winery, which had a license and a few pieces of equipment, although no land. They renamed the company Magnotta Winery and launched

their new business in late 1990. The business has been very successful, and is now the third-largest winery in Ontario. Its net earnings were $2.6 million on net sales of $24 million for the year ending January 31, 2009. The winery has received over 3000 awards, and has also been voted one of Canada's 50 Best Managed Companies eight years in a row, starting in 1999.

Think About It

What does it mean to be a leader for today's organizations? Put yourself in Rossana Di Zio Magnotta's shoes: What kinds of challenges does she face as a leader in the male-dominated winery business? What can she do to encourage support for her leadership style from both men and women?

Why is leadership so important? Because it's the leaders in organizations who make things happen.

If leadership is so important, it's only natural to ask: What differentiates leaders from nonleaders? What is the most appropriate style of leadership? And what can you do if you want to be seen as a leader? In this chapter, we try to answer these and other questions about what it means to be a leader.

Exhibit 8-1

Distinguishing Managership From Leadership

Managership	Leadership
1. Engages in day-to-day caretaker activities; maintains and allocates resources	Formulates long-term objectives for reforming the system; plans strategy and tactics
2. Exhibits supervisory behaviour; acts to make others maintain standard job behaviour	Exhibits leading behaviour; acts to bring about change in others congruent with long-term objectives
3. Administers subsystems within organizations	Innovates for the entire organization
4. Asks how and when to engage in standard practice	Asks what and why to change standard practice
5. Acts within established culture of the organization	Creates vision and meaning for the organization
6. Uses transactional influence; induces compliance in manifest behaviour using rewards, sanctions, and formal authority	Uses transformational influence; induces change in values, attitudes, and behaviour using personal examples and expertise
7. Relies on control strategies to get things done by subordinates	Uses empowering strategies to make followers internalize values
8. Status quo supporter and stabilizer	Status quo challenger and change creator

Source: R. N. Kanungo, "Leadership in Organizations: Looking Ahead to the 21st Century," *Canadian Psychology* 39, nos. 1–2 (1998), p. 77. Copyright 1998 The Canadian Psychological Association.

Managers vs. Leaders

1 How do leaders and managers differ?

Let's begin by clarifying the distinction between managers and leaders. *Leadership* and *management* are two terms that are often confused. What is the difference between them?

Professor Rabindra Kanungo at McGill University finds that management scholars are beginning to reach a consensus that leadership and supervision/management are different.[2] Exhibit 8-1 illustrates the distinctions Kanungo sees between managership and leadership. **Leaders** provide vision and strategy to the organization; managers implement that vision and strategy, coordinate and staff the organization, and handle day-to-day problems. **Leadership** is the process of influencing individuals or groups toward the achievement of goals.

leader
Someone who can influence others and provide vision and strategy to the organization.

leadership
The process of influencing individuals or groups toward the achievement of goals.

PRISM 2

Can managers be leaders? Should leaders be managers? Because no one yet has shown that leadership ability is a handicap to a manager, we believe that all managers should ideally be leaders. One of the major functions of management is to lead. However, not all leaders have the capabilities or skills of effective managers, and thus not all leaders should be managers. The fact that an individual can set vision and strategy does not mean that he or she can also plan, organize, and control.

Early Leadership Theories

When Rossana Di Zio Magnotta and her husband, Gabe, decided to start Magnotta Winery, their intention was to sell their wine through the Liquor Control Board of Ontario (LCBO).[3] Their timing for the opening of the business could not have been worse. The economy was in the midst of a downturn. As Magnotta explains, "On December 7th, 1990, we opened up shop and immediately got hit with the recession that was rolling across the country." At the same time, the LCBO informed Magnotta and her husband that there was no room in the stores to shelve Magnotta wine. These obstacles had not been part of their business planning.

Magnotta and her husband ended up waging a 10-year battle with the LCBO. She explains, "We had no choice, it was either fight or die."

Think About It

A president and CEO of any company has to manage people effectively. Are there specific traits or behaviours that leaders such as Rossana Di Zio Magnotta should have?

Leadership has been of interest since the early days of people gathering together in groups to accomplish goals. However, it was not until the early part of the twentieth century that researchers began to study leadership. These early leadership theories focused on the *leader* (trait theories) and how the *leader interacted* with his or her group members (behavioural theories).

2 What do trait and behavioural theories tell us about leadership?

Trait Theories

Think about some of the managers you have encountered. How did their traits affect whether they were good or bad managers?

Leadership research in the 1920s and 1930s focused on leader traits—characteristics that might be used to differentiate leaders from nonleaders. The intent was to isolate traits that leaders possessed and nonleaders did not. Some of the traits studied included physical stature, appearance, social class, emotional stability, fluency of speech, and sociability. Despite the best efforts of researchers, it proved to be impossible to identify a set of traits that would *always* differentiate leaders (the person) from nonleaders. Maybe it was a bit optimistic to think that there could be consistent and unique traits that would apply universally to all effective leaders, whether they were in charge of Toyota Motor Corporation, the Moscow Ballet, Ted's Outfitters Shop, or Queen's University. However, more recent attempts to identify traits consistently associated with leadership (the process, not the person) have been more successful. Seven traits associated with effective leadership include drive, the desire to lead, honesty and integrity, self-confidence, intelligence, job-relevant knowledge, and extraversion.[4] These traits are briefly described in Exhibit 8-2.

Q&A 12.1

Researchers have begun organizing traits around the Big Five personality framework.[5] They have found that most of the dozens of traits that emerged in various leadership reviews fall under one of the Big Five personality traits (extraversion, agreeableness,

---

Exhibit 8-2

Seven Traits Associated With Leadership

1. **Drive.** Leaders exhibit a high effort level. They have a relatively high desire for achievement; they are ambitious; they have a lot of energy; they are tirelessly persistent in their activities; and they show initiative.

2. **Desire to lead.** Leaders have a strong desire to influence and lead others. They demonstrate the willingness to take responsibility.

3. **Honesty and integrity.** Leaders build trusting relationships between themselves and followers by being truthful or nondeceitful and by showing high consistency between word and deed.

4. **Self-confidence.** Followers look to leaders for an absence of self-doubt. Leaders, therefore, need to show self-confidence in order to convince followers of the rightness of their goals and decisions.

5. **Intelligence.** Leaders need to be intelligent enough to gather, synthesize, and interpret large amounts of information, and they need to be able to create visions, solve problems, and make correct decisions.

6. **Job-relevant knowledge.** Effective leaders have a high degree of knowledge about the company, industry, and technical matters. In-depth knowledge allows leaders to make well-informed decisions and to understand the implications of those decisions.

7. **Extraversion.** Leaders are energetic, lively people. They are sociable, assertive, and rarely silent or withdrawn.

Sources: S. A. Kirkpatrick and E. A. Locke, "Leadership: Do Traits Really Matter?" *Academy of Management Executive*, May 1991, pp. 48–60; and T. A. Judge, J. E. Bono, R. Ilies, and M. Werner, "Personality and Leadership: A Qualitative and Quantitative Review," *Journal of Applied Psychology*, August 2002, pp. 765–780.

Conservative MP Steven Fletcher (Charleswood–St. James–Assiniboia, Manitoba) is driven to be a leader. A car accident left him quadriplegic when he was 23, and this inspired him to take charge of his life. He won his first political campaign to become president of the University of Manitoba Students' Union. He later became president of the Progressive Conservative Party of Manitoba. When he was elected MP, he defeated his riding's incumbent Liberal candidate. He says many of his constituents are not aware that he is quadriplegic until they meet him.

conscientiousness, emotional stability, and openness to experience). This approach has resulted in consistent and strong support for traits as predictors of leadership.

Q&A 12.2

Researchers agreed that traits alone were not sufficient for explaining effective leadership because explanations based solely on traits ignored the interactions of leaders and their group members as well as situational factors. Possessing the appropriate traits only made it more likely that an individual would be an effective leader. Therefore, leadership research from the late 1940s to the mid-1960s concentrated on the preferred behavioural styles that leaders demonstrated. Researchers wondered whether there was something unique in what effective leaders *did*—in other words, in their *behaviour*.

Behavioural Theories

behavioural theories
Leadership theories that identify behaviours that differentiate effective leaders from ineffective leaders.

Behavioural theories of leadership identify behaviours that differentiate effective leaders from ineffective leaders. Researchers hoped that the behavioural theories approach would provide more definitive answers about the nature of leadership than did the trait theories. There are four main leader behaviour studies we need to examine. (Exhibit 8-3 provides a summary of the major leader behavioural dimensions and the conclusions of each of the studies.)

autocratic style
A leadership style where the leader tends to centralize authority, dictate work methods, make unilateral decisions, and limit employee participation.

University of Iowa Studies

democratic style
A leadership style where the leader tends to involve employees in decision making, delegate authority, encourage participation in deciding work methods and goals, and use feedback as an opportunity for coaching employees.

The University of Iowa studies (conducted by Kurt Lewin and his associates) explored three leadership styles.[6] The **autocratic style** describes a leader who tends to centralize authority, dictate work methods, make unilateral decisions, and limit employee participation. The **democratic style** describes a leader who tends to involve employees in decision making, delegate authority, encourage participation in deciding work methods and goals, and use feedback as an opportunity for coaching employees. Finally, the **laissez-faire style** describes a leader who generally gives the group complete freedom to make decisions and complete the work in whatever way it sees fit.

laissez-faire style
A leadership style where the leader tends to give the group complete freedom to make decisions and complete the work in whatever way it sees fit.

Lewin and his associates researched which one of the three leadership styles was most effective. Their results seemed to indicate that the democratic style contributed to both good quantity and quality of work. Had the answer to the question of the most effective leadership style been found? Unfortunately, it was not that simple. Later studies of the autocratic and democratic styles showed mixed results. The democratic style sometimes

Exhibit 8-3

Behavioural Theories of Leadership

	Behavioural Dimension	Conclusion
University of Iowa	*Democratic style:* involving subordinates, delegating authority, and encouraging participation *Autocratic style:* dictating work methods, centralizing decision making, and limiting participation *Laissez-faire style:* giving group freedom to make decisions and complete work	Democratic style of leadership was most effective, although later studies showed mixed results.
Ohio State	*Consideration:* being considerate of followers' ideas and feelings *Initiating structure:* structuring work and work relationships to meet job goals	High-high leader (high in consideration and high in initiating structure) achieved high subordinate performance and satisfaction, but not in all situations.
University of Michigan	*Employee-oriented:* emphasizes interpersonal relationships and taking care of employees' needs *Production-oriented:* emphasized technical or task aspects of job	Employee-oriented leaders were associated with high group productivity and higher job satisfaction.
Managerial Grid	*Concern for people:* measures leader's concern for subordinates on a scale of 1 to 9 (low to high) *Concern for production:* measures leader's concern for getting job done on a scale of 1 to 9 (low to high)	Leaders performed best with a 9,9 style (high concern for production and high concern for people).

produced higher performance levels than the autocratic style, but at other times it produced lower or equal performance levels. More consistent results were found, however, when a measure of subordinate satisfaction was used. Group members' satisfaction levels were generally higher under a democratic leader than under an autocratic one.[7] To learn more about your leadership style, see *Self-Assessment—What's My Leadership Style?* on pages 257–259, at the end of the chapter.

Q&A 12.3

Now leaders faced a dilemma! Should they focus on achieving higher performance or on achieving higher member satisfaction? This recognition of the dual nature of a leader's behaviour—that is, focusing on the task and on the people—was also a key characteristic of the other behavioural studies.

Ohio State Studies

The Ohio State studies identified two important dimensions of leader behaviour.[8] Beginning with more than 1000 behavioural dimensions, the researchers eventually narrowed the list down to just two categories that accounted for most of the leadership behaviour described by individuals: initiating structure and consideration.

Initiating structure refers to the extent to which a leader is likely to define and structure his or her role and the roles of group members in the search for goal attainment. It includes behaviour that attempts to organize work, work relationships, and goals. **Consideration** refers to the extent to which a leader has job relationships characterized by mutual trust and respect for group members' ideas and feelings. A leader who is high in consideration helps group members with personal problems, is friendly and approachable, and treats all group members as equals. He or she shows concern for (is considerate of) his or her followers' comfort, well-being, status, and satisfaction.

Were these behavioural dimensions adequate descriptions of leader behaviour? Research found that a leader who is high in both initiating structure and consideration behaviours (a **high-high leader**) achieved high group task performance and satisfaction more frequently than one who is low on either dimension or both. However, the high-high style

initiating structure
The extent to which a leader is likely to define and structure his or her role and the roles of group members in the search for goal attainment.

consideration
The extent to which a leader has job relationships characterized by mutual trust and respect for group members' ideas and feelings.

high-high leader
A leader high in both initiating structure and consideration behaviours.

did not always yield positive results. Enough exceptions were found to indicate that perhaps situational factors needed to be integrated into leadership theory.

University of Michigan Studies

Leadership studies conducted at the University of Michigan's Survey Research Center at about the same time as those being done at Ohio State had a similar research objective: Identify behavioural characteristics of leaders that are related to performance effectiveness. The Michigan group also came up with two dimensions of leadership behaviour, which they labelled employee oriented and production oriented.[9] *Employee-oriented* leaders tend to emphasize interpersonal relationships; they take a personal interest in the needs of their followers and accept individual differences among group members. In contrast, *production-oriented* leaders tend to emphasize the technical or task aspects of the job; they are concerned mainly with accomplishing their group's tasks and regard group members as a means to that end. The conclusions of the Michigan researchers strongly favoured leaders who are employee oriented, as they were associated with high group productivity and high job satisfaction.

The Managerial Grid

managerial grid
A two-dimensional grid of leadership behaviours based on concern for people vs. concern for production.

The behavioural dimensions from these early leadership studies provided the basis for the development of a two-dimensional grid for assessing leadership styles. This **managerial grid**, developed by R. R. Blake and Jane S. Mouton, uses the behavioural dimensions "concern for people" and "concern for production" and evaluates a leader's use of these behaviours, ranking them on a scale from 1 (low) to 9 (high).[10] Although the grid (shown in Exhibit 8-4) has 81 different categories into which a leader's behavioural style might fall, emphasis has been placed on five: impoverished management (1,1), task management (9,1), middle-of-the-road management (5,5), country club management (1,9), and team management (9,9). Of these five styles, Blake and Mouton concluded that managers performed best when using a 9,9 style. Unfortunately, the grid offers no answers to the question of what makes a manager an effective leader; it provides only a framework for conceptualizing leadership style. In fact, there has been little substantive evidence to support the conclusion that a 9,9 style is most effective in all situations.[11]

A lengthy review of the results of behavioural studies supports the idea that people-oriented behaviours are related to follower satisfaction, motivation, and leader effectiveness while production-oriented behaviours are slightly more strongly related to performance by the leader, the group, and the organization.[12]

Contingency Theories of Leadership

3 How do contingency theories of leadership improve our understanding of leadership?

Do you know what your leadership style is? What impact might your style have on how you lead?

Contingency theories of leadership developed after it became clear that identifying traits or key behaviours was not enough to understand what made good leaders. Contingency researchers considered whether different situations required different styles of leadership. To illustrate how situations might affect the ability to lead, consider the fate of some of the Americans who have been recruited to run Canadian companies. Hudson's Bay Company hired American Bill Fields and Zellers hired American Millard Barron to replicate their US retail successes in Canada. Neither was able to do so. Successful Texas oilman J. P. Bryan was given two chances to restore profitability at Canadian companies—Gulf Canada Resources (now ConocoPhillips) and Canadian 88 Energy (which later became Esprit Exploration)—and failed in both attempts.[13] These examples suggest that one's leadership style may need to be adjusted for different companies and employees, and perhaps even for different countries. This is consistent with research findings that not all leaders can lead in any situation.[14]

In this section, we examine four contingency theories of leadership—Fiedler contingency model, Hersey and Blanchard's Situational Leadership®, leader participation

Exhibit 8-4

The Managerial Grid

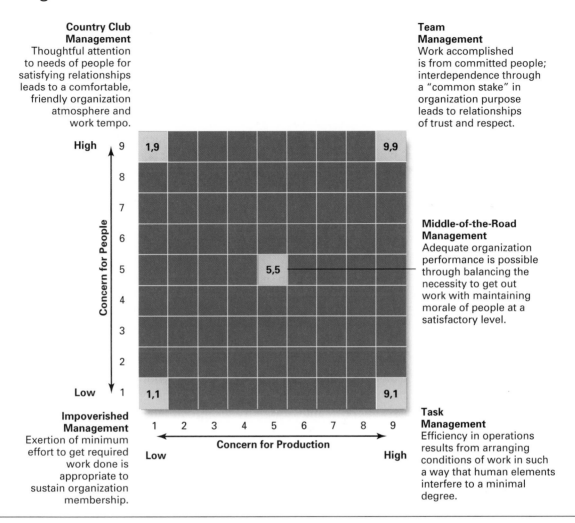

Country Club Management
Thoughtful attention to needs of people for satisfying relationships leads to a comfortable, friendly organization atmosphere and work tempo.

Team Management
Work accomplished is from committed people; interdependence through a "common stake" in organization purpose leads to relationships of trust and respect.

Middle-of-the-Road Management
Adequate organization performance is possible through balancing the necessity to get out work with maintaining morale of people at a satisfactory level.

Impoverished Management
Exertion of minimum effort to get required work done is appropriate to sustain organization membership.

Task Management
Efficiency in operations results from arranging conditions of work in such a way that human elements interfere to a minimal degree.

Source: Reprinted by permission of Harvard Business Review. An exhibit from R. R. Blake, J. S. Mouton, L. B. Barnes, and L. E. Greiner, "Breakthrough in Organization Development," *Harvard Business Review*, November–December 1964, p. 136. Copyright © 1964 by the President and Fellows of Harvard College. All rights reserved.

model, and path-goal theory. All of these theories focus on the relationship of the leader to followers, and there is broad support for the idea that this relationship is important.[15] Each theory attempts to answer *if-then* contingencies (that is, *if* this is the situation, *then* this is the best leadership style to use).

Fiedler Contingency Model

The first comprehensive contingency model for leadership was developed by Fred Fiedler.[16] The **Fiedler contingency model** proposes that effective group performance depends on the proper match between the leader's style of interacting with his or her followers and the degree to which the situation gives the leader control and influence. The model was based on the premise that a certain leadership style would be most effective in specific types of situations. The key was to define different leadership styles and types of situations and then determine the combinations of style and situation that were well matched.

Fiedler proposed that an important factor in leadership success is an individual's basic leadership style, which is either task oriented or relationship oriented. To measure a leader's orientation, Fiedler developed the **least-preferred co-worker (LPC) questionnaire**.

Fiedler contingency model
A leadership theory proposing that effective group performance depends on the proper match between the leader's style of interacting with followers and the degree to which the situation gives the leader control and influence.

least-preferred co-worker (LPC) questionnaire
A questionnaire that measures whether a leader is task oriented or relationship oriented.

Leaders who describe the least-preferred co-worker in relatively positive terms are primarily interested in good personal relations with co-workers (that is, they are *relationship oriented*). Leaders who describe the least-preferred co-worker in relatively unfavourable terms (a low LPC score), are primarily interested in productivity and getting the job done (that is, they are *task oriented*). Fiedler did acknowledge that there was a small group of people who fell in between these two extremes and who did not have a cut-and-dried leadership style. It's important to point out that Fiedler assumed a person's leadership style was always the same (fixed), regardless of the situation. In other words, a relationship-oriented leader would always be one, and the same was true for a task-oriented leader.

Q&A 12.4

Fiedler identified three contingency dimensions that together define the situation a leader faces:

- *Leader–member relations.* The degree of confidence, trust, and respect employees have for their leader; rated as either good or poor.

- *Task structure.* The degree to which job assignments are formalized and procedurized; rated as either high or low.

- *Position power.* The degree of influence a leader has over power-based activities such as hiring, firing, discipline, promotions, and salary increases; rated as either strong or weak.

Fiedler evaluated leadership situations in terms of these three contingency variables, and concluded that there are eight possible situations in which a leader could find himself or herself (see the bottom of the chart in Exhibit 8-5). Each of these situations was described in terms of its favourableness (or situational control) for the leader. Situations I, II, and III were classified as very favourable for the leader. Situations IV, V, and VI were moderately favourable for the leader. Situations VII and VIII were very unfavourable for the leader.

Fiedler concluded that task-oriented leaders performed better in either very favourable situations or very unfavourable situations. (See the top of Exhibit 8-5 where performance is shown on the vertical axis and situation favourableness is shown on the horizontal axis.) In a high control situation, a leader can "get away" with task orientation, because the relationships are good, and followers are easily influenced.[17] In a low control situation

Exhibit 8-5

Findings of the Fiedler Contingency Model

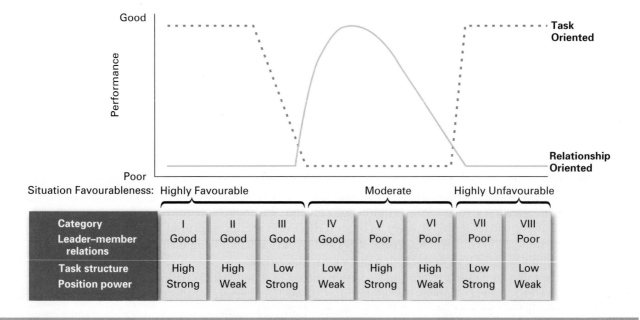

Category	I	II	III	IV	V	VI	VII	VIII
Leader–member relations	Good	Good	Good	Good	Poor	Poor	Poor	Poor
Task structure	High	High	Low	Low	High	High	Low	Low
Position power	Strong	Weak	Strong	Weak	Strong	Weak	Strong	Weak

(which is characterized by poor relations, ill-defined tasks, and low influence), task orientation may be the only thing that makes it possible to get something done. On the other hand, relationship-oriented leaders performed better in moderately favourable situations. In a moderate control situation, being relationship oriented may smooth the way to getting things done.

Since Fiedler treated an individual's leadership style as fixed, there were only two ways to improve leader effectiveness. First, you could bring in a new leader whose style better fit the situation. For example, if the group situation was rated as highly unfavourable but was led by a relationship-oriented leader, the group's performance could be improved by replacing that person with a task-oriented leader. The second alternative was to change the situation to fit the leader. This could be done by restructuring tasks or increasing or decreasing the power that the leader had over factors such as salary increases, promotions, and disciplinary actions.

Reviews of the major studies undertaken to test the overall validity of Fiedler's model have shown considerable evidence to support the model.[18] However, this theory was not without criticism. For example, additional variables are probably needed to fill in some gaps in the model. Moreover, there were problems with the LPC, and the practicality of it needed to be addressed. In addition, it's probably unrealistic to assume that a person cannot change his or her leadership style to fit the situation. Effective leaders can, and do, change their styles to meet the needs of a particular situation. Finally, the contingency variables were difficult for practitioners to assess.[19] Despite its shortcomings, the Fiedler contingency model showed that effective leadership style needed to reflect situational factors.

Hersey and Blanchard's Situational Leadership®

Paul Hersey and Ken Blanchard developed a leadership theory that has gained a strong following among management development specialists.[20] This contingency theory of leadership, called **Situational Leadership® (SL)**, focuses on followers' readiness. Hersey and Blanchard argue that successful leadership is achieved by selecting the right leadership style, which is contingent on the level of the followers' readiness. Before we proceed, there are two points we need to clarify: Why a leadership theory focuses on the followers, and what is meant by the term *readiness*.

The emphasis on the followers in leadership effectiveness reflects the reality that it is the followers who accept or reject the leader. Regardless of what the leader does, effectiveness depends on the actions of his or her followers. This is an important dimension that has been overlooked or underemphasized in most leadership theories. **Readiness**, as defined by Hersey and Blanchard, refers to the extent to which people have the ability and willingness to accomplish a specific task.

SL uses the same two leadership dimensions that Fiedler identified: task and relationship behaviours. However, Hersey and Blanchard go a step further by considering each as either high or low and then combining them into four specific leadership styles (see Exhibit 8-6 on page 242), described as follows:

- *Telling* (high task–low relationship): The leader defines roles and tells people what, how, when, and where to do various tasks.

- *Selling* (high task–high relationship): The leader provides both directive and supportive behaviour.

- *Participating* (low task–high relationship): The leader and follower share in decision making; the main role of the leader is facilitating and communicating.

- *Delegating* (low task–low relationship): The leader provides little direction or support.

The final component in the theory is the four stages of follower readiness:

- *R1:* People are both *unable* and *unwilling* to take responsibility for doing something. They are neither competent nor confident.

Situational Leadership® (SL)
A leadership theory that focuses on the readiness of followers.

Q&A 12.5

readiness
The extent to which people have the ability and willingness to accomplish a specific task.

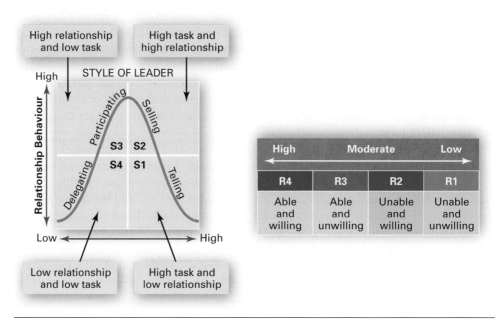

Exhibit 8-6

Hersey and Blanchard's Situational Leadership®

- *R2:* People are *unable* but *willing* to do the necessary job tasks. They are motivated but currently lack the appropriate skills.

- *R3:* People are *able* but *unwilling* to do what the leader wants.

- *R4:* People are both *able* and *willing* to do what is asked of them.

SL essentially views the leader–follower relationship as similar to that of a parent and a child. Just as a parent needs to give up control as a child becomes more mature and responsible, so, too, should a leader. As followers reach high levels of readiness, the leader responds not only by continuing to decrease control over their activities, but also by continuing to decrease relationship behaviour. SL says if followers are *unable* and *unwilling* to do a task, the leader needs to give clear and specific directions; if followers are *unable* and *willing*, the leader needs to display high task orientation to compensate for the followers' lack of ability and high relationship orientation to get followers to "buy into" the leader's desires; if followers are *able* and *unwilling*, the leader needs to use a supportive and participative style; and if employees are both *able* and *willing*, the leader does not need to do much.

SL has intuitive appeal. It acknowledges the importance of followers and builds on the logic that leaders can compensate for ability and motivational limitations in their followers. Yet research efforts to test and support the theory generally have been disappointing.[21] Why? Possible explanations include internal inconsistencies in the model itself as well as problems with research methodology. So despite its appeal and wide popularity, any endorsement should be made with caution.

Leader Participation Model

leader participation model
A leadership theory that relates leadership behaviour and participation to decision making.

Another early contingency theory of leadership, developed by Victor Vroom and Phillip Yetton, is the **leader participation model**, which relates leadership behaviour and participation to decision making.[22] Developed in the early 1970s, the model argued that leader

Many leaders in Vancouver have had to change their management style because of changes in the economic environment in recent years. With many large construction projects under way because of the upcoming 2010 Olympics, organizations are struggling to hire qualified employees. There are more jobs than employees, or that is what many managers believe when they cannot find someone to hire. Because of the boom in business, managers have to work hard to keep their best employees from accepting better offers from competing firms.

behaviour must adjust to reflect the task structure—whether it is routine, nonroutine, or in between. Vroom and Yetton's model is what we call *normative*. That is, it provides a sequential set of rules (norms) to follow in determining the form and amount of participation a leader should exercise in decision making in different types of situations.

The leader participation model has changed as research continues to provide additional insights into effective leadership style.[23] The current model reflects *how* and *with whom* decisions are made and uses variations of the same five leadership styles identified in the original model:[24]

- *Decide.* Leader makes the decision alone and either announces or sells it to the group.

- *Consult individually.* Leader presents the problem to group members individually, gets their suggestions, and then makes the decision.

- *Consult group.* Leader presents the problem to group members in a meeting, gets their suggestions, and then makes the decision.

- *Facilitate.* Leader presents the problem to the group in a meeting and, acting as facilitator, defines the problem and the boundaries within which a decision must be made.

- *Delegate.* Leader permits the group to make the decision within prescribed limits.

The contingencies that affect the leadership style chosen are decision significance, importance of commitment, leader expertise, likelihood of commitment, group support, group expertise, and team competence.[25]

Path-Goal Theory

Currently, one of the most respected approaches to understanding leadership is **path-goal theory**, which states that it's the leader's job to assist his or her followers in attaining their goals and to provide the necessary direction and support to ensure that their goals are compatible with the overall objectives of the group or organization. Developed by University of Toronto Professor Martin Evans in the late 1960s, it was subsequently expanded upon by Robert House (formerly at the University of Toronto, and now at the Wharton School of Business). Path-goal theory is a contingency model of leadership that takes key elements from the expectancy theory of motivation (see Chapter 9, pages 275–276).[26] The term *path-goal* is derived from the belief that effective leaders clarify the path to help their

path-goal theory
A leadership theory that says it's the leader's job to assist his or her followers in attaining their goals and to provide the necessary direction and/or support to ensure that their goals are compatible with the overall objectives of the group or organization.

followers get from where they are to the achievement of their work goals and make the journey along the path easier by reducing roadblocks and pitfalls.

Path-goal theory identifies four leadership behaviours:

- *Directive leader.* Leader lets subordinates know what is expected of them, schedules work to be done, and gives specific guidance on how to accomplish tasks.

- *Supportive leader.* Leader is friendly and shows concern for the needs of followers.

- *Participative leader.* Leader consults with group members and uses their suggestions before making a decision.

- *Achievement-oriented leader.* Leader sets challenging goals and expects followers to perform at their highest level.

In contrast to Fiedler's view that a leader could not change his or her behaviour, House assumed that leaders are flexible. In other words, path-goal theory assumes that the same leader can display any or all of these leadership styles, depending on the situation.

Path-goal theory proposes two situational or contingency variables that moderate the leadership behaviour–outcome relationship: *environmental* factors that are outside the control of the follower (including task structure, formal authority system, and the work group) and factors that are part of the personal characteristics of the *follower* (including locus of control, experience, and perceived ability). Environmental factors determine the type of leader behaviour required if subordinate outcomes are to be maximized; personal characteristics of the follower determine how the environment and leader behaviour are interpreted. The theory proposes that leader behaviour will not be effective if it's redundant with what the environmental structure is providing or is incongruent with follower characteristics. Exhibit 8-7 gives some illustrations of leadership behaviour tailored to the situation.

Q&A 12.6   Research on the path-goal theory is generally encouraging. Although not every study has found support, the majority of the evidence supports the logic underlying the

Exhibit 8-7

Path-Goal Situations and Preferred Leader Behaviours

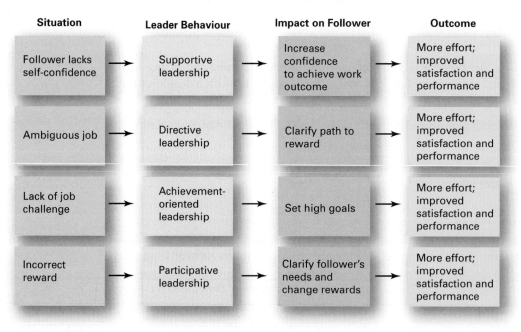

Source: R. L. Daft, *The Leadership Experience*, 3e. © 2005 South-Western, a part of Cengage Learning, Inc. Reproduced by permission, www.cengage.com/permissions.

theory.[27] In summary, employee performance and satisfaction are likely to be positively influenced when the leader compensates for shortcomings in either the employee or the work setting. However, if the leader spends time explaining tasks that are already clear or when the employee has the ability and experience to handle them without interference, the employee is likely to see such directive behaviour as redundant or even insulting.

Leading Change

When the Liquor Control Board of Ontario (LCBO) decided not to give Magnotta Winery any shelf space, Rossana Di Zio Magnotta and her husband, Gabe, settled on two strategies.[28] They decided to sell the wine themselves, and also wage a battle against the LCBO.

To gain customers, the Magnottas used an innovative marketing strategy, selling their wine at $3.95 a bottle. This was significantly less than the price of wine of similar quality selling at the LCBO. Their strategy got publicity in the newspapers, and soon people were travelling to their winery in Vaughan, Ontario, to purchase wine.

The battle against the LCBO lasted 10 years, but by 2001, the LCBO started carrying some Magnotta icewines.

Think About It

Mobilizing people to work toward a leader's vision is a difficult task. How do leaders such as Rossana Di Zio Magnotta get individuals to support their vision and help carry it out?

Most of the leadership theories presented so far in this chapter have described **transactional leaders**; that is, leaders who guide or motivate their followers in the direction of established goals by clarifying role and task requirements.[29] But another kind of leadership is needed for leading change in organizations. Two types of leadership that have been identified in situations where leaders have inspired change are charismatic–visionary leadership and transformational leadership.

4 What do charismatic and transformational leaders do?

transactional leaders Leaders who guide or motivate their followers in the direction of established goals by clarifying role and task requirements.

Charismatic–Visionary Leadership

Have you ever encountered a charismatic leader? What was this person like?

Jeff Bezos, founder and CEO of Amazon.com, is a person who exudes energy, enthusiasm, and drive.[30] He is fun-loving (his legendary laugh has been described as a flock of Canada geese on nitrous oxide), but has pursued his vision for Amazon with serious intensity and has demonstrated an ability to inspire his employees through the ups and downs of a rapidly growing company. Bezos is what we call a **charismatic leader**—that is, an enthusiastic, self-confident leader whose personality and actions influence people to behave in certain ways.

Q&A 12.7

charismatic leader An enthusiastic, self-confident leader whose personality and actions influence people to behave in certain ways.

Characteristics of Charismatic Leaders

Several authors have attempted to identify the personal characteristics of charismatic leaders.[31] The most comprehensive analysis identified five such characteristics that differentiate charismatic leaders from noncharismatic ones: They have a vision, are able to articulate that vision, are willing to take risks to achieve that vision, are sensitive to both environmental constraints and follower needs, and exhibit behaviours that are out of the ordinary.[32]

Q&A 12.8

Effects of Charismatic Leadership

What can we say about the charismatic leader's effect on his or her followers? There is an increasing body of evidence that shows impressive correlations between charismatic leadership and high performance and satisfaction among followers.[33] Research shows that people who work for charismatic leaders are motivated to exert extra work effort and express greater satisfaction, because they like their leaders.[34] One of the most cited studies of the effects of charismatic leadership was done at the University of British Columbia in the early 1980s by Jane Howell (now at the University of Western Ontario) and Peter Frost.[35] They found that those who worked under a charismatic leader generated more ideas, produced better results, reported higher job satisfaction, and showed stronger bonds of loyalty. Howell concludes, "Charismatic leaders know how to inspire people to think in new directions."[36]

Charismatic leadership also affects overall company performance. Robert House and colleagues studied 63 American and 49 Canadian companies (including Nortel Networks, Molson, Gulf Canada, and Manulife Financial) and found that "between 15 and 25 percent of the variation in profitability among the companies was accounted for by the leadership qualities of their CEO."[37] Charismatic leaders led more profitable companies. However, a recent study of the impact of a charismatic CEO on subsequent organizational performance found no relationship.[38] Despite this, charisma is still believed to be a desirable leadership quality.

Charismatic leadership may have a downside, however, as we see from the recent accounting scandals and high-profile bankruptcies of North American companies. WorldCom's Bernard Ebbers and Enron's Kenneth Lay "seemed almost a breed apart, blessed with unique visionary powers" when their companies' stock prices were growing at phenomenal rates in the 1990s.[39] After the scandals, however, there was some agreement that CEOs with less vision and more ethical and corporate responsibility might be more desirable.

Becoming Charismatic

Can people learn to be charismatic leaders? Or are charismatic leaders born with their qualities? Although a small number of experts still think that charisma cannot be learned, most believe that individuals can be trained to exhibit charismatic behaviours.[40] For example, researchers have succeeded in teaching undergraduate students to "be" charismatic. How? They were taught to articulate a sweeping goal, communicate high performance expectations, exhibit confidence in the ability of subordinates to meet those expectations, and empathize with the needs of their subordinates; they learned to project a powerful, confident, and dynamic presence; and they practised using a captivating and engaging voice tone. The researchers also trained the student leaders to use charismatic nonverbal behaviours including leaning toward the follower when communicating, maintaining direct eye contact, and having a relaxed posture and animated facial expressions. In groups with these "trained" charismatic leaders, members had higher task performance, higher task adjustment, and better adjustment to the leader and to the group than did group members who worked in groups led by non-charismatic leaders.

One last thing we need to say about charismatic leadership is that it may not always be needed to achieve high levels of employee performance. It may be most appropriate when the follower's task has an ideological purpose or when the environment involves a high degree of stress and uncertainty.[41] This may explain why, when charismatic leaders surface, it's more likely to be in the arenas of politics, religion, or war; or when a business firm is starting up or facing a survival crisis. For example, Martin Luther King Jr. used his charisma to bring about social equality through nonviolent means, and Steve Jobs achieved unwavering loyalty and commitment from Apple Computer's technical staff in the early 1980s by articulating a vision of personal computers that would dramatically change the way people lived.

Visionary Leadership

visionary leadership
The ability to create and articulate a realistic, credible, and attractive vision of the future that improves on the present situation.

Although the term *vision* is often linked with charismatic leadership, **visionary leadership** goes beyond charisma since it's the ability to create and articulate a realistic, credible, and attractive vision of the future that improves on the present situation.[42] This vision, if properly selected and implemented, is so energizing that it "in effect jump-starts the future by calling forth the skills, talents, and resources to make it happen."[43]

A vision should offer clear and compelling imagery that taps into people's emotions and inspires enthusiasm to pursue the organization's goals. It should be able to generate possibilities that are inspirational and unique and offer new ways of doing things that are clearly better for the organization and its members. Visions that are clearly articulated and have powerful imagery are easily grasped and accepted. For example, Michael Dell (founder of Dell) created a vision of a business that sells and delivers a finished personal computer directly to a customer in less than a week. The late Mary Kay Ash's vision of women as entrepreneurs selling products that improved their self-image guided her cosmetics company, Mary Kay Cosmetics.

What skills do visionary leaders have? Once the vision is identified, these leaders appear to have three skills that are related to effectiveness in their visionary roles.[44] First is the *ability to explain the vision to others* by making the vision clear in terms of required goals and actions through clear oral and written communication. The second skill is the *ability to express the vision not just verbally but through behaviour*, which requires behaving in ways that continuously convey and reinforce the vision. The third skill is the *ability to extend or apply the vision to different leadership contexts.* For example, the vision has to be as meaningful to the people in accounting as it is to those in production, and to employees in Halifax as it is to those in Toronto.

Transformational Leadership

Some leaders are able to inspire followers to transcend their own self-interests for the good of the organization, and are capable of having a profound and extraordinary effect on their followers. These are **transformational leaders**, and examples include Frank Stronach, chair of Aurora, Ontario-based Magna International; and Mogens Smed, CEO of Calgary-based DIRTT (Doing It Right This Time) and former CEO of SMED International. Prime Minister Stephen Harper was named *Time* magazine's 2006 Canadian Newsmaker of the Year, in part because of his transformational style. *Time* contributing editor Stephen Handelman explained the choice as follows: "[Harper] has set himself the messianic tasks of remaking Canadian federalism by curbing Ottawa's spending powers and overhauling Canada's health care and social welfare system." Handelman predicted that should Harper win a Conservative majority in the next election, "he may yet turn out to be the most transformational leader since Trudeau."[45]

Transformational leaders pay attention to the concerns and developmental needs of individual followers; they change followers' awareness of issues by helping those followers look at old problems in new ways; and they are able to excite, arouse, and inspire followers to put out extra effort to achieve group goals.[46]

Transformational leaders turn followers into believers on a mission, working toward what they believe is really important. "The transforming leader provides followers with a cause around which they can rally."[47] Transformational leadership is more than charisma since the transformational leader attempts to empower followers to question not only established views but even those views held by the leader.[48] The four factors that characterize transformational leadership (the "four I's") are presented in *Tips for Managers—How to Be a Transformational Leader.*

The evidence supporting the superiority of transformational leadership over transactional leadership is overwhelmingly impressive. Studies that looked at managers in different settings, including the military and business, found that transformational leaders were evaluated as more effective, higher performers, and more promotable than their transactional counterparts.[50] In addition, evidence indicates that transformational leadership is strongly correlated with

transformational leaders
Leaders who inspire followers to transcend their own self-interests for the good of the organization, and who have a profound and extraordinary effect on their followers.

TIPS FOR MANAGERS

How to Be a Transformational Leader

- **Individualized consideration:** Pay attention to the needs of individual followers to help them reach their full potential.

- **Intellectual stimulation:** Provide "ways and reasons for followers to change the way they think about" things.

- **Inspirational motivation:** "Set an example of hard work, give 'pep' talks, [and] remain optimistic in times of crisis."

- **Idealized influence:** Show respect for others, building confidence and trust about the mission in followers.[49]

lower turnover rates, higher productivity, and higher employee satisfaction.[51] Finally, sub-ordinates of transformational leaders may trust their leaders and their organizations more and feel that they are being fairly treated, which in turn may positively influence their work motivation (see Chapter 9).[52] However, transformational leadership should be used with some caution in non-North American contexts because its effectiveness may be affected by cultural values concerning leadership.[53]

Current Issues in Leadership

When Rossana Di Zio Magnotta first started trying to help her customers learn how to make wine, she ran into a significant hurdle.[54] Her customers, many of whom were first-generation Italian and Portuguese male immigrants, did not believe that a woman could know how to make wine. They constantly told her stories that implied that they knew more about wine-making than she did.

Magnotta knew that if she simply asserted her knowledge, her customers might become resentful. Instead, she wrote a step-by-step guide on winemaking, and then started distrib-uting it with each purchase of winemaking materials. This way, her customers would not feel threatened by her expertise, and were able to make better wine. The booklet significantly increased her business. "One Italian would bring three of his brothers and when I got one Portuguese guy I got five of his cousins, so all of a sudden my business became an instant success," she explains. All by leading behind the scenes.

Think About It

Do men and women lead differently? Do men and women face different challenges in mov-ing to the top of an organization? What factors might have affected Rossana Di Zio Mag-notta's ability to be seen as an effective leader?

⑤ What are some current issues in leadership?

In this section, we look at some of the issues that face leaders today, including managing power, developing trust, providing moral leadership, providing online leadership, and understanding gender differences in leadership.

Managing Power

Q&A 12.9

Where do leaders get their power—that is, their capacity to influence work actions or decisions? Five sources of leader power have been identified: legitimate, coercive, reward, expert, and referent.[55]

legitimate power
The power a leader has as a result of his or her position in the organization.

Legitimate power and authority are the same. Legitimate power represents the power a leader has as a result of his or her position in the organization. People in positions of authority are also likely to have reward and coercive power, but legitimate power is broader than the power to coerce and reward.

coercive power
The power a leader has through his or her ability to punish or control.

Coercive power is the power that rests on the leader's ability to punish or control. Fol-lowers react to this power out of fear of the negative results that might occur if they do not comply. As a manager, you typically have some coercive power, such as being able to sus-pend or demote employees or to assign them work they find unpleasant or undesirable.

reward power
The power a leader has to give positive benefits or rewards.

Reward power is the power to give positive benefits or rewards. These rewards can be anything that another person values. In an organizational context, that might include money, favourable performance appraisals, promotions, interesting work assignments, friendly colleagues, and preferred work shifts or sales territories.

expert power
The influence a leader has based on his or her expertise, special skills, or knowledge.

Expert power is influence that is based on expertise, special skills, or knowledge. As jobs have become more specialized, managers have become increasingly dependent on staff "experts" to achieve the organization's goals. If an employee has skills, knowledge, or expertise that is critical to the operation of a work group, that person's expert power is enhanced.

referent power
The power a leader has because of his or her desirable resources or personal traits.

Finally, **referent power** is the power that arises because of a person's desirable re-sources or personal traits. If I admire and identify with you, you can exercise power over me because I want to please you. Referent power develops out of admiration of another and a desire to be like that person. If you admire someone to the point of modelling your behaviour and attitudes after him or her, that person has referent power over you.

Most effective leaders rely on several different forms of power to affect the behaviour and performance of their followers. For example, Lieutenant Commander Geoffrey Wadley, commanding officer of one of Australia's state-of-the-art submarines, the HMAS *Sheean*, employs different types of power in managing his crew and equipment. He gives orders to the crew (legitimate), praises them (reward), and disciplines those who commit infractions (coercive). As an effective leader, he also strives to have expert power (based on his expertise and knowledge) and referent power (based on his being admired) to influence his crew.[56] To learn more about acquiring and using power, see *Developing Your Interpersonal Skills—Acquiring Power* on pages 262–263, at the end of the chapter.

PRISM 5

Developing Trust

After union members reluctantly agreed to $850 million a year in concessions that they believed were necessary to keep their company from bankruptcy, Air Canada's employees were stunned at president and CEO Robert Milton's after-the-fact disclosure of lucrative compensation policies and pension protections designed to retain key executives. Milton and his chief restructuring officer, Calin Rovinescu, were to receive 1 percent of the airline's shares, potentially worth an estimated $21 million, if the proposed takeover by Victor Li was successful. Any trust that employees had in Milton's ability to lead the airline into the future was eroded. In the end, the deal with Li collapsed when union members could not agree to further concessions relating to their pension plans.[57]

Milton's behaviour illustrates how fragile leader trust can be. In today's uncertain environment, an important consideration for leaders is building trust and credibility. Before we can discuss ways leaders can build trust and credibility, we have to know what trust and credibility are and why they are so important.

The main component of credibility is honesty. Surveys show that honesty is consistently singled out as the number-one characteristic of admired leaders. "Honesty is absolutely essential to leadership. If people are going to follow someone willingly, whether it be into battle or into the boardroom, they first want to assure themselves that the person is worthy of their trust." In addition to being honest, credible leaders are competent and inspiring.[58] They are personally able to effectively communicate their confidence and enthusiasm. Thus, followers judge a leader's **credibility** in terms of his or her honesty, competence, and ability to inspire.

Trust is closely entwined with the concept of credibility, and, in fact, the terms are often used interchangeably. **Trust** is defined as the belief in the integrity, character, and ability of a person. Followers who trust a leader are willing to be vulnerable to the leader's actions because they are confident that their rights and interests will not be abused.[59] Research has identified five dimensions that make up the concept of trust:[60]

credibility
The degree to which someone is perceived as honest, competent, and able to inspire.

trust
The belief in the integrity, character, and ability of a person.

- *Integrity:* Honesty and truthfulness
- *Competence:* Technical and interpersonal knowledge and skills
- *Consistency:* Reliability, predictability, and good judgment in handling situations
- *Loyalty:* Willingness to protect a person, physically and emotionally
- *Openness:* Willingness to share ideas and information freely

Of these five dimensions, integrity seems to be the most critical when someone assesses another's trustworthiness.[61] However, both integrity and competence were seen in our earlier discussion of leadership traits as consistently associated with leadership.

Workplace changes have reinforced why such leadership qualities are so important. For example, the trend toward empowerment and self-managed work teams has reduced or eliminated many of the traditional control mechanisms used to monitor employees. If a work team is free to schedule its own work, evaluate its own performance,

TIPS FOR MANAGERS

Suggestions for Building Trust

✔ Practise **openness**.

✔ Be **fair**.

✔ Speak your **feelings**.

✔ Tell the **truth**.

✔ Show **consistency**.

✔ Fulfill your **promises**.

✔ Maintain **confidences**.

✔ Demonstrate **competence**.

PRISM 4

and even make its own hiring decisions, trust becomes critical. Employees have to trust managers to treat them fairly, and managers have to trust employees to conscientiously fulfill their responsibilities.

Also, leaders have to increasingly lead others who may not be in their immediate work group—members of cross-functional teams, individuals who work for suppliers or customers, and perhaps even people who represent other organizations through strategic alliances. These situations do not allow leaders the luxury of falling back on their formal positions for influence. Many of these relationships, in fact, are fluid and fleeting; the ability to develop trust quickly is crucial to the success of the relationship.

Why is it important that followers trust their leaders? Research has shown that trust in leadership is significantly related to positive job outcomes, including job performance, job satisfaction, and organizational commitment.[62] Given the importance of trust in effective leadership, how should leaders build trust? See *Tips for Managers—Suggestions for Building Trust*.[63]

Providing Ethical Leadership

The topic of leadership and ethics has received surprisingly little attention. Only recently have ethics and leadership researchers begun to consider the ethical implications of leadership.[64] Visit your local bookstore and you will find quite a few books on ethics and leadership. Why now? One reason is a growing general interest in ethics throughout the field of management. Another, without a doubt, is the recent corporate and government financial scandals that have increased the public's and politicians' concerns about ethical standards.

Ethics is part of leadership in a number of ways. For example, transformational leaders have been described as fostering moral virtue when they try to change the attitudes and behaviours of followers.[65] We can also see an ethical component to charisma. Unethical leaders may use their charisma to enhance their power over followers and use that power for self-serving purposes. On the other hand, ethical leaders may use their charisma in more socially constructive ways to serve others.[66] We also see a lack of ethics when leaders abuse their power and give themselves large salaries and bonuses while, at the same time, they seek to cut costs by laying off employees. And, of course, trust, which is important to ethical behaviour, explicitly deals with the leadership traits of honesty and integrity.

As we have seen recently, leadership is not value-free. Providing moral leadership involves addressing the *means* that a leader uses in trying to achieve goals as well as the content of those goals. As a recent study concluded, ethical leadership is more than being ethical; it's reinforcing ethics through organizational mechanisms such as communication and the reward system.[67] Thus, before we judge any leader to be effective, we should consider both the moral content of his or her goals *and* the means used to achieve those goals.

Providing Online Leadership

Would you expect your job as a leader to be more difficult if employees are working from home, connected by computer?

How do you lead people who are physically separated from you and where interactions are essentially reduced to written online communications? Pat O'Day, manager of a five-person virtual team at KPMG International, understands the challenges of providing online leadership. To help his team be more effective, O'Day says, "We communicate through email and conference calls and meet in person four times a year."[68]

What little research has been done in online leadership has focused on managing virtual teams.[69] This research suggests that there are three fundamental challenges in providing online leadership: communication, performance management, and trust.

Communication

In a virtual setting, leaders may need to learn new communication skills in order to be seen as effective. To effectively convey online leadership, managers must realize that they have choices in words, structure, tone, and style of their online communications and be alert to expressions of emotions. In face-to-face communications, harsh *words* can be softened by nonverbal action. A smile and comforting gestures, for example, can lessen the blow behind words such as *disappointed, unsatisfactory, inadequate,* or *below expectations.* In online interactions, that nonverbal aspect does not exist.

The *structure* of words in online communication has the power to motivate or demotivate the receiver. Is the message made up of full sentences or just phrases? The latter is likely to be seen as curt and more threatening. Similarly, a message in ALL CAPS is the equivalent of shouting.

Leaders also need to be sure the *tone* of their message correctly conveys the emotions they want to send. Is the message formal or informal? Does it convey the appropriate level of importance or urgency? Also, is the leader's writing style consistent with his or her oral style? For example, if a leader's written communication is more formal than his or her oral style, it will likely create confusion for employees and hinder the effectiveness of the message.

Online leaders must also choose a *style.* Do they use emoticons, abbreviations, jargon, and the like? Do they adapt their style to their audience? Observation suggests that some managers have difficulty adjusting to computer-based communications. For instance, they use the same style with their bosses that they use with their staff. Or they selectively use online communication to "hide" when delivering bad news. Finally, online leaders need to develop the skills of "reading between the lines" in the messages they receive so they can decipher the emotional components.

Performance Management

Another challenge of online leadership is managing performance. How? By defining, facilitating, and encouraging it.[70] As leaders *define* performance, it's important to ensure that all members of a virtual team understand the team's goals, their responsibilities in achieving those goals, and how goal achievement is going to be assessed. There should be no surprises or uncertainties about performance expectations. Although these are important managerial responsibilities in all situations, they are particularly critical in virtual work environments as there are no face-to-face interactions to convey expectations or address performance problems.

Online leaders also have a responsibility to *facilitate* performance. This means reducing or eliminating obstacles to successful performance and providing adequate resources to get the job done. This can be particularly challenging, especially if the virtual team is global, since the physical distance separating the leader and the team means it's not easy to get team members the resources they may need.

Finally, online leaders are responsible for *encouraging* performance by providing sufficient rewards that virtual employees really value. As we will see in Chapter 9, motivating employees can be difficult, even in work settings where there is face-to-face interaction. In a virtual setting, the motivational challenge can be even greater because the leader is not there in person to encourage, support, and guide. So what can online leaders do? They can ask virtual employees what rewards are most important to them—pay, benefits, technology upgrades, opportunities for professional development, or whatever. Then, they can make sure the rewards are provided in a timely manner after major work goals have been achieved. Finally, any rewards program must be perceived as fair. This expectation is not any different from that of leaders in nonvirtual settings—employees want and expect rewards to be distributed fairly.

Trust

The final challenge of providing online leadership is the trust issue. In a virtual setting, there are numerous opportunities to violate trust. One possible trust issue is whether the system is being used to monitor and evaluate employees. The technology is there to do so, but leaders must consider whether that is really the best way to influence employee behaviour. T. J. Rodgers, founder and CEO of Cypress Semiconductor, found out the hard way that it might not be.[71] He built an in-house system that tracked goals and deadlines. If a department missed its target, the software shut down its computers and cancelled the manager's next paycheque. After realizing the system encouraged dishonesty, Rodgers ditched it. The experience made him understand that it was more important to create a culture in which trust among all participants is expected and required. In fact, the five dimensions of trust we described earlier—integrity, competence, consistency, loyalty, and openness—would be vital to the development of such a culture.

Team Leadership

Q&A 12.10

Since leadership is increasingly taking place within a team context and more organizations are using work teams, the role of the leader in guiding team members has become increasingly important. The role of team leader *is* different from the traditional leadership role. Many leaders are not equipped to handle the change to employee teams. As one consultant noted, "Even the most capable managers have trouble making the transition because all the command-and-control type things they were encouraged to do before are no longer appropriate. There's no reason to have any skill or sense of this."[72] This same consultant estimated that "probably 15 percent of managers are natural team leaders; another 15 percent could never lead a team because it runs counter to their personality—that is, they're unable to sublimate their dominating style for the good of the team. Then there's that huge group in the middle: Team leadership doesn't come naturally to them, but they can learn it."[73]

The challenge for many managers is learning how to become an effective team leader. They have to learn skills such as having the patience to share information, being able to trust others and to give up authority, and understanding when to intervene. Effective team leaders have mastered the difficult balancing act of knowing when to leave their teams alone and when to get involved. New team leaders may try to retain too much control at a time when team members need more autonomy, or they may abandon their teams at times when team members need support and help.[74] (To learn more about teams, see *Self-Assessment—How Good Am I at Building and Leading a Team?* on pages 312–313, in Chapter 10.)

One study of organizations that had reorganized themselves around employee teams found certain common responsibilities of all leaders. These included coaching, facilitating,

When Eva Aariak spoke to the Nunavut legislative assembly to explain why she should be elected the territory's premier, she emphasized that her leadership style included the ability to listen and encourage others to share their ideas. She considers herself a team player, which will work well with the territory's consensus style of government built from the principles of parliamentary democracy and Aboriginal values.

Exhibit 8-8

Specific Team Leadership Roles

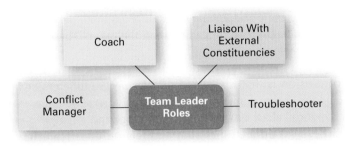

What has been your biggest challenge when trying to lead team members?

handling disciplinary problems, reviewing team and individual performance, training, and communication.[75] However, a more meaningful way to describe the team leader's job is to focus on two priorities: (1) managing the team's external boundary and (2) facilitating the team process.[76] These priorities entail four specific leadership roles (see Exhibit 8-8).

Team leaders are *liaisons with external constituencies.* These may include upper management, other organizational work teams, customers, or suppliers. The leader represents the team to other constituencies, secures needed resources, clarifies others' expectations of the team, gathers information from the outside, and shares that information with team members.

Team leaders are *troubleshooters.* When the team has problems and asks for assistance, team leaders sit in on meetings and try to help resolve the problems. Troubleshooting rarely involves technical or operational issues because the team members typically know more about the tasks being done than does the leader. The leader is most likely to contribute by asking penetrating questions, helping the team talk through problems, and getting needed resources to tackle problems.

Team leaders are *conflict managers.* They help identify issues such as the source of the conflict, who is involved, the issues, the resolution options available, and the advantages and disadvantages of each. By getting team members to address questions such as these, the leader minimizes the disruptive aspects of intrateam conflicts.

Finally, team leaders are *coaches.* They clarify expectations and roles, teach, offer support, and do whatever else is necessary to help team members keep their work performance high.

Understanding Gender Differences and Leadership

There was a time when the question "Do males and females lead differently?" could be accurately characterized as a purely academic issue—interesting, but not very relevant. That time has certainly passed! Many women now hold management positions, and many more around the world will continue to join the management ranks. Women fill 37 percent of managerial roles in Canada, although only 22 percent of the senior management roles (down from 27 percent in 1996), and 6.7 percent of the highest corporate titles—CEO, chief financial officer, or chief operating officer.[77] They are highly involved in smaller companies, however. Industry Canada reports that in 2004, 47 percent of all small to medium-sized enterprises had some degree of female ownership.[78] Moreover, a study by the Canadian Imperial Bank of Commerce estimates that since 1989, women-run businesses have increased 60 percent faster than those run by men.[79]

In other economically developed countries, the percentage of female managerial/administrative employees is as follows: Australia—37 percent; France—37 percent;

Germany—37 percent; Japan—10 percent; Poland—33 percent; and Sweden—30 percent.[80] Misconceptions about the relationship between leadership and gender can adversely affect hiring, performance evaluation, promotion, and other human resource decisions for both men and women. For example, evidence indicates that a "good" manager is still perceived as predominantly masculine.[81] A warning before we proceed: This topic is controversial. If male and female styles differ, is one inferior? If there is a difference, is one gender more effective in leading than the other? These are important questions and we will address them shortly.

A number of studies focusing on gender and leadership style have been conducted.[82] Their general conclusion is that males and females *do* use different styles. Specifically, women tend to adopt a more democratic or participative style. Women are more likely to encourage participation, share power and information, and attempt to enhance followers' self-worth. They lead through inclusion and rely on their charisma, expertise, contacts, and interpersonal skills to influence others. Women tend to use transformational leadership, motivating others by transforming their self-interest into organizational goals. Men are more likely to use a directive, command-and-control style. They rely on formal position authority for their influence. Men use transactional leadership, handing out rewards for good work and punishment for bad.[83] There is an interesting qualifier to the above findings. The tendency of female leaders to be more democratic than males declines when women are in male-dominated jobs. In such jobs, apparently, group norms and male stereotypes influence women, and they are likely to act more autocratically.[84]

Another issue to consider is how male and female leaders are perceived in the workplace. A recent study sheds some light on this topic.[85] One major finding of this research was that men consider women to be less skilled at problem solving, which is one of the qualities often associated with effective leadership. Another finding was that both men and women believed women to be superior to men at "take care" behaviours and men superior to women at "take charge" behaviours. Such gender-based stereotyping creates challenges both for organizations and for leaders within those organizations. Organizations need effective leaders at all levels, but they need to ensure that stereotypical perceptions do not limit who those leaders might be.[86]

Although it's interesting to see how male and female leadership styles differ, a more important question is whether they differ in effectiveness. Although some researchers have shown that males and females tend to be equally effective as leaders,[87] an increasing number of studies have shown that women executives, when rated by their peers, employees, and bosses, score higher than their male counterparts on a wide variety of measures, including getting extra effort from subordinates and overall effectiveness in leading. Subordinates also reported more satisfaction with the leadership given by women.[88] See Exhibit 8-9 for a scorecard on where female managers do better, based on a summary of five studies. Why these differences? One possible explanation is that in today's organizations,

Yale graduate Indra Nooyi, who played in an all-girl rock band while growing up in Chennai, India, is the savvy and irreverent chair and CEO of PepsiCo Inc. Drawn to PepsiCo as chief strategist almost 15 years ago by the chance to help turn around the company, she has helped the company double net profits to more than $5.6 billion by focusing on better nutrition and by promoting workforce diversity. "Indra can drive as deep and hard as anyone I've ever met," says former CEO Roger Enrico, "but she can do it with a sense of heart and fun." Nooyi still sings in the office and has been known to go barefoot at work.

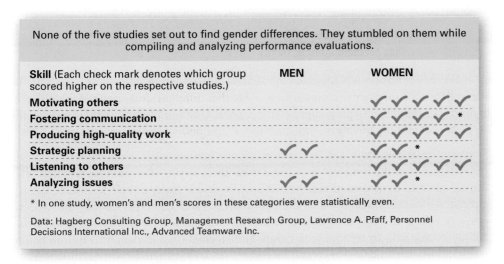

Exhibit 8-9

Where Female Managers Do Better: A Scorecard

None of the five studies set out to find gender differences. They stumbled on them while compiling and analyzing performance evaluations.

Skill (Each check mark denotes which group scored higher on the respective studies.)	MEN	WOMEN
Motivating others		✓ ✓ ✓ ✓ ✓
Fostering communication		✓ ✓ ✓ ✓ *
Producing high-quality work		✓ ✓ ✓ ✓ ✓
Strategic planning	✓ ✓	✓ ✓ *
Listening to others		✓ ✓ ✓ ✓ ✓
Analyzing issues	✓ ✓	✓ ✓ *

* In one study, women's and men's scores in these categories were statistically even.

Data: Hagberg Consulting Group, Management Research Group, Lawrence A. Pfaff, Personnel Decisions International Inc., Advanced Teamware Inc.

Source: R. Sharpe, "As Leaders, Women Rule," *BusinessWeek*, November 20, 2000, p. 75.

flexibility, teamwork and partnering, trust, and information sharing are rapidly replacing rigid structures, competitive individualism, control, and secrecy. In these types of workplaces, effective managers must use more social and interpersonal behaviours. They listen, motivate, and provide support to their people. They inspire and influence rather than control. And women seem to do those things better than men.[89]

Although women seem to rate highly on those leadership skills needed to succeed in today's dynamic global environment, we do not want to fall into the same trap as the early leadership researchers who tried to find the "one best leadership style" for all situations. We know that there is no one *best* style for all situations. Instead, which leadership style is effective will depend on the situation. So even if men and women differ in their leadership styles, we should not assume that one is always preferable to the other.

Tips for Managers—Being a Better Leader gives some suggestions for being a better leader.

TIPS FOR MANAGERS

Being a Better Leader

- **Be clear** about expectation for business practices: What is and is not acceptable? How can unacceptable behaviours be changed?

- **Spend time with people** at all levels and positions in the organization.

- Create a workplace that **makes people want to come to work.**

- **Support your organization's people.** Be loyal.

SUMMARY AND IMPLICATIONS

❶ How do leaders and managers differ? Managers are appointed to their positions. They have formal authority, and it is this authority that gives them their ability to influence employees. In contrast, leaders can be appointed or can emerge from within a work group. They provide vision and strategy and are able to influence others for reasons beyond formal authority. Though ideally all managers should be leaders, not all leaders can be managers, because they do not all have the ability to plan, organize, and control.

○○○○ Rossana Di Zio Magnotta has demonstrated the ability to both lead and manage at
○○○○ Magnotta Winery.

② **What do trait and behavioural theories tell us about leadership?** Researchers agree that traits alone are not sufficient for explaining effective leadership. Possessing the appropriate traits makes it only more likely that an individual would be an effective leader. In general, behavioural theories have identified useful behaviours that managers should have, but the research could not identify when these behaviours were most useful.

> Rossana Di Zio Magnotta notes that one of her most useful leadership traits is being tough and willing to stand up to adversity.

③ **How do contingency theories of leadership improve our understanding of leadership?** Contingency theories acknowledge that different situations require different leadership styles. The theories suggest that leaders may need to adjust their style to the needs of different organizations and employees, and perhaps different countries.

④ **What do charismatic and transformational leaders do?** While most leaders are transactional, guiding followers to achieve goals by clarifying role and task requirements, charismatic and transformational leaders inspire and influence their followers. Charismatic leaders are enthusiastic and self-confident leaders whose personality and actions motivate followers. They are known for having and articulating a vision, and for being willing to take risks to achieve that vision. Transformational leaders turn followers into believers on a mission, and encourage followers to go beyond their own self-interests for the greater good. Transformational leadership is more than charisma since the transformational leader attempts to empower followers to question established views and even those views held by the leader.

> Rossana Di Zio Magnotta found that motivating customers to help with the winery's dispute with the Liquor Control Board of Ontario reinforced the idea that the wines should be carried in the stores. By mobilizing customers, she caught the attention of the LCBO.

⑤ **What are some current issues in leadership?** The major leadership issues today include managing power, developing trust, providing moral leadership, providing online leadership, and understanding gender differences and leadership.

> Rossana Di Zio Magnotta's experience with Italian and Portuguese male customers illustrates the differences men and women can face in the workplace. She had to find a way to make her male customers comfortable with her expertise, something a man in her position would probably not have had to do.

Management @ Work

READING FOR COMPREHENSION

1. Discuss the strengths and weaknesses of the trait theory of leadership.

2. What is the managerial grid? Contrast this approach to leadership with that developed by the Ohio State and Michigan groups.

3. How is a least-preferred co-worker (LPC) determined? What is the importance of one's LPC for the Fiedler contingency model for leadership?

4. What are the two contingency variables of the path-goal theory of leadership?

5. What similarities, if any, can you find among Fiedler's contingency model, Hersey and Blanchard's Situational Leadership®, and path-goal theory?

6. What sources of power are available to leaders? Which ones are most effective?

7. What are the five dimensions of trust?

LINKING CONCEPTS TO PRACTICE

1. "All managers should be leaders, but not all leaders should be managers." Do you agree or disagree with this statement? Support your position.

2. If you ask people why a given individual is a leader, they tend to describe the person using terms such as *competent*, *consistent*, *self-assured*, *inspiring a shared vision*, and *enthusiastic*. How do these descriptions fit with leadership concepts presented in the chapter?

3. Do you think that most managers in real life use a contingency approach to increase their leadership effectiveness? Discuss.

4. Do you think trust evolves out of an individual's personal characteristics or out of specific situations? Explain.

5. "Charismatic leadership is always appropriate in organizations." Do you agree or disagree? Support your position.

6. What kinds of campus activities could a full-time student do that might lead to the perception that he or she is a charismatic leader? In pursuing those activities, what might the student do to enhance this perception of being charismatic?

SELF-ASSESSMENT

What's My Leadership Style?

The following items describe aspects of leadership behaviour. Respond to each item according to the way you would be most likely to act if you were the leader of a work group. Use this scale for your responses:[90]

A = Always
F = Frequently
O = Occasionally
S = Seldom
N = Never

1. I would most likely act as the spokesperson of the group. A F O S N

2. I would encourage overtime work. A F O S N

3. I would allow group members complete freedom in their work. A F O S N

4. I would encourage the use of uniform procedures. A F O S N

5. I would permit group members to use their own judgment in solving problems. A F O S N

6. I would stress being ahead of competing groups. A F O S N

7. I would speak as a representative of the group.	A	F	O	S	N
8. I would needle group members for greater effort.	A	F	O	S	N
9. I would try out my ideas in the group.	A	F	O	S	N
10. I would let group members do their work the way they think best.	A	F	O	S	N
11. I would be working hard for a promotion.	A	F	O	S	N
12. I would be able to tolerate postponement and uncertainty.	A	F	O	S	N
13. I would speak for the group when visitors were present.	A	F	O	S	N
14. I would keep the work moving at a rapid pace.	A	F	O	S	N
15. I would turn group members loose on a job and let them go to it.	A	F	O	S	N
16. I would settle conflicts when they occur in the group.	A	F	O	S	N
17. I would get swamped by details.	A	F	O	S	N
18. I would represent the group at outside meetings.	A	F	O	S	N
19. I would be reluctant to allow group members any freedom of action.	A	F	O	S	N
20. I would decide what shall be done and how it shall be done.	A	F	O	S	N
21. I would push for increased production.	A	F	O	S	N
22. I would let some group members have authority that I should keep.	A	F	O	S	N
23. Things would usually turn out as I predicted.	A	F	O	S	N
24. I would allow the group a high degree of initiative.	A	F	O	S	N
25. I would assign group members to particular tasks.	A	F	O	S	N
26. I would be willing to make changes.	A	F	O	S	N
27. I would ask group members to work harder.	A	F	O	S	N
28. I would trust group members to exercise good judgment.	A	F	O	S	N
29. I would schedule the work to be done.	A	F	O	S	N
30. I would refuse to explain my actions.	A	F	O	S	N
31. I would persuade group members that my ideas are to their advantage.	A	F	O	S	N
32. I would permit the group to set its own pace.	A	F	O	S	N
33. I would urge the group to beat its previous record.	A	F	O	S	N
34. I would act without consulting the group.	A	F	O	S	N
35. I would ask that group members follow standard rules and regulations.	A	F	O	S	N

Scoring Key

1. Circle the numbers 8, 12, 17, 18, 19, 30, 34, and 35.

2. Write a 1 in front of the circled number if you responded Seldom or Never.

3. Also write a 1 in front of any remaining (uncircled) items if you responded Always or Frequently to these.

4. Circle the 1s that you have written in front of the following questions: 3, 5, 8, 10, 15, 18, 19, 22, 24, 26, 28, 30, 32, 34, and 35.

5. Count the circled 1s. This is your score for "Concern for People."

6. Count the uncircled 1s. This is your score for "Task."

Analysis and Interpretation

This leadership instrument taps the degree to which you are task or people oriented. Task orientation is concerned with getting the job done, whereas people orientation focuses on group interactions and the needs of individual members.

The cutoff scores separating high and low scores are approximately as follows. For task orientation, high is a score above 10; low is below 10. For people orientation, high is a score above 7; low is below 7.

The best leaders are ones who can balance their task/people orientation to various situations. A high score on both would indicate this balance. If you are too task oriented, you tend to be autocratic. You get the job done but at a high emotional cost. If you are too people oriented, your leadership style may be overly laissez-faire. People are likely to be happy in their work but sometimes at the expense of productivity.

Your score should also help you put yourself in situations that increase your likelihood of success. So, for instance, evidence indicates that when employees are experienced and know their jobs well, they tend to perform best with a people-oriented leader. If you are people oriented, then this is a favourable situation for you. But if you are task oriented, you might want to pass on this situation.

More Self-Assessments

To learn more about your skills, abilities, and interests, take the following self-assessments on MyManagementLab at www.pearsoned.ca/mymanagementlab:

- II.B.2.—How Charismatic Am I?
- II.B.4.—Do Others See Me as Trustworthy?
- II.B.6.—How Good Am I at Building and Leading a Team? (This exercise also appears in Chapter 10 on pages 312–313.)

MANAGEMENT FOR YOU TODAY

Dilemma

Your school is developing a one-day orientation program for new students majoring in business. You have been asked to consider leading the group of students who will design and implement the orientation program. Develop a 2- to 3-page handout that shows whether the position is a natural fit for you. To do this, (1) identify your strengths and weaknesses in the sources of power you can bring to the project; and (2) discuss whether you would be a transactional or transformational leader and why. Provide a strong concluding statement about whether or not you would be the best leader for this task.

Becoming a Manager

- As you interact with various organizations, note different leadership styles.
- Think of people that you would consider effective leaders and try to determine why they are effective.
- If you have the opportunity, take leadership development courses.

- Practise building trust in relationships that you have with others.
- Read books on great leaders (not just business leaders) and on leadership development topics.

WORKING TOGETHER: TEAM-BASED EXERCISE

The Pre–Post Leadership Assessment

Objective

To compare characteristics intuitively related to leadership with leadership characteristics found in leadership theory.

Procedure

Identify 3 people (e.g., friends, relatives, previous boss, public figures) whom you consider outstanding leaders. List why you feel each individual is a good leader. Compare your lists of the 3 people. Which traits, if any, are common to all 3? Your instructor will lead the class in a discussion of leadership characteristics based on your lists. Students will call out what they identified, and your instructor will write the traits on the chalkboard. When all students have shared their lists, class discussion will focus on the following:

- What characteristics consistently appeared on students' lists?

- Were these characteristics more trait oriented or behaviour oriented?
- In what situations were these characteristics useful?
- What, if anything, does this exercise suggest about leadership attributes?

ETHICS IN ACTION

Ethical Dilemma Exercise: Is an Eye for an Eye Fair Play?

What happens when a charismatic leader's relentless pursuit of a vision encourages extreme or even ethically questionable behaviour? Consider the CEO of a company that hired an investigator to dive into other firms' dumpsters for information about their dealings with a major competitor. The same CEO's company has used precisely timed news releases as strategic weapons against particular rivals. And the same CEO's company once announced a hostile takeover bid for a direct competitor with the stated intention of not actively selling its products but acquiring its best customers and employees. This CEO, described by the *Wall Street Journal* as "a swashbuckling figure in Silicon Valley," is Larry Ellison of Oracle.

Ellison's charismatic leadership has built Oracle into a software powerhouse. Although it is locked in fierce competition with Microsoft and other giants, it does not ignore smaller rivals such as i2 Technologies. Oracle once issued a news release belittling i2's attempt to develop a certain type of software only minutes before i2's CEO was to meet with influential analysts. Such hardball tactics are hardly random or spontaneous. "We definitely sit down with a

calendar and work out which week we're going to pick on Siebel and which week we're going to pick on i2," says Oracle's chief marketing officer. When Oracle pursued an unwelcome acquisition bid for rival PeopleSoft, the two CEOs traded barbed quotes for weeks as the companies battled in courtrooms and in the media. PeopleSoft's CEO, a former Oracle executive, described the situation as "enormously bad behavior from a company that's had a history of it."[91] Nevertheless, Oracle finally bought PeopleSoft in 2005.

Imagine that you are the CEO of i2 Technologies, which makes inventory and supply tracking systems that compete with Oracle's large-scale business software suites. In five minutes, you will be meeting with a roomful of financial analysts who make buy or sell recommendations to investors. Your goal is to showcase your company's accomplishments, outline your vision for its future, and encourage a positive recommendation so your stock price will go even higher. You just heard about Oracle's news release belittling your product in development—and you suspect the analysts also know about it. How will you handle the news release?

Thinking Critically About Ethics

Your boss is not satisfied with the way one of your colleagues is handling a project and she reassigns the project to you. She tells you to work with this person to find out what he has done already and to discuss any other necessary information that he might have. She wants your project report by the end of the month. This person is quite upset and angry over the reassignment and will not give you the

information you need to even start, much less complete, the project. You will not be able to meet your deadline unless you get this information.

What type of power does your colleague appear to be using? What type of influence could you possibly use to gain his cooperation? What could you do to resolve this situation successfully, yet ethically?

CASE APPLICATION

Grafik Marketing Communications

When more seasoned employees take less experienced employees under their wings, we call this mentoring.[92] The wisdom and guidance of these seasoned individuals serve to assist less-experienced employees in obtaining the

necessary skills and socialization to succeed in the organization. It is also helpful in facilitating an individual's career progress. Technology, however, is starting to change some of this traditional mentoring process in terms of who does the mentoring. For Judy Kirpich, for example, technological advancements have resulted in significant increases in mentoring in her organization, Grafik Marketing Communications. However, the company's senior managers are the ones who need to be mentored. They do not have the technological savvy of the younger employees who have grown up on computers, resulting in what is called reverse mentoring.

Kirpich is considering introducing reverse mentoring, a practice started years ago at General Electric. Then CEO Jack Welch recognized that his senior managers needed to become more proficient with technology—especially the Internet. Accordingly, Welch had several hundred senior managers partner with younger employees in the organization. Not only were these managers able to learn about the Internet, but reverse mentoring also enhanced intergenerational understanding and gave senior decision makers a new perspective on younger consumer products and service needs. It also helped the organization brainstorm new and creative ideas.

Reverse mentoring, however, is not without drawbacks. For these younger employees to mentor properly, they must be trained. They must understand how to be patient with those individuals who may have a technology phobia. These reverse mentors need to recognize that their mentoring is limited to offering advice solely on relevant technology topics. They must also understand and acknowledge the need for confidentiality because many senior managers may be reluctant to have this mentoring relationship widely known. Reverse mentoring can also lead to a problem of subordinates forgetting that the leaders are still in charge. Furthermore, when reverse mentors exist, organizational members must be made aware that problems arising out of favouritism are a reality.

Kirpich wants to move reverse mentoring forward at Grafik Marketing Communications. However, she is aware of the many problems that could arise. What advice would you give her about successfully implementing reverse mentoring?

DEVELOPING YOUR DIAGNOSTIC AND ANALYTICAL SKILLS

Radical Leadership

Ricardo Semler, CEO of Semco Group of São Paulo, Brazil, is considered by many to be a radical. He has never been the type of leader that most people might expect to be in charge of a multimillion-dollar business.[93] Why? Semler breaks all the traditional "rules" of leading and managing. He is the ultimate hands-off leader who does not even have an office at the company's headquarters. As the "leading proponent and most tireless evangelist" of participative management, Semler says his philosophy is simple: Treat people like adults and they will respond like adults.

Underlying the participative management approach is the belief that "organizations thrive best by entrusting employees to apply their creativity and ingenuity in service of the whole enterprise, and to make important decisions close to the flow of work, conceivably including the selection and election of their bosses." According to Semler, his approach works . . . and works well. But how does it work in reality?

At Semco, you will not find most of the trappings of organizations and management. There are no organization charts, no long-term plans, no corporate values statements, no dress codes, and no written rules or policy manuals. The company's 3000 employees decide their work hours and their pay levels. Subordinates decide who their bosses will

be and they also review their boss's performance. The employees also elect the corporate leadership and decide most of the company's new strategic initiatives. Each person has one vote—including Ricardo Semler.

At one of the company's plants outside São Paulo, there are no supervisors telling employees what to do. On any given day, an employee may decide to "run a grinder or drive a forklift, depending on what needs to be done." João Vendramin Neto, who is in charge of Semco's manufacturing, says that "the workers know the organization's objectives and they use common sense to decide for themselves what they should do to hit those goals."

Why did Semler decide that his form of radical leadership was necessary, and does it work? Semler did not pursue such radical self-governance out of some altruistic ulterior motive. Instead, he felt it was the only way to build an organization that was flexible and resilient enough to flourish in chaotic and turbulent times. He maintains that this approach has enabled Semco to survive the roller-coaster nature of Brazilian politics and the Brazilian economy. Although the country's political leadership and economy have gone from one extreme to another and countless Brazilian banks and companies have failed, Semco has survived. And not just survived—prospered. Semler says, "If you look at Semco's numbers, we've grown 27.5 percent a year for 14 years." Semler attributes this fact to flexibility . . . of his company and, most importantly, of his employees.

Questions

1. Describe Ricardo Semler's leadership style. What do you think the advantages and drawbacks of his style might be?

2. What challenges might a radically "hands-off" leader face? How could those challenges be addressed?

3. How could future leaders be identified in this organization? Would leadership training be important to this organization? Discuss.

4. What could other businesses learn from Semler's approach to leadership?

DEVELOPING YOUR INTERPERSONAL SKILLS

Acquiring Power

About the Skill

The exercise of power is a natural process in any group or organization, and to perform their jobs effectively managers need to know how to acquire and use power—the capacity of a leader to influence work actions or decisions. We discussed the concept of power earlier in the chapter and identified five different sources of power for leaders, including legitimate, coercive, reward, expert, and referent. Why is having power important? Because power makes you less dependent on others. When a manager has power, he or she is not as dependent on others for critical resources. If the resources managers control are important, scarce, and nonsubstitutable, their power will increase because others will be more dependent on them for those resources.

Steps in Developing the Skill

You can be more effective at acquiring and using power if you accept the following eight suggestions:[94]

1. **Frame arguments in terms of organizational goals.** To be effective at acquiring power means camouflaging your self-interests. Discussions over who controls what resources should be framed in terms of the benefits that will accrue to the organization; do not point out how you personally will benefit.

2. **Develop the right image.** If you know your organization's culture, you already understand what the organization wants and values from its employees in terms of dress, associates to cultivate and those to avoid, whether to appear risk taking or risk averse, the preferred leadership style, the importance placed on getting along well with others, and so forth. With this knowledge, you are equipped to project the appropriate image. Because the assessment of your performance is not always a fully objective process, you need to pay attention to style as well as substance.

3. **Gain control of organizational resources.** Controlling organizational resources that are scarce and important is a source of power. Knowledge and expertise are particularly effective resources to control. They make you more valuable to the organization and, therefore, more likely to have job security, chances for advancement, and a receptive audience for your ideas.

4. **Make yourself appear indispensable.** Because we are dealing with appearances rather than objective facts, you can enhance your power by appearing to be indispensable. You do not really have to be indispensable as long as key people in the organization believe that you are.

5. **Be visible.** If you have a job that brings your accomplishments to the attention of others, that is great. However, if you do not have such a job, you will want to find ways to let others in the organization know what you are doing by highlighting successes in routine reports, having satisfied customers relay their appreciation to senior executives, being seen at social functions, being active in your professional associations, and developing powerful allies who speak positively about your accomplishments. Of course, you will want to be on the lookout for those projects that will increase your visibility.

6. **Develop powerful allies.** To get power, it helps to have powerful people on your side. Cultivate contacts with potentially influential people above you, at your own level, and at lower organizational levels. These allies often can provide you with information that is otherwise not readily available. In addition, having allies can provide you with a coalition of support if and when you need it.

7. **Avoid "tainted" members.** In almost every organization, there are fringe members whose status is questionable.

Their performance and/or loyalty may be suspect. Keep your distance from such individuals.

8. **Support your manager.** Your immediate future is in the hands of your current manager. Because he or she evaluates your performance, you will typically want to do whatever is necessary to have your manager on your side. You should make every effort to help your manager succeed, make her look good, support her if she is under siege, and spend the time to find out the criteria she will use to assess your effectiveness. Do not speak negatively of your manager to others, or undermine her in any way.

Practising the Skill

You used to be the star marketing manager for Hilton Electronics. But for the past year you have been outpaced again and again by Conor, a new manager in the design department, who has been accomplishing everything expected of her and more. Meanwhile, your best efforts to do your job well have been sabotaged and undercut by Leonila—your and Conor's manager. For example, before last year's international consumer electronics show, Leonila moved $30 000 from your budget to Conor's. Despite your best efforts, your marketing team could not complete all the marketing materials normally developed to showcase all of your organization's new products at this important industry show. Leonila has chipped away at your staff and budget ever since. Although you have been able to meet most of your goals with fewer staff and a reduced budget, Leonila has continued to slice resources away from your group. Just last week, she eliminated two positions in your team of eight marketing specialists to make room for a new designer and some extra equipment for Conor. Leonila is clearly taking away your resources while giving Conor whatever she wants and more. You think it's time to do something or soon you will not have any team members or resources left. How should you approach the problem?

Motivating Employees

How do I motivate people to accomplish
organizational goals?

1   What is motivation?

2   How can needs help one be motivated?

3   What are the contemporary theories
of motivation?

4   What are some current issues in motivation?

5   What can managers learn from motivation
theories?

How do you motivate employees in an industry where absenteeism rates average 5 percent of all working hours, but can be as high as 10 percent in urban areas?[1]

What do you do when the turnover rate of managers averages 20 percent, and the turnover rate of nonmanagerial employees averages 30 percent?

Sir Terry Leahy, CEO of UK-based Tesco, faces these problems daily. The company has over 3700 supermarkets, hypermarkets, and convenience stores in the United Kingdom, Ireland, Central Europe, Asia, and the United States. Once a discount supermarket, Tesco has redesigned itself as a dressier, mid-market retailer while becoming the number-one food retailer in the United Kingdom.

The company is trying to keep its Generation-Y employees (Generation Y includes those born between 1979 and 1994) motivated, while also trying to accommodate the needs of other groups of employees, including ethnic minorities and mothers returning to the workplace. Not all of the jobs are interesting, and many can be quite repetitive, such as stocking shelves, or running groceries past scanners for hours on end.

Leahy believes in starting with the basics in dealing with employees. "We've built Tesco around sound values and principles," he says. Therefore, he makes sure that employees are treated with respect. But he is also concerned about performance: "If that's bad and there's no good reason, I get cross."

Think About It

What are the different motivation tools that managers use? Put yourself in Sir Terry Leahy's shoes. How should he motivate his managers so that he will have lower turnover? What can he do to keep his shelf-stockers and cashiers motivated?

Motivating and rewarding employees is one of the most important, and one of the most challenging, activities that managers perform. Successful managers, such as Sir Terry Leahy, understand that what motivates them personally may have little or no effect on others. Just because *you* are motivated by being part of a cohesive work team, do not assume everyone is. Or the fact that you are motivated by challenging work does not mean everyone is. Effective managers who want their employees to put forth maximum effort recognize that they need to know how and why employees are motivated and to tailor their motivational practices to satisfy the needs and wants of those employees.

In this chapter, we first look at some early motivation theories and then at the contemporary theories. We finish by looking at some current motivation issues and some practical suggestions that managers can use in motivating employees.

What Is Motivation?

All managers need to be able to motivate their employees, and that requires an understanding of what motivation is. Many people incorrectly view motivation as a personal trait—that is, a trait that some people have and others do not. Our knowledge of motivation tells us that we cannot label people that way. What we *do* know is that motivation is the result of the interaction between a person and a situation. Certainly, individuals differ in motivational drive but, overall, motivation varies from situation to situation. For

1 What is motivation?

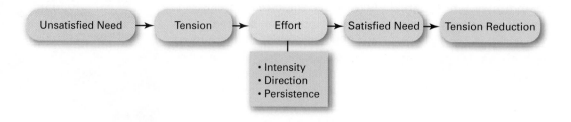

Exhibit 9-1

The Motivation Process

Unsatisfied Need → Tension → Effort → Satisfied Need → Tension Reduction

Effort:
• Intensity
• Direction
• Persistence

example, your level of motivation probably differs among the various courses you take each term. As we analyze the concept of motivation, keep in mind that the level of motivation varies both between individuals and within individuals at different times.

motivation
An individual's willingness to exert high levels of effort to reach organizational goals, conditioned by the degree to which that effort satisfies some individual need.

Motivation refers to an individual's willingness to exert high levels of effort to reach organizational goals, conditioned by the degree to which that effort satisfies some individual need. Although, in general, motivation refers to effort exerted toward any goal, here it refers to organizational goals because our focus is on work-related behaviour.

The three key elements in the definition of motivation are effort, organizational goals, and need. The *effort* element is a measure of intensity or drive.[2] A motivated person tries hard. But high levels of effort are unlikely to lead to favourable job performance unless the effort is channelled in a direction that benefits the organization.[3] Therefore we must consider the quality of the effort as well as its intensity. Effort that is directed toward, and consistent with, *organizational goals* is the kind of effort that we should be seeking. Finally, we will treat motivation as a *need-satisfying* process, as shown in Exhibit 9-1.

need
An internal state that makes certain outcomes appear attractive.

A **need** is an internal state that makes certain outcomes appear attractive. An unsatisfied need creates tension, which an individual reduces by exerting effort. Because we are interested in work behaviour, this tension-reduction effort must be directed toward organizational goals. Therefore, inherent in our definition of motivation is the requirement that the individual's needs be compatible with the organization's goals. When the two do not match, individuals may exert high levels of effort that run counter to the interests of the organization. Incidentally, this is not all that unusual. Some employees regularly spend a lot of time talking with friends at work to satisfy their social need. There is a high level of effort, but little if any is being directed toward work.

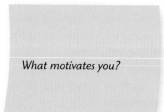

What motivates you?

Finding ways to motivate employees to achieve high levels of performance is an important organizational problem, and managers keep looking for a solution. A Canadian Policy Research Network survey found that only 40 percent of Canadians are very satisfied with their jobs. By comparison, 47 percent of American workers are happy with their work, and 54 percent of Danish workers report high satisfaction.[4] In light of these results, it's no wonder that both academic researchers and practising managers want to understand and explain employee motivation.

⭕ Early Theories of Motivation

Management at Tesco was interested in discovering what concerns their employees had and how these might be addressed.[5] They conducted research on their employees and found that many of their staff were single and worked mainly to have the money to travel overseas and participate in leisure activities. Their research also found that these employees "were unlikely to take much pride in their work, would lack commitment and would have little hesitation about going to work elsewhere if the pay were better."

Think About It

What kinds of needs do employees have? How can they be addressed?

We begin by looking at needs theories of motivation, which are probably the most widely known approaches to employee motivation. Below, we briefly review Maslow's hierarchy of needs, McGregor's Theory X and Theory Y, Herzberg's motivation-hygiene theory, and McClelland's theory of needs.

② How can needs help one be motivated?

Q&A 13.1

Maslow's Hierarchy of Needs Theory

The best-known theory of motivation is probably Abraham Maslow's **hierarchy of needs theory**.[6] Maslow was a psychologist who proposed that within every person is a hierarchy of five needs:

1. *Physiological needs*. Food, drink, shelter, sexual satisfaction, and other physical requirements.

2. *Safety needs*. Security and protection from physical and emotional harm, as well as assurance that physical needs will continue to be met.

3. *Social needs*. Affection, belongingness, acceptance, and friendship.

4. *Esteem needs*. Internal esteem factors such as self-respect, autonomy, and achievement, and external esteem factors such as status, recognition, and attention.

5. *Self-actualization needs*. Growth, achieving one's potential, and self-fulfillment; the drive to become what one is capable of becoming.

Maslow argued that each level in the needs hierarchy must be substantially satisfied before the next is activated and that once a need is substantially satisfied, it no longer motivates behaviour. In other words, as each need is substantially satisfied, the next need becomes dominant. In terms of Exhibit 9-2, an individual moves up the needs hierarchy. From the standpoint of motivation, Maslow's theory proposed that, although no need is ever fully satisfied, a substantially satisfied need will no longer motivate an individual. Therefore, according to Maslow, if you want to motivate someone, you need to understand what level that person is on in the hierarchy and focus on satisfying needs at or above that level.

hierarchy of needs theory
Maslow's theory that there is a hierarchy of five human needs: physiological, safety, social, esteem, and self-actualization; as each need becomes satisfied, the next need becomes dominant.

physiological needs
A person's need for food, drink, shelter, sexual satisfaction, and other physical requirements.

safety needs
A person's need for security and protection from physical and emotional harm; as well as assurance that physical needs will continue to be met.

social needs
A person's need for affection, belongingness, acceptance, and friendship.

esteem needs
A person's need for internal esteem factors such as self-respect, autonomy, and achievement, and external esteem factors such as status, recognition, and attention.

self-actualization needs
A person's need to grow and become what he or she is capable of becoming.

Exhibit 9-2

Maslow's Hierarchy of Needs

The practical significance of Maslow's theory is widely accepted.[7] However, Maslow provided no empirical support for his theory, and several studies that sought to validate it could not.[8]

McGregor's Theory X and Theory Y

extrinsic motivation
Motivation that comes from outside the person and includes such things as pay, bonuses, and other tangible rewards.

intrinsic motivation
Motivation that comes from the person's internal desire to do something, due to such things as interest, challenge, and personal satisfaction.

Theory X
The assumption that employees have little ambition, dislike work, want to avoid responsibility, and must be closely controlled to perform effectively.

Theory Y
The assumption that employees can exercise self-direction, accept and seek out responsibility, and consider work a natural activity.

Q&A 13.2

Do you need to be rewarded by others or are you a self-motivator?

Are individuals intrinsically or extrinsically motivated? Douglas McGregor tried to uncover the answer to this question through his discussion of Theory X and Theory Y.[9] **Extrinsic motivation** comes from outside the person and includes such things as pay, bonuses, and other tangible rewards. **Intrinsic motivation** reflects an individual's internal desire to do something, with motivation coming from interest, challenge, and personal satisfaction. Individuals show intrinsic motivation when they deeply care about their work, look for ways to improve the work, and are fulfilled by doing it well.[10]

McGregor's **Theory X** offers an essentially negative view of people. It assumes that employees have little ambition, dislike work, want to avoid responsibility, and need to be closely controlled to work effectively. It suggests that people are almost exclusively driven by extrinsic motivators. **Theory Y** offers a positive view. It assumes that employees can exercise self-direction, accept and actually seek out responsibility, and consider work a natural activity. It suggests that people are more intrinsically motivated. McGregor believed that Theory Y assumptions best captured the true nature of employees and should guide management practice, and he proposed that participation in decision making, responsible and challenging jobs, and good group relations would maximize employee motivation.

Our knowledge of motivation tells us that neither theory alone fully accounts for employee behaviour. What we know is that motivation is the result of the interaction of the individual and the situation. Individuals differ in their basic motivational drive. As well, while you may find completing a homework assignment boring, you might enthusiastically plan a surprise party for a friend. These points underscore the idea that the level of motivation varies both *between* individuals and *within* individuals at different times. They also suggest that managers should try to make sure that situations are motivating for employees.

Herzberg's Motivation-Hygiene Theory

motivation-hygiene theory
Herzberg's theory that intrinsic factors are related to job satisfaction and motivation, whereas extrinsic factors are related to job dissatisfaction.

Frederick Herzberg's **motivation-hygiene theory** proposes that intrinsic factors are related to job satisfaction and motivation, whereas extrinsic factors are related to job dissatisfaction.[11] Believing that individuals' attitudes toward work determined success or failure, Herzberg investigated the question "What do people want from their jobs?" He asked people for detailed descriptions of situations in which they felt exceptionally good or bad about their jobs. These findings are shown in Exhibit 9-3.

Herzberg concluded from his analysis that the replies people gave when they felt good about their jobs were significantly different from the replies they gave when they felt bad. Certain characteristics were consistently related to job satisfaction (factors on the left side of the exhibit), and others to job dissatisfaction (factors on the right side). Those factors associated with job satisfaction were intrinsic and included things such as achievement, recognition, and responsibility. When people felt good about their work, they tended to attribute these characteristics to themselves. On the other hand, when they were dissatisfied with their work, they tended to cite extrinsic factors such as supervision, company policy, interpersonal relationships, and working conditions.

Exhibit 9-3

Herzberg's Motivation-Hygiene Theory

Motivators	Hygiene Factors
• Achievement • Recognition • Work itself • Responsibility • Advancement • Growth	• Supervision • Company policy • Relationship with supervisor • Working conditions • Salary • Relationship with peers • Personal life • Relationship with subordinates • Status • Security
Extremely Satisfied	Neutral Extremely Dissatisfied

In addition, Herzberg believed that the data suggested that the opposite of satisfaction was not dissatisfaction, as traditionally had been believed. Removing dissatisfying characteristics from a job would not necessarily make that job more satisfying (or motivating). As shown in Exhibit 9-4, Herzberg proposed that his findings indicated the existence of a dual continuum: The opposite of "satisfaction" is "no satisfaction," and the opposite of "dissatisfaction" is "no dissatisfaction."

According to Herzberg, the factors that led to job satisfaction were separate and distinct from those that led to job dissatisfaction. Therefore, managers who sought to eliminate factors that created job dissatisfaction could bring about workplace harmony but not necessarily motivation. The extrinsic factors that eliminate job dissatisfaction were called **hygiene factors**. When these factors are adequate, people will not be dissatisfied, but they will not be satisfied (or motivated) either. To motivate people in their jobs, Herzberg suggested emphasizing **motivators**, the intrinsic factors such as achievement, recognition, and challenge that increase job satisfaction.

Herzberg's theory enjoyed wide popularity from the mid-1960s to the early 1980s, but criticisms arose concerning his procedures and methodology. Although today we say the theory is simplistic, it has had a strong influence on how we currently design jobs, as the following *Management Reflection* shows.

hygiene factors
Factors that eliminate job dissatisfaction, but do not motivate.

motivators
Factors that increase job satisfaction and motivation.

Exhibit 9-4

Contrasting Views of Satisfaction–Dissatisfaction

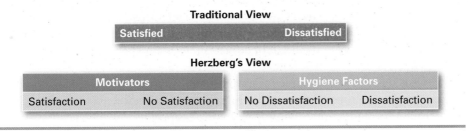

MANAGEMENT REFLECTION

Machine Shop Cleans Up Its Act

Can the design of a machine shop affect employee morale? Langley, BC-based Pazmac Enterprises uses insights from Herzberg's theory to organize its workplace.[12] The employees at the machine shop enjoy perks often associated with employees in the high-tech industry. Owner Steve Scarlett provides opportunities for his employees to be involved in decision making. "I believe business needs to be planned diplomatically—we talk things out," says Scarlett. He ensures good relationships among employees, and he also shows concern about employees' hygiene needs, reflecting Herzberg. Usually machine shops are noisy and messy, the floors are covered with oil, and employees wear dirty overalls. Pazmac, however, is spotlessly clean. The lunchroom is tastefully designed, and the men's washroom is plush, with potpourri bowls and paintings on the walls.

Scarlett believes that employees should be treated the way he himself would like to be treated, which explains why he provides an on-site swimming pool, personal trainers, weekly yoga classes, and professional counselling services for employees. Scarlett clearly considers both hygiene factors and motivator factors in dealing with his employees. His strategy has paid off. The company has had very little employee turnover in recent years, and a number of employees have worked there for more than 15 years.[13] ∎

McClelland's Theory of Needs

theory of needs
McClelland's theory that the needs for achievement, power, and affiliation are major motives in work.

need for achievement (nAch)
The drive to excel, to achieve in relation to a set of standards, and to strive to succeed.

need for power (nPow)
The need to make others behave in a way that they would not have behaved otherwise.

need for affiliation (nAff)
The desire for friendly and close interpersonal relationships.

David McClelland and his associates proposed the **theory of needs**, which says there are three acquired (not innate) needs that motivate work performance.[14] These three needs are the **need for achievement (nAch)**, which is the drive to excel, to achieve in relation to a set of standards, and to strive to succeed; the **need for power (nPow)**, which is the need to make others behave in a way that they would not have behaved otherwise; and the **need for affiliation (nAff)**, which is the desire for friendly and close interpersonal relationships. Of these three needs, the need for achievement has been researched the most. What does this research show?

People with a high need for achievement are striving for personal achievement rather than for the trappings and rewards of success. They have a desire to do something better or more efficiently than it's been done before.[15] They prefer jobs that offer personal responsibility for finding solutions to problems, in which they can receive rapid and unambiguous feedback on their performance in order to tell whether they are improving, and in which they can set moderately challenging goals. High achievers avoid what they perceive to be very easy or very difficult tasks. Also, a high need to achieve does not necessarily lead to being a good manager, especially in large organizations. That is because high achievers focus on their *own* accomplishments, while good managers emphasize helping *others* accomplish their goals.[16] McClelland showed that employees can be trained to stimulate their achievement need by being in situations where they have personal responsibility, feedback, and moderate risks.[17]

The other two needs in this theory have not been researched as extensively as the need for achievement. However, we do know that the best managers tend to be high in the need for power and low in the need for affiliation.[18]

While needs theories give us some insights into motivating employees, they do not provide a complete picture of motivation. Moreover, additional needs seem to motivate some employees. For example, employees are increasingly feeling the need for work–life balance. They need time to take care of their loved ones while managing their workloads. Having some time during the day when one can at least see nature may be another important need. Research suggests that being exposed to nature (even just being able to see some trees from your office window) has many beneficial effects. A lack of such exposure can actually impair well-being and performance.[19] We now turn to some contemporary theories of motivation that explain the processes managers can use to motivate employees.

Contemporary Theories of Motivation

One of the challenges of motivating employees is linking productivity to rewards. Compounding this challenge for Tesco is the fact that some jobs are very boring.[20] Clare Chapman, Tesco's director of human resources, says, "We're trying to take the routine out of the workplace, and build in more interest." The company eliminated the boring task of unloading soft drinks by ordering merchandising units that come fully stocked, ready to be wheeled into the store.

Tesco also encourages employees to buy shares of the company, so that staff can "share in the success they helped to create," says reward manager Helen O'Keefe. To help employees understand the potential benefits of shares, the annual benefit report includes share price graphs and a reward statement for staff. The benefit report helps employees see how the share price performs over the longer term and in comparison with the shares of other companies.

Sir Terry Leahy says he wants his employees to take four things from the job: "They find it interesting, they're treated with respect, they have the chance to get on, and they find their boss is helpful and not their biggest problem." All of these rewards make it easier for employees to perform well.

Think About It
How can you link productivity to rewards so that employees feel motivated? What other things can be done at Tesco to ensure that employees feel motivated?

The theories we discuss in this section represent contemporary explanations of employee motivation. Although they may not be as well known as some of the theories we just discussed, they do have reasonable degrees of valid research support.[21] What are the contemporary theories of motivation? We look at four: reinforcement theory, job characteristics model, equity theory, and expectancy theory.

③ What are the contemporary theories of motivation?

Reinforcement Theory

Reinforcement theory says that behaviour is influenced by consequences. Reinforcement theory argues that behaviour is externally caused by **reinforcers**, which are consequences that, when given immediately following a behaviour, increase the probability that the behaviour will be repeated.

Reinforcement theory focuses solely on what happens to a person when he or she takes some action. According to B. F. Skinner, reinforcement theory can be explained as follows: People will most likely engage in desired behaviours if they are rewarded for doing so; these rewards are most effective if they immediately follow a desired behaviour, and behaviour that is not rewarded, or is punished, is less likely to be repeated.[22]

In keeping with reinforcement theory, managers can influence employees' behaviour by reinforcing actions they deem desirable. However, the emphasis is on positive reinforcement, which means managers should ignore, not punish, unfavourable behaviour. Even though punishment eliminates undesired behaviour faster than nonreinforcement does, its effect is often only temporary and may result in workplace conflicts, absenteeism, and turnover. Research has shown that reinforcement is an important influence on employee behaviour, but it is not the only explanation for differences in employee motivation.[23]

reinforcement theory
The theory that behaviour is influenced by consequences.

reinforcers
Consequences that, when given immediately following a behaviour, increase the probability that the behaviour will be repeated.

Job Characteristics Model (JCM)

Q&A 13.3

job characteristics model (JCM)
A framework for analyzing jobs and designing motivating jobs that identifies five core job dimensions, their interrelationships, and their impact on employees.

Have you ever had a job that was really motivating? What were its characteristics?

Because managers are primarily interested in how to motivate individuals on the job, we need to look at ways to design motivating jobs. The **job characteristics model (JCM)** provides a conceptual framework for analyzing jobs and for guiding managers in designing motivating jobs.[24] It identifies five core job dimensions, their interrelationships, and their impact on employee productivity, motivation, and satisfaction.

According to the JCM, any job can be described in terms of the following five core dimensions:

1. *Skill variety*. The degree to which the job requires a variety of activities so the employee can use a number of different skills and talents.

2. *Task identity*. The degree to which the job requires completion of a whole and identifiable piece of work.

3. *Task significance*. The degree to which the job affects the lives or work of other people.

4. *Autonomy*. The degree to which the job provides substantial freedom, independence, and discretion to the individual in scheduling the work and determining the procedures to be used in carrying it out.

5. *Feedback.* The degree to which carrying out the work activities required by the job results in the individual's obtaining direct and clear information about the effectiveness of his or her performance.

Exhibit 9-5 presents the model. Notice how the first three dimensions—skill variety, task identity, and task significance—combine to create meaningful work. What we mean is that if these three characteristics exist in a job, we can predict that the person will view his or her job as important, valuable, and worthwhile. Notice, too, that jobs that possess autonomy give the job incumbent a feeling of personal responsibility for the results, and

skill variety
The degree to which the job requires a variety of activities so the employee can use a number of different skills and talents.

task identity
The degree to which the job requires completion of a whole and identifiable piece of work.

task significance
The degree to which the job affects the lives or work of other people.

autonomy
The degree to which the job provides substantial freedom, independence, and discretion to the individual in scheduling the work and determining the procedures to be used in carrying it out.

feedback
The degree to which carrying out the work activities required by the job results in the individual's obtaining direct and clear information about the effectiveness of his or her performance.

Exhibit 9-5

Job Characteristics Model

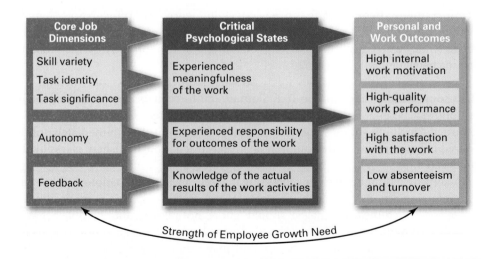

Source: J. R. Hackman and J. L. Suttle, eds., *Improving Life at Work* (Glenview, IL: Scott, Foresman, 1977). With permission of the authors.

Exhibit 9-6

Guidelines for Job Redesign

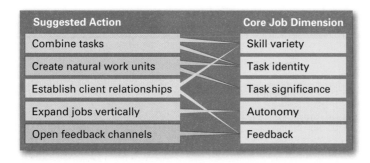

Suggested Action	Core Job Dimension
Combine tasks	Skill variety
Create natural work units	Task identity
Establish client relationships	Task significance
Expand jobs vertically	Autonomy
Open feedback channels	Feedback

Source: J. R. Hackman and J. L. Suttle, eds., *Improving Life at Work* (Glenview, IL: Scott, Foresman, 1977). With permission of the authors.

that if a job provides feedback the employee will know how effectively he or she is performing.

From a motivational standpoint, the JCM suggests that internal rewards are obtained when an employee *learns* (knowledge of results through feedback) that he or she *personally* (experienced responsibility through autonomy of work) has performed well on a task that he or she *cares about* (experienced meaningfulness through skill variety, task identity, and/or task significance).[25]

The more these three conditions characterize a job, the greater the employee's motivation, performance, and satisfaction and the lower his or her absenteeism and likelihood of resigning. As the model shows, the links between the job dimensions and the outcomes are moderated by the strength of the individual's growth need (the person's desire for self-esteem and self-actualization). This means that individuals with a high growth need are more likely to experience the critical psychological states and respond positively when their jobs include the core dimensions than are individuals with a low growth need. This may explain the mixed results with job enrichment: Individuals with low growth need do not tend to achieve high performance or satisfaction by having their jobs enriched. For further insights into motivating employees, see *Developing Your Interpersonal Skills—Maximizing Employee Effort* on pages 292–293, at the end of the chapter.

PRISM 1

The JCM provides specific guidance to managers for job redesign. These guidelines are shown in Exhibit 9-6, which specifies the types of changes in jobs that are most likely to lead to improvement in each of the five core job dimensions.

Equity Theory

Have you ever thought someone else's pay was unfair compared with yours?

After graduating from the University of New Brunswick, Mike Wilson worked in Northern Alberta as a civil engineer. He liked his job, but he became frustrated with his employer. "If you did a great job you were treated just the same as if you did a poor job," he says.[26] Wilson decided to return home to work in the business his father had started in 1965—Dorchester, New Brunswick-based Atlantic Industries, which designs, fabricates, and builds corrugated steel structures. At Atlantic Industries, Wilson's hard work has paid off: He received the 2005 Ernst & Young Entrepreneur of the Year Award for the Atlantic Region.

Wilson's decision to leave his job in Northern Alberta can be explained by equity theory. The term *equity* is related to the concept of fairness and equal treatment compared

Q&A 13.4

Exhibit 9-7

Equity Theory

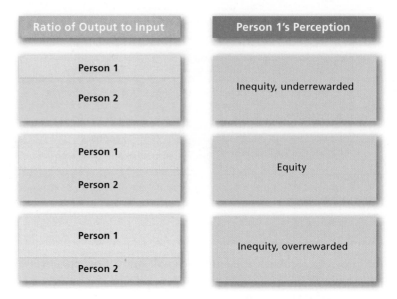

with others who behave in similar ways. There is considerable evidence that employees compare their job inputs and outcomes relative to others' and that inequities influence the degree of effort that employees exert.[27]

equity theory
The theory that an employee compares his or her job's inputs–outcomes ratio with that of relevant others and then responds to correct any inequity.

Equity theory, developed by J. Stacey Adams, proposes that employees perceive what they get from a job situation (outcomes) in relation to what they put into it (inputs) and then compare their inputs–outcomes ratio with the inputs–outcomes ratio of relevant others (see Exhibit 9-7). If employees perceive their ratios as equal to those of relevant others, a state of equity exists. In other words, they perceive that their situations are fair—that justice prevails. However, if the ratio is perceived as unequal, inequity exists and they view themselves as underrewarded or overrewarded. Not all inequity (or equity) is real. It is important to underscore that it is the individual's *perception* that determines the equity of the situation.

What will employees do when they perceive an inequity? Equity theory proposes that employees might (1) distort either their own or others' inputs or outcomes, (2) behave in some way to induce others to change their inputs or outcomes, (3) behave in some way to change their own inputs or outcomes, (4) choose a different comparison person, or (5) quit their jobs. These types of employee reactions have generally proved to be accurate.[28] A review of the research consistently confirms the equity thesis: Whenever employees perceive inequity, they will act to correct the situation.[29] The result might be lower or higher productivity, improved or reduced quality of output, increased absenteeism, or voluntary resignation.

Diversity in Action 4

When Toronto city councillors faced inequity in their pay, they responded by voting themselves a raise, as the following *Management Reflection* shows.

MANAGEMENT REFLECTION

City Councillors End "Inequitable" Pay

What is fair pay for city councillors? Toronto city councillors voted themselves an 8.9 percent pay raise effective January 2007, shortly before it became obvious that extensive budget cuts were going to be needed to manage the city.[30] On a percentage basis, the pay raise seems high compared to what the average Ontarian received as a pay raise in 2006. Other government employees might have wondered if they should raise their salaries as well.

But what should a municipal councillor be paid? In 2007, members of the Quebec Parliament earned annual salaries of $82 073, heads of federal Crown corporations started at $109 000, Ontario's premier, Dalton McGuinty, earned $198 620 and members of the BC legislature earned $98 000, plus expenses. With the raise, Toronto's councillors earn $95 000 a year. Despite working at different levels of government—federal, provincial, and local—all of these officials make complex decisions, and need many of the same skills. Many of them could make more money working in the private sector.

When the Toronto councillors voted themselves a pay raise, they were not thinking about possible budget shortfalls. Instead, they were responding to the idea that they were underpaid compared to other government decision makers who performed duties similar to their own. As councillors for the largest city in the country, with the largest budget, they were advised by a consulting firm that they should rank in the "top 25 per cent of salaries of councillors across the country." Their salary before the raise was one of the lowest in the country. ■

The **referent** against which individuals compare themselves is an important variable in equity theory.[31] Three referent categories have been defined: other, system, and self. The *other* category includes other individuals with similar jobs in the same organization but also includes friends, neighbours, or professional associates. On the basis of what they hear at work or read about in newspapers or trade journals, employees compare their pay with that of others. The *system* category includes organizational pay policies and procedures and the administration of the system. Whatever precedents have been established by the organization regarding pay allocation are major elements of this category. The *self* category refers to the inputs–outcomes ratios that are unique to the individual. It reflects personal experiences and contacts and is influenced by criteria such as previous jobs or family commitments. The choice of a particular set of referents is related to the information available about the referents as well as to their perceived relevance. At Surrey, BC-based Back in Motion Rehab (named the #1 Best Workplace in Canada for 2007 by *Canadian Business*), management decided that the highest-paid director's base salary should be less than two times the salary of the average staff member.[32] Because this policy uses the average staff member's pay as a referent, it sends the message that the output of the average staff member is truly valued.

Originally, equity theory focused on **distributive justice**, which is the perceived fairness of the amount and allocation of rewards among individuals. More recent research has focused on looking at issues of **procedural justice**, which is the perceived fairness of the process used to determine the distribution of rewards. This research shows that distributive justice has a greater influence on employee satisfaction than procedural justice, while procedural justice tends to affect an employee's organizational commitment, trust in his or her boss, and intention to quit.[33] What are the implications for managers? They should consider openly sharing information on how allocation decisions are made, follow consistent and unbiased procedures, and engage in similar practices to increase the perception of procedural justice. Employees who have an increased perception of procedural justice are likely to view their bosses and the organization as positive even if they are dissatisfied with pay, promotions, and other personal outcomes.

referents
Those things individuals compare themselves against in order to assess equity.

distributive justice
Perceived fairness of the amount and allocation of rewards among individuals.

procedural justice
Perceived fairness of the process used to determine the distribution of rewards.

Expectancy Theory

The most comprehensive and widely accepted explanation of employee motivation to date is Victor Vroom's expectancy theory.[34] Although the theory has its critics,[35] most research evidence supports it.[36]

Exhibit 9-8

Simplified Expectancy Model

Individual Effort → (A) → Individual Performance → (B) → Organizational Rewards → (C) → Individual Goals

(A) = Effort-performance linkage
(B) = Performance-reward linkage
(C) = Attractiveness of reward

expectancy theory
The theory that an individual tends to act in a certain way based on the expectation that the act will be followed by a given outcome and on the attractiveness of that outcome to the individual.

Expectancy theory states that an individual tends to act in a certain way based on the expectation that the act will be followed by a given outcome and on the attractiveness of that outcome to the individual. It includes three variables or relationships (see Exhibit 9-8):

- *Expectancy, or effort–performance linkage.* The probability perceived by the individual that exerting a given amount of effort will lead to a certain level of performance.

- *Instrumentality, or performance–reward linkage.* The degree to which the individual believes that performing at a particular level is instrumental in attaining the desired outcome.

- *Valence, or attractiveness of reward.* The importance that the individual places on the potential outcome or reward that can be achieved on the job. Valence considers both the goals and needs of the individual. (See also *Self-Assessment—What Rewards Do I Value Most?* on pages 288–289, at the end of the chapter.)

This explanation of motivation might sound complex, but it really is not. It can be summed up in these questions: How hard do I have to work to achieve a certain level of performance, and can I actually achieve that level? What reward will I get for working at that level of performance? How attractive is the reward to me, and does it help me achieve my goals? Whether you are motivated to put forth effort (that is, to work) at any given time depends on your particular goals and your perception of whether a certain level of performance is necessary to attain those goals.

The key to expectancy theory is understanding an individual's goal and the link between effort and performance, between performance and rewards, and finally, between rewards and individual goal satisfaction. Expectancy theory recognizes that there is no universal principle for explaining what motivates individuals and thus stresses that managers need to understand why employees view certain outcomes as attractive or unattractive. After all, we want to reward individuals with those things they value as positive. Also, expectancy theory emphasizes expected behaviours. Do employees know what is expected of them and how they will be evaluated? Finally, the theory is concerned with perceptions; reality is irrelevant. An individual's own perceptions of performance, reward, and goal outcomes, not the outcomes themselves, will determine his or her motivation (level of effort). Exhibit 9-9 suggests how managers might increase employee motivation, using expectancy theory.

Q&A 13.5

Integrating Contemporary Theories of Motivation

We have presented four contemporary motivation theories. You might be tempted to view them independently, but doing so would be a mistake. Many of the ideas underlying the theories are complementary, and you will better understand how to motivate people if you see how the theories fit together.[37]

Exhibit 9-9

Steps to Increasing Motivation, Using Expectancy Theory

Improving Expectancy	Improving Instrumentality	Improving Valence
Improve the ability of the individual to perform	**Increase the individual's belief that performance will lead to reward**	**Make sure that the reward is meaningful to the individual**
• Make sure employees have skills for the task. • Provide training. • Assign reasonable tasks and goals.	• Observe and recognize performance. • Deliver rewards as promised. • Indicate to employees how previous good performance led to greater rewards.	• Ask employees what rewards they value. • Give rewards that are valued.

Expectancy theory predicts that an employee will exert a high level of effort if he or she perceives that there is a strong relationship between effort and performance, performance and rewards, and rewards and satisfaction of personal goals. Each of these relationships is, in turn, influenced by certain factors. The level of individual performance is determined not only by the level of individual effort, but also by the individual's ability to perform and by whether the organization has a fair and objective performance evaluation system. The performance–reward relationship will be strong if the individual perceives that it is performance (rather than seniority, personal favourites, or some other criterion) that is rewarded. The final link in expectancy theory is the rewards–goal relationship. Needs theories come into play at this point. Motivation is high to the degree that the rewards an individual receives for his or her high performance satisfy the dominant needs consistent with his or her individual goals.

Rewards also play a key part in equity theory. Individuals will compare the rewards (outcomes) they have received from the inputs or efforts they made with the inputs–outcomes ratio of relevant others. Any inequities may influence the effort expended.

The JCM suggests that task characteristics (job design) influence job motivation at two places. First, jobs that are designed around the five core dimensions are likely to lead to higher actual job performance because the individual's motivation will be stimulated by the job itself—that is, he or she will increase the link between effort and performance. Second, jobs that are designed around the five core dimensions also increase an employee's control over key elements in his or her work. Therefore, jobs that offer autonomy, feedback, and similar task characteristics help satisfy the individual goals of employees who desire greater control over their work.

Reinforcement theory says that behaviour is influenced by consequences, which is consistent with expectancy theory. The theory argues that when consequences are given immediately following a behaviour, the behaviour is more likely to be repeated. Thus, much like expectancy theory, the emphasis is on linking rewards (consequences) directly to performance.

Current Issues in Motivation

One of the challenges managers at Tesco faced was how to motivate its many different employee groups: students, new graduates, mothers returning to the workplace, and ethnic minorities.[38] In a survey of its employees, the company found that older female employees wanted flexible hours and stimulating work, but they were not looking to be promoted. Young college graduates working in head office wanted a challenging, well-paid career and time to pursue personal interests and family life. Many employees noted they wanted managers who helped them.

Tesco has come up with a variety of practices to meet employee needs, including career breaks of up to eight months, discounts on family holidays, driving lessons, and magazine subscriptions. Tesco has a website that offers career and financial advice and discounts on meals, cinema tickets, and travel for its 16- to 24-year-old employees who are in school or have recently left school. The company created the "A-Level Options" program to give young people who did not want a post-secondary education the opportunity to be fast-tracked into management. Clare Chapman, Tesco's director of human resources, says the company has not limited specific rewards for specific groups. "It's more a question of being mindful of the needs of all staff instead of catering for one or two types of attitude."

Think About It
What factors need to be considered when motivating employees who have very different needs? Is there anything else Tesco can do to motivate young people?

④ What are some current issues in motivation?

So far, we have covered a lot of the theoretical bases of employee motivation. Understanding and predicting employee motivation continues to be one of the most popular areas in management research. However, even current studies of employee motivation are influenced by several significant workplace issues—issues such as motivating a diverse workforce, designing effective rewards programs, and improving work–life balance. Let's take a closer look at each of these issues.

Motivating a Diverse Workforce

To maximize motivation in today's workforce, managers need to think in terms of *flexibility.* For example, studies tell us that men place more importance on having autonomy in their jobs than do women. In contrast, the opportunity to learn, convenient and flexible work hours, and good interpersonal relations are more important to women.[39] Baby Boomers may need more flextime as they manage the needs of their children and their aging parents. Gen-Xers want employers to add to their experience so they develop portable skills. Meanwhile, Gen-Yers want more opportunities, and the ability to work in teams.[40] Managers need to recognize that what motivates a single mother with two dependent children who is working full time to support her family may be very different from the needs of a single part-time employee or an older employee who is working only to supplement his or her retirement income. A diverse array of rewards is needed to motivate employees with such diverse needs.

Motivating Employees from Diverse Cultures

In today's global business environment, managers cannot automatically assume that motivational programs that work in one location are going to work in others. Most current motivation theories were developed in the United States by Americans about Americans.[41] Maybe the most obviously American characteristic in these theories is the strong emphasis on individualism and quantity-of-life cultural characteristics. For example, both goal-setting and expectancy theories emphasize goal accomplishment as well as rational and individual thought. Let's look at several theories to see if there is any cross-cultural transferability.

Maslow's hierarchy of needs proposes that people start at the physiological level and then move progressively up the hierarchy in order. This hierarchy, if it has any application at all, aligns with American culture. In countries such as Japan, Greece, and Mexico, where uncertainty-avoidance characteristics are strong (that is, individuals prefer structured situations), security needs would be on the top of the needs hierarchy. Countries that score high on quality-of-life characteristics (that is, individuals value relationships and are concerned with the welfare of others)—Denmark, Sweden, Norway, the Netherlands, and Finland—would have social needs on top.[42] We would predict, for example, that group work will motivate employees more when a country's culture scores high on quality-of-life characteristics.

Equity theory has a relatively strong following in the United States. That is not surprising given that US-style reward systems are based on the assumption that employees are highly sensitive to equity in reward allocations. In the United States, equity is meant to closely tie pay to performance. However, recent evidence suggests that even in collectivist cultures (where individuals expect that others will look after and protect them), especially in the former socialist countries of Central and Eastern Europe, employees expect rewards to reflect their individual needs as well as their performance.[43] Moreover, consistent with a legacy of communism and centrally planned economies, employees exhibited a greater "entitlement" attitude—that is, they expected outcomes to be greater than their inputs.[44] These findings suggest that US-style pay practices may need modification, especially in Russia and other former communist countries, in order to be perceived as fair by employees.

Despite these cross-cultural differences in motivation, do not assume there are no cross-cultural consistencies. For example, the desire for interesting work seems important to almost all employees, regardless of their national culture. In a study of seven countries, employees in Belgium, Britain, Israel, and the United States ranked "interesting work" number one among 11 work goals, and this factor was ranked either second or third in Japan, the Netherlands, and Germany.[45] Similarly, in a study comparing job-preference outcomes among graduate students in the United States, Canada, Australia, and Singapore, growth, achievement, and responsibility were rated the top three and had identical rankings.[46] Both of these studies suggest some universality to the importance of intrinsic factors identified by Herzberg in his motivation-hygiene theory. Another recent study examining workplace motivation trends in Japan also seems to indicate that Herzberg's model is applicable to Japanese employees.[47] For a discussion of diversity initiatives in the workplace, see *Managing Workforce Diversity—Developing Employee Potential: The Bottom Line of Diversity* on page 293, at the end of the chapter.

It can be difficult or even misleading to apply Western theories of motivation to employees such as Rina Masuda of Sharp Corp. Masuda uses a soldering iron to quickly and delicately repair tiny computer chips, a task so extraordinarily precise that she is among only a few thousand of all Japan's workers honoured with the title of "super technician," or supaa ginosha. These workers receive certificates and pins, but seldom money. "The soldering I do by hand is far superior to anything that machines can do," says Masuda, her pride expressing the common view that recognition and honour are enough.

Motivating Minimum-Wage Employees

Suppose that in your first managerial position after graduating, you are responsible for managing a work group composed of minimum-wage employees. Offering more pay to these employees for high levels of performance is out of the question: Your company just cannot afford it.[48] In addition, these employees have limited education and skills. What are your motivational options at this point? One of the toughest motivational challenges facing many managers today is how to achieve high performance levels from minimum-wage employees.

Q&A 13.6

One trap we often fall into is thinking that people are motivated only by money. Although money is important as a motivator, it's not the only reward that people seek and that managers can use. What are some other types of rewards? Many companies use employee recognition programs such as employee of the month, quarterly employee performance award ceremonies, or other celebrations of employee accomplishment. For instance, at many fast-food restaurants such as McDonald's and Wendy's, you will often see plaques hanging in prominent places that feature the "Crew Member of the Month." These types of programs highlight employees whose performance has been of the type and level the organization wants to encourage. Many managers also recognize the power of praise, but you need to be sure that these "pats on the back" are sincere and done for the right reasons; otherwise, employees can interpret such actions as manipulative.

We know from the motivation theories presented earlier that rewards are only part of the motivation equation. We need to look at other elements such as empowerment and

Nancy Gray-Starkebaum, director of human resources at Vancouver-based Electronic Arts Canada, finds that companies have to pay attention to employee needs in order to motivate them. The cafeteria at Electronic Arts is well stocked with employee favourites, and employees can purchase takeout dinners at good prices for their families if they do not have time to cook dinner.

career development assistance. We can look to job design and expectancy theories for these insights. In service industries such as travel and hospitality, retail sales, child care, and maintenance, where pay for front-line employees generally does not get much higher than the minimum-wage level, successful companies are empowering these front-line employees with more authority to address customers' problems. If we use the JCM to examine this change, we can see that this type of job redesign provides enhanced motivating potential because employees now experience increased skill variety, task identity, task significance, autonomy, and feedback. Also, employees facing this situation often want to better themselves professionally. They need guidance, assistance in self-assessment, and training. By providing these to minimum-wage employees, you are preparing them for the future—one that ideally promises better pay. For many, this is a strong motivator![49]

Motivating Professional and Technical Employees

In contrast to a generation ago, the typical employee today is more likely to be a highly trained professional with a post-secondary degree than a blue-collar factory worker. What special concerns should managers be aware of when trying to motivate a team of engineers at London, Ontario-based EllisDon, software designers at Vancouver-based Electronic Arts, or a group of consultants at Accenture?

Professionals are typically different from nonprofessionals.[50] They have a strong and long-term commitment to their field of expertise. Their loyalty is more often to their profession than to their employer. To keep current in their field, they need to regularly update their knowledge, and because of their commitment to their profession they rarely define their workweek as 8:00 a.m. to 5:00 p.m., five days a week.

What motivates professionals? Money and promotions typically are low on their priority list. Why? They tend to be well paid and enjoy what they do. In contrast, job challenge tends to be ranked high. They like to tackle problems and find solutions. Their chief reward in their jobs is the work itself. Professionals also value support. They want others to think that what they are working on is important.[51] That may be true for all employees, but professionals tend to be focused on their work as their central life interest, whereas nonprofessionals typically have other interests outside work that can compensate for needs not met on the job. The preceding points imply that managers should provide professional and technical employees with new assignments and challenging projects. Give them autonomy to follow their interests and allow them to structure their

To attract, motivate, and retain employees, Google offers many different perks, including chef-prepared food, a gym, a masseuse, on-site car washes, haircuts, dry cleaning, free on-site doctor and dentist, and child care next door.

work in ways they find productive. Reward them with educational opportunities—training, workshops, conferences—that allow them to keep current in their field and to network with their peers. Also reward them with recognition. Managers should ask questions and engage in other actions that demonstrate to their professional and technical employees that they are sincerely interested in what they are doing.

Motivating Contingent Workers

As many full-time jobs have been eliminated through downsizing and other organizational restructurings, the number of openings for part-time, contract, and other forms of temporary work have increased. Contingent workers do not have the security or stability that permanent employees have, and they do not identify with the organization or display the commitment that other employees do. Temporary workers also typically get little or no benefits such as health care or pensions.[52]

There is no simple solution for motivating contingent employees. For that small set of individuals who prefer the freedom of their temporary status—for example, some students, working mothers, retirees—the lack of stability may not be an issue. In addition, temporariness might be preferred by highly compensated physicians, engineers, accountants, or financial planners who do not want the demands of a full-time job. But these are the exceptions. For the most part, temporary employees are not temporary by choice.

What will motivate involuntarily temporary employees? An obvious answer is the opportunity to become a permanent employee. In cases in which permanent employees are selected from a pool of temps, the temps will often work hard in hopes of becoming permanent. A less obvious answer is the opportunity for training. The ability of a temporary employee to find a new job is largely dependent on his or her skills. If the employee sees that the job he or she is doing can help develop marketable skills, then motivation is increased. From an equity standpoint, you should also consider the repercussions of mixing permanent and temporary workers when pay differentials are significant. When temps work alongside permanent employees who earn more, and get benefits, too, for doing the same job, the performance of temps is likely to suffer. Separating such employees or perhaps minimizing interdependence between them might help managers decrease potential problems.[53]

Designing Effective Rewards Programs

Employee rewards programs play a powerful role in motivating for appropriate employee behaviour. In this section, we look at how managers can design effective rewards programs by using employee recognition programs and pay-for-performance programs. First, though, we should examine the issue of the extent to which money motivates.

The Role of Money

The most commonly used reward in organizations is money. As one author notes, "Money is probably the most emotionally meaningful object in contemporary life: only food and sex are its close competitors as common carriers of such strong and diverse feelings, significance, and strivings."[54]

Little research attention has been given to individual differences in people's feelings about money, although some studies indicate that money is not employees' top priority.[55] A survey of 2000 Canadians discovered that trustworthy senior management and a good balance between work and personal or family life mattered more than pay or benefits when it came to employee satisfaction.[56] In another survey that looked at Canadian attitudes about work, one respondent explained, "Of course money is important, but that's not what's going to make you jump out of bed in the morning." Another noted, "Everyone here would take more money and more time off—that's a given. But some of the things that really make the job a good or bad one are your relations with your boss."[57]

Employee recognition plays an important role in motivating the employees at Nichols Foods in Merseyside, England, where the average wage is only a little above the norm. The main hallway in the production department is hung with "bragging boards" on which the accomplishments of employee teams are noted. Monthly awards are presented to employees recognized for their efforts by their peers, and plant-floor supervisors make presentations about their results at every annual meeting. "To deliver really great customer service," says operations manager Martin Lee, "you need really great, motivated people."

employee recognition programs
Reward programs that provide managers with opportunities to give employees personal attention and express interest, approval, and appreciation for a job well done.

A number of studies suggest that an individual's attitude toward money is correlated with personality traits and demographic factors.[58] People who value money score higher on "attributes like sensation seeking, competitiveness, materialism, and control." People who desire money score higher on self-esteem, need for achievement, and Type A personality measures. Men seem to value money more than women. These studies suggest that individuals who value money will be more motivated by it than individuals who value other things.

What these findings suggest is that when organizations develop reward programs, they need to consider very carefully what individuals value.

Employee Recognition Programs

Employee recognition programs provide managers with opportunities to give employees personal attention and express interest, approval, and appreciation for a job well done.[59] These programs can take many forms. For instance, you can personally congratulate an employee in private for a good job. You can send a handwritten note or an email message acknowledging something positive that the employee has done. For employees with a strong need for social acceptance, you can publicly recognize accomplishments. To enhance group cohesiveness and motivation, you can celebrate team successes, perhaps by throwing a pizza party to celebrate a team's accomplishments.

A survey of Canadian firms in 2006 by Hewitt Associates found that 35 percent of companies recognized individual or group achievements with cash or merchandise.[60] Do employees think employee recognition programs are important? You bet! One of the consistent themes that has emerged in the six years that Hewitt Associates has studied the 50 Best Companies to work for in Canada is the importance of recognition. A large number of the winning companies show appreciation for their employees frequently and visibly.[61]

Pay-for-Performance Programs

What's in it for me? That is a question every person consciously or unconsciously asks before engaging in any form of behaviour. Our knowledge of motivation tells us that people act in order to satisfy some need. Before they do anything, therefore, they look for a payoff or reward. Although many different rewards may be offered by organizations, most of us are concerned with earning an amount of money that allows us to satisfy our needs and wants. In fact, a large body of research suggests that pay is far more motivational than some motivation theorists such as Maslow and Herzberg suggest.[62] Because pay is an important variable in motivation, we need to look at how we can use pay to motivate high levels of employee performance. This concern explains the logic behind pay-for-performance programs.

pay-for-performance programs
Variable compensation plans that pay employees on the basis of some performance measure.

Pay-for-performance programs are variable compensation plans that pay employees on the basis of some performance measure.[63] Piece-rate pay plans, wage-incentive plans, profit-sharing, and lump-sum bonuses are examples. What differentiates these forms of pay from more traditional compensation plans is that instead of paying a person for time on the job, pay is adjusted to reflect some performance measure. These performance measures might include such things as individual productivity, team or work-group productivity, departmental productivity, or the overall organization's profit performance.

Q&A 13.7   Pay for performance is probably most compatible with expectancy theory. Specifically, if motivation is to be maximized, individuals should perceive a strong relationship between their performance and the rewards they receive. If rewards are allocated only on nonperformance factors—such as seniority, job title, or across-the-board pay raises—then employees are likely to reduce their efforts.

Pay-for-performance programs are popular; the number of employees affected by variable-pay plans has been rising in Canada. A 2007 survey of 314 firms by Hewitt Associates found that 80 percent of respondents have variable-pay programs in place, compared with 43 percent in 1994.[64] Pay-for-performance programs are more common for non-unionized employees than unionized ones, although more than 30 percent of unionized companies had such plans in 2002.[65] Prem Benimadhu, former vice-president of governance and human resource management with The Conference Board of Canada, noted, "Canadian unions have been very allergic to variable compensation."[66] In addition to wage uncertainty, employees may object to pay for performance if they feel that factors out of their control might affect the extent to which bonuses are possible.

In 2005, some 78 percent of large US companies had some form of variable-pay plan.[67] About 22 percent of Japanese companies have company-wide pay-for-performance plans.[68] However, one Japanese company, Fujitsu, dropped its performance-based program after eight years because it proved to be "flawed and a poor fit with Japanese culture."[69] Management found that some employees set goals as low as possible for fear of falling short. Others set extremely short-term goals. As a result, Fujitsu executives felt that ambitious projects that could produce hit products were being avoided.

Do pay-for-performance programs work? The evidence is mixed, at best.[70] One recent study that followed the careers of 1000 top economists found that they put in more effort early in their careers, at a time when productivity-related incentives had a larger impact.[71] A recent study of Finnish white-collar employees found that higher levels of payment and more frequent payments positively affected productivity, while lower levels of payment did not improve productivity.[72] A recent study in Canada looked at both unionized and non-unionized workplaces, and found that variable-pay plans result in "increased productivity, a safer work environment, a better understanding of the business by employees, and little risk of employees losing base pay," according to Prem Benimadhu.[73] But there are also studies that question the effectiveness of pay-for-performance approaches, suggesting they can lead to less group cohesiveness in the workplace.[74]

If the organization uses work teams, managers should consider group-based performance incentives that will reinforce team effort and commitment. But whether these programs are individual based or team based, managers do need to ensure that they are specific about the relationship between an individual's pay and his or her expected level of appropriate performance. Employees must clearly understand exactly how performance—theirs and the organization's—translates into dollars on their paycheques.[75] Ottawa-based Lee Valley Tools uses quarterly newsletters to employees to let them know how much profit is forecast. This helps employees understand how hard work will pay off for them. Robin Lee, the company's president, says that "sharing information and profits promotes an atmosphere in which hard work, innovation and efficiency pay off for everybody."[76]

The sometimes weak link between pay and performance is nowhere more evident than in the final type of rewards program we are going to look at—employee stock options.

Stock Option Programs

During 2003, Lino Saputo, chair of Montreal-based Saputo, one of the largest cheese producers in North America, received a salary of $600 000, bonuses of $330 000, and no stock options. Eugene Melnyk, former chair of Mississauga, Ontario-based Biovail, a pharmaceutical company, received a salary of $830 463, no bonus, and $56.4 million in long-term incentives. Total compensation for the two men over the period 2000–2003 was quite different: Saputo received $2.43 million, just a little more than 10 percent of the $202 million Melnyk received. Yet by March 2004, Biovail's shares had declined 74 percent from their high in December 2001, while Saputo's share price was similar to what it was at its high in early 2002.[77] These results mirror a 2006 study of the largest Canadian public companies by the Teachers Pension Plan, which found little evidence that the amount paid to Canada's top executives was related to the performance of their companies.[78]

Executive bonus and stock option programs have come under fire because they seem to fly in the face of the belief that executive pay aligns with the organization's performance. What are stock option programs and what are they designed to do?

Stock options are a financial incentive that gives employees the right to purchase shares of company stock, at some time in the future, at a set price. The original idea behind employee stock option plans was to turn employees into owners and give them strong motivation to work hard to make the company successful.[79] If the company was successful, the value of the stock went up, making the stock options valuable. In other words, there was a link between performance and reward. The popularity of stock options as a motivational and compensation tool skyrocketed during the dot-com boom in the late 1990s. Because many dot-coms could not afford to pay employees the going market-rate salaries, stock options were offered as performance incentives. However, the shake-out among dot-com stocks in 2000 and 2001 illustrated one of the inherent risks of offering stock options. As long as the market was rising, employees were willing to give up large salaries in exchange for stock options. However, when stock prices tanked, many individuals who joined and stayed with a dot-com for the opportunity to get rich through stock options found those stock options had become worthless. The declining stock market became a powerful demotivator.

Despite the risk of potential lost value and the widespread abuse of stock options, managers might want to consider them as part of their overall motivational program. An appropriately designed stock option program can be a powerful motivational tool for the entire workforce.[80]

Improving Work–Life Balance

While many employees continue to work an eight-hour day, five days a week, with fixed start and end times, organizations have started to implement programs to help employees manage their lives outside work. Many of the work–life balance programs that organizations have implemented are a response to the varied needs of a diverse workforce. At Electronic Arts Canada, employees are given help with their family and personal needs, as the following *Management Reflection* shows.

stock options
A financial incentive that gives employees the right to purchase shares of company stock, at some time in the future, at a set price.

MANAGEMENT REFLECTION

Electronic Arts Canada Meets Family Needs

Can your workplace really make life easier? It is not always easy to make sure that employees working in the computer game–designing industry do not decide to take a job elsewhere.[81] Nancy Gray-Starkebaum's job as director of human resources at Vancouver-based Electronic Arts Canada (EA), the world's leading game developer, is to make sure that the employees do not think about looking for jobs elsewhere.

"Demographics are shifting and companies have learned they need to pay attention to employees' needs across the demographic scale," says Gray-Starkebaum. During the 1990s, it became commonplace for high-tech firms to offer free beverages, including lattes, and other perks that suited 20-something employees. EA has found that different perks are needed now that these same employees have moved into their thirties and beyond.

One emphasis at EA is having more family-friendly policies in the workplace. During spring break, children accompany their parents to work, and there are high chairs in the company cafeteria. New parents get generous leave time. Employees can even take dinner home to their families. Gray-Starkebaum says she was able to buy a chicken and rice dish and spareribs and found it "a comparative bargain at $18 to feed her family." The cafeteria offers breakfast, lunch, dinner, and snacks, and even provides Atkins, HeartSmart, and vegetarian meals.

The firm tries to make it easier for its employees to balance work life with family life. It takes care of many of the errands people might have to do at night or on weekends by providing drop-off dry cleaning services, a hairdresser and a barber who regularly show up to give haircuts, and a seamstress who does alterations. On Fridays, employees can have their cars washed.

EA also has a gym, with Pilates classes and a personal trainer, and a massage therapist is on site several days a week. ■

In addition to helping with errands and meals, contemporary companies are looking at a variety of scheduling options, including flextime, job sharing, and telecommuting to help employees balance work and personal life.

Flexible Work Schedules

Many organizations have developed flexible working schedules that recognize different needs. For instance, a **compressed workweek** is a workweek in which employees work longer hours per day but fewer days per week. The most common form is four 10-hour days (a 4-40 program). However, organizations could design whatever schedules they wanted to fit employees' needs. Another alternative is **flexible work hours** (also popularly known as **flextime**), a scheduling option in which employees are required to work a specific number of hours per week but are free to vary those hours within certain limits. In a flextime schedule, there are certain common core hours when all employees are required to be on the job, but starting, ending, and lunch-hour times are flexible. Flextime is one of the most desired benefits among employees.[82] Employers have responded; a survey shows that 82 percent of Canadian employers expect to have flexible work arrangements by 2015 if not earlier.[83]

> **compressed workweek**
> A workweek in which employees work longer hours per day but fewer days per week.

> **flexible work hours (flextime)**
> A scheduling option in which employees are required to work a specific number of hours per week but are free to vary those hours within certain limits.

Job Sharing

Another scheduling option that can be effective in motivating a diverse workforce is **job sharing**—the practice of having two or more people split a full-time job. This type of job schedule might be attractive to individuals who want to work but do not want the demands and hassles of a full-time position.

> **job sharing**
> The practice of having two or more people split a full-time job.

Telecommuting

Another alternative made possible by information technology is **telecommuting**, in which employees work at home and are linked to the workplace by computer and other technology. Since many jobs are computer- and Internet-oriented, this job arrangement might be considered ideal for some people as there is no commuting, the hours are flexible, there is freedom to dress as you please, and there are few or no interruptions from colleagues. However, keep in mind that not all employees embrace the idea of telecommuting. A number of employees enjoy the informal interactions at work that satisfy their social needs and provide a source of new ideas.

> **telecommuting**
> A job arrangement in which employees work at home and are linked to the workplace by computer and other technology.

Q&A 13.8

From Theory to Practice: Suggestions for Motivating Employees

We have covered a lot of information about motivation in this chapter. If you are a manager concerned with motivating your employees, what specific recommendations can you draw from the theories and issues discussed so far? Although there is no simple, all-encompassing set of guidelines, the following suggestions draw on what we know about motivating employees:

> ⑤ What can managers learn from motivation theories?

- *Recognize individual differences.* Almost every contemporary motivation theory recognizes that employees are not identical. They have different needs, attitudes, personalities, and other important individual variables. Managers may not be giving enough consideration to what employees really want in terms of pay and benefits from the workplace. A recent survey of 446 employers by Western Compensation and Benefits Consultants found that 94 percent listed competitive base salary as an important incentive. Only 52 percent of employers listed flexible scheduling as a good incentive.[84] Meanwhile, a Statistics Canada survey found that employees want "challenging work, continuous learning, flexible work arrangements and better communication with their employers."[85] Eighty-seven percent of companies in the Western Compensation survey reported having difficulties attracting new employees in 2006. Companies may need to pay more attention to what their employees say that they want.

- *Match people to jobs.* There is a great deal of evidence showing the motivational benefits of carefully matching people to jobs. For example, high achievers should have jobs that let them participate in setting moderately challenging goals and give them autonomy and feedback. Also, keep in mind that not everybody is motivated by jobs that are high in autonomy, variety, and responsibility.

- *Individualize rewards.* Because employees have different needs, what acts as a reinforcer for one may not for another. Managers should use their knowledge of employee differences to individualize the rewards they control, such as pay, promotions, recognition, desirable work assignments, autonomy, and participation.

- *Link rewards to performance.* Managers need to make rewards contingent on performance. Rewarding factors other than performance will reinforce only those other factors. Important rewards such as pay increases and promotions should be given for the attainment of specific goals. Managers should also look for ways to increase the visibility of rewards, making them potentially more motivating.

- *Check the system for equity.* Employees should perceive that rewards or outcomes are equal to the inputs. On a simple level, experience, ability, effort, and other obvious inputs should explain differences in pay, responsibility, and other obvious outcomes. And remember that one person's equity is another's inequity, so an ideal reward system should probably weigh inputs differently in arriving at the proper rewards for each job.

- *Use recognition.* Recognize the power of recognition. In an economy where cost-cutting and layoffs are widespread (as we are experiencing in the current economy), using recognition is a low-cost means to reward employees. And it's a reward that most employees consider valuable.

- *Don't ignore money.* It's easy to get so caught up in setting goals, creating interesting jobs, and providing opportunities for participation that you forget that money is a major reason why most people work. Some studies indicate that money is not the top priority of employees. Professor Graham Lowe at the University of Alberta and a colleague found that relationships in the workplace are more important than pay or benefits in determining job satisfaction.[86] Nevertheless, the allocation of performance-based wage increases, piecework bonuses, and other pay incentives is important in determining employee motivation. We are not saying that managers should focus solely on money as a motivational tool; rather, we are simply stating the obvious—that is, if money is removed as an incentive, people are not going to show up for work. The same cannot be said for removing performance goals, enriched work, or participation.

SUMMARY AND IMPLICATIONS

① What is motivation? Motivation refers to an individual's willingness to exert high levels of effort to reach organizational goals, conditioned by the degree to which that effort satisfies some individual need.

○ ○ ○   At Tesco, one challenge was to motivate employees so that there would be less
○ ○ ○   turnover.

② How can needs help one be motivated? Needs theories point out that individuals have needs that, when fulfilled, will motivate individuals to perform well. While the theories do not account for all aspects of motivation, they do inform managers that individuals have different needs that should be considered when developing reward plans.

○ ○ ○   Managers at Tesco discovered that different employee groups, such as students and
○ ○ ○   mothers returning to the workplace, had different needs, and tried to address these
          needs to keep employees motivated.

③ What are the contemporary theories of motivation? Equity theory proposes that employees compare their rewards and their productivity with others, and then determine whether they have been treated fairly. Individuals who perceive that they are underrewarded will try to adjust their behaviour to correct this imbalance. Expectancy theory explores the link between people's belief in whether they can do the work assigned, their belief in whether they will get the rewards promised, and the extent to which the reward is something they value. Most research evidence supports expectancy theory.

○ ○ ○   Tesco encourages employees to buy shares of the company, so that they can "share in
○ ○ ○   the success they helped to create" and see the link between performance and reward.

④ What are some current issues in motivation? Current issues in motivation include motivating a diverse workforce, designing effective rewards programs, and improving work–life balance.

○ ○ ○   One of Tesco's challenges was motivating employees who had somewhat repetitive
○ ○ ○   jobs.

⑤ What can managers learn from motivation theories? Managers can motivate employees by recognizing individual differences, matching people to jobs, individualizing rewards, linking rewards to performance, checking the system for equity, using recognition, and not ignoring that money is a major reason why most people work.

○ ○ ○   Tesco has worked hard to recognize the different needs of students and mothers re-
○ ○ ○   turning to the workplace. The company also uses recognition to motivate employees
          and reduce turnover.

Management @ Work

READING FOR COMPREHENSION

1. How do needs affect motivation?

2. Contrast lower-order and higher-order needs in Maslow's needs hierarchy.

3. Describe the three needs in McClelland's theory of needs.

4. Define the five core dimensions of the job characteristics model.

5. What are some of the possible consequences of employees' perceiving an inequity between their inputs and outcomes and those of others?

6. What are some advantages of using pay-for-performance programs to motivate employee performance? Are there drawbacks? Explain.

7. What are the advantages of flextime from an employee's perspective? From management's perspective?

8. What can organizations do to create more motivating environments for their employees?

LINKING CONCEPTS TO PRACTICE

1. Most of us have to work for a living, and a job is a central part of our lives. So why do managers have to worry so much about employee motivation issues?

2. What role would money play in (1) the hierarchy of needs theory, (2) motivation-hygiene theory, (3) equity theory, and (4) expectancy theory?

3. If you accept Theory Y assumptions, how would you be likely to motivate employees? What would you do if you accept Theory X assumptions?

4. What difficulties do you think workforce diversity causes for managers who are trying to use equity theory?

5. Describe a task you have done recently for which you exerted a high level of effort. Explain your behaviour

using the following motivation approaches: (1) the hierarchy of needs theory, (2) motivation-hygiene theory, (3) equity theory, and (4) expectancy theory.

6. Describe several means that you might use to motivate (1) minimum-wage employees working for a small company that makes tortillas or (2) professional and technical employees working for a software design firm. Which of your suggestions do you think is best? Support your position.

7. Many job design experts who have studied the changing nature of work say that people do their best work when they are motivated by a sense of purpose rather than by the pursuit of money. Do you agree? Explain your position.

SELF-ASSESSMENT

What Rewards Do I Value Most?

Below are 10 work-related rewards.[87] For each, identify the number that best describes the value that a particular reward has for you personally. Use the following scale to express your feelings:

1 = No Value at All 2 = Slight Value 3 = Moderate Value 4 = Great Value 5 = Extremely Great Value

1. Good pay   1 2 3 4 5

2. Prestigious title   1 2 3 4 5

3. Vacation time   1 2 3 4 5

4. Job security   1 2 3 4 5

5. Recognition	1 2 3 4 5
6. Interesting work	1 2 3 4 5
7. Pleasant conditions	1 2 3 4 5
8. Chances to advance	1 2 3 4 5
9. Flexible schedule	1 2 3 4 5
10. Friendly co-workers	1 2 3 4 5

Scoring Key

To assess your responses, prioritize them into groups. Put all the rewards you gave a 5 together. Do the same for your other responses. The rewards you gave 5s or 4s are the ones that you most desire and that your employer should emphasize with you.

Analysis and Interpretation

What motivates you does not necessarily motivate me. So employers that want to maximize employee motivation should determine what rewards each employee individually values. This instrument can help you understand which work-related rewards have the greatest value to you. Compare the rewards that your employer offers with your scores. The greater the disparity, the more you might want to consider looking for opportunities at another organization with a reward structure that better matches your preferences.

More Self-Assessments

To learn more about your skills, abilities, and interests, take the following self-assessments on MyManagementLab at www.pearsoned.ca/mymanagementlab:

- I.C.1—What Motivates Me?
- I.C.4—What's My View on the Nature of People?
- IV.B.1—Am I Engaged?

MANAGEMENT FOR YOU TODAY

Dilemma

You are in a team with 6 other management students, and you have a major case analysis due in 4 weeks. The case project will count for 25 percent of the course mark. You are the team's leader. Several team members are having difficulty getting motivated to get started on the project. Identify ways you could motivate your team members, using needs theories, expectancy theory, and equity theory. How will you motivate yourself?

Becoming a Manager

- Start paying attention to times when you are highly motivated and times when you are not as motivated. What accounts for the difference?

- When working on teams for class projects or on committees in student organizations, try different approaches to motivating others.

- If you are working, assess your job using the job characteristics model. How might you redesign your job to make it more motivating?

- As you visit various businesses, note what, if any, employee recognition programs these businesses use.

- Talk to practising managers about their approaches to employee motivation. What have they found works?

WORKING TOGETHER: TEAM-BASED EXERCISE

How Can You Motivate Others?

This exercise is designed to help increase your awareness of how and why you motivate others and to help focus on the needs of those you are attempting to motivate.

Step 1

Break into groups of 5 to 7 people. Each group member is to respond individually to the following:

Situation 1: You are the owner and president of a 50-employee organization that provides call-centre services to a number of local businesses. There are 2 major units. *Customer care* answers questions from customers about malfunctioning technology (computers, cellphones, and home networks). *Sales and marketing* makes telemarketing calls to people's homes. Employees who work in sales and marketing phone people and try to sell them cellphone plans and/or Internet access at reduced prices. They also conduct market research via phone, calling people to ask them to answer survey questions. Employees who work in customer care often receive calls from irate customers who are having technical difficulties. Employees who work in sales and marketing often encounter irate people when they phone to sell them something or conduct a survey, particularly at dinner time. Your goal is to motivate all 50 employees to their highest level of effort.

Task 1: On a separate piece of paper, list the factors you would use to motivate your employees. Avoid general

statements such as "give them a raise." Rather, be as specific as possible, such as "give them a 5 percent raise."

Task 2: Rank (from most important to least important) all the factors listed in Task 1.

Situation 2: Consider now that you are 1 of the 50 employees who have been given insight into what motivates you.

Task 3: As an employee, list those factors that would motivate you most effectively. Again, be as specific as possible.

Task 4: Rank (from most important to least important) all the factors listed in Task 3.

Step 2

Each member should share his or her prioritized lists (the lists from tasks 2 and 4) with the other members of the group.

Step 3

After each member has presented his or her lists, the group should respond to the following questions:

1. Are each individual's lists (Task 2 and Task 4) similar or dissimilar to the others? What do the differences or similarities suggest to you?

2. What have you learned about how and why to motivate others, and how can you apply these data?

ETHICS IN ACTION

Ethical Dilemma Exercise: Are Some Employees More Deserving Than Others?

Employees who feel unfairly forced into accepting deep cuts in salary and benefits may not be the most motivated employees. This is the situation many major North American airlines have faced as they struggle for survival. To stay in business, management at Air Canada and other carriers have pressured unionized pilots, mechanics, and flight attendants for concessions on pay and work rules again and again.

Still, many North American airline employees fear that their compensation will not return to previous levels. Air Canada employees wonder about the survivability of the airline. Moreover, employees cynically believe that cuts in management's compensation will be restored faster than those of unionized employees. Many employees resent this inequitable treatment. "We know we had to help the airline," says one flight attendant. "But we think they took more than they needed from us." This sense of inequity could dampen

motivation and affect the way employees work together and deal with customers.[88]

Imagine that you were just promoted and now manage one of your airline's mechanical maintenance facilities at a regional airport. Your manager just told you that the airline has lost many managers to jobs outside the industry. To stop defections and retain good managers, your company has decided to return managers to full pay and benefits within 12 months. However, employees must wait much longer. You sympathize with your employees' gripes about compensation cuts, and you know they have little hope of getting maintenance jobs at other airlines. Although you like your new job and would welcome full pay, you could easily move to another industry. What, if anything, would you do about the nonmanagerial employees who will continue working with the pay cuts? (Look back at this chapter's discussion of equity theory as you consider this ethical challenge.)

Thinking Critically About Ethics

You have been hired as a phone sales representative at G.A.P Adventures in Toronto. In this job, you help customers who call in to book vacations by finding what works best for them and their needs. You check airline flights, times, and fares, and also help with rental car and hotel reservations.

Most car rental firms and hotels run contests for the sales representative who books the most cars or most hotel rooms. The contest winners receive very attractive rewards! For example, if you book just 50 clients for one rental car company, your name is put in a draw for $1000. If you book 100 clients, the draw is for $2500. And if you book 200 clients, you receive an all-expenses-paid, one-week Caribbean vacation. So the incentives are attractive enough to encourage you to "steer" customers toward one of those companies even though it might not be the best or cheapest for them. Your manager does not discourage participation in these programs.

Do you see anything wrong with this situation? Explain. What ethical issues do you see for (a) the employee, (b) the organization, and (c) the customer? How could an organization design performance incentive programs that encourage high levels of performance without compromising ethics?

CASE APPLICATION

Best Buy

Customer-centricity.[89] That is the new strategic focus that Brad Anderson, CEO of Best Buy, is betting on to keep the company from becoming a retailing casualty like Woolworth or Kmart. What is customer-centricity? Simply put, it's figuring out which customers are the most profitable and doing whatever it takes to please them so they want to come back often and spend money. As the biggest consumer electronics retailer in North America, Best Buy has a lot at stake. And its 100 000-plus employees will play a crucial role in this new approach, which shifts the focus from "pushing gadgets to catering to customers."

"At Best Buy, People Are the Engines That Drive Our Success." That is the up-front-and-central phrase on the company's web-based career centre. And to Best Buy, it's not an empty slogan. The company has tried to create an environment in which employees, wherever they are, have numerous opportunities to learn, work, play, and achieve. One way they do that is by providing facts and figures to employees on everything from new technology to industry changes to company actions. At store meetings or on the intranet, employees can get the information they need to do their jobs and do them well.

Like many other companies, Best Buy has "struggled to meet the demands of its business—how to do things better, faster, and cheaper than its competitors—with an increasingly stressed-out workforce." Its culture has always rewarded long hours and sacrifice. One manager used a plaque to recognize the employee "who turns on the lights in the morning and turns them off at night." However, that approach has been taking its toll on employees. Best Buy is having difficulty retaining its best and brightest managers and executives.

Anderson wants to know why the company does not have an "innovative incentive program to foster our innovative culture." He has come to you for advice. What is the best way for the company to get employees on board so that they will be more customer-centric in their approach?

DEVELOPING YOUR DIAGNOSTIC AND ANALYTICAL SKILLS

Paradise Lost . . . Or Gained?

A massage every other week, on-site laundry, swimming pool and spa, free delicious all-you-can-eat gourmet meals.[90] What more could an employee want? Sounds like an ideal job, doesn't it? However, at Google, many people are demonstrating by their decisions to leave the company that all those perks (and these are just a few) are not enough to keep them there. As one analyst put it, "Yes, Google's making gobs of money. Yes, it's full of smart people. Yes, it's a wonderful place to work. So why are so many people leaving?"

Google has been named the "best company to work for" by *Fortune* magazine for two years running, but make no mistake: Google's executives made the decision to offer all those fabulous perks in order to attract the best knowledge workers it can in an intensely competitive, cut-throat market; to help employees work long hours and not have to deal with time-consuming personal chores outside work; to show employees they are valued; and to have employees remain Googlers (the name used for employees) for many years. Nevertheless, a number of Googlers have jumped ship and given up these fantastic benefits to go out on their own.

For example, Sean Knapp and two colleagues, brothers Bismarck and Belsasar Lepe, came up with an idea about how to handle web video. They left Google in April 2007, or as one person put it, "expelled themselves from paradise to start their own company." When the threesome made the decision to leave the company, Google desperately wanted them and their project to stay, and offered them a "blank cheque." But Knapp and his colleagues realized they would still be doing all the hard work, and Google would own the product. So off they went, for the excitement of a start-up.

If this were an isolated occurrence, it would be easy to write off. But it's not. Other talented Google employees have done the same thing. In fact, so many of them have left that they have created an informal alumni club of ex-Googlers turned entrepreneurs.

Questions

1. What's it like to work at Google? (Hint: Go to Google's website and click on About Google. Find the section Jobs at Google.) What is your assessment of the company's work environment?

2. Google is doing a lot for its employees, but obviously it has not done enough to retain a number of its talented employees. Using what you have learned from studying the various motivation theories, what does this situation tell you about employee motivation?

3. What do you think is Google's biggest challenge in keeping employees motivated?

4. If you were managing a team of Google employees, how would you keep them motivated?

DEVELOPING YOUR INTERPERSONAL SKILLS

Maximizing Employee Effort

About the Skill

There is no simple, all-encompassing set of motivational guidelines, but the following suggestions draw on the essence of what we know about motivating employees.[91]

Steps in Developing the Skill

You can be more effective at maximizing employee effort if you apply the following eight suggestions:

1. **Recognize individual differences.** Almost every contemporary motivation theory recognizes that employees are not homogeneous. They have different needs. They also differ in terms of attitudes, personality, and other important individual variables.

2. **Match people to jobs.** There is a great deal of evidence showing the motivational benefits of carefully matching people to jobs. People who lack the necessary skills to perform successfully will be disadvantaged.

3. **Use goals.** You should ensure that employees have hard, specific goals and feedback on how well they are doing in pursuit of those goals. In many cases, these goals should be participatively set.

4. **Ensure that goals are perceived as attainable.** Regardless of whether goals are actually attainable, employees who see goals as unattainable will reduce their effort. Be sure, therefore, that employees feel confident that increased effort can lead to achieving performance goals.

5. **Individualize rewards.** Because employees have different needs, what acts as a reinforcer for one may not do so for another. Use your knowledge of employee differences to individualize the rewards over which you have control. Some of the more obvious rewards that you can allocate include pay, promotions, autonomy, and the opportunity to participate in goal setting and decision making.

6. **Link rewards to performance.** You need to make rewards contingent on performance. Rewarding factors other than performance will reinforce only the importance of those other factors. Key rewards such as pay increases and promotions should be given for the attainment of employees' specific goals.

7. **Check the system for equity.** Employees should perceive that rewards or outcomes are equal to the inputs given. On a simplistic level, experience, ability, effort, and other obvious inputs should explain differences in pay, responsibility, and other obvious outcomes.

8. **Don't ignore money.** It's easy to get so caught up in setting goals, creating interesting jobs, and providing opportunities for participation that you forget that money is a major reason why most people work. Thus, the allocation of performance-based wage increases, piecework bonuses, employee stock ownership plans, and other pay incentives are important in determining employee motivation.

Practising the Skill

Employees at Radialpoint in Montreal can get their laundry washed, dried, and folded for them at work. At trucking company Groupe Robert, based in Rougemont, Quebec, employees are entered into monthly draws for concerts and shows; each employee receives a Christmas food basket; and birthday cards are personally signed by the CEO. At Brantford, Ontario-based S. C. Johnson & Son, employees and their families can take holidays at the company's resort in the Muskokas. The company also provides an on-site massage therapist. All of these companies believe that there is more to rewards than just cash.

All of the following traditional and offbeat benefits are currently offered at various Canadian firms. Rank-order them for yourself, putting those that are most likely to motivate you at the top of your list. Now look at your top five choices. How do you think you will rank them in 10 years? Why?

Flextime
Telecommuting
Dental insurance
Tuition refund
Vision insurance
Health club
Life insurance
On-site daycare

Employee assistance program
Laundry/dry cleaning service
Company car
Subsidized cafeteria
Paid vacation
Profit sharing
Stock purchase plan
Ability to keep frequent flier miles
Pets at work
Management program
Daily naptime
Free snacks/candy
Year-end bonus
Clothing allowance
Flexible spending plan
Free lunch
Retirement plan
Paid sick days
Children's college/university tuition
Annual birthday gift
Non-work-related courses
Company-sponsored sports team
Free uniform
Transportation voucher
Family picnics and parties
Child and elder care referral services
Benefits for unmarried domestic partners

MANAGING WORKFORCE DIVERSITY

Developing Employee Potential: The Bottom Line of Diversity

One of a manager's more important goals is helping employees develop their potential.[92] This is particularly important in managing talented employees from a variety of cultures who can bring new perspectives and ideas to the business but who may find that the workplace environment is not as conducive as it could be to accepting and embracing these different perspectives. For example, managers at Alcatel-Lucent's distinguished Bell Labs have worked hard to develop an environment in which the ideas of nonwhite employees are encouraged openly.

What can managers do to ensure that employees from different cultures have the opportunity to develop their potential? One thing they can do is to make sure that there are role models of different cultures in leadership positions so that others see that there are opportunities to grow and advance. Having motivated, talented, hard-working, and enthusiastic diverse employees who excel in decision-making roles can be a powerful motivator to other employees of the same or similar backgrounds to work hard to develop their own potential. A mentoring program in which diverse employees are given the opportunity to work closely with organizational leaders can be a powerful tool. At Silicon

Graphics, for example, new employees become part of a mentoring group called "Horizons." Through this mentoring group, diverse employees have the opportunity to observe and learn from key company decision makers.

Another way for managers to develop the potential of their diverse employees is to offer developmental work assignments that provide a variety of learning experiences in different organizational areas. DaimlerChrysler, for example, started its Corporate University, which offers a comprehensive series of learning opportunities for all employees. The company's director of diversity and work/family says that employees who are provided the opportunity to learn new processes and how to use new technology are more likely to excel at their work and to stay with the company. These types of developmental opportunities are particularly important for diverse employees because they empower employees with tools that are critical to professional development.

Consider organizations for which you have worked. Did any of them have diversity initiatives? What did they do to either recruit employees from various cultures, or to make them feel more welcome? Were the company's policies effective in managing diversity?

CHAPTER

10

Understanding Groups and Teams

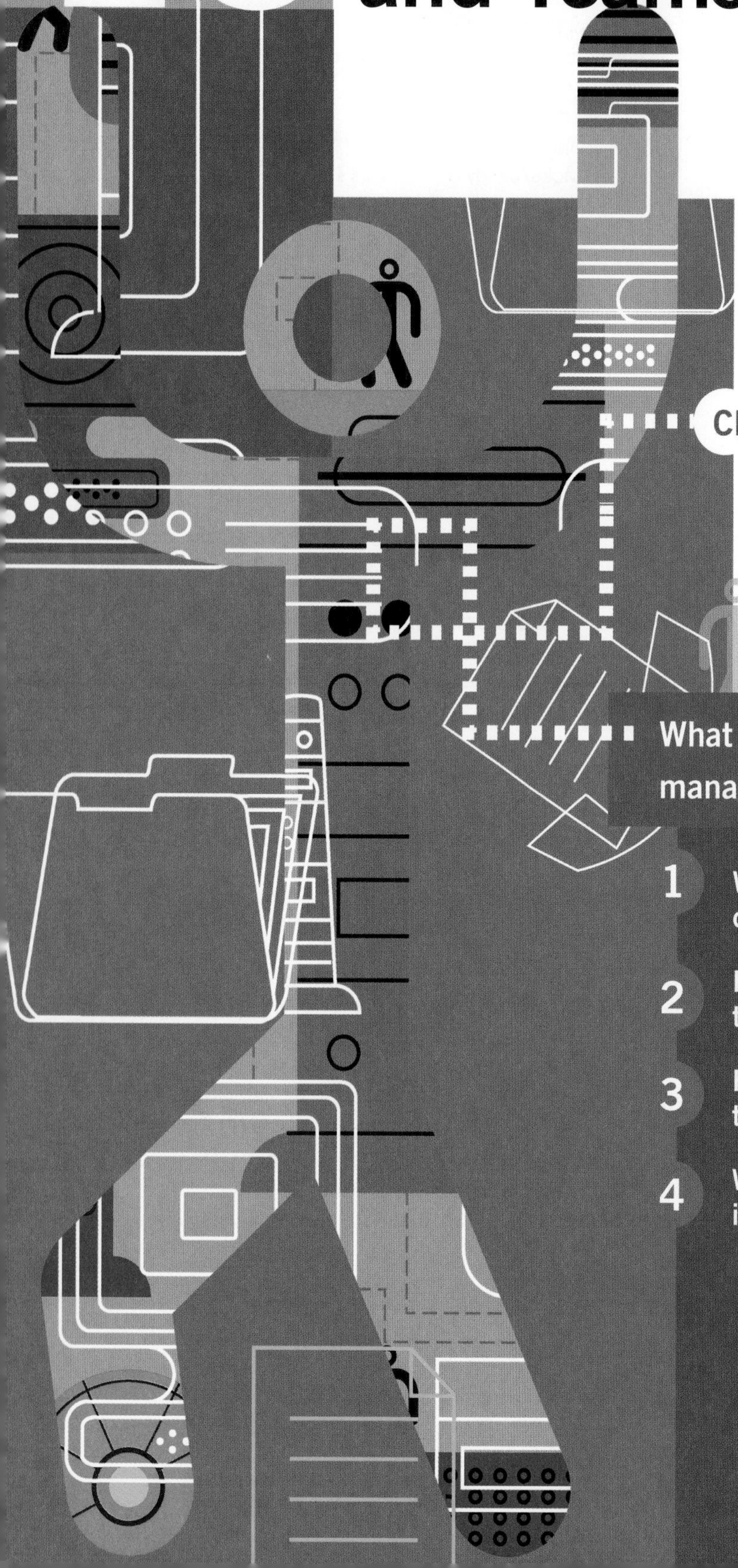

What is the best way to create and manage teams?

1   What are the stages of team development?

2   How do individuals become team players?

3   How can groups become effective teams?

4   What are some of the current challenges in managing teams?

When you are putting together the Canadian team for the 2006 Winter Olympics in Turin, do you go with the proven winners of the 2004 World Cup of Hockey and the 2002 Winter Olympics or put together a new team?[1]

That was the challenge facing Wayne Gretzky and management as they prepared to announce the 24-man roster for Team Canada on December 21, 2005.

Gretzky's 2004 World Cup hockey team beat Finland 3 to 2 in Toronto, taking first place. His 2002 Olympic hockey team beat the Americans 5 to 2 in Salt Lake City, winning the gold medal. It was the first time Canada had won Olympic gold since 1952.

When Steve Tambellini, filling in for Gretzky, whose mother's funeral had been earlier that week, announced the new team in December 2005, 20 of the players had played for either the World Cup team, the 2002 Olympic team, or both. Only three new players were added to the team. There were certainly questions about some of the decisions. Was it right to leave off Pittsburgh Penguin Sidney Crosby, who was having a strong debut season in the NHL? Why include controversial Canuck Todd Bertuzzi, after he attacked Colorado Avalanche player Steve Moore, ending his career? Most importantly, what about 2010? Shouldn't there be some younger players getting experience now in preparation for playing for Olympic gold in Vancouver?

Team Canada assistant coach Wayne Fleming defended against those who complained that there were not enough new faces on the team. This would be a team that would have "instant chemistry, with very little preparation time." Better to go with experience, in other words.

Think About It

What is the best way to choose an effective team? Put yourself in Wayne Gretzky's shoes. Are there other players he should have chosen instead? Could he have put together a better team?

Work teams are one of the realities—and challenges—of managing in today's dynamic global environment. Teams are widely used in Canada. Thousands of organizations have made the move to restructure work around teams rather than individuals. Why? What do these teams look like? What stages of development do teams go through? And, like the challenge Wayne Gretzky faced, how can managers create effective teams? These are a few of the types of questions we answer in this chapter. First, however, let's begin by developing our understanding of group behaviour.

Understanding Groups and Teams

Because most organizational work is done by individuals who are part of a work group, it's important for managers to understand group behaviour. The behaviour of a group is not simply the sum total of the behaviours of all the individuals in the group. Why? Because individuals act differently in groups than they do when they are alone. Therefore, if we want to understand organizational behaviour more fully, we need to study groups.

① What are the stages of team development?

What Is a Group?

A **group** is defined as two or more interacting and interdependent individuals who come together to achieve particular goals. Groups can be either formal or informal. *Formal*

group
Two or more interacting and interdependent individuals who come together to achieve particular goals.

Exhibit 10-1

Examples of Formal Groups

Command Groups: Groups that are determined by the organizational chart and composed of individuals who report directly to a given manager.

Task Groups: Groups composed of individuals brought together to complete a specific job task; their existence is often temporary because once the task is completed, the group disbands.

Cross-Functional Teams: Groups that bring together the knowledge and skills of individuals from various work areas, or groups whose members have been trained to do one another's jobs.

Self-Managed Teams: Groups that are essentially independent and, in addition to their own tasks, take on traditional managerial responsibilities such as hiring, planning and scheduling, and performance evaluations.

---

groups are work groups defined by the organization's structure that have designated work assignments and specific tasks. In formal groups, appropriate behaviours are established by and directed toward organizational goals. Exhibit 10-1 provides some examples of different types of formal groups in today's organizations.

Diversity in Action 3

In contrast, *informal groups* are social. These groups occur naturally in the workplace in response to the need for social contact. For example, three employees from different departments who regularly eat lunch together are an informal group. Informal groups tend to form around friendships and common interests.

What Is a Team?

Most of you are already familiar with teams, especially if you have watched organized sports events. Although a sports team has many of the same characteristics as a work team, work teams *are* different from work groups and have their own unique traits. (See Exhibit 10-2 for a description of the differences.) Work groups interact primarily to share information and to make decisions to help each member do his or her job more efficiently and effectively. These groups have no need or opportunity to engage in collective work that requires joint effort. On the other hand, **work teams** are groups whose members work intensely on a specific, common goal using their positive **synergy** (combined efforts that are greater than the sum of individual efforts), individual and mutual accountability, and complementary skills. In a work team, the combined individual efforts of team members result in a level of performance that is greater than the sum of those individual inputs, by generating positive synergy through coordinated effort.

work teams
Groups whose members work intensely on a specific, common goal using their positive synergy, individual and mutual accountability, and complementary skills.

synergy
Combined efforts that are greater than the sum of individual efforts.

Exhibit 10-2

Groups vs. Teams

Work Group	Work Team
• Strong, clearly focused leader	• Shared leadership roles
• Individual accountability	• Individual and mutual accountability
• The group's purpose is the same as the broader organizational mission	• Specific team purpose that the team itself delivers
• Individual work products	• Collective work products
• Runs efficient meetings	• Encourages open-ended discussion and active problem-solving meetings
• Measures its effectiveness indirectly by its influence on others (such as financial performance of the business)	• Measures performance directly by assessing collective work products
• Discusses, decides, and delegates together	• Discusses, decides, and does real work

Source: J. R. Katzenbach and D. K. Smith, "The Discipline of Teams," *Harvard Business Review*, July–August 2005, p. 164. With permission from Harvard Business School Publishing.

Though teams and groups do differ, we sometimes use "groups" and "teams" interchangeably in our theoretical discussions below (conforming to how scholars have written their research). This simply underscores that in some cases the processes for groups and teams are similar, although teams involve more synergy.

Types of Teams

Teams can do a variety of things. They can design products, provide services, negotiate deals, coordinate projects, offer advice, and make decisions.[2] The four most common types of teams you are likely to find in an organization are problem-solving teams, self-managed teams, cross-functional teams, and virtual teams.

Google's website explains the company looks for exceptional people, and one of the skills they need is the ability to work as a team member. "We work in small teams, which we believe promotes spontaneity, creativity, and speed," the company says, "and team achievements are highly valued." Pictured here are some of Google's employees at its R & D centre in India.

Problem-Solving Teams

If we look back to when work teams were just beginning to gain in popularity, most were what we call **problem-solving teams**, which are teams of 5 to 12 employees from the same department or functional area who are involved in efforts to improve work activities or to solve specific problems. In problem-solving teams, members share ideas or offer suggestions on how work processes and methods can be improved. However, these teams are rarely given the authority to unilaterally implement any of their suggested actions.

problem-solving teams
Work teams of 5 to 12 employees from the same department or functional area who are involved in efforts to improve work activities or to solve specific problems.

Self-Managed Teams

Self-managed teams are formal groups of employees that operate without a manager and are responsible for a complete work process or segment. Unlike a problem-solving team, the self-managed team is responsible for getting the work done *and* for managing itself. This usually includes planning and scheduling work, assigning tasks to members, collectively controlling the pace of work, making operating decisions, and taking action on problems. For example, a self-managed team operates Muskoseepi Park in Grand Prairie, Alberta. Team members are accountable to each other and do not have direct supervision on a daily basis.

How effective are self-managed teams? Most organizations that use them find them successful and plan to expand their use in the coming years.[3] The evidence indicates that self-managed work teams often perform better than teams with formally appointed leaders.[4] Leaders can obstruct high performance when they interfere with self-managed teams.[5] However, managers cannot forget to consider cultural differences when deciding whether to use self-managed teams. For example, evidence suggests that these types of teams have not fared well in Mexico largely due to that culture's low tolerance for ambiguity and uncertainty and employees' strong respect for hierarchical authority.[6]

self-managed teams
Work teams that operate without a manager and are responsible for a complete work process or segment.

Cross-Functional Teams

Cross-functional teams, which we introduced in Chapter 5, are work teams made up of individuals who are experts in various functional specialties. Many organizations use cross-functional teams. For example, Calgary-based Canadian Pacific Railway (CPR) uses cross-functional teams to figure out ways to cut costs. Individuals from all of the functional areas affected by the spending review (such as supply services, operations, and finance) make up the team.[7] Organic organizations, which we discussed in Chapter 5, are generally structured around cross-functional teams.

cross-functional teams
Work teams made up of individuals who are experts in various functional specialties.

Q&A 14.1

Virtual Teams

Virtual teams are teams that use computer technology to link physically dispersed members in order to achieve a common goal. Microsoft's staff in Richmond, BC, are part of a virtual team that works for managers in Redmond, Washington, and other global centres.

virtual teams
Work teams that use computer technology to link physically dispersed members in order to achieve a common goal.

They collaborate with colleagues throughout the world.[8] Virtual teams can do all the things that other teams can—share information, make decisions, and complete tasks; however, they can suffer from the absence of paraverbal (the way in which language is communicated, such as volume and tone) and nonverbal cues and limited social contact. Professor Mark Mortensen of McGill University's Faculty of Management notes a major difficulty in working long distance. "You may be in Montreal and are working with someone in Bangalore, India. You send an email to someone there and get no response. You send another and get no response and then you get annoyed. Later, you find out that it was a national holiday and no one was working."[9] An additional concern about virtual teams is whether members are able to build the same kind of trust that face-to-face teams build.[10]

However, two recent studies examining how virtual teams work on projects indicate that virtual teams can develop close interaction and trust; these qualities simply develop differently than in face-to-face groups.[11] The researchers found that initial electronic messages set the tone and determined the extent to which trust developed on a virtual team. On one team the appointed leader sent an introductory message that had a distrustful tone. This team suffered low morale and poor performance throughout the project. Virtual teams should start with an electronic form of "courtship," with members providing some personal information early on. Teams should assign clear roles to members, so members can identify with each other. By engaging in spontaneous communication with virtual team members, managers can also reduce the likelihood and impact of conflict.[12]

Managing virtual teams effectively has become more important as more employees engage in telecommuting, an alternative work arrangement we discussed in Chapter 9.

Stages of Team Development

Have you ever noticed the stages a team goes through in learning how to work together?

Team development is a dynamic process. Most teams and groups are in a continual state of change, although there is a general pattern that describes how most of them develop. Professor Bruce Tuckman of Ohio State University developed a five-stage model of small group development.[13] As shown in Exhibit 10-3, these five stages are *forming*, *storming*, *norming*, *performing*, and *adjourning*.

Stage I, **forming**, has two aspects. First, people join the team either because of a work assignment or for some other benefit desired (such as status, self-esteem, affiliation, power, or security).

Once the team's membership is in place, the second part of the forming stage begins: the task of defining the team's purpose, structure, and leadership. This phase is characterized by a great deal of uncertainty. Members are "testing the waters" to determine what types of behaviour are acceptable. This stage is complete when members begin to think of themselves as part of a team.

Stage II, **storming**, is one of intragroup conflict. Members accept the existence of the team but resist the control that the team imposes on individuality. Further, there is conflict over who will control the team. When this stage is complete, there will be a relatively clear hierarchy of leadership within the team and agreement on the team's direction.

Stage III is one in which close relationships develop and the team demonstrates cohesiveness. There is now a strong sense of team identity and camaraderie. This **norming** stage is complete when the team structure solidifies and the team has assimilated a common set of expectations of what defines correct member behaviour.

Stage IV is **performing**. The team structure at this point is fully functional and accepted by team members. Team energy has moved from getting to know and understand each other to performing the task at hand.

Performing is the last stage in the development of permanent work teams. Temporary teams—such as project teams, task forces, and similar groups that have a limited task to perform—have a fifth stage, **adjourning**. In this stage, the team prepares to disband. High levels of task performance are no longer the team's top priority. Instead, attention is directed at wrapping up activities. Responses of team members vary at this stage. Some

forming
The first stage of team development in which people join the group and then define the team's purpose, structure, and leadership.

Q&A 14.2

storming
The second stage of team development, which is characterized by intragroup conflict.

norming
The third stage of team development, which is characterized by close relationships and cohesiveness.

performing
The fourth stage of team development, in which the team structure is fully functional and accepted by team members.

adjourning
The final stage of team development for temporary teams, in which members are concerned with wrapping up activities rather than task performance.

Exhibit 10-3

Stages of Team Development

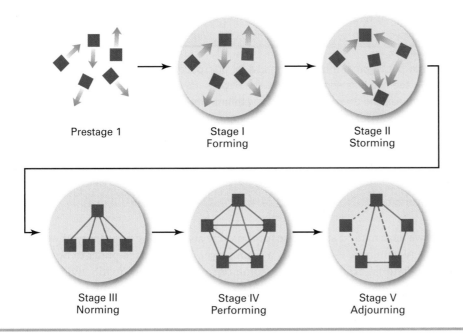

Prestage 1

Stage I
Forming

Stage II
Storming

Stage III
Norming

Stage IV
Performing

Stage V
Adjourning

are upbeat, basking in the team's accomplishments. Others may be saddened by the loss of camaraderie and friendships gained during the work team's life.

Many of you have probably experienced each of these stages in working on a class team project. Team members are selected and then meet for the first time. There is a "feeling out" period to assess what the team is going to do and how it's going to do it. This is usually rapidly followed by a battle for control: Who is going to be in charge? Once this issue is resolved and a "hierarchy" agreed on, the team identifies specific aspects of the task, who is going to do them, and dates by which the assigned work needs to be completed. General expectations are established and agreed on by each member. These decisions form the foundation for what you hope will be a coordinated team effort culminating in a project well done. Once the team project is completed and turned in, the team breaks up. Of course, some teams do not get far beyond the first or second stage; these teams typically have serious interpersonal conflicts, turn in disappointing work, and get lower grades.

Should you assume from the preceding discussion that a team becomes more effective as it progresses through the first four stages? Some researchers argue that effectiveness of work teams increases at advanced stages, but that is not always the case.[14] Also, teams do not always proceed clearly from one stage to the next. Sometimes, in fact, several stages may be going on simultaneously, as when teams are storming and performing at the same time. Individuals within a team may also be at different stages, with some performing while others are still in the forming or norming stage. When individuals are shy, it may take them longer to reach the performing stage, and it may be helpful for team members to support and encourage each other through the stages. Teams sometimes regress to previous stages. Therefore, do not always assume that all teams precisely follow this development process or that Stage IV (performing) is always the most desirable stage. It's better to think of this model as a general framework. It underscores the fact that teams are dynamic entities, and it can help you better understand the problems and issues that are most likely to surface during a team's life.

Diversity in Action 1

Senior Vice-President Dadi Perlmutter leads a chip design group in Haifa, Israel, for the foremost semiconductor maker in the world, Intel. Perlmutter's group thrives on the kind of debate and confrontation typical of the storming stage of group development, but it achieves the kind of real-world results that usually characterize the performing stage. Recently, for example, the group came up with a winning design for a processor chip for wireless computers that consumes half the power of other chips without sacrificing processing speed.

⚪⚪⚪ Turning Individuals into Team Players

When Wayne Gretzky put together Team Canada for the 2006 Winter Olympics, he had to balance out many considerations.[15] His 2002 Winter Olympics team and his 2004 World Cup of Hockey team had each done a terrific job in representing Canada. Still, having some younger players gain experience for the 2010 Winter Olympics in Vancouver might be a consideration.

Gretzky put together a team that had a lot of experience, particularly international experience. He seemed less concerned with the players' recent performance in the league. Since Mario Lemieux and Steve Yzerman, two veterans whom Gretzky had relied on for leadership roles in the previous Team Canada, were unavailable, Gretzky might have felt experienced players would fill the leadership void. Choosing the players was not the end of the task, however. Gretzky had to get the collection of individuals to play like a team.

Think About It

What does it take to turn an individual into a team player?

❷ How do individuals become team players?

So far, we have made a strong case for the value and growing popularity of work teams, but not every employee is inherently a team player. Some people prefer to be recognized for their individual achievements. In some organizations, too, work environments are such that only the strong survive. Creating teams in such an environment may meet some resistance. Countries differ in terms of the degree to which individuals are encouraged by societal institutions to be integrated into groups. Teams fit well in countries that score high on collectivism, where working together is encouraged. But what if an organization wants to introduce teams into an individualistic society, like that of Canada? The job becomes more difficult.

Q&A 14.3

The Challenges of Creating Team Players

One substantial barrier to work teams is the individual resistance that may exist. Employees' success, when they are part of teams, is no longer defined in terms of individual performance. Instead, success is a function of how well the team as a whole performs. To perform well as team members, individuals must be able to communicate openly and honestly with one another, to confront differences and resolve conflicts, and to place lower priority on personal goals for the good of the team. For many employees, these are difficult and sometimes impossible assignments. *Ethical Dilemma Exercise: Does Everyone Have to Be a Team Player?* on page 314 looks at a situation in which an employee does not want to be a team member.

The challenge of creating team players will be greatest when the national culture is highly individualistic and the teams are being introduced into an established organization that has historically valued individual achievement.[16] These organizations prospered by hiring and rewarding corporate stars, and they bred a competitive work climate that encouraged individual achievement and recognition. In this context, employees can experience culture shock caused by a sudden shift in the focus to teamwork.[17]

Team players do not just appear. There is a lot of hard work required to get team members to gel. That is why baseball players, like the Toronto Blue Jays, go to spring training every year—to prepare themselves as a team for the upcoming season.

In contrast, the challenge for management is less demanding when teams are introduced in places in which employees have strong collectivist values—such as Japan or Mexico. The challenge of forming teams will also be less in new organizations that use teams as their initial means of structuring work. For instance, Saturn Corporation (an American organization owned by General Motors) was designed around teams from its start. Everyone at Saturn was hired on the understanding that they would be working in teams, and the ability to be a good team player was a hiring prerequisite. *Managing Workforce Diversity—The Challenge of Managing Diverse Teams* on page 317 considers how you can help team members from different cultures work together more effectively.

What Roles Do Team Members Play?

A **role** refers to a set of expected behaviour patterns attributed to someone who occupies a given position in a social unit. In a group, individuals are expected to perform certain roles because of their positions in the group. **Task-oriented roles** tend to be oriented toward task accomplishment, while **maintenance roles** are oriented toward maintaining group member satisfaction and relationships.[18] Think about groups that you have been in and the roles that you played. Were you continually trying to keep the group focused on getting its work done? If so, you were filling a task accomplishment role. Or were you more concerned that group members had the opportunity to offer ideas and that they were satisfied with the experience? If so, you were performing a maintenance role to preserve the harmony of the group. Both roles are important to the ability of a group to function effectively and efficiently, and some group members are flexible and play both roles. One study found that the most effective teams had a leader who performed both the task-oriented and the maintenance roles.[19] In some groups, unfortunately, there are people who take on neither role, and participate very little in the team functions. It is not helpful if there are too many people who do not take on a role.

role
A set of expected behaviour patterns attributed to someone who occupies a given position in a social unit.

task-oriented roles
Roles performed by group members to ensure that group tasks are accomplished.

maintenance roles
Roles performed by group members to maintain good relations within the group.

Q&A 14.4

Shaping Team Behaviour

There are several options available for managers who are trying to turn individuals into team players. The three most popular ways include proper selection, employee training, and rewarding the appropriate team behaviours. Let's look at each of these.

Selection

Some individuals already possess the interpersonal skills to be effective team players. When hiring team members, in addition to checking on the technical skills required to successfully perform the job, the organization should ensure that applicants can fulfill team roles.

As we have mentioned before, some applicants have been socialized around individual contributions and, consequently, lack team skills, as might some current employees whose jobs are being restructured into teams. When faced with such candidates, a manager can do several things. First, and most obvious, if a candidate's team skills are woefully lacking, do not hire that candidate. If successful performance requires interaction, rejecting such a candidate is appropriate. On the other hand, a good candidate who has only some basic team skills can be hired on a probationary basis and required to undergo training to shape him or her into a team player. If the skills are not learned or practised, the individual may have to be let go for failing to master the skills necessary for performing successfully on the job.

Training

Performing well in a team involves a set of behaviours. As we discussed in the preceding chapter, new behaviours can be learned. Even a large portion of people who were raised on the importance of individual accomplishment can be trained to become team players. Training specialists can conduct workshops that allow employees to experience the satisfaction that teamwork can provide. The workshops usually cover such topics as team problem solving, communications, negotiations, conflict resolution, and coaching skills. It's not unusual, too, for these employees to be exposed to the five stages of team development that we discussed earlier.[20] At Verizon Communications, for example, trainers focus on how a team goes through various stages before it gels. Employees are reminded of the importance of patience, because teams take longer to do some things—such as make decisions—than do employees acting alone.[21]

Rewards

The organization's reward system needs to encourage cooperative efforts rather than competitive ones. For example, Lockheed Martin Aeronautics Company has organized its 20 000-plus employees into teams. Rewards are structured to return a percentage increase in the bottom line to the team members on the basis of achievements of the team's performance goals.

Promotions, pay raises, and other forms of recognition should be given to employees who are effective collaborative team members. This does not mean that individual contribution is ignored, but rather that it is balanced with selfless contributions to the team. Examples of behaviours that should be rewarded include training new colleagues, sharing information with teammates, helping resolve team conflicts, and mastering new skills in which the team is deficient.[22] Finally, managers cannot forget the inherent rewards that employees can receive from teamwork. Work teams provide camaraderie. It's exciting and satisfying to be an integral part of a successful team. The opportunity to engage in personal development and to help teammates grow can be a very satisfying and rewarding experience for employees.[23]

Turning Groups into Effective Teams

Wayne Gretzky had many excellent players to choose from for the team that would play in the 2006 Winter Olympics.[24] One strategy for choosing players might have been to pick the absolute best players for each position, examining their records during the previous season. Alternatively, it might have made sense to pick very good players, who also know how to work well with other team members. Gretzky chose the latter strategy, picking 20 players who had been on either the 2004 World Cup of Hockey team or the 2002 Winter Olympics team.

Hockey Canada president Bob Nicholson explained the thinking behind Gretzky's strategy: "We've always stated that we want to have players with experience at the Olympics, world championships and players who have won a Cup. You want players around [the Olympics] who have won."

Clearly Gretzky felt that a team, particularly the Olympic team, was more than just the sum of its parts. Gretzky's choice of team members did not pay off, however. Unlike Team Canada's performance in the 2004 World Cup, going undefeated in the six playoff games and never once trailing in a game, Canada was eliminated in the quarter-finals of the 2006 Winter Olympics, and played three scoreless games on the way to Olympic defeat. Hockey Canada president Bob Nicholson summarized what went wrong: "Seventeen power plays (in the three shutout losses) and zero goals, who would have ever expected that? It wasn't one player, it was a group of individuals that couldn't put the puck in the net."

Think About It
How can managers create effective teams?

3 How can groups become effective teams?

Teams are not automatic productivity enhancers. They can also be disappointments. So the challenge is to create effective teams. Effective teams have a number of characteristics, which we review below. In addition, teams need to build group cohesiveness, manage group conflict, and prevent social loafing to perform well. For more insights into creating effective teams, see *Developing Your Interpersonal Skills—Creating Effective Teams* on page 316, at the end of the chapter.

PRISM 9

Characteristics of Effective Teams

How do you build an effective team? Have you ever done so?

Research on teams provides insights into the characteristics associated with effective teams.[25] Let's look more closely at these characteristics, which are shown in Exhibit 10-4.

Clear Goals

High-performance teams have a clear understanding of the goals to be achieved. Members are committed to the team's goals; they know what they are expected to accomplish and understand how they will work together to achieve these goals.

Exhibit 10-4

Characteristics of Effective Teams

Relevant Skills

Effective teams are composed of competent individuals who have the necessary technical and interpersonal skills to achieve the desired goals while working well together. This last point is important since not everyone who is technically competent has the interpersonal skills to work well as a team member.

Mutual Trust

Effective teams are characterized by high levels of mutual trust among members. That is, members believe in each other's ability, character, and integrity. But as you probably know from personal relationships, trust is fragile. For team members to have mutual trust, they must believe that the team is capable of getting the task done and that "the team will not harm the individual or his or her interests."[26] Maintaining this trust requires careful attention by managers.

Unified Commitment

Unified commitment is characterized by dedication to the team's goals and a willingness to expend extraordinary amounts of energy to achieve them. Members of an effective team exhibit intense loyalty and dedication to the team and are willing to do whatever it takes to help their team succeed.

Good Communication

Not surprisingly, effective teams are characterized by good communication. Members convey messages, verbally and nonverbally, to each other in ways that are readily and clearly understood. Also, feedback helps to guide team members and to correct misunderstandings. Like a couple who has been together for many years, members on high-performing teams are able to quickly and efficiently share ideas and feelings.

Negotiating Skills

Effective teams are continually making adjustments as to who does what. This flexibility requires team members to possess negotiating skills. Since problems and relationships are regularly changing in teams, members need to be able to confront and reconcile differences.

All the work that employees do at Whole Foods Market is based around teamwork. Characteristics of effective teams like job skills, commitment, trust, communication, and effective training and support are important for making this kind of structure successful and contributing to the rapid growth of the organic-food retailer.

Appropriate Leadership

Effective leaders can motivate a team to follow it through the most difficult situations. How? By clarifying goals, demonstrating that change is possible by overcoming inertia, increasing the self-confidence of team members, and helping members to more fully realize their potential. Increasingly, effective team leaders act as coaches and facilitators. They help guide and support the team but do not control it. See also *Self-Assessment—How Good Am I at Building and Leading a Team?* on pages 312–313, at the end of the chapter.

group cohesiveness
The degree to which group members are attracted to each other and share the group's goals.

TIPS FOR MANAGERS

Increasing Group Cohesiveness

Increasing socio-emotional cohesiveness

 ✔ Keep the group relatively **small**.

 ✔ Strive for a **favourable public image** to increase the status and prestige of belonging.

 ✔ Encourage **interaction** and **cooperation**.

 ✔ Emphasize members' **common characteristics** and interests.

 ✔ **Point out environmental threats** (e.g., competitors' achievements) to rally the group.

Increasing instrumental cohesiveness

 ✔ Regularly update and **clarify the group's goal(s)**.

 ✔ Give every group member a **vital "piece of the action."**

 ✔ Channel each group member's special talents toward the **common goal(s)**.

 ✔ **Recognize** and equitably reinforce **every member's contributions**.

 ✔ Frequently remind group members **they need each other** to get the job done.[31]

Internal and External Support

The final condition necessary for an effective team is a supportive climate. Internally, the team should have a sound infrastructure, which means having proper training, a clear and reasonable measurement system that team members can use to evaluate their overall performance, an incentive program that recognizes and rewards team activities, and a supportive human resource system. The right infrastructure should support members and reinforce behaviours that lead to high levels of performance. Externally, managers should provide the team with the resources needed to get the job done.

Building Group Cohesiveness

Intuitively, it makes sense that groups in which there is a lot of internal disagreement and lack of cooperation are less effective in completing their tasks than are groups in which members generally agree, cooperate, and like each other. Research in this area has focused on **group cohesiveness**, or the degree to which members are attracted to each other and share the group's goals. Cohesiveness is important because it has been found to be related to a group's productivity.[27]

Research has generally shown that highly cohesive groups are more effective than are less cohesive ones.[28] However, this relationship between cohesiveness and effectiveness is more complex. A key moderating variable is the degree to which the group's attitude aligns with its goals or with the goals of the organization.[29] The more cohesive a group is, the more its members will follow its goals. If the goals are desirable (e.g., high output, quality work,

Exhibit 10-5

The Relationship Between Cohesiveness and Productivity

		Cohesiveness	
		High	**Low**
Alignment of Group and Organizational Goals	**High**	Strong increase in productivity	Moderate increase in productivity
	Low	Decrease in productivity	No significant effect on productivity

cooperation with individuals outside the group), a cohesive group is more productive than a less cohesive group. But if cohesiveness is high and attitudes are unfavourable, productivity decreases. If cohesiveness is low and goals are supported, productivity increases, but not as much as when both cohesiveness and support are high. When cohesiveness is low and goals are not supported, cohesiveness has no significant effect on productivity. These conclusions are illustrated in Exhibit 10-5.

Most studies of cohesiveness focus on *socio-emotional cohesiveness*: the "sense of togetherness that develops when individuals derive emotional satisfaction from group participation."[30] There is also *instrumental cohesiveness*: the "sense of togetherness that develops when group members are mutually dependent on one another because they believe they could not achieve the group's goal by acting separately." Teams need to achieve a balance of these two types of cohesiveness to function well. *Tips for Managers—Increasing Group Cohesiveness* indicates how to increase both socio-emotional and instrumental cohesiveness.

Managing Group Conflict

Another important group process is how a group manages conflict. As a group performs its assigned tasks, disagreements inevitably arise. When we use the term **conflict**, we are referring to *perceived* differences that result in some form of interference or opposition. Whether the differences are real or not is irrelevant. If people in a group perceive that differences exist, then there is conflict. Our definition encompasses the full range of conflict—from subtle or indirect acts to overt acts such as strikes, riots, or wars.

Over the years, three different views have evolved regarding conflict.[32] One view argues that conflict must be avoided—that it indicates a problem within the group. We call this the **traditional view of conflict**. A second view, the **human relations view of conflict**, argues that conflict is a natural and inevitable outcome in any group and need not be negative but, rather, has the potential to be a positive force in contributing to a group's performance. The third and most recent perspective proposes that not only can conflict be a positive force in a group, but also that some conflict is *absolutely necessary* for a group to perform effectively. This third approach is called the **interactionist view of conflict**.

The interactionist view does not suggest that all conflicts are good. Some conflicts are seen as supporting the goals of the work group and improving its performance; these are **functional conflicts** of a constructive nature. Other conflicts are destructive and prevent a group from achieving its goals. These are **dysfunctional conflicts**. Exhibit 10-6 on page 306 illustrates the challenge facing managers. They want to create an environment in which there is healthy conflict that will help the group reach a high level of performance.

Q&A 14.5

Q&A 14.6

conflict
Perceived differences that result in some form of interference or opposition.

traditional view of conflict
The view that all conflict is bad and must be avoided.

human relations view of conflict
The view that conflict is a natural and inevitable outcome in any group and has the potential to be a positive force in contributing to a group's performance.

interactionist view of conflict
The view that some conflict is absolutely necessary for a group to perform effectively.

functional conflicts
Conflicts that support the goals of the work group and improve its performance.

dysfunctional conflicts
Conflicts that are destructive and prevent a group from achieving its goals.

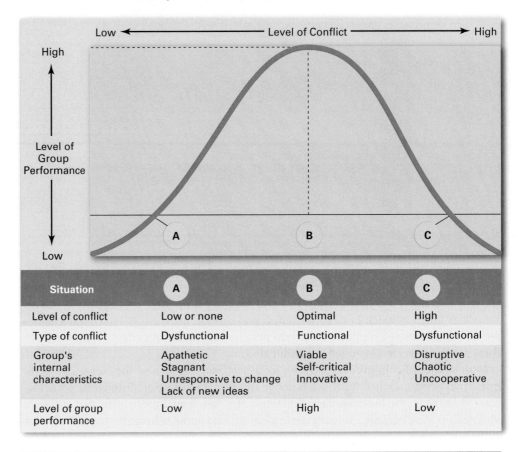

Exhibit 10-6

Conflict and Group Performance

Situation	A	B	C
Level of conflict	Low or none	Optimal	High
Type of conflict	Dysfunctional	Functional	Dysfunctional
Group's internal characteristics	Apathetic Stagnant Unresponsive to change Lack of new ideas	Viable Self-critical Innovative	Disruptive Chaotic Uncooperative
Level of group performance	Low	High	Low

task conflict
Conflict over content and goals of the work.

relationship conflict
Conflict based on interpersonal relationships.

process conflict
Conflict over how the work gets done.

Q&A 14.7, Q&A 14.8

What differentiates functional from dysfunctional conflict? The evidence indicates that you need to look at the *type* of conflict.[33] Three types have been identified: task, relationship, and process.

Task conflict relates to the content and goals of the work. **Relationship conflict** is based on interpersonal relationships. **Process conflict** relates to how the work gets done. Studies demonstrate that relationship conflicts are almost always dysfunctional. Why? It appears that the friction and interpersonal hostilities inherent in relationship conflicts increase personality clashes and decrease mutual understanding, thereby hindering the completion of organizational tasks. On the other hand, low levels of process conflict and low-to-moderate levels of task conflict are functional. For process conflict to be productive, it must be kept to a minimum. Intense arguments about who should do what become dysfunctional when they create uncertainty about task roles, increase the time taken to complete tasks, and lead to members working at cross-purposes. A low-to-moderate level of task conflict consistently demonstrates a positive effect on group performance because it stimulates discussions of ideas that help groups be more innovative.[34] Because we have yet to devise a sophisticated measuring instrument for assessing whether a given task, relationship, or process conflict level is optimal, too high, or too low, the manager must make intelligent judgments.

When group conflict becomes dysfunctional, what can managers do? They can select from five conflict-resolution options: avoiding, accommodating, forcing, compromising, and collaborating.[35] (See Exhibit 10-7 for a description of each of these techniques.) Keep in mind that no one option is ideal for every situation. Which approach to use depends on the manager's desire to be more or less cooperative and more or less assertive.

Exhibit 10-7

Conflict-Resolution Techniques

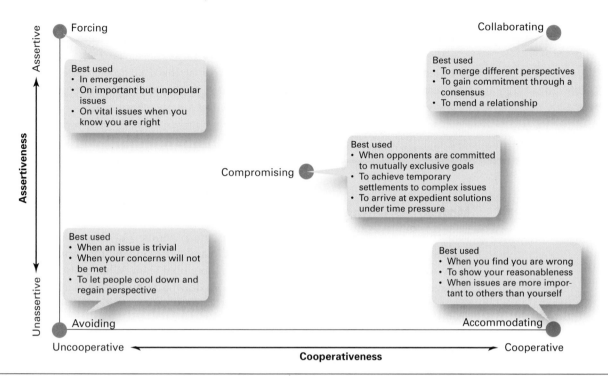

Forcing

Best used
- In emergencies
- On important but unpopular issues
- On vital issues when you know you are right

Collaborating

Best used
- To merge different perspectives
- To gain commitment through a consensus
- To mend a relationship

Compromising

Best used
- When opponents are committed to mutually exclusive goals
- To achieve temporary settlements to complex issues
- To arrive at expedient solutions under time pressure

Best used
- When an issue is trivial
- When your concerns will not be met
- To let people cool down and regain perspective

Best used
- When you find you are wrong
- To show your reasonableness
- When issues are more important to others than yourself

Avoiding

Accommodating

Assertive

Unassertive

Assertiveness

Uncooperative ← **Cooperativeness** → Cooperative

Sources: Adapted from K. W. Thomas, "Conflict and Negotiation Processes in Organizations," in *Handbook of Industrial and Organizational Psychology*, vol. 3, 2nd ed., ed. M. D. Dunnette and L. M. Hough (Palo Alto, CA: Consulting Psychologists Press, 1992), p. 668; and C. K. W. De Dreu, A. Evers, B. Beersma, E. S. Kluwer, and A. Nauta, "A Theory-Based Measure of Conflict Management Strategies in the Workplace," *Journal of Organizational Behavior* 22, no. 6 (September 2001), pp. 645–668. With permission.

Preventing Social Loafing

One of the more important findings related to group size is **social loafing**, which is the tendency of individuals to expend less effort when working with others than when working individually.[36] Social loafing is much more likely to happen in larger groups. This finding directly challenges the logic that the group's productivity should at least equal the sum of the productivity of each group member. What causes social loafing? It may be caused by a belief that others in the group are not doing their fair share. If you see others as lazy or inept, you can reestablish equity by reducing your effort. Another explanation is the dispersion of responsibility. Because the results of the group cannot be attributed to any one person, the relationship between an individual's input and the group's output is clouded. In such situations, individuals may be tempted to become "free riders" and coast on the group's efforts. In other words, there will be a reduction in efficiency when individuals think that their contribution cannot be measured.

For managers, the implications of social loafing are significant. When managers use collective work situations to enhance morale and teamwork, they must also have a way to identify individual efforts. If this is not done, they must weigh the potential losses in productivity from using groups against any possible gains in employee satisfaction.[37]

social loafing
The tendency of individuals to expend less effort when working collectively than when working individually.

Current Challenges in Managing Teams

Managers also face some current challenges in managing global teams. They also have to determine when it is best to use a team.

4 What are some of the current challenges in managing teams?

Exhibit 10-8

Drawbacks and Benefits of Global Teams

Drawbacks	Benefits
• Dislike team members • Mistrust team members • Stereotyping • Communication problems • Stress and tension	• Greater diversity of ideas • Limited groupthink • Increased attention on understanding others' ideas, perspectives, etc.

Source: Based on N. Adler, *International Dimensions in Organizational Behavior*, 4th ed. (Cincinnati, OH: South-Western College Publishing, 2002), pp. 141–147.

Managing Global Teams

Two characteristics of today's organizations are obvious: (1) they are global; and (2) work is increasingly done by groups or teams. This means that any manager is likely, at some point in time, to have to manage a global team. What do we know about managing global teams? We know there are both drawbacks and benefits in using global teams (see Exhibit 10-8). We will look at some of the issues associated with managing global teams.

Group Member Resources in Global Teams

In global organizations, understanding the relationship between group performance and group member resources is more challenging because of the unique cultural characteristics represented by members of a global team. In addition to recognizing team members' abilities, skills, knowledge, and personality, managers need to be familiar with and clearly understand the cultural characteristics of the groups and the group members they manage.[38] For example, is the global team from a culture in which uncertainty avoidance is high? If so, members will not be comfortable dealing with unpredictable and ambiguous tasks. Also, as managers work with global teams, they need to be aware of the potential for stereotyping, which has been shown to be a problem with global teams.[39]

Group Structure

Some of the structural areas where we see differences in managing global teams include conformity, status, social loafing, and cohesiveness.

Conformity Research suggests that conformity to social norms tends to be higher in collectivist cultures than in individualistic cultures.[40] Despite this, however, groupthink (discussed in Chapter 4) tends to be less of a problem in global teams because members are less likely to feel pressured to conform to the ideas, conclusions, and decisions of the group.[41]

Status The importance of status varies between cultures. The French, for example, are extremely status conscious. Also, countries differ on the criteria that confer status. Status for Latin Americans and Asians tends to come from family position and formal roles held in organizations. In contrast, although status is important in countries such as Canada and Australia, it tends to be less "in your face." Also, it tends to be given based on accomplishments rather than on titles and family history. Managers should be sure to understand who and what holds status when interacting with people from a culture different from their own. A Canadian manager who does not understand that office size is not a measure of a Japanese executive's position or who fails to grasp the importance the

British place on family genealogy and social class is likely to unintentionally offend others and lessen his or her interpersonal effectiveness.

Social loafing Social loafing has a Western bias. It is consistent with individualistic cultures, such as Canada and the United States, which are dominated by self-interest. It is not consistent with collectivistic societies, in which individuals are motivated by in-group goals. In studies comparing employees from the United States with employees from the People's Republic of China and Israel (both collectivistic societies), the Chinese and Israelis did not tend to engage in social loafing. In fact, they actually performed better in a group than when working alone.[42]

Cohesiveness Cohesiveness is another group structural element where managers may face special challenges. In a cohesive group, members are unified and "act as one." There is a great deal of camaraderie and group identity is high. In global teams, however, cohesiveness is often more difficult to achieve because of higher levels of mistrust, miscommunication, and stress.[43]

Group Processes

The processes global teams use to do their work can be particularly challenging for managers. For one thing, communication problems often arise because not all team members may be fluent in the team's working language. This can lead to inaccuracies, misunderstandings, and inefficiencies.[44] However, research has also shown that a multicultural global team is better able to make use of the diversity of ideas represented if a wide range of information is used.[45]

Managing conflict in global teams, especially when those teams are virtual teams, is not easy. Conflict in multicultural teams can interfere with how information is used by the team. However, research shows that in collectivistic cultures, a collaborative conflict management style can be most effective.[46]

The Manager's Role

Despite the challenges associated with managing global teams, there are things managers can do to provide the group with an environment in which efficiency and effectiveness are enhanced.[47] First, because communication skills are vital, managers should focus on developing those skills. Also, as we have said earlier, managers must consider cultural differences when deciding what type of global team to use. For example, evidence suggests that self-managed teams have not fared well in Mexico largely due to that culture's low tolerance for ambiguity and uncertainty and employees' strong respect for hierarchical authority.[48] Finally, it is vital that managers be sensitive to the unique differences of each member of the global team. But, it is also important that team members be sensitive to each other.

Beware! Teams Are Not Always the Answer

Do you ever find you are tired of working in a team?

Despite considerable success in the use of teams, they are not necessarily appropriate in all situations. Teamwork takes more time and often more resources than individual work; also, it has increased communication demands, and an increased number of conflicts to be managed and meetings to be run. In the rush to enjoy the benefits of teams, some managers have introduced them into situations in which the work is better done by individuals. A 2003 study by Statistics Canada found that the introduction of teamwork lowered job turnover in the service industries, for both high- and low-skilled employees. However, manufacturing companies experienced higher job turnover if they introduced teamwork and formal teamwork training, compared with not doing so (15.8 percent vs. 10.7 percent).[49]

How do you know if the work of your group would be better done in teams? Three questions can help determine whether a team fits the situation:[50]

- *Can the work be done better by more than one person?* Simple tasks that do not require diverse input are probably better left to individuals.

- *Does the work create a common purpose or set of goals for the people in the group that is more than the sum of individual goals?* For example, many new-car dealer service departments have introduced teams that link customer service personnel, mechanics, parts specialists, and sales representatives. Such teams can better manage collective responsibility for ensuring that customer needs are properly met.

- *Are the members of the group interdependent?* Teams make sense where there is interdependence between tasks; where the success of the whole depends on the success of each one; and where the success of each one depends on the success of the others. Soccer, for example, is an obvious *team* sport because of the interdependence of the players. Swim teams, by contrast, are not really teams, but groups of individuals whose total performance is merely the sum of the individual performances.

Researchers have outlined the conditions under which organizations would find teams more useful: "when work processes cut across functional lines; when speed is important (and complex relationships are involved); when the organization mirrors a complex, differentiated, and rapidly changing market environment; when innovation and learning have priority; when the tasks that have to be done require online integration of highly interdependent performers."[51]

SUMMARY AND IMPLICATIONS

❶ What are the stages of team development? The five stages are forming, storming, norming, performing, and adjourning. These stages describe how teams evolve over time, although teams do not necessarily go through these stages in a completely linear fashion. Some researchers argue that the effectiveness of work teams increases at advanced stages, but it's not that simple. That assumption may be generally true, but what makes a team effective is a complex issue. It's better to think of this model as a general framework of how teams develop.

When Team Canada started practising for the 2006 Winter Olympics, individual hockey players knew how to play the game, but team members needed to learn how to work together, even though they were usually opponents.

❷ How do individuals become team players? Many individuals resist being team players. To improve the odds that a team will function well, managers can select the right people to be on a team, train individuals in how to work on teams, and make sure that rewards encourage individuals to be cooperative team players.

For the 2006 Winter Olympics, Wayne Gretzky put together a group of players who had international playing experience, hoping this would be enough to create a winning team.

❸ How can groups become effective teams? The characteristics associated with effective teams include clear goals, relevant skills, mutual trust, unified commitment, good communication, negotiating skills, appropriate leadership, and internal and external support. Teams also need to build group cohesiveness, manage group conflict, and prevent social loafing to be effective.

○ ○ ○   For Team Canada players, perhaps the most important factors in working toward win-
○ ○ ○   ning the 2004 World Cup of Hockey were learning to trust each other, communicating well, and having the right leadership. The same team chemistry was not apparent in the 2006 Winter Olympics.

❹ What are some of the current challenges in managing teams? Managers face a variety of challenges in managing global teams. The cultural differences of the team members may lead to more conflict, at least initially. As well, there may be an increase in communication difficulties. Another challenge that managers face is to consider whether a team is really necessary to get the work done.

Management @ Work

READING FOR COMPREHENSION

1. Contrast (1) self-managed and cross-functional teams; and (2) virtual and face-to-face teams.

2. How do virtual teams enhance productivity?

3. What problems might surface in teams during each of the five stages of team development?

4. Describe three ways managers can try to encourage individuals to become team players.

5. Why do you believe mutual trust is important in developing high-performing work teams?

6. Why might a manager want to stimulate conflict in a group or team? How could conflict be stimulated?

LINKING CONCEPTS TO PRACTICE

1. How do you explain the rapidly increasing popularity of work teams in countries such as Canada and the United States, whose national cultures place a high value on individualism?

2. Think of a team to which you belong (or have belonged). Trace its development through the five stages of team development shown in Exhibit 10-3 on page 299. How closely did its development parallel the team development model? How might the team development model have been used to improve the team's effectiveness?

3. "All work teams are work groups, but not all work groups are work teams." Do you agree or disagree with this statement? Discuss.

4. Would you prefer to work alone or as part of a team? Why? Support your response with data from your self-assessments.

5. Describe a situation in which individuals, acting independently, outperform teams in an organization.

SELF-ASSESSMENT

How Good Am I at Building and Leading a Team?

Use the following rating scale to respond to the 18 statements on building and leading an effective team:[52]

1 = Strongly Disagree 2 = Disagree 3 = Slightly Disagree 4 = Slightly Agree 5 = Agree 6 = Strongly Agree

1. I am knowledgeable about the different stages of development that teams can go through in their life cycles.	1 2 3 4 5 6
2. When a team forms, I make certain that all team members are introduced to one another at the outset.	1 2 3 4 5 6
3. When the team first comes together, I provide directions, answer team members' questions, and clarify goals, expectations, and procedures.	1 2 3 4 5 6
4. I help team members establish a foundation of trust among one another and between themselves and me.	1 2 3 4 5 6
5. I ensure that standards of excellence, not mediocrity or mere acceptability, characterize the team's work.	1 2 3 4 5 6
6. I provide a great deal of feedback to team members regarding their performance.	1 2 3 4 5 6
7. I encourage team members to balance individual autonomy with interdependence among other team members.	1 2 3 4 5 6

8. I help team members become at least as committed to the success of the team as to their own personal success.   1 2 3 4 5 6

9. I help members learn to play roles that assist the team in accomplishing its tasks as well as building strong interpersonal relationships.   1 2 3 4 5 6

10. I articulate a clear, exciting, passionate vision of what the team can achieve.   1 2 3 4 5 6

11. I help team members become committed to the team vision.   1 2 3 4 5 6

12. I encourage a win/win philosophy in the team; that is, when one member wins, every member wins.   1 2 3 4 5 6

13. I help the team avoid groupthink or making the group's survival more important than accomplishing its goal.   1 2 3 4 5 6

14. I use formal process management procedures to help the group become faster, more efficient, and more productive, and to prevent errors.   1 2 3 4 5 6

15. I encourage team members to represent the team's vision, goals, and accomplishments to outsiders.   1 2 3 4 5 6

16. I diagnose and capitalize on the team's core competence.   1 2 3 4 5 6

17. I encourage the team to achieve dramatic breakthrough innovations as well as small continuous improvements.   1 2 3 4 5 6

18. I help the team work toward preventing mistakes, not just correcting them after the fact.   1 2 3 4 5 6

Scoring Key

To calculate your total score, add up your scores on the 18 individual items.

Analysis and Interpretation

The authors of this instrument propose that it assesses team development behaviours in 5 areas: diagnosing team development (statements 1, 16); managing the forming stage (2–4); managing the norming stage (6–9, 13); managing the storming stage (10–12, 14, 15); and managing the performing stage (5, 17, 18). Your score will range between 18 and 108, with higher scores indicating greater ability at building and leading an effective team.

Based on a norm group of 500 business students, the following can help estimate where you are in relation to others:

Total score of 95 or more = You are in the top quartile

72–94 = You are in the second quartile
60–71 = You are in the third quartile
Less than 60 = You are in the bottom quartile

More Self-Assessments

To learn more about your skills, abilities, and interests, take the following self-assessments on MyManagementLab at www.pearsoned.ca/mymanagementlab:

- II.A.2.—How Good Are My Listening Skills?
- II.B.4.—Do Others See Me as Trustworthy?

MANAGEMENT FOR YOU TODAY

Dilemma

One of your instructors has just informed your class that you will be working on a new major assignment worth 30 percent of your course mark. The assignment is to be done in teams of 7. Realistically you will need to function as a virtual team, as it turns out that each of you has a different work and class schedule, so that there is almost no time when more than 3 people could meet face to face. As you know, virtual teams have benefits, but they can also face problems. How will you build group cohesiveness in this team? What norms might help the team function, and how should the norms be decided? What will you do to prevent social loafing?

Becoming a Manager

- Use any opportunities that come up to work in a group. Note things such as stages of team development, roles, norms, social loafing, and so forth.

- When confronted with conflicts, pay attention to how you manage or resolve them.

- In group projects, try different techniques for improving the group's creativity.

- When you see a successful team, try to assess what makes it successful.

WORKING TOGETHER: TEAM-BASED EXERCISE

Puzzle Building

What happens when a group is presented with a task that must be completed within a certain time frame? Does the group exhibit characteristics of the stages of team development? Your instructor will divide the class into groups and give you instructions about building a puzzle or watching others do so.

Note: Instructors can find the instructions for this exercise in the Instructor's Resource Manual.

ETHICS IN ACTION

Ethical Dilemma Exercise: Does Everyone Have to Be a Team Player?

You are a production manager at a Saturn plant. One of your newest employees is Barbara Petersen, who has a bachelor's degree in engineering and a recently completed master's degree in business. You hired Barbara for a position in supply chain management.

You have recently been chosen to head up a cross-functional team to look at ways to reduce inventory costs. This team would essentially be a permanent task force. You have decided to have team members come from supplier relations, cost accounting, transportation, and production systems. You have also decided to include Barbara on the team. While she has been at Saturn only for four months, you have been impressed with her energy, intelligence, and industriousness. You think this would be an excellent assignment for her to increase her visibility in the company and expand her understanding of the company's inventory system.

When you called Barbara into your office to give her the good news, you were quite surprised by her response. "I'm not a team player," she said. "I didn't join clubs in high school. I was on the track team and I did well, but track is an individual sport. We were a team only in the sense that we rode together in the same bus to away meets. In university, I avoided the whole sorority thing. Some people may call me a loner. I don't think that's true. I can work well with others, but I hate meetings and committees. To me, they waste so much time. And anything you're working on with a group, you've got all these different personalities that you have to adjust for. I'm an independent operator. Give me a job and I'll get it done. I work harder than anyone I know—and I give my employer 150 percent. But I don't want my performance to be dependent on the other people in my group. They may not work as hard as I will. Someone is sure to shirk some of their responsibilities. I just don't want to be a team player."

What do you do? Should you give Barbara the option of joining the inventory cost reduction team? Is it unethical for you to require someone like Barbara to do his or her job as part of a team?

Thinking Critically About Ethics

You have been hired as a summer intern in the events planning department of a public relations firm in Calgary. After working there about a month, you conclude that the attitude in the office is "anything goes." Employees know that supervisors will not discipline them for ignoring company rules. For example, employees have to turn in expense reports, but the process is a joke; nobody submits receipts to verify reimbursement, and nothing is ever said. In fact, when you tried to turn in your receipts with your expense report, you were told, "Nobody else turns in receipts and you don't really need to, either." You know that no expense cheque has ever been denied because of failure to turn in a receipt, even though the employee handbook says that receipts are required. Also, your co-workers use company phones for personal long-distance calls even though that is prohibited by the employee handbook. And one permanent employee told you to "help yourself" to any paper, pens, or pencils you might need here or at home. What are the norms of this group? Suppose that you were the supervisor in this area. How would you go about changing the norms?

CASE APPLICATION

Samsung Electronics

Samsung Electronics is now the world's largest and most profitable consumer electronics company.[53] In 2006, it ranked higher than Sony as the world's most valuable consumer electronics brand, according to the most recent valuable global brands survey done by the Interbrand Consulting Group. Its clever product designs have won over consumers and won numerous awards.

Samsung Group was founded as a trucking company in the 1930s and in the 1960s became one of several *chaebol* (large conglomerates) "shaped by the Korean government and protected from foreign competition by import duties and other government-sponsored regulations." The electronics division, Samsung Electronics, is by far the largest and most global of the Samsung businesses.

At the company's design centre just a few blocks away from headquarters, in Seoul, designers work in small teams with three to five members coming from various specialty areas and levels of seniority. Even though Korean culture has

loosened up somewhat, respect for elders and a reluctance to speak out of turn are still the norm. But here at Samsung's design centre, there is no dress code and team members work as equals. Everyone—even the younger staffers who often have their hair dyed green or pink—is encouraged to speak up and challenge their superiors.

Although Samsung Electronics is sitting on top now, Kim Byung Cheol, a senior executive, is worried about his company's future. Why? Because Samsung "still has not mastered one crucial factor: originality." Much of Samsung's success in electronics can be traced to its ability to mimic and enhance others' inventions, but it has never been the design innovator. Kim says, "We are at a pivotal moment for the company. If we don't become an innovator, we could end up like one of those Japanese companies, mired in difficulties." What can Kim and his managers do to encourage innovation and originality with the design centre teams?

DEVELOPING YOUR DIAGNOSTIC AND ANALYTICAL SKILLS

Mixing It Up

How do you combine two packaged-food companies, both with very well-known household brand names, and make the new company work?[54] That's the challenge managers at General Mills faced when it acquired Pillsbury. The company's chief learning officer, Kevin Wilde, said, "Let's get the best out of both of our marketing organizations. And let's not stop there." So they decided to identify, share, and integrate the best practices from both companies. And employee teams played a major role in how the company proceeded.

An intensive training program called Brand Champions was created and launched. The program was designed not just for marketing specialists but for all employees from different functional areas who worked on particular brands. These cross-functional teams attended the in-house training together as a unified group. According to one of the program developers, specific benefits of including these teams soon became evident. "A person from human resources, for instance, would ask a provocative question precisely because she wasn't a marketer. And you'd see the look on the marketers' faces: Whoa, I never thought of that." It helped employees understand and appreciate different perspectives.

Another benefit of including people from different functional areas was improved communication throughout the company. People were no longer griping about what other functional areas were doing. Employees began to understand how the other functional areas worked and how each

area's contribution was important to the overall success of the company.

The training program has been so successful that now General Mills's production plants have asked for a mini-version of the course. "They want to understand the language marketers speak and why things are done as they are." Oh . . . and there's one other example of how successful the program has been. Betty Crocker is well known for packaged cake mixes and less so for cookie mixes. Inspired by input from the group, the cookie-mix team decided to go after scratch bakers (people who bake from scratch rather than from a boxed mix). As one person said, they were "taking on grandma." The cookie mixes were reformulated, and now the brand owns 90 percent of the dry cookie mix category.

Questions

1. What benefits did the cross-functional teams bring to General Mills?

2. What challenges would there be in creating an effective cross-functional team? How could managers deal with these challenges?

3. Explain how each of the characteristics of effective teams (see Exhibit 10–3 on page 299) would be important for an effective cross-functional team.

DEVELOPING YOUR INTERPERSONAL SKILLS

Creating Effective Teams

About the Skill

A team is different from a group because its members are committed to a common purpose, have a set of specific performance goals, and hold themselves mutually accountable for the team's results. Teams can produce outputs that are greater than the sum of the individual contributions of its members. The primary force that makes a work group an effective team—that is, a real high-performing team—is its emphasis on performance.

Steps in Developing the Skill

Managers and team leaders have a significant impact on a team's effectiveness. You can be more successful at creating an effective team if you use the following nine suggestions:[55]

1. **Establish a common purpose.** An effective team needs a common purpose to which all members aspire. This purpose is a vision. It's broader than any specific goals. This common purpose provides direction, momentum, and commitment for team members.

2. **Assess team strengths and weaknesses.** Team members will have different strengths and weaknesses. Knowing these strengths and weaknesses can help the team leader build on the strengths and compensate for the weaknesses.

3. **Develop specific individual goals.** Specific individual goals help lead team members to achieve higher performance. In addition, specific goals facilitate clear communication and help maintain the focus on getting results.

4. **Get agreement on a common approach for achieving goals.** Goals are the ends a team strives to attain. Defining and agreeing on a common approach ensures the team's unity regarding the means for achieving those ends.

5. **Encourage acceptance of responsibility for both individual and team performance.** Successful teams make members individually and jointly accountable for the team's purpose, goals, and approach. Members understand what they are individually responsible for and what they are jointly responsible for.

6. **Build mutual trust among members.** When there is trust, team members believe in the integrity, character, and ability of each other. When trust is lacking, members are unable to depend on each other. Teams that lack trust tend to be short-lived.

7. **Maintain an appropriate mix of team member skills and personalities.** Team members come to the team with different skills and personalities. To perform effectively, teams need three types of skills. First, teams need people with technical expertise. Next, they need people with problem-solving and decision-making skills to identify problems, generate alternatives, evaluate those alternatives, and make competent choices. Finally, teams need people with good interpersonal skills.

8. **Provide needed training and resources.** Team leaders need to make sure that their teams have both the training and the resources they need to accomplish their goals.

9. **Create opportunities for small achievements.** Building an effective team takes time. Team members have to learn to think and work as a team. New teams cannot be expected to hit home runs every time they come to bat, especially at the beginning. Instead, team members should be encouraged to try for small achievements at the beginning.

Practising the Skill

You are the leader of a five-member project team that has been assigned the task of moving your engineering firm into the new booming area of high-speed rail construction. You and your team members have been researching the field, identifying specific business opportunities, negotiating alliances with equipment vendors, and evaluating high-speed rail experts and consultants from around the world. Throughout the process, Tonya, a highly qualified and respected engineer, has challenged everything you say during team meetings and in the workplace. For example, at a meeting two weeks ago, you presented the team with a list of 10 possible high-speed rail projects that had been identified by the team, and started evaluating your organization's ability to compete for them. Tonya contradicted virtually all your comments, questioned your statistics, and was quite pessimistic about the possibility of contracts. After this latest display of displeasure, two other group members, Liam and Ahmed, came to you and complained that Tonya's actions were damaging the team's effectiveness. You originally put Tonya on the team for her unique expertise and insight. What should you say to Tonya, and how can you help get the team on the right track to reach its full potential?

MANAGING WORKFORCE DIVERSITY

The Challenge of Managing Diverse Teams

Understanding and managing teams composed of people who are similar can be difficult! Add in diverse members and managing teams can be even more of a challenge. However, the benefits to be gained from the diverse perspectives, skills, and abilities often more than offset the extra effort.[56] How can you meet the challenge of coordinating a diverse work team? It's important to stress four critical interpersonal behaviours: understanding, empathy, tolerance, and communication.

You know that people are not the same, yet they need to be treated fairly and equitably. And differences (cultural, physical, or other) can cause people to behave in different ways. Team leaders need to understand and accept these differences. Each and every team member should be encouraged to do the same.

Empathy is closely related to understanding. As a team leader, you should try to understand others' perspectives.

Tolerance is another important interpersonal behaviour in managing diverse teams. The fact that you understand that people are different and you empathize with them does not mean that it's any easier to accept different perspectives or behaviours. But it's important to be tolerant in dealing with diverse ages, gender, and cultural backgrounds—to allow team members the freedom to be themselves. Part of being tolerant is being open-minded about different values, attitudes, and behaviours.

Finally, open communication is important to managing a diverse team. Diversity problems may intensify if people are afraid or unwilling to openly discuss issues that concern them. Communication within a diverse team needs to be two-way. If a person wants to know whether a certain behaviour is offensive to someone else, it's best to ask. Likewise, a person who is offended by a certain behaviour of someone else should explain his or her concerns and ask that person to stop. As long as these communication exchanges are handled in a non-threatening, low-key, and friendly manner, they generally will have positive outcomes. Finally, it helps to have an atmosphere within the team that supports and celebrates diversity.

Put yourself in the place of an Asian woman who has joined a team of Caucasian and Hispanic men. How can you be made to feel more welcome and comfortable with the team? As the Asian woman, what could you do to help the team get along well together and also help your transition to the team?

Continuing Case: Starbucks

Once people are hired or brought into organizations, managers must oversee and coordinate their work so that organizational goals can be pursued and achieved.[1] This is the leading function of management, and it's an important one! However, it also can be quite challenging. Managing people successfully means understanding their attitudes, behaviours, personalities, individual and team work efforts, motivation, conflicts, and so forth. That is not an easy thing to do. In fact, understanding how people behave and why they do the things they do is downright difficult at times. Starbucks has worked hard to create a workplace environment in which employees (partners) are encouraged to and want to put forth their best efforts. President, chair, and CEO Howard Schultz says, "We all want the same thing as people—to be respected and valued as employees and appreciated as customers."

Starbucks—Focus on Individuals and Teamwork

Even with some 170 000 full- and part-time partners around the world, one thing that has been important to Schultz from day one is the relationship he has with employees. He says, "We know that our people are the heart and soul of our success." And one way that Starbucks demonstrates the concern it has for the relationship with its partners is through an attitude survey that is administered approximately every 18 months. This survey "gives partners a voice in shaping their partner experience." It also measures "overall satisfaction and, more important, partner engagement—the degree to which partners are connected to the company." It's been an effective way for Starbucks to show that it cares about what its employees think.

The most recent partner view survey was conducted in fiscal 2006 with partners around the globe. About 84 percent of the partners responded to the survey—much higher than the number of respondents to the previous survey in 2005 in which the partner response rate was only 64 percent. Responses to questions about partner satisfaction and partner engagement were quite positive,

although they showed a drop from the 2005 survey: In 2006, 86 percent of partners said they were satisfied or very satisfied, and 69 percent said they were engaged with the company. (The numbers in 2005 were 87 percent satisfied and 73 percent engaged.) In addition, partners specifically said they "Know what is expected of them at work; believe someone at work cares about them; and work for managers who promote work/life balance." But partners identified some areas where they felt improvements were needed. These included, "Pay and benefits; communication within and between groups; and future job opportunities." Starbucks' managers took specific actions to address these concerns.

Every organization needs employees who will be able to do their jobs efficiently and effectively. Starbucks states that it wants employees who are "adaptable, self-motivated, passionate, creative team players." As you can see, this "ideal" Starbucks' partner should have individual strengths and should be able to work as part of a team. In the retail store setting, especially, individuals must work together as a team to provide the experience that customers expect when they walk into a Starbucks. If that does not happen, the company's ability to pursue its mission and goals is likely to be affected.

Starbucks—Motivating Employees

A story from Schultz's childhood provides some clues into what has shaped his philosophy about how to treat people. Schultz's father worked hard at various blue-collar jobs. However, when he did not work, he did not get paid. Schultz was seven years old when his father broke his ankle, and the family "had no income, no health insurance, no worker's compensation, nothing to fall back on." The image of his father "slumped on the couch with his leg in a cast unable to work or earn money left a lasting impression." Many years later, when his father died of lung cancer, "he had no savings, no pension, and more important, he had never attained fulfillment and dignity from work he found meaningful." The

Locals and tourists alike enjoy Starbucks beverages in Shanghai, China.

sad realities of the types of work environments his father endured had a powerful effect on Schultz, and he vowed that if he were "ever in a position where I could make a difference, I wouldn't leave people behind." And those personal experiences have shaped the way that Starbucks cares for its partners—the relationships and commitments the company has with each and every employee.

One of the best reflections of how Starbucks treats its eligible part- and full-time partners is its Total Pay package, which includes competitive base pay, bonuses, a comprehensive health plan, paid time-off plans, stock options, a savings program, and partner perks (which includes a pound of coffee each week). Although specific benefits differ among regions and countries, all Starbucks international partners share the "Total Pay" philosophy. For instance, in Malaysia and Thailand, partners are provided extensive training opportunities to further their careers, in addition to health insurance, paid vacation,

sick leave, and other benefits. In Turkey, the "Total Pay" package for Starbucks' partners includes transportation subsidies and access to a company doctor who provides free treatment.

Partner (employee) recognition is important to Starbucks. The company currently has 18 formal recognition programs in place that partners can use as tools to encourage, reward, and inspire one another. These programs range from formal company awards to informal special acknowledgments given by co-workers. One of the newest "tools"—developed in response to suggestions on the partner survey—is an on-the-spot recognition card that celebrates partner and team successes.

To assist partners who are facing particularly difficult circumstances (such as natural disaster, fire, illness), the company has a CUP (Caring Unites Partners) fund that provides financial support. After hurricanes Katrina and Rita in 2005, more than 300 partners from the Gulf Coast region

Partner recognition is important to Starbucks.

received approximately $260 000 in assistance from the CUP fund. This is the type of caring and compassion that Schultz vowed to provide after seeing his father not able to work and without an income because of a broken ankle.

In 2006, Starbucks Canada ranked ninth among the "Most Admired Corporate Cultures" in a study conducted by Waterstone Human Capital and *Canadian Business* and in 2005 was named one of "Canada's Most Responsible Companies" by *Report on Business* magazine.

Starbucks—Fostering Leadership

Not surprisingly, Schultz has some definite views about leading and leadership. He says, "Being a great leader means finding the balance between celebrating success and not embracing the status quo. Being a great leader also means identifying a path we need to go down and creating enough confidence in our people so they follow it and don't veer off course because it's an easier route to go." He also has this to say about leadership: "The art of leadership is making sure we don't allow the scale and size of the company to change the methodology of how we conduct ourselves. We have to be careful not to let our values be compromised by an ambition to grow."

Since 1982, Schultz has led Starbucks in a way that has allowed the company to successfully grow and meet and exceed its goals and to do so ethically and responsibly. From the creation of the company's Guiding Principles to the various innovative strategic initiatives, Schultz has never veered from his belief about what Starbucks, the company, could be and should be.

Starbucks also recognizes the importance of having individuals with excellent leadership skills throughout the company. In addition to the leadership development training for upper-level managers, Starbucks offers a program called Learning to Lead for hourly employees (baristas) to develop leadership skills. This training program also covers store operations and effective management practices. In addition, Starbucks offers to managers at all organizational levels additional training courses on coaching and providing feedback to help managers improve their people skills.

Questions

1. Do the overwhelmingly positive results from the partner view survey surprise you? Why or why not? Do you think giving employees an opportunity to express their opinions in something like an attitude survey is beneficial? Why or why not?

2. How might the results of the partner survey affect the way a local store manager does his or her job? How about a district manager? How about the senior vice-president of store development? Do you think there are differences in the impact of employee surveys on how managers at different organizational levels lead? Why or why not?

3. Discuss the "ideal" Starbucks employee in terms of the various personality trait theories.

4. Describe in your own words the workplace environment that Starbucks has tried to create. What impact might such an environment have on motivating employees?

5. Using the job characteristics model in Exhibit 9-5 on page 272, redesign a part-time hourly employee's job to be more motivating. Do the same with a store manager's job.

6. Does Starbucks "care" too much for its partners? Can a company ever treat its employees too well? Why or why not?

7. Howard Schultz says, "We all want the same thing as people—to be respected and valued as employees and appreciated as customers." Does the company respect and value its partners (employees)? Explain. What do you think this implies for its employee relationships?

8. Describe Howard Schultz's leadership style. Would his approach be appropriate in other types of organizations? Why or why not?

9. Do you agree that leadership succession planning is important? Why or why not?

10. What is Starbucks doing "right" with respect to the leading function? Are they doing anything "wrong?" Explain.

11. Which of the company's Guiding Principles influence the leading function of management? Explain how the one(s) you chose would affect how Starbucks' managers deal with (a) work team behaviour issues; (b) motivational techniques; and (c) leadership styles or approaches.

VIDEO CASE INCIDENTS

Work–Life Balance and Motivation: Ernst & Young

Ernst & Young, the third-largest US accounting firm, increased its employee retention rate by 5 percent as a result of a human resource initiative to put "people first." By creating a feedback-rich culture, building great résumés for its 160 000 employees in New York City and around the world, and giving employees time and freedom to pursue personal goals, Ernst & Young has reaped the benefits of a highly motivated workforce. The company uses mandatory goal setting, provides employees with learning opportunities in areas of interest, and measures human resource processes using an employee survey to evaluate the workplace environment. While conceding that everyone is somewhat motivated by money, Jim Freer, vice-chair of people, believes that the way a person is treated is the determining factor in a person's level of performance. "People don't leave organizations," he says. "They leave managers."

QUESTIONS

1. *For analysis:* How might the job characteristics model be useful to managers at Ernst & Young?

2. *For analysis:* Recently, Ernst & Young was barred from accepting any new audit clients in the United States for six months after an SEC administrative judge called Ernst & Young "reckless," "highly unreasonable," and "negligent" in forming a business relationship with an audit client, PeopleSoft. As a student intern at the firm, how might this affect your career plans? Explain.

3. *For application:* In light of the damage to the firm's public image and the consequential six-month ban on new business, what steps would you take as a manager to maintain employee motivation at Ernst & Young?

4. *For application:* How would you suggest that diversity initiative managers at Ernst & Young create an inclusive environment that will motivate employees from diverse cultural backgrounds to excel?

5. *For debate:* According to Richard Whiteley, author of Love the Work You're With, by discovering your purpose in life, you can increase your job satisfaction. Would you agree that Ernst & Young's "people first" initiative supports this viewpoint? Explain why you feel the human resource initiative either supports or contradicts Richard Whiteley's premise.

Sources: "Ernst & Young" (video), Pearson Prentice Hall Management Video Library; and M. Goldstein, "Ernst & Young Hit Hard in PeopleSoft Case," *TheStreet.com*, April 16, 2004, www.thestreet.com/story/10154603/ernst-young-hit-hard-in-peoplesoft-case.html (accessed August 31, 2009).

Millionaire on a Mission

Bill Young is a millionaire with a heart. After making millions leading high-growth entrepreneurial organizations, he decided to invest in helping others. He founded Toronto-based Social Capital Partners (SCP) in 2001. SCP provides support to businesses that hire people who often have difficulties finding employment: youths, single mothers, Aboriginal peoples, new immigrants, people with disabilities, and those with substance abuse issues.

SCP provides start-up capital to business ventures that it thinks will be able to grow and turn a profit within about three years. The business owners must commit to helping improve the lives of their employees by making them financially self-sufficient while providing training and other support as necessary.

The types of businesses supported by SCP are known as "social enterprises." They look like typical businesses, except most of their employees come from groups that rely heavily on government assistance to live and have found it nearly impossible to get full-time jobs for a variety of reasons. These businesses have a "double bottom line": "a financial bottom line like traditional businesses but also a social bottom line—getting people who have traditionally faced significant employment barriers back into the economic mainstream."

SCP funds a number of social enterprises, including Winnipeg-based Inner City Renovation (ICR). ICR, founded in August 2002, is a construction and renovation company that works mainly on nonprofit housing projects. The company's work helps address the lack of affordable housing in Winnipeg, and also provides employment to Aboriginal peoples who live in the inner city. Employees often work on houses in their own neighbourhoods, which means that their work is also improving their local environment. ICR's employees earn a steady income, and also learn a skilled trade that they can use in the future. An Aboriginal social worker on staff helps employees address personal problems, including alcohol and chemical dependency.

By mid-2004, SCP and Winnipeg-based Community Ownership Solutions had invested $100 000 in ICR. The company generated almost $1 million in revenue after its first year, but also suffered a $350 000 loss. By the end of 2005, however, the company generated more than $1 million in revenue, with a loss of only $3000. Young acknowledges that ICR is a "wonderful learning experience. It's not like it's gone smoothly. It's such an exciting model, this notion of combining housing and employment. It's taking a radically different approach to structural social problems in a lot of urban areas. There are exciting implications, if we can make this work."

QUESTIONS

1. *For analysis:* What leadership style(s) might be effective when dealing with employees who have personal challenges, such as those who are employed by Inner City Renovation?

2. *For analysis:* From a leadership perspective, what are the advantages and disadvantages of leading a company identified as a social enterprise?

3. *For application:* Inner City Renovation would like to reduce the absenteeism and turnover rates of its employees. How should it go about doing this?

4. *For application:* What are some of the challenges that Bill Young faces in trying to identify social enterprises to invest in?

5. *For debate:* "Only money motivates employees. Inner City Renovation should pay its employees more in order to solve its turnover problems." Do you agree or disagree with this statement? Explain.

Sources: "Social Capitalist," *CBC Venture*, February 29, 2004, 916, VA–2050 D; Social Capital Partners website, www.socialcapitalpartners.ca (accessed August 31, 2009); M. Cook, "Chasing the Double Bottom Line: Series: The Charity Industry," *Ottawa Citizen*, March 1, 2004, p. D7; and http://socialcapitalpartners.ca/images/uploads/docs/ICR_SROI_2005.ppt#258,1,Slide 1 (accessed August 31, 2009).

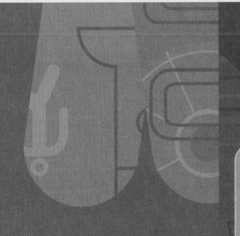

After you have completed your study of Part 4, do the following exercises on MyManagementLab at www.pearsoned.ca/mymanagementlab:

- *You're the Manager: Putting Ethics into Action* (**Avon Products**)

- *Passport, Scenario 1* (**Robert Mathis, DaimlerChrysler**), *Scenario 2* (**Mary Chang**), and *Scenario 3* (**Jean Claude Moreau, Bon Appétit**)

Foundations of Control

How do I evaluate the effectiveness of my plans?

1   What is control?

2   What is the control process?

3   When should controls be introduced?

4   What methods of control do managers use?

5   How do financial and information controls help managers monitor performance?

6   What are some current issues in control?

When Li Ka-shing first invested in Calgary-based Husky Oil (now Husky Energy) in 1986, buying 52 percent of its shares, the company had just posted its first year-end loss in the company's history.[1] The company had no cash on hand, shares had dropped to half of their 1981 value, and the company's debt was growing. Bob Blair, then the CEO at Husky, turned to Li. "We required a lot of capital, more than Husky could generate from its own cash flow," says Blair, in explaining why he approached his friend Li, a wealthy Hong Kong businessman, to invest in the company. In 1991, Li and his holding company bought 43 percent more of the company.

After the 1991 investment, Li immediately sent John Chin-Sung Lau (at right) to Calgary to turn the company around. Li wanted to halt the company's large losses and the "wild expansions" of Husky's previous management. Appointed vice-president at the time, Lau had difficulty working with Husky president Art Price. Lau found Price to be "a hopeless free-spender,"

just trying to maintain his position as president.

Lau had a difficult task in front of him to make Husky profitable.

Think About It

What is organizational control? Put yourself in John Lau's shoes. How can he use control to make Husky successful? What did he need to do to turn Husky Energy into one of Canada's largest oil and gas enterprises?

In today's competitive global marketplace, managers want their organizations to achieve high levels of performance, and one way they can do that is by searching out the best practices successful organizations are using. By comparing themselves against the best, managers look for specific performance gaps and areas for improvement—areas where better controls over the work being done are needed.

As we will see in this chapter, John Lau understands the importance of management controls. No matter how thorough the planning, a decision still may be poorly implemented without a satisfactory control system in place. This chapter describes controls for monitoring and measuring performance. It also looks at how to create a well-designed organizational control system.

What Is Control?

Both the viewing public and NASA officials were devastated by the tragic *Columbia* shuttle disaster in February 2003. Investigations of the tragedy suggest that organizational safety controls may not have been as thorough as they should have been.[2] When problems were spotted, managers might have been too quick to dismiss them as non-life-threatening,

1 What is control?

and in this situation that choice might have led to disastrous consequences. Although most managers will not face such tragic consequences if they ignore signs that something may be wrong, this example does point out the importance of control.

What is **control**? It's the process of monitoring activities to ensure that they are being accomplished as planned, and correcting any significant deviations. All managers should be involved in the control function even if their units are performing as planned. Managers cannot really know whether their units are performing properly until they have evaluated what activities have been done and have compared the actual performance with the desired standard.[3] An effective control system ensures that activities are completed in ways that lead to the attainment of the organization's goals. The criterion that determines the effectiveness of a control system is how well it facilitates goal achievement. The more it helps managers achieve their organization's goals, the better the control system.[4]

> **control**
> The process of monitoring activities to ensure that they are being accomplished as planned, and correcting any significant deviations.

Q&A 15.1, Q&A 15.2

Performance Standards

To achieve control, performance standards must exist. These standards are the specific goals created during the planning process. **Performance** is the end result of an activity. Whether that activity is hours of intense practice before a concert or race or whether it's carrying out job responsibilities as efficiently and effectively as possible, performance is what results from that activity.

> **performance**
> The end result of an activity.

Managers are concerned with **organizational performance**—the accumulated end results of all the organization's work activities. It's a complex but important concept. Managers need to understand the factors that contribute to a high level of organizational performance. After all, they do not want (or intend) to manage their way to mediocre performance. They *want* their organizations, work units, or work groups to achieve high levels of performance, no matter what mission, strategies, or goals are being pursued.

> **organizational performance**
> The accumulated end results of all the organization's work activities.

Q&A 15.3

Measures of Organizational Performance

All managers must know what organizational performance measures will give them the information they need. The most frequently used organizational performance measures include organizational productivity, organizational effectiveness, and industry and company rankings.

Organizational Productivity

Productivity is the overall output of goods or services produced divided by the inputs needed to generate that output. Organizations strive to be productive. They want the most goods and services produced using the least amount of inputs. Output is measured by the sales revenue an organization receives when those goods and services are sold (selling price × number sold). Input is measured by the costs of acquiring and transforming the organizational resources into the outputs.

> **productivity**
> The overall output of goods or services produced divided by the inputs needed to generate that output.

Organizational Effectiveness

In Chapter 1, we defined managerial effectiveness as goal attainment. Can the same interpretation apply to organizational effectiveness? Yes, it can. **Organizational effectiveness** is a measure of how appropriate organizational goals are and how well an organization is achieving those goals. It's a common performance measure used by managers in designing strategies, work processes, and work activities, and in coordinating the work of employees.

> **organizational effectiveness**
> A measure of how appropriate organizational goals are and how well an organization is achieving those goals.

Q&A 15.4

Industry and Company Rankings

There is no shortage of different types of industry and company rankings. The rankings for each list are determined by specific performance measures. For example, the companies listed in *Report on Business Magazine*'s Top 1000: Canada's Power Book are measured by assets. They are ranked according to after-tax profits in the most recent fiscal year, excluding extraordinary gains or losses.[5] The companies listed in the 50 Best Employers in Canada are ranked based on answers given by managers to a leadership team survey, an employee opinion survey, and a human resource survey designed by Hewitt Associates, a compensation and benefits consultant.[6] The companies listed in the *PROFIT* 100: Canada's Fastest Growing Companies are ranked based on their percentage sales growth over the past five years. Private and publicly traded companies that are over 50 percent Canadian-owned and are headquartered in Canada nominate themselves, and then *PROFIT* editors collect further information about eligible companies.[7]

Q&A 15.5, Q&A 15.6

Why Is Control Important?

Planning can be done, an organizational structure can be created to efficiently facilitate the achievement of goals, and employees can be motivated through effective leadership. Still, there is no assurance that activities are going as planned and that the goals managers are seeking are, in fact, being attained. Control is important, therefore, because it's the final link in the four management functions. It's the only way managers know whether organizational goals are being met and, if not, the reasons why. The value of the control function lies in its relation to planning, empowering employees, and protecting the organization and workplace.

Q&A 15.7

How can control help a team perform better on a course project?

In Chapter 3, we described goals as the foundation of planning. Goals give specific direction to managers. However, just stating goals or having employees accept your goals is no guarantee that the necessary actions to accomplish those goals have been taken. As the old saying goes, "The best-laid plans often go awry." The effective manager needs to follow up to ensure that what others are supposed to do is, in fact, being done and that their goals are, in fact, being achieved. In reality, managing is an ongoing process, and controlling activities provide the critical link back to planning (see Exhibit 11-1). If managers did not control, they would have no way of knowing whether their goals and plans were on target and what future actions to take.

Q&A 15.8

Exhibit 11-1

The Planning–Controlling Link

Another reason control is important is employee empowerment. Many managers are reluctant to empower their employees because they fear employees will do something wrong for which the manager will be held responsible. Thus, many managers are tempted to do things themselves and avoid empowering. This reluctance, however, can be reduced if managers develop an effective control system that provides information and feedback on employee performance.

The final reason that managers control is to protect the organization and the physical workplace.[8] Given today's environment, with heightened security alerts and surprise financial scandals, managers must have plans in place to protect the organization's employees, data, and infrastructure.

The Control Process

2 What is the control process?

control process
A three-step process that includes measuring actual performance, comparing actual performance against a standard, and taking managerial action to correct deviations or inadequate standards.

The **control process** is a three-step process: measuring actual performance, comparing actual performance against a standard, and taking managerial action to correct deviations or inadequate standards (see Exhibit 11-2). The control process for managers is similar to what you might do as a student at the beginning of the term: set goals for yourself for studying and marks, and then evaluate your performance after midterms, determining whether you have studied enough or need to study more in order to meet whatever goals you set for your marks. (To learn more about how proactive you are, see *Self-Assessment—How Proactive Am I?* on pages 354–355, at the end of the chapter.)

Measuring Performance

To determine what actual performance is, a manager must acquire information about it. The first step in control, then, is measuring. Let's consider how we measure and what we measure.

How We Measure

Four sources of information frequently used by managers to measure actual performance are personal observations, statistical reports, oral reports, and written reports. Exhibit 11-3 summarizes the advantages and drawbacks of each approach. For most managers, using a combination of approaches increases both the number of input sources and the probability of getting reliable information.

Exhibit 11-2

The Control Process

Exhibit 11-3

Common Sources of Information for Measuring Performance

	Advantages	Drawbacks
Personal observations (Management by walking around)	• Get first-hand knowledge • Information is not filtered • Intensive coverage of work activities	• Subject to personal biases • Time-consuming • Can distract employees
Statistical reports	• Easy to visualize • Effective for showing relationships	• Provide limited information • Ignore subjective factors
Oral reports	• Fast way to get information • Allow for verbal and nonverbal feedback	• Information is filtered • Information cannot be documented
Written reports	• Comprehensive • Formal • Easy to file and retrieve	• Take more time to prepare

What We Measure

What we measure is probably more critical to the control process than *how* we measure. Why? The selection of the wrong criteria can result in serious dysfunctional consequences. Besides, what we measure determines, to a great extent, what people in the organization will attempt to excel at.[9] For example, if employees are evaluated by the number of big-ticket items they sell, they may not help customers who are looking for less expensive items.

Some control criteria are applicable to any management situation. For example, because all managers, by definition, coordinate the work of others, criteria such as employee satisfaction or turnover and absenteeism rates can be measured. Most managers also have budgets set in dollar costs for their areas of responsibility. Keeping costs within budget is, therefore, a fairly common control measure. However, any comprehensive control system needs to recognize the diversity of activities that managers do. A production manager at a paper tablet manufacturer might use measures such as quantity of paper tablets produced per day and per labour-hour, scrap rate, and/or percentage of rejects returned by customers. On the other hand, the manager of an administrative unit in a government agency might use the number of client requests processed per hour or the average time required to process paperwork. Marketing managers often use measures such as percentage of market held, average dollars per sale, number of customer visits per salesperson, or number of customer impressions per advertising medium.

Most jobs and activities can be expressed in tangible and measurable terms. However, when a performance indicator cannot be stated in quantifiable terms, managers should use subjective measures. Although subjective measures have significant limitations, they are better than having no standards at all and ignoring the control function. If an activity is important, the excuse that it's difficult to measure is unacceptable.

Comparing Performance Against Standard

The comparing step determines the degree of variation between actual performance and the standard. Although some variation in performance can be expected in all activities, it's critical to determine the acceptable **range of variation** (see Exhibit 11-4 on page 330). Deviations that exceed this range become significant and need the manager's attention. In the comparison stage, managers are particularly concerned with the size and direction of the variation. An example can help make this concept clearer.

Chris Tanner is sales manager for Beer Unlimited, a distributor of specialty beers in the Prairies. Chris prepares a report during the first week of each month that describes sales

range of variation

The acceptable degree of variation between actual performance and the standard.

Exhibit 11-4

Defining the Acceptable Range of Variation

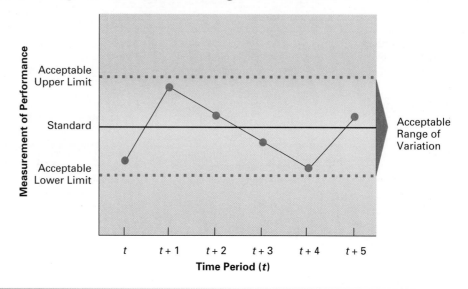

---

for the previous month, classified by brand name. Exhibit 11-5 displays both the sales goal (standard) and the actual sales figures for the month of July.

Should Chris be concerned about July's sales performance? Sales were a bit higher than originally targeted, but does that mean there were no significant deviations? Even though overall performance was generally quite favourable, several brands might need to be examined more closely by Chris. However, the number of brands that deserve attention depends on what Chris believes to be *significant*. How much variation should Chris allow before corrective action is taken?

Q&A 15.9

Exhibit 11-5

Sales Performance Figures for July, Beer Unlimited

Brand	(number of cases)		
	Standard	Actual	Over (Under)
Premium Lager (Okanagan Spring, Vernon, BC)	1075	913	(162)
India Pale Ale (Alexander Keith's, Halifax)	800	912	112
Maple Brown Ale (Upper Canada Brewery, Toronto)	620	622	2
Blanche de Chambly (Brasseries Unibroue, Quebec)	160	110	(50)
Full Moon (Alley Kat, Edmonton)	225	220	(5)
Black Cat Lager (Paddock Wood Brewing, Saskatoon, Saskatchewan)	80	65	(15)
Bison Blonde Lager (Agassiz, Winnipeg)	170	286	116
Total cases	**3130**	**3128**	**(2)**

The deviation on three brands (Maple Brown Ale, Full Moon, Black Cat Lager) is very small and does not need special attention. On the other hand, are the shortages for Premium Lager and Blanche de Chambly brands significant? That is a judgment Chris must make. Premium Lager sales were 15 percent below Chris' goal. This deviation is significant and needs attention. Chris should look for a cause. In this instance, Chris attributes the decrease to aggressive advertising and promotion programs by the big domestic producers, Anheuser-Busch and Miller. Because Premium Lager is his company's number-one selling microbeer, it's most vulnerable to the promotion clout of the big domestic producers. If the decline in sales of Premium Lager is more than a temporary slump (that is, if it happens again next month), then Chris will need to cut back on inventory stock.

An error in understating sales can be as troublesome as an overstatement. For example, is the surprising popularity of Bison Blonde Lager (up 68 percent) a one-month anomaly, or is this brand becoming more popular with customers? If the brand is increasing in popularity, Chris will want to order more product to meet customer demand, so as not to run short and risk losing customers. Again, Chris will have to interpret the information and make a decision. Our Beer Unlimited example illustrates that both overvariance and undervariance in any comparison of measures may require managerial attention.

Benchmarking of Best Practices

We first introduced the concept of benchmarking in Chapter 3. Remember that **benchmarking** is the search for the best practices among competitors or noncompetitors that lead to their superior performance. The **benchmark** is the standard of excellence against which to measure and compare.[10] At its most fundamental level, benchmarking means learning from others.[11] As a tool for monitoring and measuring organizational performance, benchmarking can be used to help identify specific performance gaps and potential areas for improvement.[12] To ensure the company is on track, Montreal-based BouClair, a home-decorating store, benchmarks everything against past performance and also against what other leading retailers are doing. "If a particular department or category is up 40% in sales over last year but we said we expected it to grow at 60%, then we are going to investigate and find out why," Gerry Goldberg, president and CEO, says.[13] "Then we look at our own same-store sales increases and compare them to the best companies out there. That's how we measure our efficiency and our productivity."

Managers should not look just at external organizations for best practices. It is also important for them to look inside their organization for best practices that can be shared. Research shows that best practices frequently already exist within an organization but usually go unidentified and unused.[14] In today's environment, organizations striving for high performance levels cannot afford to ignore such potentially valuable information. Some companies already have recognized the potential of internally benchmarking best practices as a tool for monitoring and measuring performance. For example, to improve diversity within the company, Saskatoon, Saskatchewan-based Yanke Group, a trucking

benchmarking
The search for the best practices among competitors or noncompetitors that lead to their superior performance.

benchmark
The standard of excellence against which to measure and compare.

Southwest Airlines calls itself "first and foremost, a Customer Service organization. We simply use aircraft to deliver this product." To produce high-quality service in the airline industry means, among other things, to be on time, so Southwest benchmarked Indy 500 racing crews for ways to generate faster turnaround of planes (cleaning, refuelling, and so on) at the various locations it flies to. Here a mechanic refuels one of the company's aircraft at Love Field in Dallas.

Exhibit 11-6

Steps to Successfully Implement an Internal Benchmarking Best-Practices Program

1. *Connect best practices to strategies and goals.* The organization's strategies and goals should dictate what types of best practices might be most valuable to others in the organization.

2. *Identify best practices throughout the organization.* Organizations must have a way to find out what practices have been successful in different work areas and units.

3. *Develop best-practices reward and recognition systems.* Individuals must be given an incentive to share their knowledge. The reward system should be built into the organization's culture.

4. *Communicate best practices throughout the organization.* Once best practices have been identified, that information needs to be shared with others in the organization.

5. *Create a best-practices knowledge-sharing system.* There needs to be a formal mechanism for organizational members to continue sharing their ideas and best practices.

6. *Nurture best practices on an ongoing basis.* Create an organizational culture that reinforces a "we can learn from everyone" attitude and emphasizes sharing information.

Source: Based on T. Leahy, "Extracting Diamonds in the Rough," *Business Finance,* August 2000, pp. 33–37.

---

company, is committed to hiring Aboriginal peoples and people with disabilities. Yanke reviews its employment equity benchmarks quarterly.[15] Toyota Motor Corporation developed a suggestion-screening system to prioritize best practices based on potential impact, benefits, and difficulty of implementation. General Motors sends employees—from upper management to line employees—to different plants where they learn about internal and external best practices.[16] Exhibit 11-6 provides a summary of what managers must do to implement an internal benchmarking best-practices program.

Q&A 15.10

Taking Managerial Action

The third and final step in the control process is taking managerial action. Managers can choose among three possible courses of action: They can do nothing; they can correct the actual performance; or they can revise the standard. Because "doing nothing" is fairly self-explanatory, let's look more closely at the other two options.

Correct Actual Performance

If the source of the performance variation is unsatisfactory work, the manager will want to take corrective action. Examples of such corrective action might include changing strategy, structure, compensation practices, or training programs; redesigning jobs; or firing employees. Toronto-based Celestica redesigned its manufacturing process to cut waste, as the following *Management Reflection* shows.

MANAGEMENT REFLECTION

Celestica Works to Improve the Bottom Line

Can changing the manufacturing process reduce the bottom line? Toronto-based Celestica, an electronics manufacturer, has spent most of this decade introducing control mechanisms to improve the company's fortunes.[17] Between 2001 and 2005, the company cut 29 600 jobs and restructured its operations five times. The company saw its revenues decline significantly between 2001 and 2003, and finally started to see a profit at the end of 2006. The introduction of a number of controls is given credit for the turnaround.

One of the areas that Celestica worked on was improving manufacturing operations. It did so by watching how factory workers carried out their duties, and then designing more efficient processes. Workers at its Monterrey, Mexico, plant "reduced equipment setup time by 85 percent, shortened time between receiving an order and shipping it by 71 percent, reduced floor space used by 34 percent, reduced consumables by 25 percent, reduced scrap by 66 percent and reduced the investment in surface-mount technology (SMT) lines by 49 percent." ■

A manager who decides to correct actual performance has to make another decision: Should immediate or basic corrective action be taken? **Immediate corrective action** corrects problems at once to get performance back on track. **Basic corrective action** looks at how and why performance has deviated and then proceeds to correct the source of deviation. It's not unusual for managers to rationalize that they do not have the time to take basic corrective action and therefore must be content to perpetually "put out fires" with immediate corrective action. Effective managers, however, analyze deviations and, when the benefits justify it, take the time to pinpoint and correct the causes of variance.

To return to our Beer Unlimited example, taking immediate corrective action on the negative variance for Premium Lager, Chris might contact the company's retailers and have them immediately drop the price on Premium Lager by 5 percent. However, taking basic corrective action would involve more in-depth analysis by Chris. After assessing how and why sales deviated, Chris might choose to increase in-store promotional efforts, increase the advertising budget for this brand, or reduce future purchases from the brewery. The action Chris takes will depend on the assessment of the brand's potential profitability.

Revise the Standard

It's possible that the variance was a result of an unrealistic standard; that is, the goal may have been too high or too low. In such instances, it's the standard that needs corrective attention, not the performance. For example, if individuals are exceeding the standard, or have no problem meeting the standard, this might suggest that the standard should be raised. In our example, Chris might need to raise the sales goal (standard) for Bison Blonde Lager to reflect its growing popularity.

The more troublesome problem is revising a performance standard downward. If an employee, work team, or work unit falls significantly short of reaching its goal, their natural response is to shift the blame for the variance to the goal. For example, students who

immediate corrective action
Corrective action that corrects problems at once to get performance back on track.

basic corrective action
Corrective action that looks at how and why performance deviated and then proceeds to correct the source of deviation.

Q&A 15.11

Employees at the Cordis de Mexico S.A. de C.V. production facility in Ciudad Juarez, Mexico, make medical devices used to treat various circulatory system problems. The facility has a rapid-response team that gets called into action when Mozart's Symphony no. 40 blares through the overhead speakers. When a production-line employee discovers a problem on the line, the employee activates the music, and the team races toward the work area to find out what's happened and how it can be corrected quickly.

Exhibit 11-7

Managerial Decisions in the Control Process

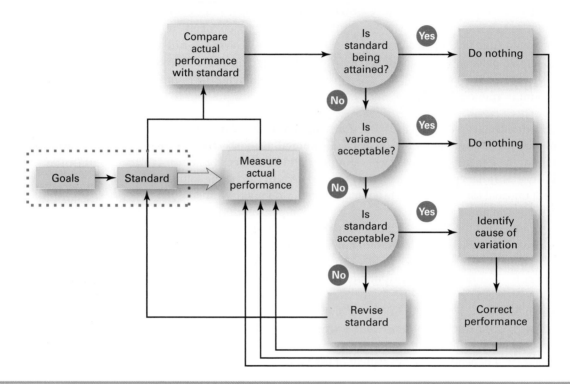

make a low grade on a test often attack the grade cut-off standards as too high. Rather than accept the fact that their performance was inadequate, students argue that the standards are unreasonable. Similarly, salespeople who fail to meet their monthly quotas may attribute the failures to unrealistic quotas. It may be true that when a standard is too high, it can result in a significant variation and may even contribute to demotivating those employees being measured. But keep in mind that if employees or managers do not meet the standard, the first thing they are likely to attack is the standard. If you believe that the standard is realistic, fair, and achievable, hold your ground. Explain your position, reaffirm to the employee, team, or unit that you expect future performance to improve, and then take the necessary corrective action to turn that expectation into reality.

Summary of Managerial Decisions

Exhibit 11-7 summarizes the manager's decisions in the control process. Standards evolve out of goals that are developed during the planning process. These goals then provide the basis for the control process, which is essentially a continuous flow between measuring, comparing, and taking managerial action. Depending on the results of comparing, a manager's decision about what course of action to take might be to do nothing, revise the standard, or correct the performance.

When to Introduce Control

3 When should controls be introduced?

Managers can implement controls *before* an activity begins, *during* the time the activity is going on, and *after* the activity has been completed. The first type is called *feedforward control*, the second is *concurrent control*, and the last is *feedback control* (see Exhibit 11-8).

Exhibit 11-8

Types of Control

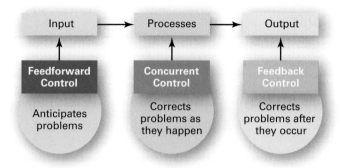

Feedforward Control

The most desirable type of control—**feedforward control**—prevents anticipated problems since it takes place before the actual activity.[18] Let's look at some examples of feedforward control.

When McDonald's Canada opened its first restaurant in Moscow, it sent company quality control experts to help Russian farmers learn techniques for growing high-quality potatoes and to help bakers learn processes for baking high-quality breads. Why? Because McDonald's strongly emphasizes product quality no matter what the geographical location. It wants a cheeseburger in Moscow to taste like one in Winnipeg. Still another example of feedforward control is the scheduled preventive maintenance programs on aircraft done by airlines. These are designed to detect and, it is hoped, to prevent structural damage that might lead to an accident.

When working on a project, do you anticipate problems ahead of time or wait until they occur?

The key to feedforward controls is taking managerial action *before* a problem occurs. Feedforward controls are desirable because they allow managers to prevent problems rather than having to correct them later after the damage (such as poor-quality products, lost customers, lost revenue, and so forth) has already been done. Unfortunately, these controls require timely and accurate information that often is difficult to obtain. As a result, managers frequently end up using the other two types of control. (The *Video Case Incident—Creativity and the Bottom Line: Mullen PR* on page 390 shows the controls that are used in the advertising industry.)

feedforward control
A type of control that focuses on preventing anticipated problems, since it takes place before the actual activity.

Concurrent Control

Concurrent control, as its name implies, takes place while an activity is in progress. When control is enacted while the work is being performed, management can correct problems before they become too costly.

The best-known form of concurrent control is direct supervision. When managers use **management by walking around**, which is a term used to describe a manager being out in the work area, interacting directly with employees, they are using concurrent control. When a manager directly oversees the actions of employees, he or she can monitor their actions and correct problems as they occur. Although, obviously, there is some delay between the activity and the manager's corrective response, the delay is minimal. Problems usually can be addressed before much resource waste or damage has been done. Also, technical equipment (computers, computerized machine controls, and so forth) can be programmed for concurrent controls. You may have experienced concurrent control

concurrent control
A type of control that takes place while an activity is in progress.

management by walking around
A term used to describe a manager being out in the work area, interacting directly with employees.

when using a computer program such as word-processing software that alerts you to misspelled words or incorrect grammatical usage as you type. In addition, many organizational quality programs rely on concurrent controls to inform employees if their work output is of sufficient quality to meet standards.

Q&A 15.12

Feedback Control

feedback control
A type of control that takes place after a work activity is done.

The most popular type of control relies on feedback. In **feedback control**, the control takes place *after* the activity is done. For example, when McDonald's executives learned that a suspected criminal ring had allegedly stolen millions of dollars in top prizes in their customer games, it was discovered through feedback control.[19] Even though the company took corrective action once it was discovered, the damage had already occurred.

Have you used feedback with team members after completing a team project?

As the McDonald's example shows, the major drawback of this type of control is that by the time the manager has the information, the problems have already occurred—leading to waste or damage. But for many activities, feedback is the only viable type of control available. Financial statements are an example of feedback controls. If, for example, the income statement shows that sales revenues are declining, the decline has already occurred. So at this point, the manager's only option is to try to determine why sales have decreased and to correct the situation.

Feedback controls do have two advantages.[20] First, feedback provides managers with meaningful information on how effective their planning efforts were. Feedback that indicates little variance between standard and actual performance is evidence that the planning was generally on target. If the deviation is significant, a manager can use that information when formulating new plans to make them more effective. Second, feedback control can enhance employee motivation. People want information on how well they have performed and feedback control provides that information. However, managers should be aware that recent research suggests that while individuals raise their goals when they receive positive feedback, they lower their goals when they receive negative feedback.[21] (To learn how to give feedback effectively, see *Developing Your Interpersonal Skills—Providing Feedback* on pages 358–359, at the end of the chapter.)

⣿ Methods of Control

Everyone seems to agree that John Lau, president and CEO of Husky Energy, is a difficult and demanding boss.[22] He represents the Li family's interests in the company, and the Li family "favours a top down, autocratic environment, crammed with checks and balances." As one former executive of the company noted, "If you want to learn manufacturing cost control, unit cost measurement, they are great at it." Lau, trained as an accountant, brought to Husky the financial models that Li uses with his own companies to control costs and improve performance. Husky gets top shareholder returns as a result, but the company is viewed as tough on its employees.

Think About It

What methods of control are available to managers? How do managers introduce controls? What impact might controls have on employees?

❹ What methods of control do managers use?

Ideally, every organization would like to efficiently and effectively reach its goals. Does this mean that the control systems organizations use are identical? In other words, would Matsushita, Husky Energy, and WestJet Airlines have the same types of control systems? Probably not. There are generally three approaches to designing control systems: market, bureaucratic, and clan controls (see Exhibit 11-9).[23]

Exhibit 11-9

Characteristics of Three Approaches to Designing Control Systems

Type of Control	Characteristics
Market	Uses external market mechanisms, such as price competition and relative market share, to establish standards used in system. Typically used by organizations whose products or services are clearly specified and distinct and that face considerable marketplace competition.
Bureaucratic	Emphasizes organizational authority. Relies on administrative and hierarchical mechanisms, such as rules, regulations, procedures, policies, standardization of activities, well-defined job descriptions, and budgets to ensure that employees exhibit appropriate behaviours and meet performance standards.
Clan	Regulates employee behaviour by the shared values, norms, traditions, rituals, beliefs, and other aspects of the organization's culture. Often used by organizations in which teams are common and technology is changing rapidly.

Market Control

Market control is an approach to control that emphasizes the use of external market mechanisms, such as price competition and relative market share, to establish the standards used in the control system. Organizations that use the market control approach often have divisions that are set up as profit centres and evaluated by the percentage of total corporate profits contributed. For instance, at Japan's Matsushita, which supplies a wide range of products throughout the world, the various divisions (audiovisual and communication networks, components and devices, home appliances, and industrial equipment) are evaluated according to the profit each generates.

market control
An approach to control that emphasizes the use of external market mechanisms, such as price competition and relative market share, to establish the standards used in the control system.

Bureaucratic Control

Another approach to control is **bureaucratic control**, which emphasizes organizational authority and relies on administrative rules, regulations, procedures, and policies. Husky Energy provides a good example of bureaucratic control. Although managers at Husky's various divisions are allowed some freedom to run their units as they see fit, they are expected to adhere closely to their budgets and to stay within corporate guidelines.

bureaucratic control
An approach to control that emphasizes organizational authority and relies on administrative rules, regulations, procedures, and policies.

Clan Control

Clan control is an approach to control in which employee behaviour is regulated by the shared values, norms, traditions, rituals, beliefs, and other aspects of the organization's culture. While market control relies on external standards and bureaucratic control is based on strict hierarchical mechanisms, clan control is dependent on the individuals and the groups in the organization (the clan) to identify appropriate and expected behaviours and performance measures. At Calgary-based WestJet Airlines, individuals are well aware of the expectations regarding appropriate work behaviour and performance standards, as the following *Management Reflection* shows.

clan control
An approach to control in which employee behaviour is regulated by the shared values, norms, traditions, rituals, beliefs, and other aspects of the organization's culture.

MANAGEMENT REFLECTION

WestJet Airlines' Employees Control Costs

Can employees be encouraged to think just like owners? WestJet Airlines' founder and former CEO, Clive Beddoe, encouraged his employees to keep costs low.[24] The airline has a much better profit margin than Air Canada and its other rivals. Beddoe introduced a generous profit-sharing plan to ensure that employees felt personally responsible for the profitability of the airline. The company's accountants insist that profit-sharing turns employees into "cost cops" looking for waste and savings. "We are one of the few companies that has to justify [to employees] its Christmas party every year," Derek Payne, vice-president of finance, boasts ruefully.

WestJet encourages teamwork and gives employees a lot of freedom to determine and carry out their day-to-day duties. There are no rigid job descriptions for positions, and employees are required to help with all tasks. Sometimes pilots are recruited to load baggage. When a plane reaches its destination, all employees onboard, even those not working the flight, are expected to prepare the plane for its next takeoff. The company saves $2.5 million annually in cleaning costs by having everyone work together. Planes get turned around much more quickly as well, usually within about a half-hour. When necessary, though, the employees have been able to do it in as little as six minutes. WestJet's profit-sharing program encourages employees to do their best because they see a clear link between their performance, the profits of the company, and their rewards. Not all companies that have profit-sharing programs provide employees with such clear links between behaviour and performance. ■

Most organizations do not rely totally on just one of these approaches to design an appropriate control system. Instead, they choose to emphasize either bureaucratic or clan control, and then add some market control measures. The key is to design an appropriate control system that helps the organization efficiently and effectively reach its goals. We consider clan culture in more detail than the other types of control systems because it provides control that is both more flexible and more enduring than either market or bureaucratic control. As we mentioned earlier, clan control is regulated by organizational culture. When employees are guided by a strong set of organizational values and norms, they can be empowered to make decisions that will benefit the organization in the long run.

Organizational Culture

organizational culture
A system of shared meaning and beliefs held by organizational members that determines, in large degree, how employees act.

How does the culture of your college or university differ from that of your high school?

Q&A 2.3, Q&A 2.4

Organizational culture is a system of shared meaning and beliefs held by organizational members that determines, in large degree, how they act. It represents a common perception held by an organization's members that influences how they behave. In every organization, there are values, symbols, rituals, myths, and practices that have evolved over time.[25] These shared values and experiences determine, in large degree, what employees perceive and how they respond to their world.[26] When faced with problems or issues, the organizational culture—the "way we do things around here"—influences what employees can do and how they conceptualize, define, analyze, and resolve issues.

Our definition of organizational culture implies three things:

- Culture is a *perception*. Individuals perceive the organizational culture on the basis of what they see, hear, or experience within the organization.

- Culture is *shared*. Even though individuals may have different backgrounds or work at different organizational levels, they tend to describe the organization's culture in similar terms.

- Culture is a *descriptive* term. It's concerned with how members perceive the organization, not with whether they like it. It describes rather than evaluates.

Q&A 2.5

Research suggests that there are seven dimensions that capture the essence of an organization's culture.[27] These dimensions are described in Exhibit 11-10. Each dimension ranges from low (it's not very typical of the culture) to high (it's very typical of the culture). Appraising an organization on these seven dimensions gives a composite picture of the organization's culture. In many organizations, often one of these cultural dimensions is emphasized more than the others and essentially shapes the organization's personality and the way organizational members work. For example, at Sony Corporation the focus is on product innovation. The company "lives and breathes" new-product development

Exhibit 11-10

Dimensions of Organizational Culture

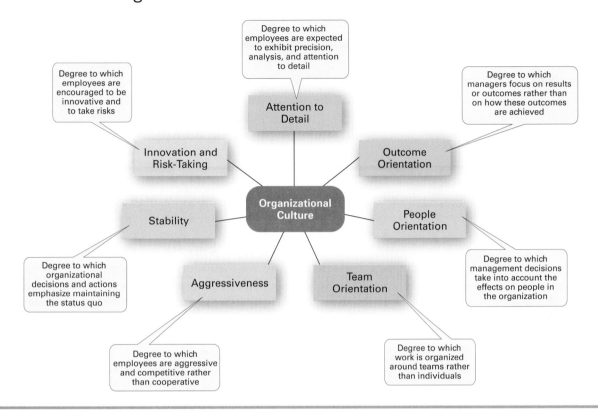

(outcome orientation), and employees' work decisions, behaviours, and actions support that goal. In contrast, WestJet Airlines has made its employees a central part of its culture (people orientation). However, its admission in 2006 of engaging in corporate espionage against Air Canada may cause employees to question WestJet's corporate values.

Strong vs. Weak Cultures

Although all organizations have cultures, not all cultures have an equal impact on employees' behaviours and actions. **Strong cultures**—cultures in which the key values are deeply held and widely shared—have a greater influence on employees than do weak cultures. The more employees accept the organization's key values and the greater their commitment to those values, the stronger the culture is.

Whether an organization's culture is strong, weak, or somewhere in between depends on factors such as the size of the organization, how long it has been around, how much turnover there has been among employees, and the intensity with which the culture started.

Some organizations do not make clear what is important and what is not, and this lack of clarity is a characteristic of weak cultures. In such organizations, culture is unlikely to greatly influence managers. Most organizations, however, have moderate to strong cultures. There is relatively high agreement on what is important, what defines "good" employee behaviour, what it takes to get ahead, and so forth. *Tips for Managers—Creating a More Ethical Culture* provides some suggestions for managers who want to build and maintain a more ethical culture in the workplace.

A growing body of evidence suggests that strong cultures are associated with high organizational performance.[28] It's easy to

strong cultures
Organizational cultures in which the key values are deeply held and widely shared.

Q&A 2.6

TIPS FOR MANAGERS

Creating a More Ethical Culture

- Be a **visible role model**.
- Communicate **ethical expectations**.
- Provide **ethics training**.
- Visibly **reward ethical acts and punish unethical ones**.
- Provide **protective mechanisms** so employees can discuss ethical dilemmas and report unethical behaviour without fear.

Exhibit 11-11

How an Organization's Culture Is Established and Maintained

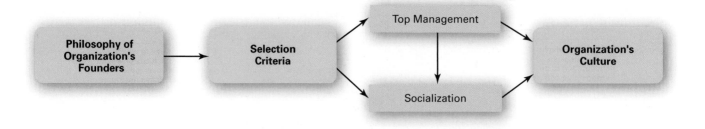

understand why a strong culture enhances performance. After all, when values are clear and widely accepted, employees know what they are supposed to do and what is expected of them, so they can act quickly to take care of problems, thus preventing any potential performance decline. However, the drawback is that the same strong culture also might prevent employees from trying new approaches, especially during periods of rapid change.[29] Strong cultures do not always yield *positive* results, however.[30] Enron had a very strong, and unethical, culture. This enabled employees and top management to engage in unethical behaviour that was concealed from public scrutiny.

Q&A 2.7
PRISM 3

Developing an Organization's Culture

Exhibit 11-11 summarizes how an organization's culture is established and maintained. The original culture is derived from the founders' philosophy. This, in turn, strongly influences the selection criteria used to hire new employees. Clan control requires careful selection and socialization of employees who will support the organization's culture. This includes making sure to manage diversity in the workforce (see *Managing Workforce Diversity—Diversity Success Stories* on page 359).

The actions of the current top managers set the general expectations as to what is acceptable behaviour and what is not. Through the socialization process, new employees learn the organization's way of doing things. If socialization is successful, new employees will learn the values of the organization and behave accordingly, and the organization's culture will be preserved.

How Employees Learn Culture

Culture is transmitted to employees in a number of ways. The most significant are stories, rituals, material symbols, and language.

Stories An organization's "stories" typically are related to significant people or events, such as the organization's founders, rule breaking, reactions to past mistakes, and so forth.[31] They help employees learn the culture by anchoring the present in the past, providing explanations and legitimacy for current practices, and showing what is important to the organization.[32]

Rituals An organization's rituals are repetitive sequences of activities that express and reinforce the values of the organization, the goals that are most important, and the people who are most important.[33] One well-known ritual is Walmart's company chant that employees say at the beginning of each workday.

Material Symbols An organization's material symbols convey to employees who is important, the degree of equality desired by top management, and the kinds of behaviour (for example, risk-taking, conservative, authoritarian, participative, individualistic) that are expected and appropriate. The layout of an organization's facilities, how employees

Exhibit 11-12

Managerial Decisions Affected by Organizational Culture

Planning

- The degree of risk that plans should contain
- Whether plans should be developed by individuals or teams
- The degree of environmental scanning in which management will engage

Organizing

- How much autonomy should be designed into employees' jobs
- Whether tasks should be done by individuals or in teams
- The degree to which department managers interact with each other

Leading

- The degree to which managers are concerned with increasing employee job satisfaction
- The appropriate leadership style(s)
- Whether all disagreements—even constructive ones—should be eliminated

Controlling

- Whether to impose external controls or to allow employees to control their own actions
- What criteria should be emphasized in employee performance evaluations
- What repercussions will result from exceeding one's budget

dress, the types of automobiles provided to top executives, and the availability of corporate aircraft are examples of material symbols.

Language Many organizations and units within organizations use language as a way to identify members of a culture. By learning this language, members attest to their acceptance of the culture and their willingness to help preserve it. New employees are frequently overwhelmed with acronyms and jargon that, after a short period of time, become a natural part of their language. Once learned, this language acts as a common denominator that unites members of a given culture. *Managing Workforce Diversity— Diversity Success Stories* on page 359 discusses companies that have integrated employees from different cultures into the workplace.

How Culture Affects Managers

An organization's culture does more than influence employee behaviour; it also constrains a manager's decision-making options in all management functions. Exhibit 11-12 shows the major areas of a manager's job that are affected by the culture in which he or she operates.

Q&A 2.8

Financial and Information Controls

For Husky Energy president and CEO John Lau, the bottom line is the measure of organizational performance.[34] When he started at Husky in 1991, it was not doing well financially. By 1993, it had a loss of $250 million on the books. In 2006, the company had $2.7 billion in net earnings, clearly an outstanding turnaround. Judith Romanchuk, an investment banker, notes that Lau has taken the company from "minor league player with a 'crumbling foundation'" to a major producer" with holdings in both Canada and China.

Lau also measures performance by the number of barrels of oil equivalent (BOE) produced daily. When he started, Husky was producing 28 000 barrels daily. In 2008, the company produced 355 900 BOE daily. Lau has grown volume 10 percent a year since 2004; by

2020, he expects the company will extract half a million BOEs daily from the Alberta oil sands alone.

Think About It
How can managers use financial and information controls to make sure that their organizations are performing well?

❺ How do financial and information controls help managers monitor performance?

One of the primary purposes of every business is to earn a profit. To achieve this goal, managers need financial controls and accurate information. Managers might, for example, carefully analyze quarterly income statements for excessive expenses. They might also perform several financial ratio tests to ensure that sufficient cash is available to pay ongoing expenses, that debt levels have not risen too high, or that assets are being used productively. Or they might look at some newer financial control tools such as EVA (economic value added) to see if the company is creating economic value. Managers can control information and use it to control other organizational activities.

Traditional Financial Control Measures

Q&A 15.13   Traditional financial control measures include ratio analysis and budget analysis. Exhibit 11-13 summarizes some of the most popular financial ratios used in organizations. Liquidity ratios measure an organization's ability to meet its current debt obligations. Leverage ratios examine the organization's use of debt to finance its assets and whether it's able to meet the interest payments on the debt. Activity ratios assess how

Exhibit 11-13

Popular Financial Ratios

Objective	Ratio	Calculation	Meaning
Liquidity	Current ratio	$\frac{\text{Current assets}}{\text{Current liabilities}}$	Tests the organization's ability to meet short-term obligations
	Acid test	$\frac{\text{Current assets less inventories}}{\text{Current liabilities}}$	Tests liquidity more accurately when inventories turn over slowly or are difficult to sell
Leverage	Debt to assets	$\frac{\text{Total debt}}{\text{Total assets}}$	The higher the ratio, the more leveraged the organization
	Times interest earned	$\frac{\text{Profits before interest and taxes}}{\text{Total interest charges}}$	Measures how far profits can decline before the organization is unable to meet its interest expenses
Activity	Inventory turnover	$\frac{\text{Sales}}{\text{Inventory}}$	The higher the ratio, the more efficiently inventory assets are being used
	Total asset turnover	$\frac{\text{Sales}}{\text{Total assets}}$	The fewer assets used to achieve a given level of sales, the more efficiently management is using the organization's total assets
Profitability	Profit margin on sales	$\frac{\text{Net profit after taxes}}{\text{Total sales}}$	Identifies the profits that various products are generating
	Return on investment	$\frac{\text{Net profit after taxes}}{\text{Total assets}}$	Measures the efficiency of assets to generate profits

efficiently the firm is using its assets. Finally, profitability ratios measure how efficiently and effectively the firm is using its assets to generate profits.

These ratios are calculated using information from the organization's two primary financial statements: the balance sheet and the income statement. They compare two figures and express them as a percentage or ratio. Because you have undoubtedly discussed these ratios in introductory accounting and finance courses, or you will in the near future, we are not going to elaborate on how they are calculated. Instead, we mention these ratios only briefly here to remind you that managers use such ratios as internal control devices for monitoring how efficiently and profitably the organization uses its assets, debt, inventories, and the like.

Budgets are used for control as they provide managers with quantitative standards against which to measure and compare resource consumption. By pointing out deviations between standard and actual consumption, they become control tools. If the deviations are judged to be significant enough to require action, the manager will want to examine what has happened and try to uncover the reasons behind the deviations. With this information, he or she can take whatever action is necessary. For example, if you use a personal budget for monitoring and controlling your monthly expenses, you might find one month that your miscellaneous expenses were higher than you had budgeted for. At that point, you might cut back spending in another area or work extra hours to try to get more income.

Other Financial Control Measures

In addition to the traditional financial tools, managers are using measures such as EVA (economic value added) and MVA (market value added). The fundamental concept behind these financial tools is that companies are supposed to take in capital from investors and make it worth more. When managers do that, they have created wealth. When they take in capital and make it worth less, they have destroyed wealth.

Economic value added (EVA) is a tool that measures corporate and divisional performance. It's calculated by taking after-tax operating profit minus the total annual cost of capital.[35] EVA is a measure of how much economic value is being created by what a company does with its assets, less any capital investments the company has made in its assets. As a performance control tool, EVA focuses managers' attention on earning a rate of return over and above the cost of capital. About 30 percent of Canadian companies use EVA, including Montreal-based Rio Tinto Alcan, Montreal-based Domtar, Markham, Ontario-based Robin Hood Multifoods, and Montreal-based cable company Cogeco.[36] When EVA is used as a performance measure, employees soon learn that they can improve their organization's or business unit's EVA either by using less capital (that is, figuring out how to spend less) or by investing capital in high-return projects (that is, projects that will bring in more money, with fewer expenses). Former Molson CEO Daniel O'Neill was well rewarded for EVA improvement to the company in 2002. He "closed several breweries, laid off hundreds of staff and slashed overhead costs, using the savings to modernize remaining breweries," all of which sent Molson shares soaring. O'Neill received a $2.4 million bonus for his efforts.[37]

economic value added (EVA)
A financial tool that measures corporate and divisional performance, calculated by taking after-tax operating profit minus the total annual cost of capital.

Market value added (MVA) adds a market dimension because it is a tool that measures the stock market's estimate of the value of a firm's past and expected capital investment projects. If the company's market value (value of all outstanding stock plus the company's debt) is greater than all the capital invested in it (from shareholders, bondholders, and retained earnings), it has a positive MVA, indicating that managers have created wealth. If the company's market value is less than all the capital invested in it, the MVA will be negative, indicating that managers have destroyed wealth. Studies have shown that EVA is a predictor of MVA and that consecutive years of positive EVA generally lead to a high MVA.[38]

market value added (MVA)
A financial tool that measures the stock market's estimate of the value of a firm's past and expected capital investment projects.

Q&A 15.14

To understand that EVA and MVA measure different things, let's consider three companies that had the highest MVA in the United States in 2006 and the amount of wealth they created for their shareholders (in US dollars): General Electric ($281 billion), Exxon Mobil ($223 billion), and Microsoft ($221 billion). While these three companies had relatively similar MVA, they had very different real profits (measured by EVA). Exxon Mobil had the highest EVA ($28.9 billion), followed by Microsoft ($9.1 billion), and then GE ($8.2 billion). Microsoft, with a lower MVA than General Electric, delivered a higher EVA.[39]

Information Controls

In April 2007, Gordon Bobbitt found hundreds of phone records from Rogers littering the streets of Toronto. These records contained contact information, financial details, and, in some cases, social insurance numbers. This case was just one instance of consumer records that were not handled properly. Earlier in 2007, CIBC and retailer TJX Companies (operator of Winners and HomeSense) had breaches of security with consumer data. In 2006, the RCMP processed about 7800 cases of identity theft, which represented $16.3 million in individual losses.[40]

There are two ways to view information: (1) as a tool to help managers control other organizational activities and (2) as an organizational area that managers need to control. Let's look first at information as a control tool.

How Is Information Used in Controlling?

Information is critical to monitoring and measuring an organization's activities and performance. Managers need the right information at the right time and in the right amount. Without information, they would find it difficult to measure, compare, and take action as part of the controlling process. Inaccurate, incomplete, excessive, or delayed information will seriously impede performance.

For example, in measuring actual performance, managers need information about what is, in fact, happening within their area of responsibility, about what the standards are in order to be able to compare actual performance with the standard, and to help them determine acceptable ranges of variation within these comparisons. And they rely on information to help them develop appropriate courses of action if there are or are not significant deviations between actual and standard. Information can also be used to control costs, as the following *Management Reflection* shows.

MANAGEMENT REFLECTION

Air Canada Improves Maintenance Procedures

How can wireless technology make maintenance more efficient? Air Canada's former vice-president of IT and CIO, Alice Keung, found that maintenance costs at Air Canada were skyrocketing because line maintenance (unscheduled repairs to a plane's equipment, instruments, or body) was not handled very effectively.[41] In particular, pilots or mechanics would send a note to the Toronto maintenance facility by teletype or fax or put a note in the plane's log, noting a repair issue. Mechanics often would not get these notes, or the plane would arrive but the mechanic would not have the necessary parts to perform a quick maintenance procedure.

Keung realized that maintenance procedures could be significantly streamlined if mechanics had easy and immediate access to information about repairs that needed to be made, as well as maintenance manuals and diagrams. Mechanics were given tablet-sized display screens mounted on their trucks and connected to a wireless local area network. This made the information easily available, and the display was large enough to show maintenance diagrams when needed.

The technology significantly improved maintenance productivity. Mechanics spent less time travelling back and forth to the hangar to get additional parts, since they could determine what they needed more quickly. Mechanics could also make sure that parts were waiting when planes landed, so simple repairs could be performed without delaying flights. "That all has a bottom-line impact," Keung says. ■

As you can see, information is an important tool in monitoring and measuring organizational performance. Most of the information tools that managers use arise out of the organization's management information system.

Although there is no universally agreed-upon definition of a **management information system (MIS)**, we will define it as a system used to provide management with needed information on a regular basis. In theory, this system can be manual or computer-based, although all current discussions focus on computer-supported applications. The term *system* in MIS implies order, arrangement, and purpose. Further, an MIS focuses specifically on providing managers with *information,* not merely *data*. These two points are important and require elaboration.

A library provides a good analogy. Although it can contain millions of volumes, a library does not do users much good if they cannot find what they want quickly. That is why librarians spend a great deal of time cataloguing a library's collections and ensuring that materials are returned to their proper locations. Organizations today are like well-stocked libraries. There is no lack of data. There is, however, an inability to process that data so that the right information is available to the right person when he or she needs it. Likewise, a library is almost useless if it has the book you need immediately but either you cannot find it or the library takes a week to retrieve it from storage. An MIS, on the other hand, has organized data in some meaningful way and can access the information in a reasonable amount of time. **Data** are raw, unanalyzed facts, such as numbers, names, or quantities. Raw unanalyzed facts are relatively useless to managers. When data are analyzed and processed, they become **information**. An MIS collects data and turns them into relevant information for managers to use.

management information system (MIS)
A system used to provide management with needed information on a regular basis.

data
Raw, unanalyzed facts.

information
Processed and analyzed data.

Controlling Information

As critically important as an organization's information is to everything it does, managers must have comprehensive and secure controls in place to protect that information. Such controls can range from data encryption to system firewalls to data backups, and other techniques as well.[42] Problems can lurk in places that an organization might not even have considered, such as search engines. Sensitive, defamatory, confidential, or embarrassing organizational information has found its way into search engine results. For example, detailed monthly expenses and employee salaries on the National Speleological Society's website turned up in a Google search.[43] Laptop computers are also proving to be a weak link in an organization's data security. For example, Boston-based mutual fund company Fidelity Investments disclosed that a stolen laptop had the personal information of almost 200 000 current and former Hewlett-Packard employees.[44] Even RFID (radio frequency identification) tags, now being used by more and more organizations to track and control products, may be vulnerable to computer viruses.[45] Needless to say, whatever information controls are used must be monitored regularly to ensure that all possible precautions are in place to protect the organization's important information.

Current Issues in Control

Husky Energy, like all public organizations, has a board of directors that looks after the interests of shareholders.[46] In recent years, corporate governance has come under scrutiny because of corporate scandals. Many boards were not overseeing management as well as they might have.

Husky has strengthened its board policies in recent years. The primary duty of Husky's board is to "approve, monitor and provide guidance on the strategic planning process." While the president and CEO and senior management team create the strategic plan, the board has to review and approve it. The board's role also includes identifying the principal risks of Husky's business and managing and monitoring these risks, as well as approving Husky's strategic plans, annual budget, and financial plans.

Think About It
Why has corporate governance become so important in recent years? What are the advantages of having a strong corporate board? Would there be any disadvantages?

⑥ What are some current issues in control?

The employees of Tempe, Arizona-based Integrated Information Systems thought there was nothing wrong with exchanging copyrighted digital music over a dedicated office server they had set up. Like office betting on college basketball games, it was technically illegal, but harmless—or so they thought. But after the company had to pay a $1.5 million settlement to the Recording Industry Association of America, managers wished they had controlled the situation better.[47]

Control is an important managerial function. What types of control issues do today's managers face? We look at five: balanced scorecard, corporate governance, cross-cultural differences, workplace concerns, and customer interactions.

Balanced Scorecard

The balanced scorecard approach to performance measurement was introduced as a way to evaluate organizational performance from more than just the financial perspective.[48] The **balanced scorecard** is a performance measurement tool that examines four areas—financial, customer, internal business process, and learning and growth assets—that contribute to an organization's performance. Exhibit 11-14 illustrates how the balanced scorecard is measured. The financial area looks at activities that improve the short- and long-term performance of the organization. The customer area looks at the customer's view of the organization, whether customers return, and whether they are satisfied. The internal business process looks at how production and operations, such as order fulfillment, are carried out. The learning and growth area looks at how well the company's employees are being managed for the company's future.

Q&A 15.15 According to this approach, managers should develop goals in each of the four areas and then measure to determine if these goals are being met. For example, a company might include cash flow, quarterly sales growth, and return on investment (ROI) as

balanced scorecard
A performance measurement tool that looks at four areas—financial, customer, internal business process, and learning and growth assets—that contribute to an organization's performance.

Exhibit 11-14

The Balanced Scorecard

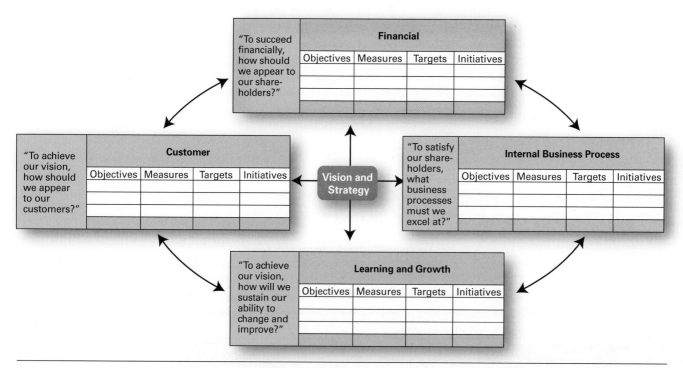

Source: R. S. Kaplan and D. P. Norton, "Using the Balanced Scorecard as a Strategic Management System," *Harvard Business Review* 74, no. 1 (January–February 1996), pp. 75–85. With permission from Harvard Business School Publishing.

measures for success in the financial area. It might include percentage of sales coming from new products as a measure of customer goals. It might include dollars spent toward training, or number of courses taken by employees, as a measure of learning and growth. The intent of the balanced scorecard is to emphasize that all of these areas are important to an organization's success and that there should be a balance among them.

Although a balanced scorecard makes sense, managers still tend to focus on areas that drive their organization's success.[49] Their scorecards reflect their strategies. If those strategies centre on the customer, for example, then the customer area is likely to get more attention than the other three areas. Yet you really cannot focus on measuring only one performance area because, ultimately, other performance areas will be affected.

Many companies are starting to use the balanced scorecard as a control mechanism, including Bell Canada, British Airways, and Hilton Hotels. In 2003, the Ontario Hospital Association developed a scorecard for 89 hospitals, designed to evaluate four main areas: clinical use and outcomes, financial performance and financial condition of the hospital, patient satisfaction, and how the hospital was investing for the future. The scorecard was purposefully designed to recognize the synergies among each of these measures. After hospitals were evaluated on the scorecard measures, the results of the scorecard evaluations were made available to patients, giving them an objective basis for choosing a hospital. The association has provided the reports for every year since then, except 2004, on its website.[50]

Corporate Governance

Although Andrew Fastow, Enron's former chief financial officer, had an engaging and persuasive personality, that still does not explain why Enron's board of directors failed to raise even minimal concerns about management's questionable accounting practices. The board even allowed Fastow to set up off-balance-sheet partnerships for his own profit at the expense of Enron's shareholders.

Corporate governance, the system used to govern a corporation so that the interests of corporate owners are protected, failed abysmally at Enron, as it did at many of the other companies caught in recent financial scandals. In the aftermath of these scandals, there have been increased calls for better corporate governance. Two areas in which corporate governance is being reformed are the role of boards of directors and financial reporting. The concern over corporate governance exists in Canada and globally.[51] For example, 75 percent of senior executives at US and Western European corporations expect their boards of directors to take a more active role in improving corporate governance.[52]

corporate governance
The system used to govern a corporation so that the interests of corporate owners are protected.

The Role of Boards of Directors

The original purpose of a board of directors was to have a group, independent from management, looking out for the interests of shareholders who, because of the corporate structure, were not involved in the day-to-day management of the organization. However, it has not always worked that way in practice. Board members often enjoy a cozy relationship with managers in which board members "take care" of the CEO and the CEO "takes care" of the board members.

This quid pro quo arrangement is changing. In the United States, since the passage of the Sarbanes-Oxley Act in 2002, demands on board members of publicly traded companies in the United States have increased considerably.[53] The Canadian Securities Administrators rules, which came into effect in March 2004, strive to tighten board responsibility somewhat, though these rules are not as stringent as those developed in the United States. To help boards do their job better, researchers at the Corporate Governance Center at Kennesaw State University, Georgia, developed 10 governance principles for American public companies that have been endorsed by the Institute of Internal Auditors in the United States. These principles are equally relevant for Canadian public companies (see Exhibit 11-15 on page 348 for a list of these principles).

Exhibit 11-15

Twenty-First Century Governance Principles for Public Companies

1. *Interaction:* Sound governance requires effective interaction among the board, management, the external auditor, and the internal auditor.

2. *Board purpose:* The board of directors should understand that its purpose is to protect the interests of the corporation's stockholders, while considering the interests of other stakeholders (for example, creditors and employees).

3. *Board responsibilities:* The board's major areas of responsibility should be monitoring the CEO, overseeing the corporation's strategy, and monitoring risks and the corporation's control system. Directors should employ healthy skepticism in meeting these responsibilities.

4. *Independence:* The major stock exchanges should define an "independent" director as one who has no professional or personal ties (either current or former) to the corporation or its management other than service as a director. The vast majority of the directors should be independent in both fact and appearance so as to promote arm's-length oversight.

5. *Expertise:* The directors should possess relevant industry, company, functional area, and governance expertise. The directors should reflect a mix of backgrounds and perspectives. All directors should receive detailed orientation and continuing education to ensure they achieve and maintain the necessary level of expertise.

6. *Meetings and information:* The board should meet frequently for extended periods of time and should have access to the information and personnel it needs to perform its duties.

7. *Leadership:* The roles of board chair and CEO should be separate.

8. *Disclosure:* Proxy statements and other board communications should reflect board activities and transactions (e.g., insider trades) in a transparent and timely manner.

9. *Committees:* The nominating, compensation, and audit committees of the board should be composed only of independent directors.

10. *Internal audit:* All public companies should maintain an effective, full-time internal audit function that reports directly to the audit committee.

Source: P. D. Lapides, D. R. Hermanson, M. S. Beasley, J. V. Carcello, F. T. DeZoort, and T. L. Neal. Corporate Governance Center, Kennesaw State University, March 26, 2002. Used with permission.

Financial Reporting

In addition to expanding the role of boards of directors, the Canadian Securities Administrators rules require more financial disclosure by organizations, but, unlike the Sarbanes-Oxley Act of the United States, do not require senior managers to provide a qualitative assessment of an organization's internal compliance control. Still, these types of changes should lead to somewhat better information—that is, information that is more accurate and reflective of the firm's financial condition.

Cross-Cultural Differences

The concepts of control that we have discussed so far are appropriate for an organization whose units are not geographically separated or culturally distinct. But what about global organizations? Will control systems be different, and what should managers know about adjusting controls for cross-cultural differences?

Methods of controlling people and work can be quite different in different countries. The differences we see in organizational control systems of global organizations are primarily in the measurement and corrective action steps of the control process. In a global corporation, managers of foreign operations tend to be less directly controlled by the home office, if for no other reason than that distance keeps managers from being able to observe work directly. Because distance creates a tendency to formalize controls, the home office of a global company often relies on extensive formal reports for control. The global company also may use the power of information technology to control work activities. For instance, the Japanese-based retailer Seven & i Holdings, which owns the 7-Eleven convenience store chain, uses automated cash registers not only to record sales and monitor inventory, but also to schedule tasks for store managers and to track managers' use of the built-in analytical graphs and forecasts. If managers do not use them enough, they are told to increase their activities.[54]

Technology's impact on control is most evident in comparisons of technologically advanced nations with those that are less technologically advanced. In countries such as Canada, the United States, Japan, Great Britain, Germany, and Australia, global managers use indirect control devices—especially computer-generated reports and analyses—in addition to standardized rules and direct supervision to ensure that work activities are going as planned. In less technologically advanced countries, managers tend to rely more on direct supervision and highly centralized decision making as means of control.

Also, constraints on what corrective actions managers can take may affect managers in foreign countries because laws in some countries do not allow managers the option of closing facilities, laying off employees, taking money out of the country, or bringing in a new management team from outside the country.

Finally, another challenge for global companies in collecting data for measurement and comparison is comparability. For instance, a company's manufacturing facility in Mexico might produce the same products as a facility in Scotland, however, the Mexican facility might be much more labour intensive than its Scottish counterpart (to take strategic advantage of lower labour costs in Mexico). If the top-level executives were to control costs by, for example, calculating labour costs per unit or output per employee, the figures would not be comparable. Global managers must address these types of control challenges.

Workplace Concerns

Today's workplace presents considerable control challenges for managers. From monitoring employees' computer use at work to protecting the workplace from disgruntled employees, managers must control the workplace to ensure that the organization's work can be carried out efficiently and effectively as planned. In this section, we look at two major workplace concerns: workplace privacy and employee theft.

Workplace Privacy

If you work, do you think you have a right to privacy at your workplace? What can your employer find out about you and your work? You might be surprised by the answers!

Employers can (and do), among other things, read your email (even those marked "personal" or "confidential"), tap your telephone, monitor your work by computer, store and review computer files, and monitor you in an employee washroom or dressing room. And these actions are not all that uncommon. Nearly 57 percent of Canadian companies have Internet-use policies restricting employees' personal use of the Internet.[55] Employees of the City of Vancouver are warned that their computer use is monitored, and a desktop agent icon of a spinning head reminds them that they are being watched. Exhibit 11-16 summarizes the percentage of employers engaging in different forms of workplace monitoring.

Why do managers feel they must monitor what employees are doing? A big reason is that employees are hired to work, not to surf the web checking stock prices, placing bets

---

Exhibit 11-16

Types of Workplace Monitoring by Employers

Internet use	54.7%
Telephone use	44.0%
Email messages	38.1%
Computer files	30.8%
Job performance using video cameras	14.6%
Phone conversations	11.5%
Voice mail messages	6.8%

Source: Based on S. McElvoy, "E-Mail and Internet Monitoring and the Workplace: Do Employees Have a Right to Privacy?" *Communications and the Law*, June 2002, p. 69.

Do you think it is right for your employer to monitor your email and web surfing at work?

at online casinos, or shopping for presents for family or friends. An Ipsos Reid poll found Canadians spend 1.6 billion hours a year online at work for personal reasons, an average of 4.5 hours a week per employee.[56] That is a significant cost to businesses. Conservative estimates suggest that personal use of the Internet at work costs Canadian businesses more than $16 billion annually in lost productivity.[57]

Another reason that managers monitor employee email and computer use is that they do not want to risk being sued for creating a hostile workplace environment because of offensive messages or an inappropriate image displayed on a co-worker's computer screen. Concern about racial or sexual harassment is one of the reasons why companies might want to monitor or keep backup copies of all email. This electronic record can help establish what actually happened and can help managers react quickly.[58]

Finally, managers want to ensure that company secrets are not being leaked.[59] Although protecting intellectual property is important for all businesses, it's especially important in high-tech industries. Managers need to be certain that employees are not, even inadvertently, passing information on to others who could use that information to harm the company.

Even with the workplace monitoring that managers can do, Canadian employees do have some protection through the Criminal Code, which prohibits unauthorized interception of electronic communication. The Personal Information Protection and Electronic Documents Act, which went into effect in early 2004, gives employees some privacy protection, but it does not make workplace electronic monitoring illegal. Under existing laws, if an individual is aware of a corporate policy of surveillance and does not formally object, or remains at the job, the monitoring is acceptable.[60] Unionized employees may have a bit more privacy with respect to their computers. The Canada Labour Code requires employers operating under a collective agreement to disclose information about plans for technological change. This might provide unions with an opportunity to bargain over electronic surveillance.

Because of the potentially serious costs, and given the fact that many jobs now entail work that involves using a computer, many companies are developing and enforcing workplace monitoring policies. The responsibility for this falls on managers. It's important to develop some type of viable workplace monitoring policy. What can managers do to maintain control but do so in a way that is not demeaning to employees? They should develop a clear and unambiguous computer-use policy and make sure that every employee knows about it. For example, managers should tell employees upfront that their computer use may be monitored at any time and provide clear and specific guidelines as to what constitutes acceptable use of company email systems and the web. The Bank of Montreal blocks access to "some of the dubious sites that are high risk," such as Playboy.com and other pornographic sites. The bank has developed policies about appropriate and inappropriate use of the Internet, which are emailed to all employees several times a year.[61]

Employee Theft

Would you be surprised to find out that up to 75 percent of Canadian organizations have reported experiencing employee theft and fraud?[62] It's a costly problem—Air Canada, which has run a campaign against employee theft, noted that the airline "is right in line with industry standards for employee theft, and that means as much as 9 per cent of stock such as office supplies and on-board products is taken each year."[63] A study found that employee theft cost Canadian retail businesses $1.6 billion in 2006.[64]

Employee theft is defined as any unauthorized taking of company property by employees for their personal use.[65] It can range from embezzlement to fraudulent filing of expense reports to removing equipment, parts, software, and office supplies from company premises. While retail businesses have long faced serious potential losses from

employee theft
Any unauthorized taking of company property by employees for their personal use.

Exhibit 11-17

Control Measures for Deterring or Reducing Employee Theft or Fraud

Feedforward	Concurrent	Feedback
Use careful prehiring screening.	Treat employees with respect and dignity.	Make sure employees know when theft or fraud has occurred—not naming names but letting people know this is not acceptable.
Establish specific policies defining theft and fraud and discipline procedures.	Openly communicate the costs of stealing.	
Involve employees in writing policies.	Let employees know on a regular basis about their successes in preventing theft and fraud.	Use the services of professional investigators.
Educate and train employees about the policies.	Use video surveillance equipment if conditions warrant.	Redesign control measures.
Have professionals review your internal security controls.	Install "lock-out" options on computers, telephones, and email.	Evaluate your organization's culture and the relationships of managers and employees.
	Use corporate hotlines for reporting incidences.	
	Set a good example.	

Sources: Based on A. H. Bell and D. M. Smith, "Protecting the Company Against Theft and Fraud," *Workforce Online,* December 3, 2000, www.workforce.com; J. D. Hansen, "To Catch a Thief," *Journal of Accountancy,* March 2000, pp. 43–46; and J. Greenberg, "The Cognitive Geometry of Employee Theft," in *Dysfunctional Behavior in Organizations: Nonviolent and Deviant Behavior,* eds. S. B. Bacharach, A. O'Leary-Kelly, J. M. Collins, and R. W. Griffin (Stamford, CT: JAI Press, 1998), pp. 147–193.

employee theft, loose financial controls at start-ups and small companies and the ready availability of information technology have made employee stealing an escalating problem in all kinds and sizes of organizations. It's a control issue that managers need to educate themselves about and with which they must be prepared to deal.[66]

Why do employees steal? The answer depends on whom you ask.[67] Experts in various fields—industrial security, criminology, clinical psychology—all have different perspectives. Industrial security people propose that people steal because the opportunity presents itself through lax controls and favourable circumstances. Criminologists say that it's because people have financial pressures (such as personal financial problems) or vice-based pressures (such as gambling debts). Clinical psychologists suggest that people steal because they can rationalize whatever they are doing as correct and appropriate behaviour ("everyone does it," "they had it coming," "this company makes enough money and they will never miss anything this small," "I deserve this for all that I put up with," and so forth).[68] Although each of these approaches provides compelling insights into employee theft and has been instrumental in program designs to deter it, unfortunately employees continue to steal.

What can managers do to deter or reduce employee theft or fraud? We can use the concepts of feedforward, concurrent, and feedback controls to identify actions managers can take.[69] Exhibit 11-17 summarizes several possible control measures.

Customer Interactions

Every month, each local branch of Enterprise Rent-a-Car conducts telephone surveys with customers.[70] Each branch earns a ranking based on the percentage of its customers who say they were "completely satisfied" with their last Enterprise experience—a level of satisfaction referred to as "top box." Top box performance is important to Enterprise because completely satisfied customers are far more likely to be repeat customers. And by using

One of the many ways in which L.L.Bean controls interactions with its customers is by providing outstanding customer service. Not only are the company's store staff and telephone order takers trained to handle all inquiries with exceptional courtesy and efficiency, but also every item purchased, from clothing to kayaks, is 100 percent guaranteed. Continuing a tradition of customer satisfaction that is almost 100 years old, L.L.Bean promises to accept returns for refund or replacement of "anything purchased from us at any time" if it is not completely satisfactory in every way.

Exhibit 11-18

The Service Profit Chain

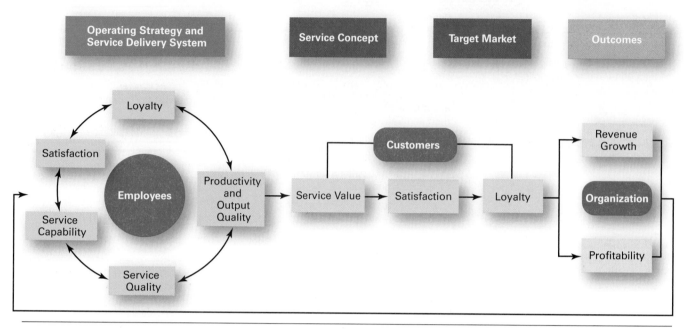

Sources: An exhibit from J. L. Heskett, T. O. Jones, G. W. Loveman, W. E. Sasser Jr., and L. A. Schlesinger, "Putting the Service Profit Chain to Work," *Harvard Business Review,* March–April 1994, p. 166. With permission from Harvard Business School Publishing. See also J. L. Heskett, W. E. Sasser, and L. A. Schlesinger, *The Service Profit Chain* (New York: Free Press, 1997).

this service-quality index measure, employees' careers and financial aspirations are linked with the organizational goal of providing consistently superior service to each and every customer. Managers at Enterprise understand the connection between employees and customers and the importance of controlling these interactions.

There is probably no better area to see the link between planning and controlling than in customer service. If a company proclaims customer service as one of its goals, it quickly and clearly becomes apparent whether or not that goal is being achieved by seeing how satisfied customers are with their service. How can managers control the interactions between the goal and the outcome when it comes to customers? The concept of a service profit chain can help (see Exhibit 11-18).

service profit chain
The service sequence from employees to customers to profit.

The **service profit chain** is the service sequence from employees to customers to profit.[71] According to this concept, the company's strategy and service delivery system influences how employees serve customers—their attitudes, behaviours, and service capability. Service capability, in turn, enhances how productive employees are in providing service and the quality of that service. The level of employee service productivity and service quality influences customer perceptions of service value. When service value is high, it has a positive impact on customer satisfaction, which leads to customer loyalty. And customer loyalty improves organizational revenue growth and profitability.

So what does the concept of a service profit chain mean for managers? Managers who want to control customer interactions should work to create long-term and mutually beneficial relationships among the company, employees, and customers. How? By creating a work environment that not only enables employees to deliver high levels of quality service, but also makes them feel they are capable of delivering top-quality service. In such a service climate, employees are motivated to deliver superior service.

There is no better example of the service profit chain in action than WestJet Airlines. WestJet is the most consistently profitable Canadian airline, and its customers are fiercely loyal. This is because the company's operating strategy (hiring, training, rewards and recognition, teamwork, and so forth) is built around customer service. Employees consistently deliver outstanding service value to customers. And WestJet's customers reward the company by coming back. It's through efficiently and effectively controlling these customer interactions that companies such as WestJet and Enterprise have succeeded.

SUMMARY AND IMPLICATIONS

❶ What is control? Control is the process of monitoring activities to ensure that they are being accomplished as planned and of correcting any significant deviations. Managers can measure a variety of performances, but the most frequently used ones are organizational productivity, organizational effectiveness, and industry rankings.

○○○ When Li Ka-shing first bought Husky Energy, he immediately introduced financial con-
○○○ trols to improve the company's bottom line. He also hired John Lau to stop the losses and halt the expansions that previous managers had introduced. These measures were put in place to make the company profitable.

❷ What is the control process? The control process is a three-step process: measuring actual performance, comparing actual performance against a standard, and taking managerial action to correct deviations or inadequate standards.

❸ When should controls be introduced? Managers can implement controls before an activity begins (feedforward control), during the time the activity is going on (concurrent control), and after the activity has been completed (feedback control).

❹ What methods of control do managers use? There are three different approaches to designing control systems: market, bureaucratic, and clan control. Market control emphasizes the use of external market mechanisms, such as price competition and relative market share, to establish the standards used in the control system. Bureaucratic control emphasizes organizational authority and relies on administrative rules, regulations, procedures, and policies. Under clan control, employee behaviours are regulated by the shared values, norms, traditions, rituals, beliefs, and other aspects of the organization's culture.

○○○ Control is often needed to improve organizational performance, as John Lau found
○○○ when he took over Husky Energy and had to halt the company's large losses and the "wild expansions" of the company's previous management.

❺ How do financial and information controls help managers monitor performance? Financial ratio analysis allows managers to monitor how efficiently and profitably the organization uses its assets, debt, inventories, and the like. Budget analysis provides managers with quantitative standards against which to measure and compare resource consumption. Economic value added (EVA) is a tool that measures corporate and divisional performance, while market value added (MVA) measures the stock market's estimate of the value of a firm's past and expected capital investment projects. Information may be used both as a tool to help managers control other organizational activities and as an organizational area that managers need to control.

○○○ At Husky Energy, John Lau uses traditional financial controls, as well as other measures,
○○○ including the number of barrels of oil equivalent (BOE) produced by the company daily.

❻ What are some current issues in control? Some important current issues in control include the balanced scorecard (looking at financial, customer, internal business process, and learning and growth assets), corporate governance, cross-cultural differences, workplace concerns, and customer interactions.

○○○ Husky Energy has a board of directors that looks after the interests of shareholders.
○○○ The primary duty of Husky's board is to "approve, monitor and provide guidance on the strategic planning process." The board also approves Husky's strategic plans, annual budget, and financial plans.

Snapshot Summary

1 What Is Control?
Performance Standards
Measures of Organizational Performance
Why Is Control Important?

2 The Control Process
Measuring Performance
Comparing Performance Against Standard
Taking Managerial Action
Summary of Managerial Decisions

3 When to Introduce Control
Feedforward Control
Concurrent Control
Feedback Control

4 Methods of Control
Market Control
Bureaucratic Control
Clan Control

5 Financial and Information Controls
Traditional Financial Control Measures
Other Financial Control Measures
Information Controls

6 Current Issues in Control
Balanced Scorecard
Corporate Governance
Cross-Cultural Differences
Workplace Concerns
Customer Interactions

Management @ Work

READING FOR COMPREHENSION

1. What is the role of control in management?

2. What are three approaches to designing control systems?

3. Explain the source of an organization's culture and how that culture is maintained.

4. Describe how culture is transmitted to employees.

5. Name four methods managers can use to acquire information about actual organizational performance.

6. Contrast immediate and basic corrective action.

7. What are the advantages and disadvantages of feedforward control?

8. Describe the financial control measures managers can use.

9. What can management do to implement a benchmarking best-practices program?

10. What challenges do managers of global organizations face with their control systems?

LINKING CONCEPTS TO PRACTICE

1. How are planning and control linked? Is the control function linked to the organizing and leading functions of management? Explain.

2. Why do you think feedback control is the most popular type of control? Justify your response.

3. How could you use the concept of control in your own personal life? Be specific. (Think in terms of feedforward, concurrent, and feedback controls as well as controls for the different areas of your life.)

4. Why is it that what is measured probably is more critical to the control process than how it is measured?

5. When do electronic surveillance devices such as computers, video cameras, and telephone monitoring step over the line from "effective management controls" to "intrusions on employee rights"?

6. What would an organization have to do to change its dominant control approach from bureaucratic to clan? From clan to bureaucratic?

7. "Every individual employee in the organization plays a role in controlling work activities." Do you agree or do you think control is something that only managers are responsible for? Explain.

SELF-ASSESSMENT

How Proactive Am I?

For each of the following statements, circle the level of agreement or disagreement that you personally feel:[72]

1 = Strongly Disagree 2 = Moderately Disagree 3 = Slightly Disagree 4 = Neither Agree nor Disagree
5 = Slightly Agree 6 = Moderately Agree 7 = Strongly Agree

1. I am constantly on the lookout for new ways to improve my life.   1 2 3 4 5 6 7

2. I feel driven to make a difference in my community, and maybe the world.   1 2 3 4 5 6 7

3. I tend to let others take the initiative to start new projects.   1 2 3 4 5 6 7

4. Wherever I have been, I have been a powerful force for constructive change.   1 2 3 4 5 6 7

5. I enjoy facing and overcoming obstacles to my ideas.   1 2 3 4 5 6 7

6. Nothing is more exciting than seeing my ideas turn into reality.   1 2 3 4 5 6 7

7. If I see something I don't like, I fix it.   1 2 3 4 5 6 7

8. No matter what the odds, if I believe in something I will make it happen.   1 2 3 4 5 6 7

9. I love being a champion for my ideas, even against others' opposition.   1 2 3 4 5 6 7

10. I excel at identifying opportunities.   1 2 3 4 5 6 7

11. I am always looking for better ways to do things.   1 2 3 4 5 6 7

12. If I believe in an idea, no obstacle will prevent me from making it happen.   1 2 3 4 5 6 7

13. I love to challenge the status quo.   1 2 3 4 5 6 7

14. When I have a problem, I tackle it head-on.   1 2 3 4 5 6 7

15. I am great at turning problems into opportunities.   1 2 3 4 5 6 7

16. I can spot a good opportunity long before others can.   1 2 3 4 5 6 7

17. If I see someone in trouble, I help out in any way I can.   1 2 3 4 5 6 7

Scoring Key

Add up the numbers for each of your responses to get your total score.

Analysis and Interpretation

This instrument assesses proactive personality. Research finds that the proactive personality is positively associated with entrepreneurial intentions.

Your proactive personality score will range between 17 and 119. The higher your score, the stronger your proactive personality. High scores on this questionnaire suggest you have strong inclinations toward becoming an entrepreneur.

More Self-Assessments

To learn more about your skills, abilities, and interests, take the following self-assessments on MyManagementLab at www.pearsoned.ca/mymanagementlab:

- I.E.2.—What Time of Day Am I Most Productive?
- II.B.5.—How Good Am I at Disciplining Others?
- III.A.2.—How Willing Am I to Delegate?
- III.A.3.—How Good Am I at Giving Performance Feedback? (This exercise also appears in Chapter 7 on pages 221–222.)

MANAGEMENT FOR YOU TODAY

Dilemma

Your parents have let you know that they are expecting a big party for their twenty-fifth wedding anniversary, and that you are in charge of planning it. Develop a timeline for carrying out the project, and then identify ways to monitor progress toward getting the party planned. How will you know that your plans have been successful? At what critical points do you need to examine your plans to make sure that everything is on track?

Becoming a Manager

- Identify the types of controls you use in your own personal life and whether they are feedforward, concurrent, or feedback controls.

- When preparing for major class projects, identify some performance measures that you can use to help you determine whether or not the project is going as planned.
- Try to come up with some ways to improve your personal efficiency and effectiveness.

WORKING TOGETHER: TEAM-BASED EXERCISE

Applying Feedforward, Concurrent, and Feedback Controls

You will be assigned 1 or more of the following tasks:

1. You are a consultant to a manager of a small retail clothing store. Over the past six months the manager has noticed that a significant amount of inventory has gone missing. The manager is not sure whether it is employees or customers who are taking things from the store. The manager has a somewhat limited budget, but wants to know what possibilities there are for controlling inventory. You have agreed to present a set of recommendations, identifying feedforward, concurrent, and feedback mechanisms that the manager might use.

2. You are a student in a business program at a local college or university. Several of your professors have expressed an interest in developing some specific controls to minimize opportunities for students to cheat on homework assignments and exams. Because you find cheating offensive, you and some other students have volunteered to write a report outlining some

suggestions that might be used to control possible cheating (1) before it happens, (2) while in-class exams or assignments are being completed, and (3) after it has happened.

3. Devise control measures for each of the tasks involved in delivering a beverage to a Starbucks customer. Determine whether the measure is a feedforward, concurrent, or a feedback control.

Be prepared to present your suggestions before the rest of the class.

ETHICS IN ACTION

Ethical Dilemma Exercise: Should Surfing Adult Websites on a Personal Laptop at Work Be Considered Private?

Pornography and offensive email are two major reasons why many companies establish strict policies and monitor their employees' use of the Internet.[73] Citing legal and ethical concerns, managers are determined to keep inappropriate images and messages out of the workplace. "As a company, if we don't make some effort to keep offensive material off our network, we could end up on the wrong end of a sexual harassment lawsuit or other legal action that could cost the company hundreds of thousands of dollars," says the technology manager at one small business. "To a company our size, that would be devastating." Another reason is cost. Unauthorized Internet activity not only wastes valuable work time, but also ties up network resources. Thus, many companies have installed electronic systems to screen email messages and monitor what employees do online. In some companies, one person is designated to review incoming emails and delete offensive messages.

Having a clear policy and a monitoring system are only first steps. Management must be sure that employees are aware of the rules—and understand that the company is se-

rious about cleaning up any ethics violations. British Telecom (BT), for example, twice sent emails to remind all its employees that looking at online pornography was grounds for dismissal. Despite the warnings, management had to fire 200 employees in an 18-month period. Going further, the company told police about 10 employees' activities, and one has already been sentenced to prison. "We took this decision for the good of BT," explained a spokesperson, "and since we have taken this action, the problem has reduced dramatically."

Imagine that you are the administrative assistant for a high-ranking executive at BT. One afternoon you receive an urgent phone call for your manager. You knock on his office door but get no answer, so you open the door, thinking you will leave a note on his desk. Then you notice that your manager is absorbed in watching a very graphic adult website on his personal laptop. As you quietly back out of the office, you wonder how to handle this situation. Review this chapter's "Workplace Privacy" section on pages 349–350 as you consider this ethical challenge.

Thinking Critically About Ethics

Duplicating software for co-workers and friends is a widespread practice, but software in Canada is protected by copyright laws. Copying software is punishable by fines of up to $20 000. Businesses can be held accountable if their employees use unlicensed software on company computers.

Is reproducing copyrighted software ever an acceptable practice? Explain. Is it wrong for employees of a business to pirate software but permissible for struggling students who cannot afford to buy their own software? As a manager, what types of ethical guidelines could you establish for software use? What if you were a manager in another country where software piracy was an accepted practice?

CASE APPLICATION

Air Canada and WestJet Airlines

Without information, managers cannot make good decisions.[74] In order to make good decisions, then, companies need to protect their information. Executives at Air Canada thought they had. However, managers were shocked when

they discovered that outsiders had penetrated their website to steal data. Their experience raises some troubling questions about the security of company information in the Internet age.

One of Air Canada's former employees, Jeffrey Lafond, had a password for an Air Canada employee travel website that listed all of the company's flights and passenger loads. The password had been given to him as part of a severance package in 2000. It was meant to enable Lafond to book two free flights of his choice a year through 2005.

Lafond subsequently became a financial analyst at WestJet Airlines, and Mark Hill, WestJet co-founder and vice-president of strategic planning, learned of Lafond's ability to access the Air Canada website. Hill asked for Lafond's password, so that he could access the website himself.

Hill used the password to count Air Canada's load factors, spending about 90 minutes an evening doing so. Because it was so time-consuming to do this by hand, Don Bell, WestJet's vice-president of customer service and another airline co-founder, asked a WestJet IT staff member to create a program to automatically download and analyze Air Canada's load factors. Air Canada claims that WestJet entered Air Canada's website 240 000 times between May 2003 and March 2004, using Lafond's password.

Air Canada filed a lawsuit against WestJet. In a countersuit, WestJet accused Air Canada of collecting garbage from Hill's house in an effort to determine exactly how he was using Air Canada's data.

In May 2006, to put an end to the lawsuits, WestJet admitted that senior executives stole confidential information and apologized to Air Canada. They agreed to pay Air Canada $5.5 million for its legal fees and donate $10 million to children's charities.

Should Lafond have given Hill his password? What other ethical issues do you see in this case? What should Air Canada's chief information officer do to ensure that information is available to those who need it, but not available to outsiders who may use the information for competitive advantage?

DEVELOPING YOUR DIAGNOSTIC AND ANALYTICAL SKILLS

Baggage Blunders

Terminal 5, built by British Airways for $8.6 billion, is Heathrow Airport's newest state-of-the-art facility.[75] Made of glass, concrete, and steel, it's the largest freestanding building in the United Kingdom. At the terminal's unveiling on March 15, 2008, Queen Elizabeth II called it a "twenty-first-century gateway to Britain." Alas . . . the accolades didn't last long! After two decades of planning and 100 million hours of labour, opening day didn't work out as planned. Endless lines and severe baggage handling delays led to numerous flight cancellations, stranding many irate passengers. Airport operators said the problems were triggered by glitches in the terminal's high-tech baggage-handling system.

With its massive automation features, Terminal 5 was planned to ease congestion at Heathrow and improve the flying experience of the 30 million passengers expected to pass through it annually. However, despite 96 self-service check-in kiosks, more than 90 check-in fast bag drops, 54 standard check-in desks, and over 16 kilometres of suitcase-moving belts that were supposed to be able to process 12 000 bags per hour, the facility's design did not seem to support those goals.

Within the first few hours of the terminal's operation, problems developed. Baggage workers, presumably understaffed, were unable to clear incoming luggage fast enough. Many arriving passengers had to wait more than an hour to get their bags. There were problems for departing passengers, as well, as many tried in vain to check in for flights. Flights were allowed to leave with empty cargo holds. At one point that first day, the airline had no choice but to check in only those with no luggage. And it did not help matters that the moving belt system jammed at one point. Lesser problems also became apparent: a few broken escalators, some hand dryers that did not work, a gate that would not function at the new Underground station, and inexperienced ticket sellers who did not know the fares between Heathrow and various stations on the Piccadilly line. By the end of the first full day of operation, Britain's Department of Transportation released a statement calling for British Airways and the airport operator BAA to "work hard to resolve these issues and limit disruptions to passengers."

You might be tempted to think that all this could have been prevented if British Airways had only tested the system. But thorough runs of all systems "from toilets to check in and seating" took place six months before opening, including four full-scale test runs using 16 000 volunteers.

Questions

1. What type of control—feedforward, concurrent, or feedback—do you think would be most important in this situation? Explain your choice.

2. How might immediate corrective action have been used in this situation? How about basic corrective action?

3. Could British Airways' controls have been more effective? How?

4. What role would information controls play in this situation? Customer interaction controls? Benchmarking?

DEVELOPING YOUR INTERPERSONAL SKILLS

Providing Feedback

About the Skill

In this chapter, we introduced several suggestions for providing feedback. One of the more critical feedback sessions will occur when you, as a manager, are using feedback control to address performance issues.

Steps in Developing the Skill

You can be more effective at providing feedback if you use the following 10 suggestions:[76]

1. **Schedule the feedback session in advance and be prepared.** One of the biggest mistakes you can make is to treat feedback control lightly. Simply calling in an employee and giving feedback that is not well organized serves little purpose for you and your employee. For feedback to be effective, you must plan ahead. Identify the issues you wish to address and cite specific examples to reinforce what you are saying. Furthermore, set aside the time for the meeting with the employee. Make sure that what you do is done in private and can be completed without interruptions. That may mean closing your office door (if you have one), holding phone calls, and the like.

2. **Put the employee at ease.** Regardless of how you feel about the feedback, you must create a supportive climate for the employee. Recognize that giving and getting this feedback can be an emotional event even when the feedback is positive. By putting your employee at ease, you begin to establish a supportive environment in which understanding can take place.

3. **Make sure the employee knows the purpose of this feedback session.** What is the purpose of the meeting? That is something any employee will wonder. Clarifying what you are going to do sets the appropriate stage for what is to come.

4. **Focus on specific rather than general work behaviours.** Feedback should be specific rather than general. General statements are vague and provide little useful information—especially if you are attempting to correct a problem.

5. **Keep comments impersonal and job-related.** Feedback should be descriptive rather than judgmental or evaluative, especially when you are giving negative feedback. No matter how upset you are, keep the feedback job-related and never criticize someone personally because of an inappropriate action. You are censuring job-related behaviour, not the person.

6. **Support feedback with hard data.** Tell your employee how you came to your conclusion about his or her performance. Hard data help your employees identify with specific behaviours. Identify the "things" that were done correctly and provide a detailed critique. If you do need to criticize, state the basis of your conclusion that a good job was not completed.

7. **Direct the negative feedback toward work-related behaviour that the employee controls.** Negative feedback should be directed toward work-related behaviour that the employee can do something about. Suggest what he or she can do to improve the situation. This practice helps take the sting out of the criticism and offers guidance to an individual who understands the problem but does not know how to resolve it.

8. **Let the employee speak.** Get the employee's perceptions of what you are saying, especially if you are addressing a problem. Of course, you are not looking for excuses, but you need to be empathetic to the employee. Get his or her side. Maybe there is something that has contributed to the issue. Letting the employee speak involves your employee and just might provide information you were unaware of.

9. **Ensure that the employee has a clear and full understanding of the feedback.** Feedback must be concise and complete enough that your employee clearly and fully understands what you have said. Consistent with active listening techniques, have your employee rephrase the content of your feedback to check whether it fully captures your meaning.

10. **Detail a future plan of action.** Performing does not stop simply because feedback occurred. Good performance must be reinforced and new performance goals set. However, when there are performance deficiencies, time must be devoted to helping your employee develop a detailed, step-by-step plan to correct the situation. This plan includes what has to be done, when, and how you will monitor the activities. Offer whatever assistance you can to help the employee, but make it clear that it is the employee, not you, who has to make the corrections.

Practising the Skill

This exercise can help you learn how managers might use feedback control when starting a project. Think of a skill you would like to acquire or improve, or a habit you would like to break. Perhaps you would like to learn a foreign language, start exercising, quit smoking, ski better, or spend less. For the purpose of this exercise, assume you have 3 months to make a start on your project and all the necessary funds.

Draft a plan of action that outlines what you need to do, when you need to do it, and how you will know that you have successfully completed each step of your plan. Be realistic, but do not set your sights too low either. Review your plan.

What outside help or resources will you require? How will you get them? Add these to your plan. Ask someone to follow the steps in your plan. What modifications did the person suggest you make, if any?

MANAGING WORKFORCE DIVERSITY

Diversity Success Stories

Canadian companies are making progress in their diversity programs.[77] Although many still have a long way to go, some companies are doing their best to make employees of all races into full and active participants in their businesses. *Canadian Business* and Rogers OMNI TV recently identified top places for visible minorities and Aboriginal peoples to work. Each of the companies on this list has made a strong commitment to diversity at every organizational level and in every aspect—from new hires to suppliers, and even to the charitable causes supported. Who are some of these diversity champions? The top 10 are Call-Net Enterprises (now part of Rogers), Canadian Imperial Bank of Commerce, TD Bank Financial Group, Bank of Nova Scotia, Bank of Montreal, HSBC Bank Canada, TELUS Mobility, Canadian Western Bank, Citizens Bank of Canada, and Westcoast Energy (now Duke Energy Gas Transmission Canada).

At Vancouver-based HSBC Bank Canada, 43.3 percent of the employees are from visible minorities. "Diversity is core to our business," says former executive vice-president Sarah Morgan-Silvester.

Canadian Business recently recognized Ottawa-based Nasittuq Corporation, which monitors 47 radar stations that protect Canadian skies from threats, as one of Canada's most inclusive workplaces for Aboriginal peoples. Nasittuq runs a training program that introduces Inuit to the North Warning System. Graduates are then hired by Nasittuq or find jobs with other companies because of the skills they have acquired.

How can companies use control mechanisms to make sure that they have a diverse workforce? Do you think companies should make special efforts to recruit employees with diverse characteristics? Why or why not? What would be the business advantages of doing so?

CHAPTER

12

Managing Change

How can I manage and encourage change?

1   What factors create the need for change?

2   Is change ongoing or episodic?

3   How do organizations manage change and resistance to change?

4   What are current issues in managing change?

Carol Bartz took on the challenging task of being CEO of Yahoo! in early 2009, after the company had suffered a sharp decline in fortunes over the previous several years. In 2005, Yahoo! and Google had the same market share, about 19 percent. By late 2006 Yahoo! was starting to lose its top position in providing web services to Internet users, facing stiff competition for visitors and advertisers from Google, Microsoft's MSN, America Online, and even MySpace.[1] Yahoo!'s shares were slumping, revenue growth was slowed, staff were leaving in alarming numbers, and a crucial project code-name "Panama," was delayed. More importantly, Google's market share was about 25 percent of US online-ad revenue, and Yahoo!'s had fallen to 18 percent at the end of 2006.

Concerns about the company's problems at the time were so high that a Yahoo! senior vice-president, Brad Garlinghouse, wrote a memo later dubbed "The Peanut Butter Manifesto" to Yahoo!'s top executives, noting that Yahoo! was losing ground. Garlinghouse argued that Yahoo! was spreading its resources too thin, "thus we focus on nothing in particular." He recommended that the company undergo a deep reorganization, lay off 15 to 20 percent of the workforce, and make executives accountable for poor performance.

About eight months after "The Peanut Butter Manifesto" was written,
Yahoo! finally made a change industry analysts hoped would make the difference. On June 18, 2007, Terry Semel stepped down as Yahoo! CEO. In his place, the company appointed Jerry Yang, one of Yahoo!'s co-founders, as CEO and Susan Decker as president. High hopes were placed on the two to "cut through the bureaucracy and indecision," and lead Yahoo! back to the front of the pack. Six months later, Microsoft made an unsolicited bid to take over Yahoo! Many wondered: Would Yang be able to turn Yahoo! around and lead it back to its position of leadership in the industry?

Think About It

Can large organizations be innovative at the same speed as smaller organizations? Put yourself in Jerry Yang's shoes. You are faced with major competition from several newer, smaller, and innovative organizations. Meanwhile, Yahoo! has grown so bureaucratic in recent years, that it has stopped acting rapidly in the face of opportunities. How would you go about making Yahoo! respond more quickly?

Big companies and small businesses, universities and colleges, and governments at all levels are being forced to significantly change the way they do things. Although change has always been a part of the manager's job, it has become even more important in recent years. In this chapter, we describe the forces that lead to change and how managers can manage change. We conclude by looking at the critical concerns managers face when managing change today.

Forces for Change

❶ What factors create the need for change?

If it were not for change, the manager's job would be relatively easy. Planning would be simple because tomorrow would be no different from today. The issue of effective organizational design would also be solved because the environment would be free from uncertainty and there would be no need to adapt. Similarly, decision making would be dramatically streamlined because the outcome of each alternative could be predicted with almost certain accuracy. It would, indeed, simplify the manager's job if, for example, competitors did not introduce new products or services, if customers did not demand new and improved products, if government regulations were never modified, or if employees' needs never changed. But that is not the way it is. Change is an organizational reality.[2] And managing change is an integral part of every manager's job. In Chapter 2, we pointed out the external and internal forces that constrain managers. These same forces also bring about the need for change. Let's look briefly at these forces.

External Forces

Are there external forces that might suggest to you that your college or university might think about doing things differently?

The external forces that create the need for change come from various sources. In recent years, the *marketplace* has affected companies such as Yahoo! as competition from Google, MySpace, and Ask Jeeves intensified. These companies constantly adapt to changing consumer desires as they develop new search capabilities.

Government laws and regulations are a frequent impetus for change. For example, the Canadian Securities Administrators rules, which came into effect in 2004, require Canadian companies to change the way they disclose financial information and enact corporate governance.

Technology also creates the need for change. For example, technological improvements in diagnostic equipment have created significant economies of scale for hospitals. Assembly-line technology in other industries is changing dramatically as organizations replace human labour with robots. In the greeting card industry, email and the Internet have changed the way people exchange greeting cards. Technological change from analogue to digital recording has meant the shift from records to CDs, videotapes to DVDs, and film to digital cameras. In just 10 years, DVD players have gone from the test stage to virtually eliminating the videotape rental market. The companies that produce videotapes and the companies that rent them have had to develop new strategies or go out of business.

The fluctuation in *labour markets* also forces managers to change. Organizations that need certain kinds of employees must change their human resource management activities to attract and retain skilled employees in the areas of greatest need. For example, health care organizations facing severe nursing shortages have had to change the way they schedule work hours.

Economic changes, of course, affect almost all organizations. For example, global recessionary pressures force organizations to become more cost-efficient. But even in a strong economy, uncertainties about interest rates, federal budget deficits, and currency exchange rates create conditions that may force organizations to change.

Internal Forces

In addition to the external forces just described, internal forces also create the need for change. These internal forces tend to originate primarily from the internal operations of the organization or from the impact of external changes.

A redefinition or modification of an organization's *strategy* often introduces a variety of changes. For instance, when Steve Bennett took over as president and CEO of Intuit (Quicken, QuickBooks, and QuickTax are its best-known products), the company was losing money. By orchestrating a series of well-planned and dramatic strategic changes, he turned Intuit into a profitable company with extremely committed employees, as the following *Management Reflection* shows.

MANAGEMENT REFLECTION

Steve Bennett Transforms Intuit

Can a company stay entrepreneurial and become more structured? When Steve Bennett was hired as Intuit's president and CEO in 2000, he had never worked for a high-tech firm.[3] He had spent all of his career with General Electric. Intuit's founder, Scott Cook, was looking for someone who could take Intuit to the next level. The company was struggling to break through the $1 billion (US) revenue wall, and Cook wanted the company to reach $10 billion (US) in revenue.

After he was hired, Bennett spent five weeks interviewing employees at more than 12 of Intuit's locations. He found a company still being run as haphazardly as a start-up venture. "The operation was a mess. It was losing money. Its technology was outdated. Execution was grindingly slow, and nothing was documented."[4] He discovered the organization had a democratic culture that nurtured employees to make sure they felt good. Managers chose whatever brand of PC they wanted to use, the employees were always holding meetings, and different units were responsible for the same product's development and sales support. Bennett felt the employees had to change how they viewed their work: "I wanted them to know that a company can be focused on high performance and still be a good place to work," he says.

Bennett introduced a number of changes, including putting business units in charge of development and customer service, introducing zero-based budgeting, and ordering the same computers for everyone to manage costs. He also flattened the organization, taking on 18 direct reports, rather than 8, so that he could drive change faster. "If you have that many direct reports, you don't have time to meddle in their business. My job is to conduct the orchestra, not to play all the instruments." He also introduced a new motto: "Mind your minutes." Employees were not to be involved in endless meetings, and they were to focus on the things that were really important. ■

In addition, an organization's *workforce* is rarely static. Its composition changes in terms of age, education, ethnic background, sex, and so forth. Take, for example, an organization in which a large number of older executives, for financial reasons, decide to continue working instead of retiring. There might be a need to restructure jobs in order to retain and motivate younger managers. Also, the compensation and benefits system might need to be adapted to reflect the needs of this older workforce.

The introduction of new *equipment* represents another internal force for change. Employees may have their jobs redesigned, need to undergo training on how to operate the new equipment, or be required to establish new interaction patterns within their work groups.

Finally, *employee attitudes* such as job dissatisfaction may lead to increased absenteeism, more voluntary resignations, and even labour strikes. Such events often lead to changes in management policies and practices.

This chapter's *Managing Workforce Diversity—The Paradox of Diversity*, on page 385, notes the challenge managers face when they are balancing competing goals under change: to encourage employees to accept the organization's dominant values and to encourage employees to accept differences.

Two Views of the Change Process

For years Yahoo!—which helped give birth to the commercial Internet in 1994—dominated the Internet services market.[5] By 2005, however, the company started to lose its competitive edge.

The company, well known for its banner and video ads, was targeted by both Google (who bought online ad firm DoubleClick) and Microsoft (who bought digital marketing firm aQuantive). Yahoo! tried to make a deal with Facebook but was not successful, while Google bought the leading video-sharing site YouTube. Yahoo!'s response to competition has been comparatively slow, although it did buy 80 percent of advertising network RightMedia in April 2007.[6]

Because Yahoo! delayed its response to competition from Google, it faced even bigger challenges. In 2007, Google was worth $158 billion on the stock market while Yahoo! was valued at $42 billion. By late 2008, after a bruising battle with Microsoft, which had tried to buy the company, Yahoo!'s shares were trading at historic lows, and its valuation was down to $16 billion.[7]

> **Think About It**
>
> How does change happen in organizations? Is change a constant process, or can organizations take breaks from worrying about change, as Yahoo! seems to have done in the last few years?

❷ Is change ongoing or episodic?

We can use two very different metaphors to describe the change process.[8] One metaphor envisions the organization as a large ship crossing calm waters. The ship's captain and crew know exactly where they are going because they have made the trip many times before. Change comes in the form of an occasional storm, a brief distraction in an otherwise calm and predictable trip. In the other metaphor, the organization is seen as a small raft navigating a raging river with uninterrupted white-water rapids. Aboard the raft are half a dozen people who have never worked together before, who are totally unfamiliar with the river, who are unsure of their eventual destination, and who, as if things were not bad enough, are travelling at night. In the white-water rapids metaphor, change is an expected and natural state, and managing change is a continuous process. These two metaphors present very different approaches to understanding and responding to change. Let's take a closer look at each one.

The Calm Waters Metaphor

Up until the late 1980s, the calm waters metaphor pretty much described the situation that managers faced. It's best illustrated by Kurt Lewin's three-step description of the change process (see Exhibit 12-1).[9]

According to Lewin, successful change can be planned and requires *unfreezing* the status quo, *changing* to a new state, and *refreezing* to make the change permanent. The status quo can be considered an equilibrium state. To move from this equilibrium, unfreezing is necessary. Unfreezing can be thought of as preparing for the needed change. It can be achieved by increasing the *driving forces*, which are forces that drive change and direct behaviour away from the status quo; decreasing the *restraining forces*, which are forces

Exhibit 12-1

The Change Process

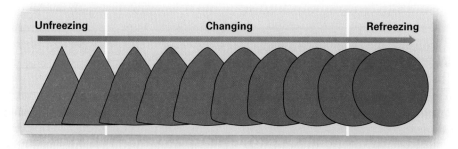

that resist change and push behaviour toward the status quo; or combining the two approaches.

Once unfreezing is done, the change itself can be implemented. However, merely introducing change does not ensure that the change will take hold. The new situation needs to be *refrozen* so that it can be sustained over time. Unless this last step is taken, there is a strong chance that the change will be short-lived as employees revert back to the old equilibrium state—that is, the old ways of doing things. The objective of refreezing, then, is to stabilize the new situation by reinforcing the new behaviours.

Note how Lewin's three-step process treats change simply as a break in the organization's equilibrium state. The status quo has been disturbed and change is necessary to establish a new equilibrium state. However, a calm waters environment is not what most managers face today.[10]

Q&A 16.1

The White-Water Rapids Metaphor

The white-water rapids metaphor is consistent with our discussion of uncertain and dynamic environments in Chapters 2 and 3. It's also consistent with a world that is increasingly dominated by information, ideas, and knowledge.[11] We can see how the metaphor applies to Microsoft, which is currently facing an uncertain and dynamic environment after dominating the software industry for many years.

To get a feeling of what managing change might be like when you have to continuously manoeuvre in uninterrupted and uncertain rapids, consider attending a college or university that has the following rules: Courses vary in length. Unfortunately, when you sign up, you do not know how long a course will run. It might go for 2 weeks or 30 weeks. Furthermore, the instructor can end a course any time he or she wants, with no prior warning. If that is not bad enough, the length of the class changes each time it meets: Sometimes the class lasts 20 minutes; other times it runs for 3 hours. The time of the next class meeting is set by the instructor during this class. There is one more thing. All exams are unannounced, so you have to be ready for a test at any time. To succeed in this type of environment, you would have to be incredibly flexible and able to respond quickly to changing conditions. Students who are overly structured, slow to respond, or uncomfortable with change would not survive.

Growing numbers of managers are coming to accept that their jobs are very much like what students would face in such a college or university. The stability and predictability of the calm waters metaphor do not exist. Disruptions in the status quo are not occasional and temporary, and they are not followed by a return to calm waters. Many managers never get out of the rapids. They face constant change, bordering on chaos.

Is the white-water rapids metaphor an exaggeration? No! Although you would expect this type of chaotic and dynamic environment in high-tech industries, even organizations in non-high-tech industries are faced with constant change.

To learn about your response to working in a changing workplace, see *Self-Assessment—How Well Do I Respond to Turbulent Change?* on pages 379–380, at the end of the chapter.

When Dr. George Saleh switched his medical practice to a digital paperless system, the initial results were chaotic as he and his staff learned to work with the new software, entering patient information on a screen with drop-down menus, for example, instead of on a clipboard. After a few months, however, Dr. Saleh found himself seeing the same number of patients in less time, reducing his secretarial expenses, and being reimbursed by insurance companies in days instead of months. He can access his patient records from home or from the hospital, search his patient database to find out who is taking which drug, and spend time asking patients important questions about partner abuse or sexual dysfunction. The new system "has made me a better doctor," says Dr. Saleh. "It has changed the way I work every day."

Putting the Two Views in Perspective

Does *every* manager face a world of constant and chaotic change? No, but the number who do not is dwindling. Managers in such businesses as telecommunications, computer software, and women's clothing have long confronted a world of white-water rapids. These managers used to envy their counterparts in industries such as banking, utilities, oil exploration, publishing, and air transportation, where the environment was historically more stable and predictable. However, those days of stability and predictability are long gone!

Today, any organization that treats change as an occasional disturbance in an otherwise calm and stable world runs a great risk. Too much is changing too fast for an organization or its managers to be complacent. It's no longer business as usual. Managers must be ready to efficiently and effectively manage the changes facing their organizations or their work areas. Nevertheless, managers have to be certain that change is the right thing to do at any given time. Law firm Brobeck, Phleger & Harrison had a disastrous strategy for change, as the following *Management Reflection* shows.

MANAGEMENT REFLECTION

To Change or Not to Change?

How important is a company's strategy for change? Brobeck, Phleger & Harrison had been a prominent San Francisco law firm for 70 years when the technology boom happened in the late 1990s.[12] Located in the heart of California's Silicon Valley, the firm saw great opportunity to engage in dot-com and venture capital deals. At first the strategy paid off, with the company handling 74 initial public offerings (IPOs) in 1999. Many new lawyers were added to the firm, and they were offered huge salaries. Average compensation increased more than 50 percent. The company expanded the number of offices it had throughout the United States, and signed very expensive leases for very large buildings to house the offices. Two years later, the firm handled just three IPOs, but Brobeck continued to increase expenses dramatically. By 2003 Brobeck had lost many of its best performing partners and was in debt to Citibank for $140 million.

Why did everything go so wrong? When Brobeck developed its plan for the technology boom, the firm decided that it would handle only the corporate side of business: "buying and selling shares, taking options in companies." Brobeck refused any business on the commercial side, which might have balanced things when the technology bubble burst. ∎

As Brobeck's experience shows, companies need to carefully consider change strategies, as change can lead to failure. If change is the appropriate course of action, how should it be managed? That is what we discuss next.

Q&A 16.2

Managing Change

When Jerry Yang returned to the helm of Yahoo! it was hoped that he would be able to inspire the company's employees in a way that former CEO Terry Semel did not seem able to do.[13] Many felt that Semel's background did not help him steer Yahoo! to a more visionary future. Semel was a Warner Bros. movie executive before joining Yahoo! in 2001. Yang is much quieter, but many of the successful Silicon Valley firms, such as Apple and Oracle, are run by their founders. "He's no Steve Jobs," said Ned May, an industry analyst. "But he's a founder. Putting a founder back in the reins will create excitement inside Yahoo!"

Think About It

What advantages might come from bringing back a co-founder to help with the changes needed at Yahoo!? Could there be any disadvantages?

3 How do organizations manage change and resistance to change?

organizational change
Any alteration of people, structure, or technology in an organization.

change agent
Someone who acts as a catalyst and assumes the responsibility for managing the change process.

What Is Organizational Change?

Most managers, at one point or another, will have to make changes in some aspects of their workplace. We classify these changes as **organizational change**—which is any alteration of people, structure, or technology. Organizational changes often need someone to act as a catalyst and assume the responsibility for managing the change process—that is, a **change agent**. Who can be change agents?

We assume that changes are initiated and coordinated by a manager within the organization. However, the change agent could be a nonmanager—for example, a change specialist from the HR department or even an outside consultant whose expertise is in change implementation. For major system-wide changes, an organization often hires outside consultants to provide advice and assistance. Because they are from the outside, they offer an objective perspective that insiders may lack. However, outside consultants are usually at a disadvantage because they have a limited understanding of the organization's history, culture, operating procedures, and people. Outside consultants also are likely to initiate more drastic change than insiders would (which can be either a benefit or a disadvantage) because they do not have to live with the repercussions after the change is implemented. In contrast, internal managers who act as change agents may be more thoughtful, but possibly overcautious, because they must live with the consequences of their decisions.

As change agents, managers are motivated to initiate change because they are committed to improving their organization's performance. Initiating change involves identifying what types of changes might be needed and putting the change process in motion. But that is not all there is to managing organizational change. Managers must manage employee resistance to change. What types of organizational change might managers need to make, and how do managers deal with resistance to change?

Types of Change

What *can* a manager change? The manager's options fall into three categories: structure, technology, and people (see Exhibit 12-2). Changing *structure* includes any alteration in authority relations, coordination mechanisms, employee empowerment, job redesign, or similar structural variables. Changing *technology* encompasses modifications in the way work is performed or the methods and equipment that are used. Changing *people* refers to changes in employee attitudes, expectations, perceptions, and behaviour.

Changing Structure

We discussed organizational structure issues in Chapter 5. Managers' organizing responsibilities include such activities as choosing the organization's formal design, allocating authority, and determining the degree of formalization. Once those structural decisions have been made, however, they are not final. Changing conditions or changing strategies brings about the need to make structural changes.

Exhibit 12-2

Three Categories of Change

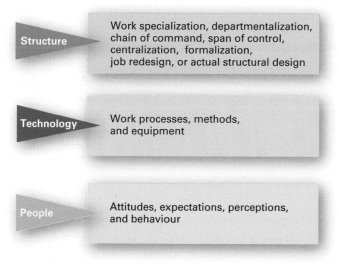

Structure — Work specialization, departmentalization, chain of command, span of control, centralization, formalization, job redesign, or actual structural design

Technology — Work processes, methods, and equipment

People — Attitudes, expectations, perceptions, and behaviour

What options does the manager have for changing structure? The manager has the same ones we introduced in our discussion of organizational structure and design. A few examples should make this clearer. Recall from Chapter 5 that an organization's structure is defined in terms of work specialization, departmentalization, chain of command, span of control, centralization and decentralization, and formalization. Managers can alter one or more of these *structural elements.*

Another option would be to make major changes in the actual *structural design.* For example, this might involve a shift from a functional to a product structure or the creation of a project structure design. Hamilton, Ontario-based Dofasco became a more profitable steel producer after changing its traditional functional structure to a new design that arranges work around cross-functional teams. Some government agencies and private organizations are looking to new organizational ventures, forming public–private partnerships to deal with change, as the following *Management Reflection* shows.

MANAGEMENT REFLECTION

New Ways for Government to Get Jobs Done

Can public–private partnerships work? Federal and provincial governments are trying to come up with new ways to get much-needed projects completed.[14] Tony Fell, chair of Toronto-based RBC Capital Markets, notes that governments need help financing transportation, water, health care, and education systems, which are "deteriorating at an alarming rate." There is much talk about an innovative way of handling these projects: public–private partnerships (P3s), by which the government and the private sector form companies to get things done. Unfortunately, to date most have not been successful. Almost four out of five P3s fail.

Whether they fail because the idea is unworkable or because they suffer from an inability of the public sector and the private sector to figure out appropriate ways to work together is not entirely clear. Gordon Campbell, premier of British Columbia, has been trying to find a successful model to make P3s work. Despite trying to get P3s started that would help with the "$2 billion in public capital projects built annually across the province," only one project has been signed. The private sector seems unwilling to take on risks that the government also does not want to assume.

BC's Canada Line, a rail-based rapid transit line to be built between Vancouver International Airport and downtown Vancouver before the 2010 Olympic Winter Games, was the first BC P3 project to launch, but gaining acceptance for the project was not easy. The provincial government was seen as pushing the project through, while labour unions fought it and Vancouver residents were divided on whether the project should be given a go-ahead.

One successful P3 is Toronto-based Teranet Enterprises, formed in 1995 to create an electronic database of all of the property title records in Ontario, so that lawyers could research and transfer titles in property deals from their office computers. The company has been profitable from the beginning. "The trouble was if government tried it alone, it would probably take 30 to 40 years to get done and cost tens of millions of dollars," says Bonnie Foster, vice-president of corporate affairs and an original member of the Teranet management team.

The difficulties governments face in raising money for and managing large projects suggest that innovative ways to build public infrastructure need to be found. Teranet is one example of how to create a joint public–private venture that works. ■

Changing Technology

Managers can also change the technology used to convert inputs into outputs. This generally involves the introduction of new equipment, tools, or methods; automation (replacing certain tasks done by people with machines); or computerization.

Exhibit 12-3

Organizational Development Techniques

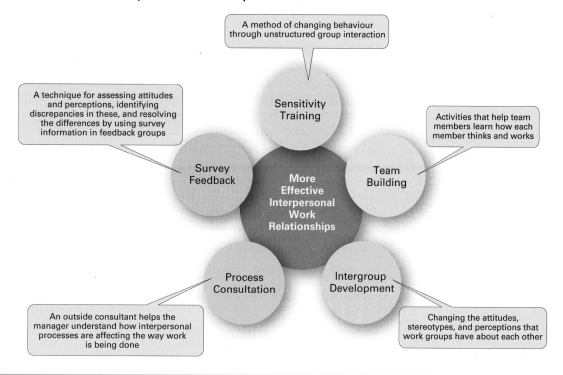

A method of changing behaviour through unstructured group interaction

A technique for assessing attitudes and perceptions, identifying discrepancies in these, and resolving the differences by using survey information in feedback groups

Activities that help team members learn how each member thinks and works

Sensitivity Training

Survey Feedback

More Effective Interpersonal Work Relationships

Team Building

Process Consultation

Intergroup Development

An outside consultant helps the manager understand how interpersonal processes are affecting the way work is being done

Changing the attitudes, stereotypes, and perceptions that work groups have about each other

Changing People

Changing people—that is, changing their attitudes, expectations, perceptions, and behaviours—is not easy. Yet, for over 30 years now, academic researchers and actual managers have been interested in finding ways for individuals and groups within organizations to work together more effectively. The term **organizational development (OD)**, although occasionally used to refer to all types of change in an organization, essentially describes techniques or programs that are meant to change people and the nature and quality of interpersonal work relationships.[15] The most popular OD techniques are described in Exhibit 12-3. The common thread in these techniques is that each seeks to bring about changes in the organization's people. For example, executives at Scotiabank, Canada's second-largest bank, knew that the success of a new customer sales and service strategy depended on changing employee attitudes and behaviours. Managers used different OD techniques during the strategic change including team building, survey feedback, and intergroup development. One indicator of how well these techniques worked in getting people to change was that every branch in Canada implemented the new strategy on or ahead of schedule.[16]

organizational development (OD)
Techniques or programs meant to change people and the nature and quality of interpersonal work relationships.

Making Change Happen Successfully

When changes are needed, who makes them happen? Who manages them? Although you may think that it's the responsibility of top managers, actually managers at *all* organizational levels are involved in the change process.

Even with the involvement of all levels of managers in change efforts, change processes do not always work the way they should. In fact, a global study of organizational change concludes that "Hundreds of managers from scores of U.S. and European companies [are] satisfied with their operating prowess . . . [but] dissatisfied with their ability to implement change."[17] One of the reasons that change fails is that managers do not really know how to introduce change in organizations. Professor John Kotter of Harvard Business School identifies a number of places where managers make mistakes when leading change. These are illustrated in Exhibit 12-4 on page 370. We should also note that recent

Exhibit 12-4

Mistakes Managers Make When Leading Change

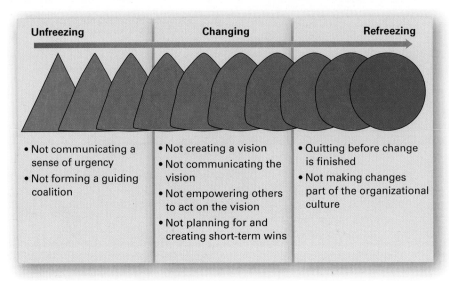

Unfreezing	Changing	Refreezing
• Not communicating a sense of urgency • Not forming a guiding coalition	• Not creating a vision • Not communicating the vision • Not empowering others to act on the vision • Not planning for and creating short-term wins	• Quitting before change is finished • Not making changes part of the organizational culture

Sources: J. P. Kotter, "Leading Change: Why Transformation Efforts Fail," *Harvard Business Review*, March–April 1995, pp. 59–67. With permission from Harvard Business School Publishing. *Management*, First Canadian Edition by Williams/Kondra/Vibert. © 2004. Reprinted with permission of Nelson, a division of Thomson Learning: www.thomsonrights.com. Fax: 800-730-2215.

research emphasizes the need in change processes to manage the "hard stuff" as well as the "soft" or people issues in order to be successful.[18]

How can managers make change happen successfully? Managers can increase the likelihood of making change happen successfully in three ways. First, they should focus on making the organization ready for change. Exhibit 12-5 summarizes the characteristics of organizations that are ready for change.

Exhibit 12-5

Characteristics of Change-Capable Organizations

• *Link the present and the future.* Think of work as more than an extension of the past; think about future opportunities and issues and factor them into today's decisions.

• *Make learning a way of life.* Change-friendly organizations excel at knowledge sharing and management.

• *Actively support and encourage day-to-day improvements and changes.* Successful change can come from the small changes as well as the big ones.

• *Ensure diverse teams.* Diversity ensures that things won't be done the way they are always done.

• *Encourage mavericks.* Since their ideas and approaches are outside the mainstream, mavericks can help bring about radical change.

• *Shelter breakthroughs.* Change-friendly organizations have found ways to protect those breakthrough ideas.

• *Integrate technology.* Use technology to implement changes.

• *Build and deepen trust.* People are more likely to support changes when the organization's culture is trusting and managers have credibility and integrity.

Source: Based on P. A. McLagan, "The Change Capable Organization," *Training & Development*, January 2003, pp. 50–58.

Second, managers need to understand their own role in the change process. They do this by creating a simple, compelling statement of the need for change; communicating constantly and honestly throughout the process; getting as much employee participation as possible; respecting employees' apprehension about the change but encouraging them to be flexible; removing those who resist but only after all possible attempts have been made to get their commitment to the change; aiming for short-term change successes since large-scale change can take a long time; and setting a positive example.[19]

Third, managers need to encourage employees to be change agents—to look for those day-to-day improvements and changes that individuals and teams can make. For example, a recent study of organizational change found that 77 percent of changes at the work-group level were reactions to a specific, current problem or to a suggestion from someone outside the work group; and 68 percent of those changes occurred in the course of employees' day-to-day work.[20]

Communicating Effectively When Undergoing Change

One study examined employee communications programs in 10 leading companies that had successfully undertaken major restructuring programs.[21] Eight factors were found to be related to the effectiveness of employee communications in these companies during times of change: (1) CEOs were committed to communication; (2) management matched their actions to their words; (3) two-way communication between managers and employees was encouraged; (4) the organization emphasized face-to-face communication; (5) managers shared responsibility for employee communication; (6) positive ways were found to deal with bad news; (7) messages were shaped for their intended audience; and (8) communication was treated as an ongoing process. Because the companies studied came from a variety of industries and organizational settings, the authors propose that these eight factors should apply to many types of organizations.

Perhaps the most important lesson from this research is that employees facing change need to be told what is happening and why, in very direct language, in order to reduce their fears. Good communication makes the process of change go more smoothly.

Global OD

Much of what we know about OD practices has come from North American research. However, managers need to recognize that although there may be some similarities in the types of OD techniques used, some techniques that work for North American organizations may not be appropriate for organizations or organizational divisions based in other countries.[22] For example, a study of OD interventions showed that "multirater (survey) feedback as practiced in the United States is not embraced in Taiwan" because the cultural value of "saving face is simply more powerful than the value of receiving feedback from subordinates."[23] What is the lesson for managers? Before using the same techniques to implement behavioral changes, especially across different countries, managers need to be sure that they have taken into account cultural characteristics and whether the techniques "make sense for the local culture."

Managing Resistance to Change

Change can be a threat to people in an organization. Organizations can build up inertia that motivates people to resist changing their status quo, even though change might be beneficial. Why do people resist change and what can be done to minimize their resistance?   **Q&A 16.3**

Why People Resist Change

Resistance to change is well documented.[24] Why *do* people resist change? An individual is likely to resist change for the following reasons: uncertainty, habit, concern over personal loss, and the belief that the change is not in the organization's best interest.[25]

How would you feel if your company, two years after your started there, changed the software you used to enter your contract and sales information?

Change replaces the known with ambiguity and uncertainty. When you finish school, you will be leaving an environment where you know what is expected of you to join an organization where things are uncertain. Employees in organizations are faced with similar uncertainty. For example, when quality control methods based on sophisticated statistical models are introduced into manufacturing plants, many quality control inspectors have to learn the new methods. Some inspectors may fear that they will be unable to do so and may, therefore, develop a negative attitude toward the change or behave poorly if required to use the methods.

Another cause of resistance is that we do things out of habit. Every day, when you go to school or work you probably go the same way. If you are like most people, you find a single route and use it regularly. Human beings are creatures of habit. Life is complex enough—we do not want to have to consider the full range of options for the hundreds of decisions we make every day. To cope with this complexity, we rely on habits or programmed responses. But when confronted with change, this tendency to respond in our accustomed ways becomes a source of resistance.

The third cause of resistance is the fear of losing something already possessed. Change threatens the investment you have already made in the status quo. The more that people have invested in the current system, the more they resist change. Why? They fear the loss of status, money, authority, friendships, personal convenience, or other economic benefits that they value. This helps explain why older employees tend to resist change more than younger employees. Older employees have generally invested more in the current system and thus have more to lose by changing.

A final cause of resistance is a person's belief that the change is incompatible with the goals and interests of the organization. An employee who believes that a proposed new job procedure will reduce product quality or productivity can be expected to resist the change.

Exhibit 12-6

Helping Employees Accept Change

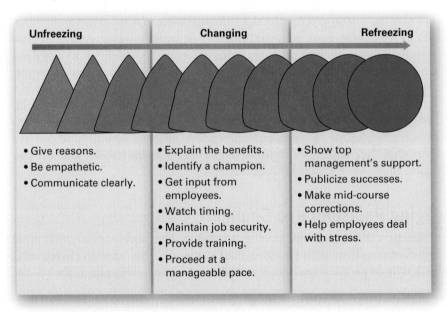

Unfreezing	Changing	Refreezing
• Give reasons. • Be empathetic. • Communicate clearly.	• Explain the benefits. • Identify a champion. • Get input from employees. • Watch timing. • Maintain job security. • Provide training. • Proceed at a manageable pace.	• Show top management's support. • Publicize successes. • Make mid-course corrections. • Help employees deal with stress.

Source: J. Liebowitz and G. J. Iskat, "What to Do When Employees Resist Change," *Supervision* 57, no. 8 (August 1996), pp. 3–5.

Techniques for Reducing Resistance

When managers see resistance to change as dysfunctional, they can use a variety of actions to deal with it.[26] Exhibit 12-6 shows how to manage resistance at the unfreezing, changing, and refreezing stages. Actions include communicating the reasons for change, getting input from employees, choosing the timing of change carefully, and showing management support for the change process. Providing support to employees to deal with the stress of the change is also important. The actions a manager chooses depend on the type and source of the resistance. In general, resistance is likely to be lower if managers involve people in the change, offer training where needed, and are open to revisions once the change has been implemented. For more suggestions on reducing resistance, see *Developing Your Interpersonal Skills—Managing Resistance to Change* on pages 384–385, at the end of the chapter.

PRISM 5

⊙⊙⊙ Current Issues in Managing Change

One of the most difficult challenges Yahoo! CEO Jerry Yang faced in moving the company forward was recapturing the organization's entrepreneurial culture, which it lost under the previous CEO.[27] The culture had become bureaucratic, with lots of separate silos, when what was needed was a sleek, well-run organization. "Jerry won't be able to do much unless he can bring back that entrepreneurial spirit," noted Professor John Sullivan of San Francisco State University's business school.

One of Yang's major challenges in taking over the company was that Microsoft had extended an offer to buy Yahoo! around the time he became CEO. Microsoft's offer was viewed as a hostile takeover attempt, and Yang insisted that the price to sell Yahoo! to Microsoft was considerably higher than Microsoft was prepared to offer. Yang then faced a proxy fight by shareholder Carl Icahn, who had lost confidence in the direction Yahoo! was headed. Microsoft eventually dropped its bid, and Icahn dropped his proxy fight, but the damage to Yahoo! (and Yang) had been done. A large number of senior executives left the company in 2008, and Yahoo! announced a layoff of 10 percent of the company, effective in late 2008.

Yang's vision to restore Yahoo! did not happen, and he stepped down from his position in November 2008. A few months later, in January 2009, Carol Bartz was named his successor.

Think About It
What can companies do to stimulate and nurture innovation?

Today's change issues—changing organizational culture and handling employee stress— are critical concerns for managers. What can managers do to change an organization's culture when that culture no longer supports the organization's mission? What can managers do to handle the stress created by today's dynamic and uncertain environment? These are the topics we look at in this section.

❹ What are current issues in managing change?

Changing Organizational Culture

When W. James McNerney Jr. took over as CEO of 3M Company, he brought with him managerial approaches from his old employer, General Electric. He soon discovered that what was routine at General Electric was unheard of at 3M. For example, he was the only one who showed up at meetings without a tie. His blunt, matter-of-fact, and probing style of asking questions caught many 3M managers off guard. McNerney soon realized that he would need to address the cultural issues before tackling any needed organizational changes.[28]

Q&A 16.6

The fact that an organization's culture is made up of relatively stable and permanent characteristics (see Chapter 11) tends to make that culture very resistant to change.[29] A culture takes a long time to form, and once established it tends to become entrenched. Strong cultures are particularly resistant to change because employees have become so committed to them.

The toy industry is very competitive and picking the next great toy is not easy. Still, Toronto-based Spin Master is better than most at finding the most innovative new toys. Co-CEOs Anton Rabie and Ronnen Harary and Executive Vice-President Ben Varadi rely on intuition. They have also created a "culture of ideas," and pick everyone's brains for new ideas, "from inventors and licensing companies to distributors and retailers around the world." They also give a prize to one employee each month for the best idea.

The explosion of the space shuttle *Columbia* in 2003 highlights how difficult changing an organization's culture can be. An investigation of the explosion found that the causes were remarkably similar to the reasons given for the *Challenger* disaster 20 years earlier.[30] Although foam striking the shuttle was the technical cause, NASA's organizational culture was the real problem. Joseph Grenny, a NASA engineer, noted that "The NASA culture does not accept being wrong." The culture does not accept that "there's no such thing as a stupid question." Instead, "the humiliation factor always runs high."[31] Consequently, people do not speak up. As this example shows, if, over time, a certain culture becomes inappropriate to an organization and a handicap to management, there might be little a manager can do to change it, especially in the short run. Even under favourable conditions, cultural changes have to be viewed in years, not weeks or even months.

Understanding the Situational Factors

What "favourable conditions" might facilitate cultural change? The evidence suggests that cultural change is most likely to take place when most or all of the following conditions exist:

- *A dramatic crisis occurs.* This can be the shock that weakens the status quo and makes people start thinking about the relevance of the current culture. Examples are a surprising financial setback, the loss of a major customer, or a dramatic technological innovation by a competitor.

- *Leadership changes hands.* New top leadership, who can provide an alternative set of key values, may be perceived as more capable of responding to the crisis than the old leaders were. Top leadership includes the organization's chief executive but might include all senior managers.

- *The organization is young and small.* The younger the organization, the less entrenched its culture. Similarly, it's easier for managers to communicate new values in a small organization than in a large one.

- *The culture is weak.* The more widely held the values and the higher the agreement among members on those values, the more difficult it will be to change. Conversely, weak cultures are more receptive to change than are strong ones.[32]

These situational factors help explain why a company such as Microsoft faces challenges in reshaping its culture. For the most part, employees like the old ways of doing things and do not always see the company's problems as critical.

How Can Cultural Change Be Accomplished?

Now we ask the question: If conditions are right, how do managers go about changing culture? The challenge is to unfreeze the current culture, implement the new "ways of doing things," and reinforce those new values. No single action is likely to have the impact necessary to change something that is widely accepted and highly valued. Thus, there needs to be a comprehensive and coordinated strategy for managing cultural change, as shown in *Tips for Managers— Strategies for Managing Cultural Change*.

As you can see, these suggestions focus on specific actions that managers can take to change the ineffective culture. Following these suggestions, however, is no guarantee that a manager's change efforts will succeed. Organizational members do not quickly let go of values that they understand and that have worked well for them in the past. Managers must, therefore, be patient. Change, if it comes, will be slow. And managers must stay constantly alert to protect against any return to old familiar practices and traditions.

Handling Employee Stress

As a student, you have probably experienced stress when finishing class assignments and projects, taking exams, or finding ways to pay rising tuition costs, which may mean juggling a job and school. Then, there is the stress associated with getting a decent job after graduation. Even after you have landed that job, your stress is not likely to stop. For many employees, organizational change creates stress. A dynamic and uncertain environment characterized by mergers, restructurings, forced retirements, and downsizing has created a large number of employees who are overworked and stressed out.[33] In fact, Ipsos Reid recently did a survey of 1500 Canadians with employer-sponsored health care plans. It found that 62 percent reported experiencing "a great deal of stress on the job." Workplace stress was bad enough to cause 34 percent of those surveyed to say that it had made them physically ill.[34] In this section, we review what stress is, what causes it, how to identify its symptoms, and what managers can do to reduce it.

What Is Stress?

What are the things that cause you stress?

Stress is the adverse reaction people have to excessive pressure placed on them from extraordinary demands, constraints, or opportunities.[35] Let's look more closely at what stress is.

Stress is not necessarily bad. Although it's often discussed in a negative context, stress does have a positive value, particularly when it offers a potential gain. Functional stress enables an athlete, stage performer, or employee to perform at his or her highest level in crucial situations.

However, stress is more often associated with fear of loss. When you take a test at school or have your annual performance review at work, you feel stress because you know that there can be either positive or negative outcomes. A good performance review may lead to a promotion, greater responsibilities, and a higher salary. But a poor review may keep you from getting the promotion. An extremely poor review might lead to your being fired.

stress
The adverse reaction people have to excessive pressure placed on them from extraordinary demands, constraints, or opportunities.

Q&A 16.7

Exhibit 12-7

Causes of Stress

Just because the conditions are right for stress to surface does not always mean it will. Stress is highest for individuals who are uncertain whether they will win or lose and lowest for individuals who think that winning or losing is a certainty. In addition, if winning or losing is unimportant, there is no stress. An employee who believes that keeping a job or earning a promotion is unimportant will experience no stress before a performance review.

Causes of Stress

As shown in Exhibit 12-7, the causes of stress can be found in issues related to the organization or in personal factors that evolve out of the employee's private life. Clearly, change of any kind has the potential to cause stress. It can present opportunities, constraints, or demands. Moreover, changes are frequently created in a climate of uncertainty and around issues that are important to employees. It's not surprising, then, that change is a major stressor.

Symptoms of Stress

What signs indicate that an employee's stress level might be too high? Stress shows itself in a number of ways. For example, an employee who is experiencing a high level of stress may become depressed, accident prone, or argumentative; may have difficulty making routine decisions; may be easily distracted, and so on. As Exhibit 12-8 shows, stress

Exhibit 12-8

Symptoms of Stress

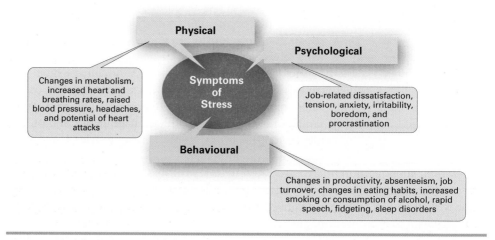

symptoms can be grouped under three general categories: physical, psychological, and behavioural. Of these, the physical symptoms are least relevant to managers. Of greater importance are the psychological and behavioural symptoms since these directly affect an employee's work.

In Japan, there is a stress phenomenon called karoshi (pronounced kah-roe-she), which is translated literally as "death from overwork." During the late 1980s, "several high-ranking Japanese executives still in their prime years suddenly died without any previous sign of illness."[36] As public concern increased, even the Japanese Ministry of Labour got involved, and it now publishes statistics on the number of karoshi deaths. As Japanese multinational companies expand operations to China, Korea, and Taiwan, it's feared that the karoshi culture may follow.

Reducing Stress

As we mentioned earlier, not all stress is dysfunctional. Since stress can never be totally eliminated from a person's life, either off the job or on, managers are concerned with reducing the stress that leads to dysfunctional work behaviour. How? Through controlling certain organizational factors to reduce organizational stress, and to a more limited extent, offering help for personal stress.

Things that managers can do in terms of organizational factors begin with employee selection. Managers need to make sure that an employee's abilities match the job requirements. When employees are in over their heads, their stress levels typically will be high. A realistic job preview during the selection process can minimize stress by reducing ambiguity about job expectations. Improved organizational communications will keep ambiguity-induced stress to a minimum. Similarly, a performance planning program such as management by objectives (see Chapter 3) will clarify job responsibilities, provide clear performance goals, and reduce ambiguity through feedback. Job redesign is also a way to reduce stress. If stress can be traced to boredom or to work overload, jobs should be redesigned to increase challenge or to reduce the workload. Redesigns that increase opportunities for employees to participate in decisions and to gain social support have also been found to reduce stress.[37]

Stress from an employee's personal life raises two problems. First, it's difficult for the manager to control directly. Second, there are ethical considerations. Specifically, does the manager have the right to intrude—even in the subtlest ways—in an employee's personal life? If the manager believes it's ethical and the employee is receptive, there are a few approaches the manager can consider. Employee *counselling* can provide stress relief. Employees often want to talk to someone about their problems, and the organization—through its managers, in-house human resource counsellors, or free or low-cost outside professional help—can meet that need. Companies such as BC Hydro and the University of British Columbia are just two of many organizations that provide extensive counselling services for their employees. A *time management program* can help employees sort out their priorities if their personal lives suffer from a lack of planning that, in turn, creates stress.[38]

Still another approach is organizationally sponsored *wellness programs.* For example, Montreal-based Ericsson Canada, a telecommunications firm, insists that all employees take two weeks of holidays a year, in week-long increments. Peter Buddo, vice-president of human resources, explains his company's policy: "One day off a week is not going to do anyone any good." Hamilton, Ontario-based Dofasco's employees have access to three gyms, one at the plant, and the other two a 15-minute drive from the plant. There are 4000 visits a month to the three gyms combined. Montreal-based Hewlett-Packard Canada gives all of its employees ergonomics training so that they will sit properly at their computer screens and avoid neck, shoulder, and arm injuries from keyboarding. The company also has four subsidized on-site fitness centres for staff in the Toronto area. Employees pay $20 a month for use of the centres at any time of the day, to take breaks and reduce stress.[39]

SUMMARY AND IMPLICATIONS

❶ What factors create the need for change? Organizations are confronted with the need for change from both external and internal forces. Externally, the marketplace, government laws and regulations, technology, labour markets, and economic changes all put pressure on organizations to change. Internally, organizations may decide to change strategies. The introduction of new equipment can also lead to change. The workforce, both in terms of composition and attitudes, can also lead to demands for change.

Yahoo! faces changes because it is a large organization experiencing challenges from ever-changing technology and fast-moving, smaller, and more aggressive organizations.

❷ Is change ongoing or episodic? Up until the late 1980s, change was viewed as episodic, something that could be planned and managed readily. In between periods of change, organizations "stayed the course." In more recent years, environments have become more uncertain and dynamic, and this has led to more continuous demands for change.

As the company moves forward, it has to be able to identify new opportunities on an ongoing basis and figure out a way to provide services that its competitors do not in order to regain its leadership edge.

❸ How do organizations manage change and resistance to change? Managers can change an organization's structure, technology, and people. People tend to resist change, and there are a variety of reasons why they do so. The main reason is that change replaces the known with ambiguity and uncertainty. As well, people do not necessarily like their habits changed; they may fear losing something already possessed (e.g., status, money, friendships); and they may believe that the change could actually reduce product quality or productivity.

One of the challenges Yahoo! needs to manage is that employees have been used to working in separate silos, not always aware of the big picture of the organization. They may resist working "outside of the box" initially because they have been rewarded for working within subunits, rather than thinking of the overall strategic plan of the organization.

❹ What are current issues in managing change? One main consideration in managing change is determining how to introduce change in an existing organizational culture. An organization's culture can make it difficult to introduce change because employees are sometimes committed to old ways of doing things. The other major consideration is how to deal with employee stress while undergoing change.

Yahoo!'s culture has been one of separate silos, and now it needs more teamwork from employees. This may create difficulties for new CEO Carol Bartz, who, as an outsider to Yahoo!, will have to figure out how to reward team activities rather than individual actions.

Management @ Work

READING FOR COMPREHENSION

1. Define organizational change.

2. Discuss the external and internal forces for change.

3. Why is handling change an integral part of every manager's job?

4. Describe Lewin's three-step change process. How is it different from the change process needed in the white-water rapids metaphor of change?

5. Discuss what it takes to make change happen successfully.

6. Explain why people resist change and how resistance might be managed.

LINKING CONCEPTS TO PRACTICE

1. Who are change agents? Do you think that a low-level employee could act as a change agent? Explain.

2. Why is organization development planned change? Explain how planned change is important for organizations in today's dynamic environment.

3. Which organization—DaimlerChrysler or Apple—do you believe would have more difficulty changing its culture? Explain your position.

4. "Managers have a responsibility to their employees who are suffering serious ill effects from work-related stress." Do you agree or disagree with the statement? Support your position.

5. Do you think changes can occur in an organization without a champion to foster new and innovative ways of doing things? Explain.

6. Organizations typically have limits to how much change they can absorb. As a manager, what signs would you look for that might suggest that your organization has exceeded its capacity to change?

SELF-ASSESSMENT

How Well Do I Respond to Turbulent Change?

Listed below are a set of statements describing the characteristics of a managerial job.[40] If your job had these features, how would you react to them? Use the following rating scale for your answers:

1 = This feature would be very unpleasant for me.

2 = This feature would be somewhat unpleasant for me.

3 = I would have no reaction to this feature one way or another; or it would be about equally enjoyable and unpleasant.

4 = This feature would be enjoyable and acceptable most of the time.

5 = I would enjoy this feature very much; it's completely acceptable.

1. I regularly spend 30 to 40 percent of my time in meetings.   1 2 3 4 5

2. A year and a half ago, my job did not exist, and I have been essentially inventing it as I go along.   1 2 3 4 5

3. The responsibilities I either assume or am assigned consistently exceed the authority I have for discharging them.   1 2 3 4 5

4. I am a member of a team and I have no more authority than anyone else on the team.   1 2 3 4 5

5. At any given moment in my job, I have on the average about a dozen phone calls or emails to be returned.   1 2 3 4 5

6. My job performance is evaluated by not only my boss but also by my peers and subordinates.   1 2 3 4 5

7. About three weeks a year of formal management training is needed in my job just to stay current. 1 2 3 4 5

8. My job consistently brings me into close working contact at a professional level with people of many races, ethnic groups, and nationalities, and of both sexes. 1 2 3 4 5

9. For many of my work colleagues, English is their second language. 1 2 3 4 5

10. My boss is from another country and has been in this country only for six months. 1 2 3 4 5

11. There is no objective way to measure my effectiveness. 1 2 3 4 5

12. I report to three different bosses for different aspects of my job, and each has an equal say in my performance appraisal. 1 2 3 4 5

13. On average, about one-third of my time is spent dealing with unexpected emergencies that force all scheduled work to be postponed. 1 2 3 4 5

14. On average, I spend about a week every month out of town on business. 1 2 3 4 5

15. I frequently have to work until 8 p.m. to get my day's work completed. 1 2 3 4 5

16. When I have a meeting with the people who report to me, at least one or two will participate by phone or electronic conferencing. 1 2 3 4 5

17. The degree I earned in preparation for this type of work is now obsolete, and I probably should go back for another degree. 1 2 3 4 5

18. My job requires me to read 100 to 200 pages per week of technical materials. 1 2 3 4 5

19. My department is so interdependent with several other departments in the organization that all distinctions about which departments are responsible for which tasks are quite arbitrary. 1 2 3 4 5

20. I am unlikely to get a promotion anytime in the near future. 1 2 3 4 5

21. There is no clear career path for me in this job and organization. 1 2 3 4 5

22. During the period of my employment here, either the entire organization or the division I worked in has been reorganized every year or so. 1 2 3 4 5

23. While I have many ideas about how to make things work better, I have no direct influence on either the business policies or the personnel policies that govern my division. 1 2 3 4 5

24. My organization is a defendant in an antitrust suit, and if the case comes to trial I will probably have to testify about some decisions that were made a few years ago. 1 2 3 4 5

25. Sophisticated new technological equipment and software are continually being introduced into my division, necessitating constant learning on my part. 1 2 3 4 5

26. The computer I have in my office can be monitored by my bosses without my knowledge. 1 2 3 4 5

Scoring Key

To calculate your tolerance of change score, add up your responses to all 26 items.

Analysis and Interpretation

This instrument describes a number of characteristics of the changing workplace. The higher your score, the more comfortable you are with change.

The author of this instrument suggests an "average" score is around 78. If you scored over 100, you seem to be accepting the "new" workplace fairly well. If your score was below 70, you are likely to find the manager's job in the twenty-first century unpleasant, if not overwhelming.

More Self-Assessments

To learn more about your skills, abilities, and interests, take the following self-assessments on MyManagementLab at www.pearsoned.ca/mymanagementlab:

- I.A.4—How Well Do I Handle Ambiguity?
- I.A.5—How Creative Am I?
- III.C.2—How Stressful Is My Life?
- III.C.3—Am I Burned Out?

MANAGEMENT FOR YOU TODAY

Dilemma

Think of something that you would like to change in your personal life. It could be your study habits, your fitness and nutrition, the way you interact with others, or anything else that is of interest to you. What values and assumptions have encouraged the behaviour that currently exists (that is, the one you want to change)? What driving and restraining forces can you address in order to make the desired change?

Becoming a Manager

- Pay attention to how you handle change. Figure out why you resist certain changes and not others.

- Practise using different approaches to managing resistance to change at work or in your personal life.

- Read material that has been written about how to be a more creative person.

- Find ways to be innovative and creative as you complete class projects or work projects.

WORKING TOGETHER: TEAM-BASED EXERCISE

The Celestial Aerospace Company

Objectives

1. To illustrate how forces for change and stability must be managed in organizations.

2. To illustrate the effects of alternative change techniques on the relative strength of forces for change and forces for stability.

The Situation

The marketing division of the Celestial Aerospace Company (CAP) has gone through two major reorganizations in the past seven years. Initially, the structure changed from a functional to a matrix form (see Chapter 5), which did not satisfy some functional managers nor did it lead to organizational improvements. The managers complained that the structure confused the authority and responsibility relationships. In reaction to these complaints, senior management returned to the functional form, which maintained market and project teams that were managed by project managers with a few general staff personnel. No functional specialists were assigned to these groups. After the change, some problems began to surface. Project managers complained that they could not obtain the necessary assistance from functional staff. It not only took more time to obtain necessary assistance but also created problems in establishing stable relationships with functional staff members. Because these problems affected customer service, project managers demanded a change in the organizational structure.

Faced with these complaints and demands from project managers, senior management is pondering yet another reorganization for the division. They have requested an outside consultant (you) to help them in their reorganization plan—one that will provide some stability to the structure, address their issues, and help the organization achieve its strategic goals.

Procedure

1. Divide into groups of 5 to 7 and take the role of consultants.

2. Each group should identify the forces necessitating the change and the resistance to that change in the company.

3. Each group should develop a set of strategies for dealing with the resistance to change and for implementing those strategies.

4. Reassemble the class and hear each group's recommendations and explanations.

5. After each group has presented, the other consulting groups should pose probing questions about the presenting group's recommendations.

ETHICS IN ACTION

Ethical Dilemma Exercise: How Can Managers Help Employees Accept Change?

What is the most ethical way to deal with change that will take away some employees' jobs or completely alter the work environment?[41] Managers at the Boots chain, which operates 1400 drugstores and employs 60 000 people in the United Kingdom, faced this issue not long ago. They had just formulated a long-term plan to cut costs and increase efficiency by replacing a group of older distribution facilities with a new automated warehouse. Closing the facilities would take years and save the company millions of dollars—but it would also mean displacing more than 2000 workers. The challenge was to manage the change in a sensitive way and minimize resistance while maintaining high productivity.

To reduce the stress on its workforce, Boots announced the change three years in advance and emphasized that the employees affected by the closures would be offered other jobs in the company. To increase participation and support, the company also held talks with the main union representing employees. Going further, management praised employee performance and kept on communicating about the progress toward constructing the new warehouse and closing individual facilities. Productivity has not suffered so far, although the combination of changing structure and technology will probably add some stress and encounter a degree of internal resistance. This is just the beginning, notes a senior executive: "Boots is changing very fast, probably faster than any other large U.K. retailer."

Imagine you are the manager of a Boots store. During a staff meeting, one of your employees suggests that the store remain open one hour later on Thursday nights. This would increase sales and help your store compete with a drugstore two blocks away. Although you like the idea, your assistant manager—an outstanding employee—raises a number of objections and keeps complaining even after the meeting ends. What should you do? (Review Exhibit 12-6 on page 372 as you consider this ethical challenge.)

Thinking Critically About Ethics

Although numerous organizations provide stress-reduction programs, many employees choose not to participate. Why? Many employees are reluctant to ask for help, especially if a major source of that stress is job insecurity. After all, there is still a stigma associated with stress. Employees do not want to be perceived as unable to handle the demands of their jobs. Although they may need stress management now more than ever, few employees want to admit that they are stressed. What can be done about this paradox? Do organizations even have an ethical responsibility to help employees deal with stress?

CASE APPLICATION

1-800-GOT-JUNK?

Eighteen thousand expired cans of sardines.[42] Fifty garden gnomes. A mechanical bull. An antique silver set (worth a lot of money). These are just some of the weird items that Vancouver-based 1-800-GOT-JUNK? customers have asked the uniformed people in the freshly scrubbed blue trucks to haul away. Company founder and CEO Brian Scudamore discovered there was a lucrative niche between "trash cans and those big green bins dropped off by" the giant waste haulers. But even in such an uncomplicated business as hauling people's junk, Scudamore must be concerned with managing change and managing innovation.

1-800-GOT-JUNK?, named one of the Best Employers in Canada for 2007 by *Canadian Business*, has a corporate staff of about 300 individuals. "With a vision of creating the 'FedEx' of junk removal," says Scudamore, "I dropped out of university with just 1 year left to become a full-time JUNKMAN! Yes, my father, a liver transplant surgeon, was not impressed to say the least." However, in 2006, the company had about 250 franchises and system-wide revenues were over $105 million. Not surprisingly, Scudamore's father is a little more understanding these days about his son's business! Since 1997, the company has grown exponentially. In fact, the company made the list of *Entrepreneur* magazine's 100 fastest-growing franchises in 2005 and 2006.

Hauling junk would be, to most people's minds at least, a pretty simple business. However, the company Scudamore founded is a "curious hybrid." It's been described as a blend of "old economy and new economy." The company's service—hauling away trash—has been done for hundreds, if not thousands, of years. But 1-800-GOT-JUNK? also relies heavily on up-to-date information technology and has the kind of organizational culture that most people associate with high-tech start-ups. The company uses its 1-800-GOT-JUNK? call centre to do the booking and dispatching for all its franchise partners. The franchise partners also use the company's proprietary intranet and customer-relationship management site—dubbed JunkNet—to access schedules, customer information, real-time reports, and so forth. Scudamore's philosophy was that this approach allowed franchise partners to "work on the business" instead of "work in the business." On any given day, all a franchisee has to do is open up JunkNet to see the day's schedule. If a new job comes in during a workday, the program automatically sends an alert to the franchisee. Needless to say, the company's franchisees tend to be quite tech-savvy. In fact, some of them have installed GPS devices in their trucks to help find the most efficient routes on a job. Others use online navigation sites. With the price of gas continuing to increase, this type of capability is important.

1-800-GOT-JUNK? also has a culture that would rival any high-tech start-up. The head office is known as the Junktion. Grizzly, Scudamore's dog, comes to the office every day and helps employees relieve stress by playing catch anytime, anywhere. Each morning at exactly 10:55, all employees at the Junktion meet for a five-minute huddle, where they share good news, announcements, metrics, and prob-

lems they are encountering. Visitors to the Junktion have to join the group huddle also. One of the most conspicuous features of the Junktion—"the first thing one sees upon entering—is the Vision Wall," which contains the "fruits of Scudamore's brainstorms." Other members of the executive team have visions for the company's future as well. Periodically they will "wander through the offices of Genome Sciences Centre, the tenant occupying the space above them, to visualize a future when Got-Junk has expanded so sufficiently" that it will take over that office space. Company franchisees are also encouraged to take initiative and be creative. For example, the Toronto franchise, which has 12 trucks, sometimes gets a blue truck motorcade going down Yonge Street through the heart of the city as a way to be noticed and to publicize its services. Despite the company's success to date, Scudamore is wondering whether he is prepared to face whatever changes may happen in the environment in the years to come. How would you advise him to be a "change-capable" organization?

DEVELOPING YOUR DIAGNOSTIC AND ANALYTICAL SKILLS

Changes in the Health Care Industry

When you think about the significant changes that have occurred in people's lives over the past five decades, clearly the advances in medical science would be at the top of such a list. Diseases have been eradicated and medical procedures and devices have helped save thousands of lives. But do not be too quick to conclude that the health care industry is a model of innovation and efficiency.[43]

Hospitals, in general, have one of the most archaic and costly operating systems of any group of large organizations. Nearly 95 percent of all hospitals currently use procedures and record-keeping systems that were implemented more than 50 years ago. It's the way it's always been done, and that is how most doctors and technicians prefer it. Individuals in this industry have been highly reluctant to accept and use new technologies.

Doctors and hospital administrators at Prairie General Hospital, however, refuse to be part of "the old guard." Consider the following incident that happened in the emergency room at Prairie General. A middle-aged patient was brought in by his wife to the emergency room. The patient, who was very overweight, was complaining of shortness of breath and dizziness. Although the patient claimed he was okay, his wife made him go to the hospital. Immediately the staff at Prairie General went to work. While nurses hooked the patient up to heart monitoring equipment and checked his vital signs, a resident wheeled over an emergency room cart, which contained a laptop computer. Logging in the patient's identification number, the ER doctor noticed that the patient had had an EKG in the past year. Immediately

reviewing the past EKG records and comparing it with current heart monitoring results, the doctor determined the patient was in the middle of a heart attack. Within 10 minutes of seeing the patient, doctors had determined that he was suffering from a blocked artery. Clot-busting drugs were swiftly administered, and the patient was immediately taken to the cardiac lab where an emergency angioplasty was performed to open up the clogged artery. Within a day, the patient was back on his feet and ready to go home. In most other hospitals, the patient might not have been so lucky!

Prairie General is unusual in the health care industry. This hospital is investing money in technology that enables it to provide better service at a lower cost. Through its system, called CareWeb, more than 1 million patient records are available. In each of these records are all previous medical orders, such as lab test results and prescriptions, for each patient. When a patient comes to the hospital, that individual's health history is easily retrievable and can be used to assist in the current diagnosis.

What has been the effect of this technology change on Prairie General? The system is saving the hospital more than $1 million each year. It has reduced errors in patient care by more than 90 percent and reduced prescription errors and potential adverse drug interactions by more than 50 percent. Patient charts are now available in moments rather than hours or days. Patients are now discharged more than 30 minutes faster than they had been before CareWeb was implemented.

Cost savings, time savings, increased patient care, and saved lives—all this makes you wonder why every hospital is not making such changes!

Questions

1. Describe the types of changes that have occurred at Prairie General in terms of structure, technology, and people. Cite examples.

2. Why do you believe there is resistance by the medical profession to systems such as CareWeb? Explain.

3. Assume you were going to make a presentation to a group of hospital staff (doctors and administrators) on why they should invest in technology such as CareWeb. How would you attempt to overcome their resistance to change and their attitude about continuing to do what they have always done? Discuss.

DEVELOPING YOUR INTERPERSONAL SKILLS

Managing Resistance to Change

About the Skill

Managers play an important role in organizational change—that is, they often serve as change agents. However, managers may find that change is resisted by employees. After all, change represents ambiguity and uncertainty, or it threatens the status quo. How can this resistance to change be effectively managed?[44]

Steps in Developing the Skill

You can be more effective at managing resistance to change if you use the following three suggestions:[45]

1. **Assess the climate for change.** One major factor why some changes succeed and others fail is the readiness for change. Assessing the climate for change involves asking several questions. The more affirmative answers you get, the more likely it is that change efforts will succeed.

   ■ Is the sponsor of the change high enough in the hierarchy to have power to effectively deal with resistance?

   ■ Is senior management supportive of the change and committed to it?

   ■ Is there a strong sense of urgency from senior managers about the need for change, and is this feeling shared by others in the organization?

   ■ Do managers have a clear vision of how the future will look after the change?

   ■ Are there objective measures in place to evaluate the change effort, and have reward systems been explicitly designed to reinforce them?

   ■ Is the specific change effort consistent with other changes going on in the organization?

   ■ Are managers willing to sacrifice their personal self-interests for the good of the organization as a whole?

   ■ Do managers pride themselves on closely monitoring changes and actions by competitors?

   ■ Are managers and employees rewarded for taking risks, being innovative, and looking for new and better solutions?

   ■ Is the organizational structure flexible?

   ■ Does communication flow both down and up in the organization?

   ■ Has the organization successfully implemented changes in the recent past?

   ■ Are employee satisfaction with and trust in management high?

   ■ Is there a high degree of interaction and cooperation between organizational work units?

   ■ Are decisions made quickly, and do decisions take into account a wide variety of suggestions?

2. **Choose an appropriate approach for managing the resistance to change.** There are five tactics that have been suggested for dealing with resistance to change. Each is designed to be appropriate for different conditions of resistance. These include *education and communication* (used when resistance comes from lack of information or inaccurate information); *participation* (used when resistance stems from people not having all the information they need or when they have the power to resist); *facilitation and support* (used when those with power will lose out in a change); *manipulation and cooptation* (used when any other tactic will not work or is too expensive); and *coercion* (used when speed is essential and change agents possess considerable power). Which one of these tactics will be most effective depends on the source of the resistance to the change.

3. **During the time the change is being implemented and after the change is completed, communicate with employees regarding what support you may be able to provide.** Your employees need to know that you are there to support them during change efforts. Be prepared to

offer the assistance that may be necessary to help your employees enact the change.

Practising the Skill

You are the nursing supervisor at a local hospital that employs both emergency room and floor nurses. Each of these teams of nurses tends to work almost exclusively with others doing the same job. In your professional reading, you have come across the concept of cross-training nursing teams and giving them more varied responsibilities, which in turn has been shown to improve patient care while lowering costs. You call the two team leaders, Sue and Scott, into your office to explain that you want the nursing teams to move to this approach. To your surprise, they are both opposed to the idea. Sue says she and the other emergency

room nurses feel they are needed in the ER, where they fill the most vital role in the hospital. They work special hours when needed, do whatever tasks are required, and often work in difficult and stressful circumstances. They think the floor nurses have relatively easy jobs for the pay they receive. Scott, the leader of the floor nurse team, tells you that his group believes the ER nurses lack the special training and extra experience that the floor nurses bring to the hospital. The floor nurses claim they have the heaviest responsibilities and do the most exacting work. Because they have ongoing contact with patients and families, they believe they should not be called away from vital floor duties to help the ER nurses complete their tasks. What should you do about your idea to introduce more cross-training for the nursing teams?

MANAGING WORKFORCE DIVERSITY

The Paradox of Diversity

When organizations bring diverse individuals in and socialize them into the culture, a paradox is created.[46] Managers want these new employees to accept the organization's core cultural values. Otherwise, the employees may have a difficult time fitting in or being accepted. At the same time, managers want to openly acknowledge, embrace, and support the diverse perspectives and ideas that these employees bring to the workplace.

Strong organizational cultures put considerable pressure on employees to conform, and the range of acceptable values and behaviours is limited. Therein lies the paradox. Organizations hire diverse individuals because of their

unique strengths, yet their diverse behaviours and strengths are likely to diminish in strong cultures as people attempt to fit in.

A manager's challenge in this paradox of diversity is to balance two conflicting goals: to encourage employees to accept the organization's dominant values and to encourage employees to accept differences. When changes are made in the organization's culture, managers need to remember the importance of keeping diversity alive.

How difficult do you think it is for managers to encourage employees to accept differences while also trying to get them to all be part of the same organizational culture?

Continuing Case: Starbucks

Once managers have established goals and plans, organized and structured work activities, and developed programs to motivate and lead people to put forth effort to accomplish those goals, the manager's job is not done.[1] Quite the opposite! Managers must now monitor work activities to make sure they are being done as planned and correct any significant deviations. This process is called controlling. It's the final link in the management process, and although controlling happens last in the process, that does not make it any less important than any of the other managerial functions. At Starbucks, managers control various functions, activities, processes, and procedures to ensure that desired performance standards are achieved at all organizational levels.

Controlling the Coffee Experience

Why has Starbucks been so successful? Although there are many factors that have contributed to its success, one significant factor has been its ability to provide customers with a unique product of the highest quality delivered with exceptional service. Everything that each Starbucks partner does, from top level to bottom level, contributes to the company's ability to do that efficiently and effectively. Managers need to have controls in place to help monitor and evaluate what is being done and how it is being done. Starbucks' managers use different types of controls to ensure that Starbucks remains, as its mission states, "the premier purveyor of the finest coffee in the world while maintaining our uncompromising principles as we grow." These controls include transaction controls, security controls, employee controls, and organizational performance controls.

A legal recruiter stops by Starbucks on her way to her office in downtown Calgary and orders her daily Caffè Mocha tall. A construction site supervisor pulls into the drive-through line at the Starbucks store in Montreal, for a cinnamon chip scone and grande Caffè Americano. It's 11 p.m. and, needing a break from studying for her next-day's management exam, a student heads to the local Starbucks for a tasty treat—Tazo® Chai Tea Latte. Now she is ready again to tackle that chapter material on managerial controls.

A customer places an order at a Starbucks drive-through.

Each week, about 50 million transactions take place in its nearly 17 000 stores, in 49 countries. The average sale per transaction is $4.05. These transactions between partners (employees) and customers—the exchange of products for money—are the major source of sales revenue for Starbucks. Measuring and evaluating the efficiency and effectiveness of these transactions for both walk-in customers and customers at drive-through windows is important. As Starbucks has been doing walk-in transactions for a number of years, numerous procedures and processes are in place to make those transactions go smoothly. However, as Starbucks adds more drive-through windows, the focus of the transaction is on being fast as well as on quality, a different metric than for walk-in transactions. When a customer walks into a store and orders, he or she can step aside while the order is being prepared; that is not possible in a drive-through line. Recognizing these limitations, the company is taking steps to improve its drive-through ser-vice. For example, digital timers are placed where employees can easily see them to measure service times; order confirmation screens are used to help keep accuracy rates high; and additional pastry racks have been conveniently located by the drive-through windows.

Security is also an important issue for Starbucks. Keeping company assets (such as people, equipment, products, financial information, and so forth) safe and secure requires security controls. The company's Standards of Business Conduct document states, "Starbucks is committed to providing all partners with a clean, safe and healthy work environment. To achieve this goal, we must recognize our shared responsibilities to follow all safety rules and practices, to cooperate with officials who enforce those rules and practices, to take necessary steps to protect ourselves and other partners, to attend required safety training and to report immediately all accidents, injuries and unsafe practices or conditions." When hired, each partner is provided with a Safety, Security, and Health Standards manual and trained on the requirements outlined in the manual. In addition, managers receive ongoing training about these issues and are expected to keep employees trained and up-to-date on any changes. And at any time, any partner can contact the partner and asset protection department for information and advice.

Starbucks has been particularly concerned with security issues surrounding its hugely popular gift cards. (Review the information on Starbucks Cards in the continuing case at the end of Part 2.) With these gift cards, there are lots of opportunities for an unethical employee to "steal" from the company. The company's director of compliance says that "detecting such fraud can be difficult because there is no visibility from an operations standpoint." However, Starbucks uses transactional data analysis technology to detect multiple card redemptions in a single day and has identified other "telltale" activities that pinpoint possible fraud. When the company's technology detects transaction activity outside the norm, Starbucks' corporate staff is alerted and a panel of company experts reviews the data. Investigators have found individuals at stores who confess to stealing as much as $42 000. When smaller exceptions are noted, the individuals are sent letters asking them to explain what is going on. The director of compliance says, "I view this as a gentle touch on the shoulder saying we can see what is happening." Employees who have been so "notified" often quit.

Starbucks' part-time and full-time hourly partners are the primary—and most important—source of contact between the company and the customer, and outstanding customer service is a top priority at Starbucks. The Standards of Business Conduct document states, "We strive to make every customer's experience pleasant and fulfilling, and we treat our customers as we treat one another, with respect and dignity." What kinds of employee controls does Starbucks use to ensure that this happens? Partners are trained in and are required to follow all proper procedures relating to the storage, handling, preparation, and service of Starbucks' products. In addition, partners are told to notify their managers immediately if they see anything that suggests a product may pose a danger to the health or safety of themselves or customers. Partners are also taught the warning signs associated with possible workplace violence and how to reduce their vulnerability if faced with a potentially violent situation. In either circumstance, where product or partner safety and security are threatened, store managers have been trained in the appropriate steps to take if such a situation occurs.

The final types of control that are important to Starbucks' managers are the organizational performance and financial controls. Starbucks uses the typical financial control measures, but also looks at growth in sales at stores open at least one year as a performance standard. One

issue with which company executives are dealing is that store operating costs have increased. One contributing factor is the health care packages offered to every employee who puts in more than 20 hours a week. Another factor is that, as the company continues to expand, there are more employees. There is a fine balance the company has to achieve between keeping costs low and keeping quality high. However, there are steps the company has taken to control costs. For example, new, thinner garbage bags will save the company half a million dollars a year. As chair, president, and CEO Howard Schultz notes, "I think when you get large and very successful, you have to balance creativity and entrepreneurship with process and strategy."

In addition to the typical financial measures, corporate governance procedures and guidelines are an important part of Starbucks' financial controls, as they are at any public corporation that is covered by Sarbanes-Oxley legislation. The company has identified guidelines for its board of directors with respect to responsibilities, processes, procedures, and expectations.

Starbucks' Value Chain: From Bean to Cup

The steaming cup of coffee placed in a customer's hand at any Starbucks store location starts as coffee beans (berries) plucked from fields of coffee plants. From harvest to storage to roasting to retail to cup, Starbucks understands the important role each participant in its value chain plays.

Starbucks offers a selection of coffees from around the world, and its coffee buyers personally travel to the coffee-growing regions of Latin America, Africa/Arabia, and Asia/

Pacific in order to select and purchase the highest-quality arabica beans. Once the beans arrive at any one of the four roasting facilities (in Washington, Pennsylvania, Nevada, or Amsterdam), Starbucks' master professional roasters do their "magic" in creating the company's rich signature roast coffee, a process that is the "cumulative result of expert roasters knowing coffee and bringing balance to all of its flavor attributes." There are many potential challenges to "transforming" the raw material into the quality product and experience that customers have come to expect at Starbucks. Weather, shipping and logistics, technology, political instability, and so forth all could potentially impact what Starbucks is in business to do.

One issue of great importance to Starbucks is environmental protection. Starbucks has taken actions throughout its entire supply chain to minimize its "environmental footprint." For example, suppliers are asked to sign a Supplier Code of Conduct that deals with business standards and practices that "produce social, environmental, and economic benefits for the communities where Starbucks does business." Even company stores are focused on the environmental impact of their store operations. Partners at stores around the world have found innovative ways to reuse coffee grounds. For example, in Japan, a team of Starbucks partners realized that coffee grounds could be used as an ingredient to make paper. A local printing company uses this paper to print the official Starbucks Japan newsletter. In Bahrain, partners dry coffee grounds in the sun, package them, and give them to customers as fertilizer for house plants.

Questions

1. What control criteria might be useful to a retail store manager? What control criteria might be appropriate for a barista at one of Starbucks' retail stores (walk-in only)? How about for a store that has a drive-through window?

2. What types of feedforward, concurrent, and feedback controls does Starbucks use? Are there others that might be important to use? If so, describe.

3. What "red flags" might indicate significant deviations from standard for (a) an hourly employee; (b) a store manager; (c) a district manager; (d) the executive vice-president of finance; and (e) the CEO? Are there any similarities? Why or why not?

4. Would it be easy to keep costs low and quality high? Discuss.

5. Evaluate the control measures Starbucks is using with its gift cards from the standpoint of the three steps in the control process.

6. Using the company's most current financial statements, calculate the following financial ratios: current ratio, debt to assets, inventory turnover, total asset turnover, profit margin on sales, and return on investment (see Exhibit 11-13 on page 342). What do these ratios tell managers?

7. Describe and evaluate Starbucks' operations in terms of the service profit chain illustrated in Exhibit 11-18 on page 352.

8. Would you describe Starbucks' production/operations technology in its retail stores as unit, mass, or process? How about in its roasting plants? Explain. (Hint: You might need to review material in Chapter 5, as well, in order to answer this question.)

9. Describe the things Starbucks is doing to manage its value chain. Are these activities appropriate? Why or why not?

10. Can Starbucks manage the uncertainties in its value chain? If so, how? If not, why not?

11. Go to the company's website (**www.starbucks.com**) and find the information on the company's environmental activities from bean to cup. Select one of the steps in the chain (or your instructor may assign one). Describe and evaluate what environmental actions Starbucks is taking. How might these affect the planning, organizing, and leading that take place in these areas?

12. Look at the company's mission and Guiding Principles. How might these affect the way Starbucks uses controls? How do the ways Starbucks controls contribute to pursuing or achieving its mission and Guiding Principles?

13. Would you classify Starbucks' environment as more calm waters or white-water rapids? Explain. How does the company manage change in this type of environment?

VIDEO CASE INCIDENTS

Creativity and the Bottom Line: Mullen PR

Mullen is a full-service advertising and public relations firm located north of Boston and housed in a 1920s mansion. Its staff of 300 employees bills $640 million a year and has created some of the United States' most compelling commercials and print ads. Mullen's clients include Nextel, Arby's, Lending Tree, Orbitz, and General Motors. Since the dot-com bust, concurrent control has been replaced by preventive control, or "account planning," in the advertising industry. Although he acknowledges the importance of measuring the bottom line, Chief Creative Director Edward Boches, who began his career in the 1970s, still maintains allegiance to the following corporate mission: "to generate enduring creative ideas, to do beautifully crafted work, and to expect the best." After this video was filmed, it was reported in *AdWeek* that the $150 million Nextel Communications account, which Mullen had held since 1996, was under review. Mullen competed against three rival advertising agencies in an effort to keep the account. Ultimately, Nextel awarded its advertising business jointly to TBWA\Chiat\Day New York and MindShare.

QUESTIONS

1. *For analysis:* Why was concurrent control popular in the advertising industry during the dot-com boom of the 1990s?

2. *For analysis:* How does using feedforward control give Mullen a competitive advantage in today's dynamic and unpredictable business environment?

3. *For application:* What financial controls would you advise Mullen to use in analyzing its yearly billing to clients for commercials? Use the Nextel spot starring Dennis Franz as a guide.

4. *For application:* What steps can managers take to maintain control over sensitive corporate information?

5. *For debate:* Mullen operates in the bucolic setting of New England in a 1920s mansion, far from the buzz of Madison Avenue and Wall Street. For 30 years, it has based its business on individual excellence, responsibility, integrity, and care. The firm's image has remained pristine during the recent financial scandals. As a result, there is no reason for management at Mullen to be concerned about the renewed zeal for more stringent corporate governance. Do you agree or disagree? Support your position.

Sources: "Mullen PR" (video), Pearson Prentice Hall Management Video Library; D. Gianatasio, "Nextel Cuts to Four," *AdWeek*, March 5, 2003, www.adweek.com/aw/esearch/article_display.jsp?vnu_content_id=1830360 (accessed August 31, 2009); Mullen website, www.mullen.com (accessed August 31, 2009); and Z. Rodgers, "Execs and Accounts for June 11, 2003," *ClickZ*, June 11, 2003, www.clickz.com/2220811 (accessed August 31, 2009).

Organizational Change at Air Canada

In early 2003, Canada's national airline was in crisis. The downturn in air travel caused Air Canada to post a $428 million annual loss. Air Canada executives decided to restructure the company and approached its employee unions to talk about ways of cutting $650 million in labour costs from its 35 000-employee workforce. By April 2003, the corporation had restructured the company and cut more than 4000 jobs. However, the airline continued to sink further into debt and filed for protection from its creditors. The CEO, Robert Milton, communicated to employees that the company was in financial crisis and that all employees were expected to "make significant concessions" in order to save the company. Unions representing Air Canada staff agreed to over $1 billion in cuts to compensation and benefits. The corporation's major investor, Victor Li, proposed an injection of $650 million into Air Canada in return for an equity stake in the airline, on the condition that the employees agree to further concessions. Employees were asked to agree to additional reductions to their pension plan.

Air Canada employees then discovered that, while they had agreed to major cuts in benefits and compensation, the restructuring plan provided Milton with a $20 million pay raise if he remained CEO of the company for five years. Employees were outraged that Milton had not also made concessions in his own pay and benefits. Morale at Air Canada was driven to an all-time low. Organizational performance declined. Industry experts commented that the airline business was one in which employee morale is critical to organizational performance: unhappy employees lead to unhappy customers.

A similar situation occurred at American Airlines a year earlier. American Airlines' employees agreed to $2.2 billion in pay cuts in order to rescue the company. Just as employees were about to sign agreements to prevent bankruptcy, they discovered that the CEO, Don Carty, had secretly accepted a $1.65 million bonus to remain with the company. Employees were outraged and threatened to back out of the deal. Don Carty resigned, the agreements were signed, and the company turned around. Carty's advice to the Air Canada CEO was that credibility with employees is crucial to the ability to lead the company through times of crisis. Credibility cannot be demanded—it must be earned.

QUESTIONS

1. *For analysis:* Describe the organizational change that Air Canada was going through and what the forces for this change were.

2. *For application:* Why were the employees at Air Canada resisting the change that corporate executives proposed, and what could account for the decline in organizational performance?

3. *For application:* What steps would you have recommended the corporation take to turn around the company and successfully implement change?

4. *For debate:* Outside consultants make the best change agents for most corporations. Do you agree? Explain.

Sources: "Air Canada Employee Morale—The Hostile Skies," *CBC Venture*, February 15, 2004, 914, VA-2070 D; "Air Canada Timeline," June 20, 2005, www.cbc.ca/news/background/aircanada/timeline.html (accessed August 24, 2009).

After you have completed your study of Part 5, do the following exercises on MyManagementLab at www.pearsoned.ca/mymanagementlab:

- *You're the Manager: Putting Ethics into Action* (**Boston Scientific**)
- *Passport, Scenario 1* (**Nelson Naidoo, Diamonds International**), *Scenario 2* (**Kristen Mesicek, Global One Cellular**), and *Scenario 3* (**Danny Lim, 88WebCom**)

Management Cases

The case "The YMCA of London, Ontario" focuses on the need to engage in long-term strategic planning, while developing community relations. At the same time, the organization is facing a number of internal struggles because of the different business models of the core service areas. What can management do to effectively address the internal and external concerns raised in this case?

MC-1   The YMCA of London, Ontario

As Shaun Elliott, chief executive officer, prepared for the last senior management planning session in 2005, he reflected on what the YMCA of London (the London Y or the association) had achieved in the last four years. Since joining in 2001, Elliott had led the organization from a deficit of $230,000[1] to a projected surplus of almost $1 million by the end of this fiscal year. This turnaround had been accomplished through a careful balance of internal cost cutting and growth through partnering and program expansion. Innovative partnerships with other organizations had allowed the London Y to expand its programs and facilities with minimal capital investment. In addition to its now solid financial performance, the London Y was on track to exceed its targeted participation level of 46,500 individuals by the end of 2005. It was now time for Elliott to turn his attention to achieving the next level of growth: participation levels of 102,000 individuals by 2010. He knew that to achieve an increase of this magnitude, senior management would need to increase their focus and its capacity and that he would need to spend more time on longer term strategic initiatives and community relations. He wondered if this was possible given the current situation.

The YMCA

The Young Men's Christian Association (YMCA) was an international federation of autonomous not-for-profit community service organizations dedicated to meeting the health and human service needs of men, women and children in their communities. The YMCA was founded in London, England in 1844, in response to the unhealthy social conditions resulting from the industrial revolution. Its founder, George Williams, hoped to substitute Bible study and prayer for life on the streets for the many rural young men who had moved to the cities for jobs. By 1851, there were 24 YMCAs in Great Britain and the first YMCA in North America had opened in Montreal. Three years later, in 1854, there were 397 separate YMCAs in seven nations, with a total of 30,400 members.[2]

From its start, the YMCA was unusual in that it crossed the rigid lines that separated the different churches and social classes in England at the time. This openness was a trait that would lead eventually to YMCAs including all men, women and children regardless of race, religion or nationality. In 2005, the YMCA was in more than 120 countries around the world and each association was independent and reflected its own unique social, political, economic and cultural situation. YMCAs worldwide shared a commitment to growth in spirit, mind and body, as well as a focus on community service, social change, leadership development and a passion for youth.[3]

A similar, although separate organization, the Young Women's Christian Association (YWCA) was founded in 1855 in England.[4] It remained a separate organization; however, some YMCA and YWCAs chose to affiliate in order to best serve the needs in their communities.

The YMCA in Canada

The London Y was a member of YMCA Canada, the national body of the 61 Canadian member associations. YMCA Canada's role was to foster and stimulate the development of strong member associations and advocate on their behalf regionally, nationally and internationally. YMCA Canada was a federation governed by a national voluntary board of directors which oversaw national plans and priorities. Volunteer board members were nominated by the member associations. YMCA Canada's President and CEO was accountable to the board for national operations. The national office had only

---

[1]All funds in Canadian dollars unless specified otherwise.

[2]http://www.ymca.net/about_the_ymca/history_of_the_ymca.html. Accessed February 23, 2006.

[3]http://www.ymca.ca/eng_worldys.htm. Accessed Feb. 23, 2006.

[4]http://www.ywca.org/site/pp.asp?c=djISI6PIKpG&b=281379. Accessed February 23, 2006.

20 employees in 2005, reflecting the relative autonomy of the member associations.

As in the rest of the world, YMCAs in Canada served people of all ages, backgrounds and abilities and through all stages of life. They were dedicated to helping people attain a healthy lifestyle and encouraging them to get involved in making their community a better place. As charities, the YMCA member associations relied on the support of their communities, the private sector, governments and other agencies. YMCA fundraising campaigns helped to provide better programs and facilities, as well as greater accessibility and financial assistance to include as many people as possible.[5]

Earlier in 2005, YMCA Canada, in conjunction with its member associations, had developed a strong association profile, which comprised a wide range of performance measures similar to a balanced scorecard. Implementation of this measurement tool was voluntary, although YMCA Canada encouraged individual associations to use it to assess their performance and to compare their performance with other associations. According to the YMCA Canada strong association profile, a strong YMCA position profile is as follows:

- demonstrates that it is having an impact on individuals' spirits, minds and bodies, while building strong kids, strong families and strong communities;

- assists people to participate in the YMCA who otherwise could not afford to be involved;

- is seen as a valued contributor to the community;

- has the capacity to influence the community relative to its strategic priorities;

- has quality programs that help members meet their personal goals;

- demonstrates growth in participation over time;

- offers a variety of programs that are accessible to the community;

- has a culture of involving their members continually by encouraging them to give their time, talent and treasure to the YMCA;

- has identified key audiences and has a communications plan that addresses each audience.

The London Y had piloted an earlier version of the strong association profile and had already set annual targets for 2005 through to 2010 (see Exhibit 1). The London Y planned to implement these targets and measures as part of its 2005 strategic planning cycle.

Exhibit 1

The YMCA of London Participation Targets

	2005	2006	2007	2008	2009	2010	5 yr inc	Avg inc
Childcare								
Infant	70	70	70	70	70	70	0%	0%
Toddler	140	140	140	140	140	140	0%	0%
Preschool	608	672	736	832	928	1,024	68%	14%
School Age	316	316	316	316	316	316	0%	0%
Childcare Total	**1,134**	**1,198**	**1,262**	**1,358**	**1,454**	**1,550**	**37%**	**7%**
Camping and Educational Services								
CQE	1,815	2,215	2,215	2,439	2,471	2,471	36%	7%
Day Camp	5,350	5,457	5,566	5,677	5,791	5,907	10%	2%
Outdoor Education	5,800	6,960	9,048	9,953	10,948	12,043	108%	22%
Children's Safety Village	12,000	13,500	14,000	14,000	14,000	14,000	17%	3%
Community School Programs	1,630	1,880	2,130	2,380	2,630	2,880	77%	15%
Camping Total	**26,595**	**30,012**	**32,959**	**34,449**	**35,840**	**37,301**	**40%**	**8%**
Health Fitness and Recreation								
CBY full fee	5,450	5,580	5,750	5,825	6,000	6,200	14%	3%
CBY assisted	2,210	2,330	2,450	2,500	2,525	2,650	20%	4%
CBY programs	4,200	4,580	4,975	5,750	6,875	8,050	92%	18%
BHY full fee	1,500	1,525	1,900	2,100	2,400	2,700	80%	16%
BHY assisted	300	305	380	420	480	540	80%	16%

(Continued)

---

[5]http://www.ymca.ca/eng_abouty.htm. Accessed February 23, 2006.

Exhibit 1 (continued)

	2005	2006	2007	2008	2009	2010	5 yr inc	Avg inc
BHY programs	1,600	7,565	9,100	10,195	11,480	13,125	720%	144%
ELY full fee		1,025	1,050	1,050	1,075	1,200		
ELY assisted		205	210	210	215	240		
ELY programs		4,085	5,010	5,280	5,755	6,225		
SCY full fee	481	865	1,155	1,155	1,155	1,155	140%	28%
SCY assisted	26	74	100	110	110	110	323%	65%
SCY programs	773	826	865	905	925	945	22%	4%
WDY full fee	1,822	1,844	1,879	1,913	2,400	3,040	67%	13%
WDY assisted	373	405	426	449	600	760	104%	21%
WDY programs	4,900	5,680	6,480	6,935	8,140	9,375	91%	18%
New location full fee	n/a	n/a	n/a	5,000	7,000	7,000		
New location assisted	n/a	n/a	n/a	1,250	1,750	1,750		
HFR Total	**18,735**	**31,214**	**35,250**	**49,797**	**57,135**	**63,315**	**238%**	**48%**
Grand Total of Participants	**46,464**	**62,424**	**69,471**	**85,604**	**94,429**	**102,166**	**120%**	**24%**
Volunteers								
Childcare								
Camping								
CBY								
BHY		55	60	65	70	75		
ELY		15	20	25	30	35		
SCY	20	23	27	30	35	40	100%	20%
WDY	35	38	42	45	60	80		
Total	**55**	**131**	**149**	**165**	**195**	**230**		
Member Retention Rate								
CBY		76%	76%	76%	76%	76%		
BHY		55%	64%	68%	69%	70%		
ELY		55%	64%	68%	69%	70%		
SCY		55%	65%	68%	72%	75%		
WDY		80%	80%	82%	82%	82%		
New Location								

Source: YMCA of London, 2005 Strategic Planning Documents.

The YMCA of London

Founded in 1856, the YMCA of London was a multi-service charity that described its mission as providing "opportunities for personal growth in spirit, mind and body for people of all backgrounds, beliefs and abilities."[6] Its articulated values and the principles by which it operates were:

- **Honesty:** to tell the truth, to act in such a way that you are worthy of trust, to have integrity, making sure your actions match your words.

- **Caring:** to accept others, to be sensitive to the well-being of others, to help others.

- **Respect:** to treat others as you would have them treat you, to value the worth of every person, including yourself.

- **Responsibility:** to do what is right, what you ought to do, to be accountable for your behaviour and obligations.

The association served almost 28,000 children annually through childcare and camping at 16 childcare locations, two

---

[6]http://www.londony.ca/. Accessed February 24, 2006.

Exhibit 2

The YMCA of London Growth 2001 to 2005

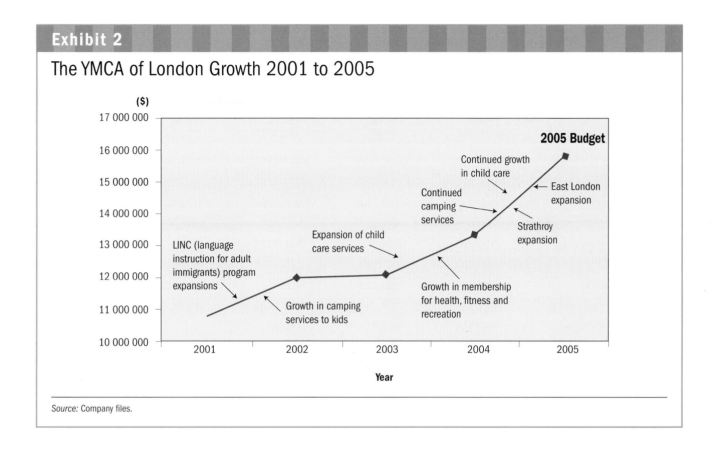

Source: Company files.

residential camps, one outdoor education centre and numerous summer day camps and after school program locations. In 2004, the London Y had provided 13,025 health, fitness and recreation (HFR) memberships for children and adults at five branches: three in London, one in Strathroy and one in Woodstock. In addition, the St. Thomas YMCA was operated by London Y senior management under contract. To ensure that no one was turned away because of an inability to pay, in 2004, the association provided 2,994 assisted HFR memberships, 1,100 assisted "camperships" and assistance to 310 children in childcare. The association had a very positive brand position in the community and its internal research had shown that referrals were the number one source of new members and participants.

The last four years had been a time of renewal and change for the London Y (see Exhibit 2). Revenue had increased by 50 per cent and the association had transformed an operating deficit of $230,000 in 2001 to an expected $1 million operating surplus by the end of 2005 (see Exhibit 3). In 2004, childcare contributed 38 per cent of total revenue, HFR contributed 27 per cent and 16 per cent of revenue came from camping (see Exhibit 4 for The YMCA of London—Revenue). The remaining revenue sources included government programs and contracts, community programs, donations and the United Way. Almost 90 per cent of the London Y's revenue was self-generated through program and participation fees.

The responsibility for all development and fundraising activity was in the process of being moved into the YMCA of London Foundation, an affiliated but separate organization which had a strong record of investing and securing grants.

In its newly expanded role, the foundation was expected to support capital campaigns, conduct annual campaigns and enhance planned giving.

The London Y's structure included the CEO who was accountable to a volunteer board of directors (the board). Seven general managers and one manager reported to the CEO along with three senior directors and one director. The general managers and manager were responsible for service areas or locations including camping and outdoor education, childcare, community services, London HFR, the Woodstock District YMCA, the St. Thomas Elgin Family YMCA, the Strathroy-Caradoc Family YMCA, overall facilities, and employment initiatives. The senior directors and director were responsible for finance, development, human resources and communications, respectively (see Exhibit 5). The number of senior managers had not increased in the last four years.

With the introduction of the strong association profile framework for performance measurement, all senior managers would have performance agreements and work-plans that they had planned together. Measures of participation, program quality and financial performance would be tracked and accountability would be to the group. Once the measures and targets were well established, it was expected that compensation decisions would be based on each senior manager's performance against their plans.

In 2005, the association had over 500 permanent staff with an additional 200 seasonal staff. Full-time employees made up 35 to 40 per cent of the total and the remaining 60 to 65 per cent were part-time employees. Annual staff satisfaction surveys consistently showed high levels of both satisfaction

Exhibit 3

The YMCA of London Schedule of Operations

REVENUE	2005 Projected	Year ended Dec. 31, 2004	Year ended Dec. 31, 2003	Year ended Dec. 31, 2002	Year ended Dec. 31, 2001
Memberships	3,647,014	3,560,527	3,364,190	3,139,980	3,183,699
Childcare	6,811,401	4,958,138	4,037,612	4,516,214	4,576,632
Camp Fees	2,192,237	2,121,787	2,023,885	2,020,531	1,978,414
Community Programs	260,676	442,927	532,606	863,573	414,659
Program Service Fees	328,495	228,500	342,727	302,069	299,177
United Way	205,999	185,250	169,989	164,619	178,818
Ancillary Revenue	544,748	519,225	458,768	633,102	252,935
Donations & Fundraising	341,701	297,917	371,996	416,779	128,190
Employment Initiatives	989,141	891,815	792,983		
International Contributions & Grants				41,239	46,023
Total Revenue	15,321,412	13,206,086	12,094,756	12,098,106	11,058,547
EXPENSES					
Salaries & Benefits	9,550,594	8,525,862	7,663,975	7,718,093	7,288,194
Program Costs	973,935	1,357,277	1,237,143	946,329	1,013,640
Facilities	2,060,400	1,830,450	1,746,122	1,918,676	1,878,400
Promotion	165,180	178,053	140,143	183,441	164,600
Association Dues	163,543	157,570	137,985	136,795	132,777
Travel & Development	214,130	222,013	238,060		
Office Expenses	285,302	276,835	284,382		
Professional & Other Fees	247,592	247,430	302,695		
Miscellaneous	149,741	168,117	128,503		
Administration				840,048	763,095
International Development				41,239	46,023
Total expenses	14,399,676	12,963,607	11,879,008	11,784,621	11,286,729
EXCESS (DEFICIENCY) OF REVENUE OVER EXPENSES	921,736	242,279	215,748	313,485	-228,182

Source: The London YMCA Annual Reports 2004, 2003, 2002, 2001.

and commitment to the association. However, wages were a persistent issue with staff in the childcare centres and finding suitable HFR staff had been particularly challenging.

During the last four years, the board and senior management of the London Y had identified partnering as a key strategy to achieve the association's long term strategic objectives in its three core service areas: HFR, childcare, and camping and outdoor education. Senior management moved quickly to seize opportunities for a number of new partnerships.[7] A new HFR facility in East London was developed in partnership with the London Public Library. Partnerships were established with Kellogg Canada Inc. and John Labatt Ltd. for the London Y to operate their on-site HFR facilities. Childcare services had grown more than 50 per cent,

---

[7] All of the London Y's partnering relationships have approximately the same legal structure which involves a facilities lease and an operating or service provision agreement. There are no fees paid to the partners as all services are provided on a fee for service basis and the London Y covers the operating costs of the facility.

The YMCA London Revenue 2004

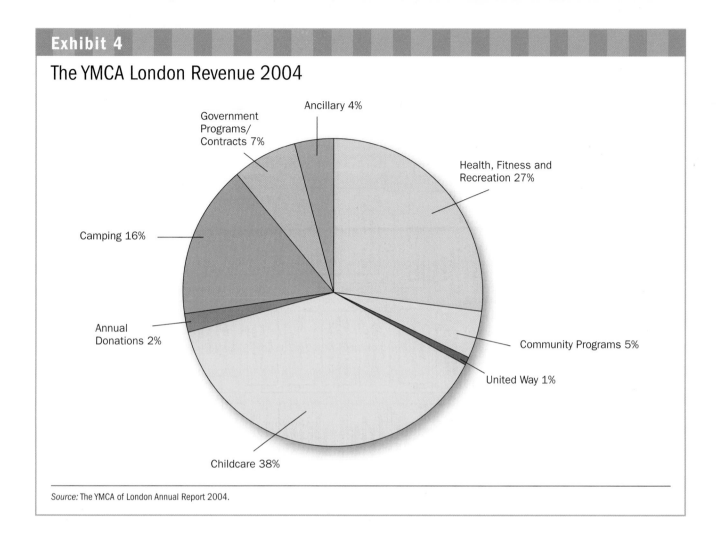

Government
Programs/
Contracts 7%

Ancillary 4%

Health, Fitness and
Recreation 27%

Camping 16%

Community Programs 5%

Annual
Donations 2%

United Way 1%

Childcare 38%

Source: The YMCA of London Annual Report 2004.

primarily as a result of a partnership with the University of Western Ontario.

Some partnerships were opportunistic or tactical but were nonetheless guided by their fit with the long term goals and values of the London Y. For example, a partnership with the Children's Safety Village made resources available to pursue a new full service HFR location in an underserved area of the city, thus expanding service and programs. In the absence of a significant capital infusion, senior management believed that new partnerships were critical to the London Y achieving its participation target of 102,000 individuals by 2010.

Core Service Areas

Health, Fitness and Recreation

One of the longest standing services that the London Y provided was HFR. These services were offered through five branches each led by a general manager. These included the London Centre YMCA (CBY), the Bob Hayward (BHY) and East London (ELY) all located in London; the Strathroy-Caradoc Family YMCA (SCY) located 40 kilometres west of London; and the YMCA of Woodstock and District (WDY) located 50 kilometres east of London. By 2005, the London Y had served more than 18,700 individuals through its HFR

programs and by 2010 the association had a target of serving more than 63,000 in six locations, an increase of 238 per cent. The St. Thomas Y was located 35 kilometres south of London.

The branches were membership-based and offered health and fitness programs for children, families and adults. Twenty-five per cent of the London Y's members received an assisted membership and paid one-third of the cost on average. Programs for children and youth were estimated to cost more than four times the association's programs for adults, yet generated lower fees. Children's programs and services often ran at a loss. The London Y depended on full fee paying adult HFR members to cross-subsidize assisted memberships and children's programs.

The largest challenge to the London Y attracting full fee adult members was the proliferation of fitness facilities for adults. Market-research commissioned by the London Y in 2002, indicated that approximately 30 per cent of the 193,845 adults in London would join a fitness facility and that 25.5 per cent of adults were already members of a fitness club. The potential for market growth was assessed as limited. The research also showed significant penetration of the market by private sector providers with the primary competition in London coming from the Good Life Clubs with 37 per cent market share and The Athletic Club with 22 per cent of

Exhibit 5

The YMCA of London Organization Chart, September 2005

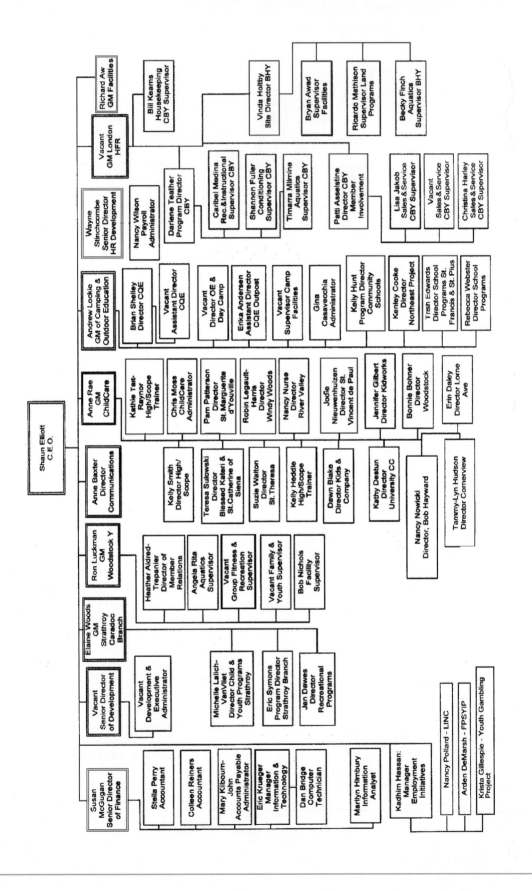

the market. The London Y was third in the London market with a share of 12 per cent. The competition had increased recently with the entrance of the Premier/Mademoiselle chain of fitness clubs into the City of London.

The private clubs operated under a very different economic model than the London Y, typically leasing equipment and facilities. They targeted the adult market only and they did not offer pools or as wide a range of programming as the London Y. In contrast to the private operators, the London Y owned relatively large facilities with pools. Only the two newest branches in London and Strathroy (ELY and SCY) did not have pools, although interest in adding a pool to the SCY had already been raised in the community.

A number of the London Y facilities were aging and required significant capital reinvestment or replacement. The CBY was 25 years old and required ongoing maintenance and refurbishment. The BHY in East London and the WDY were each 50 years old and were not wheelchair accessible. Both buildings required significant capital investment to meet and maintain modern standards. Unfortunately, the BHY was not ideally located so the potential for new members would be limited. More positively, the City of Woodstock had expressed an interest in partnering with the association to develop a new community facility as part of the city's master recreational plan. Replacing the WDY building was considered to be an imperative and partnering with the city was the association's preferred strategy.

Senior management of the London Y believed that to remain relevant in the HFR market as well as meet its targets, the association must develop new facilities in London's north and west ends. The City of London's master recreational plan supported partnership in the delivery of recreational programs and the association had begun discussions with the city regarding development of a new HFR facility in the north end. The city's plan also identified the southwest of the city as a priority site for a HFR facility.

Retention was a key part of membership growth as research showed that two-thirds of new members leave within the first year. Currently, the London Y had relatively high retention rates for members that lasted beyond one year at CBY (76 per cent), WDY (80 per cent) and BHY (75 per cent). ELY and SCY had been in operation less than two years, and retention rates while high were expected to decrease. The association had targeted overall HFR retention rates of 55 per cent at BHY, ELY and SCY next year increasing to more than 70 per cent by 2010. While the association planned to continue its focus on families and to differentiate itself as a values-based organization, it also planned to offer specialized programs targeted at specific groups such as cardiac rehabilitation, weight loss, osteoporosis treatment, etc., to enhance both member retention and new member attraction. This would require increased staff with increased qualifications, resulting in increased costs. To offset these expected cost increases HFR management would need to determine ways to increase revenues or fees.

Although the CEO managed most of the HFR facilities, each facility was run as a separate unit by its general manager. Each branch did its own hiring, staff training, uniform purchasing, program development, and sales and promotion materials. This had resulted in inconsistencies in program quality, program delivery, member service, staff management, facility maintenance and house-keeping between branches. There were significant economic and operational inefficiencies as well. Senior management believed that increased consistency would contribute to increased efficiency, allowing the association to serve more members and to retain more of the existing members. However, there were no coordinating mechanisms for HFR other than the CEO. With financial stability and revenue growth as his priorities, he had not had sufficient time to work with each of the HFR general managers. Also, the CEO was not himself an experienced HFR manager, having spent his career in financial services prior to joining the association.

HFR staff tended to be young and at the beginning of their careers. Finding and retaining appropriate HFR staff had been challenging for the London Y. Work had begun on developing relationships with the local community college and university to establish a placement/apprentice program to identify strong candidates. Also a skill/aptitude profile of HFR staff was in development based on YMCA Canada's standards and training for HFR staff.

The senior management team had developed a number of strategic initiatives for HFR for the coming year. In summary they were:

- develop a new facility in London in partnership with the city of London

- develop a new facility in Woodstock

- manage and promote the Bob Hayward and East London facilities as one branch

- initiate discussions with the town of Strathroy for the development of a pool

- focus on program development and quality, and develop a new revenue structure to support increased quality of service

Childcare Services

Childcare services were the London Y's largest source of revenue. These services were offered through 16 childcare centres located in London (12 locations), Strathroy (two locations), St. Thomas and Woodstock (one location each). The centres were mostly located in leased premises with only the Woodstock centre operating in a facility owned by the association. In 2004, the London Y had served 1,139 children in three categories: infant, toddler and preschooler. By 2010, the association planned to serve an additional 415 preschoolers, for a total of 1,554 children. The London Y childcare centres were similar to other providers in offering full-time, part-time and flexible care options and its fees were set between the midpoint and the high end of fees charged in London. Infants are considerably more expensive to serve due to the higher staff to child ratios required.

Childcare is highly regulated through Ontario's Day Nursery Act (DNA). The DNA prescribes staff to children ratios by age, as well as physical space design, procedures, food preparation and all other aspects of operations. Wage enhancement subsidies were established by the provincial government 10 years ago, as private centres were made public and regulations were established. The subsidies were considered to be necessary for the financial feasibility of centres; however, they had remained at the same levels since their introduction in the early 1990s. Many levels of government were involved with the regulation and funding of childcare, including the Province of Ontario, the Ministry of Community and Social Services, the Ministry of Health, cities and counties, and in some instances, boards of education. It was expected that the landscape of childcare would undergo significant change in 2006 and beyond based on provincial initiatives and programs resulting from proposed increases in federal funding.

Subsidies for childcare fees are available to low income families through the cities and counties. These subsidies did not typically cover all of the fees and the London Y absorbed the shortfall as part of its support to the community.

There were two other large childcare providers in London: London Children's Connection with 13 centres and London Bridge with 11 centres. Unlike these service providers, the London Y offered unique programming through its use of the High Scope curriculum and its values-based programming. In fact, the London Y's curriculum and values focus were key reasons that The University of Western Ontario decided to partner with the association. In addition to the High Scope curriculum, the London Y also offered HFR memberships to each full-time child, discounts for HFR family memberships, summer day camp discounts for customers, swimming as part of their programs and family input through parent advisory committees.

The number of children aged zero to four was expected to decline until the year 2012 in the communities the association currently served. However, senior management believed that opportunities for expansion existed in some of the rural communities and counties that were near existing locations. To continue to maintain full enrollment, the association would need to closely monitor local demographics, competitors' expansion and new subdivision development.

The London Y employed a large number of early childhood educators. Wage scales in the industry were lower than in many other industries. While the London Y had made every effort to provide reasonable compensation and reward good performance, staff satisfaction surveys consistently identified wages as an issue. It was now suspected that the London Y was paying slightly below the average childcare wages in the City of London. Management realized that they must carefully balance wage increases and additional managers against their goal of maintaining a surplus.

Communication and consistency among the centres seemed to require constant attention. Some operational processes had been centralized, such as subsidies and collections, while most processes remained with each centre, including the purchasing of supplies and food preparation. Procedures had been standardized with a common operation manual, although there were still many opportunities for greater consistency and standardization.

With more than 50 per cent growth in childcare since 2001, the general manager's scope of authority had become very large. By 2005, she had 18 people reporting directly to

her, including all 16 centre directors. This created significant barriers to relationship-building, both internally with staff and externally with parents, potential partners, funding organizations and regulators. It was also a challenge during budget review when the general manager of childcare had to review 16 centre budgets and the overall childcare budget in the same time frame as, for example, a general manager in HFR whose one budget might be smaller than one of the larger child care centres.

While the nature and the extent of the changes in programs and program funding were unclear, senior management believed that the complex regulatory environment gave a distinct advantage to an experienced and competent childcare provider. The London Y was confident that it had good working relationships with the cities of London, Woodstock, Strathroy and St. Thomas, the counties in which it operated, and with both the Public and the Roman Catholic School Boards.

Partially in response to the changes expected in the childcare environment, the London Y had begun to explore partnership or merger opportunities with other service providers. In addition to operating advantages, management believed a partnership might also enhance their ability to influence government funding.

The senior management team had developed a number of strategic initiatives for childcare services in the coming year. In summary they were:

- explore partnerships or mergers with other providers
- identify and initiate opportunities in rural areas
- enhance wage structure in balance with budget limitations
- monitor changes in government policy, acquire the best and earliest information and develop appropriate contingency plans.

Camping and Outdoor Education

The London Y expected to serve more than 26,500 participants through camping and education programs in 2005. Residential camping programs were delivered in July and August to almost 2,000 children aged six to 17 at two sites in Northern Ontario, Camp Queen Elizabeth and Camp Queen Elizabeth (CQE) Outpost. Summer day camps served more than 5,000 children aged three to 15 with a variety of programs running from traditional day camps to sports camps and other specialty camps. During the school year more than 1,500 children were served through community school programs delivered in cooperation with school boards. Another 12,000 children were served annually through programs given by police and firefighters at the Children's Safety Village located in the Upper Thames Conservation Authority area near the city of London. Finally, almost 6,000 children and adults participated in outdoor education programs including leadership and team building programs offered at various locations.

Camp Queen Elizabeth had been in operation for 50 years and had an excellent reputation. Each year the Camp was booked to capacity and each year those bookings occurred earlier. Similar to other residential camps, much of the activity was outdoors and programming included water sports, crafts and climbing. Fees were amongst the highest in YMCA camping and the return rate of campers was the highest of all YMCA camps in Ontario. Campers tended to be more homogeneous and from higher income families; however, assisted spots were made available for those unable to afford the fees.

Camp Queen Elizabeth was located on land leased from Parks Canada, a federal department. The current lease was due to expire in 2007 and the London Y had postponed capital investment in the facilities pending renewal of the lease. The association had now received assurance from Parks Canada that the lease would be renewed so a long-overdue refurbishment of the camp's infrastructure could be planned.

The CQE Outpost property had been purchased as a hedge against renewal of the Camp Queen Elizabeth lease as well as for additional capacity to serve older youth with adventure and canoe trips. Service to older youth had not increased as planned and there appeared to be little demand for this type of service. Management was now exploring the possibility of selling the property and using the proceeds towards the renovation of Camp Queen Elizabeth.

The London Y offered a wide variety of day camp and outdoor education programs during all weeks of the summer and, to a limited extent, in the shoulder seasons of spring and fall. During the summer, the association ran a bussing network throughout the City of London to collect and return participants to designated drop-off points. Programming was value-based and emphasized character development more than skill development. Other summer day camp providers included the local university, the City of London, a variety of private businesses and not-for-profit organizations, and churches. The London Y day camps offered the same size groups and staff ratios as other day camp providers and in some cases the offerings were quite undifferentiated. The service needs and selection processes for families and children were not clearly understood by the London Y, although it appeared to management that there were a number of different segments such as skills-based camps, traditional camps and camps that were more like a childcare service.

The association had recently invested some capital dollars in its outdoor education program and developed two new sites in partnership with Spencer Hall, run by the Richard Ivey School of Business and Spencer Lodge, run by the Boy Scouts of Canada. With these new partners and facilities the association hoped to increase the number of its outdoor education program participants by more than 100 per cent by 2010.

The community school program, funded by the United Way and the London Y, was an after school program aimed at improving the academic performance and the social skills of children in higher risk neighbourhoods. The focus was on literacy, social skills and recreation, and the programs were delivered in a number of designated schools. London Y staff worked closely with teachers to identify children who would benefit from participation in the program. This program continued to expand as much as funding and staffing would allow.

Each school year the Children's Safety Village targeted students in grades one to four with its programs on broad safety topics including pedestrian safety, bike safety, fire safety, electrical safety and other household hazards.[8] As a result of their partnership agreement, the London Y's Camping and Outdoor Education operations moved from their dilapidated offices at the association's outdoor education centre to the Children's Safety Village site and the London Y took over management of the site. While the London Y was responsible for the physical operation, the Children's Safety Village Board continued to govern the organization, resulting in some overlapping responsibilities.

Camping and outdoor education offered a wide variety of programs in a large number of locations under a number of different names. Each program produced its own sales and promotion materials and parent communications. A number of programs and facilities were not clearly identified as part of the YMCA, such as Camp Queen Elizabeth or the Children's Safety Village. Management believed that there were a number of opportunities to send a more consistent message to the community and to strengthen the London Y's brand.

The senior management team had developed a number of strategic initiatives for camping and outdoor education in the coming year. In summary they were:

- identify day camp market segments and deliver programs to meet identified needs
- sell the CQE Outpost site and use the proceeds to improve Camp Queen Elizabeth, ensuring that current and expected demand can be accommodated
- negotiate a new governance model and transfer governance of the YMCA Children's Safety Village to the YMCA of London
- ensure that all facilities and programs are clearly identified as part of the London YMCA
- leverage opportunities to serve more individuals in outdoor education programs

Elliott's Consideration of the Situation

Elliott realized that each of the association's three main service areas had very different business models and dynamics and that this created challenges for organizational focus and expertise, resource allocation and communication. He also knew that while the challenges coming from this multi-service approach were abundant and the synergies limited, neither the board of the London Y nor the senior management wished to reduce the range of services that the association provided to the community. Elliott's challenge was how to best manage the association as a whole while appropriately nurturing each of the core service areas. He had a number of concerns.

---

[8]http://www.safetyvillage.ca/about.htm. Accessed February 28, 2006.

The recent growth had put significant strain on both the capacity and capabilities of the senior managers. Elliott was concerned that there were simply not enough managers to deliver the targeted growth and, particularly, the new partnership relationships that would need to be established. Over the last few years Elliott felt that he was the "chief business development officer," searching out partnering opportunities with external organizations and developing both the opportunity and the relationship through to the final agreement. The service area leaders had been focusing on operations and did not have the time, or perhaps the inclination, to think about innovative ways for their areas to serve more people. He believed that it was now time for the service area leaders to take on the development role and to identify and create their own growth opportunities.

In addition to greater capacity, Elliott believed that the senior management team needed to increase its focus on higher level strategic issues affecting the whole association. With 12 people at the table, senior management team meetings were not as effective as they might have been and in fact some members only contributed when the discussion was about their specific location. Also, the meetings tended to over-emphasize day-to-day HFR operations simply because there were so many HFR general managers at the table. This meant that they were perhaps under-emphasizing the association's other key service areas of childcare and camping.

Along with decreasing senior management's focus on HFR, Elliott knew that he too needed to spend less time on day-to-day HFR operations and more time on strategic initiatives and community relations. However, with four HFR general managers reporting to him and with HFR representing the biggest operational challenges and the largest growth target, he knew that HFR needed the undivided attention of a capable senior manager. Also, he did not know how the HFR general managers would respond to any changes that might be perceived as a loss of status or position.

Elliott had real fears about creating a potentially unnecessary layer of management or, even worse, an elite group that became out of touch with the staff and the various locations. He worried about becoming out of touch with the operations himself. One of the first things that Elliott had done when he joined the association in 2001 was to eliminate most of the so called "head office" positions, including the chief operating officer, the head of HFR and the head of development. He did not think that the association could afford those roles at that time and he still believed in carefully balancing expenses and overhead with the need for resources to support expansion. Elliott also had concerns about how the community would perceive a charitable organization that significantly increased its senior management personnel. Finally, he worried about moving too quickly.

Conclusion

Elliott recognized that in trying to determine what was best for the London Y, he must consider the business model and strategy of each of the core service areas while taking into account the overall mission and values of the association. He needed to be confident that any changes would increase the management capacity and focus within each area as well as free him up to focus on longer term strategic initiatives. Elliott was concerned about introducing more overhead expense just when the association's financial performance was stable. He did not have much time left to ponder as he wanted the senior management team to consider any potential organizational changes in the last planning session which was scheduled for next week.

The case "Sarnia Food Fresh Grocery Store" focuses on the experiences of Krysta Lee Becker, a part-time cake decorator. She encounters a number of obstacles in learning to do her job, and then carrying it out. What organizational problems might lead to the experiences Becker has? What could the Assistant Bakery Department Manager and the Bakery Department Manager do to make sure that the next new employee does not have a similar negative experience at Food Fresh?

MC-2 Sarnia Food Fresh Grocery Store: The Icing on the Cake

In July 2002, Krysta Lee Becker, a part-time cake decorator, was working her usual Saturday shift at the local Food Fresh grocery store in Sarnia, Ontario, a shift she had worked regularly since the new store had opened four months before. Her duties for the day required her to complete custom cake orders for Sunday morning pick-up. At approximately 1:00 p.m., she had glanced at the order forms for cakes still to be completed and had realized that one of them, which had been prepared by another employee, had not been completely filled out. See Exhibit 1 for a sample order form. The order form did not specify the type of cake (chocolate or vanilla) or the flavour of icing (chocolate or vanilla). Becker knew this type of problem could often be resolved with a quick phone call to the customer, as the customer's phone number was required on the cake order form; however, on this particular form, no contact information for the customer had been recorded and the employee who took the order had not even written his or her name on the form. Unfortunately, this was not the first time that Becker had been caught in such a situation. The custom cake was due to be picked up at 10:00 a.m. the following day. Carrie Smith, the Bakery Department Manager, and Samantha Ochej, the Bakery Department Assistant Manager, were both also working this particular Saturday shift. This problem was simply the most recent that Becker had encountered in trying to do her job well since the store had opened—it was the "icing on the cake." Becker did not know how to complete the order as the customer required by the time the customer required it and, later in the shift at 2:30 p.m., she was still wondering what to do about it and all the other problems she had been experiencing on her job.

The City and the Competition

Sarnia is a relatively small city of 69,000 citizens located in Southwestern Ontario on the Canada–United States border. At the mouth of the St. Clair River where the river entered Lake Huron, Sarnia is a city surrounded by water. This superb geographic location has attracted a large segment of seniors who have felt that Sarnia is an ideal community in which to retire. Historically, Sarnia has been known for its large oil refineries and manufacturing facilities. More recently, however, the tourism industry has been steadily increasing. When the Sarnia Food Fresh opened its doors for business in November 2001, it was in direct competition locally with eight other large grocery stores, namely, four discount retailers and four full-serve retailers.

Sarnia Food Fresh Grocery Store

Food Fresh's purpose was to create enduring value for customers, employees, suppliers and shareholders. In addition, Food Fresh was founded upon company values which consistently considered customers' interests as primary, as well as the need for employees to complete their tasks with passion and integrity. The Sarnia Food Fresh store was part of one of the two major national retail grocers in Canada, and when rumors that a Food Fresh store would be opening in Sarnia began to circulate, considerable hype and excitement was generated in the city. In November 2001, after much anticipation, Sarnia Food Fresh opened for business.

At the top of the Sarnia Food Fresh store hierarchy was the store manager to whom each of six department managers reported. The six departments included bakery as well as produce, seafood, deli, grocery, and customer service.

The Bakery Department

The bakery department manager, Carrie Smith, supervised the bakers, who completed all the daily baking of breads and pastries, the cake decorators, who maintained the display cases and filled custom cake orders, and the front end bakery clerks, who packaged all the goods and performed general cleaning in the department. Samantha Ochej, a full-time cake decorator, was also the assistant bakery manager and managed the department when Carrie Smith was not in the store. There was a mix of full-time and part-time staff. Five full-time employees worked the day shift, 7:00–16:00, Monday through Friday, and two or three part-time employees worked the night shift, 16:00–21:00, and the day shift on weekends. No bakery employees had been trained to perform the duties of more than one of the three jobs in the department.

Krysta Lee Becker and Her First Job in the Front End Bakery Clerk Position

When Krysta Lee Becker was hired, in October 2001, as a part-time Front End Bakery Clerk for the new Food Fresh, she was seventeen years old and in high school with one more year to go before graduation. Her rate of pay when hired was the student minimum wage of $6.40. She actively participated in community and high school functions. Many of her teachers and supervisors at previous part-time jobs knew her to be an ambitious, independent, and responsible young individual, who fully intended to go on to university in a couple of years upon completion of high school. The front end bakery clerk tasks included slicing and wrapping freshly baked breads, packaging and labeling baked goods, doing general clean-up of the bakery department, as well as providing consistent customer service. Becker was comfortable performing these tasks from the start because she had had previous bakery experience in a small independently owned bakery.

Grand Opening of Food Fresh Grocery Store Sarnia

On opening day, in November of 2001, the new Sarnia Food Fresh was brimming with excited customers who had been waiting many months in anticipation for the grand opening. That day, the bakery department was staffed by the regional manager, experienced bakery employees from other Food Fresh stores who had been relocated temporarily to Sarnia to assist with the grand opening, and by employees newly hired to work in the Sarnia Food Fresh store.

Becker's first shift was 16:00 to 22:00 on opening day. She was one of several newly hired front end bakery clerks working that shift. Within seconds of stepping on to the department floor, each of the clerks was bombarded by questions from excited customers: "Can you slice my bread?" "What are the ingredients in these muffins?" "How much is this cake?" "How many will it feed?" "Do you recommend it?" The new clerks had received no previous training regarding product description, or how to slice and bag bread, or how to complete cake orders. As a result, the new clerks continually had to ask the experienced Food Fresh bakery personnel for advice and recommendations.

Later on her first shift, Becker was asked by the regional manager to complete a series of tasks. She quickly completed all the tasks and asked for additional work. The regional manager noticed that Becker was a hard-working individual and took her aside to ask her if she wanted to work as a cake decorator for the bakery department. He promised Becker that she would be formally trained for her position. Becker quickly agreed, believing that, with training, she could excel on that job, and started work immediately as a cake decorator.

The Training

One month following grand opening, Samantha Ochej, who was a full-time cake decorator and the Assistant Bakery Department Manager, decided that the time had come to train Becker formally to decorate cakes. On Becker's first day of formal training, Ochej took a large pile of chocolate 8-inch round cakes, one 45 pound container of chocolate fudge, a plastic container of chocolate cake garnish, a pile of cake containers, and a picture of a fully decorated chocolate fudge cake and placed all of these in front of Becker. Then she told Becker, "Have fun. If you have any questions, I will be counting inventory." Becker looked at the pile of cakes and simply did what she was told to the best of her ability.

Becker quickly noticed that the fudge was extremely difficult to spread on the cakes. Nevertheless, she continued the slow and tedious process of spreading fudge on cakes until her department manager, Carrie Smith, came by to check on her progress. Smith took one look at the pile of cakes and said, "You *do* know that you can warm the fudge before spreading it on the cakes, don't you?" Becker looked at her manager and shook her head, "no," in response. Smith said, "Oh, Ochej was probably just testing you." After this brief conversation with Smith, Becker began to warm the fudge before using it, and this made the task of decorating chocolate fudge cakes much easier and faster.

After three weeks of decorating only chocolate fudge cakes, and with no offer of further formal training, Becker was getting bored by the repetition and was looking for her next challenge. She noticed that Ochej was decorating classic birthday cakes, which included a flat base coat icing, icing roses, and trim. See Exhibit 2. Rather than decorating more of the chocolate fudge cakes that she had been assigned, Becker grabbed an icing bag and pin and stood watching Ochej create icing roses. Becker caught onto this method very quickly and, within a few minutes, she was able to create her own roses. The tough part for Becker now was to get the rose from the pin to the cake. Again, with a few failed attempts, Becker's roses were making it successfully onto the tops of birthday cakes. Becker's own method of learning by doing and watching enabled her to ice and trim cakes, to create icing roses, as well as to use all of the other required decorating techniques, without any further formal training.

Classic Food Fresh Birthday Cake

The Inventories

By the end of June 2002, after nine months on the job, Becker was working the busiest shifts in the bakery department, that is, Thursday and Friday evenings, and during the day on Saturdays and Sundays. Because she was working these busy shifts, Becker was able to identify the products that sold well and those that did not, and she notified the bakery department manager of the inventories that required replenishment. For instance, on one occasion, Becker predicted that over the weekend there would be an increase in customer requests for specific *LaRocca Specialty Cakes*, such as *Brownie Chocolate Cheesecake* or *Chocolate Truffle Cake*. See Exhibit 3. Becker suggested to her manager prior to the start of the weekend that she reorder these specific popular cakes because inventories were low. To Becker's dismay, Smith replied that there were other kinds of cakes in the refrigerator or freezer for customers to select. Not surprisingly, over the course of the weekend, there were many customers who requested those specific popular cakes, who were annoyed to discover none were available, and who had to settle for a less desirable alternative.

In addition, on another occasion Becker informed Samantha Ochej, the full-time cake decorator and Assistant Bakery Department Manager, that DecoPacs, including Disney Princess and Winnie-the-Pooh cakes, were low in inventory. Becker was aware of the animated figures children favoured at the time because she would listen when children visited the bakery with their parents to look at the DecoPac cake catalogue. Rather than ordering additional popular DecoPacs, Ochej told Becker that the current inventory was still too

Chocolate Truffle Cake

Chocolate Brownie Cheesecake

high and, therefore, that an order would not be placed. Consequently, Becker had to turn customers away because the desired DecoPac was not in stock.

Time-Off

Other part-time employees were allowed to swap shifts with one another to accommodate social and school related schedules without giving the department manager any notice. When other Bakery Department employees requested a scheduled shift off, their requests were usually granted even when their requests were made with just one week's notice.

If Becker ever wanted to have a scheduled day shift off, she was not permitted to simply swap shifts with other employees and she was required to give Smith three weeks notice. When Becker questioned these procedures, she was told by Smith that no other part-time bakery employee was cross-trained to decorate cakes. In addition, when Becker was granted the day off, the following week she would be scheduled for only four and a half hours rather than her usual twenty-four hours. Becker thought that this pattern of scheduling was a form of punishment by her manager for requesting a day off.

On more than one occasion, the scheduled part-time front end bakery clerk did not report to work. Consequently, Becker was required to work late, as she was expected to perform the duties of the front end bakery clerk, as well as the duties of a cake decorator.

To provide a solution to these scheduling problems, Smith had attempted to cross-train interested part-time front end bakery clerks to decorate cakes. Although they wanted the prestige of becoming a cake decorator, the other part-time employees never wanted to put in the time and effort to learn how to perform the cake decorating job properly. As a result,

Becker received more hours and more shifts than any other part-time worker in the department because no other part-time employee was qualified to perform her job. However, the scheduling problems continued.

Day-to-day Work

When selecting icing colours to decorate cakes, Becker would typically use bright blues, oranges, yellows, pinks and greens. Her manager told her to use "dull" colours, rather than the bright colours that she had been using because customers preferred pastel coloured cakes to brightly coloured cakes. However, Becker refused to create cakes with pastel colours because she knew colourful cakes with bright colours were more popular among customers.

One Saturday in June, Smith asked Becker to make eight quarter-slab birthday cakes for the self-serve cake area. This was one of Becker's favourite tasks and she completed the cakes quickly, using her bright colour pallet. She then took her one-hour lunch break. When she returned, all but one of her cakes had been sold. Her manager approached her and said, "I thought I told you to make eight cakes and *then* take your lunch break." Becker responded, "I did. I am making more now to restock." Smith answered, "We sold seven of *your* cakes in an hour?" Becker replied, "Yes. Now do you believe me?" Smith said, "Fine," and walked away.

On another occasion, a distressed customer returned to the bakery department with a recently purchased cake. She told Becker, "I just purchased this cake and had asked another employee to have 'Congratulations Ashley' written on it." Becker quickly noticed that "Congratulations" had been spelled incorrectly, "Congradulations," with a "d", rather than a "t". This was not the first time in Becker's experience

Airbrush Machine Top

that a bakery employee had spelled "Congratulations" incorrectly. Becker retrieved the cake from the customer and told her that it would be fixed immediately.

On another occasion, Becker was required to use the bakery department's airbrush machine to spray coloured dye onto cakes. See Exhibit 4. Becker disliked using this particular airbrush machine for numerous reasons. The machine often dripped dye haphazardly onto the surface of the cake and many times the bottle which held the dye would drop from the machine onto the cake, ruining the cake. Becker would have to strip the icing completely off the cake and start again. Becker had repeatedly told Smith that she was not satisfied with the airbrush machine, but Smith always replied that the department could not afford a new one.

In spite of all these problems, Becker continued to work hard, doing her part to ensure that the bakery department was operating as efficiently and effectively as possible. She sometimes forgot to take her mandatory fifteen-minute breaks during her shift because she was so busy. In addition, many times she did not take all of her one-hour lunch break

because she was bored sitting around and wanted to get back to work. Returning to work early before the end of her break did not bother Becker because she truly enjoyed her job and the customers she served. Becker sometimes became annoyed with other employees in the department when they took extended breaks and lunch hours or additional smoke breaks during their shifts. These employees often did this during bakery rush hours, leaving Becker to serve more than one customer at a time. However, Becker did not let these employees know how she felt about their behaviour, and she did not tell her manager what was going on.

Becker also cleaned and organized the cake cupboards, washed the small cake refrigerators and swept floors. She went out of her way to help the other bakery employees if she noticed they were falling behind in their work. Becker was extremely proud of her position at the Sarnia Food Fresh, and would go "above and beyond" to ensure that each customer she served was satisfied with the product and with their entire shopping experience within the store.

The Decision

It was now 2:30 p.m. near the end of Becker's Saturday shift. She still had a number of custom cake orders to complete for Sunday morning pick up by customers, and she knew how to complete all of them except the cake on the order form that had been incorrectly filled out. Both Samantha Ochej, the full-time cake decorator and Assistant Bakery Department Manager, and Carrie Smith, the Bakery Department Manager, were working that particular Saturday shift. Becker knew that if she was going to do anything about the problem of the incomplete order form, she would have to do it within the hour. She also wondered what, if anything, she could do about the many other problems she had been experiencing at work.

Endnotes

Chapter 1

1. Based on S. Whittaker, "The Junk Man Cometh," *Gazette* (Montreal), June 5, 2006, p. B1; and M. Haiken, "Employees: The Ultimate Partners," *Business 2.0 Magazine*, November 27, 2006; www.1800gotjunk.com/us_en/Files/PRESS_KIT.pdf (accessed June 1, 2009).

2. Based on S. Whittaker, "The Junk Man Cometh," *Gazette* (Montreal), June 5, 2006, p. B1; and M. Villano, "Making a Cache of Cash Cleaning Up Others' Trash," *Globe and Mail*, May 5, 2006, p. G7.

3. K. A. Tucker and V. Allman, "Don't Be a Cat-and-Mouse Manager," The Gallup Organization, http://gmj.gallup.com, September 9, 2004.

4. www.kpmg.ca/en/news/pr20060130.html?zoom_highlight= human+resources+investment+value (accessed June 10, 2009).

5. "WorkUSA 2004/2005: Effective Employees Drive Financial Results," Watson Wyatt Worldwide, Washington, DC.

6. D. J. Campbell, "The Proactive Employee: Managing Workplace Initiative," *Academy of Management Executive*, August 2000, pp. 52–66.

7. J. S. McClenahen, "Prairie Home Champion," *IndustryWeek*, October 2005, pp. 45–47.

8. B. Scudamore, "The Out-of-Towners," *PROFIT*, May 2007, www.canadianbusiness.com/entrepreneur/columnists/brian_scudamore/article.jsp?content=20070405_145004_6148 (accessed July 2, 2009).

9. P. Drucker, *Management: Tasks, Responsibilities, Practices* (New York: Harper & Row, 1974).

10. H. Fayol, *Industrial and General Administration* (Paris: Dunod, 1916).

11. For a comprehensive review of this question, see C. P. Hales, "What Do Managers Do? A Critical Review of the Evidence," *Journal of Management*, January 1986, pp. 88–115.

12. H. Mintzberg, *The Nature of Managerial Work* (New York: Harper & Row, 1973); and J. T. Straub, "Put on Your Manager's Hat," *USA Today*, October 29, 2002, www.usatoday.com.

13. S. J. Carroll and D. A. Gillen, "Are the Classical Management Functions Useful in Describing Managerial Work?" *Academy of Management Review*, January 1987, p. 48.

14. H. Koontz, "Commentary on the Management Theory Jungle—Nearly Two Decades Later," in *Management: A Book of Readings*, 6th ed., ed. H. Koontz, C. O'Donnell, and H. Weihrich (New York: McGraw-Hill, 1984); S. J. Carroll and D. A. Gillen, "Are the Classical Management Functions Useful in Describing Managerial Work?" *Academy of Management Review*, January 1987, p. 48; and P. Allan, "Managers at Work: A Large-Scale Study of the Managerial Job in New York City Government," *Academy of Management Journal*, September 1981, pp. 613–619.

15. E. White, "Firms Step Up Training for Front-Line Managers," *Wall Street Journal*, August 27, 2007, p. B3.

16. R. L. Katz, "Skills of an Effective Administrator," *Harvard Business Review*, September–October 1974, pp. 90–102.

17. D. Nebenzahl, "People Skills Matter Most," *Gazette* (Montreal), September 20, 2004, p. B1.

18. H. G. Barkema, J. A. C. Baum, and E. A. Mannix, "Management Challenges in a New Time," *Academy of Management Journal*, October 2002, pp. 916–930; M. A. Hitt, "Transformation of Management for the New Millennium," *Organizational Dynamics*, Winter 2000, pp. 7–17; T. Aeppel, "Power Generation," *Wall Street Journal*, April 7, 2000, p. A11; "Rethinking Work," *Fast Company*, April 2000, p. 253; "Workplace Trends Shifting over Time," *Springfield News Leader*, January 2, 2000, p. 7B1; "Expectations: The State of the New Economy," *Fast Company*, September 1999, pp. 251–264; T. J. Tetenbaum, "Shifting Paradigms: From Newton to Chaos," *Organizational Dynamics*, Spring 1998, pp. 21–33; T. A. Stewart, "Brain Power: Who Owns It . . . How They Profit from It," *Fortune*, March 17, 1997, pp. 105–110; G. P. Zachary, "The Right Mix," *Wall Street Journal*, March 13, 1997, p. A11; W. H. Miller, "Leadership at a Crossroads," *IndustryWeek*, August 19, 1996, pp. 42–56; M. Scott, "Interview with Dee Hock," *Business Ethics*, May–June 1996, pp. 37–41; J. O. C. Hamilton, S. Baker, and B. Vlasic, "The New Workplace," *BusinessWeek*, April 29, 1996, pp. 106–117.

19. R. Spence, "Entrepreneurial Nation: How the Rise of Entrepreneurship Saved Canada's Economy," *Profit*, May 2007.

20. Statistics Canada, "Latest Release from the Labour Force Survey," June 8, 2007, www.statcan.ca/english/Subjects/Labour/LFS/lfs-en.htm.

21. These figures are from August 2006 and based on information in Statistics Canada, "Latest Release from the Labour Force Survey," September 8, 2006, www.statcan.ca/english/Subjects/Labour/LFS/lfs-en.htm.

22. Canada Post, *Annual Report*, 2005, www.canadapost.ca/corporate/about/annual_report/contents _EN/introduction-e.html (accessed September 24, 2006); and "50 Biggest Employers (2005)," *Report on Business*, www.theglobeandmail.com/v5/content/tp1000/index.php?view=top_50_employers (accessed September 24, 2006).

23. Based on J. B. Miner and N. R. Smith, "Decline and Stabilization of Managerial Motivation Over a 20-Year Period," *Journal of Applied Psychology*, June 1982, pp. 297–305; and J. B. Miner, B. Ebrahimi, and J. M. Wachtel, "How Deficiencies in Motivation to Manage Contribute to the United States' Competitiveness Problem (and What Can Be Done About It)," *Human Resource Management*, Fall 1995, pp. 363–386.

24. H. Mackenzie (Canadian Centre for Policy Alternatives), *Banner Year for Canada's CEOs: Record High Pay Increase*, January 2009, p. 3.

25. See, for example, "Executive Hires and Compensations: Performance Rules," *HRfocus*, July 2003, p. 1; and H. B. Herring, "At the Top, Pay and Performance Are Often Far Apart," *New York Times*, August 17, 2003, p. B9.

26. L. Lavelle, "CEO Pay: Nothing Succeeds Like Failure," *BusinessWeek*, September 11, 2000, p. 48.

27. C. Perkel, "Top CEOs Need Just 12 Hours to Earn Average Canadian Annual Salary," *The Canadian Press*, January 1, 2009, www.finance.sympatico.msn.ca/investing/insight/article.aspx?cp-documentid=16485314&ucpg=a4b2dce363117474ef89dc3890913c58469#_uca_list (accessed June 8, 2009).

28. Information from company website, www.thethinkers.com (accessed March 15, 2003); and N. K. Austin, "Tear Down the Walls," *Inc.*, April 1999, pp. 66–76.

29. Information from Symantec website, www.symantec.com, February 23, 2008; J. Cox, "Cyber Threats Get Personal," *CNN-Money.com*, September 18, 2007; N. Rothbaum, "The Virtual

Battlefield," *Smart Money*, January 2006, pp. 76 –80; S. H. Wildstrom, "Viruses Get Smarter—and Greedy," *BusinessWeek* online, November 22, 2005; and S. Kirsner, "Sweating in the Hot Zone," *Fast Company*, October 2005, pp. 60–65.

30. Based on H. Rothman, "The Boss as Mentor," *Nation's Business*, April 1993, pp. 66–67; J. B. Cunningham and T. Eberle, "Characteristics of the Mentoring Experience: A Qualitative Study," *Personnel Review*, June 1993, pp. 54–66; S. Crandell, "The Joys of Mentoring," *Executive Female*, March–April 1994, pp. 38–42; and W. Heery, "Corporate Mentoring Can Break the Glass Ceiling," *HRfocus*, May 1994, pp. 17–18.

Supplement 1

1. Based on "Coffee Crisis Prompts Action from Aid Groups," *CTV News*, September 19, 2002; www.wd.gc.ca/eng/8271.asp (accessed June 11, 2009); and G. Shaw, "No Turning Back Once the Money Rolls In: $30,000 Loan from a Friend Puts Jazzed-Up Coffee Van on the Road with Espresso Machine at the Ready," *Vancouver Sun*, August 21, 2004, p. J1.

2. C. S. George Jr., *The History of Management Thought*, 2nd ed. (Upper Saddle River, NJ: Prentice Hall, 1972), p. 4.

3. F. W. Taylor, *The Principles of Scientific Management* (New York: Harper, 1911), p. 44. For other information on F. W. Taylor, see M. Banta, *Taylored Lives: Narrative Productions in the Age of Taylor, Veblen, and Ford* (Chicago: University of Chicago Press, 1993); and R. Kanigel, *The One Best Way: Frederick Winslow Taylor and the Enigma of Efficiency* (New York: Viking, 1997).

4. See, for example, F. B. Gilbreth, *Motion Study* (New York: Van Nostrand, 1911); and F. B. Gilbreth and L. M. Gilbreth, *Fatigue Study* (New York: Sturgis and Walton, 1916).

5. G. Colvin, "Managing in the Info Era," *Fortune*, March 6, 2000, pp. F6–F9; and A. Harrington, "The Big Ideas," *Fortune*, November 22, 1999, pp. 152–153.

6. H. Fayol, *Industrial and General Administration* (Paris: Dunod, 1916).

7. M. Weber, *The Theory of Social and Economic Organizations*, ed. T. Parsons, trans. A. M. Henderson and T. Parsons (New York: Free Press, 1947).

8. E. Mayo, *The Human Problems of an Industrial Civilization* (New York: Macmillan, 1933); and F. J. Roethlisberger and W. J. Dickson, *Management and the Worker* (Cambridge, MA: Harvard University Press, 1939).

9. See, for example, A. Carey, "The Hawthorne Studies: A Radical Criticism," *American Sociological Review*, June 1967, pp. 403–416; R. H. Franke and J. Kaul, "The Hawthorne Experiments: First Statistical Interpretations," *American Sociological Review*, October 1978, pp. 623–643; B. Rice, "The Hawthorne Defect: Persistence of a Flawed Theory," *Psychology Today*, February 1982, pp. 70–74; J. A. Sonnenfeld, "Shedding Light on the Hawthorne Studies," *Journal of Occupational Behavior*, April 1985, pp. 111–130; S. R. G. Jones, "Worker Interdependence and Output: The Hawthorne Studies Reevaluated," *American Sociological Review*, April 1990, pp. 176–190; S. R. Jones, "Was There a Hawthorne Effect?" *American Sociological Review*, November 1992, pp. 451–468; and G. W. Yunker, "An Explanation of Positive and Negative Hawthorne Effects: Evidence from the Relay Assembly Test Room and Bank Wiring Observation Room Studies" (paper presented at Academy of Management annual meeting, Atlanta, Georgia, August 1993).

10. With thanks to a reviewer who provided this example.

11. K. B. DeGreene, *Sociotechnical Systems: Factors in Analysis, Design, and Management* (Englewood Cliffs, NJ: Prentice Hall, 1973), p. 13.

Chapter 2

1. Based on D. Tetley, "Tension Rises as Recall List Grows," *Calgary Herald*, April 3, 2007, p. A3; and C. Gillis and A. Kingston, "The Great Pet Food Scandal," *Maclean's*, April 30, 2007, www.macleans.ca/business/companies/article.jsp?content=20070430_104326_104326 (accessed July 8, 2007).

2. T. M. Hout, "Are Managers Obsolete?" *Harvard Business Review*, March–April 1999, pp. 161–168; and J. Pfeffer, "Management as Symbolic Action: The Creation and Maintenance of Organizational Paradigms," in *Research in Organizational Behavior*, vol. 3, ed. L. L. Cummings and B. M. Staw (Greenwich, CT: JAI Press, 1981), pp. 1–52.

3. B. Cooper, "Blue Mantle Will Close on April 30: Other Closures Hurt Business," *Leader Post*, March 20, 2004, p. B2.

4. "U.S. Legislators Could Side-Swipe Canada With Measures to Protect Food Supply," *Alaska Highway News*, May 11, 2007, p. C2; and R. Myers, "Food Fights: As Supply Chains Stretch to All Corners of the Globe, Producers Struggle To," *CFO Magazine*, June 1, 2007.

5. A. Kingston, "Green Report: It's So Not Cool," *macleans.ca*, May 14, 2007.

6. A. Martin, "Is It Healthy? Food Rating Systems Battle It Out," *NYtimes.com*, December 1, 2007.

7. J. Greenwood, "Home Depot Runs into Vancouver Red Tape," *Financial Post* (*National Post*), May 10, 2004, pp. FP1, FP11.

8. D. Calleja, "Equity or Else," *Canadian Business*, March 19, 2001, p. 31.

9. R. Annan, "Merger Remedies in Canada," Competition Bureau, June 20, 2006, www.competitionbureau.gc.ca/internet/index.cfm?itemID=2134&lg=e#25 (accessed June 3, 2009).

10. T. S. Mescon and G. S. Vozikis, "Federal Regulation—What Are the Costs?" *Business*, January–March 1982, pp. 33–39.

11. J. Thorpe, "Inter-Provincial Trade Barriers Still a Concern for Executives 'Handicapping Country Economically,'" *Financial Post* (*National Post*), September 13, 2004, p. FP2.

12. See www.canada.com/nationalpost/entrepreneur/savoie.html (accessed June 7, 2009).

13. See www.fritolay.ca/fritolay/nutrition/press.html (accessed June 11, 2009).

14. See www.ctv.ca/servlet/ArticleNews/story/CTVNews/1069789271153_26//# (accessed June 11, 2009).

15. G. Bonnell, "Food Industry Rushes to Drop Trans Fats," *Calgary Herald*, March 11, 2004, p. D1.

16. C. Gillis and A. Kingston, "The Great Pet Food Scandal," *Maclean's*, April 30, 2007, www.macleans.ca/business/companies/article.jsp?content=20070430_104326_104326 (accessed June 3, 2009); see http://investing.businessweek.com/research/stocks/snapshot/snapshot.asp?capId=3206215 (accessed June 3, 2009); D. George-Cosh, "Menu Foods Hammered as Customer Walks," *Globe and Mail*, June 13, 2007, p. B15; and www.menufoods.com/about_us/distribution.html (accessed June 3, 2009).

17. "Is Corporate Canada Being 'Hollowed Out'?" *CBC News*, May 27, 2007.

18. See http://money.cnn.com/magazines/fortune/global500/2006/countries/C.html (accessed June 3, 2009).

19. See http://money.cnn.com/magazines/fortune/global500/2006/countries/C.html (accessed June 3, 2009).

20. A. Shama, "Management Under Fire: The Transformation of Management in the Soviet Union and Eastern Europe," *Academy of Management Executive* 7, no. 1 (1993), pp. 22–35.

21. "WTO Policy Issues for Parliamentarians," World Trade Organization, www.wto.org/english/res_e/booksp_e/parliamentarians_e.pdf (accessed June 7, 2009), p. 1.

22. B. Mitchener, "Ten New Members to Weigh in on Future of EU," *Wall Street Journal*, April 16, 2003, p. A16; C. Taylor, "Go East, Young Man," *Smart Money*, January 2003, p. 25; S. Miller and B. Grow, "A Bigger Europe? Not So Fast," *Wall Street Journal*, December 12, 2002, p. A15; http://europa.eu/abc/european_countries/index_ en.htm (accessed June 3, 2009); and http://europa.eu/abc/ european_countries/candidate_countries/index_en.htm (accessed June 3, 2009).

23. B. Mitchener, "A New EU, But No Operating Manual," *Wall Street Journal*, December 16, 2002, p. A10; and https://www.cia.gov/ library/publications/the-world-factbook/print/ee.html (accessed June 3, 2009).

24. US Census Bureau, *Foreign Trade Statistics*, www.census.gov/ foreign-trade/statistics/highlights/index.html.

25. Statistics Canada, "International Merchandise Trade: Annual Review," *The Daily*, May 8, 2007.

26. "Goods Going South? Think Mexico," www.edc.ca/english/ publications_9432.htm (accessed June 3, 2009).

27. Information from ASEAN website, www.aseansec.org/stat/ Table5.pdf (accessed June 3, 2009).

28. This section is based on materials from the World Trade Organization website, www.wto.org.

29. G. Abramovich, "Google's China Syndrome," DM News, June 20, 2006, www.dmnews.com/cms/dm-news/search-marketing/37089. html (accessed June 3, 2009).

30. G. Hofstede, *Culture's Consequences: International Differences in Work-Related Values*, 2nd ed. (Thousand Oaks, CA: Sage, 2001), pp. 9–15; and G. Hofstede, "The Cultural Relativity of Organizational Practices and Theories," *Journal of International Business Studies*, Fall 1983, pp. 75–89.

31. Hofstede called this dimension *masculinity versus femininity*, but we have changed his terms because of their strong sexist connotation.

32. The five usual criticisms and Hofstede's responses (in parentheses) are: (1) Surveys are not a suitable way to measure cultural differences (answer: they should not be the only way); (2) Nations are not the proper units for studying cultures (answer: they are usually the only kind of units available for comparison); (3) A study of the subsidiaries of one company cannot provide information about entire national cultures (answer: what was measured were differences among national cultures; any set of functionally equivalent samples can supply information about such differences); (4) The IBM data are old and therefore obsolete (answer: the dimensions found are assumed to have centuries-old roots; they have been validated against all kinds of external measurements; recent replications show no loss of validity); (5) Four or five dimensions are not enough (answer: additional dimensions should be statistically independent of the dimensions defined earlier; they should be valid on the basis of correlations with external measures; candidates are welcome to apply). See A. Harzing and G. Hofstede, "Planned Change in Organizations: The Influence of National Culture," in *Research in the Sociology of Organizations*, p. 14: *Cross Cultural Analysis of Organizations*, ed. P. A. Bamberger, M. Erez, and S. B. Bacharach (Greenwich, CT: JAI Press, 1996), pp. 297–340.

33. G. Hofstede, *Culture's Consequences: Comparative Values, Behaviors, Institutions and Organizations Across Nations*, 2nd ed. (Thousand Oaks, CA: Sage), 2001.

34. Based on C. Gillis and A. Kingston, "The Great Pet Food Scandal," *Maclean's*, April 30, 2007, www.macleans.ca/business/ companies/article.jsp?content=20070430_104326_104326 (accessed June 3, 2009); and D. Barboza and A. Barrionuevo, "Filler in Animal Feed Is Open Secret in China," *New York Times*, April 30, 2007.

35. C. A. Barlett and S. Ghoshal, *Managing Across Borders: The Transnational Solution*, 2nd ed. (Boston: Harvard Business School Press, 2002); and N. J. Adler, *International Dimensions of Organizational Behavior*, 4th ed. (Cincinnati, OH: South-Western College Publishing, 2002), pp. 9–11.

36. D. A. Aaker, *Developing Business Strategies*, 5th ed. (New York: John Wiley & Sons, 1998); and J. A. Byrne, "Borderless Management," *BusinessWeek*, May 23, 1994, pp. 24–26.

37. G. A. Knight and S. T. Cavusgil, "A Taxonomy of Born-Global Firms," *Management International Review* 45, no. 3 (2005), pp. 15–35; S. A. Zahra, "A Theory of International New Ventures: A Decade of Research," *Journal of International Business Studies*, January 2005, pp. 20–28; and B. M. Oviatt and P. P. McDougall, "Toward a Theory of International New Ventures," *Journal of International Business Studies*, January 2005, pp. 29–41.

38. See www.blonnet.com/2006/10/17/stories/ 2006101701390400.htm (accessed June 3, 2009).

39. Mega Brands, *Annual Report*, 2006; and http://communities. canada.com/nationalpost/blogs/tradingdesk/archive/2007/01/23/ good-news-for-mega-brands-put-in-context.aspx (figure is for 2006; accessed June 3, 2009).

40. Statistics Canada, "International Merchandise Trade," *The Daily*, April 3, 2009, www.statcan.gc.ca/daily-quotidien/090403/ dq090403a-eng.htm (accessed June 8, 2009).

41. L. Frost, "Starbucks Lures French Café Society," Associated Press, January 16, 2004.

42. T. Donaldson and L. E. Preston, "The Stakeholder Theory of the Corporation: Concepts, Evidence, and Implications," *Academy of Management Review*, January 1995, pp. 65–91.

43. J. S. Harrison and C. H. St. John, "Managing and Partnering With External Stakeholders," *Academy of Managing Executive*, May 1996, pp. 46–60.

44. A. J. Hillman and G. D. Keim, "Shareholder Value, Stakeholder Management, and Social Issues: What's the Bottom Line?" *Strategic Management Journal*, March 2001, pp. 125–139; and J. Kotter and J. Heskett, *Corporate Culture and Performance* (New York: Free Press, 1992).

45. O. Ward, "Pop Goes Globalization," *Toronto Star*, March 13, 2004, p. A18.

46. A. Kreamer, "America's Yang Has a Yen for Asia's Yin," *Fast Company*, July 2003, p. 58; D. Yergin, "Globalization Opens Door to New Dangers," *USA Today*, May 28, 2003, p. 11A; K. Lowrey Miller, "Is It Globaloney?" *Newsweek*, December 16, 2002, pp. E4–E8; L. Gomes, "Globalization Is Now a Two-Way Street—Good News for the U.S.," *Wall Street Journal*, December 9, 2002, p. B1; J. Kurlantzick and J. T. Allen, "The Trouble with Globalism," *U.S. News & World Report*, February 11, 2002, pp. 38–41; J. Guyon, "The American Way," *Fortune*, November 26, 2001, pp. 114–120.

47. J. Guyon, "The American Way," *Fortune*, November 26, 2001, pp. 114–120.

48. Adapted from G. M. Spreitzer, M. W. McCall Jr., and J. D. Mahoney, "Early Identification of International Executive Potential," *Journal of Applied Psychology*, February 1997, pp. 6–29.

49. Information from company website, www.inditex.com (accessed January 5, 2003); and M. Helft, "Fashion Fast-Forward," *Business 2.0*, May 2002, pp. 60–66.

50. Based on M. R. Cohn, "Indian Villagers Set to Battle Alcan," *Toronto Star*, July 3, 2004, pp. A1, A10–A12; A. Swift, "Alcan to Do Well in 2004, Says CEO," *Trail Times*, April 23, 2004, p. 14; L. Moore, "Alcan Sees Bright Year Ahead," *Gazette* (Montreal), April 23, 2004, p. B1; and www.alcan.com/web/publishing.nsf/Content/Alcan+Facts+2006 (accessed June 3, 2009).

51. Based on www.nba.com/canada/Canadians_in_the_NBA-Canada_Generic_Article-18022.html (accessed June 9, 2009); D. Eisenberg, "The NBA's Global Game Plan," *Time*, March 17, 2003, pp. 59–63; J. Tyrangiel, "The Center of Attention," *Time*, February 10, 2003, pp. 56–60; "Spin Master Stern," *Latin Trade*, July 2000, p. 32; Information from NBA website, www.nba.com (accessed July 1, 2004); J. Tagliabue, "Hoop Dreams, Fiscal Realities," *New York Times*, March 4, 2000, p. B11; D. Roth, "The NBA's Next Shot," *Fortune*, February 21, 2000, pp. 207–216; A. Bianco, "Now It's NBA All-the-Time TV," *BusinessWeek*, November 15, 1999, pp. 241–242; and D. McGraw and M. Tharp, "Going Out on Top," *U.S. News & World Report*, January 25, 1999, p. 55.

52. See www.nba.com/schedules/international_nba_tv_schedule.html (accessed June 3, 2009).

53. M. A. Prospero, "Attitude Adjustment," *Fast Company*, December 2005, p. 107; D. Roberts and M. Arndt, "It's Getting Hotter in the East," *BusinessWeek*, August 22/29, 2005, pp. 78–81; M. Champion, "Scotland Looks East for Labor," *Wall Street Journal*, July 7, 2005, p. A11; L. Bower, "Cultural Awareness Aids Business Relations," *Springfield Business Journal*, April 4–10, 2005, p. 59; R. Rosmarin, "Mountain View Masala," *Business 2.0*, March 2005, pp. 54–56; and P.-W. Tam, "Culture Course," *Wall Street Journal*, May 25, 2004, pp. B1+.

54. C. Harvey and M. J. Allard, *Understanding and Managing Diversity: Readings, Cases, and Exercises*, 2nd ed. (Upper Saddle River, NJ: Prentice Hall, 2002); P. L. Hunsaker, *Training in Management Skills* (Upper Saddle River, NJ: Prentice Hall, 2001); and J. Greenberg, *Managing Behavior in Organizations: Science in Service to Practice*, 2nd ed. (Upper Saddle River, NJ: Prentice Hall, 1999).

Part 1 Continuing Case: Starbucks

1 Based on information from Starbucks website, www.starbucks.com; Hoover's Online, www.hoovers.com (accessed June 14, 2006); J. Simmons, *My Sister's a Barista: How They Made Starbucks a Home Away from Home* (London: Cyan Books, 2005); A. Serwer and K. Bonamici, "Hot Starbucks to Go," *Fortune*, January 26, 2004, pp. 60–74; S. Holmes, I. M. Kunii, J. Ewing, and K. Capell, "For Starbucks, There's No Place Like Home," *BusinessWeek*, June 9, 2003, p. 48; H. Schultz and D. Jones Yang, *Pour Your Heart into It; How Starbucks Built a Company One Cup at a* Time (New York: Hyperion, 1997); R. Gulati, S. Huffman, and G. Neilson, "The Barista Principle," *Strategy+Business*, Third Quarter 2002, pp. 58–69; J. Cummings, "Legislative Grind," *Wall Street Journal*, April 12, 2005, pp. A1+; B. Horovitz, "Starbucks Nation," *USA Today*, May 29, 2006, pp. A1+; J. Lawless, "Historian Studies Impact of Starbucks Globally," *Marketing News*, May 15, 2006, p. 44; K. M. Butler, "Examining the Benefits of Corporate Social Responsibility," *Employee Benefit News*, May 2006, p. 16; R. Tiplady, "Can Starbucks Blend into France?" *BusinessWeek*, April 21, 2006; A. Serwer, "Interview with Howard Schultz," *Fortune* (Europe), March 20, 2006, pp. 35–36; E. Barraclough, "Starbucks and Ferrero Celebrate China Victories," *Managing*

Intellectual Property, February 2006, p. 12; K. Bonamici, S. Herman, and P. Jarvis, "Decoding the Dress Code," *Fortune*, January 23, 2006, pp. 130–131; A. Lustgarten, "A Hot, Steaming Cup of Customer Awareness," *Fortune*, November 15, 2004, p. 192; W. Meyers, "Conscience in a Cup of Coffee," *U.S. News & World Report*, October 31, 2005, pp. 48–50; M. Berglind and C. Nakata, "Cause-Related Marketing: More Buck Than Bang?" *Business Horizons*, September–October 2005, pp. 443–453; I. Mochari, "Coffee with Cream, Sugar, and Interest," *CFO*, September 2005, p. 23; C. Williamson, "Starbucks, Calvert Support Fair Trade," *Pensions & Investments*, July 11, 2005, p. 8; T. Howard, "Starbucks Takes Up Cause for Safe Drinking Water," *USA Today*, August 3, 2005, p. 5B; P. Orsi, "Selling Charity in a Bottle," *Business 2.0*, October 2005, p. 38; P. L. Green, "US Firms Widen the Net," *Global Finance*, January 2006, pp. 28–29; www.starbucks.ca/en-ca/_About+Starbucks/Starbucks+in+Canada.htm (accessed June 9, 2009); www.starbucks.com/aboutus/Company_Factsheet.pdf (accessed June 9, 2009); Starbucks 2006 Annual Report, http://investor.starbucks.com/phoenix.zhtml?c=99518&p=irol-IRHome (accessed June 9, 2009); and "Hero's Goodbye for McNaughton," *Province* (Vancouver), February 8, 2000, p. A4.

Chapter 3

1. Based on H. Shaw, "Indigo Pens Next Chapter," *Financial Post (National Post)*, June 22, 2007, www.canada.com; Indigo Books & Music website, www.chapters.indigo.ca (accessed June 8, 2009); and www.cb-bc.gc.ca/eic/site/cb-bc.nsf/eng/00494.html (accessed June 17, 2009).

2. V. Pilieci, "The Lost Generation of Business Talent," *Vancouver Sun*, May 2, 2001, pp. D1, D9.

3. See, for example, J. A. Pearce II, K. K. Robbins, and R. B. Robinson Jr., "The Impact of Grand Strategy and Planning Formality on Financial Performance," *Strategic Management Journal*, March–April 1987, pp. 125–134; L. C. Rhyne, "Contrasting Planning Systems in High, Medium, and Low Performance Companies," *Journal of Management Studies*, July 1987, pp. 363–385; J. A. Pearce II, E. B. Freeman, and R. B. Robinson Jr., "The Tenuous Link Between Formal Strategic Planning and Financial Performance," *Academy of Management Review*, October 1987, pp. 658–675; D. K. Sinha, "The Contribution of Formal Planning to Decisions," *Strategic Management Journal*, October 1990, pp. 479–492; N. Capon, J. U. Farley, and J. M. Hulbert, "Strategic Planning and Financial Performance: More Evidence," *Journal of Management Studies*, January 1994, pp. 22–38; C. C. Miller and L. B. Cardinal, "Strategic Planning and Firm Performance: A Synthesis of More Than Two Decades of Research," *Academy of Management Journal*, March 1994, pp. 1649–1685; and P. J. Brews and M. R. Hunt, "Learning to Plan and Planning to Learn: Resolving the Planning School/Learning School Debate," *Strategic Management Journal*, December 1999, pp. 889–913.

4. R. Molz, "How Leaders Use Goals," *Long Range Planning*, October 1987, p. 91.

5. P. N. Romani, "MBO by Any Other Name Is Still MBO," *Supervision*, December 1997, pp. 6–8; and A. W. Schrader and G. T. Seward, "MBO Makes Dollar Sense," *Personnel Journal*, July 1989, pp. 32–37.

6. P. N. Romani, "MBO by Any Other Name Is Still MBO," *Supervision*, December 1997, pp. 6–8; and R. Rodgers and J. E. Hunter, "Impact of Management by Objectives on Organizational Productivity," *Journal of Applied Psychology*, April 1991, pp. 322–336.

7. For additional information on goals, see, for example, P. Drucker, *The Executive in Action* (New York: HarperCollins Books, 1996), pp. 207–214; and E. A. Locke and G. P. Latham, *A Theory of Goal Setting and Task Performance* (Upper Saddle River, NJ: Prentice Hall, 1990).

8. See www.canada.com/nationalpost/entrepreneur/transat.html (accessed June 8, 2009).

9. J. D. Hunger and T. L. Wheelen, *Strategic Management*, 7th ed. (Upper Saddle River, NJ: Prentice Hall, 2000).

10. Several of these factors were suggested by J. S. Armstrong, "The Value of Formal Planning for Strategic Decisions: Review of Empirical Research," *Strategic Management Journal*, July–September 1982, pp. 197–211; and R. K. Bresser and R. C. Bishop, "Dysfunctional Effects of Formal Planning: Two Theoretical Explanations," *Academy of Management Review*, October 1983, pp. 588–599.

11. P. J. Brews and M. R. Hunt, "Learning to Plan and Planning to Learn: Resolving the Planning School/Learning School Debate," *Strategic Management Journal*, December 1999, pp. 889–913.

12. P. J. Brews and M. R. Hunt, "Learning to Plan and Planning to Learn: Resolving the Planning School/Learning School Debate," *Strategic Management Journal*, December 1999, pp. 889–913.

13. H. Mintzberg, *The Rise and Fall of Strategic Planning* (New York: Free Press, 1994).

14. H. Mintzberg, *The Rise and Fall of Strategic Planning* (New York: Free Press, 1994).

15. H. Mintzberg, *The Rise and Fall of Strategic Planning* (New York: Free Press, 1994).

16. G. Hamel and C. K. Prahalad, *Competing for the Future* (Boston: Harvard Business School Press, 1994).

17. D. Miller, "The Architecture of Simplicity," *Academy of Management Review*, January 1993, pp. 116–138.

18. Based on J. McElgunn, "Staying on a Kicking Horse," *PROFIT Magazine*, November 2006.

19. Based on H. Shaw, "Indigo Pens Next Chapter," *Financial Post (National Post)*, June 22, 2007, www.canada.com/nationalpost/financialpost/story.html?id=d1bc522d-712c-42f4-b2e4-fe71c0c5d0ba&k=68292 (accessed June 8, 2009).

20. J. W. Dean Jr. and M. P. Sharfman, "Does Decision Process Matter? A Study of Strategic Decision-Making Effectiveness," *Academy of Management Journal*, April 1996, pp. 368–396.

21. Based on A. A. Thompson, Jr., A. J. Strickland III, and J. E. Gamble, *Crafting and Executing Strategy*, 14th ed. (New York: McGraw-Hill Irwin), 2005.

22. J. Magretta, "Why Business Models Matter," *Harvard Business Review*, May 2002, pp. 86–92.

23. "About Us," *WorkSafeBC*, www.worksafebc.com/about_us/default.asp (accessed June 8, 2009).

24. See www.worksafebc.com/about_us/our_mandate/default.asp (accessed June 8, 2009).

25. C. K. Prahalad and G. Hamel, "The Core Competence of the Corporation," *Harvard Business Review*, May–June 1990, pp. 79–91.

26. A. Taylor, "How Toyota Does It," *Fortune*, March 6, 2006, pp. 107–124; C. Woodyard, "Slow and Steady Drives Toyota's Growth," *USA Today*, December 21, 2005, pp. 1B+; I. M. Kunii, C. Dawson, and C. Palmeri, "Toyota Is Way Ahead of the Hybrid Pack," *BusinessWeek*, May 5, 2003, p. 48; and S. Spear and H. K. Bowen, "Decoding the DNA of the Toyota Production System," *Harvard Business Review*, September–October 1999, pp. 96–106.

27. See, for example, H. J. Cho and V. Pucik, "Relationship Between Innovativeness, Quality, Growth, Profitability, and Market Value," *Strategic Management Journal* 26, no. 6 (2005), pp. 555–575; W. F. Joyce,

"Building the 4+2 Organization," *Organizational Dynamics*, May 2005, pp. 118–129; R. S. Kaplan and D. P. Norton, "Measuring the Strategic Readiness of Intangible Assets," *Harvard Business Review*, February 2004, pp. 52–63; C. M. Fiol, "Managing Culture as a Competitive Resource: An Identity-Based View of Sustainable Competitive Advantage," *Journal of Management*, March 1991, pp. 191–211; T. Kono, "Corporate Culture and Long-Range Planning," *Long Range Planning*, August 1990, pp. 9–19; S. Green, "Understanding Corporate Culture and Its Relation to Strategy," *International Studies of Management and Organization*, Summer 1988, pp. 6–28; C. Scholz, "Corporate Culture and Strategy—The Problem of Strategic Fit," *Long Range Planning*, August 1987, pp. 78–87; and J. B. Barney, "Organizational Culture: Can It Be a Source of Sustained Competitive Advantage?" *Academy of Management Review*, July 1986, pp. 656–665.

28. K. E. Klein, "Slogans That Are the Real Thing," *BusinessWeek Online*, www.businessweek.com, August 4, 2005; and T. Mucha, "The Payoff for Trying Harder," *Business 2.0*, July 2002, pp. 84–85.

29. A. Carmeli and A. Tischler, "The Relationships Between Intangible Organizational Elements and Organizational Performance"; P. W. Roberts and G. R. Dowling, "Corporate Reputation and Sustained Financial Performance," *Strategic Management Journal*, December 2002, pp. 1077–1093; and C. J. Fombrun, "Corporate Reputations as Economic Assets," in *Handbook of Strategic Management*, ed. M. A. Hitt, R. E. Freeman, and J. S. Harrison (Malden, MA: Blackwell Publishers, 2001), pp. 289–312.

30. "Johnson & Johnson Ranks No. 1 in National Corporate Reputation Survey for Seventh Consecutive Year," Harris Interactive Press Release, www.harrisinteractive.com, December 7, 2005.

31. Based on G. Pitts, "Tide Turns for P&G Canada President," *Globe and Mail*, October 14, 2002, p. B3; S. Heinrich, "P&G Still the Best Step Up," *National Post*, April 14, 2003, p. FP4; and www.pg.com/en_CA/index.jhtml (accessed June 8, 2009).

32. H. Mintzberg, "The Strategy Concept I: Five Ps for Strategy," *California Management Review*, Fall 1987, pp. 11–24.

33. Based on H. Shaw, "Indigo Pens Next Chapter," *Financial Post (National Post)*, June 22, 2007, www.canada.com/nationalpost/financialpost/story.html?id=d1bc522d-712c-42f4-b2e4-fe71c0c5d0ba&k=68292 (accessed June 8, 2009); and Indigo Books & Music website, www.chapters.indigo.ca.

34. M. Bustillo, "New Chief at Wal-Mart Looks Abroad For Growth," *Wall Street Journal*, February 2, 2009, p. B1.

35. P. Marck, "Tim Hortons Brews Up Record Sales: No Holes in Doughnut Business in Canada," *Edmonton Journal*, January 7, 2004, p. A1.

36. A. Swift, "Quebec Drugstore Chain Acquires 1539 Outlets in Eastern U.S.," *Vancouver Sun*, April 6, 2004, p. F6.

37. www.jeancoutu.com/finance/english/Profil/main.cfm?ID=0 (accessed June 8, 2009).

38. G. Pitts, "Small Is Beautiful, Conglomerates Signal," *Globe and Mail*, April 1, 2002, pp. B1, B4; Brookfield Asset Management website, www.brookfield.com (accessed June 8, 2009); and *Brookfield Asset Management 2006 Annual Report*, www.brookfield.com/userfiles/file/Annual Reports/2006/2006 Annual Report.pdf (accessed June 8, 2009).

39. V. Ramanujam and P. Varadarajan, "Research on Corporate Diversification: A Synthesis," *Strategic Management Journal* 10 (1989), pp. 523–551. See also A. Shleifer and R. W. Vishny, "Takeovers in the 1960s and 1980s: Evidence and Implications," in *Fundamental Issues in Strategy*, ed. R. P. Rumelt, D. E. Schendel, and D. J. Teece (Boston: Harvard Business School Press, 1994).

40. J. A. Pearce, II, "Retrenchment Remains the Foundation of Business Turnaround," *Strategic Management Journal* 15 (1994), pp. 407–417.

41. www.nasrecruitment.com/TalentTips/NASinsights/CANLayoff07_08.pdf (accessed June 16, 2009.)

42. See, for example, M. E. Porter, *Competitive Strategy: Techniques for Analyzing Industries and Competitors* (New York: Free Press, 1980); M. E. Porter, *Competitive Advantage: Creating and Sustaining Superior Performance* (New York: Free Press, 1985); G. G. Dess and P. S. Davis, "Porter's (1980) Generic Strategies as Determinants of Strategic Group Membership and Organizational Performance," *Academy of Management Journal*, September 1984, pp. 467–488; G. G. Dess and P. S. Davis, "Porter's (1980) Generic Strategies and Performance: An Empirical Examination With American Data—Part I: Testing Porter," *Organization Studies* 7, no. 1 (1986), pp. 37–55; G. G. Dess and P. S. Davis, "Porter's (1980) Generic Strategies and Performance: An Empirical Examination With American Data—Part II: Performance Implications," *Organization Studies* 7, no. 3 (1986), pp. 255–261; M. E. Porter, "From Competitive Advantage to Corporate Strategy," *Harvard Business Review*, May–June 1987, pp. 43–59; A. I. Murray, "A Contingency View of Porter's 'Generic Strategies,'" *Academy of Management Review*, July 1988, pp. 390–400; C. W. L. Hill, "Differentiation Versus Low Cost or Differentiation and Low Cost: A Contingency Framework," *Academy* of Management Review, July 1988, pp. 401–412; I. Bamberger, "Developing Competitive Advantage in Small and Medium-Sized Firms," *Long Range Planning*, October 1989, pp. 80–88; D. F. Jennings and J. R. Lumpkin, "Insights Between Environmental Scanning Activities and Porter's Generic Strategies: An Empirical Analysis," *Strategic Management Journal* 18, no. 4 (1992), pp. 791–803; N. Argyres and A. M. McGahan, "An Interview with Michael Porter," *Academy of Management Executive*, May 2002, pp. 43–52; and A. Brandenburger, "Porter's Added Value: High Indeed!" *Academy of Management Executive*, May 2002, pp. 58–60.

43. G. Pitts, "Ganong Boss Aims for Sweet Spot," *Globe and Mail*, March 3, 2003, p. B4.

44. Based on W. Hanley, "Mowat's Lefty Ways Pay Big Dividends," *National Post*, February 28, 2004, p. IN01.

45. www.peicreditunions.com/news/article.php?ID=594 (accessed June 8, 2009).

46. D. Miller and J. Toulouse, "Strategy, Structure, CEO Personality, and Performance in Small Firms," *American Journal of Small Business*, Winter 1986, pp. 47–62.

47. C. W. L. Hill, "Differentiation versus Low Cost or Differentiation and Low Cost: A Contingency Framework," *Academy of Management Review*, July 1988, pp. 401–412; R. E. White, "Organizing to Make Business Unit Strategies Work," in *Handbook of Business Strategy*, 2nd ed., ed. H. E. Glass (Boston: Warren Gorham and Lamont, 1991), pp. 24.1–24.14; D. Miller, "The Generic Strategy Trap," *Journal of Business Strategy*, January–February 1991, pp. 37–41; S. Cappel, P. Wright, M. Kroll, and D. Wyld, "Competitive Strategies and Business Performance: An Empirical Study of Select Service Businesses," *International Journal of Management*, March 1992, pp. 1–11; and J. W. Bachmann, "Competitive Strategy: It's O.K. to Be Different," *Academy of Management Executive*, May 2002, pp. 61–65.

48. See, for example, B. Krone, "Total Quality Management: An American Odyssey," *The Bureaucrat*, Fall 1990, pp. 35–38; A. Gabor, *The Man Who Discovered Quality* (New York: Random House, 1990); J. W. Dean Jr. and D. E. Bowen, "Management Theory and Total Quality: Improving Research and Practice through Theory Development," *Academy of Management Review*, July 1994, pp. 392–418; C. A. Reeves and D. A. Bednar, "Defining Quality: Alternatives and Implications," *Academy of Management Review*, July 1994, pp. 419–445;

R. K. Reger, L. T. Gustafson, S. M. Demarie, and J. V. Mullane, "Reframing the Organization: Why Implementing Total Quality Is Easier Said Than Done," *Academy of Management Review*, July 1994, pp. 565–584; T. C. Powell, "Total Quality Management as Competitive Advantage: A Review and Empirical Study," *Strategic Management Journal*, January 1995, pp. 15–37; J. R. Hackman and R. Wageman, "Total Quality Management: Empirical, Conceptual, and Practical Issues," *Administrative Science Quarterly*, June 1995, pp. 309–342; T. A. Stewart, "A Conversation With Joseph Juran," *Fortune*, January 11, 1999, pp. 168–170; and J. Jusko, "Tried and True," *IW*, December 6, 1999, pp. 78–84.

49. T. C. Powell, "Total Quality Management as Competitive Advantage: A Review and Empirical Study," *Strategic Management Journal*, January 1995, pp. 15–37.

50. See R. J. Schonenberger, "Is Strategy Strategic? Impact of Total Quality Management on Strategy," *Academy of Management Executive*, August 1992, pp. 80–87; C. A. Barclay, "Quality Strategy and TQM Policies: Empirical Evidence," *Management International Review*, Special Issue (1993), pp. 87–98; T. E. Benson, "A Business Strategy Comes of Age," *IndustryWeek*, May 3, 1993, pp. 40–44; R. Jacob, "TQM: More Than a Dying Fad?" *Fortune*, October 18, 1993, pp. 66–72; R. Krishnan, A. B. Shani, R. M. Grant, and R. Baer, "In Search of Quality Improvement Problems of Design and Implementation," *Academy of Management Executive*, November 1993, pp. 7–20; B. Voss, "Quality's Second Coming," *Journal of Business Strategy*, March–April 1994, pp. 42–46; M. Barrier, "Raising TQM Consciousness," *Nation's Business*, April 1994, pp. 62–64; and a special issue of *Academy of Management Review* devoted to TQM, July 1994, pp. 390–584.

51. F. Jossi, "Take a Peek Inside," *HR Magazine*, June 2002, pp. 46–52; and R. A. Martins, "Continuous Improvement Strategies and Production Competitive Criteria: Some Findings in Brazilian Industries," *Total Quality Management*, May 2001, pp. 281–291.

52. Ford Motor Company, "New Range Rover Debuts at North American International Auto Show," news release, January 7, 2002, www.pcnewswire.net/cgi-bin/stories.pl?ACCT=104&STORY=/www/story/01-07-2002/0001642696&EDATE= (accessed June 17, 2009).

53. See, for example, J. P. Wilson, M. A. T. Walsh, and K. L. Needy, "An Examination of the Economic Benefits of ISO 9000 and the Baldrige Award to Manufacturing Firms," *Engineering Management Journal*, December 2003, pp. 3–5; and International Organization for Standardization, "ISO 9000 and ISO 14000," International Organization for Standardization, www.iso.org/iso/iso_catalogue/management_standards/iso_9000_iso_14000.htm (accessed June 8, 2009).

54. T. B. Schoenrock, "ISO 9000: 2000 Gives Competitive Edge," *Quality Progress*, May 2002, p. 107.

55. See, for example, L. P. Dodd Jr., "The Team Approach to ISO 9000: 2000 at Standard Aero Alliance," *Journal for Quality and Participation*, Spring 2002, pp. 41–44; and S. Smith, "The Cutting Edge of Environmental Management," *Occupational Hazards*, February 2002, pp. 33–37.

56. C. Mitman, "Get ISO Certified on Time and Within Budget," *Quality*, November 2001, pp. 46–48.

57. "Green Belt Training Starts February 4; Other Courses On-Line," *Quality Progress*, February 2002, p. 13; J. M. Lucas, "The Essential Six Sigma," *Quality Progress*, January 2002, pp. 27–31; and D. Treichler, R. Carmichael, A. Kusmanoff, J. Lewis, and G. Berthiez, "Design for Six Sigma: 15 Lessons Learned," *Quality Progress*, January 2002, p. 33.

58. T. Aeppel, "Career Journal: Nicknamed 'Nag,' She's Just Doing Her Job," *Wall Street Journal*, May 14, 2002, p. B1.

59. L. Heuring, "Six Sigma in Sight," *HR Magazine*, March 2004, pp. 76–80; G. Eckes, "Making Six Sigma Last (and Work)," *Ivey Business Journal*, January–February 2002, pp. 77–81.

60. "Six Sigma Gets Its Day," *Quality*, January 2002, p. 48.

61. "Is 99.9% Good Enough?" *Training*, March 1991, p. 38. See also J. Petty, "When Near Enough Is Not Good Enough," *Australian CPA*, May 2000, pp. 34–35.

62. M. Arndt, "Quality Isn't Just for Widgets," *BusinessWeek*, July 22, 2002, pp. 72–74.

63. R. E. Quinn, S. R. Faerman, M. P. Thompson, and M. R. McGrath, *Becoming a Master Manager: A Competency Framework* (New York: Wiley, 1990), pp. 33–34. Reproduced by permission of John Wiley & Sons Inc.

64. Situation adapted from information in S. Leith, "Coke Faces Damage Control," *Atlanta Journal-Constitution*, June 19, 2003, p. C1; C. Terhune, "Coke Employees Acted Improperly in Marketing Test," *Wall Street Journal*, June 18, 2003, pp. A3, A6; and T. Howard, "Burger King, Coke May Face Off in Frozen Coke Suit," *USA Today*, June 6, 2003, www.usatoday.com/money/industries/food/_2003-06-04.bk_x.htm (accessed June 17, 2009).

65. Based on company information from Haier websites: www.haier.com, www.haieramerica.com, and www.haier.com.au (accessed June 8, 2009); S. Hamm and I. Rowley, "Speed Demons," *BusinessWeek*, March 27, 2006, pp. 68–76; E. Esfahani, "Thinking Locally, Succeeding Globally," *Business 2.0*, December 2005, pp. 96–98; Interbrand, "The Strategy for Chinese Brands," October 2005, www.brandchannel.com/images/papers/250_ChinaBrandStrategy.pdf (accessed June 8, 2009); Agence France-Presse, "Chinese Brands Coming to a Market Near You," *IndustryWeek*, April 14, 2005; and "Leadership in China: Haier's Zhang Ruimin," *Wharton Leadership Digest* 9, no. 6 (March 2005).

66. Based on Live Nation website, www.livenation.com, April 28, 2008; E. Smith, "Live Nation Sings a New Tune," *Wall Street Journal*, July 11, 2008, pp. B1+; B. Sisario, "Nickelback Signs Up with Live Nation," *New York Times* online, www.nytimes.com, July 9, 2008; E. Smith, "Live Nation's Leaders Battle Over Strategy," *Wall Street Journal*, June 12, 2008, p. B1; C. Robertson, "Live Nation Finds a Buyer for Its Theater Business," *New York Times* online, www.nytimes.com, January 25, 2008; P. Sloan, "Keep on Rocking in the Free World," *Fortune*, December 10, 2007, pp. 156–160; and E. Smith, "Live Nation's New Act," *Wall Street Journal*, November 30, 2007, pp. B1+.

67. Based on L. M. Fuld, *Monitoring the Competition* (New York: Wiley, 1988); E. H. Burack and N. J. Mathys, "Environmental Scanning Improves Strategic Planning," *Personnel Administrator*, 1989, pp. 82–87; and R. Subramanian, N. Fernandes, and E. Harper, "Environmental Scanning in U.S. Companies: Their Nature and Their Relationship to Performance," *Management International Review*, July 1993, pp. 271–286.

Chapter 4

1. Based on W. Stueck, "Builder of Toddler Shoe Empire Nudges Her Baby Out of the Nest," *Globe and Mail*, September 7, 2006, p. B1; D. Drew, "She Turned a Crisis into a Success," *Cowichan Valley Citizen*, November 29, 2006, p. 12; and G. Shaw, "Robeez Shoes Sold for $30.5 Million," *Vancouver Sun*, September 7, 2006, p. C1.

2. I. Wylie, "Who Runs This Team Anyway?" *Fast Company*, April 2002, pp. 32–33.

3. D. A. Garvin and M. A. Roberto, "What You Don't Know About Making Decisions," *Harvard Business Review*, September 2001, pp. 108–116.

4. W. Pounds, "The Process of Problem Finding," *Industrial Management Review*, Fall 1969, pp. 1–19.

5. P. C. Nutt, *Why Decisions Fail: Avoiding the Blunders and Traps That Lead to Debacles* (San Francisco, CA: Berrett-Koehler Publishers, 2002).

6. W. Stueck, "Builder of Toddler Shoe Empire Nudges Her Baby Out of the Nest," *Globe and Mail*, September 7, 2006, p. B1; and Strategis, "Robeez Footwear, Better by Design," http://strategis.ic.gc.ca/epic/site/mfbs-gprea.nsf/en/lu00062e.html (accessed June 10, 2009).

7. See H. A. Simon, "Rationality in Psychology and Economics," *Journal of Business*, October 1986, pp. 209–224; A. Langley, "In Search of Rationality: The Purposes Behind the Use of Formal Analysis in Organizations," *Administrative Science Quarterly*, December 1989, pp. 598–631.

8. See, for example, J. G. March, *A Primer on Decision Making* (New York: Free Press, 1994), pp. 8–25; and A. Langley, H. Mintzberg, P. Pitcher, E. Posada, and J. Saint-Macary, "Opening Up Decision Making: The View from the Black Stool," *Organization Science*, May–June 1995, pp. 260–279.

9. See N. McK. Agnew and J. L. Brown, "Bounded Rationality: Fallible Decisions in Unbounded Decision Space," *Behavioral Science*, July 1986, pp. 148–161; B. E. Kaufman, "A New Theory of Satisficing," *Journal of Behavioral Economics*, Spring 1990, pp. 35–51; and D. R. A. Skidd, "Revisiting Bounded Rationality," *Journal of Management Inquiry*, December 1992, pp. 343–347.

10. W. Cole, "The Stapler Wars," *Time Inside Business,* April 2005, p. A5.

11. See K. R. Hammond, R. M. Hamm, J. Grassia, and T. Pearson, "Direct Comparison of the Efficacy of Intuitive and Analytical Cognition in Expert Judgment," in *IEEE Transactions on Systems, Man, and Cybernetics* SMC-17 no. 5 (1987): pp. 753–770; W. H. Agor, ed., *Intuition in Organizations* (Newbury Park, CA: Sage Publications, 1989); O. Behling and N. L. Eckel, "Making Sense Out of Intuition," *The Executive*, February 1991, pp. 46–47; L. A. Burke and M. K. Miller, "Taking the Mystery Out of Intuitive Decision Making," *Academy of Management Executive*, October 1999, pp. 91–99; A. L. Tesolin, "How to Develop the Habit of Intuition," *Training & Development*, March 2000, p. 76; and T. A. Stewart, "How to Think with Your Gut," *Business 2.0*, November 2002, pp. 98–104.

12. A. Dijksterhuis, M. W. Bos, L. F. Nordgren, R. B. van Baaren, "On Making the Right Choice: The Deliberation-Without-Attention Effect," *Science*, February 17, 2006, Vol. 311. no. 5763, pp. 1005-1007.

13. S. Maich, "Promises, Promises but Tax Bill Grows," *Financial Post (National Post)*, June 1, 2004, p. FP1.

14. K. R. Brousseau, M. J. Driver, G. Hourihan, and R. Larsson, "The Seasoned Executive's Decision-Making Style," *Harvard Business Review,* February 2006, pp. 111–121.

15. A. J. Rowe, J. D. Boulgarides, and M. R. McGrath, *Managerial Decision Making, Modules in Management Series* (Chicago: SRA, 1984), pp. 18–22.

16. C. Shaffran, "Mind Your Meeting: How to Become the Catalyst for Culture Change," *Communication World*, February–March 2003, pp. 26–29.

17. I. L. Janis, *Victims of Groupthink* (Boston: Houghton Mifflin, 1972); R. J. Aldag and S. Riggs Fuller, "Beyond Fiasco: A Reappraisal of the Groupthink Phenomenon and a New Model of Group Decision Processes," *Psychological Bulletin*, May 1993, pp. 533–552; T. Kameda and S. Sugimori, "Psychological Entrapment in Group Decision Making: An Assigned Decision Rule and a Groupthink

Phenomenon," *Journal of Personality and Social Psychology*, August 1993, pp. 282–292.

18. R. G. Vleeming, "Machiavellianism: A Preliminary Review," *Psychology Reports*, February 1979, pp. 295–310.

19. Based on J. Brockner, *Self Esteem at Work* (Lexington, MA: Lexington Books, 1988), chapters 1–4.

20. See, for example, L. K. Michaelson, W. E. Watson, and R. H. Black, "A Realistic Test of Individual vs. Group Consensus Decision Making," *Journal of Applied Psychology* 74, no. 5 (1989), pp. 834–839; R. A. Henry, "Group Judgment Accuracy: Reliability and Validity of Postdiscussion Confidence Judgments," *Organizational Behavior and Human Decision Processes*, October 1993, pp. 11–27; P. W. Paese, M. Bieser, and M. E. Tubbs, "Framing Effects and Choice Shifts in Group Decision Making," *Organizational Behavior and Human Decision Processes*, October 1993, pp. 149–165; N. J. Castellan Jr., ed., *Individual and Group Decision Making* (Hillsdale, NJ: Lawrence Erlbaum Associates, 1993); and S. G. Straus and J. E. McGrath, "Does the Medium Matter? The Interaction of Task Type and Technology on Group Performance and Member Reactions," *Journal of Applied Psychology*, February 1994, pp. 87–97.

21. E. J. Thomas and C. F. Fink, "Effects of Group Size," *Psychological Bulletin*, July 1963, pp. 371–384; F. A. Shull, A. L. Delbecq, and L. L. Cummings, *Organizational Decision Making* (New York: McGraw-Hill, 1970), p. 151; A. P. Hare, *Handbook of Small Group Research* (New York: Free Press, 1976); M. E. Shaw, *Group Dynamics: The Psychology of Small Group Behavior*, 3rd ed. (New York: McGraw-Hill, 1981); P. Yetton and P. Bottger, "The Relationships Among Group Size, Member Ability, Social Decision Schemes, and Performance," *Organizational Behavior and Human Performance*, October 1983, pp. 145–159.

22. D. Kahneman and A. Tversky, "Judgment Under Uncertainty: Heuristics and Biases," *Science* 185 (1974), pp. 1124–1131.

23. Information for this section is taken from S. P. Robbins, *Decide & Conquer* (Upper Saddle River, NJ: Financial Times/Prentice Hall, 2004).

24. See, for example, B. M. Staw, "The Escalation of Commitment to a Course of Action," *Academy of Management Review*, October 1981, pp. 577–587; D. R. Bobocel and J. P. Meyer, "Escalating Commitment to a Failing Course of Action: Separating the Roles of Choice and Justification," *Journal of Applied Psychology*, June 1994, pp. 360–363; C. F. Camerer and R. A. Weber, "The Econometrics and Behavioral Economics of Escalation of Commitment: A Re-examination of Staw's Theory," *Journal of Economic Behavior and Organization*, May 1999, pp. 59–82; V. S. Rao and A. Monk, "The Effects of Individual Differences and Anonymity on Commitment to Decisions," *Journal of Social Psychology*, August 1999, pp. 496–515; and G. McNamara, H. Moon, and P. Bromiley, "Banking on Commitment: Intended and Unintended Consequences of an Organization's Attempt to Attenuate Escalation of Commitment," *Academy of Management Journal*, April 2002, pp. 443–452.

25. K. Davis and W. C. Frederick, *Business and Society: Management, Public Policy, Ethics*, 5th ed. (New York: McGraw-Hill, 1984), pp. 28–41, 76.

26. G. F. Cavanagh, D. J. Moberg, and M. Valasquez, "The Ethics of Organizational Politics," *Academy of Management Journal*, June 1981, pp. 363–374. See also F. N. Brady, "Rules for Making Exceptions to Rules," *Academy of Management Review*, July 1987, pp. 436–444, for an argument that the theory of justice is redundant with the prior two theories. See also T. Donaldson and T. W. Dunfee, "Toward a Unified Conception of Business Ethics: Integrative Social Contracts Theory," *Academy of Management Review*, April 1994, pp. 252–284; M. Douglas, "Integrative Social Contracts Theory: Hype Over Hyper-

norms," *Journal of Business Ethics*, July 2000, pp. 101–110; and E. Soule, "Managerial Moral Strategies—In Search of a Few Good Principles," *Academy of Management Review*, January 2002, pp. 114–124, for discussions of integrative social contracts theory.

27. E. Soule, "Managerial Moral Strategies—In Search of a Few Good Principles," *Academy of Management Review*, January 2002, p. 117.

28. F. D. Sturdivant, *Business and Society: A Managerial Approach*, 3rd ed. (Homewood, IL: Richard D. Irwin, 1985), p. 128.

29. L. Bogomolny, "Good Housekeeping," *Canadian Business*, March 1, 2004, pp. 87–88; and www.rbc.com/responsibility/ (accessed June 10, 2009).

30. See www.csa-acvm.ca/html_CSA/about.html (accessed June 10, 2009).

31. W. Dabrowski, "Tighter Guidelines Issued on Disclosure: Canada's 'Sarbanes,'" *Financial Post* (*National Post*), March 30, 2004, p. FP1.

32. L. Bogomolny, "Good Housekeeping," *Canadian Business*, March 1, 2004, pp. 87–88.

33. "Global Ethics Codes Gain Importance as a Tool to Avoid Litigation and Fines," *Wall Street Journal*, August 19, 1999, p. A1; and J. Alexander, "On the Right Side," *World Business*, January–February 1997, pp. 38–41.

34. P. Richter, "Big Business Puts Ethics in Spotlight," *Los Angeles Times*, June 19, 1986, p. 29.

35. F. R. David, "An Empirical Study of Codes of Business Ethics: A Strategic Perspective" (paper presented at the 48th Annual Academy of Management Conference, Anaheim, California, August 1988).

36. "Ethics Programs Aren't Stemming Employee Misconduct," *Wall Street Journal*, May 11, 2000, p. A1.

37. L. Bogomolny, "Good Housekeeping," *Canadian Business*, March 1, 2004, pp. 87–88.

38. A. K. Reichert and M. S. Webb, "Corporate Support for Ethical and Environmental Policies: A Financial Management Perspective," *Journal of Business Ethics*, May 2000; G. R. Weaver, L. K. Trevino, and P. L. Cochran, "Corporate Ethics Programs as Control Systems: Influences of Executive Commitment and Environmental Factors," *Academy of Management Journal*, February 1999, pp. 41–57; G. R. Weaver, L. K. Trevino, and P. L. Cochran, "Integrated and Decoupled Corporate Social Performance: Management Commitments, External Pressures, and Corporate Ethics Practices," *Academy of Management Journal*, October 1999, pp. 539–552; and B. Z. Posner and W. H. Schmidt, "Values and the American Manager: An Update," *California Management Review*, Spring 1984, pp. 202–216.

39. L. Nash, "Ethics Without the Sermon," *Harvard Business Review*, November–December 1981, p. 81.

40. See, for example, R. A. Buccholz, *Essentials of Public Policy for Management*, 2nd ed. (Upper Saddle River, NJ: Prentice Hall, 1990).

41. M. Friedman, *Capitalism and Freedom* (Chicago: University of Chicago Press, 1962); and M. Friedman, "The Social Responsibility of Business Is to Increase Profits," *New York Times Magazine*, September 13, 1970, p. 33.

42. J. Bakan, *The Corporation* (Toronto: Big Picture Media Corporation, 2003).

43. Information from Avon's website, www.avoncompany.com/women/avoncrusade/ (accessed June 10, 2009).

44. E. P. Lima, "Seeding a World of Transformation," *IndustryWeek*, September 6, 1999, pp. 30–31.

45. E. White, "PR Firms Advise Corporations on Social Responsibility Issues," *Wall Street Journal*, November 13, 2002, p. B10.

46. The Triple Bottom Line was first introduced in J. Elkington, *Cannibals with Forks: The Triple Bottom Line of 21st Century Business* (Stony Creek, CT: New Society Publishers, 1998).

47. See, for example, A. B. Carroll, "The Pyramid of Corporate Social Responsibility: Toward the Moral Management of Organizational Stakeholders," *Business Horizons*, July–August 1991, pp. 39–48.

48. This section has been influenced by E. Gatewood and B. Carroll, "The Anatomy of Corporate Social Response," *Business Horizons*, September–October 1981, pp. 9–16.

49. See, for example, P. Cochran and R. A. Wood, "Corporate Social Responsibility and Financial Performance," *Academy of Management Journal*, March 1984, pp. 42–56; K. Aupperle, A. B. Carroll, and J. D. Hatfield, "An Empirical Examination of the Relationship Between Corporate Social Responsibility and Profitability," *Academy of Management Journal*, June 1985, pp. 446–463; J. B. McGuire, A. Sundgren, and T. Schneeweis, "Corporate Social Responsibility and Firm Financial Performance," *Academy of Management Journal*, December 1988, pp. 854–872; D. M. Georgoff and J. Ross, "Corporate Social Responsibility and Management Performance" (paper presented at the National Academy of Management Conference, Miami, Florida, August 1991); S. A. Zahra, B. M. Oviatt, and K. Minyard, "Effects of Corporate Ownership and Board Structure on Corporate Social Responsibility and Financial Performance" (paper presented at the National Academy of Management Conference, Atlanta, Georgia, August 1993); "Social Responsibility and the Bottom Line," *Business Ethics*, July–August 1994, p. 11; D. B. Turban and D. W. Greening, "Corporate Social Performance and Organizational Attractiveness to Prospective Employees," *Academy of Management Journal*, June 1996, pp. 658–672; S. A. Waddock and S. B. Graves, "The Corporate Social Performance–Financial Performance Link," *Strategic Management Journal*, April 1997, pp. 303–319; S. L. Berman, A. C. Wicks, S. Kotha, and T. M. Jones, "Does Stakeholder Orientation Matter? The Relationship Between Stakeholder Management Models and Firm Financial Performance," *Academy of Management Journal*, October 1999, pp. 488–506.

50. D. J. Wood and R. E. Jones, "Stakeholder Mismatching: A Theoretical Problem in Empirical Research on Corporate Social Performance," *International Journal of Organizational Analysis* 3, no. 3 (1995), pp. 229–267.

51. See A. A. Ullmann, "Data in Search of a Theory: A Critical Examination of the Relationships Among Social Performance, Social Disclosure, and Economic Performance of U.S. Firms," *Academy of Management Review*, July 1985, pp. 540–557; R. E. Wokutch and B. A. Spencer, "Corporate Saints and Sinners: The Effects of Philanthropic and Illegal Activity on Organizational Performance," *California Management Review*, Winter 1987, pp. 62–77; R. Wolfe and K. Aupperle, "Introduction to Corporate Social Performance: Methods for Evaluating an Elusive Construct," ed. J. E. Post, *Research in Corporate Social Performance and Policy* 13 (1991), pp. 265–268; and D. J. Wood and R. E. Jones, "Stakeholder Mismatching: A Theoretical Problem in Empirical Research on Corporate Social Performance," *International Journal of Organizational Analysis* 3 (1995), pp. 229–267.

52. D. Macfarlane, "Why Now?" *Report on Business Magazine*, March 2004, pp. 45–46.

53. Adapted from W. H. Agor, *AIM Survey* (El Paso, TX: ENP Enterprises, 1989), Part I. With permission.

54. Situation adapted from information in N. Weinberg, "Holier Than Whom?" *Forbes*, June 23, 2003, p. 711; and E. Baum, "Schwab

Campaign Bundles Controversy, Consistency," *Fund Marketing Alert*, March 10, 2003, p. 10.

55. Information from C. F. Martin's website, www.mguitar.com (accessed June 10, 2009); D. Lieberman, "Guitar Sales Jam Despite Music Woes," *USA Today*, December 16, 2002, p. 2B; and S. Fitch, "Stringing Them Along," *Forbes*, July 26, 1999, pp. 90–91.

56. Based on B. Breen, "No Accounting for Design," *Fast Company*, February 2007, pp. 38–39; and R. Siegel, "Meet the Whirlwind of Whirlpool," *BusinessWeek* online, www.businessweek.com, April 11, 2006.

57. J. V. Anderson, "Mind Mapping: A Tool for Creative Thinking," *Business Horizons*, January–February 1993, pp. 42–46; M. Loeb, "Ten Commandments for Managing Creative People," *Fortune*, January 16, 1995, pp. 135–136; M. Henricks, "Good Thinking," *Entrepreneur*, May 1996, pp. 70–73; H.-S.Choi and L. Thompson, "Old Wine in a New Bottle: Impact of Membership Change on Group Creativity," *Organizational Behavior and Human Decision Processes* 98, no. 2 (2005), pp. 121–132; R. Florida and J. Goodnight, "Managing for Creativity," *Harvard Business Review* 83, no. 7 (2005), pp. 124+; L. L. Gilson, J. E. Mathieu, C. E. Shalley, and T. M. Ruddy, "Creativity and Standardization: Complementary or Conflicting Drivers of Team Effectiveness?" *Academy of Management Journal* 48, no. 3 (2005), pp. 521–531; and K. G. Smith, C. J. Collins, and K. D. Clark, "Existing Knowledge, Knowledge Creation Capability, and the Rate of New Product Introduction in High-Technology Firms," *Academy of Management Journal* 48, no. 2 (2005), pp. 346–357.

58. Information for this box comes from B. C. McDonald and D. Hutcheson, "Dealing With Diversity Is Key to Tapping Talent," *Atlanta Business Chronicle*, December 18, 1998, p. 45A1; P. M. Elsass and L. M. Graves, "Demographic Diversity in Decision-Making Groups: The Experience of Women and People of Color," *Academy of Management Review*, October 1997, pp. 946–973; and N. J. Adler, ed., *International Dimensions of Organizational Behavior*, 4th ed. (Cincinnati, OH: South-Western College Publishing, 2001).

Part 2 Continuing Case: Starbucks

1. Based on "Coffee Penetration," *Springfield Business Journal*, June 12–18, 2006, p. 70; B. Horovitz, "Starbucks Nation," *USA Today*, May 29, 2006, pp. A1+; "Starbucks Details Strategy for Profitable Strategy," Reuters, March 18, 2009, www.reuters.com/article/pressRelease/idUS192069+18-Mar-2009+BW20090318 (accessed June 23, 2009); S. E. Lockyer, "Operators Aim to Build More Than Restaurants When Adding Locations," *Nation's Restaurant News*, May 22, 2006, pp. 72–74; N. Ramachandran, "Java and a Shot of Hip-Hop, *U.S. News & World Report*, May 22, 2006, pp. EE14–EE15; The Associated Press, "Starbucks Profit Climbs 27% in Quarter," *New York Times*, May 4, 2006, www.nytimes.com (accessed June 17, 2009); S. Bradbury, "Rethinking Every Rule of Reinvention," *Advertising Age*, May 1, 2006, pp. 14–16; S. Waxman, "A Small Step at Starbucks from Mocha to Movies," *New York Times*, May 1, 2006, www.nytimes.com (accessed June 17, 2009); Interview with Jim Donald, *Smart Money*, May 2006, pp. 31–32; P. R. LaMonica, "Coffee and Popcorn," *CNNMoney.com*, April 28, 2006, www.money.cnn.com/2006/04/21/news/companies/starbucks_movies/index.htm (accessed June 17, 2009); "Industry News," *National Petroleum News*, April 2006, p. 44; K. Macarthur, "Latte Reward: Cards Add Up at Starbucks," *Advertising Age*, March 20, 2006, p. S2; Starbucks Corporation, "Starbucks Unveils New Strategic Initiatives To Transform and Innovate the Customer Experience," March 19, 2008, www.starbucks.com/aboutus/pressdesc.asp?id=850 (accessed July 1, 2009); Starbucks Corporation, *Company Factsheet,* Company Fact Sheet, February 2008, www.starbucks.com/aboutus/company_factsheet.pdf (accessed July 1, 2009); B. G. Francella, "Coffee Clash," *Convenience Store News*, March 6, 2006, pp. 43–46;

D. Anderson, "Starbucks, Yahoo! Make a Match," *Brandweek*, February 20, 2006, p. 23; C. J. Farley, "A Tall Skinny Latte, a Nice, Comfy Chair and Now Kid Tunes," *Wall Street Journal*, February 14, 2006, pp. B1+; D. Anderson, "Starbucks Eyes Good Will from Times' Crosswords," *Brandweek*, February 13, 2006, p. 8; S. Thompson and K. MacArthur, "Starbucks, Kellogg Plot Cereal Killing," *Advertising Age*, February 6, 2006, pp. 1+; S. Gray and K. Kelly, "Starbucks Plans to Make Debut in Movie Business," *Wall Street Journal*, January 12, 2006, pp. A1+; "Hot Drink in the United States: Industry Profile," *DataMonitor*, December 2005; M. Moran, "Starbucks to Shutter Torrefazione Coffee Bars," *Gourmet Retailer*, August 2005, p. 10; interview with Jim Donald, *Fortune*, April 4, 2005, p. 30; A. Serwer and K. Bonamici, "Hot Starbucks to Go," *Fortune*, January 26, 2004, pp. 60–74; www.starbucks.com/aboutus/Company_Factsheet.pdf (accessed June 17, 2009); www.starbucks.com/aboutus/Company_Timeline.pdf (accessed June 17, 2009); www.starbucks.ca/en-ca/_About+Starbucks/Starbucks+in+Canada.htm; and www.secondcup.com/eng/about_us.php (accessed June 17, 2009); Starbucks Corporation, *Fiscal 2008 Annual Report*, p. 3, www.investor.starbucks.com/phoenix.zhtml?c=99518&p=irol-reportsAnnual (accessed July 1, 2009).

Chapter 5

1. Based on "Company Facts," *Air Canada Centre*, www.theaircanadacentre.com/corporate/CompanyFacts.asp (accessed June 10, 2009); "Richard Peddie, President and CEO, Maple Leaf Sports & Entertainment," *Raptors*, www.nba.com/raptors/news/richardpeddie_bio.html (accessed August 2, 2007); "Ownership," *MLSnet*, MLSnet.com, http://toronto.fc.mlsnet.com/t280/about/ownership/(accessed June 10, 2009); City of Toronto, "BMO Field Opens at Exhibition Place," news release, May 11, 2007, http://wx.toronto.ca/inter/it/newsrel.nsf/9da959222128b9e885256618006646d3/41b84cf6c5ef64fe852572db004bc010?OpenDocument (accessed June 10, 2009); "Maple Leaf Sports & Entertainment Unveils Toronto FC as 13th Major League Soccer Team," *CanadaSoccer.com*, May 11, 2006, www.canadasoccer.com/eng/media/viewArtical.asp?Press_ID=2445 (accessed June 10, 2009); and "Contact Us," *Ricoh Coliseum*, www.ricohcoliseum.com/contact/(accessed June 10, 2009).

2. See, for example, R. L. Daft, *Organization Theory and Design*, 6th ed. (St. Paul, MN: West Publishing, 1998).

3. S. Melamed, I. Ben-Avi, and M. S. Green, "Objective and Subjective Work Monotony: Effects on Job Satisfaction, Psychological Distress, and Absenteeism in Blue-Collar Workers," *Journal of Applied Psychology*, February 1995, pp. 29–42.

4. W. Hillier, "BC Forest Fires: A Time Of Need," *Canadian Underwriter*, January 2004, Vol. 71, Iss. 1, pp. 22–23.

5. For a discussion of authority, see W. A. Kahn and K. E. Kram, "Authority at Work: Internal Models and Their Organizational Consequences," *Academy of Management Review*, January 1994, pp. 17–50.

6. B. Arthur, "Peddie Gives New GM 'Autonomy' for Change," *National Post*, June 8, 2004, p. S2.

7. M. Grange, "So What, Exactly, Has Changed?" *Globe and Mail*, March 11, 2006, p. S1.

8. "Senators Fire GM John Muckler: Report," *CBCnews.ca*, June 17, 2007, www.cbc.ca/sports/hockey/story/2007/06/17/senators-fire-muckler.html (accessed June 10, 2009); and D. Cox, "Ripples from Ottawa Shuffle," *TheStar.com*, June 19, 2007, www.thestar.com/article/226850 (accessed June 18, 2009).

9. Tips for Managers based on R. L. Daft, *The Leadership Experience,* 3e. © 2005 South-Western, a part of Cengage Learning, Inc. Reproduced by permission, www.cengage.com/permissions.

10. R. Ashkenas, "Simplicity-Minded Management," *Harvard Business Review*, December 2007, pp. 101–109; and P. Glader, "It's Not Easy Being Lean," *Wall Street Journal*, June 19, 2006, pp. B1+.

11. R. C. Morais, "The Old Lady Is Burning Rubber," *Forbes*, November 26, 2007, pp. 146–150.

12. D. Van Fleet, "Span of Management Research and Issues," *Academy of Management Journal*, September 1983, pp. 546–552.

13. Based on L. Millan, "Who's Scoffing Now? The Lemaire Brothers Started Out Using Recycled Fibre in One Small Paper Mill in Rural Quebec," *Canadian Business*, March 27, 1998, pp. 74–77; "Profile," *Cascades*, www.cascades.com/profile (accessed June 18, 2009); and *Cascades 2008 Annual Report*, www.cascades.com/investors/financial-documents (accessed June 18, 2009).

14. See, for example, H. Mintzberg, *Power in and Around Organizations* (Upper Saddle River, NJ: Prentice Hall, 1983); and J. Child, *Organization: A Guide to Problems and Practices* (London: Kaiser & Row, 1984).

15. E. W. Morrison, "Doing the Job Well: An Investigation of Pro-Social Rule Breaking," *Journal of Management,* February 2006, pp. 5–28.

16. E. W. Morrison, "Doing the Job Well: An Investigation of Pro-Social Rule Breaking," *Journal of Management,* February 2006, pp. 5–28.

17. T. Burns and G. M. Stalker, *The Management of Innovation* (London: Tavistock, 1961); D. A. Morand, "The Role of Behavioral Formality and Informality in the Enactment of Bureaucratic Versus Organic Organizations," *Academy of Management Review*, October 1995, pp. 831–872.

18. K. Shimizu and M. A. Hitt, "Strategic Flexibility: Organizational Preparedness to Reverse Ineffective Decisions," *Academy of Management Executive*, November 2004, p. 44.

19. J. Dee, "All the News That's Fit to Print Out," *New York Times Magazine*, July 1, 2007, pp. 34–39; and www.wikipedia.com.

20. See, for example, R. E. Miles and C. C. Snow, *Organizational Strategy, Structure, and Process* (New York: McGraw-Hill, 1978); D. Miller, "The Structural and Environmental Correlates of Business Strategy," *Strategic Management Journal*, January–February 1987, pp. 55–76; H. L. Boschken, "Strategy and Structure: Reconceiving the Relationship," *Journal of Management*, March 1990, pp. 135–150; H. A. Simon, "Strategy and Organizational Evolution," *Strategic Management Journal*, January 1993, pp. 131–142; R. Parthasarthy and S. P. Sethi, "Relating Strategy and Structure to Flexible Automation: A Test of Fit and Performance Implications," *Strategic Management Journal* 14, no. 6 (1993), pp. 529–549; D. C. Galunic and K. M. Eisenhardt, "Renewing the Strategy-Structure-Performance Paradigm," in *Research in Organizational Behavior*, vol. 16, ed. B. M. Staw and L. L. Cummings (Greenwich, CT: JAI Press, 1994), pp. 215–255; and D. Jennings and S. Seaman, "High and Low Levels of Organizational Adaptation: An Empirical Analysis of Strategy, Structure, and Performance," *Strategic Management Journal*, July 1994, pp. 459–475.

21. See, for example, P. M. Blau and R. A. Schoenherr, *The Structure of Organizations* (New York: Basic Books, 1971); D. S. Pugh, "The Aston Program of Research: Retrospect and Prospect," in *Perspectives on Organization Design and Behavior*, ed. A. H. Van de Ven and W. F. Joyce, pp. 135–166 (New York: John Wiley, 1981); and R. Z. Gooding and J. A. Wagner III, "A Meta-Analytic Review of the Relationship between Size and Performance: The Productivity and Efficiency of Organizations and Their Subunits," *Administrative Science Quarterly*, December 1985, pp. 462–481.

22. J. Woodward, *Industrial Organization: Theory and Practice* (London: Oxford University Press, 1965).

23. See, for example, C. Perrow, "A Framework for the Comparative Analysis of Organizations," *American Sociological Review*, April 1967, pp. 194–208; J. D. Thompson, *Organizations in Action* (New York: McGraw-Hill, 1967); J. Hage and M. Aiken, "Routine Technology, Social Structure, and Organizational Goals," *Administrative Science Quarterly*, September 1969, pp. 366–377; and C. C. Miller, W. H. Glick, Y. D. Wang, and G. P. Huber, "Understanding Technology-Structure Relationships: Theory Development and Meta-Analytic Theory Testing," *Academy of Management Journal*, June 1991, pp. 370–399.

24. D. Gerwin, "Relationships Between Structure and Technology," in *Handbook of Organizational Design*, vol. 2, ed. P. C. Nystrom and W. H. Starbuck, pp. 3–38 (New York: Oxford University Press, 1981); and D. M. Rousseau and R. A. Cooke, "Technology and Structure: The Concrete, Abstract, and Activity Systems of Organizations," *Journal of Management*, Fall–Winter 1984, pp. 345–361.

25. F. E. Emery and E. Trist, "The Causal Texture of Organizational Environments," *Human Relations*, February 1965, pp. 21–32; P. Lawrence and J. W. Lorsch, *Organization and Environment: Managing Differentiation and Integration* (Boston: Harvard Business School, Division of Research, 1967); and M. Yasai-Ardekani, "Structural Adaptations to Environments," *Academy of Management Review*, January 1986, pp. 9–21.

26. L. A. Perlow, G. A. Okhuysen, and N. P. Repenning, "The Speed Trap: Exploring the Relationship Between Decision Making and Temporal Context," *Academy of Management Journal* 45, 2002, pp. 931–995.

27. Based on www.nba.com/raptors/news/mlsel_management.html; http://mapleleafs.nhl.com/team/app/?service=page&page= NHLPage&id=12778; http://mapleleafs.nhl.com/team/app/ ?service=page&page=NHLPage&id=12839; www.torontomarlies. com/news/News.asp?story_id=14; and www.torontomarlies.com/ news/news.asp?story_id=433 (all accessed June 10, 2009).

28. H. Mintzberg, *Structure in Fives: Designing Effective Organizations* (Upper Saddle River, NJ: Prentice Hall, 1983), p. 157.

29. R. J. Williams, J. J. Hoffman, and B. T. Lamont, "The Influence of Top Management Team Characteristics on M-Form Implementation Time," *Journal of Managerial Issues*, Winter 1995, pp. 466–480.

30. See, for example, R. E. Hoskisson, C. W. L. Hill, and H. Kim, "The Multidivisional Structure: Organizational Fossil or Source of Value?" *Journal of Management* 19, no. 2 (1993), pp. 269–298; I. I. Mitroff, R. O. Mason, and C. M. Pearson, "Radical Surgery: What Will Tomorrow's Organizations Look Like?" *Academy of Management Executive*, February 1994, pp. 11–21; T. Clancy, "Radical Surgery: A View from the Operating Theater," *Academy of Management Executive*, February 1994, pp. 73–78; M. Hammer, "Processed Change: Michael Hammer Sees Process as 'the Clark Kent of Business Ideas'—A Concept That Has the Power to Change a Company's Organizational Design," *Journal of Business Strategy*, November–December 2001, pp. 11–15; D. F. Twomey, "Leadership, Organizational Design, and Competitiveness for the 21st Century," *Global Competitiveness*, Annual 2002, pp. S31–S40; and G. J. Castrogiovanni, "Organization Task Environments: Have They Changed Fundamentally over Time?" *Journal of Management* 28, no. 2 (2002), pp. 129–150.

31. T. Starner, "Room for Improvement," *IQ Magazine*, March–April 2003, pp. 36–37.

32. Q. Hardy, "Google Thinks Small," *Forbes,* November 14, 2005, pp. 198–202.

33. See, for example, H. Rothman, "The Power of Empowerment," *Nation's Business*, June 1993, pp. 49–52; B. Dumaine, "Payoff from the New Management," *Fortune*, December 13, 1993, pp. 103–110; J. A. Byrne, "The Horizontal Corporation," *BusinessWeek*, December 20, 1993, pp. 76–81; J. R. Katzenbach and D. K. Smith, *The Wisdom of Teams* (Boston: Harvard Business School Press, 1993); L. Grant,

"New Jewel in the Crown," *U.S. News & World Report*, February 28, 1994, pp. 55–57; D. Ray and H. Bronstein, *Teaming Up: Making the Transition to a Self-Directed Team-Based Organization* (New York: McGraw Hill, 1995); and D. R. Denison, S. L. Hart, and J. A. Kahn, "From Chimneys to Cross-Functional Teams: Developing and Validating a Diagnostic Model," *Academy of Management Journal*, December 1996, pp. 1005–1023.

34. C. Fishman, "Whole Foods Is All Teams," *Fast Company*, Greatest Hits, vol. 1, 1997, pp. 102–113.

35. W. Hillier, "BC Forest Fires: A Time of Need," *Canadian Underwriter*, January 2004, pp. 22–23.

36. P. LaBarre, "This Organization Is Dis-Organization," *Fast Company*, www.fastcompany.com/magazine/03/oticon.html (accessed June 10, 2009).

37. See, for example, G. G. Dess et al., "The New Corporate Architecture," *Academy of Management Executive*, August 1995, pp. 7–20.

38. For additional readings on boundaryless organizations, see M. Hammer and S. Stanton, "How Process Enterprises Really Work," *Harvard Business Review*, November–December 1999, pp. 108–118; T. Zenger and W. Hesterly, "The Disaggregation of Corporations: Selective Intervention, High-Powered Incentives, and Modular Units," *Organization Science* 8 (1997), pp. 209–222; R. Ashkenas, D. Ulrich, T. Jick, and S. Kerr, *The Boundaryless Organization: Breaking the Chains* of Organizational Structure (San Francisco: Jossey-Bass, 1997); R. M. Hodgetts, "A Conversation With Steve Kerr," *Organizational Dynamics*, Spring 1996, pp. 68–79; and J. Gebhardt, "The Boundaryless Organization," *Sloan Management Review*, Winter 1996, pp. 117–119. For another view of boundaryless organizations, see B. Victor, "The Dark Side of the New Organizational Forms: An Editorial Essay," *Organization Science*, November 1994, pp. 479–482.

39. S. C. Certo and S. T. Certo, *Modern Management*, 10th edition, (Upper Saddle River, NJ: Prentice Hall, 2006), p. 316; P. M. J. Christie and R. R. Levary, "Virtual Corporations: Recipe for Success," *Industrial Management*, July/August 1998, pp. 7–11; and C. C. Snow, R. E. Miles, and H. J. Coleman Jr., "Managing 21st Century Network Organizations," *Organizational Dynamics*, Winter, 1992, pp. 5–20.

40. See, for example, W. H. Davidow and M. S. Malone, *The Virtual Corporation* (New York: HarperCollins, 1992); H. Chesbrough and D. Teece, "When Is Virtual Virtuous? Organizing for Innovation," *Harvard Business Review*, January–February 1996, pp. 65–73; G. G. Dess, A. Rasheed, K. J. McLaughlin, and R. L. Priem, "The New Corporate Architecture," *Academy of Management Executive*, August 1995, pp. 7–20; M. Sawhney and D. Parikh, "Break Your Boundaries," *Business 2.0*, May 2000, pp. 198–207; D. Pescovitz, "The Company Where Everybody's a Temp," *New York Times Magazine*, June 11, 2000, pp. 94–96; W. F. Cascio, "Managing a Virtual Workplace," *Academy of Management Executive*, August 2000, pp. 81–90; D. Lyons, "Smart and Smarter," *Forbes*, March 18, 2002, pp. 40–41; and B. Hedberg, G. Dahlgren, J. Hansson, and N. Goran Olve, *Virtual Organizations and Beyond: Discovering Imaginary Systems* (New York: John Wiley, 2001).

41. Based on G. Shaw, "Vancouver Law Firm Opens Virtual Branch Office," *Vancouver Sun*, September 26, 2007, p. F4.

42. R. E. Miles and C. C. Snow, "Causes of Failures in Network Organizations," *California Management Review* 34, no. 4 (1992), pp. 53–72; R. E. Miles and C. C. Snow, "The New Network Firm: A Spherical Structure Built on Human Investment Philosophy," *Organizational Dynamics*, Spring 1995, pp. 5–18; C. Jones, W. Hesterly, and S. Borgatti, "A General Theory of Network Governance: Exchange Conditions and Social Mechanisms," *Academy of Management Review*, October 1997, pp. 911–945; and R. E. Miles, C. C. Snow, J. A. Mathews, G. Miles, and H. J. Coleman, "Organizing in the Knowledge

Age: Anticipating the Cellular Form," *Academy of Management Executive*, November 1997, pp. 7–24.

43. S. Reed, A. Reinhardt, and A. Sains, "Saving Ericsson," *BusinessWeek*, November 11, 2002, pp. 64–68.

44. J. Barthelemy and D. Adsit, "The Seven Deadly Sins of Outsourcing," *Academy of Management Executive* 17, no. 2 (2003), pp. 87–100.

45. K. Restivo, "Most Canadian Tech Firms Prefer Not to Outsource, Study Shows," *Financial Post (National Post)*, June 11, 2004, p. FP5.

46. C. E. Connelly and D. G. Gallagher, "Emerging Trends in Contingent Work Research," *Journal of Management,* November 2004, pp. 959–983.

47. P. Olson, "Tesco's Landing," *Forbes*, June 4, 2007, pp. 116–118; and P. M. Senge, *The Fifth Discipline: The Art and Practice of Learning Organizations* (New York: Doubleday, 1990).

48. D. A. Garvin, A. C. Edmondson, and F. Gino, "Is Yours a Learning Organization?" *Harvard Business Review*, March 2008, pp. 109–116; A. N. K. Chen and T. M. Edgington, "Assessing Value in Organizational Knowledge Creation: Considerations for Knowledge Workers," *MIS Quarterly*, June 2005, pp. 279–309; K. G. Smith, C. J. Collins, and K. D. Clark, "Existing Knowledge, Knowledge Creation Capability, and the Rate of New Product Introduction in High-Technology Firms," *Academy of Management Journal*, April 2005, pp. 346–357; R. Cross, A. Parker, L. Prusak, and S. P. Borgati, "Supporting Knowledge Creation and Sharing in Social Networks," *Organizational Dynamics*, Fall 2001, pp. 100–120; M. Schulz, "The Uncertain Relevance of Newness: Organizational Learning and Knowledge Flows," *Academy of Management Journal*, August 2001, pp. 661–681; G. Szulanski, "Exploring Internal Stickiness: Impediments to the Transfer of Best Practice within the Firm," *Strategic Management Journal*, Winter Special Issue, 1996, pp. 27–43; and J. M. Liedtka, "Collaborating Across Lines of Business for Competitive Advantage," *Academy of Management Executive*, April 1996, pp. 20–37.

49. N. M. Adler, *International Dimensions of Organizational Behavior,* 4th ed. (Cincinnati, OH: South-Western College Publishing), 2002, p. 66.

50. P. B. Smith and M. F. Peterson, "Demographic Effects on the Use of Vertical Sources of Guidance by Managers in Widely Differing Cultural Contexts," *International Journal of Cross Cultural Management,* April 2005, pp. 5–26.

51. Based on J. F. Veiga and J. N. Yanouzas, *The Dynamics of Organization Theory: Gaining a Macro Perspective* (St. Paul, MN: West, 1979), pp. 158–160.

52. Situation adapted from information in "HR Pressured to Breach Ethics Policies, Says Survey," *HR Briefing*, June 1, 2003, p. 1; S. Pulliam, "A Staffer Ordered to Commit Fraud Balked, Then Caved," *Wall Street Journal*, June 23, 2003, pp. A1, A6; and J. Gilbert, "A Matter of Trust," *Sales & Marketing Management,* March 2003, pp. 30–31.

53. P. W. Tam, "System Reboot," *Wall Street Journal*, April 3, 2006, pp. A1+; A. Lashinsky, "Can HP Win Doing It the Hurd Way?" *Fortune*, April 3, 2006, p. 65; P. Burrows, "H-P Says Goodbye to Drama," *BusinessWeek*, September 12, 2005, pp. 83–86; A. Lashinsky, "Mark Hurd Takes His First Swing at H-P," *Fortune*, August 8, 2005, p. 24; P. Burrows and B. Elgin, "The Un-Carly Unveils His Game Plan," *BusinessWeek*, June 27, 2005, p. 36; and A. Lashinsky, "Take a Look at H-P," *Fortune*, June 13, 2005, pp. 117–120.

54. FAST COMPANY by A. Cohen. Copyright 2008 by Mansueto Ventures LLC. Reproduced with permission of Mansueto Ventures LLC in the format Textbook via Copyright Clearance Center.

55. Based on P. L. Hunsaker, *Training in Management Skills* (Upper Saddle River, NJ: Prentice Hall, 2001), pp. 135–136 and 430–432;

R. T. Noel, "What You Say to Your Employees When You Delegate," *Supervisory Management*, December 1993, p. 13; and S. Caudron, "Delegate for Results," *IndustryWeek*, February 6, 1995, pp. 27–30.

Chapter 6

1. Based on Hoover's Online; "Canada Embraces Facebook as Web Site Reports 'Explosive' Growth," *National Post*, June 14, 2007, p. A6; B. McCrea, "A New Kind of Hookup," *Black Enterprise*, July 2007, p. 52; J. N. Hoover, "Facebook, MySpace Become Work Tools For Some," *InformationWeek*, July 17, 2007, www.informationweek.com/internet/showArticle.jhtml?articleID=201001803 (accessed June 17, 2009).

2. T. Dixon, *Communication, Organization, and Performance* (Norwood, NJ: Ablex Publishing Corporation, 1996), p. 281; P. G. Clampitt, *Communicating for Managerial Effectiveness* (Newbury Park, CA: Sage Publications, 1991); L. E. Penley, E. R. Alexander, I. E. Jernigan, and C. I. Henwood, "Communication Abilities of Managers: The Relationship to Performance," *Journal of Management*, March 1991, pp. 57–76.

3. "Electronic Invective Backfires," *Workforce*, June 2001, p. 20; and E. Wong, "A Stinging Office Memo Boomerangs," *New York Times*, April 5, 2001, p. C11.

4. C. O. Kursh, "The Benefits of Poor Communication," *Psychoanalytic Review*, Summer–Fall 1971, pp. 189–208.

5. W. G. Scott and T. R. Mitchell, *Organization Theory: A Structural and Behavioral Analysis* (Homewood, IL: Richard D. Irwin, 1976).

6. Based on A. Shimo, "Why Is T.O. the Capital of Facebook?" *Toronto Star*, June 30, 2007, p. ID3; and "City of Toronto Disconnects Workers from Facebook," *CBCnews.ca*, May 10, 2007, www.cbc.ca/technology/story/2007/05/10/facebook-toronto-city.html (accessed June 17, 2009).

7. www.gm.tv/index.cfm?articleid=26462 (accessed June 17, 2009).

8. D. K. Berlo, *The Process of Communication* (New York: Holt, Rinehart & Winston, 1960), pp. 30–32.

9. T. R. Kurtzberg, C. E. Naquin, and L. Y. Belkin, "Electronic Performance Appraisals: The Effects of E-Mail Communication on Peer Ratings in Actual and Simulated Environments," *Organizational Behavior and Human Decision Processes* 98, no. 2 (2005), pp. 216–226.

10. J. Kruger, N. Epley, J. Parker, and Z.-W. Ng, "Egocentrism Over E-Mail: Can We Communicate as Well as We Think?" *Journal of Personality and Social Psychology* 89, no. 6 (2005), pp. 925–936.

11. Thanks to an anonymous reviewer for providing this elaboration.

12. P. G. Clampitt, *Communicating for Managerial Effectiveness* (Newbury Park, CA: Sage Publications, 1991).

13. A. Warfield, "Do You Speak Body Language?" *Training & Development*, April 2001, pp. 60–61; D. Zielinski, "Body Language Myths," *Presentations*, April 2001, pp. 36–42; and "Visual Cues Speak Loudly in Workplace," *Springfield News-Leader*, January 21, 2001, p. 8B.

14. C. Cavanagh, *Managing Your E-Mail: Thinking Outside the Inbox* (Hoboken, NJ: John Wiley & Sons, 2003).

15. K. Macklem, "You've Got Too Much Mail," *Maclean's*, January 30, 2006, pp. 20–21.

16. K. Macklem, "You've Got Too Much Mail," *Maclean's*, January 30, 2006, pp. 20–21.

17. D. K. Berlo, *The Process of Communication* (New York: Holt, Rinehart & Winston, 1960), p. 103.

18. Based on G. Robertson, "Goodbye, Buttonhole Makers. Hello, Tapas," *Globe and Mail*, May 22, 2007, p. B1.

19. A. Mehrabian, "Communication Without Words," *Psychology Today*, September 1968, pp. 53–55.

20. See, for example, S. P. Robbins and P. L. Hunsaker, *Training in Interpersonal Skills*, 3rd ed. (Upper Saddle River, NJ: Prentice Hall, 2003); M. Young and J. E. Post, "Managing to Communicate, Communicating to Manage: How Leading Companies Communicate with Employees," *Organizational Dynamics*, Summer 1993, pp. 31–43; J. A. DeVito, *The Interpersonal Communication Book*, 6th ed. (New York: HarperCollins, 1992); and A. G. Athos and J. J. Gabarro, *Interpersonal Behavior* (Upper Saddle River, NJ: Prentice Hall, 1978).

21. O. Thomas, "Best-Kept Secrets of the World's Best Companies: The Three Minute Huddle," *Business 2.0,* April 2006, p. 94.

22. Tips for Managers based on R. Kreitner and A. Kinicki, *Organizational Behavior*, 6th ed. (New York: McGraw-Hill/Irwin, 2004), p. 335. Reprinted by permission of McGraw-Hill Education.

23. V. Galt, "Top-Down Feedback," *Vancouver Sun*, February 15, 2003, pp. E1, E2.

24. Cited in "Heard It Through the Grapevine," *Forbes*, February 10, 1997, p. 22.

25. See, for example, A. Bruzzese, "What to Do About Toxic Gossip," *USA Today*, March 14, 2001, www.usatoday.com; N. B. Kurland and L. H. Pelled, "Passing the Word: Toward a Model of Gossip and Power in the Workplace," *Academy of Management Review*, April 2000, pp. 428–438; N. DiFonzo, P. Bordia, and R. L. Rosnow, "Reining in Rumors," *Organizational Dynamics*, Summer 1994, pp. 47–62; M. Noon and R. Delbridge, "News from Behind My Hand: Gossip in Organizations," *Organization Studies* 14, no. 1 (1993), pp. 23–26; and J. G. March and G. Sevon, "Gossip, Information and Decision Making," in *Decisions and Organizations*, ed. G. March (Oxford: Blackwell, 1988), pp. 429–442.

26. "Effective Communication: A Leading Indicator of Financial Performance—2005/2006 Communication ROI Study," 2006, Watson Wyatt Worldwide, Washington, DC.

27. B. McCrea, "A New Kind of Hookup," *Black Enterprise*, July 2007, p. 52.

28. G. Buckler, "Instant Messaging Replacing Pagers in the Enterprise," *Computing Canada*, March 26, 2004, p. 18.

29. J. Rohwer, "Today, Tokyo: Tomorrow, the World," *Fortune*, September 18, 2000, pp. 140–152; J. McCullam and L. Torres, "Instant Enterprising," *Forbes*, September 11, 2000, p. 28; J. Guyon, "The World Is Your Office," *Fortune*, June 12, 2000, pp. 227–234; S. Baker, N. Gross, and I. M. Kunii, "The Wireless Internet," *BusinessWeek*, May 29, 2000, pp. 136–144; R. Lieber, "Information Is Everything . . ." *Fast Company*, November 1999, pp. 246–254.

30. M. Vallis, "Nasty E-mail from the Boss May Mean More Sick Days," *National Post*, January 9, 2004, pp. A1, A9. Study was done by George Fieldman, a psychologist at Buckinghamshire Chilterns University College, and presented at the 2004 Annual Occupational Psychology Conference of the British Psychological Society.

31. Derived from P. Kuitenbrouwer, "Office E-Mail Runs Amok," *Financial Post*, October 18, 2001, p. FP11.

32. "AP-AOL Instant Messaging Trends Survey Reveals Popularity of Mobile Instant Messaging," www.businesswire.com/news/google/20071115005196/en (accessed June 28, 2009).

33. Information on *Second Life* based on A. Athavaley, "A Job Interview You Don't Have to Show Up For," *Wall Street Journal*, June 20, 2007, p. D1.

34. "Be Careful about Your E-Trail," *Prince George Citizen*, June 22, 2007, p. 36.

35. M. Blanchard, "Johnson Inc. Relies on IP Telephony," *Globe and Mail*, May 13, 2004.

36. K. Hafner, "For the Well Connected, All the World's an Office," *New York Times*, March 30, 2000, p. D11.

37. Adapted from Norton, R., "Foundation of a Communicator Style Construct," *Human Communication Research*, 4, 1978, pp. 99–112.

38. Situation adapted from information in T. Weidlich, "The Corporate Blog Is Catching On," *New York Times*, June 22, 2003, sec. 3, p. 12; "CNN Shuts Down Correspondent's Blog," *EuropeMedia*, March 24, 2003.

39. Based on E. Frauenheim, "Stop Reading This Headline and Get Back to Work," *C/Net*, July 13, 2005, www.news.com.com/Stop+reading+this+headline+and+get+back+to+work/2100-1022_3-5783552.html (accessed June 17, 2009); and R. Breeden, "More Employees Are Using the Web at Work," *Wall Street Journal*, May 10, 2005, p. B4.

40. Information on company from Hoover's Online, www.hoovers.com (accessed May 29, 2003); and S. Clifford, "How to Get the Geeks and the Suits to Play Nice," *Business 2.0*, May 2002, pp. 92–93.

41. E. Anderssen and M. Valpy, "Face the Nation: Canada Remade," *Globe and Mail*, June 7, 2003, pp. A10–A11.

42. G. Schellenberg, *Immigrants in Canada's Census Metropolitan Areas*, Catalogue no. 89-613-MIE—No. 003 (Ottawa: Statistics Canada, August 2004); and Statistics Canada, 2006 Census, www12.statcan.ca/census-recensement/2006/dp-pd/hlt/97-557/T403-eng.cfm?Lang=E&T=403&GH=8&GF=0&G5=0&SC=1&RPP=144&SR=1&S=0&O=A&D1=1(accessed June 26, 2009).

43. Statistics Canada, 2006 Census, www12.statcan.ca/census-recensement/2006/dp-pd/hlt/97-555/T401-eng.cfm?Lang=E&T=401&GH=8&GF=0&G5=0&SC=1&RPP=144&SR=1&S=0&O=A&D1=1 (accessed June 26, 2009).

44. Case based on D. D. Hatch, J. E. Hall, and M. T. Miklave, "New EEOC Guidance on National-Origin Discrimination," *Workforce*, April 2003, p. 76; and A. Piech, "Going Global: Speaking in Tongues," *Inc.*, June 2003, p. 50.

45. Based on C. R. Rogers and R. E. Farson, *Active Listening* (Chicago: Industrial Relations Center of the University of Chicago, 1976); and P. L. Hunsaker, *Training in Management Skills* (Upper Saddle River, NJ: Prentice Hall, 2001), pp. 61–62.

46. J. Langdon, "Differences Between Males and Females at Work," *USA Today*, February 5, 2001, www.usatoday.com; J. Manion, "He Said, She Said," *Materials Management in Health Care*, November 1998, pp. 52–62; G. Franzwa and C. Lockhart, "The Social Origins and Maintenance of Gender Communication Styles, Personality Types, and Grid-Group Theory," *Sociological Perspectives* 41, no. 1 (1998), pp. 185–208; D. Tannen, *Talking from 9 to 5: Women and Men in the Workplace* (New York: Avon Books, 1995).

Chapter 7

1. Based on Hoover's Online, www.hoovers.com; R. Waugh, "Getting More Leaders Is Hard Enough, but the Job Skills Needed Are Changing, Too," *Canadian HR Reporter*, January 26, 2004, p. 18; J. Kirby, "In the Vault," *Canadian Business*, March 1–14, 2004, pp. 68–72; S. Greengard, "Brett Ellison," *IQ Magazine*, November–December 2002, p. 52; www.scotiabank.com/cda/content/0,1608,CID821_LIDen,00.html; http://cgi.scotiabank.com/annrep2006/en/pdf/ScotiaAR06_ConsolidatedFinancialStatements.pdf; and www.scotiabank.com/cda/content/0,1608,CID11095_LIDen,00.html (all accessed June 19, 2009).

2. See, for example, Y. Y. Kor and H. Leblebici, "How Do Interdependencies Among Human-Capital Deployment, Development, and Diversification Strategies Affect Firms' Financial Performance?" *Strategic Management Journal,* October 2005, pp. 967–985; D. E. Bowen and C. Ostroff, "Understanding HRM–Firm Performance Linkages: The Role of the 'Strength' of the HRM System," *Academy of Management Review,* April 2004, pp. 203–221; R. Batt, "Managing Customer Services: Human Resource Practices, Quit Rates, and Sales Growth," *Academy of Management Journal,* June 2002, pp. 587–597; A. S. Tsui, J. L. Pearce, L. W. Porter, and A. M. Tripoli, "Alternative Approaches to the Employee–Organization Relationship: Does Investment in Employees Pay Off?" *Academy of Management Journal*, October 1997, pp. 1089–1121; M. A. Huselid, S. E. Jackson, and R. S. Schuler, "Technical and Strategic Human Resource Management Effectiveness As Determinants of Firm Performance," *Academy of Management Journal*, January 1997, pp. 171–188; J. T. Delaney and M. A. Huselid, "The Impact of Human Resource Management Practices on Perceptions of Organizational Performance," *Academy of* Management Journal, August 1996, pp. 949–969; B. Becker and B. Gerhart, "The Impact of Human Resource Management on Organizational Performance: Progress and Prospects," *Academy of Management Journal*, August 1996, pp. 779–801; M. J. Koch and R. G. McGrath, "Improving Labor Productivity: Human Resource Management Policies Do Matter," *Strategic Management Journal*, May 1996, pp. 335–354; and M. A. Huselid, "The Impact of Human Resource Management Practices on Turnover, Productivity, and Corporate Financial Performance," *Academy of Management Journal*, June 1995, pp. 635–672.

3. "Maximizing the Return on Your Human Capital Investment: The 2005 Watson Wyatt Human Capital Index® Report," "WorkAsia 2004/2005: A Study of Employee Attitudes in Asia," and "European Human Capital Index 2002," Watson Wyatt Worldwide (Washington, D.C.).

4. J. N. Baron and D.M. Kreps, "Consistent Human Resource Practices," *California Management Review* 41 no. 3, Spring 1999, pp. 29–53.

5. Statistics Canada, "Fact-sheet on Unionization in Canada," *The Daily*, August 28, 2003.

6. J. Visser, "Union Membership Statistics in 24 Countries," *Monthly Labor Review*, January 2006, pp. 38–49; and "Foreign Labor Trends—Mexico," *US Department of Labor*, 2002.

7. S. Premack and J. E. Hunter, "Individual Unionization Decisions," *Psychological Bulletin* 103, no. 2 (1988), pp. 223–234.

8. Based on M. King, "Union at Indigo," *Gazette* (Montreal), February 11, 2003, p. B3.

9. S. Armour, "Lawsuits Pin Target on Managers," *USA Today*, October 1, 2002, www.usatoday.com.

10. R. Waugh, "Getting More Leaders Is Hard Enough, But the Job Skills Needed Are Changing, Too," *Canadian HR Reporter*, January 26, 2004, p. 18.

11. E. Beauchesne, "Skills Training Rebounds: But Labour Shortage May Still Be Looming," *Telegram*, November 21, 2003, p. D1.

12. J. Sullivan, "Workforce Planning: Why to Start Now," *Workforce*, September 2002, pp. 46–50.

13. Based on A. Tomlinson, "The Many Benefits of Online Job Boards," *Canadian HR Reporter*, July 15, 2002, pp. 17–18. The Career webpage is at www.scotiabank.com/cda/content/0,1608,CID9031_LIDen,00.html (accessed June 19, 2009).

14. T. J. Bergmann and M. S. Taylor, "College Recruitment: What Attracts Students to Organizations?" *Personnel*, May–June 1984, pp. 34–46; and A. S. Bargerstock and G. Swanson, "Four Ways to Build Cooperative Recruitment Alliances," *HR Magazine*, March 1991, p. 49.

15. J. R. Gordon, *Human Resource Management: A Practical Approach* (Boston: Allyn & Bacon, 1986), p. 170.

16. F. Loyie, "Police in a Rush to Lure New Recruits," *Edmonton Journal*, April 24, 2004, p. B3.

17. S. Burton and D. Warner, "The Future of Hiring—Top 5 Sources for Recruitment Today," *Workforce Vendor Directory*, 2002, p. 75.

18. C. Eustace, "VPD: Virtual Police Department," *Vancouver Sun*, May 29, 3007, pp. A1–A2.

19. G. Shaw, "An Offer That's Hard to Refuse," *Vancouver Sun*, November 12, 2003, p. D5.

20. See, for example, J. P. Kirnan, J. E. Farley, and K. F. Geisinger, "The Relationship Between Recruiting Source, Applicant Quality, and Hire Performance: An Analysis by Sex, Ethnicity, and Age," *Personnel Psychology*, Summer 1989, pp. 293–308; and R. W. Griffeth, P. Hom, L. Fink, and D. Cohen, "Comparative Tests of Multivariate Models of Recruiting Sources Effects," *Journal of Management* 23, no. 1 (1997), pp. 19–36.

21. K. Harley, "Zero Churn," *Progress*, May 2001, pp. 30–33.

22. G. W. England, *Development and Use of Weighted Application Blanks*, rev. ed. (Minneapolis: Industrial Relations Center, University of Minnesota, 1971); J. J. Asher, "The Biographical Item: Can It Be Improved?" *Personnel Psychology*, Summer 1972, p. 266; G. Grimsley and H. F. Jarrett, "The Relation of Managerial Achievement to Test Measures Obtained in the Employment Situation: Methodology and Results," *Personnel Psychology*, Spring 1973, pp. 31–48; E. E. Ghiselli, "The Validity of Aptitude Tests in Personnel Selection," *Personnel Psychology*, Winter 1973, p. 475; I. T. Robertson and R. S. Kandola, "Work Sample Tests: Validity, Adverse Impact, and Applicant Reaction," *Journal of Occupational Psychology* 55, no. 3 (1982), pp. 171–183; A. K. Korman, "The Prediction of Managerial Performance: A Review," *Personnel Psychology*, Summer 1986, pp. 295–322; G. C. Thornton, *Assessment Centers in Human Resource Management* (Reading, MA: Addison-Wesley, 1992); C. Fernandez-Araoz, "Hiring Without Firing," *Harvard Business Review*, July–August, 1999, pp. 108–120; and A. M. Ryan and R. E. Ployhart, "Applicants' Perceptions of Selection Procedures and Decisions: A Critical Review and Agenda for the Future," *Journal of Management* 26, no. 3 (2000), pp. 565–606.

23. See, for example, R. D. Arvey and J. E. Campion, "The Employment Interview: A Summary and Review of Recent Research," *Personnel Psychology*, Summer 1982, pp. 281–322; and M. M. Harris, "Reconsidering the Employment Interview: A Review of Recent Literature and Suggestions for Future Research," *Personnel Psychology*, Winter 1989, pp. 691–726; J. H. Prager, "Nasty or Nice: 56-Question Quiz," *Wall Street Journal*, February 22, 2000, p. A4; and M. K. Zachary, "Labor Law for Supervisors," Supervision, March 2001, pp. 23–26.

24. See, for example, G. Nicholsen, "Screen and Glean: Good Screening and Background Checks Help Make the Right Match for Every Open Position," *Workforce*, October 2000, p. 70.

25. R. L. Dipboye, *Selection Interviews: Process Perspectives* (Cincinnati: South-Western College Publishing, 1992), p. 6.

26. See, for example, R. D. Arveny and J. E. Campion, "The Employment Interview: A Summary and Review of Recent Research," *Personnel Psychology*, Summer 1982, pp. 281–322; and M. M. Harris, "Reconsidering the Employment Interview: A Review of Recent Literature and Suggestions for Future Research," *Personnel Psychology*, Winter 1989, pp. 691–726.

27. Tips for Managers based on D. A. DeCenzo and S. P. Robbins, *Human Resource Management*, 7th ed. (New York: Wiley, 2002), p. 200.

28. J. Merritt, "Improv at the Interview," *BusinessWeek*, February 3, 2003, p. 63.

29. S. Caudron, "Who Are You Really Hiring?" *Workforce*, November 2002, pp. 28–32.

30. P. Johnson, "Fibbing Applicants Filtered Out," *Springfield News Leader*, August 4, 2002, p. 6E.

31. J. Middlemiss, "Bad Hires Can Be Costly," *The Province* (Vancouver), February 4, 2007, p. A46.

32. See, for example, S. L. Premack and J. P. Wanous, "A Meta-Analysis of Realistic Job Preview Experiments," *Journal of Applied Psychology*, November 1985, pp. 706–720; J. A. Breaugh and M. Starke, "Research on Employee Recruitment: So Many Studies, So Many Remaining Questions," *Journal of Management* 26, no. 3 (2000), pp. 405–434; B. M. Meglino, E. C. Ravlin, and A. S. DeNisi, "A Meta-Analytic Examination of Realistic Job Preview Effectiveness: A Test of Three Counterintuitive Propositions," *Human Resource Management Review* 10, no. 4 (2000), pp. 407–434; and Y. Ganzach, A. Pazy, Y. Ohayun, and E. Brainin, "Social Exchange and Organizational Commitment: Decision-Making Training for Job Choice as an Alternative to the Realistic Job Preview," *Personnel Psychology*, Autumn 2002, pp. 613–637.

33. A. Wahl, "People Power," *Canadian Business*, March 29–April 11, 2004, p. 58.

34. C. L. Cooper, "The Changing Psychological Contract at Work: Revisiting the Job Demands–Control Model," *Occupational and Environmental Medicine*, June 2002, p. 355; D. M. Rousseau and S. A. Tijoriwala, "Assessing Psychological Contracts: Issues, Alternatives and Measures," *Journal of Organizational Behavior* 19, S1 (1998), pp. 679–695; and S. L. Robinson, M. S. Kraatz, and D. M. Rousseau, "Changing Obligations and the Psychological Contract: A Longitudinal Study," *Academy of Management Journal*, February 1994, pp. 137–152.

35. "2006 Industry Report," *Training*, December 2006, www.trainingmag.com/managesmarter/images/pdfs/IndRep06.pdf (accessed June 19, 2009).

36. D. Sankey, "Canadian Companies Skimp on Training," *Canada.com*, June 27, 2007, www.canada.com/working/feeds/resources/atwork/story.html?id=30a5d031-8f8b-4f64-b607-2bcf11bead9d (accessed June 19, 2009); and "2006 Industry Report," *Training*, December 2006, www.trainingmag.com/managesmarter/images/pdfs/IndRep06.pdf (accessed June 19, 2009).

37. B. Hall, "The Top Training Priorities for 2003," *Training*, February 2003, p. 40; and T. Galvin, "2002 Industry Report," *Training*, October 2002, pp. 24–33.

38. H. Dolezalek, "2005 Industry Report," *Training,* December 2005, pp. 14–28.

39. B. Hall, "The Top Training Priorities for 2003," *Training*, February 2003, p. 40.

40. Based on K. Harding, "Once and Future Kings," *Globe and Mail*, April 9, 2003, pp. C1, C6.

41. V. Galt, "Training on Tap," *Globe and Mail*, November 20, 2002, pp. C1, C8.

42. U. Boser, "Gaming the System, One Click at a Time," *U.S. News & World Report*, October 28, 2002, p. 60.

43. L. Fowlie, "Online Training Takes the Slow Train: 'Next Big Thing' Fails to Live Up to Initial Hype," *Daily Townsman*, March 5, 2004, p. 11.

44. S. Purba, "When Reviews Deserve a Failing Grade," *Globe and Mail*, June 11, 2004, p. C1.

45. K. Clark, "Judgment Day," *U.S. News & World Report*, January 13, 2003, pp. 31–32; E. E. Lawler III, "The Folly of Forced Ranking," *Strategy & Business*, Third Quarter 2002, pp. 28–32; K. Cross, "The Weakest Links," *Business2.Com*, June 26, 2001, pp. 36–37; J. Greenwald, "Rank and Fire," *Time*, June 18, 2001, pp. 38–39; D. Jones, "More Firms Cut Workers Ranked at Bottom to Make Way for Talent," *USA Today*, May 30, 2001, p. B11; M. Boyle, "Performance Reviews: Perilous Curves Ahead," *Fortune*, May 28, 2001, pp. 187–188.

46. J. McGregor, "The Struggle to Measure Performance," *BusinessWeek,* January 9, 2006, pp. 26–28.

47. D. Jones, "Study: Thinning Herd from Bottom Helps," *USA Today,* March 14, 2005, p. 1B.

48. S. E. Cullen, P. K. Bergey, and L. Aiman-Smith, "Forced Distribution Rating Systems and the Improvement of Workforce Potential: A Baseline Simulation," *Personnel Psychology,* Spring 2005, pp. 1–32.

49. J. McGregor, "The Struggle to Measure Performance," *BusinessWeek,* January 9, 2006, pp. 26–28.

50. R. D. Bretz Jr., G. T. Milkovich, and W. Read, "The Current State of Performance Appraisal Research and Practice: Concerns, Directions, and Implications," *Journal of Management*, June 1992, p. 331.

51. M. Debrayen and S. Brutus, "Learning from Others' 360-Degree Experiences," *Canadian HR Reporter*, February 10, 2003, pp. 18–19.

52. M. Johne, "It's Good PR to Keep Employees Loyal," *Globe and Mail*, September 20, 2002, p. C1.

53. M. A. Peiperl, "Getting 360° Feedback Right," *Harvard Business Review*, January 2001, pp. 142–147.

54. This section based on R. I. Henderson, *Compensation Management in a Knowledge-Based World*, 9th ed. (Upper Saddle River, NJ: Prentice Hall, 2003).

55. L. R. Gomez-Mejia, "Structure and Process of Diversification, Compensation Strategy, and Firm Performance," *Strategic Management Journal* 13 no. 5 (1992), pp. 381–397; and E. Montemayor, "Congruence Between Pay Policy and Competitive Strategy in High-Performing Firms," *Journal of Management* 22, no. 6 (1996), pp. 889–908.

56. E. E. Lawler III, G. E. Ledford Jr., and L. Chang, "Who Uses Skill-Based Pay and Why," *Compensation & Benefits Review*, March–April 1993, p. 22; G. E. Ledford, "Paying for the Skills, Knowledge and Competencies of Knowledge Workers," *Compensation & Benefits Review*, July–August 1995, pp. 55–62; C. Lee, K. S. Law, and P. Bobko, "The Importance of Justice Perceptions on Pay Effectiveness: A Two-Year Study of a Skill-Based Pay Plan," *Journal of Management* 26, no. 6 (1999), pp. 851–873.

57. J. D. Shaw, N. Gupta, A. Mitra, and G. E. Ledford Jr., "Success and Survival of Skill-Based Pay Plans," *Journal of Management,* February 2005, pp. 28–49

58. M. Rowland, "It's What You Can Do That Counts," *New York Times*, June 6, 1993, p. F17.

59. Information from Hewitt Associates Studies, "Hewitt Study Shows Pay-for-Performance Plans Replacing Holiday Bonuses," December 6, 2005; "Salaries Continue to Rise in Asia Pacific," Hewitt Annual Study Reports, November 23, 2005; and "Hewitt Study Shows Base Pay Increases Flat for 2006 with Variable Pay Plans Picking Up the Slack," Hewitt Associates, LLC, www.hewitt.com, August 31, 2005.

60. D. E. Super and D. T. Hall, "Career Development: Exploration and Planning," in *Annual Review of Psychology*, vol. 29, ed. M. R. Rosenzweig and L. W. Porter (Palo Alto, CA: Annual Reviews, 1978), p. 334.

61. M. Cianni and D. Wnuck, "Individual Growth and Team Enhancement: Moving Toward a New Model of Career Development," *Academy of Management Executive*, February 1997, pp. 105–115.

62. D. E. Super, "A Life-Span Life Space Approach to Career Development," *Journal of Vocational Behavior*, Spring 1980, pp. 282–298. See also E. P. Cook, and M. Arthur, *Career Theory Handbook* (Upper Saddle River, NJ: Prentice Hall, 1991), pp. 99–131; and L. S. Richman, "The New Worker Elite," *Fortune*, August 22, 1994, pp. 56–66.

63. R. Henkoff, "Winning the New Career Game," *Fortune*, July 12, 1993, pp. 46–49; "10 Tips for Managing Your Career," *Personnel*, October 1995, p. 106; A. Fisher, "Six Ways to Supercharge Your Career," *Fortune*, January 13, 1997, pp. 46–48; A. K. Smith, "Charting Your Own Course," *U.S. News & World Report*, November 6, 2000, pp. 56–65; and D. D. Dubois, "The 7 Stages of One's Career," *Training & Development*, December 2000, pp. 45–50.

64. Based on C. Petten, "Progressive Aboriginal Relations Important to Scotiabank," *Windspeaker*, March 2002, p. B7.

65. L. Crawford, "Motivation, Not a Degree Key at Ikea," *Financial Post* (*National Post*), February 24, 2004, p. FP12.

66. A. Wahl, "Opening Doors," *Canadian Business*, March 29–April 11, 2004, p. 45.

67. J. Hickman, "50 Best Companies for Minorities," *Fortune*, June 28, 2004, http://money.cnn.com/magazines/fortune/fortune_archive/2004/06/28/374393/index.htm (accessed June 19, 2009); J. Kahn, "Diversity Trumps the Downturn," *Fortune*, July 9, 2001, pp. 114–116; www.dennys.com/en/cms/History/31.html (accessed June 19, 2009); and www.dennysdiversity.com/ (accessed June 19, 2009).

68. "Employers Underestimate Extent of Sexual Harassment, Report Says," *Vancouver Sun*, March 8, 2001, p. D6.

69. J. Monchuk, "Female Mounties Allege Sex Harassment Not Investigated to Protect RCMP," Canadian Press Newswire, September 26, 2003; and H. Polischuk, "RCMP Officer Accuses Superior of Harassment, *Leader-Post*, March 29, 2007.

70. www.ottawabusinessjournal.com/293617634517614.php (accessed June 19, 2009).

71. "Employers Underestimate Extent of Sexual Harassment, Report Says," *Vancouver Sun*, March 8, 2001, p. D6.

72. U.S. Equal Employment Opportunity Commission, *Sexual Harassment Charges: FY 1997–FY 2007*, www.eeoc.gov.

73. "U.S. Leads Way in Sex Harassment Laws, Study Says," *Evening Sun*, November 30, 1992, p. A11; and W. Hardman and J. Heidelberg, "When Sexual Harassment Is a Foreign Affair," *Personnel*, April 1996, pp. 91–97.

74. *Janzen v. Platy Enterprises Ltd.* (1989), 10 C.H.R.R. D/6205 (S.C.C.).

75. "Sexual Harassment," U.S. Equal Employment Opportunity Commission, www.eeoc.gov (accessed June 19, 2009).

76. A. Fisher, "After All This Time, Why Don't People Know What Sexual Harassment Means?" *Fortune*, January 12, 1998, p. 68; and A. R. Karr, "Companies Crack Down on the Increasing Sexual Harassment by E-Mail," *Wall Street Journal*, September 21, 1999, p. A1.

77. See T. S. Bland and S. S. Stalcup, "Managing Harassment," *Human Resource Management*, Spring 2001, pp. 51–61; K. A. Hess and D. R. M. Ehrens, "Sexual Harassment—Affirmative Defense to Employer Liability," *Benefits Quarterly*, Second Quarter 1999, p. 57; J. A. Segal, "The Catch-22s of Remedying Sexual Harassment Complaints," *HR Magazine*, October 1997, pp. 111–117; S. C. Bahls and J. E. Bahls, "Hands-Off Policy,"*Entrepreneur*, July 1997, pp. 74–76; J. A. Segal, "Where Are We Now?" *HR Magazine*, October 1996, pp. 69–73; B. McAfee and D. L. Deadrick, "Teach Employees to Just Say No," *HR Magazine*, February 1996, pp. 86–89; G. D. Block, "Avoiding Liability for Sexual Harassment," *HR Magazine*, April 1995, pp. 91–97; and J. A. Segal, "Stop Making Plaintiffs' Lawyers Rich," *HR Magazine*, April 1995, pp. 31–35.

78. C. Oglesby, "More Options for Moms Seeking Work–Family Balance," *CNN.com*, May 10, 2001.

79. J. Miller and M. Miller, "Get A Life!" *Fortune,* November 28, 2005, pp. 108–124.

80. M. Elias, "The Family-First Generation," *USA Today,* December 13, 2004, p. 5D.

81. F. Hansen, "Truths and Myths About Work/Life Balance," *Workforce*, December 2002, pp. 34–39.

82. J. H. Greenhaus and G. N. Powell, "When Work and Family Are Allies: A Theory of Work–Family Enrichment," *Academy of Management Review,* January 2006, pp. 72–92; L. Duxbury, C Higgins, and D. Coghill, "Voices of Canadians: Seeking Work–Life Balance," *HRSDC*, January 2003, www.hrsdc.gc.ca/eng/lp/spila/wlb/vcswlb/05table_of_contents.shtml (accessed June 19, 2009); and S. D. Friedman and J. H. Greenhaus, *Work and Family—Allies or Enemies?* (New York: Oxford University Press, 2000).

83. J. H. Greenhaus and G. N. Powell, "When Work and Family Are Allies: A Theory of Work–Family Enrichment," *Academy of Management Review,* January 2006, pp. 72–92.

84. L. B. Hammer, M. B. Neal, J. T. Newsom, K. J. Brockwood, and C. L. Colton, "A Longitudinal Study of the Effects of Dual-Earner Couples' Utilization of Family-Friendly Workplace Supports on Work and Family Outcomes," *Journal of Applied Psychology,* July 2005, pp. 799–810.

85. M. M. Arthur, "Share Price Reactions to Work–Family Initiatives: An Institutional Perspective," *Academy of Management Journal,* August 2003, pp. 497–505.

86. N. P. Rothbard, T. L. Dumas, and K. W. Phillips, "The Long Arm of the Organization: Work–Family Policies and Employee Preferences for Segmentation," paper presented at the 61st Annual Academy of Management meeting, Washington, D.C., August 2001.

87. "Latest Release from the Labour Force Survey," Statistics Canada, April 9, 2009, www.statcan.gc.ca/subjects-sujets/labour-travail/lfs-epa/lfs-epa-eng.htm (accessed May 5, 2009).

88. S. Alleyne, "Stiff Upper Lips," *Black Enterprise*, April 2002, p. 59; C. Hymowitz, "Getting a Lean Staff to Do 'Ghost Work' of Departed Colleagues," *Wall Street Journal*, October 22, 2002, p. B1; E. Krell, "Defusing Downsizing," *Business Finance*, December 2002, pp. 55–57.

89. P. P. Shah, "Network Destruction: The Structural Implications of Downsizing," *Academy of Management Journal*, February 2000, pp. 101–112.

90. See, for example, K. A. Mollica and B. Gray, "When Layoff Survivors Become Layoff Victims: Propensity to Litigate," *Human Resource Planning*, January 2001, pp. 22–32.

91. S. Koudsi, "You're Stuck," *Fortune*, December 10, 2001, pp. 271–274.

92. L. A. Mainiero and C. L. Tromley, *Developing Managerial Skills in Organizational Behavior* (Upper Saddle River, NJ: Prentice-Hall, 1994). Adapted by permission of Prentice-Hall, Inc.

93. Situation adapted from information in J. Russell, "Older Goodyear Workers Who Say Age Played into Evaluations Get Day in Court," *Akron Beacon Journal*, July 3, 2003; and K. Clark, "Judgment Day," *U.S. News & World Report*, January 13, 2003, pp. 31–32.

94. Information on company from Mitsubishi Motors North America website, www.mitsubishicars.com (accessed June 19, 2009); "Mitsubishi Plans Big Boost to U.S. Production," *IndustryWeek*, March 18, 2003, www.industryweek.com (accessed June 19, 2009); D. Kiley, "Workplace Woes Almost Eclipse Mitsubishi Plant," *USA Today*, October 21, 2002, p. B11; "EEOC Responds to Final Report of Mitsubishi Consent Decree Monitors," Equal Employment Opportunity Commission, http://eeoc.gov/press/5-23-01.html (accessed June 19, 2009); and S. Greengard, "Zero Tolerance: Making It Work," *Workforce*, May 1999, pp. 28–34.

95. Based on S. P. Robbins and D. A. DeCenzo, *Fundamentals of Management*, 4th ed. (Upper Saddle River, NJ: Prentice Hall, 2004), p. 194.

Part 3 Continuing Case: Starbucks

1. A. Serwer and K. Bonamici, "Hot Starbucks to Go," *Fortune*, January 26, 2004, pp. 60–74; J. Cummings, "Legislative Grind," *Wall Street Journal*, April 12, 2005, pp. A1+; interview with Jim Donald, *Smart Money*, May 2006, pp. 31–32; A. Serwer "Interview with Howard Schultz," *Fortune* (Europe), March 20, 2006, pp. 35–36; A. Lustgarten, "A Hot, Steaming Cup of Customer Awareness," *Fortune*, November 15, 2004, p. 192; W. Meyers, "Conscience in a Cup of Coffee," *U.S. News & World Report*, October 31, 2005, pp. 48–50; S. Gray, "Fill 'er Up—with Latte," *Wall Street Journal*, January 6, 2006, pp. A9+; S. Holmes, "A Bitter Aroma at Starbucks," *BusinessWeek*, June 6, 2005, p. 13; K. Maher and J. Adamy, "Do Hot Coffee and 'Wobblies' Go Together?" *Wall Street Journal*, March 21, 2006, pp. B1+; P. Sellers, "Starbucks: The Next Generation," *Fortune*, April 4, 2005, p. 20; J. M. Cohn, R. Khurana, and L. Reeves, "Growing Talent as if Your Business Depended on," *Harvard Business Review*, October 2005, pp. 62–70; B. Nussbaum, R. Berner, and D. Brady, "Get Creative," *BusinessWeek*, August 1, 2005, pp. 60–68; "Training Top 100," *Training*, March 2006, pp. 40–59 and p. 72; P. Kafka, "Bean Counter," *Forbes*, February 28, 2005, pp. 78–80; and *Beyond the Cup: Corporate Social* Responsibility, Fiscal 2005 Annual Report, Starbucks Corporation.

Chapter 8

1. Based on "Magnotta: Breaking New Ground with Innovative Marketing Strategies," *Industry Canada*, www.ic.gc.ca/eic/site/mfbs-gprea.nsf/eng/lu00057.html (accessed June 23, 2009); S. Fife, "Break the Competitive Roadblock: Three Canadian Success Stories," *Canadian Business*, May 18, 2007, www.canadianbusiness.com; G. Stimmell, "Wine's Scrappy Duo," *Toronto Star*, January 24, 2007, p. D4; "Canada's Most Award-Winning Magnotta Winery," December 8, 2008, http://thewineladies.com; and "Magnotta Winery Corporation Announces January 31, 2009 Annual Results," *Marketwire*, April 30, 2009, www.marketwire.com.

2. R. N. Kanungo, "Leadership in Organizations: Looking Ahead to the 21st Century," *Canadian Psychology* 39, nos. 1–2 (1998), p. 77. For more evidence of this consensus, see N. Adler, *International Dimensions of Organizational Behavior*, 3rd ed. (Cincinnati, OH: South-Western College Publishing, 1997); R. J. House, "Leadership in the Twenty-First Century," in *The Changing Nature of Work*, ed. A. Howard (San Francisco: Jossey-Bass, 1995), pp. 411–450; R. N. Kanungo and M. Mendonca, *Ethical Dimensions of Leadership* (Thousand Oaks, CA: Sage Publications, 1996); and A. Zaleznik, "The Leadership Gap," *Academy of Management Executive* 4, no. 1 (1990), pp. 7–22.

3. Based on "Magnotta: Breaking New Ground with Innovative Marketing Strategies," *Industry Canada*, http://strategis.ic.gc.ca/epic/site/mfbs-gprea.nsf/en/lu00057e.html (accessed June 23, 2009); S. Fife, "Break the Competitive Roadblock: Three Canadian Success Stories," *Canadian Business*, May 18, 2007, www.canadianbusiness.com/innovation/article.jsp?content=20070518_094759_4716; and G. Stimmell, "Wine's Scrappy Duo," *Toronto Star*, January 24, 2007, p. D4.

4. See S. A. Kirkpatrick and E. A. Locke, "Leadership: Do Traits Matter?" *Academy of Management Executive*, May 1991, pp. 48–60; and T. A. Judge, J. E. Bono, R. Ilies, and M. Werner, "Personality and Leadership: A Qualitative and Quantitative Review," *Journal of Applied Psychology*, August 2002, pp. 765–780.

5. See T. A. Judge, J. E. Bono, R. Ilies, and M. Werner, "Personality and Leadership: A Review" (paper presented at the 15th Annual Conference of the Society for Industrial and Organizational Psychology, New Orleans, 2000); T. A. Judge, J. E. Bono, R. Ilies, and M. W. Gerhardt, "Personality and Leadership: A Qualitative and Quantitative Review," *Journal of Applied Psychology*, August 2002, pp. 765–780; and D. A. Hofmann and L. M. Jones, "Leadership, Collective Personality, and Performance," *Journal of Applied Psychology* 90, no. 3 (2005), pp. 509–522.

6. K. Lewin and R. Lippitt, "An Experimental Approach to the Study of Autocracy and Democracy: A Preliminary Note," *Sociometry* 1 (1938), pp. 292–300; K. Lewin, "Field Theory and Experiment in Social Psychology: Concepts and Methods," *American Journal of Sociology* 44 (1939), pp. 868–896; K. Lewin, R. Lippitt, and R. K. White, "Patterns of Aggressive Behavior in Experimentally Created Social Climates," *Journal of Social Psychology* 10 (1939), pp. 271–301; R. Lippitt, "An Experimental Study of the Effect of Democratic and Authoritarian Group Atmospheres," *University of Iowa Studies in Child Welfare* 16 (1940), pp. 43–95.

7. B. M. Bass, *Stogdill's Handbook of Leadership* (New York: Free Press, 1981), pp. 289–299.

8. R. M. Stogdill and A. E. Coons, eds., *Leader Behavior: Its Description and Measurement*, Research Monograph No. 88 (Columbus: Ohio State University, Bureau of Business Research, 1951). For an updated literature review of Ohio State research, see S. Kerr, C. A. Schriesheim, C. I. Murphy, and R. M. Stogdill, "Toward a Contingency Theory of Leadership Based upon the Consideration and Initiating Structure Literature," *Organizational Behavior and Human Performance*, August 1974, pp. 62–82; and B. M. Fisher, "Consideration and Initiating Structure and Their Relationships with Leader Effectiveness: A Meta-Analysis," in *Proceedings of the 48th Annual Academy of Management Conference*, ed. F. Hoy (Anaheim, California, 1988), pp. 201–205.

9. R. Kahn and D. Katz, "Leadership Practices in Relation to Productivity and Morale," in *Group Dynamics: Research and Theory*, 2nd ed., ed. D. Cartwright and A. Zander (Elmsford, NY: Row, Paterson, 1960).

10. R. R. Blake and J. S. Mouton, *The Managerial Grid III* (Houston, TX: Gulf Publishing, 1984).

11. L. L. Larson, J. G. Hunt, and R. N. Osborn, "The Great Hi-Hi Leader Behavior Myth: A Lesson from Occam's Razor," *Academy of Management Journal*, December 1976, pp. 628–641; and P. C. Nystrom, "Managers and the Hi-Hi Leader Myth," *Academy of Management Journal*, June 1978, pp. 325–331.

12. T. A. Judge, R. F. Piccolo, and R. Ilies, "The Forgotten Ones? The Validity of Consideration and Initiating Structure in Leadership Research," *Journal of Applied Psychology* 89, no. 1 (February 2004), pp. 36–51; and R. T. Keller, "Transformational Leadership, Initiating Structure, and Substitutes for Leadership: A Longitudinal Study of Research and Development Project Team Performance," *Journal of Applied Psychology* 91, no. 1 (2006), pp. 202–210.

13. R. McQueen, "The Long Shadow of Tom Stephens: He Branded MacBlo's Crew as Losers, Then Made Them into Winners," *Financial Post* (*National Post*), June 22, 1999, pp. C1, C5.

14. A. J. Mayo and N. Nohria, "Zeitgeist Leadership," *Harvard Business Review* 83, no. 10 (2005), pp. 45–60.

15. H. Wang, K. S. Law, R. D. Hackett, D. Wang, and Z. X. Chen, "Leader–Member Exchange as a Mediator of the Relationship Between Transformational Leadership and Followers' Performance and Organizational Citizenship Behavior," *Academy of Management Journal* 48, no. 3 (June 2005), pp. 420–432.

16. F. E. Fiedler, *A Theory of Leadership Effectiveness* (New York: McGraw-Hill, 1967).

17. G. Johns and A. M. Saks, *Organizational Behaviour*, 5th ed. (Toronto: Pearson Education Canada, 2001), pp. 278–279.

18. L. H. Peters, D. D. Hartke, and J. T. Pholmann, "Fiedler's Contingency Theory of Leadership: An Application of the Meta-Analysis Procedures of Schmidt and Hunter," *Psychological Bulletin*, March 1985, pp. 274–285; C. A. Schriesheim, B. J. Tepper, and L. A. Tetrault, "Lease Preferred Co-Worker Score, Situational Control, and Leadership Effectiveness: A Meta-Analysis of Contingency Model Performance Predictions," *Journal of Applied Psychology*, August 1994, pp. 561–573; and R. Ayman, M. M. Chemers, and F. Fiedler, "The Contingency Model of Leadership Effectiveness: Its Levels of Analysis," *Leadership Quarterly*, Summer 1995, pp. 147–167.

19. See E. H. Schein, *Organizational Psychology*, 3rd ed. (Upper Saddle River, NJ: Prentice Hall, 1980), pp. 116–117; and B. Kabanoff, "A Critique of Leader Match and Its Implications for Leadership Research," *Personnel Psychology*, Winter 1981, pp. 749–764.

20. P. Hersey and K. Blanchard, "So You Want to Know Your Leadership Style?" *Training & Development*, February 1974, pp. 1–15; P. Hersey and K. Blanchard, *Management of Organizational Behavior: Leading Human Resources*, 8th ed. (Englewood Cliffs, NJ: Prentice Hall, 2001).

21. See, for example, C. F. Fernandez and R. P. Vecchio, "Situational Leadership Theory Revisited: A Test of an Across-Jobs Perspective," *Leadership Quarterly* 8, no. 1 (1997), pp. 67–84; and C. L. Graeff, "Evolution of Situational Leadership Theory: A Critical Review," *Leadership Quarterly* 8, no. 2 (1997), pp. 153–170.

22. V. H. Vroom and P. W. Yetton, *Leadership and Decision-Making* (Pittsburgh, PA: University of Pittsburgh Press, 1973).

23. V. H. Vroom and A. G. Jago, *The New Leadership: Managing Participation in Organizations* (Upper Saddle River, NJ: Prentice Hall, 1988). See especially Chapter 8.

24. Based on V. H. Vroom, "Leadership and the Decision-Making Process," *Organizational Dynamics* 28, no. 4 (2000), p. 84.

25. V. H. Vroom, "Leadership and the Decision-Making Process," *Organizational Dynamics* 28, no. 4 (2000), pp. 82–94.

26. R. J. House, "A Path-Goal Theory of Leader Effectiveness," *Administrative Science Quarterly*, September 1971, pp. 321–338; R. J. House and T. R. Mitchell, "Path-Goal Theory of Leadership," *Journal of Contemporary Business*, Autumn 1974, p. 86; R. J. House, "Path-Goal Theory of Leadership: Lessons, Legacy, and a Reformulated Theory," *Leadership Quarterly*, Fall 1996, pp. 323–352.

27. J. C. Wofford and L. Z. Liska, "Path-Goal Theories of Leadership: A Meta-Analysis," *Journal of Management*, Winter 1993, pp. 857–876; M. G. Evans, "R. J. House's 'A Path-Goal Theory of Leader Effectiveness,'" *Leadership Quarterly*, Fall 1996, pp. 305–309; C. A. Schriesheim and L. L. Neider, "Path-Goal Leadership Theory: The Long and Winding Road," *Leadership Quarterly*, Fall 1996, pp. 317–321; A. Somech, "The Effects of Leadership Style and Team Process on Performance and Innovation in Functionally Heterogeneous Teams," *Journal of Management* 32, no. 1 (2006), pp. 132–157; and S. Yun, S. Faraj, and H. P. Sims, "Contingent Leadership and Effectiveness of Trauma Resuscitation Teams," *Journal of Applied Psychology* 90, no. 6 (2005), pp. 1288–1296.

28. Based on "Magnotta: Breaking New Ground with Innovative Marketing Strategies," *Industry Canada*, http://strategis.ic.gc.ca/epic/site/mfbs-gprea.nsf/en/lu00057e.html (accessed June 23, 2009); S. Fife, "Break the Competitive Roadblock: Three Canadian Success Stories," *Canadian Business*, May 18, 2007, www.canadianbusiness.com; and G. Stimmell, "Wine's Scrappy Duo," *Toronto Star*, Jan 24, 2007, p. D4.

29. B. M. Bass and R. E. Riggio, *Transformational Leadership,* 2nd ed. (Mahwah, NJ: Lawrence Erlbaum Associates, Inc., 2006), p. 3.

30. F. Vogelstein, "Mighty Amazon," *Fortune*, May 26, 2003, pp. 60–74.

31. J. A. Conger and R. N. Kanungo, "Behavioral Dimensions of Charismatic Leadership," in *Charismatic Leadership*, ed. J. A. Conger and R. N. Kanungo (San Francisco: Jossey-Bass, 1988), pp. 78–97; G. Yukl and J. M. Howell, "Organizational and Contextual Influences on the Emergence and Effectiveness of Charismatic Leadership," *Leadership Quarterly*, Summer 1999, pp. 257–283; and J. M. Crant and T. S. Bateman, "Charismatic Leadership Viewed from Above: The Impact of Proactive Personality," *Journal of Organizational Behavior*, February 2000, pp. 63–75.

32. J. A. Conger and R. N. Kanungo, *Charismatic Leadership in Organizations* (Thousand Oaks, CA: Sage, 1998).

33. K. S. Groves, "Linking Leader Skills, Follower Attitudes, and Contextual Variables via an Integrated Model of Charismatic Leadership," *Journal of Management,* April 2005, pp. 255–277; J. J. Sosik, "The Role of Personal Values in the Charismatic Leadership of Corporate Managers: A Model and Preliminary Field Study," *Leadership Quarterly,* April 2005, pp. 221–244; A. H. B. deHoogh, D. N. den Hartog, P. L. Koopman, H. Thierry, P. T. van den Berg, J. G. van der Weide, and C. P. M. Wilderom, "Leader Motives, Charismatic Leadership, and Subordinates' Work Attitudes in the Profit and Voluntary Sector," *Leadership Quarterly,* February 2005, pp. 17–38; J. M. Howell and B. Shamir, "The Role of Followers in the Charismatic Leadership Process: Relationships and Their Consequences," *Academy of Management Review,* January 2005, pp. 96–112; J. Paul, D. L. Costley, J. P. Howell, P. W. Dorfman, and D. Trafimow, "The Effects of Charismatic Leadership on Followers' Self-Concept Accessibility," *Journal of Applied Social Psychology,* September 2001, pp. 1821–1844; J. A. Conger, R. N. Kanungo, and S. T. Menon, "Charismatic Leadership and Follower Effects," *Journal of Organizational Behavior,* vol. 21, 2000, pp. 747–767; R. W. Rowden, "The Relationship between Charismatic Leadership Behaviors and Organizational Commitment," *Leadership & Organization Development Journal*, January 2000, pp. 30–35; G. P. Shea and C. M. Howell, "Charismatic Leadership and Task Feedback: A Laboratory Study of Their Effects on Self-Efficacy," *Leadership Quarterly*, Fall 1999, pp. 375–396; S. A. Kirkpatrick and E. A. Locke, "Direct and Indirect Effects of Three Core Charismatic Leadership Components on Performance and Attitudes," *Journal of Applied Psychology*, February 1996, pp. 36–51; D. A. Waldman, B. M. Bass, and F. J. Yammarino, "Adding to Contingent-Reward Behavior: The Augmenting Effect of Charismatic Leadership," *Group & Organization Studies*, December 1990, pp. 381–394; and R. J. House, J. Woycke, and E. M. Fodor, "Charismatic and Noncharismatic Leaders: Differences in Behavior and Effectiveness," in *Charismatic Leadership*, ed. J. A. Conger and R. N. Kanungo (San Francisco: Jossey-Bass, 1988), pp. 103–104.

34. T. Dvir, D. Eden, B. J. Avolio, and B. Shamir, "Impact of Transformational Leadership on Follower Development and Performance: A Field Experiment," *Academy of Management Journal* 45, no. 4 (2002), pp. 735–744; R. J. House, J. Woycke, and E. M. Fodor, "Charismatic and Noncharismatic Leaders: Differences in Behavior and Effectiveness," in *Charismatic Leadership in Organizations*, ed. J. A. Conger and R. N. Kanungo (Thousand Oaks, CA: Sage, 1998), pp. 103–104; D. A. Waldman, B. M. Bass, and F. J. Yammarino, "Adding to Contingent-Reward Behavior: The Augmenting Effect of Charismatic Leadership," *Group & Organization Studies*, December 1990, pp. 381–394; S. A. Kirkpatrick and E. A. Locke, "Direct and Indirect Effects of Three Core Charismatic Leadership Components on Performance and Attitudes," *Journal of Applied Psychology*, February 1996, pp. 36–51; and J. A. Conger, R. N. Kanungo, and S. T. Menon, "Charismatic Leadership and Follower Outcome Effects" (paper presented at the 58th Annual Academy of Management Meetings, San Diego, CA, August 1998).

35. J. M. Howell and P. J. Frost, "A Laboratory Study of Charismatic Leadership," *Organizational Behavior & Human Decision Processes* 43, no. 2 (April 1989), pp. 243–269.

36. "Building a Better Boss," *Maclean's*, September 30, 1996, p. 41.

37. "Building a Better Boss," *Maclean's*, September 30, 1996, p. 41.

38. B. R. Agle, N. J. Nagarajan, J. A. Sonnenfeld, and D. Srinivasan, "Does CEO Charisma Matter? An Empirical Analysis of the Relationships Among Organizational Performance, Environmental Uncertainty, and Top Management Team Perceptions of CEO Charisma," *Academy of Management Journal*, February 2006, pp. 161–174.

39. A. Elsner, "The Era of CEO as Superhero Ends Amid Corporate Scandals," *Globe and Mail*, July 10, 2002, www.globeandmail.com.

40. J. A. Conger and R. N. Kanungo, "Training Charismatic Leadership: A Risky and Critical Task," in *Charismatic Leadership*, ed. J. A. Conger and R. N. Kanungo (San Francisco: Jossey-Bass, 1988), pp. 309–323; S. Caudron, "Growing Charisma," *IndustryWeek*, May 4, 1998, pp. 54–55; R. Birchfield, "Creating Charismatic Leaders," *Management*, June 2000, pp. 30–31.

41. R. J. House, "A 1976 Theory of Charismatic Leadership" in *Leadership: The Cutting Edge*, ed. J. G. Hunt and L. L. Larson (Carbondale, IL: Southern Illinois University Press, 1977); R. J. House and R. N. Aditya, "The Social Scientific Study of Leadership: Quo Vadis?" *Journal of Management* 23, no. 3 (1997), pp. 316–323; J. G. Hunt, K. B. Boal, and G. E. Dodge, "The Effects of Visionary and Crisis-Responsive Charisma on Followers: An Experimental Examination," *Leadership Quarterly*, Fall 1999, pp. 423–448.

42. This definition is based on M. Sashkin, "The Visionary Leader," in *Charismatic Leadership*, ed. J. A. Conger and R. N. Kanungo, pp. 124–125 (San Francisco: Jossey-Bass, 1988); B. Nanus, *Visionary Leadership* (New York: Free Press, 1992), p. 8; N. H. Snyder and M. Graves, "Leadership and Vision," *Business Horizons*, January–February 1994, p. 1; and J. R. Lucas, "Anatomy of a Vision Statement," *Management Review*, February 1998, pp. 22–26.

43. B. Nanus, *Visionary Leadership* (New York: Free Press, 1992), p. 8.

44. Based on M. Sashkin, "The Visionary Leader," in *Charismatic Leadership*, ed. J. A. Conger and R. N. Kanungo (San Francisco: Jossey-Bass, 1988), pp. 128–130; and J. R. Baum, E. A. Locke, and S. A. Kirkpatrick, "A Longitudinal Study of the Relation of Vision and Vision Communication to Venture Growth in Entrepreneurial Firms," *Journal of Applied Psychology*, February 1998, pp. 43–54.

45. See www.cbc.ca/canada/story/2006/12/17/time-harper.html (accessed July 2, 2009).

46. J. M. Howell and B. Shamir, "The Role of Followers in the Charismatic Leadership Process: Relationships and Their Consequences," *Academy of Management Review* 30, no. 1 (2005), pp. 96–112.

47. B. M. Bass, "Theory of Transformational Leadership Redux," *Leadership Quarterly* 6, no. 4 (Winter 1995), pp. 463–478.

48. B. J. Avolio and B. M. Bass, "Transformational Leadership, Charisma, and Beyond" (working paper, School of Management, State University of New York, Binghamton, 1985), p. 14.

49. Tips for Managers based on B. J. Avolio, D. A. Waldman, and F. J. Yammarino, "Leading in the 1990s: The Four I's of Transformational Leadership," *Journal of European Industrial Training* 15, no. 4 (1991), pp. 9–16. Copyright Emerald Group Publishing Limited. All rights reserved.

50. R. S. Rubin, D. C. Munz, and W. H. Bommer, "Leading from Within: The Effects of Emotion Recognition and Personality on Transformational Leadership Behavior," *Academy of Management Journal*, October 2005, pp. 845–858; T. A. Judge and J. E. Bono, "Five-Factor Model of Personality and Transformational Leadership," *Journal of Applied Psychology*, October 2000, pp. 751–765; B. M. Bass and B. J. Avolio, "Developing Transformational Leadership: 1992 and Beyond," *Journal of European Industrial Training*, January 1990, p. 23; and J. J. Hater and B. M. Bass, "Supervisors' Evaluation and Subordinates' Perceptions of Transformational and Transactional Leadership," *Journal of Applied Psychology*, November 1988, pp. 695–702.

51. R. F. Piccolo and J. A. Colquitt, "Transformational Leadership and Job Behaviors: The Mediating Role of Core Job Characteristics," *Academy of Management Journal*, April 2006, pp. 327–340; O. Epitropaki and R. Martin, "From Ideal to Real: A Longitudinal Study of the Role of Implicit Leadership Theories on Leader-Member Exchanges and Employee Outcomes," *Journal of Applied Psychology*, July 2005, pp. 659–676; J. E. Bono and T. A. Judge, "Self-Concordance at Work: Toward Understanding the Motivational Effects of Transformational Leaders," *Academy of Management Journal*, October 2003, pp. 554–571; T. Dvir, D. Eden, B. J. Avolio, and B. Shamir, "Impact of Transformational Leadership on Follower Development and Performance: A Field Experiment," *Academy of Management Journal*, August 2002, pp. 735–744; N. Sivasubramaniam, W. D. Murry, B. J. Avolio, and D. I. Jung, "A Longitudinal Model of the Effects of Team Leadership and Group Potency on Group Performance," *Group & Organization Management*, March 2002, pp. 66–96; J. M. Howell and B. J. Avolio, "Transformational Leadership, Transactional Leadership, Locus of Control, and Support for Innovation: Key Predictors of Consolidated-Business-Unit Performance," *Journal of Applied Psychology*, December 1993, pp. 891–911; R. T. Keller, "Transformational Leadership and the Performance of Research and Development Project Groups," *Journal of Management*, September 1992, pp. 489–501; and B. M. Bass and B. J. Avolio, "Developing Transformational Leadership: 1992 and Beyond," *Journal of European Industrial Training*, January 1990, p. 23.

52. R. Pillai, C. A. Schriesheim, and E. S. Williams, "Fairness Perceptions and Trust as Mediators of Transformational and Transactional Leadership: A Two-Sample Study," *Journal of Management* 25, 1999, pp. 897–933.

53. G. M. Spreitzer, K. H. Perttula, and K. Xin, "Traditionality Matters: An Examination of the Effectiveness of Transformational Leadership in the United States and Taiwan," *Journal of Organizational Behavior* 26, no. 3 (2005), pp. 205–227.

54. Based on "Magnotta: Breaking New Ground with Innovative Marketing Strategies," *Industry Canada*, http://strategis.ic.gc.ca/epic/site/mfbs-gprea.nsf/en/lu00057e.html (accessed June 23, 2009); S. Fife, "Break the Competitive Roadblock: Three Canadian Success Stories," *Canadian Business*, May 18, 2007, www.canadianbusiness.com/innovation/article.jsp?content=20070518_094759_4716; and G. Stimmell, "Wine's Scrappy Duo," *Toronto Star*, January 24, 2007, p. D4.

55. See J. R. P. French Jr. and B. Raven, "The Bases of Social Power," in *Group Dynamics: Research and Theory*, ed. D. Cartwright and A. F. Zander (New York: Harper & Row, 1960), pp. 607–623; P. M. Podsakoff and C. A. Schriesheim, "Field Studies of French and Raven's Bases of Power: Critique, Reanalysis, and Suggestions for Future Research,"

Psychological Bulletin, May 1985, pp. 387–411; R. K. Shukla, "Influence of Power Bases in Organizational Decision Making: A Contingency Model," *Decision Sciences*, July 1982, pp. 450–470; D. E. Frost and A. J. Stahelski, "The Systematic Measurement of French and Raven's Bases of Social Power in Workgroups," *Journal of Applied Social Psychology*, April 1988, pp. 375–389; and T. R. Hinkin and C. A. Schriesheim, "Development and Application of New Scales to Measure the French and Raven (1959) Bases of Social Power," *Journal of Applied Psychology*, August 1989, pp. 561–567.

56. See the Royal Australian Navy website, www.navy.gov.au.

57. J. Partridge and J. Saunders, "Milton's Right-Hand Man Quits Air Canada," *Globe and Mail*, April 7, 2004, p. A1.

58. J. M. Kouzes and B. Z. Posner, *Credibility: How Leaders Gain and Lose It, and Why People Demand It* (San Francisco: Jossey-Bass, 1993), p. 14.

59. Based on L. T. Hosmer, "Trust: The Connecting Link Between Organizational Theory and Philosophical Ethics," *Academy of Management Review*, April 1995, p. 393; R. C. Mayer, J. H. Davis, and F. D. Schoorman, "An Integrative Model of Organizational Trust," *Academy of Management Review*, July 1995, p. 712; and G. M. Spreitzer and A. K. Mishra, "Giving Up Control Without Losing Control," *Group & Organization Management*, June 1999, pp. 155–187.

60. P. L. Schindler and C. C. Thomas, "The Structure of Interpersonal Trust in the Workplace," *Psychological Reports*, October 1993, pp. 563–573.

61. H. H. Tan and C. S. F. Tan, "Toward the Differentiation of Trust in Supervisor and Trust in Organization," *Genetic, Social, and General Psychology Monographs*, May 2000, pp. 241–260.

62. K. T. Dirks and D. L. Ferrin, "Trust in Leadership: Meta-Analytic Findings and Implications for Research and Practice," *Journal of Applied Psychology*, August 2002, pp. 611–628.

63. This section is based on F. Bartolome, "Nobody Trusts the Boss Completely—Now What?" *Harvard Business Review*, March–April 1989, pp. 135–142; J. K. Butler Jr., "Toward Understanding and Measuring Conditions of Trust: Evolution of a Conditions of Trust Inventory," *Journal of Management*, September 1991, pp. 643–663; and K. T. Dirks and D. L. Ferrin, "Trust in Leadership: Meta-Analytic Findings and Implications for Research and Practice," *Journal of Applied Psychology*, August 2002, pp. 611–628.

64. This section is based on R. B. Morgan, "Self- and Co-Worker Perceptions of Ethics and Their Relationships to Leadership and Salary," *Academy of Management Journal*, February 1993, pp. 200–214; E. P. Hollander, "Ethical Challenges in the Leader–Follower Relationship," *Business Ethics Quarterly*, January 1995, pp. 55–65; J. C. Rost, "Leadership: A Discussion About Ethics," *Business Ethics Quarterly*, January 1995, pp. 129–142; R. N. Kanungo and M. Mendonca, *Ethical Dimensions of Leadership* (Thousand Oaks, CA: Sage Publications, 1996); J. B. Ciulla, ed., *Ethics: The Heart of Leadership* (New York: Praeger Publications, 1998); J. D. Costa, *The Ethical Imperative: Why Moral Leadership Is Good Business* (Cambridge, MA: Perseus Press, 1999); and N. M. Tichy and A. McGill, eds., *The Ethical Challenge: How to Build Honest Business Leaders* (New York: John Wiley & Sons, 2003).

65. J. M. Burns, *Leadership* (New York: Harper & Row, 1978).

66. J. M. Avolio, S. Kahai, and G. E. Dodge, "The Ethics of Charismatic Leadership: Submission or Liberation?" *Academy of Management Executive*, May 1992, pp. 43–55.

67. L. K. Trevino, M. Brown, and L. P. Hartman, "A Qualitative Investigation of Perceived Executive Ethical Leadership: Perceptions From Inside and Outside the Executive Suite," *Human Relations*, January 2003, pp. 5–37.

68. C. Kleiman, "Virtual Teams Make Loyalty More Realistic," *Chicago Tribune*, January 23, 2001, p. B1.

69. B. J. Alge, C. Wiethoff, and H. J. Klein, "When Does the Medium Matter? Knowledge-Building Experiences and Opportunities in Decision-Making Teams," *Organizational Behavior and Human Decision Processes* 91, no. 1 (2003), pp. 26–37; C. O. Grosse, "Managing Communication Within Virtual Intercultural Teams," *Business Communication Quarterly*, December 2002, pp. 22–38; M. M. Montoya-Weiss, A. P. Massey, and M. Song, "Getting It Together: Temporal Coordination and Conflict Management in Global Virtual Teams," *Academy of Management Journal*, December 2001, pp. 1251–1262; M. L. Maznevski and K. M. Chudoba, "Bridging Space Over Time: Global Virtual-Team Dynamics and Effectiveness," *Organization Science* 11 (2000), pp. 473–492; W. F. Cascio, "Managing a Virtual Workplace," *Academy of Management Executive*, August 2000, pp. 81–90; A. M. Townsend, S. M. DeMarie, and A. R. Hendrickson, "'Virtual Teams' Technology and the Workplace of the Future," *Academy of Management Executive*, August 1998, pp. 17–29.

70. W. F. Cascio, "Managing a Virtual Workplace," *Academy of Management Executive*, August 2000, pp. 88–89.

71. N. Desmond, "The CEO Dashboard," *Business 2.0*, August 2002, p. 34.

72. S. Caminiti, "What Team Leaders Need to Know," *Fortune*, February 20, 1995, p. 93.

73. S. Caminiti, "What Team Leaders Need to Know," *Fortune*, February 20, 1995, p. 100.

74. N. Steckler and N. Fondas, "Building Team Leader Effectiveness: A Diagnostic Tool," *Organizational Dynamics*, Winter 1995, p. 20.

75. R. S. Wellins, W. C. Byham, and G. R. Dixon, *Inside Teams* (San Francisco: Jossey-Bass, 1994), p. 318.

76. N. Steckler and N. Fondas, "Building Team Leader Effectiveness: A Diagnostic Tool," *Organizational Dynamics*, Winter 1995, p. 21.

77. www.statcan.ca/english/freepub/89-503-XIE/0010589-503-XIE.pdf (accessed June 23, 2009); and J. McFarland, "Women Still Find Slow Rise to Power Positions," *Globe and Mail*, March 13, 2003, pp. B1, B7.

78. www.ic.gc.ca/eic/site/sbrp-rppe.nsf/eng/rd02355.html (accessed June 27, 2009).

79. Canadian Imperial Bank of Commerce, *Women Entrepreneurs: Leading the Change*, 2005, www.cibc.com/ca/small-business/article-tools/women-entrepreneurs.html (accessed June 27, 2009).

80. All numbers are for 2005, except for Japan, which is 2004. United Nations, Statistics on Men and Women, http://mdgs.un.org/unsd/demographic/products/indwm/tab5d.htm (accessed June 23, 2009).

81. G. N. Powell, D. A. Butterfield, and J. D. Parent, "Gender and Managerial Stereotypes: Have the Times Changed?" *Journal of Management* 28, no. 2 (2002), pp. 177–193.

82. A. H. Eagly and B. T. Johnson, "Gender and Leadership Style: A Meta-Analysis," *Psychological Bulletin*, September 1990, pp. 233–256; A. H. Eagly and S. J. Karau, "Gender and the Emergence of Leaders: A Meta-Analysis," *Journal of Personality and Social Psychology*, May 1991, pp. 685–710; J. B. Rosener, "Ways Women Lead," *Harvard Business Review*, November–December 1990, pp. 119–125; A. H. Eagly, M. G. Makhijani, and B. G. Klonsky, "Gender and the Evaluation of Leaders: A Meta-Analysis," *Psychological Bulletin*, January 1992, pp. 3–22; A. H. Eagly, S. J. Karau, and B. T. Johnson, "Gender and Leadership Style Among School Principals: A Meta-Analysis," *Educational Administration Quarterly*, February 1992, pp. 76–102; L. R. Offermann and C. Beil, "Achievement Styles of Women Leaders and

Their Peers," *Psychology of Women Quarterly*, March 1992, pp. 37–56; R. L. Kent and S. E. Moss, "Effects of Size and Gender Role on Leader Emergence," *Academy of Management Journal*, October 1994, pp. 1335–1346; C. Lee, "The Feminization of Management," *Training*, November 1994, pp. 25–31; H. Collingwood, "Women as Managers: Not Just Different: Better," *Working Woman*, November 1995, p. 14; J. B. Rosener, *America's Competitive Secret: Women Managers* (New York: Oxford University Press, 1995); and J. Cliff, N. Langton, and H. Aldrich, "Walking the Talk? Gendered Rhetoric vs. Action in Small Firms," *Organizational Studies* 26, no. 1 (2005), pp. 63–91.

83. See F. J. Yammarino, A. J. Dubinsky, L. B. Comer, and M. A. Jolson, "Women and Transformational and Contingent Reward Leadership: A Multiple-Levels-of-Analysis Perspective," *Academy of Management Journal*, February 1997, pp. 205–222; M. Gardiner and M. Tiggemann, "Gender Differences in Leadership Style, Job Stress and Mental Health in Male- and Female-Dominated Industries," *Journal of Occupational and Organizational Psychology*, September 1999, pp. 301–315; C. L. Ridgeway, "Gender, Status, and Leadership," *Journal of Social Issues*, Winter 2001, pp. 637–655; W. H. Decker and D. M. Rotondo, "Relationships Among Gender, Type of Humor, and Perceived Leader Effectiveness," *Journal of Managerial Issues*, Winter 2001, pp. 450–465; J. M. Norvilitis and H. M. Reid, "Evidence for an Association Between Gender-Role Identity and a Measure of Executive Function," *Psychological Reports*, February 2002, pp. 35–45; N. Z. Selter, "Gender Differences in Leadership: Current Social Issues and Future Organizational Implications," *Journal of Leadership Studies*, Spring 2002, pp. 88–99; J. Becker, R. A. Ayman, and K. Korabik, "Discrepancies in Self/Subordinates' Perceptions of Leadership Behavior: Leader's Gender, Organizational Context, and Leader's Self-Monitoring," *Group & Organization Management*, June 2002, pp. 226–244; A. H. Eagly and S. J. Karau, "Role Congruity Theory of Prejudice Toward Female Leaders," *Psychological Review*, July 2002, pp. 573–598; and K. M. Bartol, D. C. Martin, and J. A. Kromkowski, "Leadership and the Glass Ceiling: Gender and Ethnic Influences on Leader Behaviors at Middle and Executive Managerial Levels," *Journal of Leadership & Organizational Studies*, Winter 2003, pp. 8–19.

84. M. Gardiner and M. Tiggemann, "Gender Differences in Leadership Style, Job Stress and Mental Health in Male- and Female-Dominated Industries," *Journal of Occupational and Organizational Psychology*, September 1999, pp. 301–315.

85. "Women 'Take Care,' Men 'Take Charge:' Stereotyping of U.S. Business Leaders Exposed," *Catalyst* (New York, 2005).

86. C. Hymowitz, "Too Many Women Fall for Stereotypes of Selves, Study Says," *Wall Street Journal,* October 24, 2005, p. B1; B. Kantrowitz, "When Women Lead," *Newsweek,* October 24, 2005, pp. 46–61; and "Why Can't Women Be Leaders Too?" *Gallup Management Journal,* gmj.gallup.com, October 13, 2005.

87. J. M. Norvilitis and H. M. Reid, "Evidence for an Association Between Gender-Role Identity and a Measure of Executive Function," *Psychological Reports*, February 2002, pp. 35–45; W. H. Decker and D. M. Rotondo, "Relationships Among Gender, Type of Humor, and Perceived Leader Effectiveness," *Journal of Managerial Issues*, Winter 2001, pp. 450–465; H. Aguinis and S. K. R. Adams, "Social-Role Versus Structural Models of Gender and Influence Use in Organizations: A Strong Inference Approach," *Group & Organization Management*, December 1998, pp. 414–446; A. H. Eagly, S. J. Karau, and M. G. Makhijani, "Gender and the Effectiveness of Leaders: A Meta-Analysis," *Psychological Bulletin* 117 (1995), pp. 125–145.

88. A. H. Eagly, M. C. Johannesen-Schmidt, and M. L. van Engen, "Transformational, Transactional, and Laissez-Faire Leadership Styles: A Meta-Analysis Comparing Women and Men," *Psychological Bulletin* 129, no. 4 (July 2003), pp. 569–591; K. M. Bartol, D. C. Martin, and J. A. Kromkowski, "Leadership and the Glass Ceiling:

Gender and Ethnic Influences on Leader Behaviors at Middle and Executive Managerial Levels," *Journal of Leadership & Organizational Studies*, Winter 2003, pp. 8–19; R. Sharpe, "As Leaders, Women Rule," *BusinessWeek*, November 20, 2000, pp. 74–84.

89. K. M. Bartol, D. C. Martin, and J. A. Kromkowski, "Leadership and the Glass Ceiling: Gender and Ethnic Influences on Leader Behaviors at Middle and Executive Managerial Levels," *Journal of Leadership & Organizational Studies*, Winter 2003, pp. 8–19.

90. Adapted with permission from T. Sergiovanni, R. Metzcus, and L. Burden, "Toward a Particularistic Approach to Leadership Style: Some Findings," *American Educational Research Journal* 6, no. 1 (January 1969), American Educational Research Association, Washington, D.C.

91. Situation adapted from information in J. Menn, "Ellison Talks Tough on Bid for PeopleSoft," *Los Angeles Times*, July 10, 2003, p. C11; M. Mangalindan, D. Clark, and R. Sidel, "Hostile Move Augurs High-Tech Consolidation," *Wall Street Journal*, June 9, 2003, p. A11; A. Pham, "Oracle's Merger Hurdles Get Higher," *Los Angeles Times*, June 30, 2003, p. C11; S. Pannill, "Smashmouth PR Meets High Tech," *Forbes*, May 28, 2001, p. 9; and F. Vogelstein, "Oracle's Ellison Turns Hostile," *Fortune*, June 23, 2003, p. 28.

92. Based on M. Henricks, "Kids These Days," *Entrepreneur*, May 2002, pp. 71–72.

93. L. M. Fisher, "Ricardo Semler Won't Take Control," *Strategy+Business*, Winter 2005, pp. 78–88; R. Semler, *The Seven-Day Weekend: Changing the Way Work Works* (New York: Penguin Group, 2004); A. J. Vogl, "The Anti-CEO," *Across the Board*, May–June 2004, pp. 30–36; G. Colvin, "The Anti-Control Freak," *Fortune*, November 26, 2001, p. 22; and R. Semler, "Managing without Managers," *Harvard Business Review*, September–October 1989, pp. 76–84.

94. Based on H. Mintzberg, *Power In and Around Organizations* (Upper Saddle River, NJ: Prentice Hall, 1983), p. 24; and. L. Hunsaker, *Training in Management Skills* (Upper Saddle River, NJ: Prentice Hall, 2001), pp. 339–364.

Chapter 9

1. Based on Hoover's Online, www.hoover.com; S. Butcher, "Relentless Rise in Pleasure Seekers,"*Financial Times*, July 6, 2003; C. Blackhurst, "The Chris Blackhurst Interview: Sir Terry Leahy," *Management Today*, February 2004, pp. 32–34; Tesco, *Corporate Responsibility Report 2009*, pp. 40–45, www.tescoplc.com/plc/corporate_responsibility_09/people/ (accessed June 30, 2009); and "Tesco at a Glance," *Tesco*, www.tescoreports.com/crreview08/cr-bus-ataglance.html (accessed June 25, 2009).

2. G. P. Latham and C. C. Pinder, "Work Motivation Theory and Research at the Dawn of the Twenty-First Century," *Annual Review of Psychology* 56, no. 1 (2005), pp. 485–516; and C. C. Pinder, *Work Motivation in Organizational Behavior* (Upper Saddle River, NJ: Prentice Hall, 1998), p. 11. See also E. A. Locke and G. P. Latham, "What Should We Do About Motivation Theory? Six Recommendations For the Twenty-First Century," *Academy of Management Review* 29, no. 3 (July 1, 2004), pp. 388–403.

3. See, for example, T. R. Mitchell, "Matching Motivational Strategies With Organizational Contexts," in *Research in Organizational Behavior*, vol. 19, ed. B. M. Staw and L. L. Cummings (Greenwich, CT: JAI Press, 1997), pp. 60–62; and R. Katerberg and G. J. Blau, "An Examination of Level and Direction of Effort and Job Performance," *Academy of Management Journal*, June 1983, pp. 249–257.

4. G. Shaw, "Canada Lags World on Job Quality," *Vancouver Sun*, September 18, 2004, p. F5.

5. Based on S. Butcher, "Relentless Rise in Pleasure Seekers," *Financial Times*, July 6, 2003.

6. A. Maslow, *Motivation and Personality* (New York: McGraw-Hill, 1954); A. Maslow, D. C. Stephens, and G. Heil, *Maslow on Management* (New York: John Wiley & Sons, 1998); M. L. Ambrose and C. T. Kulik, "Old Friends, New Faces: Motivation Research in the 1990s," *Journal of Management* 25, no. 3 (1999), pp. 231–292; and "Dialogue," *Academy of Management Review*, October 2000, pp. 696–701.

7. G. P. Latham and C. C. Pinder, "Work Motivation Theory and Research at the Dawn of the Twenty-First Century," *Annual Review of Psychology* 56, no. 1 (2005), pp. 485–516.

8. See, for example, D. T. Hall and K. E. Nongaim, "An Examination of Maslow's Need Hierarchy in an Organizational Setting," *Organizational Behavior and Human Performance*, February 1968, pp. 12–35; E. E. Lawler III and J. L. Suttle, "A Causal Correlational Test of the Need Hierarchy Concept," *Organizational Behavior and Human Performance*, April 1972, pp. 265–287; R. M. Creech, "Employee Motivation," *Management Quarterly*, Summer 1995, pp. 33–39; J. Rowan, "Maslow Amended," *Journal of Humanistic Psychology*, Winter 1998, pp. 81–92; J. Rowan, "Ascent and Descent in Maslow's Theory," *Journal of Humanistic Psychology*, Summer 1999, pp. 125–133; and M. L. Ambrose and C. T. Kulik, "Old Friends, New Faces: Motivation Research in the 1990s," *Journal of Management* 25, no. 3 (1999), pp. 231–292.

9. D. McGregor, *The Human Side of Enterprise* (New York: McGraw-Hill, 1960). For an updated analysis of theories X and Y, see R. J. Summers and S. F. Conshaw, "A Study of McGregor's Theory X, Theory Y and the Influence of Theory X, Theory Y Assumptions on Causal Attributions for Instances of Worker Poor Performance," in *Organizational Behavior*, ASAC 1988 Conference Proceedings, vol. 9, part 5, ed. S. L. McShaneed (Halifax, NS: ASAC, 1988), pp. 115–123.

10. K. W. Thomas, *Intrinsic Motivation at Work* (San Francisco: Berrett-Koehler, 2000); and K. W. Thomas, "Intrinsic Motivation and How It Works," *Training*, October 2000, pp. 130–135.

11. F. Herzberg, B. Mausner, and B. Snyderman, *The Motivation to Work* (New York: John Wiley, 1959); F. Herzberg, *The Managerial Choice: To Be Effective or to Be Human*, rev. ed. (Salt Lake City: Olympus, 1982); R. M. Creech, "Employee Motivation," *Management Quarterly*, Summer 1995, pp. 33–39; and M. L. Ambrose and C. T. Kulik, "Old Friends, New Faces: Motivation Research in the 1990s," *Journal of Management* 25, no. 3 (1999), pp. 231–292.

12. G. Bellett, "Firm's Secret to Success Lies in Treating Workers Right," *Vancouver Sun*, March 21, 2001, pp. D7, D11; V. Galt, "Getting Fit on the Job," *Globe and Mail*, November 6, 2002, p. C1.

13. C. Lochhead, "Healthy Workplace Programs at Pazmac Enterprises Ltd.," Canadian Labour and Business Centre, March 2002.

14. D. C. McClelland, *The Achieving Society* (New York: Van Nostrand Reinhold, 1961); J. W. Atkinson and J. O. Raynor, *Motivation and Achievement* (Washington, DC: Winston, 1974); D. C. McClelland, *Power: The Inner Experience* (New York: Irvington, 1975); and M. J. Stahl, *Managerial and Technical Motivation: Assessing Needs for Achievement, Power, and Affiliation* (New York: Praeger, 1986).

15. D. C. McClelland, *The Achieving Society* (New York: Van Nostrand Reinhold, 1961).

16. D. C. McClelland, *Power: The Inner Experience* (New York: Irvington, 1975); D. C. McClelland and D. H. Burnham, "Power Is the Great Motivator," *Harvard Business Review*, March–April 1976, pp. 100–110.

17. D. Miron and D. C. McClelland, "The Impact of Achievement Motivation Training on Small Businesses," *California Management Review*, Summer 1979, pp. 13–28.

18. "McClelland: An Advocate of Power," *International Management*, July 1975, pp. 27–29.

19. R. A. Clay, "Green Is Good for You," *Monitor on Psychology*, April 2001, pp. 40–42.

20. Based on S. Butcher, "Relentless Rise in Pleasure Seekers," *Financial Times*, July 6, 2003; A. Nottage, "Tesco," *Human Resources*, May 2003, p. 10; and C. Blackhurst, "The Chris Blackhurst Interview: Sir Terry Leahy," *Management Today*, February 2004, pp. 32–34.

21. M. L. Ambrose and C. T. Kulik, "Old Friends, New Faces: Motivation Research in the 1990s," *Journal of Management* 25, no. 3 (1999), pp. 231–292.

22. B. F. Skinner, *Science and Human Behavior* (New York: Free Press, 1953); and B. F. Skinner, *Beyond Freedom and Dignity* (New York: Knopf, 1972).

23. The same data, for example, can be interpreted in either goal-setting or reinforcement terms, as shown in E. A. Locke, "Latham vs. Komaki: A Tale of Two Paradigms," *Journal of Applied Psychology*, February 1980, pp. 16–23. Also, see M. L. Ambrose and C. T. Kulik, "Old Friends, New Faces: Motivation Research in the 1990s," *Journal of Management* 25, no. 3 (1999), pp. 231–292.

24. J. R. Hackman and G. R. Oldham, "Development of the Job Diagnostic Survey," *Journal of Applied Psychology*, April 1975, pp. 159–170; J. R. Hackman and G. R. Oldham, "Motivation Through the Design of Work: Test of a Theory," *Organizational Behavior and Human Performance*, August 1976, pp. 250–279.

25. J. R. Hackman, "Work Design," in *Improving Life at Work*, ed. J. R. Hackman and J. L. Suttle (Glenview, IL: Scott, Foresman, 1977), p. 129; M. L. Ambrose and C. T. Kulik, "Old Friends, New Faces: Motivation Research in the 1990s," *Journal of Management* 25, no. 3 (1999), pp. 231–292.

26. See www.canada.com/nationalpost/entrepreneur/ail.html (accessed June 25, 2009).

27. J. S. Adams, "Inequity in Social Exchanges," in *Advances in Experimental Social Psychology*, vol. 2, ed. L. Berkowitz (New York: Academic Press, 1965), pp. 267–300; and M. L. Ambrose and C. T. Kulik, "Old Friends, New Faces: Motivation Research in the 1990s," *Journal of Management* 25, no. 3 (1999), pp. 231–292.

28. See, for example, P. S. Goodman and A. Friedman, "An Examination of Adams' Theory of Inequity," *Administrative Science Quarterly*, September 1971, pp. 271–288; E. Walster, G. W. Walster, and W. G. Scott, *Equity: Theory and Research* (Boston: Allyn & Bacon, 1978); and J. Greenberg, "Cognitive Reevaluation of Outcomes in Response to Underpayment Inequity," *Academy of Management Journal*, March 1989, pp. 174–184.

29. See, for example, M. R. Carrell, "A Longitudinal Field Assessment of Employee Perceptions of Equitable Treatment," *Organizational Behavior and Human Performance*, February 1978, pp. 108–118; R. G. Lord and J. A. Hohenfeld, "Longitudinal Field Assessment of Equity Effects on the Performance of Major League Baseball Players," *Journal of Applied Psychology*, February 1979, pp. 19–26; and J. E. Dittrich and M. R. Carrell, "Organizational Equity Perceptions, Employee Job Satisfaction, and Departmental Absence and Turnover Rates," *Organizational Behavior and Human Performance*, August 1979, pp. 29–40.

30. Based on "Councillors Approve Own Pay Hike," *cbc.ca*, July 28, 2006; and Z. Ruryk, "Most T.O. Residents Against Council Raise," *TorontoSun.com*, September 9, 2007.

31. P. S. Goodman, "An Examination of Referents Used in the Evaluation of Pay," *Organizational Behavior and Human Performance*, October 1974, pp. 170–195; S. Ronen, "Equity Perception in Multiple Comparisons: A Field Study," *Human Relations*, April 1986, pp. 333–346; R. W. Scholl, E. A. Cooper, and J. F. McKenna, "Referent Selection in Determining Equity Perception: Differential Effects on Behavioral and Attitudinal Outcomes," *Personnel Psychology*, Spring 1987, pp. 113–127; and C. T. Kulik and M. L. Ambrose, "Personal and Situational Determinants of Referent Choice," *Academy of Management Review*, April 1992, pp. 212–237.

32. A. Wahl, "Canada's Best Workplaces: Overview," *Canadian Business*, April 26, 2007, www.canadianbusiness.com/managing/career/article.jsp?content=20070425_85420_85420 (accessed June 25, 2009).

33. See, for example, R. C. Dailey and D. J. Kirk, "Distributive and Procedural Justice as Antecedents of Job Dissatisfaction and Intent to Turnover," *Human Relations*, March 1992, pp. 305–316; D. B. McFarlin and P. D. Sweeney, "Distributive and Procedural Justice as Predictors of Satisfaction with Personal and Organizational Outcomes," *Academy of Management Journal*, August 1992, pp. 626–637; M. A. Konovsky, "Understanding Procedural Justice and Its Impact on Business Organizations," *Journal of Management* 26, no. 3, 2000, pp. 489–511; J. A. Colquitt, "Does the Justice of One Interact with the Justice of Many? Reactions to Procedural Justice in Teams," *Journal of Applied Psychology*, August 2004, pp. 633–646; J. Brockner, "Why It's So Hard to Be Fair," *Harvard Business Review*, March 2006, pp. 122–129; and B. M. Wiesenfeld, W. B. Swann, Jr., J. Brockner, and C. A. Bartel, "Is More Fairness Always Preferred? Self-Esteem Moderates Reactions to Procedural Justice," *Academy of Management Journal*, October 2007, pp. 1235–1253.

34. V. H. Vroom, *Work and Motivation* (New York: John Wiley, 1964).

35. See, for example, H. G. Heneman III and D. P. Schwab, "Evaluation of Research on Expectancy Theory Prediction of Employee Performance," *Psychological Bulletin*, July 1972, pp. 1–9; and L. Reinharth and M. Wahba, "Expectancy Theory as a Predictor of Work Motivation, Effort Expenditure, and Job Performance," *Academy of Management Journal*, September 1975, pp. 502–537.

36. See, for example, V. H. Vroom, "Organizational Choice: A Study of Pre- and Postdecision Processes," *Organizational Behavior and Human Performance*, April 1966, pp. 212–225; L. W. Porter and E. E. Lawler III, *Managerial Attitudes and Performance* (Homewood, IL: Richard D. Irwin, 1968); W. Van Eerde and H. Thierry, "Vroom's Expectancy Models and Work-Related Criteria: A Meta-Analysis," *Journal of Applied Psychology*, October 1996, pp. 575–586; and M. L. Ambrose and C. T. Kulik, "Old Friends, New Faces: Motivation Research in the 1990s," *Journal of Management* 25, no. 3 (1999), pp. 231–292.

37. See, for example, M. Siegall, "The Simplistic Five: An Integrative Framework for Teaching Motivation," *Organizational Behavior Teaching Review* 12, no. 4 (1987–1988), pp. 141–143.

38. S. Butcher, "Relentless Rise in Pleasure Seekers," *Financial Times*, July 6, 2003; "Tesco Pilots Student Benefits," *Employee Benefits*, November 7, 2003, p. P12; and Tesco, *Corporate Responsibility Report 2009*, pp. 40–45, www.tescoplc.com/plc/corporate_responsibility_09/people (accessed June 30, 2009).

39. J. R. Billings and D. L. Sharpe, "Factors Influencing Flextime Usage Among Employed Married Women," *Consumer Interests Annual*, vol. 45 (Ames, IA: American Council on Consumer Interests, 1999), pp. 89–94; and I. Harpaz, "The Importance of Work Goals: An International Perspective," *Journal of International Business Studies*, First Quarter 1990, pp. 75–93.

40. N. Ramachandran, "New Paths at Work," *US News & World Report*, March 20, 2006, p. 47; S. Armour, "Generation Y: They've Arrived at Work with a New Attitude," *USA Today*, November 6, 2005, pp. B1+; R. Kanfer and P. L. Ackerman, "Aging, Adult Development, and Work Motivation," *Academy of Management Review*, July 2004, pp. 440–458; and R. Bernard, D. Cosgrave, and J. Welsh, *Chips and Pop: Decoding the Nexus Generation* (Toronto: Malcolm Lester Books, 1998).

41. N. J. Adler, *International Dimensions of Organizational Behavior*, 4th ed. (Cincinnati: South-Western College Publishing, 2002), p. 174.

42. G. Hofstede, "Motivation, Leadership and Organization: Do American Theories Apply Abroad?" *Organizational Dynamics*, Summer 1980, p. 55.

43. J. K. Giacobbe-Miller, D. J. Miller, and V. I. Victorov, "A Comparison of Russian and U.S. Pay Allocation Decisions, Distributive Justice Judgments and Productivity Under Different Payment Conditions," *Personnel Psychology*, Spring 1998, pp. 137–163.

44. S. L. Mueller and L. D. Clarke, "Political–Economic Context and Sensitivity to Equity: Differences Between the United States and the Transition Economies of Central and Eastern Europe," *Academy of Management Journal*, June 1998, pp. 319–329.

45. I. Harpaz, "The Importance of Work Goals: An International Perspective," *Journal of International Business Studies*, First Quarter 1990, pp. 75–93.

46. G. E. Popp, H. J. Davis, and T. T. Herbert, "An International Study of Intrinsic Motivation Composition," *Management International Review*, January 1986, pp. 28–35.

47. R. W. Brislin, B. MacNab, R. Worthley, F. Kabigting Jr., and B. Zukis, "Evolving Perceptions of Japanese Workplace Motivation: An Employee-Manager Comparison," *International Journal of Cross-Cultural Management*, April 2005, pp. 87–104.

48. P. Falcone, "Motivating Staff Without Money," *HR Magazine*, August 2002, pp. 105–108.

49. P. Falcone, "Motivating Staff Without Money," *HR Magazine*, August 2002, pp. 105–108.

50. See, for example, M. Alpert, "The Care and Feeding of Engineers," *Fortune*, September 21, 1992, pp. 86–95; G. Poole, "How to Manage Your Nerds," *Forbes ASAP*, December 1994, pp. 132–136; and T. J. Allen and R. Katz, "Managing Technical Professionals and Organizations: Improving and Sustaining the Performance of Organizations, Project Teams, and Individual Contributors," *Sloan Management Review*, Summer 2002, pp. S4–S5.

51. "One CEO's Perspective on the Power of Recognition," *Workforce Management*, March 2, 2004, www.workforce.com; and R. Fournier, "Teamwork Is the Key to Remote Development—Inspiring Trust and Maintaining Motivation Are Critical for a Distributive Development Team," *InfoWorld*, March 5, 2001, p. 48.

52. R. J. Bohner Jr. and E. R. Salasko, "Beware the Legal Risks of Hiring Temps," *Workforce*, October 2002, pp. 50–57.

53. J. P. Broschak and A. Davis-Blake, "Mixing Standard Work and Nonstandard Deals: The Consequences of Heterogeneity in Employment Arrangements," *Academy of Management Journal*, April 2006, pp. 371–393; M. L. Kraimer, S. J. Wayne, R. C. Liden, and R. T. Sparrowe, "The Role of Job Security in Understanding the Relationship Between Employees' Perceptions of Temporary Workers and Employees' Performance," *Journal of Applied Psychology*, March 2005, pp. 389–398; and C. E. Connelly and D. G. Gallagher, "Emerging Trends in Contingent Work Research," *Journal of Management*, November 2004, pp. 959–983.

54. D. W. Krueger, "Money, Success, and Success Phobia," in *The Last Taboo: Money as a Symbol and Reality in Psychotherapy and Psychoanalysis*, ed. D. W. Krueger (New York: Brunner/Mazel, 1986), pp. 3–16.

55. T. R. Mitchell and A. E. Mickel, "The Meaning of Money: An Individual-Difference Perspective," *Academy of Management*, July 1999, pp. 568–578.

56. This paragraph is based on Graham Lowe, "21st Century Job Quality: Achieving What Canadians Want," Canadian Policy Research Networks, Research Report W|37, September 2007.

57. D. Grigg and J. Newman, "Labour Researchers Define Job Satisfaction," *Vancouver Sun*, February 16, 2002, p. E2.

58. This paragraph is based on T. R. Mitchell and A. E. Mickel, "The Meaning of Money: An Individual-Difference Perspective," *Academy of Management*, July 1999, pp. 568–578. The reader may want to refer to the myriad references cited in the article.

59. F. Luthans and A. D. Stajkovic, "Provide Recognition for Performance Improvement," in *Principles of Organizational Behavior*, ed. E. A. Locke (Oxford, UK: Blackwell, 2000), pp. 166–180.

60. Hewitt Associates, "Employers Willing to Pay for High Performance," news release, September 8, 2004; and www.lienmarchecnx.com/en/releases/archive/September2004/08/c7255.html (accessed June 30, 2009).

61. "Secrets of Their Success (and Failure)," *Report on Business*, January 2006, pp. 54–55.

62. S. L. Rynes, B. Gerhart, and L. Parks, "Personnel Psychology: Performance Evaluation and Pay for Performance," *Annual Review of Psychology* 56, no. 1 (2005), p. 572; and A. M. Dickinson, "Are We Motivated by Money? Some Results from the Laboratory," *Performance Improvement* 44, no. 3 (March 2005), pp. 18–24.

63. R. K. Abbott, "Performance-Based Flex: A Tool for Managing Total Compensation Costs," *Compensation and Benefits Review*, March–April 1993, pp. 18–21; J. R. Schuster and P. K. Zingheim, "The New Variable Pay: Key Design Issues," *Compensation and Benefits Review*, March–April 1993, pp. 27–34; C. R. Williams and L. P. Livingstone, "Another Look at the Relationship Between Performance and Voluntary Turnover," *Academy of Management Journal*, April 1994, pp. 269–298; and A. M. Dickinson and K. L. Gillette, "A Comparison of the Effects of Two Individual Monetary Incentive Systems on Productivity: Piece Rate Pay Versus Base Pay Plus Incentives," *Journal of Organizational Behavior Management*, Spring 1994, pp. 3–82.

64. CNW Group, "Calgary Salary Increases Reach New Heights, According to Hewitt," news release, www.newswire.ca/en/releases/archive/September2007/06/c5734.html (accessed June 25, 2009); G. Teel, "City Leads Nation in Salary Increases," *Calgary Herald*, September 7, 2007, www.canada.com (accessed June 25, 2009); Hewitt Associates, "Hewitt Study Shows Pay-for-Performance Plans Replacing Holiday Bonuses," news release, December 6, 2005; and P. Brieger, "Variable Pay Packages Gain Favour: Signing Bonuses, Profit Sharing Taking Place of Salary Hikes," *Financial Post* (*National Post*), September 13, 2002, p. FP5.

65. E. Beauchesne, "Pay Bonuses Improve Productivity, Study Shows," *Vancouver Sun*, September 13, 2002, p. D5; and The Conference Board of Canada, "Variable Pay Offers a Bonus for Unionized Workplaces," news release, September 12, 2002.

66. "Hope for Higher Pay: The Squeeze on Incomes Is Gradually Easing Up," *Maclean's*, November 25, 1996, pp. 100–101.

67. Hewitt Associates, LLC, "Hewitt Study Shows Base Pay Increases Flat for 2006 with Variable Pay Plans Picking Up the Slack," August 31, 2005.

68. E. Beauchesne, "Pay Bonuses Improve Productivity, Study Shows," *Vancouver Sun,* September 13, 2002, p. D5; and "More Than 20 Percent of Japanese Firms Use Pay Systems Based on Performance," *Manpower Argus*, May 1998, p. 7.

69. M. Tanikawa, "Fujitsu Decides to Backtrack on Performance-Based Pay," *New York Times,* March 22, 2001, p. W1.

70. G. D. Jenkins Jr., N. Gupta, A. Mitra, and J. D. Shaw, "Are Financial Incentives Related to Performance? A Meta-Analytic Review of Empirical Research," *Journal of Applied Psychology*, October 1998, pp. 777–787.

71. T. Coupé, V. Smeets, and F. Warzynski, "Incentives, Sorting and Productivity Along the Career: Evidence from a Sample of Top Economists," *Journal of Law Economics & Organization* 22, no. 1 (April 2006), pp. 137–167.

72. A. Kauhanen and H. Piekkola, "What Makes Performance-Related Pay Schemes Work? Finnish Evidence," *Journal of Management and Governance* 10, no. 2 (2006), pp. 149–177.

73. E. Beauchesne, "Pay Bonuses Improve Productivity, Study Shows," *Vancouver Sun*, September 13, 2002, p. D5.

74. P. A. Siegel and D. C. Hambrick, "Pay Disparities Within Top Management Groups: Evidence of Harmful Effects on Performance of High-Technology Firms," *Organization Science* 16, no. 3 (May–June 2005), pp. 259–276; S. Kerr, "Practical, Cost-Neutral Alternatives That You May Know, but Don't Practice," *Organizational Dynamics* 28, no. 1 (1999), pp. 61–70; E. E. Lawler, *Strategic Pay* (San Francisco: Jossey Bass, 1990); and J. Pfeffer, *The Human Equation: Building Profits by Putting People First* (Boston: Harvard Business School Press, 1998).

75. T. Reason, "Why Bonus Plans Fail," *CFO*, January 2003, p. 53; and "Has Pay for Performance Had Its Day?" *McKinsey Quarterly*, no. 4 (2002), accessed on *Forbes* website, www.forbes.com (accessed June 25, 2009).

76. V. Sanderson, "Sweetening Their Slice: More Hardware and Lumberyard Dealers Are Investing in Profit-Sharing Programs as a Way to Promote Employee Loyalty," *Hardware Merchandising*, May–June 2003, p. 66.

77. J. Gray, "A Tale of Two CEOs," *Canadian Business*, April 26–May 9, 2004, pp. 35–36.

78. J. McFarland, "Missing Link: CEO Pay and Results," *Globe and Mail*, June 1, 2006, p. B1.

79. W. J. Duncan, "Stock Ownership and Work Motivation," *Organizational Dynamics*, Summer 2001, pp. 1–11.

80. P. Brandes, R. Dharwadkar, and G. V. Lemesis, "Effective Employee Stock Option Design: Reconciling Stakeholder, Strategic, and Motivational Factors," *Academy of Management Executive*, February 2003, pp. 77–95; J. Blasi, D. Kruse, and A. Bernstein, *In the Company of Owners: The Truth About Stock Options* (New York: Basic Books, 2003).

81. G. Shaw, "Top Gamers Kept on the Job With Array of Sweet Deals," *Vancouver Sun*, March 25, 2004, p. D1.

82. "Health Club Membership, Flextime Are Most Desired Perks," *Business West*, September 1999, p. 75.

83. www.cchra.ca/Web/newsroom/content.aspx?f=30017 (accessed July 1, 2009).

84. D. Penner, "Survey: Top Pay Trumps Work-Life Balance," *The Gazette* (Montreal), March 10, 2007, p. G2.

85. "What Employees Want," *CMA Management* 75, no. 7 (October 2001), p. 8.

86. Information in this paragraph is based on D. Grigg and J. Newman, "Labour Researchers Define Job Satisfaction," *Vancouver Sun*, February 16, 2002, p. E2.

87. J. Greenberg and R. Baron, *Behavior in Organizations*, 6th ed. (Upper Saddle River, NJ: Prentice-Hall, 1995). Reprinted by permission of Prentice-Hall, Inc., Upper Saddle River, NJ.

88. Situation adapted from information in W. Zellner, "They Took More Than They Needed from Us," *BusinessWeek*, June 2, 2003, p. 58; "Coffee, Tea, or Bile?" *BusinessWeek*, June 2, 2003, p. 56; "US Airways Pilots' Stand on Management," *New York Times*, May 24, 2003, p. C2; and "US Airways Flight Attendants Delay Concession Talks," *New York Times*, December 4, 2002, p. C4.

89. Based on J. Marquez, "Best Buy Offers Choice in Its Long-term Incentive Program to Keep the Best and Brightest," *Workforce Management*, April 24, 2006, pp. 42–43; M. Boyle, "Best Buy's Giant Gamble," *Fortune*, April 3, 2006, pp. 68–75; J. S. Lublin, "A Few Share the Wealth," *Wall Street Journal*, December 12, 2005, pp. B1+; J. Thotta, "Reworking Work," *Time*, July 25, 2005, pp. 50–55; and M. V. Copeland, "Best Buy's Selling Machine," *Business 2.0*, July 2004, pp. 92–102.

90. Based on A. Lashinsky, "Where Does Google Go Next?" *CNNMoney.com*, May 12, 2008; K. Hafner, "Google Options Make Masseuse a Multimillionaire," *New York Times* online, www.nytimes.com, November 12, 2007; Q. Hardy, "Close to the Vest," *Forbes*, July 2, 2007, pp. 40–42; K. J. Delaney, "Start-ups Make Inroads with Google's Work Force," *Wall Street Journal* online, www.wsj.com, June 28, 2007; and "Perk Place: The Benefits Offered by Google and Others May Be Grand, but They're All Business," *Knowledge @ Wharton*, www.knowledge.wharton.upenn.edu, March 21, 2007.

91. K. Clark, "Perking Up the Office," *U.S. News & World Report*, November 22, 1999, p. 73: L. Brenner, "Perks That Work," *BusinessWeek Frontier*, October 11, 1999, pp. F22–F40.

92. Based on D. Jones, "Ford, Fannie Mae Tops in Diversity," *USA Today*, May 7, 2003, www.usatoday.com; S. N. Mehta, "What Minority Employees Really Want," *Fortune*, July 10, 2000, pp. 180–186; K. H. Hammonds, "Difference Is Power," *Fast Company,* July 2000, pp. 258–266; "Building a Competitive Workforce: Diversity, the Bottom Line," *Forbes*, April 3, 2000, pp. 181–194; and "Diversity: Developing Tomorrow's Leadership Talent Today," *BusinessWeek*, December 20, 1999, pp. 85–100.

Chapter 10

1. Based on D. Cox, "Team Canada Has It All: Depth, Experience and, Oh Yes, Talent," *Toronto Star*, December 22, 2005, p. 1; M. MacDonald, "Teamwork Key to Gold—On and Off the Ice," *Nanaimo Daily News*, January 27, 2003, p. A9; S. Burnside and B. Beacon, "Lafleur Says Team Canada Well Chosen, Even if There's No Canadiens," Canadian Press, May 18, 2004; and "Primeau Looks Like Conn Man," *StarPhoenix*, May 17, 2004. p. C2.

2. See, for example, E. Sunstrom, K. DeMeuse, and D. Futrell, "Work Teams: Applications and Effectiveness," *American Psychologist*, February 1990, pp. 120–133.

3. G. M. Spreitzer, S. G. Cohen, and G. E. Ledford Jr., "Developing Effective Self-Managing Work Teams in Service Organizations," *Group & Organization Management*, September 1999, pp. 340–366.

4. R. I. Beekun, "Assessing the Effectiveness of Sociotechnical Interventions: Antidote or Fad?" *Human Relations*, October 1989, pp. 877–897.

5. S. G. Cohen, G. E. Ledford, and G. M. Spreitzer, "A Predictive Model of Self-Managing Work Team Effectiveness," *Human Relations*, May 1996, pp. 643–676.

6. C. E. Nicholls, H. W. Lane, and M. Brehm Brechu, "Taking Self-Managed Teams to Mexico," *Academy of Management Executive*, August 1999, pp. 15–27.

7. R. Lepine and K. Rawson, "Strategic Savings on the Right Track: How Canadian Pacific Railway Has Saved Millions of Dollars in the Past Four Years Through Strategic Sourcing," *CMA Management*, February 2003, pp. 20–23.

8. G. Shaw, "The New Home of Microsoft in Canada," *The Vancouver Sun*, October 6, 2007, p. D1.

9. S. Whittaker, "Being Part of the Team," *The Gazette* (Montreal), April 30, 2005, p. B5.

10. See, for example, C. M. Fiol and E. J. O'Connor, "Identification in Face-to-Face, Hybrid, and Pure Virtual Teams: Untangling the Contradictions," *Organization Science* 16, no. 1 (January–February 2005), pp. 19–32; and L. L. Martins, L. L. Gilson, and M. T. Maynard, "Virtual Teams: What Do We Know and Where Do We Go from Here?" *Journal of Management* 30, no. 6 (December 2004), pp. 805–835.

11. J. M. Wilson, S. G. Straus, and B. McEvily, "All in Due Time: The Development of Trust in Computer-Mediated and Face-To-Face Teams," *Organizational Behavior and Human Decision Processes* 99, no. 1 (2006), pp. 16–33; and S. L. Jarvenpaa, K. Knoll, and D. E. Leidner, "Is Anybody Out There? Antecedents of Trust in Global Virtual Teams," *Journal of Management Information Systems*, Spring 1998, pp. 29–64.

12. P. J. Hinds and M. Mortensen, "Understanding Conflict in Geographically Distributed Teams: The Moderating Effects of Shared Identity, Shared Context, and Spontaneous Communication," *Organization Science* 16, no. 3 (2005), pp. 290–307.

13. B. W. Tuckman and M. C. Jensen, "Stages of Small-Group Development Revisited," *Group and Organizational Studies*, December 1977, pp. 419–427; and M. F. Maples, "Group Development: Extending Tuckman's Theory," *Journal for Specialists in Group Work*, Fall 1988, pp. 17–23.

14. L. N. Jewell and H. J. Reitz, *Group Effectiveness in Organizations* (Glenview, IL: Scott, Foresman, 1981); and M. Kaeter, "Repotting Mature Work Teams," *Training*, April 1994, pp. 54–56.

15. Based on B. Beacon, "Continuity Rules on Squad," *Leader-Post*, December 22, 2005, p. C2.

16. See, for example, J. E. Salk and M. Y. Brannien, "National Culture, Networks, and Individual Influence in a Multinational Management Team," *Academy of Management Journal*, April 2000, p. 191; B. L. Kirkman, C. B. Gibson, and D. L. Shapiro, "Enhancing the Implementation and Effectiveness of Work Teams in Global Affiliates," *Organizational Dynamics*, Summer 2001, pp. 12–30; and B. L. Kirkman and D. L. Shapiro, "The Impact of Cultural Values on Employee Resistance to Teams: Towards a Model of Globalized Self-Managing Work Team Effectiveness," *Academy of Management Review*, July 1997, pp. 730–757.

17. S. Stern, "Teams That Work," *Management Today*, June 2001, p. 48.

18. G. Prince, "Recognizing Genuine Teamwork," *Supervisory Management*, April 1989, pp. 25–36; R. F. Bales, *SYMOLOG Case Study Kit* (New York: Free Press, 1980); K. D. Benne and P. Sheats, "Functional Roles of Group Members," *Journal of Social Issues* 4, no. 2 (1948), pp. 41–49.

19. A. R. Jassawalla and H.C. Sashittal, "Strategies of Effective New Product Team Leaders," *California Management Review* 42, no.2 (Winter 2000), pp. 34–51.

20. R. M. Yandrick, "A Team Effort," *HR Magazine*, June 2001, pp. 136–141.

21. R. M. Yandrick, "A Team Effort," *HR Magazine*, June 2001, pp. 136–141.

22. M. A. Marks, C. S. Burke, M. J. Sabella, and S. J. Zaccaro, "The Impact of Cross-Training on Team Effectiveness," *Journal of Applied Psychology*, February 2002, pp. 3–14; and M. A. Marks, S. J. Zaccaro, and J. E. Mathieu, "Performance Implications of Leader Briefings and Team Interaction for Team Adaptation to Novel Environments," *Journal of Applied Psychology*, December 2000, p. 971.

23. C. Garvey, "Steer Teams with the Right Pay: Team-Based Pay Is a Success When It Fits Corporate Goals and Culture, and Rewards the Right Behavior," *HR Magazine*, May 2002, pp. 71–77.

24. Based on "Canada Lacked Cohesion, Chemistry," *Edmonton Journal*, February 24, 2006, p. C3; and E. Duhatschek, "Under Pressure, Gretzky Scores in Balancing Act," *Globe and Mail*, May 17, 2004, p. S1.

25. G. R. Jones and G. M. George, "The Experience and Evolution of Trust: Implications for Cooperation and Teamwork," *Academy of Management Review*, July 1998, pp. 531–546; A. R. Jassawalla and H. C. Sashittal, "Building Collaborative Cross-Functional New Product Teams," *Academy of Management Executive*, August 1999, pp. 50–63; R. Forrester and A. B. Drexler, "A Model for Team-Based Organization Performance," *Academy of Management Executive*, August 1999, pp. 36–49; V. U. Druskat and S. B. Wolff, "The Link Between Emotions and Team Effectiveness: How Teams Engage Members and Build Effective Task Processes," *Academy of Management Proceedings*, CD-ROM, 1999; M. Mattson, T. Mumford, and G. S. Sintay, "Taking Teams to Task: A Normative Model for Designing or Recalibrating Work Teams," *Academy of Management Proceedings*, CD-ROM, 1999; J. D. Shaw, M. K. Duffy, and E. M. Stark, "Interdependence and Preference for Group Work: Main and Congruence Effects on the Satisfaction and Performance of Group Members," *Journal of Management* 26, no. 2 (2000), pp. 259–279; G. L. Stewart and M. R. Barrick, "Team Structure and Performance: Assessing the Mediating Role of Intrateam Process and the Moderating Role of Task Type," *Academy of Management Journal*, April 2000, pp. 135–148; J. E. Mathieu, T. S. Heffner, G. F. Goodwin, E. Salas, and J. A. Cannon-Bowers, "The Influence of Shared Mental Models on Team Process and Performance," *Journal of Applied Psychology*, April 2000, pp. 273–283; J. M. Phillips and E. A. Douthitt, "The Role of Justice in Team Member Satisfaction With the Leader and Attachment to the Team," *Journal of Applied Psychology*, April 2001, pp. 316–325; J. A. Colquitt, R. A. Noe, and C. L. Jackson, "Justice in Teams: Antecedents and Consequences of Procedural Justice Climate," *Personnel Psychology* 55 (2002), pp. 83–100; M. A. Marks, M. J. Sabella, C. S. Burke, and S. J. Zaccaro, "The Impact of Cross-Training on Team Effectiveness," *Journal of Applied Psychology*, February 2002, pp. 3–13; and S. W. Lester, B. W. Meglino, and M. A. Korsgaard, "The Antecedents and Consequences of Group Potency: A Longitudinal Investigation of Newly Formed Work Groups," *Academy of Management Journal*, April 2002, pp. 352–368.

26. D. R. Ilgen, J. R. Hollenbeck, M. Johnson, and D. Jundt, "Teams in Organizations: From Input-Process-Output Models to IMOI Models," *Annual Review of Psychology* 56, no. 1 (2005), pp. 517–543.

27. C. R. Evans and K. L. Dion, "Group Cohesion and Performance: A Meta-Analysis," *Small Group Research*, May 1991, pp. 175–186; B. Mullen and C. Copper, "The Relation Between Group Cohesiveness and Performance: An Integration," *Psychological Bulletin*, March 1994, pp. 210–227; P. M. Podsakoff, S. B. MacKenzie, and M. Ahearne, "Moderating Effects of Goal Acceptance on the Relationship Between Group Cohesiveness and Productivity," *Journal of Applied Psychology*, December 1997, pp. 974–983.

28. See, for example, L. Berkowitz, "Group Standards, Cohesiveness, and Productivity," *Human Relations*, November 1954, pp. 509–519; and B. Mullen and C. Copper, "The Relation Between Group Cohesiveness and Performance: An Integration," *Psychological Bulletin*, March 1994, pp. 210–227.

29. S. E. Seashore, *Group Cohesiveness in the Industrial Work Group* (Ann Arbor: University of Michigan, Survey Research Center, 1954).

30. Paragraph based on R. Kreitner and A. Kinicki, *Organizational Behavior*, 6th ed. (New York: Irwin, 2004), pp. 459–461.

31. This Tips for Managers is based on R. Kreitner and A. Kinicki, *Organizational Behavior*, 6th ed. (New York: McGraw Hill/Irwin, 2004), p. 460. Reprinted by permission of McGraw-Hill Education.

32. This section is adapted from S. P. Robbins, *Managing Organizational Conflict: A Nontraditional Approach* (Upper Saddle River, NJ: Prentice Hall, 1974), pp. 11–14. Also, see D. Wagner-Johnson, "Managing Work Team Conflict: Assessment and Preventative Strategies," Center for the Study of Work Teams, University of North Texas, 1999; and M. Kennedy, "Managing Conflict in Work Teams," Center for the Study of Work Teams, University of North Texas, 1998.

33. See K. A. Jehn, "A Multimethod Examination of the Benefits and Detriments of Intragroup Conflict," *Administrative Science Quarterly*, June 1995, pp. 256–282; K. A. Jehn, "A Qualitative Analysis of Conflict Type and Dimensions in Organizational Groups," *Administrative Science Quarterly*, September 1997, pp. 530–557; K. A. Jehn, "Affective and Cognitive Conflict in Work Groups: Increasing Performance Through Value-Based Intragroup Conflict," in *Using Conflict in Organizations*, ed. C. K. W. DeDreu and E. Van deVliert (London: Sage, 1997), pp. 87–100; K. A. Jehn and E. A. Mannix, "The Dynamic Nature of Conflict: A Longitudinal Study of Intragroup Conflict and Group Performance," *Academy of Management Journal*, April 2001, pp. 238–251; and C. K. W. DeDreu and A. E. M. Van Vianen, "Managing Relationship Conflict and the Effectiveness of Organizational Teams," *Journal of Organizational Behavior*, May 2001, pp. 309–328.

34. C. K. W. DeDreu, "When Too Little or Too Much Hurts: Evidence for a Curvilinear Relationship Between Task Conflict and Innovation in Teams," *Journal of Management,* February 2006, pp. 83–107.

35. K. W. Thomas, "Conflict and Negotiation Processes in Organizations," in *Handbook of Industrial and Organizational Psychology*, vol. 3, 2nd ed., ed. M. D. Dunnette and L. M. Hough, pp. 651–717 (Palo Alto, CA: Consulting Psychologists Press, 1992).

36. See D. R. Comer, "A Model of Social Loafing in Real Work Groups," *Human Relations*, June 1995.

37. S. G. Harkins and K. Szymanski, "Social Loafing and Group Evaluation," *Journal of Personality and Social Psychology*, December 1989, pp. 934–941.

38. B. L. Kirkman, C. B. Gibson, and D. L. Shapiro, "Exporting Teams: Enhancing the Implementation and Effectiveness of Work Teams in Global Affiliates," *Organizational Dynamics,* Summer 2001, pp. 12–29; J. W. Bing and C. M. Bing, "Helping Global Teams Compete," *Training & Development,* March 2001, pp. 70–71; C. G. Andrews, "Factors That Impact Multi-Cultural Team Performance," Center for the Study of Work Teams, University of North Texas, www.workteams.unt.edu/reports, November 3, 2000; P. Christopher Earley and E. Mosakowski, "Creating Hybrid Team Cultures: An Empirical Test of Trans-national Team Functioning," *Academy of Management Journal*, February 2000, pp. 26–49; J. Tata, "The Cultural Context of Teams: An Integrative Model of National Culture, Work Team Characteristics, and Team Effectiveness," *Academy of Management Proceedings* (CD-ROM), 1999; D. I. Jung, K. B. Baik, and J. J. Sosik, "A Longitudinal Investigation of Group Characteristics and Work Group Performance: A Cross-Cultural Comparison," *Academy of Management Proceedings* (CD-ROM), 1999; and C. B. Gibson, "They Do What They Believe They Can? Group-Efficacy Beliefs and Group Performance Across Tasks and Cultures," *Academy of Management Proceedings* (CD-ROM), 1996.

39. R. Bond and P. B. Smith, "Culture and Conformity: A Meta-Analysis of Studies Using Asch's [1952, 1956] Line Judgment Task," *Psychological Bulletin,* January 1996, pp. 111–137.

40. I. L. Janis, *Groupthink,* 2nd ed. (New York: Houghton Mifflin Company, 1982), p. 175.

41. See P. C. Earley, "East Meets West Meets Mideast: Further Explorations of Collectivistic and Individualistic Work Groups," *Academy of Management Journal,* April 1993, pp. 319–348; and P. C. Earley, "Social Loafing and Collectivism: A Comparison of the United States and the People's Republic of China," *Administrative Science Quarterly,* December 1989, pp. 565–581.

42. See P. C. Earley, "Social Loafing and Collectivism: A Comparison of the United States and the People's Republic of China," *Administrative Science Quarterly,* December 1989, pp. 565–581; and P. C. Earley, "East Meets West Meets Mideast: Further Explorations of Collectivistic and Individualistic Work Groups," *Academy of Management Journal,* April 1993, pp. 319–348.

43. N. J. Adler, *International Dimensions of Organizational Behavior,* 4th ed. (Cincinnati, OH: South-Western College Publishing, 2002), p. 142.

44. K. B. Dahlin, L. R. Weingart, and P. J. Hinds, "Team Diversity and Information Use," *Academy of Management Journal,* December 2005, pp. 1107–1123.

45. N. J. Adler, *International Dimensions of Organizational Behavior,* 4th ed. (Cincinnati, OH: South-Western College Publishing, 2002), p. 142.

46. S. Paul, I. M. Samarah, P. Seetharaman, and P. P. Mykytyn, "An Empirical Investigation of Collaborative Conflict Management Style in Group Support System-Based Global Virtual Teams," *Journal of Management Information Systems,* Winter 2005, pp. 185–222.

47. S. Chang and P. Tharenou, "Competencies Needed for Managing a Multicultural Workgroup," *Asia Pacific Journal of Human Resources* 42, no. 1 (2004), pp. 57–74; and N. Adler, *International Dimensions of Organizational Behavior* (Boston, MA: Kent Publishing Co., 1986), p. 153.

48. C. E. Nicholls, H. W. Lane, and M. Brehm Brechu, "Taking Self-Managed Teams to Mexico," *Academy of Management Executive,* August 1999, pp. 15–27.

49. D. Brown, "Innovative HR Ineffective in Manufacturing Firms," *Canadian HR Reporter,* April 7, 2003, pp. 1–2.

50. A. B. Drexler and R. Forrester, "Teamwork—Not Necessarily the Answer," *HR Magazine,* January 1998, pp. 55–58.

51. R. Forrester and A. B. Drexler, "A Model for Team-Based Organization Performance," *Academy of Management Executive,* August 1999, p. 47. See also S. A. Mohrman, with S. G. Cohen and A. M. Mohrman Jr., *Designing Team-Based Organizations* (San Francisco: Jossey-Bass, 1995); and J. H. Shonk, *Team-Based Organizations* (Homewood, IL: Business One Irwin, 1992).

52. Adapted from D. A. Whetten and K. S. Cameron, *Developing Management Skills,* 3rd ed. (New York: HarperCollins, 1995), pp. 534–535.

53. M. Fackler, "Raising the Bar at Samsung," *New York Times,* April 25, 2006, www.nytimes.com/2006/04/25/technology/25samsung.html (accessed June 26, 2009); B. Breen, "The Seoul of Design," *Fast Company,* December 2005, pp. 90–97; E. Ramstad, "Standing Firm," *Wall Street Journal,* March 16, 2005, pp. A1+; D. Rocks and M. Ihlwan, "Samsung Design," *BusinessWeek,* December 6, 2004, pp. 88–96; and Interbrand Consulting Group, "Best Global Brands 2006," www.ourfishbowl.com/images/surveys/BGB06Report_072706.pdf (accessed June 26, 2009).

54. Based on L. Gratton and T. J. Erickson, "8 Ways to Build Collaborative Teams," *Harvard Business Review,* November 2007, pp. 100–109; and J. Gordon, "Building Brand Champions," *Training,* January/February 2007, pp. 14–17.

55. Based on P. L. Hunsaker, *Training in Management Skills* (Upper Saddle River, NJ: Prentice Hall, 2001), chapter 12.

56. Based on L. Copeland, "Making the Most of Cultural Differences at the Workplace," *Personnel,* June 1988, pp. 52–60; C. R. Bantz, "Cultural Diversity and Group Cross-Cultural Team Research," *Journal of Applied Communication Research,* February 1993, pp. 1–19; L. Strach and L. Wicander, "Fitting In: Issues of Tokenism and Conformity for Minority Women," *SAM Advanced Management Journal,* Summer 1993, pp. 22–25; M. L. Maznevski, "Understanding Our Differences: Performance in Decision-Making Groups With Diverse Members," *Human Relations,* May 1994, pp. 531–552; F. Rice, "How to Make Diversity Pay," *Fortune,* August 8, 1994, pp. 78–86; J. Jusko, "Diversity Enhances Decision Making," *IndustryWeek,* April 2, 2001, p. 9; and K. Lovelace, D. L. Shapiro, and L. R. Weingart, "Maximizing Cross-Functional New Product Teams' Innovativeness and Constraint Adherence: A Conflict Communications Perspective," *Academy of Management Journal,* August 2002, pp. 779–793.

Part 4 Continuing Case: Starbucks

1. A. Serwer and K. Bonamici, "Hot Starbucks to Go," *Fortune,* January 26, 2004, pp. 60–74; interview with Jim Donald, *Fortune,* April 4, 2005, p. 30; interview with Jim Donald, *Smart Money,* May 2006, pp. 31–32; A. Serwer, "Interview with Howard Schultz," *Fortune* (Europe), March 20, 2006, pp. 35–36; W. Meyers, "Conscience in a Cup of Coffee," *U.S. News & World Report,* October 31, 2005, pp. 48–50; J. M. Cohn, R. Khurana, and L. Reeves, "Growing Talent As if Your Business Depended It," *Harvard Business Review,* October 2005, pp. 62–70; P. Kafka, "Bean Counter," *Forbes,* February 28, 2005, pp. 78–80; S. Gray, "Starbucks's CEO Announces Plan to Retire in March," *Wall Street Journal,* October 13, 2004, p. A6; *Beyond the Cup: Corporate Social Responsibility, Fiscal 2005 Annual Report,* Starbucks Corporation; *My Starbucks: Corporate Social Responsibility, Fiscal 2006 Annual Report,* Starbucks Corporation; *Starbucks 2006 Annual* Report, www.investor.starbucks.com/phoenix.zhtml?c=99518&p=irol-IRHome (accessed June 24, 2009).

Chapter 11

1. Based on "Energy Roughneck," *Canadian Business,* August 1996, pp. 20+; Hoover's Online, www.hoovers.com; and C. Cattaneo, "Husky CEO Lau Reveals Intention to Retire," *National Post (Financial Post),* April 23, 2004, p. FP4.

2. J. Kluger and B. Liston, "A Columbia Culprit?" *Time,* February 24, 2003, p. 13.

3. K. A. Merchant, "The Control Function of Management," *Sloan Management Review,* Summer 1982, pp. 43–55.

4. E. Flamholtz, "Organizational Control Systems as a Managerial Tool," *California Management Review,* Winter 1979, p. 55.

5. "The Top 1000: Canada's Power Book," *Globe and Mail,* www.globeinvestor.com/series/top1000 (accessed June 27, 2009).

6. S. Brearton and J. Daly, "50 Best Employers in Canada," *Globe and Mail,* December 29, 2003, p. 33; and Hewitt Associates, "Study Guidelines," *Best Employers in Canada,* was2.hewitt.com/bestemployers/canada/pages/study_guidelines.htm (accessed July 1, 2009).

7. See www.list.canadianbusiness.com/rankings/profit100/2008/intro/Default.aspx?sp2=1&d1=d&sc1=9 (accessed July 1, 2009).

8. P. Magnusson, "Your Jitters Are Their Lifeblood," *BusinessWeek,* April 14, 2003, p. 41; S. Williams, "Company Crisis: CEO Under Fire,"

Hispanic Business, March 2003, pp. 54–56; T. Purdum, "Preparing for the Worst," *IndustryWeek*, January 2003, pp. 53–55; and S. Leibs, "Lesson from 9/11: It's Not About Data," *CFO*, September 2002, pp. 31–32.

9. S. Kerr, "On the Folly of Rewarding A, While Hoping for B," *Academy of Management Journal*, December 1975, pp. 769–783.

10. Y. F. Jarrar and M. Zairi, "Future Trends in Benchmarking for Competitive Advantage: A Global Survey," *Total Quality Management*, December 2001, pp. 906–912.

11. M. Simpson and D. Kondouli, "A Practical Approach to Benchmarking in Three Service Industries," *Total Quality Management*, July 2000, pp. S623–S630.

12. K. N. Dervitsiotis, "Benchmarking and Paradigm Shifts," *Total Quality Management*, July 2000, pp. S641–S646.

13. See www.canada.com/nationalpost/entrepreneur/bouclair.html (accessed June 27, 2009).

14. T. Leahy, "Extracting Diamonds in the Rough," *Business Finance*, August 2000, pp. 33–37.

15. "Recognizing Commitment to Diversity," *Canadian HR Reporter*, November 3, 2003, p. 12.

16. B. Bruzina, B. Jessop, R. Plourde, B. Whitlock, and L. Rubin, "Ameren Embraces Benchmarking as a Core Business Strategy," *Power Engineering*, November 2002, pp. 121–124; T. Leahy, "Extracting Diamonds in the Rough," *Business Finance*, August 2000, pp. 33–37.

17. Based on R. Luciw, "Firm's Application of New Management Practices Draws Praise From Analyst," *Globe and Mail*, March 2, 2005, p. B16; and T. Harbert, "Lean, Mean Six Sigma Machines," *Design News*, December 11, 2006.

18. H. Koontz and R. W. Bradspies, "Managing through Feedforward Control," *Business Horizons*, June 1972, pp. 25–36.

19. "An Open Letter to McDonald's Customers," *Wall Street Journal*, August 22, 2001, p. A5.

20. W. H. Newman, *Constructive Control: Design and Use of Control Systems* (Upper Saddle River, NJ: Prentice Hall, 1975), p. 33.

21. R. Ilies and T. A. Judge, "Goal Regulation across Time: The Effects of Feedback and Affect," *Journal of Applied Psychology* 90, no. 3 (May 2005), pp. 453–467.

22. Based on C. Cattaneo, "Li May Usher in Sea Change at Air Canada," *National Post* (*Financial Post*), November 24, 2003, p. FP03.

23. W. G. Ouchi, "A Conceptual Framework for the Design of Organizational Control Mechanisms," *Management Science*, August 1979, pp. 833–838; and W. G. Ouchi, "Markets, Bureaucracies, and Clans," *Administrative Science Quarterly*, March 1980, pp. 129–141.

24. Based on P. Fitzpatrick, "Wacky WestJet's Winning Ways: Passengers Respond to Stunts That Include Races to Determine Who Leaves the Airplane First," *National Post*, October 16, 2000, p. C1.

25. L. Smircich, "Concepts of Culture and Organizational Analysis," *Administrative Science Quarterly*, September 1983, p. 339; D. R. Denison, "What Is the Difference between Organizational Culture and Organizational Climate? A Native's Point of View on a Decade of Paradigm Wars" (paper presented at Academy of Management Annual Meeting, Atlanta, Georgia, 1993); and M. J. Hatch, "The Dynamics of Organizational Culture," *Academy of Management Review*, October 1993, pp. 657–693.

26. K. Shadur and M. A. Kienzle, "The Relationship Between Organizational Climate and Employee Perceptions of Involvement," *Group &*

Organization Management, December 1999, pp. 479–503; A. M. Sapienza, "Believing Is Seeing: How Culture Influences the Decisions Top Managers Make," in *Gaining Control of the Corporate Culture,* ed. R. H. Kilmann, M. J. Saxton, and R. Serpa (San Francisco: Jossey-Bass, 1985), p. 68.

27. C. A. O'Reilly III, J. Chatman, and D. F. Caldwell, "People and Organizational Culture: A Profile Comparison Approach to Assessing Person–Organization Fit," *Academy of Management Journal*, September 1991, pp. 487–516; J. A. Chatman and K. A. Jehn, "Assessing the Relationship Between Industry Characteristics and Organizational Culture: How Different Can You Be?" *Academy of Management Journal*, June 1994, pp. 522–553.

28. See, for example, D. R. Denison, *Corporate Culture and Organizational Effectiveness* (New York: Wiley, 1990); G. G. Gordon and N. DiTomaso, "Predicting Corporate Performance from Organizational Culture," *Journal of Management Studies*, November 1992, pp. 793–798; J. P. Kotter and J. L. Heskett, *Corporate Culture and Performance* (New York: Free Press, 1992), pp. 15–27; J. C. Collins and J. I. Porras, *Built to Last* (New York: HarperBusiness, 1994); J. C. Collins and J. I. Porras, "Building Your Company's Vision," *Harvard Business Review*, September–October 1996, pp. 65–77; R. Goffee and G. Jones, "What Holds the Modern Company Together?" *Harvard Business Review*, November–December 1996, pp. 133–148; and J. B. Sorensen, "The Strength of Corporate Culture and the Reliability of Firm Performance," *Administrative Science Quarterly* 47, no. 1 (2002), pp. 70–91.

29. J. B. Sorensen, "The Strength of Corporate Culture and the Reliability of Firm Performance," *Administrative Science Quarterly* 47, no. 1 (2002), pp. 70–91.

30. G. Probst and S. Raisch, "Organizational Crisis: The Logic of Failure," *Academy of Management Executive* 19, no. 1 (February 2005), pp. 90–105.

31. J. Forman, "When Stories Create an Organization's Future," *Strategy & Business*, Second Quarter 1999, pp. 6–9; D. M. Boje, "The Storytelling Organization: A Study of Story Performance in an Office-Supply Firm," *Administrative Science Quarterly*, March 1991, pp. 106–126; C. H. Deutsch, "The Parables of Corporate Culture," *New York Times*, October 13, 1991, p. F25; and T. Terez, "The Business of Storytelling," *Workforce*, May 2002, pp. 22–24.

32. A. M. Pettigrew, "On Studying Organizational Cultures," *Administrative Science Quarterly*, December 1979, p. 576.

33. A. M. Pettigrew, "On Studying Organizational Cultures," *Administrative Science Quarterly*, December 1979, p. 576.

34. C. Cattaneo, "Li May Usher in Sea Change at Air Canada," *National Post* (*Financial Post*), November 24, 2003, p. FP03; C. Cattaneo, "Stranger in a Strange Land," *National Post* (*Financial Post*), December 13, 2003, p. FP1F; Husky Energy, *Annual Report 2006*, p. 6, www.huskyenergy.ca/downloads/Investor Relations/2006/HSE_Annual2006.pdf (accessed June 27, 2009); and "Husky Energy [The Investor 500]," *Canadian Business*, www.canadianbusiness.com/rankings/investor500/index.jsp?pageID=profile&profile=16&year=2007&type=profile (accessed June 27, 2009).

35. F. Hansen, "The Value-Based Management Commitment," *Business Finance*, September 2001, pp. 2–5.

36. M. Acharya and T. Yew, "A New Kind of Top 10," *Toronto Star*, June 30, 2002, p. C01.

37. M. Acharya and T. Yew, "A New Kind of Top 10," *Toronto Star*, June 30, 2002, p. C01.

38. K. Lehn and A. K. Makhija, "EVA and MVA as Performance Measures and Signals for Strategic Change," *Strategy & Leadership*, May–June 1996, pp. 34–38.

39. S. Taub, "MVPs of MVA: Which Companies Created the Most Wealth for Shareholders Last Year? *CFO*, July 1, 2003, www.cfo.com/article.cfm/3009758/c_2984284/?f=archives (accessed June 27, 2009); and "America's Best Wealth Creators—2007 edition," EVA Dimensions, www.evadimensions.com/2007top20RankingSummary.pdf (accessed June 27, 2009).

40. Debra Black, "Rogers Data on Clients Found in Lot," *Toronto Star*, April 8, 2007, www.thestar.com/News/article/200727 (accessed June 27, 2009).

41. "When Wireless Works," *CIO*, February 12, 2002.

42. J. McPartlin, "Hackers Find Backers," *CFO*, January 2006, pp. 75–77; J. Swartz, "Data Losses Push Businesses to Encrypt Backup Tapes," *USA Today*, June 13, 2005, p. 1B; J. Goff, "New Holes for Hackers," *CFO*, May 2005, pp. 64–73; B. Grow, "Hacker Hunters," *BusinessWeek*, May 30, 2005, pp. 74–82; J. Swartz, "Crooks Slither into Net's Shady Nooks and Crannies," *USA Today*, October 21, 2004, pp. 1B+; J. Swartz, "Spam Can Hurt in More Ways Than One," *USA Today*, July 7, 2004, p. 3B; and T. Reason, "Stopping the Flow," *CFO*, September 2003, pp. 97–99.

43. D. Whelan, "Google Me Not," *Forbes*, August 16, 2004, pp. 102–104.

44. J. Levitz and J. Hechinger, "Laptops Prove Weakest Link in Data Security," *Wall Street Journal*, March 24, 2006, pp. B1+.

45. J. Markoff, "Study Says Chips in ID Tags Are Vulnerable to Viruses," *New York Times*, March 15, 2006, www.nytimes.com/2006/03/15/technology/15tag.html (accessed June 27, 2009).

46. Based on "Corporate Governance," *Husky Energy*, www.huskyenergy.ca/abouthusky/corporategovernance/ (accessed June 27, 2009).

47. J. Yaukey and C. L. Romero, "Arizona Firm Pays Big for Workers' Digital Downloads," *Springfield News-Leader*, May 6, 2002, p. 6B.

48. R. S. Kaplan and D. P. Norton, "How to Implement a New Strategy without Disrupting Your Organization," *Harvard Business Review*, March 2006, pp. 100–109; L. Bassi and D. McMurrer, "Developing Measurement Systems for Managing in the Knowledge Era," *Organizational Dynamics*, May 2005, pp. 185–196; G. M. J. de Koning, "Making the Balanced Scorecard Work (Part 2), *Gallup Brain*, August 12, 2004, http://brain.gallup.com; G. M. J. de Koning, "Making the Balanced Scorecard Work (Part 1), *Gallup Brain*, July 8, 2004, http://brain.gallup.com; Balanced Scorecard Collaborative, June 29, 2003, www.bscol.com; K. Graham, "Balanced Scorecard," *New Zealand Management*, March 2003, pp. 32–34; K. Ellis, "A Ticket to Ride: Balanced Scorecard," *Training*, April 2001, p. 50; T. Leahy, "Tailoring the Balanced Scorecard," *Business Finance*, August 2000, pp. 53–56; and R. S. Kaplan and D. P. Norton, "Using the Balanced Scorecard as a Strategic Management System," *Harvard Business Review* 74, no. 1 (January–February 1996), pp. 75–85.

49. T. Leahy, "Tailoring the Balanced Scorecard," *Business Finance*, August 2000, pp. 53–56.

50. See www.oha.ca/client/oha/oha_lp4w_lnd_webstation.nsf/page/Hospital+Report (accessed June 27, 2009); and T. Leahy, "Tailoring the Balanced Scorecard," *Business Finance*, August 2000, pp. 53–56.

51. "A Revolution Where Everyone Wins: Worldwide Movement to Improve Corporate-Governance Standards," *BusinessWeek*, May 19, 2003, p. 72.

52. J. S. McClenahen, "Executives Expect More Board Input," *IndustryWeek*, October 2002, p. 12.

53. D. Salierno, "Boards Face Increased Responsibility," *Internal Auditor*, June 2003, pp. 14–15.

54. N. Shirouzu and J. Bigness, "7-Eleven Operators Resist System to Monitor Managers," *Wall Street Journal*, June 16, 1997, p. B1.

55. E. O'Connor, "Pulling the Plug on Cyberslackers," *StarPhoenix*, May 24, 2003, p. F22.

56. E. O'Connor, "Pulling the Plug on Cyberslackers," *StarPhoenix*, May 24, 2003, p. F22.

57. "'Stealing' Time at Work on Net," *The Gazette*, April 4, 2008, www2.canada.com/montrealgazette/news/business/story.html?id=32125d78-a479-497a-ae19-4f461ea18060 (accessed July 1, 2009).

58. D. Hawkins, "Lawsuits Spur Rise in Employee Monitoring," *U.S. News & World Report*, August 13, 2001, p. 53; L. Guernsey, "You've Got Inappropriate Mail," *New York Times*, April 5, 2000, p. C11; and R. Karaim, "Setting E-Privacy Rules," *Cnnfn Online*, December 15, 1999, www.cnnfn.com.

59. E. Bott, "Are You Safe? Privacy Special Report," *PC Computing*, March 2000, pp. 87–88.

60. E. O'Connor, "Pulling the Plug on Cyberslackers," *StarPhoenix*, May 24, 2003, p. F22.

61. A. Tomlinson, "Heavy-Handed Net Policies Push Privacy Boundaries," *Canadian HR Reporter*, December 2, 2002, pp. 1–2.

62. C. Sorensen, "Canada Ranks High in Employee Theft: Global Survey Findings," *National Post*, May 28, 2004, p. FP9.

63. A. Perry, "Back-to-School Brings Pilfering: Some Employees Raid Office for Kids," *Toronto Star*, August 30, 2003, p. B01.

64. Global Retail Theft Barometer 2007, www.rsv.bifrost.is/Files/Skra_0023379.doc.

65. J. Greenberg, "The STEAL Motive: Managing the Social Determinants of Employee Theft," in *Antisocial Behavior in Organizations*, ed. R. Giacalone and J. Greenberg (Newbury Park, CA: Sage, 1997), pp. 85–108.

66. "Crime Spree," *BusinessWeek*, September 9, 2002, p. 8; B. P. Niehoff and R. J. Paul, "Causes of Employee Theft and Strategies That HR Managers Can Use for Prevention," *Human Resource Management*, Spring 2000, pp. 51–64; and G. Winter, "Taking at the Office Reaches New Heights: Employee Larceny Is Bigger and Bolder," *New York Times*, July 12, 2000, p. C11.

67. This section is based on J. Greenberg, *Behavior in Organizations: Understanding and Managing the Human Side of Work*, 8th ed. (Upper Saddle River, NJ: Prentice Hall, 2003), pp. 329–330.

68. A. H. Bell and D. M. Smith, "Why Some Employees Bite the Hand That Feeds Them," *Workforce*, May 16, 2000, www.workforce.com (accessed June 30, 2009).

69. A. H. Bell and D. M. Smith, "Protecting the Company Against Theft and Fraud," *Workforce*, May 18, 2000, www.workforce.com (accessed June 30, 2009); J. D. Hansen, "To Catch a Thief," *Journal of Accountancy*, March 2000, pp. 43–46; and J. Greenberg, "The Cognitive Geometry of Employee Theft," in *Dysfunctional Behavior in Organizations: Nonviolent and Deviant Behavior*, ed. S. B. Bacharach, A. O'Leary-Kelly, J. M. Collins, and R. W. Griffin (Stamford, CT: JAI Press, 1998), pp. 147–193.

70. Information from company website, www.enterprise.com (accessed June 29, 2003); and A. Taylor, "Driving Customer Satisfaction," *Harvard Business Review*, July 2002, pp. 24–25.

71. S. D. Pugh, J. Dietz, J. W. Wiley, and S. M. Brooks, "Driving Service Effectiveness through Employee-Customer Linkages," *Academy of Management Executive*, November 2002, pp. 73–84.

72. T. S. Bateman and J. M. Crant, "The Proactive Component of Organizational Behavior: A Measure and Correlates," *Journal of Organizational Behavior*, March 1993, p. 112; and J. M. Crant, "Proactive Behavior in Organizations," *Journal of Management* 26, no. 3 (2000), pp. 435–462.

73. Situation adapted from information in K. Cushing, "E-Mail Policy," *Computer Weekly*, June 24, 2003, p. 8; and "Spam Leads to Lawsuit Fears, Lost Time," *InternetWeek*, June 23, 2003, www.internetweek.com.

74. Based on P. Vieira, "The Airline, the Analyst and the Secret Password," *Financial Post*, June 30, 2004, p. FP1; C. Wong, "WestJet Disputes Air Canada Allegations of Corporate Espionage," *Canadian Press*, July 1, 2004; and T. Gignac, "WestJet Settles Air Canada Corporate-Espionage Suit," *Vancouver Sun*, May 30, 2006, p. D2.

75. K. Capell, "British Airways Hit by Heathrow Fiasco," *BusinessWeek*, April 3, 2008, p. 6; The Associated Press, "Problems Continue at Heathrow's Terminal 5," *New York Times* online, www.nytimes.com, March 31, 2008 (accessed June 27, 2009); M. Scott, "New Heathrow Hub: Slick, but No Savior," *BusinessWeek*, March 28, 2008, p. 11; and G. Katz, "Flights Are Canceled, Baggage Stranded, as London's New Heathrow Terminal Opens," *The Seattle Times* online, http://seattletimes.nwsource.com, March 27, 2008.

76. Based on P. L. Hunsaker, *Training in Management Skills* (Upper Saddle River, NJ: Prentice Hall, 2001), pp. 60–61.

77. Based on J. Hickman, C. Tkaczyk, E. Florian, J. Stemple, and D. Vazquez, "50 Best Companies for Minorities," *Fortune*, July 7, 2003, pp. 103–120; S. M. Mehta, "What Minority Employees Really Want," *Fortune*, July 10, 2000, pp. 180–186; and "Why Diversity Pays," *Canadian Business*, March 29–April 11, 2004, cover story.

Chapter 12

1. Based on K. J. Delaney, "Spreading Change: As Yahoo! Falters, Executive's Memo Calls for Overhaul," *Wall Street Journal*, November 18, 2006, p. A1; and R. D. Hof, "Back to the Future at Yahoo!" *BusinessWeek*, July 02, 2007, p. 34.

2. C. R. Leana and B. Barry, "Stability and Change as Simultaneous Experiences in Organizational Life," *Academy of Management Review*, October 2000, pp. 753–759.

3. Based on L. Tischler, "Sudden Impact," *Fast Company*, September 2002, pp. 106–113.

4. E. Nee, "The Hottest CEO in Tech," *Business 2.0*, June 2003, p. 86.

5. Based on R. D. Hof, "Back to the Future at Yahoo!" *BusinessWeek*, July 02, 2007, p. 34.

6. www.techcrunch.com/2007/04/29/panama-not-enough-to-battle-google-yahoo-acquires-rightmedia/ (accessed June 29, 2009).

7. K. Swisher, "Yahoo's Jerry Yang to Step Down, as a Search for New CEO Commences," www.kara.allthingsd.com/20081117/yahoos-jerry-yang-to-step-down-as-a-search-for-new-ceo-commences/, November 17, 2008 (accessed July 7, 2009).

8. The idea for these metaphors came from J. E. Dutton, S. J. Ashford, R. M. O'Neill, and K. A. Lawrence, "Moves That Matter: Issue Selling and Organizational Change," *Academy of Management Journal*, August 2001, pp. 716–736; B. H. Kemelgor, S. D. Johnson, and S. Srinivasan, "Forces Driving Organizational Change: A Business School Perspective," *Journal of Education for Business*, January–February 2000, pp. 133–137; G. Colvin, "When It Comes to Turbulence, CEOs Could Learn a Lot from Sailors," *Fortune*, March 29, 1999, pp. 194–196; and P. B. Vaill, *Managing as a Performing Art: New Ideas for a World of Chaotic Change* (San Francisco: Jossey-Bass, 1989).

9. K. Lewin, *Field Theory in Social Science* (New York: Harper & Row, 1951).

10. For contrasting views on episodic and continuous change, see K. E. Weick and R. E. Quinn, "Organizational Change and Development," in *Annual Review of Psychology*, vol. 50, ed. J. T. Spence, J. M. Darley, and D. J. Foss (Palo Alto, CA: Annual Reviews, 1999), pp. 361–386.

11. G. Hamel, "Take It Higher," *Fortune*, February 5, 2001, pp. 169–170.

12. Based on S. Rubin, "Blinded by the Dazzle of the Deal," *Financial Post* (*National Post*), February 12, 2004, pp. FP8–FP9.

13. Based on R. D. Hof, "Back to the Future at Yahoo!" *BusinessWeek*, July 2, 2007, p. 34; and J. Thaw and A. Levy, "Yahoo! CEO Digs in for Slugfest With Google, *The Vancouver Sun*, June 20, 2007, p. D3.

14. Based on T. Belford, "Half Public, Half Private, It Beats Odds," *Financial Post* (*National Post*), June 9, 2003, p. BE4; S. Tafler, "BC + X = P3: BC Struggles With the Partnering Numbers," *Summit: Canada's Magazine for Public Sector Purchasing*, September 2002, pp. 16–18; and P. Vieira, "RBC Pushes Public–Private Partnerships," *Financial Post* (*National Post*), November 26, 2002, p. FP10.

15. See, for example, T. C. Head and P. F. Sorensen, "Cultural Values and Organizational Development: A Seven-Country Study," *Leadership & Organization Development Journal*, March 1993, pp. 3–7; A. H. Church, W. W. Burke, and D. F. Van Eynde, "Values, Motives, and Interventions of Organization Development Practitioners," *Group & Organization Management*, March 1994, pp. 5–50; W. L. French and C. H. Bell Jr., *Organization Development: Behavioral Science Interventions for Organization Improvement*, 6th ed. (Upper Saddle River, NJ: Prentice Hall, 1998); N. A. Worren, K. Ruddle, and K. Moore, "From Organizational Development to Change Management," *Journal of Applied Behavioral Science*, September 1999, pp. 273–286; G. Farias, "Organizational Development and Change Management," *Journal of Applied Behavioral Science*, September 2000, pp. 376–379; W. Nicolay, "Response to Farias and Johnson's Commentary," *Journal of Applied Behavioral Science*, September 2000, pp. 380–381; S. Hicks, "What Is Organization Development?" *Training & Development*, August 2000, p. 65.

16. T. White, "Supporting Change: How Communicators at Scotiabank Turned Ideas into Action," *Communication World*, April 2002, pp. 22–24.

17. P. A. McLagan, "Change Leadership Today," *Training & Development*, November 2002, p. 29.

18. H. L. Sirkin, P. Keenan, and A. Jackson, "The Hard Side Of Change Management," *Harvard Business Review* 83, no. 10 (October 1, 2005), pp. 108–118.

19. W. Pietersen, "The Mark Twain Dilemma: The Theory and Practice for Change Leadership," *Journal of Business Strategy*, September—October 2002, pp. 32–37; C. Hymowitz, "To Maintain Success, Managers Must Learn How to Direct Change," *Wall Street Journal*, August 13, 2002, p. B1; J. E. Dutton, S. J. Ashford, R. M. O'Neill, and K. A. Lawrence, "Moves That Matter: Issue Selling and Organizational Change," *Academy of Management Journal*, August 2001, pp. 716–736.

20. P. A. McLagan, "The Change-Capable Organization," *Training & Development*, January 2003, pp. 50–58.

21. M. Young and J. E. Post, "Managing to Communicate, Communicating to Manage: How Leading Companies Communicate With Employees," *Organizational Dynamics*, Summer 1993, pp. 31–43.

22. M. Javidan, P. W. Dorfman, M. S. deLuque, and R. J. House, "In the Eye of the Beholder: Cross-Cultural Lessons in Leadership from

Project GLOBE," *Academy of Management Perspective,* February 2006, pp. 67–90; and E. Fagenson-Eland, E. A. Ensher, and W. W. Burke, "Organization Development and Change Interventions: A Seven-Nation Comparison," *The Journal of Applied Behavioral Science,* December 2004, pp. 432–464.

23. E. Fagenson-Eland, E. A. Ensher, and W. W. Burke, "Organization Development and Change Interventions: A Seven-Nation Comparison," *The Journal of Applied Behavioral Science,* December 2004, pp. 461.

24. See, for example, B. M. Staw, "Counterforces to Change," in *Change in Organizations,* ed. P. S. Goodman and Associates (San Francisco: Jossey-Bass, 1982), pp. 87–121; A. A. Armenakis and A. G. Bedeian, "Organizational Change: A Review of Theory and Research in the 1990s," *Journal of Management* 25, no. 3 (1999), pp. 293–315; C. R. Wanberg and J. T. Banas, "Predictors and Outcomes of Openness to Changes in a Reorganizing Workplace," *Journal of Applied Psychology,* February 2000, pp. 132–142; S. K. Piderit, "Rethinking Resistance and Recognizing Ambivalence: A Multidimensional View of Attitudes Toward an Organizational Change," *Academy of Management Review,* October 2000, pp. 783–794; R. Kegan and L. L. Lahey, "The Real Reason People Won't Change," *Harvard Business Review,* November 2001, pp. 85–92; M. A. Korsgaard, H. J. Sapienza, and D. M. Schweiger, "Beaten Before Begun: The Role of Procedural Justice in Planning Change," *Journal of Management* 28, no. 4 (2002), pp. 497–516; and C. E. Cunningham, "Readiness for Organizational Change: A Longitudinal Study of Workplace, Psychological and Behavioral Correlates," *Journal of Occupational and Organizational Psychology,* December 2002, pp. 377–392.

25. J. P. Kotter and L. A. Schlesinger, "Choosing Strategies for Change," *Harvard Business Review,* March–April 1979, pp. 107–109; P. Strebel, "Why Do Employees Resist Change?" *Harvard Business Review,* May–June 1996, pp. 86–92; J. Mariotti, "Troubled by Resistance to Change," *IndustryWeek,* October 7, 1996, p. 30; and A. Reichers, J. P. Wanous, and J. T. Austin, "Understanding and Managing Cynicism About Organizational Change," *Academy of Management Executive,* February 1997, pp. 48–57.

26. J. P. Kotter and L. A. Schlesinger, "Choosing Strategies for Change," *Harvard Business Review,* March–April 1979, pp. 106–111; K. Matejka and R. Julian, "Resistance to Change Is Natural," *Supervisory Management,* October 1993, p. 10; C. O'Connor, "Resistance: The Repercussions of Change," *Leadership & Organization Development Journal,* October 1993, pp. 30–36; J. Landau, "Organizational Change and Barriers to Innovation: A Case Study in the Italian Public Sector," *Human Relations,* December 1993, pp. 1411–1429; A. Sagie and M. Koslowsky, "Organizational Attitudes and Behaviors as a Function of Participation in Strategic and Tactical Change Decisions: An Application of Path-Goal Theory," *Journal of Organizational Behavior,* January 1994, pp. 37–47; V. D. Miller, J. R. Johnson, and J. Grau, "Antecedents to Willingness to Participate in a Planned Organizational Change," *Journal of Applied Communication Research,* February 1994, pp. 59–80; P. Pritchett and R. Pound, *The Employee Handbook for Organizational Change* (Dallas: Pritchett Publishing, 1994); R. Maurer, *Beyond the Wall of Resistance: Unconventional Strategies That Build Support for Change* (Austin, TX: Bard Books, 1996); D. Harrison, "Assess and Remove Barriers to Change," *HRfocus,* July 1999, pp. 9–10; L. K. Lewis, "Disseminating Information and Soliciting Input During Planned Organizational Change," *Management Communication Quarterly,* August 1999, pp. 43–75; J. P. Wanous, A. E. Reichers, and J. T. Austin, "Cynicism About Organizational Change," *Group & Organization Management,* June 2000, pp. 132–153; K. W. Mossholder, R. P. Settoon, and A. A. Armenakis, "Emotion During Organizational Transformations," *Group & Organization Management,* September 2000, pp. 220–243; and S. K. Piderit, "Rethinking Resistance and Recognizing Ambivalence: A Multidimensional View of Attitudes Toward an Organizational Change," *Academy of Management Review,* October 2000, pp. 783–794.

27. Based on K. Swisher, "Yahoo's Jerry Yang to Step Down, as a Search for New CEO Commences," www.kara.allthingsd.com/20081117/yahoos-jerry-yang-to-step-down-as-a-search-for-new-ceo-commences/, November 17, 2008 (accessed July 7, 2009); K. J. Delaney and J. S. Lublin, "Can 'Chief Yahoo' Rise to Challenges As Yahoo Chief?" *Wall Street Journal,* June 20, 2007, p. B1; and www.yodel.yahoo.com/2007/06/18/my-new-job/ (accessed June 29, 2009).

28. C. Hymowitz, "How Leader at 3M Got His Employees to Back Big Changes," *Wall Street Journal,* April 23, 2002, p. B1; and J. Useem, "Jim McNerney Thinks He Can Turn 3M from a Good Company into a Great One—With a Little Help from His Former Employer: General Electric," *Fortune,* August 12, 2002, pp. 127–132.

29. See T. H. Fitzgerald, "Can Change in Organizational Culture Really Be Managed?" *Organizational Dynamics,* Autumn 1988, pp. 5–15; B. Dumaine, "Creating a New Company Culture," *Fortune,* January 15, 1990, pp. 127–131; P. F. Drucker, "Don't Change Corporate Culture—Use It!" *Wall Street Journal,* March 28, 1991, p. A14; J. Martin, *Cultures in Organizations: Three Perspectives* (New York: Oxford University Press, 1992); D. C. Pheysey, *Organizational Cultures: Types and Transformations* (London: Routledge, 1993); C. G. Smith and R. P. Vecchio, "Organizational Culture and Strategic Management: Issues in the Strategic Management of Change," *Journal of Managerial Issues,* Spring 1993, pp. 53–70; P. Bate, *Strategies for Cultural Change* (Boston: Butterworth-Heinemann, 1994); and P. Anthony, *Managing Culture* (Philadelphia: Open University Press, 1994).

30. M. L. Wald and J. Schwartz, "Shuttle Inquiry Uncovers Flaws in Communication," *New York Times,* August 4, 2003, www.nytimes.com.

31. M. L. Wald and J. Schwartz, "Shuttle Inquiry Uncovers Flaws in Communication," *New York Times,* August 4, 2003, www.nytimes.com.

32. See, for example, R. H. Kilmann, M. J. Saxton, and R. Serpa, eds., *Gaining Control of the Corporate Culture* (San Francisco: Jossey-Bass, 1985); and D. C. Hambrick and S. Finkelstein, "Managerial Discretion: A Bridge Between Polar Views of Organizational Outcomes," in *Research in Organizational Behavior,* vol. 9, ed. B. M. Staw and L. L. Cummings (Greenwich, CT: JAI Press, 1987), p. 384.

33. M. A. Cavanaugh, W. R. Boswell, M. V. Roehling, and J. W. Boudreau, "An Empirical Examination of Self-Reported Work Stress Among U.S. Managers," *Journal of Applied Psychology,* February 2000, pp. 65–74; M. A. Verespej, "Stressed Out," *IndustryWeek,* February 21, 2000, pp. 30–34; J. Laabs, "Time-Starved Workers Rebel," *Workforce,* October 2000, pp. 26–28; and C. Daniels, "The Last Taboo," *Fortune,* October 28, 2002, pp. 137–144.

34. I. Phaneuf, "Drug Company Study Finds Rise in Work-Related Stress," *Vancouver Sun,* May 5, 2001, p. D15.

35. Adapted from R. S. Schuler, "Definition and Conceptualization of Stress in Organizations," *Organizational Behavior and Human Performance,* April 1980, p. 189. For an updated review of definitions, see R. L. Kahn and P. Byosiere, "Stress in Organizations," in *Handbook of Industrial and Organizational Psychology,* vol. 3, 2nd ed., ed. M. D. Dunnette and L. J. Hough (Palo Alto, CA: Consulting Psychologists Press, 1992), pp. 573–580.

36. B. L. de Mente, "Karoshi: Death from Overwork," Asia Pacific Management Forum, www.apmforum.com, May 2002.

37. S. E. Jackson, "Participation in Decision Making as a Strategy for Reducing Job-Related Strain," *Journal of Applied Psychology,* February 1983, pp. 3–19; C. D. Fisher, "Boredom at Work: A Neglected Concept," *Human Relations,* March 1993, pp. 395–417; C. A. Heaney, B. A. Israel, S. J. Schurman, E. A. Baker, J. S. House, and M. Hugentobler, "Industrial Relations, Worksite Stress Reduction and Employee Well-Being: A Participatory Action Research Investigation,"

Journal of Organizational Behavior, September 1993, pp. 495–510; P. Froiland, "What Cures Job Stress?" *Training*, December 1993, pp. 32–36; C. L. Cooper and S. Cartwright, "Healthy Mind, Healthy Organization—A Proactive Approach to Occupational Stress," *Human Relations*, April 1994, pp. 455–471; A. A. Brott, "New Approaches to Job Stress," *Nation's Business*, May 1994, pp. 81–82; and C. Daniels, "The Last Taboo," *Fortune*, October 28, 2002, pp. 137–144.

38. See R. S. Schuler, "Time Management: A Stress Management Technique," *Personnel Journal*, December 1979, pp. 851–855; and M. E. Haynes, *Practical Time Management: How to Make the Most of Your Most Perishable Resource* (Tulsa, OK: Penn Well Books, 1985).

39. "Employee Wellness," *Canadian HR Reporter*, February 23, 2004, pp. 9–12.

40. Adapted from P. B. Vaill, *Managing as a Performing Art: New Ideas for a World of Chaotic Change* (San Francisco: Jossey-Bass, 1989), pp. 8, 9.

41. Situation adapted from information in "HR Director Backs Team to Stay Focused During Boots Upheaval," *Personnel Today*, March 21, 2006, p. 2; "Boots' Revamp As Group to Shut 17 Depots," *Europe Intelligence Wire*, March 15, 2006.

42. Information from press kit on company's website, www.1800gotjunk.com; A. Wahl, "Canada's Best Workplaces: Overview," *Canadian Business*, April 26, 2007 (accessed May 20, 2007); "Fastest-Growing Franchises 2006 Rankings," *Entrepreneur*, April 29, 2006, www.entrepreneur.com; J. Hainsworth, The Associated Press, "Canadian Company Finds Treasures in People's Trash," *Springfield News-Leader*, April 24, 2006, p. 5B; J. Martin, "Cash from Trash," *Fortune*, November 2003, pp. 52–56; and M. Carbonaro, "1-800-GOT-JUNK? Quickly Opens Second Area Site," *CNY Business Journal*, August 10, 2007, www.findarticles.com/p/articles/mi_qa3718/is_20070810/ai_n19510769 (accessed June 29, 2009).

43. Based on M. Warner, "Under the Knife," *Business 2.0*, February 2004, www.business20.com.

44. See also T. Pollock, "Mind Your Own Business: The Gentle Art of Selling Change," *Supervision*, December 2000, p. 11; and R. M. Kanter, "The Enduring Skills of Change Leaders," *Ivey Business Journal*, May 2000, p. 31.

45. Based on J. P. Kotter and L. A. Schlesinger, "Choosing Strategies for Change," *Harvard Business Review*, March–April 1979, pp. 106–114; and T. A. Stewart, "Rate Your Readiness to Change," *Fortune*, February 7, 1994, pp. 106–110.

46. Based on C. Lindsay, "Paradoxes of Organizational Diversity: Living Within the Paradoxes," in *Proceedings of the 50th Academy of Management Conference*, ed. L. R. Jauch and J. L. Wall (San Francisco, 1990), pp. 374–378.

Part 5 Continuing Case: Starbucks

1. A. Serwer and K. Bonamici, "Hot Starbucks to Go," *Fortune*, January 26, 2004, pp. 60–74; interview with Jim Donald, *Smart Money*, May 2006, pp. 31–32; A. Serwer, "Interview with Howard Schultz," *Fortune* (Europe), March 20, 2006, pp. 35–36; W. Meyers, "Conscience in a Cup of Coffee," *U.S. News & World Report*, October 31, 2005, pp. 48–50; S. Gray, "Fill 'er Up—With Latte," *Wall Street Journal*, January 6, 2006, pp. A9+; M. Bartiromo, "Howard Schultz on Reinventing Starbucks," *Business Week*, April 9, 2008, www.businessweek.com/magazine/content/08_16/b4080000943927.htm (accessed July 2, 2009); P. Kafka, "Bean Counter," *Forbes*, February 28, 2005, pp. 78–80; J. Schnack, L. Adamson, S. Brull, L. Conger, P. Paulden, and J. Sutherland, "Starbucks Shells Out to Safeguard Schultz," *Institutional Investor*, January 2006, p. 11; R. Ruggless, "Starbucks Exec: Security from Employee Theft Important When Implementing Gift Card Strategies," *Nation's Restaurant News*, December 12, 2005, p. 24; R. Ruggless, "Transaction Monitoring Boosts Safety, Perks Up Coffee Chain Profits," *Nation's Restaurant News*, November 28, 2005, p. 35; Standards of Business Conduct, Starbucks, www.starbucks.com; and Starbucks Corporation, *Fiscal 2008 Annual Report*, http://investor.starbucks. com/phoenix.zhtml?c=99518&p=irol-reportsAnnual (accessed September 11, 2009).

Glossary/Subject Index

Note: Pages in bold refer to pages on which key terms are defined.

A

Aboriginal peoples, 37, 218, 252

absenteeism, 363

accommodative approach. Managers make choices that try to balance the interests of shareholders with those of other stakeholders. **122**

accountability. The need to report and justify work to a manager's superiors. **143**

achievement, 43

achievement-oriented leader, 244

active listening. Listening for full meaning without making premature judgments or interpretations. **177**–178, 178f, 192–193

activity ratios, 342

adjourning. The final stage of team development for temporary teams, in which members are concerned with wrapping up activities rather than task performance. **298**

adult websites at work, 356

all-channel network, 181

alternatives

    analysis of, 104–105, 104f

    development of, 104

    implementation, 105

    selection of, 105

ambiguity, tolerance for, 112

ambiguity-induced stress, 377

analytic style. A decision-making style characterized by a high tolerance for ambiguity and a rational way of thinking. **113**

anarchy, 149

anti-discrimination legislation, 198

anti-globalization groups, 52f

application forms, 203

aptitude tests, 203

assessment centres. A set of varied exercises that simulate different aspects of the work environment and are used to assess job candidates. **204**

Association of Southeast Asian Nations (ASEAN). A trading alliance of 10 Southeast Asian countries. **41**

attractiveness of reward, 276

authority. The rights inherent in a managerial position to tell people what to do and to expect them to do it. **143**

    chain of command, 143–144

    line authority, 143–144

    as principle of management, 25

    staff authority, 144

autocratic style. A leadership style where the leader tends to centralize authority, dictate work methods, make unilateral decisions, and limit employee participation. **236**

autonomy. The degree to which the job provides substantial freedom, independence, and discretion to the individual in scheduling the work and determining the procedures to be used in carrying it out. **272**, 278

avatars, 156

B

background investigations, 205

backward vertical integration, 83

balanced scorecard. A performance measurement tool that looks at four areas—financial, customer, internal business process, and learning and growth assets—that contribute to an organization's performance. **346**–347, 346f

bargaining power, 86

barriers to interpersonal communication

    active listening, 177–178, 178f

    defensiveness, 175

    emotions, 175, 178

    feedback, use of, 177

    filtering, 174–175

    generally, 174

    information overload, 175

    language, 175–176

    national culture, 176–177

    nonverbal cues, 178

    overcoming, 177–178

    selective perception, 175

    simplification of language, 177

basic corrective action. Corrective action that looks at how and why performance deviated and then proceeds to correct the source of deviation. **333**

behavioural assessment tests, 203

behavioural style. A decision-making style characterized by a low tolerance for ambiguity and an intuitive way of thinking. **113**

behavioural theories. Leadership theories that identify behaviours that differentiate effective leaders from ineffective leaders. **236**, 237f

    managerial grid, 238, 239f

    Ohio State studies, 237

    University of Iowa studies, 236–237

    University of Michigan studies, 237–238

behaviourally anchored rating scales (BARS). A performance appraisal method in which the evaluator rates an employee on examples of actual job behaviours. **211**

benchmark. The standard of excellence against which to measure and compare. **331**

benchmarking. The search for the best practices among competitors or noncompetitors that lead to their superior performance. **90, 331**, 331f

benefits, 212–213, 213f, 217, 224–225

best practices, 331

biases in decision-making, 115–117, 115f–116f

Big Five personality framework, 235

blogs, 190

board of directors, 347

body language. Gestures, facial expressions, and other body movements that convey meaning. **172**–174, 177

borderless organization. *See* transnational or borderless organization

born globals. An international company that chooses to go global from inception. **46**

boundaryless organization. An organization that is not defined by a chain of command, places no limits on spans of control, and replaces departments with empowered teams. **155**

bounded rationality. Limitations on a person's ability to interpret, process, and act on information. **108**

bragging boards, 282

breadth potential, 172

budgets, 343

bureaucracy. A form of organization characterized by division of labour, a clearly defined hierarchy, detailed rules and regulations, and impersonal relationships. **26**, 26f

bureaucratic control. An approach to control that emphasizes organizational authority and relies on administrative rules, regulations, procedures, and policies. **337**

business cycle, 37

business model. A strategic design for how a company intends to profit from its strategies, work processes, and work activities. **76**

business strategy

    competitive strategies, 85–89

    cost leadership strategy, 86–88

    differentiation strategy, 88

    focus strategy, 88–89

    generally, 85

    stuck in the middle, 89

buyers, bargaining power of, 86

C

calm waters metaphor, 364–365

Canada Labour Code, 197

Canadian Charter of Rights and Freedoms, 198

Canadian Human Rights Act, 37, 198

Canadian Human Rights Commission, 38

Canadian Securities Administrators rules, 362

capabilities. An organization's skills and abilities that enable it to do the work activities needed in its business. **77**

career. A sequence of positions held by a person during his or her lifetime. **213**

career choice, 213

conflict (contd.)

relationship conflict, 306

storming, 298

task conflict, 306

traditional view of conflict, 305

conflict resolution techniques, 307*f*

conformity, 114, 308

consideration. The extent to which a leader has job relationships characterized by mutual trust and respect for group members' ideas and feelings. **237**

consistency, 249

constraints. *See* environment

contemporary organizational design

boundaryless organization, 155

described, 153, 153*f*

matrix structure, 154, 154*f*

network organization, 157

project structure, 154–155

team structure, 153–154

virtual organization, 155–156

contemporary theories of motivation

equity theory, 273–275, 274*f*, 279

expectancy theory, 275–276, 276*f*, 277*f*

integration of, 276–277

job characteristics model (JCM), 272–273, 272*f*, 273*f*

reinforcement theory, 271

contingency approach. An approach that says that organizations are different, face different situations (contingencies), and require different ways of managing. **30**, 30*f*

contingency factors

and organizational design, 149–151

in planning, 74

contingency theories of leadership

described, 238–239

Fiedler contingency model, 239–241, 240*f*

leader participation model, 242–243

path-goal theory, 243–244, 244*f*

Situational Leadership (SL), 241–242, 241*f*

contingency variable, 30, 30*f*

contingent workers, 281

continuing case: Starbucks

controlling, 386

defining the manager's terrain, 60

leading, 318

organizing, 226

planning, 132

control. The process of monitoring activities to ensure that they are being accomplished as planned, and correcting any significant deviations. **326**

balanced scorecard, 346–347, 346*f*

bureaucratic control, 337

clan control, 337, 338

concurrent control, 335–336

corporate governance, 347–348

cross-cultural differences, 348–349

current issues, 345–353

customer interactions, 351–352

employee theft, 350–351, 351*f*

feedback control, 336

feedforward control, 335

financial controls, 342–344

importance of, 327–328

information controls, 344–345

market control, 337

methods of control, 336–341, 336*f*

and organizational culture, 338–341

performance standards, 326

service profit chain, 352, 352*f*

timing of introduction, 334–336

types of control, 334, 334*f*

workplace concerns, 349–351

workplace privacy, 349–350

control process. A three-step process that includes measuring actual performance, comparing actual performance against a standard, and taking managerial action to correct deviations or inadequate standards. **328**, 328*f*

benchmarking, 331–331*f*

control criteria, 329

corrective action, 332–333

managerial action, 332–334

managerial decisions, summary of, 334, 334*f*

performance measurement, 328–329

performance *vs.* standard, 329–331

range of variation, 329, 329*f*

revision of standards, 333

controlling. A management function that involves monitoring actual performance, comparing actual performance to a standard, and taking corrective action when necessary. **8**

see also control

and communication, 169

described, 8

planning and, 68, 327*f*

copyright, and software, 356

core competencies. An organization's major value-creating skills, capabilities, and resources that determine its competitive weapons. **77**

corporate governance. The system used to govern a corporation so that the interests of corporate owners are protected. **347**

board of directors, role of, 347

described, 347

financial reporting, 348

twenty-first century governance principles for public companies, 348*f*

corporate reputation, 79

corporate social responsibility. A business's obligation, beyond that required by law and economics, to do the right things and act in ways that are good for society. **120**

accommodative approach, 122

approaches to, 122–122*f*

classical view, 121

comparison of views of, 121–122

defensive approach, 122

and economic performance, 123

obstructionist approach, 122

proactive approach, 122

socio-economic view, 121

corporate strategy. An organizational strategy that evaluates what businesses a company is in, should be in, or wants to be in, and what it wants to do with those businesses. **82**

growth strategy, 82–84

main types of corporate strategies, 82

renewal strategies, 84–85

stability strategy, 67–84

corrective action, 332–333

cost leadership strategy. A business strategy in which the organization sets out to be the lowest-cost producer in its industry. **86–88**

cost of communication, 172

creative problem solving, 130

creativity, 74–75

credibility. The degree to which someone is perceived as honest, competent, and able to inspire. **249**

critical incidents. A performance appraisal method in which the evaluator focuses on the critical, or key, behaviours that separate effective from ineffective job performance. **210**

critical-path scheduling analysis, 27

cross-cultural differences. *See* national culture

cross-functional teams. Work teams made up of individuals who are experts in various functional specialties. 141–143, **297**

Crown corporation. A commercial company owned by the government but independently managed. **13**

cultural awareness, 58–59

cultural change, 373–375

cultural differences, 57, 177

see also national culture

cultural environment, 42–44

culture. *See* national culture; organizational culture

current-competitor rivalry, 86

customer departmentalization. Groups jobs on the basis of customers who have common needs or problems. **141**

customer interactions, 351–352

customers, 36, 90

D

data. Raw, unanalyzed facts. **345**

data encryption, 345

decentralization. The degree to which lower-level employees provide input or actually make decisions. **145**, 146–147, 146*f*

decision. A choice from two or more alternatives. **102**

effectiveness, evaluation of, 106

ethics of business decision, 119–120, 120*f*

in the management functions, 107*f*

nonprogrammed decisions, 110–111

efficiency. Getting the most output from the least amount of inputs; referred to as "doing things right.", **6**

  vs. effectiveness, 6, 7*f*

effort-performance linkage, 276

email, 182–183, 349–350, 349*f*

emotional expression, 169

emotions, 175, 178

employee attitudes, 363

employee benefits, 212–213, 213*f*, 217, 224–225

employee counselling. A process designed to help employees overcome performance-related problems. **212**

employee empowerment. Giving more authority to employees to make decisions. **146**, 328

employee-oriented leaders, 238

employee recognition programs. Reward programs that provide managers with opportunities to give employees personal attention and express interest, approval, and appreciation for a job well done. **282**

employee rewards programs. *See* rewards

employee skill obsolescence, 162

employee theft. Any unauthorized taking of company property by employees for their personal use. **350–351**, 351*f*

employees

  computer use, 349–350, 349*f*

  contingent workers, 281

  counselling, 377

  keeping employees connected, 157

  minimum-wage employees, 279–280

  monitoring, 349–350, 349*f*

  motivation. *See* motivation

  and nonwork-related websites, 191

  organizational culture, learning, 340–341

  performance. *See* performance

  privacy, 349–350

  professional employees, 280–281

  resistance to change, 371–373, 372*f*

  stress, 375–377

  technical employees, 280–281

  training, 207–209

  wellness programs, 377

Employment Equity Act, 37–38, 198

employment standards legislation, 198

encoding. Converting a message into symbols. **170**

encoding ease, 172

English-only rules, 191–192

environment

  amount of management control, 34

  dynamic environment, 48

  effect of environment, 48–51

  environmental complexity, 49

  environmental uncertainty, 48–50, 49*f*

  external environment, 35–36, 36*f*

  general environment, 37–40

  generally, 33

  global environment, 40–44

  globalization, pros and cons of, 51

  managerial discretion, parameters of, 35*f*

  scanning the environment, 98

  specific environment, 36–37

  stable environment, 48

  stakeholder relationships, 50–51

  and structure, 151

environmental complexity. The number of components in an organization's environment and the extent of the organization's knowledge about those components. **49**

environmental constraints. *See* environment

environmental uncertainty. The degree of change and the degree of complexity in an organization's environment. **48–50**, 49f, 74, 151

environmental uncertainty matrix, 49

equipment changes, 363

equity, 25

equity theory. The theory that an employee compares his or her job's inputs–outcomes ratio with that of relevant others and then responds to correct any inequity. 273–275, **274**, 274*f*, 279

errors, decision-making, 115–117, 115*f*

escalation-of-commitment. An increased commitment to a previous decision despite evidence that the decision might have been wrong. **117**

esprit de corps, 25

esteem needs. A person's need for internal esteem factors such as self-respect, autonomy, and achievement, and external esteem factors such as status, recognition, and attention. **267**

ethical dilemma exercises

  adult websites at work, 356

  change, acceptance of, 382

  charismatic leadership, 247–260

  employee compensation, 290

  executive compensation, 18

  investment advice, objectivity of, 128

  "just following orders," 162

  multiperson ranking system, 223

  opposition to expansion, reaction to, 56

  pressure to deliver results, 96

  team players, 314

  weblogs, 190

ethics. Rules and principles that define right and wrong behaviour. **117**

  codes of ethics, 119–120

  and decision making, 117–120

  duplicating software, 356

  employee skill obsolescence, 162

  ethical organizational culture, 339–340

  four views of ethics, 118–119

  improvement of ethical behaviour, 119–120

  integrative social contracts theory, 118

  and leadership, 250

  nonwork-related websites, and employees, 191

  power, use of, 260

  product labelling laws, 56

  rights view of ethics, 118

  selection process, and online investigations, 223

  stress-reduction programs, 382

  theory of justice view of ethics, 118

  utilitarian view of ethics, 118

European Union (EU). A union of 27 European countries that forms an economic and political entity. **41**

executive compensation, 18

executive vice-president, 5

expectancy-performance linkage, 276

expectancy theory. The theory that an individual tends to act in a certain way based on the expectation that the act will be followed by a given outcome and on the attractiveness of that outcome to the individual. 275–276, 276f, 277f

expert power. The influence a leader has based on his or her expertise, special skills, or knowledge. **248**

exporting. An approach to going global that involves making products at home and selling them abroad. **47**

external analysis, 79–80

external environment. Outside forces and institutions that potentially can affect the organization's performance. **35–36**, 36f, 197

external forces for change, 362

extrinsic motivation. Motivation that comes from outside the person and includes such things as pay, bonuses, and other tangible rewards. **268**

F

fairness, 273–275, 286

family, and work, 217

family-friendly benefits. Benefits that accommodate employees' needs for work–life balance. **217**

Fayol, Henri, 25

feedback. The degree to which carrying out the work activities required by the job results in the individual's obtaining direct and clear information about the effectiveness of his or her performance. **272**

  and communication channel, 172

  providing feedback, 358–359

  suggestions, 179

  360-degree feedback, 211

  use of, 177

feedback control. A type of control that takes place after a work activity is done. **336**

feedback loop, 171

feedforward control. A type of control that focuses on preventing anticipated problems, since it takes place before the actual activity. **335**

Fiedler contingency model. A leadership theory proposing that effective group performance depends on the proper match between the leader's style of interacting with followers and the degree to which the situation gives the leader control and influence. **239**–241, 240f

as primary management function, 69

purposes of planning, 68

and rigidity, 74

plans. Documents that outline how goals are going to be met and describe resource allocations, schedules, and other necessary actions to accomplish the goals. **69**

breadth, 72

contingency factors, 74

development of, 71–74

directional plans, 73, 73*f*

frequency of use, 72

long-term plans, 73

operational plans, 73

short-term plans, 73

single-use plan, 74

specific plans, 73, 73*f*

specificity, 72

standing plans, 74

strategic plans, 73

time frame, 72

types of plans, 72–74, 72*f*

plant manager, 5

policy. A guideline for making a decision. **110**

positive role models, 375

positive trends, 79

power

coercive power, 248

expert power, 248

and leadership, 248–249

legitimate power, 248

need for power, 270

referent power, 248

reward power, 248

use of, as interpersonal skill, 262–263

power distance, 43

preferred leader behaviours, 244*f*

president, 5

principles of management. Fourteen fundamental rules of management that could be taught in schools and applied in all organizational situations. 25, **26**

The Principles of Scientific Management (Taylor), 23

privacy issues, 349–350

private sector. The part of the economy that is run by organizations that are free from direct government control; operations in this sector operate to make a profit. **12–13**

privately held organization. A company whose shares are not available on the stock exchange but are privately held. **13**

pro-globalization groups, 52*f*

proactive approach. Managers go out of their way to actively promote the interests of stockholders and stakeholders, using organizational resources to do so. **122**

problem. A discrepancy between an existing and a desired state of affairs. **102**

structured problems, 110

types of problems, 109–111

unstructured problems, 110–111

problem-solving team. A work team of 5 to 12 employees from the same department or functional area who are involved in efforts to improve work activities or to solve specific problems. **297**

procedural justice. Perceived fairness of the process used to determine the distribution of rewards. **275**

procedure. A series of interrelated sequential steps that a decision maker can use to respond to a structured problem. **110**

process conflict. Conflict over how the work gets done. **306**

process departmentalization. Groups jobs on the basis of product or customer flow. **141**

process production. The production of items in continuous processes. **150**

product departmentalization. Groups jobs by product line. **141**

product labelling laws, 56

product line, 141

production-oriented leaders, 238

productivity. The overall output of goods or services produced divided by the inputs needed to generate that output. **326**

professional employees, 280–281

profit sharing, 146

profitability ratios, 342–343

programmed decision. A repetitive decision that can be handled by a routine approach. **110**

project leader, 5

project structure. An organizational structure in which employees continuously work on projects. **154–155**

public pressure groups, 37

public-private partnerships, 368

public sector. The part of the economy that is directly controlled by government. **13**

publicly held organization. A company whose shares are available on the stock exchange for public trading by brokers/dealers. **12**

Q

quality, 90–91

quality management. A philosophy of management driven by continual improvement and responding to customer needs and expectations. **90**

benchmarking, 90

characteristics of quality management, 91*f*

ISO 9000 series, 90–91

six sigma, 91, 92*f*

quantitative approach. The use of quantitative techniques to improve decision making. **27**

R

range of variation. The acceptable degree of variation between actual performance and the standard. **329**, 329*f*

rational decision making. Making decisions that are consistent and value-maximizing within specified constraints. **107**, 107*f*

ratios, financial, 342

readiness. The extent to which people have the ability and willingness to accomplish a specific task. **233**, 241

realistic job preview (RJP). A preview of a job that includes both positive and negative information about the job and the company. **206**

reality of work, 14–15

receiver, 171

recognition, power of, 286

recruitment. The process of locating, identifying, and attracting capable applicants. **200**

described, 200–201

e-recruiting, 200

major sources of potential job candidates, 200*f*

and social networking sites, 181–182, 183

and workforce diversity, 215

reference checks, 205

referent. Those things individuals compare themselves against in order to assess equity. **275**

referent power. The power a leader has because of his or her desirable resources or personal traits. **248, 275**

refreezing, 364–365

regional manager, 5

regional trading alliances, 41

regulations, 38, 362

reinforcement theory. The theory that behaviour is influenced by consequences. **271**

reinforcers. Consequences that, when given immediately following a behaviour, increase the probability that the behaviour will be repeated. **271**

related diversification. When a company grows by combining with firms in different, but related, industries. **83**

relationship conflict. Conflict based on interpersonal relationships. **306**

relationship-oriented leaders, 240–341

reliability. The ability of a selection device to measure the same thing consistently. **203**

remuneration, 25

renewal strategies. Corporate strategies designed to address organizational weaknesses that are leading to performance declines. **84**

retrenchment strategy, 84

turnaround strategy, 84

resistance to change, 371–373, 372*f*, 384–385

resource evaluation, 71

resources. An organization's assets—financial, physical, human, intangible—that are used to develop, manufacture, and deliver products or services to customers. **77**

responsibility. The obligation or expectation to perform any assigned duties. **143**

restraining forces, 364

retrenchment strategy. A short-term renewal strategy that reduces the organization's activities or operations. **84**

reward power. The power a leader has to give positive benefits or rewards. **248**

rewards

    effective rewards programs, 281–284

    employee recognition programs, 282

    individualization of rewards, 286

    money, role of, 281–282

    pay-for-performance programs, 282–283

    stock option programs, 283–284

    teams, 301–302

rights view of ethics. A view of ethics that is concerned with respecting and protecting individual liberties and privileges. **118**

rigidity, 74

risk. A condition in which a decision maker is able to estimate the likelihood of certain outcomes. **111**–112

rituals, **340**

role. A set of expected behaviour patterns attributed to someone who occupies a given position in a social unit. **301**

    maintenance roles, **301**

    management roles. See management roles

    task-oriented roles, 301

role-playing, 205

rule. An explicit statement that tells a decision maker what he or she can or cannot do. **110**

rules of thumb, 115–116, 115f–116f

rumours, 181

S

safety needs. A person's need for security and protection from physical and emotional harm; as well as assurance that physical needs will continue to be met. **267**

satisfice. To accept solutions that are "good enough.", **108**

scalar chain, 25

scanability, 172

scanning the environment, 98

scientific management. The use of the scientific method to determine the "one best way" for a job to be done. **23**

    Frank and Lillian Gilbreth, 24

    Frederick W. Taylor, 23–24

    important contributions, 23–25

    use of scientific management, 25

selection devices

    application forms, 203

    background investigations, 205

    choice of, 205–206

    interviews, 204–205

    performance-simulation tests, 204

    physical examinations, 205

    as predictors, 206f

    types of, 203–205, 204f

    written tests, 203

selection process. The process of screening job applicants to ensure that the most appropriate candidates are hired. **201**

    decision outcomes, 202f

    errors in selection, 202–203

online investigations, 223

reliability, 203

selection, generally, 202–203

selection devices, 203–206, 204f

for teams, 301

validity, 203

and workforce diversity, 215

selective perception, 175

selective perception bias, 116

self-actualization needs. A person's need to grow and become what he or she is capable of becoming. **267**

self-assessment

    "Am I well-suited for a career as a global manager?", 54–55

    "How good am I at building and leading a team?", 312–313

    "How good am I at giving performance feedback?", 221–222

    "How good am I at personal planning?", 94–95

    "How intuitive am I?", 125–126

    "How motivated am I to manage?", 16–17

    "How proactive am I?", 354–355

    "How well do I respond to turbulent change?", 379–380

    "What rewards do I value most?", 288–289

    "What type of organizational structure do I prefer?", 160–161

    "What's my face-to-face communication style?", 187–189

    "What's my leadership style?", 257–259

self-employment, 15

self-interest, 309

self-managed team. A work team that operates without a manager and is responsible for a complete work process or segment. **297**

self-serving bias, 117

selling, 241

sender, 170

service profit chain. The service sequence from employees to customers to profit. **352**, 352f

sexual harassment. Any unwelcome behaviour of a sexual nature in the workplace that negatively affects the work environment or leads to adverse job-related consequences for the employee. **216**–217

shareholders. Individuals or companies that own stocks in a business. **50**

shift managers, 4–5

short-term orientation, 43

short-term plans. Plans with a time frame of one year or less. **73**

simple structure. An organizational structure with low departmentalization, wide spans of control, authority centralized in a single person, and little formalization. **152**

simplification of language, 177

single-use plan. A one-time plan specifically designed to meet the needs of a unique situation. **74**

situational approach, 30–30f

situational interviews, 205

Situational Leadership (SL). A leadership theory that focuses on the readiness of followers. **241**–242, 241f

six sigma. A quality standard that establishes a goal of no more than 3.4 defects per million parts or procedures. **91**, 92f

size of organization, 12, 150

skill-based pay. A pay system that rewards employees for the job skills and competencies they can demonstrate. **212**

skill development, 207–209

skill variety. The degree to which the job requires a variety of activities so the employee can use a number of different skills and talents. **272**

skills

    conceptual skills, 10

    development of, 207–209

    diagnostic and analytical skills. See diagnostic and analytical skills

    employee skill obsolescence, 162

    human skills, 10

    interpersonal skills. See interpersonal skills

    interviewing skills, 225

    management skills. See management skills

    negotiation skills, 303

    relevant skills, 303

    technical skills, 10

small businesses, 12

social interaction, 169

social loafing. The tendency of individuals to expend less effort when working collectively than when working individually. **307**, 308–309

social needs. A person's need for security and protection from physical and emotional harm; as well as assurance that physical needs will continue to be met. **267**

social networking, 181

social networking websites, 183

social responsibility. See corporate social responsibility

socialization processes, 375

socio-cultural conditions, 39

socio-economic view. The view that management's social responsibility goes beyond making profits to include protecting and improving society's welfare. **121**

socio-emotional cohesiveness, 305

software, and copyright, 356

span of control. The number of employees a manager can efficiently and effectively manage. **144**–145, 144f

special-interest groups, 37

specific environment. The part of the external environment that is directly relevant to the achievement of an organization's goals. **36**

    competitors, 36–37

    customers, 36

    generally, 36

    public pressure groups, 37

    suppliers, 36

specific plans. Plans that are clearly defined and leave no room for interpretation. **73,** 73*f*

spokesperson, 9

stability of tenure of personnel, 25

stability strategy. A corporate strategy characterized by an absence of significant change in what the organization is currently doing. **67**–84

stable environment, 48

staff managers. Managers who work in the supporting activities of the organizations (such as human resources or accounting). **144**

staffing the organization

    decruitment, 201, 201*f*

    major sources of potential job candidates, 200*f*

    recruitment, 200, 201

    selection process, 201–206

stakeholder relationships, 50–51

stakeholders. Any constituencies in the organization's external environment that are affected by the organization's decisions and actions. **50,** 50*f*

standing plans. Ongoing plans that provide guidance for activities performed repeatedly. **74**

statistics, 27

status, 308

stock market fluctuations, 37

stock option programs, 283–284

stock options. A financial incentive that gives employees the right to purchase shares of company stock, at some time in the future, at a set price. **284**

stockholders, 50

stories, 340

storming. The second stage of team development, which is characterized by intragroup conflict. **298**

strategic alliance. An approach to going global that involves a partnership between a domestic and a foreign company in which both share resources and knowledge in developing new products or building production facilities. **48**

strategic design, 76

strategic management. What managers do to develop the organization's strategies. **76**

strategic management process. A six-step process that encompasses strategic planning, implementation, and evaluation. **76,** 77*f*

    evaluation of results, 81

    external analysis, 79–80

    formulation of strategies, 80–81

    identification of mission, goals and strategies, 76–77

    implementation of strategies, 81

    internal analysis, 78–79

strategic plans. Plans that apply to the entire organization, establish the organization's overall goals, and seek to position the organization in terms of its environment. **72**–73

strategies. The decisions and actions that determine the long-run performance of an organization. **76**

    business strategy, 85–89

    competitive strategies, 85–89

    corporate strategy, 82–85

    cost leadership strategy, 86–88

    differentiation strategy, 88

    evaluation of results, 81

    focus strategy, 88–89

    formulation of, 80–81

    functional strategies, 90

    growth strategy, 82–84

    and human resource management, 197

    identification of, 76–78

    implementation, 81

    and organizational structure, 149–150

    renewal strategies, 84–85

    stability strategy, 67–84

    types of organizational strategies, 81–90, 81*f*

strengths. Any activities the organization does well or any unique resources that it has. **77**

stress. The adverse reaction people have to excessive pressure placed on them from extraordinary demands, constraints, or opportunities. **375**

    ambiguity-induced stress, 377

    causes of stress, 376, 376*f*

    and change management, 375–377

    described, 375–376

    and personal life, 377

    reducing stress, 377

    symptoms, 376–377, 376*f*

strong cultures. Organizational cultures in which the key values are deeply held and widely shared. **339**

structural design, 368

    see also organizational design

structural elements, 368

structure. *See* organizational structure

structured problems. Problems that are straightforward, familiar, and easily defined. **110**

stuck in the middle. A situation in which an organization is unable to develop a competitive advantage through cost or differentiation. **89**

subcultures, 375

subordination of individual interests to general interest, 25

subsidiaries

    Canadian managers *vs.* American managers, 13

    foreign subsidiary, 48

substitutes, 86

sunk-costs error, 116

supervisors, 4–5

suppliers, 36

suppliers, bargaining power of, 86

supportive leader, 244

SWOT analysis. An analysis of the organization's strengths, weaknesses, opportunities, and threats. **80**

symbolic view of management. The view that managers have only a limited effect on substantive organizational outcomes because of the large number of factors outside their control. **34**

synergy. Combined efforts that are greater than the sum of individual efforts. **296**

system, **29**

systems approach, 29–30

T

task conflict. Conflict over content and goals of the work. **306**

task identity. The degree to which the job requires completion of a whole and identifiable piece of work. **272**

task-oriented leaders, 240–241

task-oriented roles. Roles performed by group members to ensure that group tasks are accomplished. **301**

task significance. The degree to which the job affects the lives or work of other people. **272**

Taylor, Frederick W. 23–24

team players, 300–302

team structure. An organizational structure in which the entire organization is made up of work groups or teams. **153**–154

teams

    adjourning, 298

    appropriateness of, 309–310

    cross-functional teams, 141–297

    current management issues, 307–310

    described, 296–297

    effective teams, 302–304, 303*f*

        see also effective teams

    forming, 298

    global teams, 308–309, 308*f*

    group cohesiveness, 304, 305*f*

    group conflict, management of, 305–306, 305*f*

    vs. groups, 296*f*

    norming, 298

    performing, 298

    problem-solving teams, 297

    rewards, 301–302

    roles of team members, 301

    selection, 301

    self-managed teams, 297

    shaping team behaviour, 301–302

    social loafing, 307

    stages of team development, 298–299, 299*f*

    storming, 298

    synergy, 296

    team leadership, 252–253, 253*f*

    team players, 300–302

    training, 301

    turning groups into effective teams, 302–307

    types of teams, 297–298

Name and Organization Index

List of Canadian Companies, by Province

Alberta

British Columbia

Manitoba

New Brunswick

Newfoundland

Nova Scotia

Ontario

List of International Companies, by Country

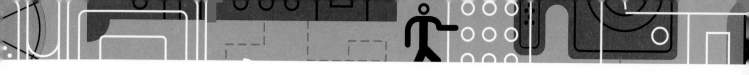

Photo Credits

Author photos
Page xviii, (top) Courtesy of Stephen P. Robbins; (bottom) Courtesy of Gary Schwartz.

Chapter 1
Page 3, Courtesy 1-800-GOT-JUNK?; page 5, H. Darr Beiser © 2007 USA Today. Reprinted with permission; page 13, Joe Gibbons/CP.

Supplement 1
Page 22, PhotoDisc.

Chapter 2
Page 33, Norm Betts/Bloomberg News/Landov; page 34, Don Healy/Leader Post; page 39, © 2009 Yvonne Berg; page 43, Andrea Greenan/W.R. Grace & Co.; page 47, Zhu Gang-Feature China/Newscom; page 61, Scott Pitts © Dorling Kindersley; page 62, AP Wide World Photos.

Chapter 3
Page 67, Wayne Cuddington/The Ottawa Citizen; page 69, Peter Battistoni/Vancouver Sun; page 79, Mark Van Manen/The Vancouver Sun; page 83, Jim Ross; page 85, Ara Koopelian Photography; page 87, Colin O'Connor; page 89, Glenn Lowson; page 90, Dave Yoder/Polaris Images.

Chapter 4
Page 101, Wayne Leidenfrost/The Province; page 104, Bill Aron/PhotoEdit, Inc.; page 111, Quentin Shih aka Shi Xiaofan; page 114, Brian Smith; page 123, Ric Ernst/The Province; page 133, David McNew/Getty Images, Inc-Liaison.

Chapter 5
Page 139, Peter Power/ The Toronto Star; page 141, Dick Hemingway; page 147, Elaine Thomson/AP Wide World Photos; page 156, Gautam Singh/AP Wide World Photos.

Chapter 6
Page 167, AP/Paul Sakuma; page 169, Frederic Jorez/Getty Images; page 174, Ann States Photography; page 184, Kim Christiansen Photography; page 185, Carlo Allegri/National Post.

Chapter 7
Page 195, Marianne Helm/CP Photo; page 201, The Vancouver Police Department; page 207, Lynsey Addario/CORBIS-NY; page 217, Bill Keay/Vancouver Sun; page 218, Dauphin Friendship Centre; page 227, AP Wide World Photos.

Chapter 8
Page 233, Magnotta Winery Corporation; page 236, Mike Aporius/CP Photo Archive; page 243, Mark Van Manen/The Vancouver Sun; page 252, Nathan Denette/CP; page 254, Manish Swarup.

Chapter 9
Page 265, Andy Shaw/Bloomberg News/Landov; page 279, The Yomiuri Shimbun; page 280 (top), Ian Lindsay/The Vancouver Sun; page 280 (bottom), Marcio Jose Sanchez/ AP Wide World Photos; page 282, Nichols Food Ltd.

Chapter 10
Page 295, Shaun Best/Reuters/Landov; page 297, Robyn Twomey/Robyn Twomey Photography; page 299, Micha Bar Am/Magnum Photos, Inc.; page 304, Mark Matson Photography; page 319, Courtesy of Nancy Langton; page 320, CP Photo/Kevin P. Casey.

Chapter 11
Page 325, Adrian Wyld/CP Photo Archive; page 331, Matt Slocum/AP Wide World Photos; page 333, Newscom; page 351, Pat Wellenbach/AP Wide World Photos.

Chapter 12
Page 361, dpa/Landov; page 365, Ron Berg Photography; page 374, Photo by Darryl James; page 386, Tim Boyle/Getty Images News; page 388, Michael Newman/PhotoEdit.

Management Cases
Page 405, Photodisc/MaXx Images; page 406 (left), Stock Food/MaXx Images; page 406 (right), FoodCollection/MaXx Images; page 407, Courtesy J. David Whitehead and Jennifer Baker.